78/-

ACCELERATING INVESTMENT
IN DEVELOPING ECONOMIES

By the same editors :

THE ECONOMICS OF UNDERDEVELOPMENT

a series of twenty-one articles and papers collected and arranged in a single volume

ACCELERATING INVESTMENT IN DEVELOPING ECONOMIES

a series of articles and papers
selected and edited by

A. N. Agarwala
and S. P. Singh

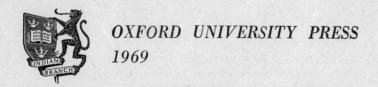

OXFORD UNIVERSITY PRESS
1969

Oxford University Press, Amen House, London E.C. 4
GLASGOW NEW YORK TORONTO MELBOURNE WELLINGTON
BOMBAY CALCUTTA MADRAS KARACHI LAHORE DACCA
CAPE TOWN SALISBURY NAIROBI IBADAN LUSAKA ADDIS ABABA
KUALA LUMPUR HONG KONG TOKYO

First published 1969

PRINTED IN INDIA BY PYARELAL SAH AT THE TIMES OF INDIA
PRESS, BOMBAY, AND PUBLISHED BY JOHN BROWN, OXFORD
UNIVERSITY PRESS, APOLLO BUNDER, BOMBAY I BR

CONTENTS

v

INTRODUCTION

In the Introduction to *The Economics of Underdevelopment**, which appeared eleven years ago, we indicated that it would be followed by two further volumes of selected readings covering other aspects of the subject. The present volume is the second in the series. The first volume comprised articles which make a general or overall approach to the various aspects of the economics of underdevelopment ; those dealing with specific aspects of the subject were, as a rule, left over for the future volumes. This second volume is devoted to investment problems and policies ; and we propose, in a final volume, to cover the remaining specific issues which, we think, can be broadly labelled problems of industrial growth.

The reasons for selecting investment policies for this special treatment are obvious. There is more than a fair measure of agreement amongst economists that investment provides kinetic force to the process of growth in a unique way. Even a primer of economic development tells us that growth depends largely on the rate of capital formation, and that the capital : output ratio plays a key role in development planning. Some of the most intractable problems which underdeveloped countries have to encounter in reaching take-off point have to do, in one way or other, with capital formation. The present volume includes only those contributions which deal with questions relating to acceleration of investment in newly developing countries.

The articles comprise a chapter from a book, two lectures, three papers read at conferences, fifteen articles published in various economics journals, and two specially written for the present volume of readings. These twenty-three items have been classified into six sections.

The first, entitled 'Investment and Economic Growth' contains contributions by Albert O. Hirschman, Paul Streeten, R. F. Kahn (now Lord Kahn), Howard S. Ellis, and A. K. Cairncross. These five papers deal with recent controversies about balanced versus unbalanced growth, the place of capital in economic progress, and expose the bold as well as the cautious approaches.

---

* Oxford University Press, Bombay, 1958.

The six papers in the second section are on investment criteria, and these have been written by Alfred E. Kahn, Hollis B. Chenery, Walter Galenson and Harvey Leibenstein, A. K. Sen, Maurice Dobb, and K. N. Raj. The first two deal with the famous criterion of social marginal productivity and have secured a place for themselves in economic literature. The third puts forward the rather controversial but interesting criterion of reinvestment quotient and also in brief the critical-minimum-effort thesis which has generally been associated with the name of Harvey Leibenstein. A. K. Sen puts forth a fresh and important approach to the problem of choice of techniques for the consumer-goods sector. The article by Maurice Dobb presents in brief his view on the conflict in policy aims of maximizing employment and maximizing growth rates and discusses the time element involved. K. N. Raj examines some important questions, particularly those relating to certain social costs and the time element pertaining to the applicability of investment criteria to choice of projects and project design in the public sector. Inevitably the question of investment criteria leads one to the question of capital intensity, and it is hoped to include articles relating to the employment-maximizing aspect of the choice of techniques in the next volume.

The third section contains three articles which deal with the issues involved in investment decisions in underdeveloped countries. W. B. Reddaway discusses the capital : output ratio, Albert O. Hirschman deals with the regional and geographical distribution of investments in the context of a dual economy, and Henry G. Aubrey with various questions which private entrepreneurs have to face in making investment decisions.

The fourth section contains two papers—one by H. W. Singer and the other by Graeme S. Dorrance. The role of deficit financing in the growth of underdeveloped economies has been a highly debatable issue, and it is not always easy to weigh capital formation against inflation. But most of the dust now seems to have settled down and the above mentioned two articles represent the general opinion fairly well. H. W. Singer provides a balanced survey of the possibilities of using deficit financing for capital formation purposes, particularly in the public sector. Dorrance deals with the dangers of inflation in the context of saving and investment processes in the developing countries.

The next section is on the role of taxation in the process of capital formation and it includes three papers. There are not many contributions to the subject, and the three which make up this section are in a sense new. The views presented here by John H. Adler, A. R. Prest, and Haskell P. Wald represent the best we could find. They deal with fiscal policy in general incentives to industry and investment, and agricultural taxation respectively.

The sixth section contains papers by T. Balogh, the late Ragnar Nurkse, Gerald M. Alter, and P. N. Rosenstein-Rodan, on foreign finance. The first, by Balogh, is an old and famous article on postwar foreign investment which makes interesting reading even today and will perhaps command more attention as time passes. Nurkse's article deals with the prospects of foreign investment in its historical context. Alter deals with the controversial question of the servicing of foreign debt by underdeveloped countries, and incidentally also makes a contribution to the theory of the Big Push. The last article on international aid is by Rodan. So far as the financing of investment is concerned, the reader who has journeyed through the contributions presented in this book will realize that we have perhaps arrived at one of the most significant problems; and one could not hope for a more exhaustive treatment of this subject than this essay provides.

We take this opportunity to state that articles have been reproduced in this volume (as in the case of the first book) as originally published, with only slight modifications to conform to the general style of the book. Again, for reasons explained in the Introduction to the first volume, we are sorry to have had to omit several articles which we would have liked to include. This, however, neither explains nor justifies any blemishes or shortcomings in this volume, for which the responsibility is clearly ours. We may add that several articles included in the first volume also discuss certain important aspects of the investment problem and these can be traced with the help of the index to that volume. Likewise some articles which we propose to include in the next volume touch upon the subject of investment, particularly investment in human capital. This duplication cannot be altogether avoided.

We have great pleasure in acknowledging a debt of gratitude to all the authors whose contributions comprise this volume and who so readily and generously allowed us to reprint them. We are also indebted to the original publishers who helped us in a similar manner. Individual acknowledgements are to be found in the foot-notes to the various articles and this explains the omission of individual names here. Particular assistance was extended to us by Dr John H. Adler, Professor E. A. G. Robinson, Professor P. N. Rosenstein-Rodan, Professor Bert F. Hoselitz, and the Secretary to the Delegates of the Clarendon Press, to whom our thanks are due.

Allahabad   A.N.A.
                                             S.P.S.

INVESTMENT AND ECONOMIC GROWTH

THE STRATEGY OF ECONOMIC DEVELOPMENT*

by Albert O. Hirschman

I will confess that the original title which I had planned for my book was The Theory of Unbalanced Growth. Eventually, however, I was persuaded that this would excessively offend the general feeling that balance is good and that imbalance is bad and alcoholic. Another reason for which I discarded that earlier title was that my espousal of unbalanced growth became more and more just one aspect of a general approach toward economic development problems and I must start here by saying a few words about this approach.

Economics deals primarily with the problems of scarce resources and the development of low-income countries should therefore be peculiarly the province in which economic reasoning can be usefully applied. But right at the start of their inquiry, economists interested in development have become divided over the question : what is the principal or original scarcity in the less developed countries? Is it natural resources? Is it capital? Is it entrepreneurship? Is it education, skills, and techniques? Is it a tradition of law enforcement and of minimum standards of public administration? Or is it all of these things at the same time? As more and more factors, conditions, and so-called prerequisites for development were discovered, the task began to look more and more hopeless. Fortunately, however, a closer examination of these various theories, permitted a more sanguine view. For anyone who was convinced of the primacy of one of these conceivable factors has usually been intent on showing that, if only this factor can somehow be generated, then the other factors, wrongly regarded by others as fundamental, will be forthcoming without much trouble. Those who think that capital is all-important show that capital can substitute for or can even generate natural resources ; those who believe in the star role of entrepreneurship show that once we have trained or imported an enterprising minority the securing of capital is no longer a problem.

* Précis of a lecture delivered at the Institute on ICA Development Programming.

The cumulative impact of these various theories is to raise doubts about the objective scarcity or outright absence of *any* of these specific factors ; in fact, one is rather made to suspect that development is held back not so much by objective scarcities of specific factors of production as by subjective man-made difficulties in mobilizing reserves in natural resources, capital, entrepreneurship, etc. . . . that are potentially available and can be called forth by a variety of pressure situations, learning processes and inducement mechanisms. My principal interest is therefore in a description of these processes and mechanisms. Primarily I am trying to understand how development actually happens, or, to put it quite simply, how one step leads to the next one. So please, during this first part of my talk at least, do not consider that I am addressing myself to the question of what *should* be done ; rather I shall try to analyse how underdeveloped societies are impelled toward development moves that bind together their various latent resources. What is most needed is a *binding agent* for these various latent resources. For reasons I cannot go into here, I consider as the basic scarcity this binding agent, or, in other words, society's ability to make development decisions or at least those decisions that economists might call autonomous in opposition to those that are induced. Now if that is the case you will see immediately that one must feel sceptical about the prescription of balanced growth. Balanced growth means to push forward simultaneously along a broad front the various sectors of an economy or, in an even more demanding version of the theory, it means that a great many new activities must be created jointly so that a market will be provided for the combined outputs of these activities through the new incomes that will have been distributed. While this construction is intellectually most satisfying it is extraordinarily expensive in terms of that scarce resource, autonomous decision making. If, on the other hand, we are interested in economizing that resource, we are bound to develop a sympathetic interest in the imbalances that invariably appear in the course of the growth process. Do these imbalances perhaps serve a purpose ? Do they perhaps have a function, are they perhaps just what the doctor ordered, do they perhaps represent society's way of calling forth more developmental energy than it could generate otherwise ?

My interest is in tracing *all* the stimuli toward development that flow from one development move toward the next one. Economists have traditionally paid attention to the subject by showing that a new activity will generate income, that this income will lead to savings and that these savings will in turn make possible the setting up of new activities. But in addition to this mechanism of expansion, many other more direct and perhaps more powerful connexions between successive development moves exist. And when we consider the problem of choosing between two alternative investments, a principal determinant of our choice must be an answer to the question: which investment, once in place, will exert most pressure towards the creation of the other one? It is from this point of view that I have developed what I call the 'model of optimum disorderliness' which is designed to show that a certain amount of disorderliness — one form of imbalance — in the course of development can be justified. As we have seen, our researchers have uncovered a discouragingly long list of 'prerequisites' for economic development, which range all the way from adequate transportation facilities to basic psychological attitudes, aptitudes and propensities. But many developing countries have a disconcerting habit of disregarding the absence of these so-called prerequisites and to put them into place a little later. They are inverting an order that seems natural to us, but their disorderliness in jumping over one stage and putting it into place in a hurry later on may actually be efficient because on balance it saves on decision-making. The other day I was told of a young woman, recently married, who had decided that before she could have any children she ought to experience some maternal feelings and since she felt entirely devoid of such feelings she proceeded to entrust herself to the cares of a psychoanalyst in the hope that his treatment would produce these feelings whereupon she would consent to have a baby. You will probably agree with me that this young lady was overly conscientious and that the more rapid and certainly the less expensive way of generating maternal feelings was to become pregnant first. But I think that it is precisely that kind of excessive orderliness which we are sometimes preaching when we are sent on missions to the less developed countries.

My interest in unbalanced growth is closely related to this point. Those who stress the importance of balanced growth have made an important contribution by recognizing that various investments and economic activities depend on each other, but from this insight they have drawn the too facile conclusion that all these interrelated activities have to be put into place *at once*. True, automotive vehicles are not much good without highways and modern highways are rather useless without vehicles. But this does not mean that the only way in which we can develop our transportation system is by expanding simultaneously and in constant proportions both the automotive industry and the highway network. Why not take advantage of the stimulus that is set up by expansion of the one toward the expansion of the other? In other words, I do not deny by any means the inter-relatedness of various economic activities of which the balanced growth theory has made so much. But I propose that we probe into the structure that is holding together these interrelated activities. As in the atom, there is much energy here that can be and is in fact being utilized in building up economic development nuclei. *Later on* these nuclei look as though they could never have separated even for a single instant when in actual fact they might never have been assembled had not a sequential solution, i.e., an unbalanced growth sequence, been found, by accident, instinct, or reasoned design.

To look at unbalanced growth means, in other words, to look at the dynamics of the development process *in the small*. But perhaps it is high time that we do just that.

In actual practice, the question balanced versus unbalanced development hardly ever arises. We are always faced with or have to opt for some kind of imbalance. But once we have rid ourselves of the taboo against imbalance, we can begin to reason about it, to differentiate various kinds and varieties of unbalanced development, and thereby come to grips with reality instead of ranting against it.

Because the subject has not been considered at all systematically, economists have stumbled on only one kind of imbalance and have ordinarily confined themselves to it. That is the one where basic facilities such as education, transportation and power are built up far ahead of existing demand on the part of industry, agriculture and commerce in the hope that the latter activities will expand in the wake of the former. Frequently, in the history of the western industrial countries and particularly in connexion with railroads, these hopes have proven well founded, but that does not mean that the same recipe is, or has been, applicable everywhere. In fact, there exist some interesting examples of the failure of railroad investment to spark the economic progress that was expected in accordance with historical precedent. In both nineteenth-century India and

Spain massive investment in railroads by the British and French respectively, had most disappointing results. In some situations, countries, or regions, the purely permissive type of unbalanced growth that banks on the railroad or highway or power station as a means of inviting the traffic may be insufficient. We may have to make sure first of the economic activity *requiring* the traffic be it even over an inadequate highway. In other words, it may be safer to rely for the building of a better highway on the clamour of the users than to rely on private entrepreneurial initiative for the creation of industrial activity in the wake of new highways. Even though this particular cart-before-the-horse sequence may conflict with our ideas of orderliness and also with our concept of the proper area within which the State should confine its economic activities, it may often be best to make sure of some ongoing economic activity first and let that activity point forcefully to the needed infrastructure. I recognize of course that there are physical limits to this procedure but I think that, here again, it is useful to understand that the shortages and bottlenecks in transportation, power, water, etc., which are such an ubiquitous feature of the more rapidly developing countries of the underdeveloped world are not just foolishness and mismanagement, but may be a necessary stage in an economic development sequence that maximizes pressures and stimuli toward action.

Now you may say: Suppose the highway does not get improved or suppose the power shortages do not get relieved? This may happen of course — because there is no 100 per cent guarantee for success. But the point is here that in some societies and environments you need stronger pressures than in others — and these bottlenecks and difficulties I am talking about at least give the developmental forces a chance to assert themselves and perhaps to carry the day — if the society does not react to these clear and present dangers, what chance is there that it would be able to perceive and grasp investment opportunities that require a fine balancing of prospective income against prospective expenditure?

You will notice that throughout this discussion I am assuming that the economy is squeezable and that it responds to the right kind and doses of stimuli, but I do not see how you can at all undertake development without this assumption. Too often we consider these stimuli and pressures as mere nuisances or as dangerous troublemakers, rather than as little helpers that permit to propel our economy forward. For instance, in discussing the role of small industry in economic development it has at times been argued that the promotion of small industry in a rural or small-town setting is advantageous because it permits to economize on the overhead capital expenditures (water, power, housing, etc.) required by urbanized industry and its labour force. This position is, of course, entirely valid on the assumption that the supply of capital is fixed. But if we drop this assumption and let ourselves be guided by the rule that during a prolonged phase the essence of development strategy consists in maximizing stimuli toward additional forward steps, then we would favour rather than oppose the establishment of industries in cities precisely because it compels additional or complementary capital formation that otherwise might never take place.

Obviously, what we are opposing here is not the principle of husbanding capital in general, but a policy which in the name of this principle would reduce the stimuli and pressures towards additional capital formation that might emanate from the investments of a given period. Such a policy would indeed economize on capital requirements in the next period, but it would equally inhibit the supply of capital; in effect, therefore, it would 'economize' on capital *formation* rather than on capital.

I shall briefly mention how the concepts I have developed can be applied to the analysis of the industrialization process. The structural interdependence of the economy provides us with the kind of direct stimuli we are looking for. Every activity that uses inputs and produces outputs sets up certain incentives or pressures for the domestic production of some of the inputs and for the setting up of ever new activities utilizing the outputs. These forces, which I call backward and forward linkage effects, can be analysed and then perhaps consciously utilized in planning development. For instance, the case for the industrialization of underdeveloped countries can in my opinion be stated far more convincingly on the grounds that industry is superior to agriculture with respect to these 'linkage' effects than because of any uniformly higher productivity in industry.

The concept of backward linkage rests to a considerable extent on the fact that for a wide range of industrial activities the size of the domestic market is an important determinant of profitability. When domestic demand in some line exceeds a 'threshold' value, it becomes economically feasible and attractive to undertake production. Now if it is true that capital formation depends largely on stimuli such as those that emanate from linkage effects, then it would be an objective of development policy to shape the process of industrialization with an eye to these thresholds, attempting to bunch them at an early stage of the development process when actual capital formation falls considerably short of the capabilities of the economy and spacing them on the contrary later on when the economic operators have learned how to call forth and mobilize savings.

Thus far, we have explored how economic progress can be communicated by one firm or one sector to another, how new economic activity can be called forth. In addition, underdeveloped countries encounter constant difficulties in *maintaining* existing activities in a good state of efficiency and in combating the corrosive forces of backwardness that still surround all new ventures. Thus opens up another important field of inquiry that is concerned with the mechanisms that induce or ensure growth and efficiency of the individual firm. In this inquiry, we should not count too much on help from the outside, whether in the form of the whip or wind of competition or in that of rapidly increasing demand stemming from other ventures arising in the course of a 'balanced growth' process; for in this way we would effectively assume away the specific difficulties of underdeveloped countries, where competition is weak and where new firms are often lonely outposts of modernism during a prolonged period. Rather, we must investigate how pressures toward efficiency, or aids in achieving it, can be built into the individual firm. Our question is really: What is the nature of the activities which underdeveloped countries are typically good at?

My earliest observation in this field was that Latin American countries as a group seemed to be so much better in running airlines than in keeping up their highway systems. I suggested as explanation for this fact that the latitude for poor performance is very narrow indeed in case of airlines. Airlines must be maintained and must be flown by highly skilled personnel whereas highways can be built by average to mediocre engineers, maestros and workmen. Lack of maintenance here leads first to a few holes, not to immediate disaster. This kind of consideration can lead to a revision of traditional ideas on the comparative advantage of the less developed countries. Perhaps they are best in industries where the nature of the process or the product compels quality and maintenance and it is possible that the technically complex and capital intensive industries toward which these considerations point are the real vocational and industrial schools for these countries. It is here that work habits important for the further industrial development are acquired and then spread to other sectors of the economy. It is therefore, in my opinion, quite wrong to criticize a government for undertaking certain industrial activities when so many other tasks that are the normal responsibility of the government remain unfulfilled. In some situation the building up of a cement industry by a government may be a necessary detour which will eventually enable it to tackle its basic problems of law and order, public administration and education.

Coming back to our subject, I will now try to anticipate and evade the question that will surely be thrown at me, namely, 'Would you actually plan imbalance if you were called upon to advise a planning agency?' I believe I have answered that question in my book[1] by saying that we must all think of ourselves as both creators of imbalance and restorers of balance. To advocate balanced growth without any consciousness of this dual function would be the economist's equivalent of the engineer's 'sticking to his blueprint' and refusing ever to get his hands dirty. Every decision in the development process means either to create an imbalance or to correct one and often both. Once we recognize this we can begin to reason about kinds of imbalance that are conducive to further growth and those that are dangerous to it, in various environments.

I believe that several other practical consequences can be drawn from the approach I have sketched:

In the first place there are some consequences for the allocation of the time and energy of economists and other social scientists that are involved in development work. In my opinion they should concentrate on identifying ventures and reform moves that are required *next* and should not worry unduly about taking care in advance of *all* the conceivable repercussions and consequential difficulties of such moves. The opposition between planning and lack of planning is far less clear cut than many planners realize. Was it lack of planning when the United States developed the

---

[1] *The Strategy of Economic Development*, Yale University Press, New Haven, 1958.

automobile without providing at the same time for smog control? And yet sometimes, it seems to me, we think that it is the proper role of the planning adviser to say, 'You can't do that because you will run into this or that difficulty or shortage', just as it has long been the role of the financial adviser to say, 'You can't do that because it leads to inflation'.

We must realize that many difficulties must be experienced as such before society will attack them in earnest; and in a rapidly changing society the only way to identify difficulties correctly and to find the appropriate remedies is often to run up against them.

Secondly, even when planning composite projects whose success ultimately depends on the coming together of their various components — multi-purpose river valley development schemes are an example — we should always think in terms of a 'second-best' sequential solution rather than in terms of the ideal simultaneous one which is unlikely to be achieved. To plan only in terms of the various components falling into place at the same time is to invite a third-best abortive sequence that may well spell failure of the whole project.

Thirdly, policy-makers or advisers should not get obsessed with one obstacle or one prerequisite or with ready-made first-things-first rules. As we have seen, obstacles can be turned and prerequisites can be put into place *ex post*. Let us learn from the industrial engineers who have recently discovered that in certain operator-controlled factory operations there is no such thing as 'one best sequence'.

I am well aware that my conclusions are perhaps most repugnant to the policy-makers in the underdeveloped countries themselves. They know well the difficulties and tensions and imbalances in which they are perennially caught and they just want to believe with all their heart that somewhere a formula exists which, if only punctiliously followed, will permit an escape from this unpleasantly dissonant reality and lead to harmonious, polyphonic, balanced growth. It is tempting for the foreign adviser (who is only human after all) to take advantage of this state of mind and to present himself as a sort of shaman who has all sorts of wonderous cures up his sleeve. Nevertheless, I believe that the real task of social scientists is to help the leaders of the newly developing countries to scrutinize their own experience and, instead of rejecting it outright, to search in it for clues to the strategy best suited to their own environment.

UNBALANCED GROWTH*

by Paul Streeten

natura facit saltus

I. INTRODUCTION

'Everything of importance has been said before, by someone who did not discover it.' Whitehead's dictum is probably also true of the doctrine of balanced growth. Friedrich List certainly formulated clearly the case for balanced national growth. In his *Nationale System der politischen Oekonomie*[1] he stressed the importance of development which is balanced between material and mental occupations,[2] between agriculture, manufacturing, and commerce,[3] and between different branches of manufacturing.[4] He saw clearly the connexion between development and complementarities both on the technical side[5] and on the side of demand.[6] He emphasized particularly the complementarity between transport and manufacturing[7] and the mutual stimulation of correctly composed production and consumption.[8] He warned, of course, above all against the dangers of lop-sided development that arise from specialization in primary production and reliance on imported manufactured goods.

Allyn Young in his famous 1928 article, elaborated Adam Smith's proposition that the division of labour is limited by the extent of the market. He replaced 'division of labour' by 'inducement to invest', i.e. inducement to produce in a more capitalistic, 'roundabout' manner, and the geographical extent by the economic size

* *Economic Integration*, Sythoff, Leiden (Holland), 1961, pp. 106-52. Reprinted by permission of Sythoff and the author.

The author is indebted to Professor Tibor Scitovsky for having aroused his interest in this subject, and for having helped with stimulating suggestions in conversation in the summer of 1956. Some of his views have since appeared in 'Growth — Balanced or Unbalanced?' in Scitovsky's *The Allocation of Economic Resources; Essays in Honor of Bernard Francis Haley*, Stanford University Press, 1959. For more specific references to his published work, see below.

[1] 1841. The page references are to the edition by Heinrich Waentig.
[2] pp. 251, 328. [3] pp. 212, 251, 328, 332, 507. [4] p. 252.
[5] p. 252. [6] pp. 279-80. [7] p. 14 *et seq.* [8] p. 332.

of the market, i.e. the level of demand. And he made the two interdependent, subject to the qualification that supply must be balanced. The inducement to invest depends upon the size of the market, and the size of the market depends on productivity. But productivity in turn depends upon the use of capital whose application yields increasing returns. In Allyn Young's article, the doctrine of balanced growth appears as a qualification to Say's law. The size of the market, i.e. the level of demand, is determined by the volume of production, but 'the conception of a market in this inclusive sense — an aggregate of productive activities tied together by trade — carries with it the notion that there must be some sort of balance, that different productive activities must be proportioned to one another'.[1] 'The rate at which one industry grows is conditioned by the rate at which other industries grow, but since the elasticities of demand and of supply will differ for different products, some industries will grow faster than others. Even with a stationary population and in the absence of new discoveries in pure or applied science there are no limits to the process of expansion except the limits beyond which demand is not elastic and returns do not increase.'[2]

Mr Rosenstein-Rodan developed the idea that the use of capital by any single entrepreneur is inhibited by the small size of the market for *his* product.[3] He modified Allyn Young's doctrine in two logically connected ways: first, investment of a largely widening type (as compared with Young's largely more 'roundabout' investment) is the generator of higher incomes: second, disguised unemployment provides the labour reserve for this increase. The market is enlarged not by improvements in productivity following investment, but by putting unemployed men to produce a balanced output. Increasing returns result not from technical economies but from external economies due to higher, mutually supporting, demand.

[1] Allyn Young, 'Increasing Returns and Economic Progress', *Economic Journal*, December 1928, p. 533.

[2] Allyn Young, loc. cit., p. 534. Young speaks here of an 'elastic demand' for a commodity 'in the special sense that a small increase in its supply will be attended by an increase in the amounts of other commodities which can be had in exchange for it'.

[3] Paul N. Rosenstein-Rodan, 'Problems of Industrialization of Eastern and South-Eastern Europe', *Economic Journal*, June-September 1943, pp. 250–7, reprinted in Agarwala and Singh (eds.), *The Economics of Underdevelopment*, Oxford University Press, Bombay, 1958, pp. 245–55.

More recently the case for balanced growth has been restated
and elaborated lucidly by Professor Ragnar Nurkse.[1] In his presentation balanced growth appears in the context of the size of the market
and the inducement to invest. In his controversy with Mr Fleming,
it became clear that Nurkse assumed a given labour force and elastic
capital supply.[2] On these assumptions the doctrine says that the
inducement to invest will be stronger if any given amount of capital
is applied to the production of a variety of products in accordance
with income elasticities of demand,[3] than in any other way. It is
fairly obvious that any *given* supply of capital is more profitably
and more sensibly used in a balanced way. To say merely that the
inducement to invest depends on the extent of the market in this
sense is not very revealing, indeed is almost tautologous. Only by
adding that the extent of the market also depends on the inducement to invest is the possibility of a process of cumulative growth
illuminated. The inducement to higher investment generates a larger
market — either because of disguised unemployment or because
investment raises productivity — and this reinforces the inducement
to invest. Either some reserve of unemployed or productivity-
raising investment or both must be assumed in order to assert more
than that any given supply of labour is used more efficiently if
applied to the production of what is wanted than of what is
unwanted.

To say that a small unbalanced investment project is worse than
a large project of balanced investment is illuminating only if we add
that several small and unprofitable projects would become profitable
if undertaken together, lending each other support, either through
cost reductions or through demand creation.

The doctrine of balanced growth is now widely accepted,[4] and
balanced growth is almost axiomatic as a desirable objective, for

[1] Ragnar Nurkse, *Problems of Capital Formation in Underdeveloped Countries*, Basil Blackwell, Oxford, 1953, pp. 11–14. Ragnar Nurkse's tragic death
occurred while an earlier version of this chapter was in the press. It will be
obvious how much it owes to him. But beyond that, Nurkse was always
patient, helpful and stimulating in his letters, allowing one to share his
thoughts and opening new vistas.

[2] R. Nurkse, ' Balanced Growth on Static Assumptions ', *Economic Journal*,
June 1956, pp. 365ff.

[3] Price elasticities would, of course, also have to be taken into account.

[4] e.g. W. A. Lewis, *Theory of Economic Growth*, George Allen & Unwin,
London, 1955, pp. 275–83 ; W. W. Lockwood, *The Economic Development of*

both developed and underdeveloped countries, on both sides of the iron curtain. Such diverse sources as the numerous reports of missions of the International Bank for Reconstruction and Development, the *Monthly Letters* of the First National City Bank of New York, and the discussions on the *Economic Report of the President* bear witness to this.[1] In the Soviet Union, the doctrine appears as the 'Law of Planned, Proportionate Development', according to which the planning commission must insure that the rates of growth of the various sectors of the economy are consistent with one another and with the rate of final output implied by the policy directives of the government.[2]

Yet, occasional rumblings of dissent can be heard. Professor Kindleberger expressed an instinctive distrust of the doctrine of balanced growth:

The choice between attacking on a wide front and storming key positions is a perennial one. . . . Without knowing which or how many priority targets must be attacked to get the dynamic process of economic development under way on a cumulative basis, instinct suggests that this may be a more fruitful method than balance. The Nurkse argument has a logical ring. But economic development in the past did not spring full blown from the brow of an economist. Nor is there any reason to think that it will be impossible to duplicate historical development which has been piece-meal in its strategic aspects, if one can duplicate the critical conditions or contrive a comparable set of interacting phenomena.[3]

Japan, Princeton University Press, Princeton, N.J., 1954, p. 227; G. M. Meier and R. E. Baldwin, *Economic Development*, John Wiley & Sons, New York, 1957, pp. 347-8, 361f, 376, 400.

[1] *Report of the Joint Committee on the January 1956 Economic Report of the President*, March 1956, p. 2. Similarly, the *Monthly Letter* of the First National City Bank of New York, e.g. November 1957, p. 122. See also the American Federation of Labour-Congress of Industrial Organizations : *The National Economy in Review, Balanced Economic Growth Needed* (1957). It must be admitted that the expression often serves merely as a fashionable empty catch-phrase.

[2] See United Nations Economic Commission for Europe, *Economic Survey of Europe in 1955*, p. 202.

[3] *Review of Economics and Statistics*, November 1952, p. 392. More recently, however, the voices of opposition have been heard more loudly and more coherently. The most important plea for unbalance has been made by Albert O. Hirschman, whose book *The Strategy of Economic Development*, Yale University Press, New Haven, 1958, reached me only after a first draft of this

Now it is obvious that development *means* disturbing an equilibrium, upsetting a balance; the equilibrium of a stable society, the balance of forces that perpetuate the *status quo*. Is there more than instinct and platitude in the notion that unbalance and disturbance are of the very nature of growth?

2. The Meaning of Balanced Growth

Balanced growth has a variety of meanings, and different aspects have been stressed by different authors. I shall try to give a general definition that comprises the different meanings and emphases.

Whenever several non-infinitesimal investment decisions (or decisions generally) depend for their success upon each other, simultaneous investment (action) in a series of industries (or firms or plants) in conformity with the pattern of consumers' demand and of different industries' (firms', plants') demand for each other's products is required.

The investment decisions must be non-infinitesimal, for if investment could be carried out in infinitesimally small steps (and if entrepreneurial attention were perfectly divisible), successive investments in different lines would be possible and profitable.

To what extent actions must be strictly simultaneous will be discussed below (see pp. 26f). Balanced growth has a horizontal and a vertical aspect. It implies a balance between, say, shoes, food, and clothing, but also between agricultural raw materials and manufacturing production, between capital goods and consumers' goods, between public utilities and other investment, between exports and production for the home market, etc. The case for balanced growth rests upon the relation of complementarity between wants, between factors, and between factors and products at various stages of production.

essay had been written. Professor Kindleberger also has elaborated his views in chapter 9 of *Economic Development*, McGraw Hill, New York, 1958. Another interesting plea for unbalanced growth is made in the Interim Report of the F.A.O. Mediterranean Project, Rome, 1957, prepared by a team headed by Mr T. Balogh. See also his ' The Strategy and Tactics of Technical Assistance ', *Public Administration*, Winter 1959. Professor J. M. Montias has permitted me to read a mimeographed copy of his ' Balanced Growth and International Specialization : A Diagrammatic Analysis ', which contains an elegant proof that in certain conditions unbalanced growth is preferable. (Now published in *Oxford Economic Papers*, June 1961.)

The definition of balanced growth can be extended from investment decisions to economic activities generally, and even to any other events whose simultaneous presence is required in order to achieve a desired result (e.g. the decision to reduce the time for national service should be accompanied by a decision to enlarge the intake at universities).

The argument that balanced growth demands planning (public or private co-ordination of decisions) is based on the correct view that in a system where decisions on the production of complementary goods are taken separately, progress may be impaired if these decisions do not dovetail.[1] *Successive* adaptation, which is the chief virtue of the price mechanism (as a system of both signals and incentives), will not work, or will work only wastefully, for the complementarity demands that several things be done simultaneously, not successively. Nor is it, as one might think, a matter of promoting information and removing ignorance.[2] Since the success of A's action depends upon B's, and *vice versa*, full knowledge by each of the other's plans is no solution. The trouble arises not from an

[1] In a lecture published in 1958, Nurkse said : ' According to some writers the balanced growth argument implies that the market mechanism is eliminated and that investments must be effected according to a co-ordinated plan. This opinion, which is widely held, seems to me dubious. . . . As a means of creating inducements to invest, balanced growth can be said to be relevant primarily to a private enterprise system. State investment can and often does go ahead without any market incentives. Planning authorities can apply capital, if they have any, wherever they may choose. . . . It is private investment that is attracted by markets and that needs the inducement of growing markets. It is here that the element of mutual support is so useful and, for rapid growth, indispensable.' ' The Conflict between " Balanced Growth " and International Specialization ', *Lectures on Economic Development*, published by the Faculty of Economics, Istanbul University, reprinted in R. Nurkse, *Equilibrium and Growth in the World Economy*, Harvard University Press, Cambridge (Mass.), 1961.

This argument is difficult to follow. Clearly both public and private investment can be and have been wasteful — where the dictates of balance are ignored (though we shall see that this need not be so). The point is that the price mechanism, by itself, does not produce that simultaneous, mutually supporting, advance that balanced growth requires. Only conscious co-ordination, which may be governmental or private, can do this.

[2] Messrs Bauer and Yamey therefore appear to be mistaken when they argue that ' on the postulated assumptions that the combined group of activities would be economic and that the government is aware of this, there is a presumption that the industries would in fact be established if the information

inconsistency of plans or from ignorance, but because, without a co-ordination of decisions (which may require central planning) no valid basis of correct anticipations of success exists.[1]

Thus the doctrine of balanced growth is right if it stresses that in certain conditions the obstacle created by one type of activity overshooting the mark *may* lead to losses and waste. There is no point in having a steel mill without fuel, or electrical equipment without power; if essential imports are needed but there are no exports (or loans), production is brought to a stop; if savings are attempted but no investment occurs, they will be abortive; if capacity accumulates but there is no demand for its output, it will be wasted, etc. Unbalanced growth may not be growth at all. If a starving and closed society raises its output of shirts by 10 per cent, but reduces its output of bread by 1 per cent, it cannot be said to have progressed. Unwanted production is not production.

But the doctrine is wrong if it maintains that unbalance *must* delay or halt progress. The tenor of the argument in this essay

is made available and is encouraging '. *The Economics of Underdeveloped Countries*, Cambridge University Press, Cambridge, 1957, p. 249.

Professor Scitovsky, in his stimulating article ' Two Concepts of External Economies ', *Journal of Political Economy*, 1954, reprinted in Agarwala and Singh (eds.), *The Economics of Underdevelopment*, Oxford University Press, Bombay, pp. 295–308, also argues that prices communicate current, not future, decisions ; but since investment relates to the future, the pricing system fails as a signalling device. He acknowledges in a footnote that trading in futures could, formally, overcome this difficulty. But the real reason for his correct conclusion is not the difficulty of foreseeing the future, but the absence of any information — whether about present or future — to be conveyed without co-ordination of decisions. Unless A invests, B will have no profits, and unless B invests, A will have none.

On the other hand, it is possible in certain conditions that a situation in which no independent information is available has yet a determinate solution, because people expect others to co-ordinate their expectations and actions. Mutual recognition of a co-ordinating signal, however ' irrational ', will increase the chances of actual co-ordination. Cf. Thomas C. Schelling, *The Strategy of Conflict*, Harvard University Press, Cambridge (Mass.), 1960, pp. 54ff. Whether these peculiar conditions are fulfilled in the case of business decisions to invest is another question.

[1] On the other hand, pseudo-information may be as good as co-ordination. Thus the announcement by governments of development plans appears to have led in several countries to an increase in investment and output in the private sector, although the plans were not implemented.

is that in certain conditions unbalance may stimulate rather than impair progress, that it may be a condition of, rather than an obstacle to, rapid growth, and that too great an emphasis on balance may cause, rather than prevent stagnation. Bottlenecks may not only, in some conditions, hold back production, but they may also, in other conditions, powerfully stimulate the growth of the complementary activity that has lagged behind.

3. COMPLEMENTARITY

Professor Nurkse writes: 'Most industries catering for mass consumption are *complementary* in the sense that they provide a market for, and thus support, each other. This basic *complementarity* stems, in the last analysis, from the diversity of human wants. The case for "balanced growth" rests on the need for a "balanced diet".'[1] At first sight it looks as if the case for balanced growth rested on the complementarity of wants, or rather of consumption goods. Yet complementarity can support the argument for unbalance.

A few words about complementarity should clarify the discussion. First, complementarity is a matter of degree. Where complementarity between two things is very strong we speak of one rather than two commodities or factors. A pair of shoes is *one* pair, not one left and one right shoe, except where one-legged markets are important. Complementarities in consumers' choice are likely to be weaker than complementarities dictated by technology,[2] although the latter can be overcome through foreign trade.

Next, we may distinguish between complementarities according to the nature of the objects of the relationship. There are not only complementarities between human wants (bread and butter) or

[1] Op. cit., p. 11. My italics.
[2] Some qualification is perhaps required. Although the plasticity of wants may be greater than that of technical requirements, postponement is much easier for the use of capital goods. Many capital goods are produced for use in the future and the supply of complementary goods can wait for a considerable time. In order to get efficient use of the investment sector in spite of an ill-balanced distribution of equipment or materials, price differentials need not be so great as they would have to be in the consumption sector. In both sectors increased availability of foreign exchange allows greater flexibility. On the relation of foreign trade to the doctrine of balanced growth, see below, pp. 41-4.

groups of wants[1] (bread and circuses, income and leisure), but also between factors of production,[2] (screws and nuts, locomotives and engine drivers), and between factors and products (usually called specificity of factors). There is also complementarity between decisions to save and to invest. If savings are attempted without investment, income reduction will wipe them out; if attempted investment expands without savings, inflation will render some of it nugatory. Complementarity prevails between exports and imports, between exports and domestic production, between the present (consumption and production) and the future, between productive capacity and consumption.[3]

Complementarities may also exist between what are usually taken to be the data and the variables of economic analysis. The existence of a market and of a legal system is a condition for the supply of factors. Similarly, technical education and entrepreneurial capacity are complementary; so are health and the supply of labour, etc.

Finally, we should distinguish between static and dynamic complementarities. Thus the complementarity of consumption goods may be due to either of two factors; the indivisibility of certain goods, or what might be called the anabolism[4] of wants. Only a static view of human nature takes the diversity of wants as given. The most important complementarities, however, arise in the process of rising consumption. Similarly, technical complementarities may arise or may become apparent only with the growth of knowledge and inventions. Investment (like consumption) may not only meet existing needs but generate new needs and new investment opportunities.

[1] Strictly speaking it is not the complementarity of wants that gives rise to the problem of balance, but the complementarity of consumption goods ministering to complementary or even the same wants. This type of complementarity has been stressed by Rosenstein-Rodan and Nurkse.

[2] e.g., in *Economic Survey of Europe in 1955*, United Nations Economic Commission for Europe, p. 76, W. Arthur Lewis, op. cit.

[3] This aspect is emphasized in the E.C.E. SURVEY quoted in the previous footnote. 'Balanced economic growth can be defined as a development in which the growth of consumption matches the growth of productive capacity in the consumer-goods sector', p. 76. Similarly, the American Federation of Labour and Congress of Industrial Organizations emphasize in their pamphlet, sub-titled 'Balanced Economic Growth Needed', the relation between investment and consumption. *The National Economy in Review* (1957), p. 3.

[4] Anabolism (= constructive metabolism) : 'The process in an organism or a single cell, by which nutritive material is built up into living matter.' *The Shorter Oxford English Dictionary*.

Progress consists in the discovery and generation of new wants clustering on each other, and of new technological gaps, as much as, or even more than, in meeting existing wants and filling existing technological gaps.

The following discussion will state the case for unbalance, first for consumption, then for production. Both will be subdivided into static arguments, concerned with indivisibilities in the face of given wants and technology, and dynamic arguments, dealing with the stimulus to new wants, new activities and technical innovations. Then the relationship between balanced or unbalanced growth and foreign transactions is examined. Finally, the argument is extended to apply to the relation between saving and investment.

4. Unbalance and Consumption

(a) Indivisibility

Common observation suggests and surveys confirm that most people think that, if their incomes were 20 per cent higher, they would be comfortably off. This opinion does not appear to depend on how much income they actually get. It seems both to confirm (dynamically) and to contradict (statically) the doctrine of the insatiability of wants. One possible explanation of this puzzle lies in the fact that many commodities can be bought only in large and expensive units, so that either we overshoot the mark that would be dictated by equalizing marginal utilities, and then feel pinched in other directions, or we refrain from buying the commodity and then feel its absence acutely. The feeling of deprivation caused by our inability to equate marginal rates of substitution is as strong as the satisfaction from the additional consumption, and leaves us with the same feeling of discontent as before. Wicksteed expressed this point as follows:

Thus, where large units come into competition with small ones and with each other, we are always vaguely conscious of either being in arrears or being in advance in our expenditure on the large units. If I have not a piano I am conscious of the pressure of an unsatisfied want which is slowly accumulating until it shall be of sufficient weight and volume to justify the whole expenditure. Meanwhile it is absolutely unsatisfied, whereas the wants to which smaller units minister are partially satisfied, though all the while I feel that they do not add as much to the value of life as an occasional hour of the piano would do if I could get it *pro rata parte* at a fraction of the price of complete command. And when I have got my piano I am conscious, from time to time, when my appetite for playing on an inferior instrument is temporarily sated, that I would very gladly curtail my opportunities of gratifying it, if I could thereby relieve the general pressure I feel at all the points at which small units might minister to unsated desires. Probably the impossibility of bringing these two classes of expenditure into perfect harmony goes a long way towards explaining that almost universal experience embodied in the aphorism, 'A competence is a little more than a man has.' Conscious of a ragged edge in our expenditure, and especially of some few things, purchasable in large units, of which we constantly feel the want, we imagine that if we had them we should be satisfied. As a matter of fact they have merely attracted to themselves our whole sense of dissatisfaction. If we got these particular articles, promontories would just at these points be substituted for bays, but the coast would be no more even than before. Certain other wants would now be realized and new voids would begin to ache. Perhaps we should be quite conscious that our general level of well-being and satisfaction was raised, but the vague uneasiness caused by the uneven edge would still be there.[1]

In fact, however, few services can be enjoyed only by purchasing indivisible commodities. Pianos and cars can be hired by the hour. The trouble is that consumption *pro rata*, though not impossible, is more expensive. An individual who equates marginal rates of substitution to price-ratios will be worse off than one who tolerates some imbalance. For the individual, just as for the nation (as we shall see later) there arises therefore a choice between higher real income (and therefore opportunity for faster growth) at the cost of imbalance, and lower real income (and risk of slower growth) with the advantage of balance.[2]

(b) Anabolism

An observation of the growth of wants in a dynamic society shows that new wants are created in the process of satisfying existing

[1] Wicksteed, *The Common Sense of Political Economy*, Routledge & Kegan Paul, London, 1933, pp. 100f.

[2] Hire-purchase would not meet the requirement for two reasons : first, though the flow of payments is divisible, the commodity bought is indivisible : we can spread payment of £1,000 or of £1,500 over time, but there may be no car for £1,250. Secondly, the instalment payments are contractual commitments, and adjustments to changing needs are impossible.

ones, and that complex consumption patterns spring from simple innovations, 'as if increase of appetite had grown by what it fed on'. A swimming-pool in the garden requires all kinds of equipments to heat the water, disinfect it, drain it, remove algae, as well as steps, a diving board, hand rails and a surface skimmer. But it also invites a flagstone terrace, the terrace demands deck-chairs and tables and the tables insist on supporting martini glasses. And perhaps one wants to build a cabana and install underwater lights for night-swimming. Some people add an outdoor bar and a juke-box. High-fidelity enthusiasts are continually improving the weakest link in the chain of tuner, amplifier, player, speaker. But the elimination of the source of trouble always shows up the relative weakness of another link, on which all attention is then concentrated. It is not a question of keeping up with the Joneses, but of keeping up with the old Adam.

Another illustration is the growth of the taste for small boats in America, in which Europe may soon follow. In a dispatch headed 'A boat in every suburban backyard', *The Times* Washington Correspondent wrote on 29 May, 1959:

Nourishing and catering for this love for messing about in boats has become big business, worth some $2,100m. (£750m.) last year and, it is confidently predicted, considerably more this year. These figures are made up not by the sale of boats or engines alone, of course, but by the many associated enterprises that have sprung up. Trailers to haul the boats to water — and some long hauls are involved in some states like Arizona — water skis, nautical equipment like compasses, small radar units and radios, petrol and petrol pumps to fuel the boats (yachtsmen are a inority), life-jackets; these account for many millions Then, of course, there are the trifles and the gew cocktail shakers for splicing the mainbrace, ya ear-rings, red for the port lobe, green for the star ship's chandler would be complete without a signal flags; the device of a glass to announce how explosive togetherness must sometimes b to show the presence on board of the capta axe, his mother-in-law.

Just as a whole commercial complex ha roads of America, so the Yacht basins electricity, telephone, freshwater outle

The correspondent sees in the lakes lines a new frontier for the leisure beckon in various directions, offe

(c) Complementarities and growth

What are the relations between these complementarities and economic growth? First, imbalance may be a condition for attaining higher income than would otherwise be possible. But it provides also one of the answers to the question why consumption has risen with income to such a surprising extent, and why the fears of under-consumptionists have proved (relatively) unjustified. In a growing and enterprising society, these complementarities in consumption budgets provide a strong incentive for investment and further production, which would be absent had there been fully balanced growth, in conformity with the pattern of consumers' demand. If wants were satisfied by balanced growth, people would have to think up new ways of spending income. Inertia or lack of imagination may then prevent a further rise. But the complementarities, whether caused by indivisibility or anabolism, create pressures and a sense of deprivation, which stimulate and guide investment, and guarantee its profitability. Investment opportunities are created by new consumption opportunities, which in turn result from unbalance.

It is true that some losses may (but need not) have to be set against these gains. The shift in demand towards the new items may be at the expense of industries from which the demand is diverted.[1] But since income grows, this need not be so, and even when there is an absolute decline in demand for a particular good or service there will be a net stimulus to investment, because dis-investment is limited to not replacing whereas net investment can be larger.

ce might lead to a curtailment of the activity d, or it might stimulate the one that was left eck can be eliminated by widening the bottle-ng the flow through it. The rise in the use of cars on on the roads. In America a $40 billion road-is in progress, which will lead to the growth ry services, and may even transform the face Britain the instinctive reaction to traffic restrict motoring. In extreme cases of ment without its complement is bound ple respond to expansionist pressures, l stimulus.

he destructive process (katabolism),

A high elasticity of supply will make it easier to accommodate unbalanced growth. But the process is cumulative. The higher rate of growth raises the elasticity of supply, which accommodates the unbalanced growth. A lower rate would present a more serious obstacle to unbalanced growth which in turn in this case would slow down growth. And the doctrine of balanced growth may well be more applicable to the initial stages of growth, though even there some arguments point the other way. For one of the objectives of development is precisely to raise supply elasticities. The pressures created by lack of balance may render factors of production, and particularly entrepreneurial decisions, more responsive to economic incentives.

The chain reactions described above need not be the result of meeting existing wants but may spring spontaneously from some discovery intended for an entirely different purpose. The wireless, the car, and the cinema may serve as illustrations. The uses foreseen by Marconi were wireless transmission between ships, and between ships and shore, where no wires could be laid. Marconi tried to recoup his outlays from royalties on apparatus hired to the fleet. The vast entertainment industry that sprang from his invention had nothing to do with the initial intention, and came to depend, after the mid-1930's, upon electricity in the home.

Similarly the first use of motor cars was on farms, and pleasure motoring sprang up rather unexpectedly. Moving pictures were a casual invention used in side-shows on fairgrounds. Again today one of the great success stories since the War has been that of the business dictating machine which has established itself as a form of do-it-yourself entertainment in the role of the tape recorder. Progress in all these instances does not consist in a response t meeting existing needs, but in creating a new sphere of needs new lack of balance (or 'promontory' to use Wicksteed's meta which later activity attempts to correct.

5. UNBALANCE AND PRODUCTION

(a) Indivisibilities

Gross investment in new capacity is under for the gross accretion of demand that res

(i) the secular rise in incomes;

(ii) the scrapping of old and obsolete capacity;

(iii) shifts in the pattern of demand.[1]

But all three sources are themselves partly determined by the rate of investment and innovation. The definition of balanced growth, it will be recalled, is simultaneous investment in several industries in conformity with the pattern of consumers' demand and of different industries' demand for each other's products. But for many economies without large markets, investment that meets these criteria will be below the size that would allow optimum use of equipment. Given the demand curves at that income level, price would have to fall to such an extent that losses would be incurred if production were to take place at the lowest cost point. But an outward shift of the demand curves (a distortion of the pattern of consumers' demand) enables the output to be absorbed. The gradual growth of income raises the demand curves and removes, in due course, the initial distortion.

Assume five different products. Each is produced by a plant with a capacity of 20,000. Assume that the gross accretion of annual demand from the sources listed above occurs at the rate of 20,000 for each product, i.e. 100,000 in total. Assume further that the technically optimum plant has a capacity of 100,000. Balanced growth requires the installation of five sub-optimum plants of 20,000 every year, unbalanced growth the installation of one optimum plant of 100,000 each year. But in this case demand might have to be temporarily distorted, or excess capacity would have to be carried, although after five years balance can be restored at a higher rate of growth. If we assume constant relative prices or zero elasticity of substitution, excess capacity and shortage of supply would be 80,000 in the first year, 120,000 in the second and ʰird years, 80,000 in the fourth, and balance could be restored in fifth year.

ⁱght be objected that the above five-year plan is really a balanced growth, only the time-period of balance is five d of one year. Since perfect simultaneity of complement- ts is impossible, we must try to average out over a

ᵈ the argument are taken from T. Scitovsky, petition, and European Integration', *American* now reprinted in his *Economic Theory and* win, London, 1958, ch. iii.

To this defence of the doctrine of balanced growth there are two replies. First, granted that ultimate balance is the aim, the doctrine leaves the period over which it is to be achieved ambiguous. It is possible to reformulate the choice between balance and imbalance in terms of choice between balance over periods of varying lengths. But the point is that there is such a choice, and the doctrine of balanced growth is either biased in favour of short-period balance or ambiguous.[1]

Secondly, balance need not be aimed at after five years. A new 5-year plan for unbalanced growth may be put up, say, for plants of 500,000 capacity, and so on, as long as economies of scale exist, so that balance is in fact never achieved. It does not appear that the concept of average balance is at all helpful here. Balanced growth, in such a situation, is neither correct as a method of procedure, nor as an ultimate objective.

We thus see that where economies of scale are important and the optimum size of equipment large, the situation is analogous to Wicksteed's piano player, faced with the choice of buying or renting a piano. It becomes a matter of choice whether balanced growth in the narrow, short-term sense, or greater economies of scale are desired. A plan directed at the full exploitation of economies of scale will be a plan for unbalanced growth. The choice lies between (1) a current sacrifice, in the form of distortion of demand[2] or shortage combined with surplus capacity, for greater cost

[1] This implicit bias in favour of short-period balance may be illustrated from the discussion of the doctrine of balanced growth in such an excellent textbook as G. M. Meier's and Robert E. Baldwin's *Economic Development*, op. cit. ' Such projects as steel mills, power plants, railways, or large manufacturing industries must be operated close to full capacity if the investment is to be most productive. This requires complementary industries to demand the output. Thus investment in one sector must always be considered with respect to the degree of complementarity among various sectors. Without sufficient complementarity, the large-scale investment project will not be economical: it will merely be an example of "conspicuous production".' p. 349.

[2] To say that distortion of demand entails a loss implies that the consumers' choice of the five products is not (a) irrational, (b) the result of habit, (c) due to other consumers' demanding these products, (d) due to lack of opportunity to choose between, on the one hand, the five products, and, on the other, fewer varieties at lower prices. If any of these assumptions is violated, concentration would not only yield gains in the future, but would impose no current sacrifice.

reductions in the future, and (2) optimum current use with higher
costs later. We have to strike a balance — or rather an imbalance —
between these two objectives. 'A system — any system, economic
or other — that at *every* given point of time fully utilizes its pos-
bilities to the best advantage may yet in the long run be inferior
to a system that does so at *no* given point of time, because the
latter's failure to do so may be a condition for the level of long-run
performance.'[1] In principle, the optimum amount of current distortion or under-utilization combined with shortages, is determined
by the time-preference of the community. If over-investment is
defined as 'failure to attain the ideal distribution of the community's
income of consumable goods through time',[2] the plan for unbalanced
growth need not imply over-investment. But even in theory, the
ideal distribution through time is an ambiguous concept, and in
practice all that can be said is that it must be a political decision
— even if only the decision to let the existing income and property
distribution settle the matter through the market forces.

A market economy too can achieve a higher rate of growth than
would be warranted by the doctrine of balanced growth. It can do
this in a variety of ways.

First, over-expansion may lead to price reductions which, however, still allow total costs to be covered. Even where a competitive
industry may not be able to cover costs, a discriminating monopoly
may do so. All this is still compatible with the doctrine of balanced
growth, which need assume neither constant prices nor competition.
But an investment may be socially justified though it cannot recover all costs even by discriminatory pricing.

[1] J. Schumpeter, *Capitalism, Socialism and Democracy*, George Allen &
Unwin, London, 1950, p. 83. The situation can be illustrated by a simple
diagram. Trace on the horizontal axis the degree of utilization of total productive capacity, as a possible index of 'balances', and on the vertical axis either
output or the rate of growth of output. The output curve may reach a
maximum at maximum utilization of capacity, but the growth curve may
reach its maximum earlier.

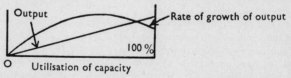

[2] D. H. Robertson, *A Study of Industrial Fluctuation*, P. S. King & Son,
Westminster, 1915, p. 180.

Secondly, advertising and other selling efforts may be used in order to switch demand into the lines in which expansion has occurred. Such distortions facilitate development and modernization. If successful, such efforts may be justified in the interest of growth. The higher the standard of living already attained, the easier it is to cajole demand into the new channels, partly because demand is more diversified because the new goods are not likely to be necessities, partly because there will be in any case the attraction of novelty.[1] An underdeveloped economy may have to use other methods than sales efforts to direct demand, e.g. discriminatory taxation and controls.

Thirdly, unexpected losses may be suffered and may be symptoms of unbalanced growth in a market economy. Those who over-optimistically over-estimated the chances of success will find that they have suffered losses, although the capacity created by them survives to serve higher production later than would otherwise have been possible. The losses during the railway mania are an outstanding example. But there is reason to suppose than an element of this is usually present. It is not those who calculate coolly the prospects of an investment, who form the entrepreneurial class, but the over-sanguine, who over-estimate their ability, their luck and the prospects. It is true that what matters is that they be more optimistic than other people, not more optimistic than the situation warrants. Hence in a situation of general gloom even the optimists may invest too little. But if spirits are buoyant, we can expect some entrepreneurs to forge ahead and create, at the cost of disappointments to themselves, the capacity that will be enjoyed later by others.

The mere fact that the lines built during the railway mania have not been torn up but are still used, although interest charges have been discarded, does not, of course, prove that the investment was

---

[1] It is easier, and less harmful, for a rich man to eat, if necessary, strawberries without cream, than for a poor man to eat chips without fish. On the other hand, certain things that do not go together in a poor society become strongly complementary as the society advances, e.g. plumbing and houses. Strength of complementarity is partly a matter of habit. 'Invention is the mother of necessity' as Veblen observed (A. O. Hirschman, *The Strategy of Economic Development*, op. cit., p. 68). This is true not only of consumption but also of production. See below, p. 36.

socially sound.[1] It might have been better had the capital been put into some other project. On the other hand, it is quite possible for the lines to be run at a loss (even if a perfectly discriminatory price policy were pursued) for a considerable time, and yet for the eventual growth in demand to be sufficient to yield interest on the principal, on the interest re-borrowed, and on any extra capital borrowed to finance losses. Even if the lines never earn sufficient income to pay these compounded charges, so that losses are permanent, they will have yielded external economies in the form of lower costs or higher demand for the products of other enterprises. It is true that they, in turn, may, after a time, reap some of the external economies of those enterprises that benefited from them. Lower transport costs will reduce the price of steel and lower the costs of railway construction. It is also true that there may be diseconomies. Nevertheless, if default occurs before the ultimate gains have had time to accrue, or in conditions in which sufficient net gains accrue to other enterprises, the investors have made socially correct decisions, though they do not reap the rewards.

In so far as it is merely a matter of waiting long enough (rather than a matter of external economies), the obvious solution would appear to be to finance these projects by adequate loans with distant maturity, or by repeated re-borrowing. But only lenders with distant time horizons would be willing to supply the capital. The span may reach beyond one generation. Moreover, in so far as the gains accrue, temporarily or permanently, to other enterprises, the full benefits can never be recouped by the industry in question.

In an economy which does not rely entirely on *laissez-faire*, there is a choice between forcing demand into line as described above, and subsidizing losses resulting from low prices or excess capacity. If the subsidies are financed by taxation, something is forgone in other directions by the taxpayers. The policy is sensible only if the ultimate benefits in cost reductions and external economies

---

[1] The argument on this and the next page is developed by Nurkse in his second Istanbul lecture ('Some Reflections on the International Financing of Public Overhead Investments', op. cit., pp. 22 and 25–8). But whilst he uses it to show that a *vertical* maladjustment, (too much overhead in relation to direct investment) can be a stimulus to growth, the crucial requirement is that the investment should be *lumpy* (static setting) and *initiatory* (dynamic setting). Cf. below, note on overhead v. direct investment.

exceed the benefits derived from the expenditures which have to
be sacrificed during the period of taxation plus subsidization. The
same is true if the subsidies are financed by loans from abroad,
unless the loans are tied to these projects, in which case their opportunity costs may be considerably lower. Whatever the method
chosen, full exploitation of large-scale economies may involve a
violation of the principle of balanced growth. Rosenstein-Rodan's
quotation from *Alice Through the Looking-Glass* is more apt to
illustrate the case of unbalanced growth in violation of the pattern
of consumers' demand:

'I should like to buy an egg, please' she said timidly. 'How
do you sell them?' 'Fivepence farthing for one — twopence for
two,' the Sheep replied. 'Then two are cheaper than one?' Alice
said in a surprised tone, taking out her purse. 'Only you *must*
eat them both, if you buy two,' said the Sheep. 'Then I'll have
one, please,' said Alice as she put the money down on the counter.
For she thought to herself, 'They mightn't be at all nice, you know.'

(b) Note on Overhead v. Direct Investment

After the bulk of this chapter had been written, Professor Ragnar
Nurkse sent me a reprint of two lectures.[1] In these very interesting
lectures Nurkse presents an argument essentially similar to the
one put forward in this section. But he attempts to maintain
consistency with the doctrine of balanced growth by drawing a
sharp distinction between what he calls overhead and direct investment.

The term 'direct investment' refers to miscellaneous business
investment and is not restricted to foreign business investment in
the present context, though of course it includes foreign direct
investment. Within a given framework of public facilities, direct
investment occurs over the whole range of industry, trade and agriculture, is suited to individual enterprise, and typically results in
quickly increased outputs of consumer or producer goods. It is within
the sphere of 'direct investment' that the balanced growth principle, which was discussed in the preceding lecture, is applicable
(in relation to the '*horizontal*' structure of consumer-goods production).

Overhead investment aims at providing the services — transport,
power, water-supply — which are *basic* for any productive activity,

[1] Op. cit.

cannot be imported from abroad, *require large and costly installations,* and in the history of western economies outside England, have usually called for *public* assistance or *public* enterprise. Because of the monopoly element that attaches to them they are now every-where subject at least to *public* regulation. Typically overhead investments take *a considerable time to reach maturity* in a growing economy. To be sure, all investments depend on expectations, but the time range of expectations is apt to be particularly long in overhead projects, because of their *lumpiness* combined with their *high* operational *capital-intensity.* (My italics.)

Nurkse goes on to argue that a *vertical* maladjustment resulting from too much overhead in relation to direct investment may be a powerful stimulus to growth. Before 1914 in countries such as America, Australia, Argentina and Canada, building overhead capacity (such as pioneer railways) ahead of demand, promoted growth and this should serve as a lesson for underdeveloped count-ries today.

Nurkse says that 'distinctions are always to some extent arbi-trary'. But the real difficulty is not where precisely to draw the distinction between 'overhead' and 'direct' investment, but to discover which distinction Nurkse considers to be crucial for se-parating the area to which the doctrine of balanced growth applies from that in which maladjustment and excess capacity serve as growth promoters. From the passage quoted above, the following distinctions can be extracted:

(1) vertical *v.* horizontal

(2) basic *v.* non-basic

(3) public *v.* private

(4) long construction period *v.* short (hence greater uncertainty *v.* smaller)

(5) long time before final goods produced *v.* short time

(6) non-importable *v.* importable

(7) capital-intensive *v.* labour intensive

(8) lumpy *v.* divisible

Now Nurkse appears to lay most stress on distinction (1):

. . . overhead investment in the provision of external economies appears as the active factor designed to induce growth in productive activity. Such investment led periodically to a state of maladjust-ment in the capital structure of the borrowing countries: too much capital in their overheads and too little in directly productive activities for export or domestic uses. *Now this is not a simple horizontal maladjustment such as an excess of toothbrushes combined with a shortage of mouth-organs. It is essentially a vertical maladjustment that tends to produce the kind of hiatus depicted by the Austrian capital and cycle theory.* (My italics.)

But it can surely not be true that vertical maladjustment is a stimulus, horizontal maladjustment a barrier to growth. For the combination of electric current, workers, machines and transport is equivalent to a balanced diet for the final consumers. His menu may have been prepared in kitchens at different floors, but the doctrine of balanced growth applies just as much to technical as to demand complementarities.

Nor are any of the other distinctions (2) to (7) relevant, if the question of growth promotion *versus* growth delay is under consideration. One crucial distinction is surely (8), viz. lumpiness. Where capacity can be added only in large blocks, excess capacity may lead (a) to lower unit costs in the longer run and hence higher incomes etc. and (b) to a clustering of complementary investments which also raise growth rates.

But lumpiness is not peculiar to public overhead investment. Worse still, for the doctrine of balanced growth, lumpiness was precisely the assumption on which this doctrine was constructed.[1] Only if investments are non-infinitesimal is simultaneous advance along a wide front needed to avoid waste. Otherwise successive adaptation in response to the price mechanism will do the trick.

Thus there appears a contradiction. Lumpiness seems to be required both for the doctrine of balanced growth, and for the doctrine of creative unbalance. In theory, the conflict can be resolved by postulating inter-temporal balance. In a static setting unbalance in any particular time period is justified if the costs of carrying excess capacity, or of distorting demand away from the balanced diet, are less than the discounted ultimate cost reductions and gains in real income. In a dynamic setting, the crucial distinction is one not found in Nurkse's list, but that between *initiatory* and *complementary* investment[2]— and initiatory investment may be in cars or swimming pools as well as in railways or roads. Indeed, in some societies the social overhead investment may occur in

---

[1] See pp. 12ff. above. [2] See below, pp. 36f.

response to pressures from direct investment in manufacturing industries having been pushed ahead. What is initiatory and what complementary depends partly on technological factors, partly on the distribution of the willingness and ability to take pioneering decisions, partly on the responses of different groups (entrepreneurs, civil servants, politicians, etc.) to different types of pressures and incentives.

(c) Dynamic Complementaries

The argument in section (a) has assumed a given rate of growth of demand, which can be pushed up by installing large-scale, under-utilized, equipment. In reality, there will be several additional forces at work, which determine the merits and drawbacks of excess capacity.

First, the advantages of building ahead of demand are not confined to economies of scale. Costs are incurred in expanding and rebuilding equipment from a smaller to a larger scale. Production may have to be interrupted, work done may have to be undone, etc. Such costs would not have been incurred if the initial outlay, instead of having been adapted to current demand, had been geared to a (future) larger demand.

On the other hand, however, it is possible that new inventions may become available, which make it appear wise to wait with heavy capital outlays. Building ahead has risks, as well as opportunities for economy.

Second, the accretion of demand may be due not only to the lowering of costs that resulted from the installation of large-scale equipment (the analogy of Wicksteed's piano player), but may be stimulated beyond that by the 'unbalanced' investment (the analogy of the swimming pools). The construction of railways in the nineteenth century and the river development schemes in this century did not merely meet existing demand, but created new demand by encouraging a whole cluster of activities: settlements along the tracks in the former case, the growth of industries and improved agriculture in the latter. The demand that arises, eventually, as a result of the initially unbalanced investment is substantially greater than that due to cost reductions from indivisibility.

It is said that the railways that Canada built in her great boom before World War I turned out to be thirty years ahead of their time. That may well be true, but the question is: would traffic requirements have increased as much as they actually did if as a matter of public policy railways had not been laid down in advance? Would the Canadian economy have grown at the same rate? Of course we must not forget the extra tax load which Canada had to carry in order to pay the 'pure tribute' of external interest before her railroads could earn their keep. This load may have tended to slow down the growth of her economy, but it seems doubtful whether this was a significant handicap. The existence of ample overheads surely brought some benefits that could not be appropriated in railway profit and loss accounts. It facilitated a great deal of direct investment later. The net effect of anticipatory overhead investment was probably to accelerate Canada's economic growth.[1]

Thirdly, there are repercussions in spheres usually considered as non-economic constants by economic analysis, but which have to be treated as variables for the present purpose since they in turn react upon the rate of growth of the economy. In the ultimate paragraph of his second Istanbul Lecture, Nurkse suggests that the beginnings of civilization were made possible by certain types of overhead investment as a means of development. The construction of roads by the Romans led to the formation of colonies and the growth of trade, and the ancient river development schemes along the Nile, the Indus, and the Euphrates and Tigris made possible the division of labour between peasants and craftsmen, which is at the root of civilization.

Furthermore, overhead expenditure on communication was the condition for the growth of government administration which made economic growth possible. Max Weber described this process in *Wirtschaft und Gesellschaft*:

Bureaucratization is occasioned more by intense and qualitative enlargement and internal deployment of the scope of administrative tasks than by their extensive and quantitative increase... Among essentially technical factors, the specifically modern means of communication enter the picture as pacemakers of bureaucratization. Public land and water-ways, railroads, the telegraph, et cetera — they must, in part, necessarily be administered in a public and collective way; in part, such administration is technically expedient. In this respect, the contemporary means of communication frequently play a role similar to that of the canals of Mesopotamia — the regulation of the Nile in the ancient Orient. The

[1] Nurkse, *Second Istanbul Lecture*, p. 28.

degree to which the means of communication have been developed is a condition of decisive importance for the possibility of bureaucratic administration, although it is not the only decisive condition. Certainly in Egypt, bureaucratic centralization, on the basis of an almost pure subsistence economy, could never have reached the actual degree which it did without the natural trade route of the Nile. In order to promote bureaucratic centralization in modern Persia, the telegraph officials were officially commissioned with reporting all occurrences in the provinces to the Shah, over the heads of the local authorities. In addition, everyone received the right to remonstrate directly by telegraph. The modern Occidental state can be administered the way it actually is only because the state controls the telegraph network and has the mails and railroads at its disposal.

Railroads, in turn, are intimately connected with the development of an inter-local traffic of mass goods. The traffic is among the causal factors in the formation of the modern state. As we have already seen, this does not hold unconditionally for the past.[1]

Finally, there are repercussions on inventions and their application: just as in consumption new voids open up as we move along the path of satisfying existing wants, so investment that is intended to fill existing gaps may lead to innovations that open up new gaps. Historically, there can be no doubt that progress has been irregular and has generated imbalance of this type. Mr. A. J. Youngson has recently drawn our attention to the distinction between initiatory and consequential investment. 'Investment . . . may well give rise to a chain of further investments whereby the initial investment is sustained, elaborated and supplemented. A classic case is the introduction of the motor car. Investment in plant to build cars gave rise to consequential investment in rubber plantations, steel presses, oil refineries, road-making equipment, petrol stations and so on'.[2] Schumpeter considered this kind of investment as the key to the understanding of economic growth. Progress depends upon the

---

[1] This extract is from part III, chapter 6 of Max Weber's *Wirtschaft und Gesellschaft*, which forms chapter VIII (entitled 'Bureaucracy') of the volume *From Max Weber — Essays in Sociology*, Routledge & Kegan Paul, London, 1948, translated by H. H. Gerth and C. Wright Mills, pp. 212–14 and section 3, chapter IX, pp. 568–9 in the new, fourth edition of Max Weber's *Wirtschaft und Gesellschaft*, edited by Johannes Winckelmann. I am indebted to Mr V. K. Ramaswami for having drawn my attention to it.

[2] 'The Disaggregation of Investment in the Study of Economic Growth', *Economic Journal*, June 1956, p. 240.

adaptation of passive sectors to the active sector in which innovations originate, i.e. on the attempts to restore balance, once it
has been destroyed, as well as on the disturbing innovation itself.

Progress — in the industrial as well as in any other sector of
social or cultural life — not only proceeds by jerks and rushes
but also by one-sided rushes. . . . We must cease to think of it as
by nature smooth and harmonious . . . On the contrary, we
must recognize that evolution is lop-sided, discontinuous, dishar-
monious by nature. . . . The history of capitalism is studded with
violent burns and catastrophes which do not accord well with the
alternative hypotheses we herewith discard. . . . Evolution is . . .
more like a series of explosions than a gentle, though incessant,
transformation.[1]

We have no satisfactory explanation of the causes of technological
discoveries and inventions. But it appears that scarcities and bottlenecks provided the stimulus to the inventions that revolutionized
England's — and the world's — economic system, and that the
inventions, in their turn, created new scarcities and bottlenecks.
Necessity was the mother of invention, but 'invention was also the
mother of necessity'.[2] On this succession rests the history of technical progress and the history of the anabolism of wants. Balanced
development, had it been possible, would have reduced or even
eliminated the incentive for discoveries, or at any rate for their
application.

From the beginning of the eighteenth century, two bottlenecks
hampered the balanced growth of production : timber and spinning.
Timber was used not only for building ships and houses, but as
fuel both in homes and in the production of iron. It was becoming
increasingly scarce and imports were both expensive and subject
to the uncertain trade policies of foreigners. The discovery of
Abraham Darby eventually emancipated the furnace owners, and
that of Henry Cort the forge-masters from their dependence on
wood. Indirectly, timber shortage also led to the invention of the
steam engine, as a method of pumping water out of coal mines. The
new source of fuel and power enabled the iron industry to raise its

---

[1] J. Schumpeter, *Business Cycles*, McGraw-Hill, New York, 1939, vol. i,
p. 102.
[2] Cf. T. S. Ashton, *The Industrial Revolution*, Oxford University Press,
London, 1948, p. 89.

output from 68,000 tons in 1788 to 3 million tons in 1855. It went far beyond breaking the timber bottlenecks and opened up a new era of investment opportunities. As a correspondent in *The Times* put it: 'The use of coke for smelting, as it were, released the world's vast stores of iron to provide the basic metal for the successively greater waves of industrial and social change in which we are swept along.'[1]

Similarly, yarn had become scarce as a result of the improvements in weaving in the beginning of the eighteenth century. The inventions of Hargreaves, Arkwright, and Crompton transferred within a few decades all spinning into factories and created a famine of weavers, which in turn led to the mechanization of weaving.

The wave of inventions which led to the Industrial Revolution originated in attempts to break through these two bottlenecks: to overcome timber shortage by coke, and shortage of yarn by the use of machinery. Similarly the pressing need for power led to the discovery of the use of steam to produce rotary motion. The railways opened up a series of new possibilities.

The requirements of railway maintenance placed a high premium on the production of cheap and good steel, because steel rails last longer than iron rails; in a sense the steel industry flowed from the railways, as in Britain the railways had flowed from the requirements of cotton. But once good cheap steel was available, many further uses for it unfolded. The history of the engineering profession tells the story in compressed form. From railway engineering it fanned out into mechanical, chemical and electrical specialities, naval construction and civil engineering. It was in the technical experience of building and operating the railways that a good part of the foundations were laid for the march of the western world into maturity.[2]

At a later date, automatic welding provides another example.

Its rise originated in Admiralty needs. The vibration and shock due to gunfire used to work rivets loose, so that many of the rivet-holes in the bulk-heads would cease to be watertight. Welding provided a joint which would remain completely watertight . . . the new process, which quickly proved economical of a particularly

---

[1] *The Times*, 17 September, 1959.

[2] W. W. Rostow, 'A Non-Communist Manifesto', *Economist*, 15 August, 1959, p. 413.

onerous type of labour, (was then) applied far more widely than the original extraordinary need would have suggested.[1]

The idea that a big advance on a few fronts is more successful than small advances on many fronts simultaneously is supported by the remarkably high correlation between rates of production growth and rates of productivity growth in manufacturing industry.[2] This relation is not merely supported by statistics, but is also plausible (or the other way round). The expansion of an industry may be a condition for raising output per man hour, whilst diversification may impede progress. In so far as this is due to internal economies of scale, the point has already been covered. But it may also be due to external economies and to the fact that when capital equipment is being extensively increased technical improvements in both products and processes are facilitated.

We have seen that a case for unbalanced development can be made out if (i) indivisibilities are important, (ii) expansion costs are important, (iii) higher incomes are created than would be by balanced growth, and (iv) incentives to invent and to apply and exploit inventions are strengthened. On what principles then should one decide upon the order in which investment is to be carried out?

This indeed is the really crucial question rather than the one mainly treated in this chapter. It is easy to argue that in certain conditions a lack of balance will have more stimulating effects than balance. It is much more important but also more difficult to show where precisely and how much to unbalance. I can offer no answer to this question, beyond the remarks in chapter 3, section 3, (pp. 57–66),[3] only some quite inadequate suggestions as to the lines along which an answer may lie.

Although the need for large fixed investment in social overhead equipment and its slow rate of obsolescence would suggest that it should always be used as the spearhead, other considerations point to different answers. Roads, railways, and river developments may not create sufficiently strong incentives to correct the unbalance which they create. One aspect of the case for unbalance is that it

[1] R. S. Sayers, 'The Springs of Technical Progress in Britain, 1919–39', *Economic Journal*, June 1950.

[2] See Colin Clark, *Conditions of Economic Progress*, 3rd ed., Macmillan & Co., London, 1960, pp. 363–72.

[3] *Economic Integration*, Sythoff, Leiden, 1961.

highlights the spots where action is needed most urgently, and thus economizes in a resource often in short supply, viz. the power to take decisions. It is therefore best to allow the pressures of un- balance to be exercised most strongly upon those who are most responsive to the signals and the incentives thus created. A keen political group in power may well provide the social overheads, hoping for response of a more sluggish private class of potential entrepreneurs. On the other hand, other societies may forge ahead in the exploitation of some natural resource or in the development of some industry and thus create the pressures upon the government to develop transport and power.

The considerations that should guide the choice of investment priorities may therefore be summed up as follows: choose projects which, (i) while advancing some sectors, concentrate the pressure of unbalance on groups and sectors whose response to a challenge is likely to be strongest; (ii) while creating bottlenecks, also break them; (iii) while providing products and services for industry, agriculture, and consumers, also induce new development to take place in other directions, directly and indirectly related to them; (iv) while providing a new product or service, require consequen- tial investments in other lines. Historical examples of (iii) are railway construction, power and raw material development. Historical examples of (iv) are the motorcar, the wireless, and the cinema.

The argument so far has been that unbalance may be a condition of and a stimulus to growth. Indivisibilities — whether of consump- tion goods or of productive equipment — and the cumulation of complementary wants or complementary technological needs may speed up growth or prevent stagnation. The justification for building ahead of demand can be found partly in technical indivisibilities, but more importantly in the cluster of complementary investments which it provokes. The concept of 'growing points', current in the literature on development, seems to express this fact. It appears to refer to a concentration of activities upon breaking through an obstacle in such a way to give a strong impetus to a series of clustering activities, all promoting growth. Only if the forward flow of energy is impeded in all directions by a succession of bottlenecks (if this were logically admissible), and if the backward pull of the passive sectors is stronger than the forward push of the active sectors, is balanced advance indicated.

But there is another side to the argument against balance. Whereas I have so far attempted to put what might be called the strong case, there is also a weak case, although the combination of the two leads to an argument that is stronger than the sum of the two cases separately. Not only may unbalance result in growth, but growth may lead to unbalance. In so far as the two interact, the result may be a cumulative process of advance, progress generating its own stimulus.

The second proposition by itself says simply that to insist on balance may slow down progress. This is the thesis of Mr Wiles.[1] To say that progress is irregular does not imply that irregularity causes growth. Similarly, to say that if we step up the rate of growth we shall make more mistakes about the correct allocation of resources does not mean that we can speed up growth by making more mistakes. All Mr Wiles says is that in order to get more rapid growth we may have to give up insisting on balance. It is possible to argue that unbalance is a necessary evil. Yet, we have seen that it can also be a source of strength. But if unbalance accelerates growth, the unbalance resulting from growth, far from being an evil, may be a further stimulus. It can become a powerful twist in a virtuous spiral.

6. FOREIGN TRADE AND FOREIGN LENDING

The doctrine of balanced growth is commonly also used to justify diversification of industries or *national* balance.[2] This may well be the correct policy today for primary producing countries which are embarking on development, but has not always been the historical pattern that led to success.

The Industrial Revolution in England is an example of how lopsided growth can lead to much more rapid economic progress than would have been possible, had investment obeyed the principle of nationally balanced growth. The innovations and the resulting rise in productivity were concentrated upon a few industries, mainly transport and textiles. Had it not been for two factors, the rise in productivity in textiles could not have led to the rise in the production of textiles that actually occurred. The workers set free would have had to be absorbed in activities such as agriculture,

---

[1] 'Growth versus Choice', *Economic Journal*, June 1956.

[2] Cf. F. List, op. cit.; R. Nurkse, op. cit., pp. 21, 84; W. W. Lockwood, op. cit., p. 228.

subject to rapidly diminishing returns (assuming that they would have been re-employed at all) and the net rate of growth would have been correspondingly smaller.

The two factors that made unbalanced excess production possible in England were foreign trade and foreign loans. The first provided a market, the second prevented the deterioration in the terms of trade that would have occurred, if exports had been sold only for imports. Between the end of the Napoleonic Wars and the outbreak of the American Civil War Britain's exports rose at a cumulative 6 per cent per annum. The ability to sell abroad the increased output for which there could have been no demand at home, without having to suffer a more substantial reduction of export prices, made a much higher rate of growth possible.

Two types of advantages followed from the concentration of investment in a few lines: first, internal and external economies of scale could be exploited that would have been absent had investment followed a more balanced pattern. Secondly, the rate of invention in those few lines, and the application of these inventions, was speeded up beyond what it would have been had there been greater dispersal. The inventions first in spinning — Hargreave's jenny, Arkwright's frame, and Crompton's mule — followed by inventions in weaving — Cartwright's loom — and in the finishing processes were related to each other and stimulated by each other, partly because the application of each overshot the mark that would have been dictated by balance. These inventions and innovations were followed by the successful search for markets in which to dispose of the increased production.

In Germany, by contrast, growth was more balanced in the sense that innovations were dispersed over a greater number of industries, and foreign trade therefore played a smaller role.

It is, of course, possible to look upon export industries as industries producing indirectly what the foreign exchange will buy — now and later. In this way what would be lop-sided growth in the absence of disposal abroad can be regarded as balanced growth. But since the inventions came first and the search for markets was a response to them, and since a part of the foreign earnings were invested abroad, it is more natural to look at the course of events as unbalanced growth combined with attempts to shape the pattern of demand and trade, rather than growth that responds to a given pattern.

It clearly does not follow that diversification may not be the right policy for some developing countries today. Against the advantages of pushing ahead in a few lines must be set two possible dangers. One is a low price elasticity of demand for exports which would inflict terms of trade losses as production for export expands. The other is the possibility that demand for the developing country's exports may not be expanding rapidly in advanced countries, so that the terms of trade would deteriorate as incomes rise. Either a low price elasticity or a low income elasticity of foreign demand may justify a programme of nationally balanced investment.

Nevertheless, there is a case for unbalanced expansion also in those countries which are trying to catch up with the more advanced countries. The reverse situation of unbalanced expansion combined with foreign lending (Industrial Revolution in England) is borrowing from abroad in order to develop a spearhead sector which activates the rest of the economy. Railway developments in the U.S.A., Canada, Argentina, and Australia in the last century, and projects for river developments, power dams, afforestation, oil or other mineral extraction, or city building, in this century fall into this category. As we have seen, not only technical indivisibilities and expansion costs may make building ahead of demand economical, but unbalance of a certain type may speed up the growth of income and demand above what it would otherwise have been.[1]

In the past, such investment led often to default on foreign loans. But we have seen that this does not necessarily mean that the projects were faulty. Although individual investors' time horizons will be too narrow, publicly financed lending institutions should be

[1] A recent illustration of conscious creation of unbalance for development is Brazil's new capital city. 'The second purpose of the new capital is to encourage development of the under-populated interior, which has vast resources waiting to be tapped.... It is hoped that the construction of a big city deep in the interior, with the markets it will create and the new movements of population it will stimulate, will start a far-reaching process of opening up the undeveloped areas. More significant even than markets and population are communications : it is chiefly the lack of communications that has held up the development of the interior. But already roads and railways link Brasilia with the coastal cities and — as important to the future development of the country — the modern highway that leads to Brasilia is being continued northwards for another thousand miles, penetrating for the first time into the tropical jungle of the Amazon basin.' J. M. Richards, ' Brazil's New Capital City ', *The Listener*, 13 November, 1958, p. 772.

expected to take a wider view. The application of strictly commercial criteria for sound lending policies does not mean that private lenders' time horizons ought to be accepted, or external economies neglected.

But it may be that the road to expansion both through an unbalanced increase in exports and through domestic spearhead development is closed: the former for terms of trade reasons, the latter because not sufficient capital from abroad is available. The choice then still remains between a domestically financed unbalanced expansion, and nationally balanced growth. Though foreign trade may fail as an 'engine of growth', interregional or inter-sectoral unbalance may provide a substitute.

7. The Conditions of Unbalanced Growth

Let us first assume that there are only two products on which income is spent, P and non-P. When the production of P is increased, unit costs of P are reduced. Real income rises and with it also the demand for non-P. The rise in the price of non-P relatively to that of P will stimulate greater production of non-P. This expansion in the production of non-P will be greater,

(1) the smaller the income elasticity of demand for P;

(2) the smaller the elasticity of substitution between P and non-P;

(3) the greater the supply elasticity of non-P.[1]

If 'complementarity' in a loose sense (in the strict sense it cannot exist if there are only two goods) is taken to mean a low elasticity of substitution at the margin, we see that complementarity in this sense can be a stimulus to the expansion of non-P.

If next we take three goods, P, Q and R, R being complementary with P and Q substitute for P, a rise in the production of P that lowers its unit costs and raises real income will stimulate the production of Q,

(1) the larger the income elasticity of demand for Q;

(2) the smaller the elasticity of substitution between P and Q;

(3) the greater the supply elasticity of Q.

And it will stimulate the expansion of R,

[1] See M. Fleming, 'External Economies and the Doctrine of Balanced Growth', *Economic Journal*, June 1955, p. 243, reprinted in Agarwala and Singh (eds.), *The Economics of Underdevelopment*, Oxford University Press, Bombay, 1958, pp. 275f.

(1) the larger the income elasticity of demand for R;
(2) the stronger the complementarity between P and R, i.e. the more the marginal rate of substitution of P for Q is raised, as R is substituted for Q, while real income is held constant;
(3) the greater the supply elasticity of R.

Zero income elasticity for P combined with infinite supply elasticity of non-P present a special case of the Keynesian multiplier. The multiplicand is the rise in real income following a cost reduction in the production of P. But even a positive or a high income elasticity for P can stimulate growth of non-P if the elasticity of substitution is low (when the price of non-P rises) or if complementarity is strong (when the price of R rises) and if the supply elasticity of non-P or R are high. From this point of view the doctrine of unbalanced growth appears as a generalization of the multiplier. Balanced growth would imply a high income elasticity of demand for P, and a high substitution elasticity between P and non-P, so that the extra income is either spontaneously spent on P, or in response to a rise in price of non-P. The net stimulus to non-P would then be minimized.

8. BALANCE BETWEEN SAVINGS AND INVESTMENT

The case for government responsibility to maintain aggregate equilibrium between savings and investment at full employment, and at a desired rate of investment, can be put in terms of the failure of the market system where complementarity is important. Decisions that should be taken simultaneously, if taken separately, may lead to waste — in this case the wastes of unemployment or inflation.

This similarity of principles has been either ignored or explicitly denied.[1] Thus Nurkse, in his Istanbul Lecture, says: 'A case for state investment may clearly arise if and when the mobilization of capital supplies discourages private investment activity and so destroys the demand for capital. But *this case is entirely separate* from the principle of balanced growth as such.' (My italics.)

But the case is, at least formally, almost identical. Just as demand from producers in the investment sector is needed in order to offset the lack of demand for consumption goods caused by saving, so

---

[1] A notable exception is the *Economic Survey for Europe in* 1955, and the publication of the American FOL-CIO. See footnote on p. 20.

demand from the producers of bread for shoes is needed in order
to offset the lack of demand for shoes caused by shoe-producers
not spending all their incomes on shoes. Furthermore, just as an
increase in consumable output must produce a balanced diet, so
the extra output must fit the community's decision as to how to
divide its resources between present consumption and larger
consumption in the future. It is part of the requirement of a balanced
diet to provide for the same or improved consumption later. There
is no difference in principle between the decision as to how much
bread and how much butter, and the decision as to how much consumption and how much saving. The same principle applies to
decisions relating to savings and investment as applied to decisions
relating to investment in different industries. But here again a
lack of co-ordination, an unbalance, *may* provide a stimulus to
growth. I shall briefly mention three cases; a free market economy,
a controlled economy with a tendency to inflation, and an economy
attempting to raise its rate of savings and investment.

(a) *The Market Economy: Investment Exceeds Profitable Investment*

As we have seen, one aspect of balanced growth is the balance
between productive capacity and consumption. The E.C.E. *Survey*
defines balanced growth 'as a development in which the growth of
consumption matches the growth of productive capacity in the
consumer-goods sector. This definition, while not implying any
particular rate of growth, does mean that consumption at any
particular time is great enough to keep up the incentive to invest'.[1]

Yet, investment that is unbalanced on this definition, can lead
to a higher rate of growth than balanced investment. Mr Kaldor
expresses this possibility:

The conclusion which emerges . . . is that so far from the trend
rate of growth determining the strength or duration of booms, it
is the strength and duration of booms which shapes the trend rate
of growth. It is the economy in which businessmen are reckless and
speculative, where expectations are highly volatile, but with an
underlying bias towards optimism, where high and growing profits
are projected into the future and lead to the hasty adoption of
'unsound' projects involving over-expansion, which is likely to
show a higher rate of progress over longer periods . . . the extent of
the 'over-expansion' in the previous boom influences to a major

[1] *Survey for 1955*, p. 76. See footnote on p. 20.

extent the degree to which the new boom surpasses the peak reached by its predecessor.[1]

Mr Kaldor is saying here that an excess of investment over savings, though destabilizing, is a force for expansion in an unplanned economy. When demand strains against capacity, more capacity may be created than is needed to accommodate demand. The principle of balanced growth is violated. This leads to the down-turn. But in the next boom more demand can be accommodated, if the surplus capacity created in the last boom has been in the right places, i.e. where there is a potential demand for it. The service that was rendered by a diversion of demand in the case of new industries with large-scale economies[2] is now rendered by buoyant entrepreneurial spirits. Had there not been over-expansion in the previous boom, the higher demand, resulting from the upward shift in the consumption function, could not have been satisfied in the succeeding boom. To build ahead of demand is one way of assisting in the achievement of a higher secular rate of growth of output.

To reverse a dictum of Sir Dennis Robertson's, what turns out to be over-investment in the sight of man, may not be over-invest-ment in the sight of God.[3] A better distribution of society's income through time may be achieved, at the cost of fluctuations, by this type of over-investment. As Sir Dennis Robertson wrote on the last page of his *Study of Industrial Fluctuation*: 'Out of the welter of industrial dislocation the great permanent riches of the future are generated.'[4]

More recently, Mr Kaldor has developed another argument for a certain kind of unbalanced growth.[5] A certain rate of inflation (i.e.

---

[1] N. Kaldor, 'Economic Growth and Cyclical Fluctuations', *Economic Journal*, March 1954, pp. 68–9. However, tucked away in a footnote on p. 62 is the assumption that the consumption function shifts upwards in time (or that autonomous investment grows at the trend rate), so that the trend ultimately depends upon the trend, not simply on the cycle. But for the present argument this makes no difference. It is the temporary disequilibrium that, later, makes possible a higher trend.

[2] See above, p. 27.

[3] It will be seen that this is not over-investment on Robertson's own defini-tion. See above, p. 28.

[4] p. 254.

[5] N. Kaldor, 'A Model of Economic Growth', *Economic Journal*, September 1957.

imbalance between total saving and total investment) may be necessary in order to achieve a given rate of investment. If the rate of inflation were reduced relatively to interest rates, the distribution or income would change in favour of wage earners and against profit earners. This in turn would reduce investment. In other words, if investment is a function of the share of profits, and if other methods of redistribution are inadequate, prices that rise in relation to money wages are the only way in which higher investment can be achieved.

(b) The Controlled Economy: Privately Desired Investment Exceeds Total Savings

In a more controlled economy which avoids the downturns and the depressions, there is also a case for imbalance resulting from excess of investment over saving. If balance and hence stability of prices can be achieved only at the expense of a lower rate of growth, we are faced with a choice between price stability (= balance) and higher growth rate. A possible explanation for the necessity of this choice might be that aggregate investment is not a smooth and continuous function of some other strategic variable such as the rate of interest or tax rates, but a function of a boom-or-bust mentality. Either business confidence prevails; then the desired rate of investment exceeds the available resources and controls have to curb the excess. While confidence is maintained, tight money would have little effect on investment decisions. Alternatively, business confidence is destroyed; then investment is too low for the desired rate of accumulation and possibly also for full employment. If the investment function is of this nature, the economy has to be run, in the familiar motoring metaphor, with one foot on the accelerator and the other on the brake. An unbalanced economy in which total demand exceeds total supply would achieve a higher rate of growth than one in which balance were aimed at.

Growth may be balanced but inadequate. A more adequate rate may conflict with stability.

(c) The Progressing Economy: Publicly Desired Investment exceeds Private Savings or Private Investment

Complementarity between investment and the consumption generated by it would seem to indicate the need for balance between rising investment and consequential consumption. Clearly, only those who believe that the rate of saving should be governed by free consumers' choice expressed in the market would accept this balance. It seems to be, for example, the view of P. T. Bauer and B. S. Yamey, who write: 'It is inherent in our concept and criterion of economic development that we attach significance to acts of choice and valuation made by individuals, including those which express individual time-preferences between present and future consumption. The role of the state is seen primarily as that of making it possible for individuals to have access to a wider range of alternatives and to more adequate knowledge of them.'[1] Such a policy would involve a budget which is always balanced. The pursuit of full employment would have to rely solely on monetary policy.

But it is difficult to see why the rate of capital accumulation and of full employment saving should be determined by the market mechanism. In a democracy, the rejection of this principle does not imply paternalism or reduced freedom of choice, but, to use the jargon, merely a reduced weight given by myself to my own individual indifference curves between present and future consumption, either because I distrust my current impulses, or because I consider that my tastes may change in time, or because saving for investment is looked upon as a collective want for which I am ready to make sacrifices only if others — and hence also I — are *forced* to contribute our proper share.

In this sense any budget surplus planned to provide savings for a higher rate of investment than the market would yield is a plan for unbalanced growth. The incomes generated by investment are not allowed to be fully spent on consumption. The poorer a country and the keener it is on development, the less balanced its plan can afford to be. All development programmes are programmes for unbalanced growth in this sense.

Somebody might possibly object that this is extending the meaning of the doctrine of balanced growth beyond permissible limits. Yet the case for altering the composition of consumption and industrial output by means of taxes and subsidies to suit the objective of growth is surely merely an extension of the principle that incomes should be taxed to provide savings for investment.

Similarly, private investment may be inadequate in a private enterprise economy. When the means to invest are there, because

---

[1] *The Economics of Underdeveloped Countries*, p. 153, op. cit.

consumption is low and factors of production are idle, the incentive is missing: when the incentive is there, because consumption and its rate of increase are high, the means are often inadequate. The case for state investment then is the case for cutting the link between consumption and investment and making investment autonomous, or unbalanced. This would be justified if the socially desirable rate of investment exceeded the investment carried out under private enterprise in obedience to the dictates of balance (viz. the accelerator in some form), and if manipulating the market mechanism (by fiscal and financial policy) could not achieve the results.[1]

In 'A Soviet Model of Growth'[2] Evsey Domar discusses and reinterprets a model in which the division of investment between the capital- and consumer-goods industries determines the rate of growth. The complementarity between savings and investment is eliminated by (a) eliminating any limitation on production other than capital, and (b) determining the ratio of investment to income by the relative capacities of the two sectors. As a result, the *allocation* of the investment thus determined between capital and consumer goods industries becomes the active force which provides the impetus of growth. The higher the ratio of investment allocated to the capital goods sector (i.e. the greater the unbalance), the faster will be the rate of growth of income, and, subject to a few qualifications, also of consumption.

9. THE TURNPIKE THEOREM AND UNBALANCED GROWTH

In their book *Linear Programming and Economic Analysis*, Dorfman, Samuelson and Solow propound a theorem which is related to the argument in this section, although their premises are more restrictive and their method of procedure more rigorous. We start with a set of capital stocks which are used to produce themselves. Von Neumann has shown that there is a path of proportional growth ('balanced growth') which maximizes the rate of growth. The intertemporal condition for optimum growth is that the marginal rates

---

[1] This point was made by Nurkse in his first *Istanbul Lecture*, p. 11, and in private correspondence where he again insisted on 'the importance of distinguishing between the vertical and the horizontal order of things'. (Cf. above, p. 30.)

[2] *Essays in the Theory of Economic Growth*, Oxford University Press, New York, 1957, chapter ix.

of substitution between any two goods regarded as outputs of the previous period must be equal to their marginal rates of substitution considered as inputs for the next period. Dorfman, Samuelson and Solow argue that if we start from a position in which the proportions are not appropriate to this path, and if we desire to reach, after a sufficiently long period, another position which again is not appropriate to the maximum growth path, the optimum path is not determined solely by the initial and the terminal position, but will move towards the von Neumann maximum path and only later veer away from it towards the specified terminal point. The required assumptions are: constant returns to scale, no consumption other than that needed to keep men productive, and no inputs other than those which also figure as outputs. (Men and rabbits are on a par.) Thus if we start with given proportions of various sectors and want to maximize production of all sectors after a period of time, keeping the same proportions between sectors, we must, for a time, deviate from these proportions towards the technical maximum path. Maximum growth is 'exactly like a turnpike paralleled by a network of minor roads. There is a fastest route between any two points; and if origin and destination are close together and far from the turnpike, the best route may not touch the turnpike. But if origin and destination are far enough apart, it will always pay to get on to the turnpike and cover distance at the best rate of travel, even if this means adding a little mileage at either end. The best intermediate capital configuration is one which will grow most rapidly; even if it is not the desired one, it is temporarily optimal'.[1]

'Unbalanced growth' in this technical sense means non-proportional growth. But it fits certain situations, such as industrialization through forced savings. If we want, after a time, the maximum of a specified ratio of goods we must, for a time, aim at a different combination. The difference between the desired terminal and the optimum ratios is prescribed by technology.

10. SUMMARY

The case against balanced growth is twofold: first, in some conditions lack of balance promotes growth. Secondly, in order to get growth, one may have to sacrifice balance. Unbalance can be a condition of, and a stimulus to, growth; or it can be the result of

[1] Op. cit., p. 331.

removing obstacles to growth. But the combination of these two arguments can yield a powerful mixture. Unbalance stimulates growth, which leads to new unbalances and further stimuli.

The relevant division here is not so much between adherents of the market economy and planners, for both balanced and unbalanced growth can, in principle, and if considered as objectives rather than procedures, be achieved by either type of system. Balance can be achieved, in the end, by successive adaptations following the signals and incentives of the price mechanism, though it must involve waste compared with a balanced process towards the goal of balance. Unbalanced growth, though it may justify the use of prices as signals and incentives, may also be more successfully pursued by planning, because surplus capacity has to be carried, because temporary losses will be incurred, and because private sights are too short.

If the road, or rather the plain, to progress is studded with obstacles, both in width and in depth, and if the removal of obstacles pushes the advance forward by less than the remaining obstacles retard it, balanced advance is advisable. If, on the other hand, obstacles, though serious, are few or of unequal strength, and if overcoming one releases forces that carry advance further, unbalanced growth is more promising.

FURTHER THOUGHTS ON BALANCED VERSUS UNBALANCED GROWTH[1]

In this section we shall attempt to show that the questions posed by the controversy over balanced versus unbalanced growth have not been very fruitful, although each doctrine contains some valuable insights. Before we enter upon a discussion of the merits and faults of the doctrines of balanced growth (BG) and of unbalanced growth (UG), it is necessary to clarify two questions to which the contributors to the debate have not given clear and satisfactory answers. The first question, most relevant in the present context

---

[1] This section is a by-product of collaboration with Professor Gunnar Myrdal on a Twentieth-Century Fund study of development in South Asia. It is printed here with the kind permission of Professor Myrdal.

of our discussion, concerns the role of planning; the second question the role of supply limitations and supply inelasticities.

11. The Role of Planning

In the controversy the role of government (or for that matter private) planning has not always been brought out clearly. In particular, it is not always clear whether the question under consideration relates to planning, or whether it relates to an attempt to explain development that takes place without planning, or with only an initial impulse of planning in the form of an investment project, while things are thereafter left to take their own course with market forces responding to demand and supply.

Nurkse thought that BG is relevant primarily to a private enterprise economy.[1] It is (he argued) private investment that needs market inducements. In his doctrine, the choice between public and private investment and between direct controls and market incentives is mainly a matter of administrative expediency. But he seems to be wrong in this. The indivisibilities assumed in BG imply the need for co-ordination, i.e. planning, although it would, in principle, be possible to have either private or public co-ordination; and this co-ordination can be explicit or tacit.[2]

UG as propounded by Hirschman is consistent with, but does not require, initial *and* continued planning. His state administrators are — or should be — subject to the same kind of pressures as private entrepreneurs. The role of the state is both to induce and to repair disequilibria. Thus state action becomes a dependent, as well as an independent variable.[3] But again, on closer inspection it would seem that UG, to be most effective, does require planning and preferably state planning, because no private firm may want or be able to carry the surplus capacity and the losses, and because private horizons are too narrow.

It is not surprising that both BG and UG should, to be most effective, presuppose each (a different kind of) planning, for they are both concerned with lumpy investments and complementaries. Co-ordination is needed in order both to get things done that otherwise

[1] *Equilibrium and Growth in the World Economy,* pp. 249–50 and p. 280.

[2] Cf. p. 17, fn. 2.

[3] A. O. Hirschman, *The Strategy of Economic Development,* op. cit., pp. 65, 202.

would not be done, and in order to reap the rewards of complementaries. Market forces look best after adjustments that can be made in infinitesimally small steps. This is why the concept 'marginal' plays such an important part in neo-classical Western economic theory. It is also one of the important differences between developed and underdeveloped countries. In the former a new profitable investment project is normally small relatively to the size of existing capital equipment (however measured), relatively to new investment, and relatively to the hinterland of facilities on which it can draw. In underdeveloped countries indivisibilities are more prominent and marginal adjustments rarer for at least four reasons. First, both the existing stock of equipment and the additions to it are small compared with those in advanced countries with comparable populations. Since plant and equipment often have to be of a minimum size for technical reasons, the addition of a plant or of a piece of equipment constitutes a greater proportion both of the stock of capital and of total investment. Second, economic development is usually directed at moving people from agriculture to industrial enterprises. This normally implies an increase in the number of indivisible units. Third, the necessary social overhead capital and the basic structure of industry (power, steel, transport, housing, government buildings) consist of large indivisible units. Fourth, complementarities between enterprises and activities are likely to be more important in the meagre economies of underdeveloped countries, so that a given investment is more liable to require complementary and supplementary investments. Both BG and UG give rise to external economies. A cost incurred by A creates profit opportunities for B. If steps are taken to seize these opportunities at once and in one type of sequence (BG), the results will be different than if they are seized later and in a different type of sequence (UG). But there is no guarantee that A will be induced by market forces to incur these costs, indeed there is a presumption that he will not be so induced.[1]

12. The Role of Supply Limitations

We next turn to the role of supply limitations and supply inelasticities in the controversy. Nurkse explicitly confined his discussion to the demand side. He assumed supplies to be available

[1] There is also more scope for *planning* income elasticities of demand than Nurkse allows.

and asked what would investment have to be like to justify itself? He wrote: 'There is no suggestion here that, by taking care of the demand side alone, any country could, as it were, lift itself up by its bootstraps. We have been considering one particular facet of our subject. The more fundamental difficulties that lie on the supply side have so far been kept off-stage for the sake of orderly discussion.'[1] Nevertheless, the position of this chapter in his book and the emphasis laid on it have led to misinterpretations. If BG stresses *markets* as the main limitation on growth, UG in the Hirschman version stresses *decisions*. The implication of Hirschman's theory is that supplies will be forthcoming with relative ease if only the lack of decision-taking can be overcome. This shift of emphasis to an attitude, usually assumed either constant or automatically adjusted to precisely the required extent, should be welcomed. Hirschman has been charged with excessive preoccupation with *investment* decisions.[2] Much of his book indeed focuses attention on them, but it is clear that he had a wider concept in mind, as is shown by his use of the terms 'development decisions' and 'developmental tasks.'[3]

In so far as BG is concerned with the creation of markets through complementary investment projects and the inducement to invest by providing complementary markets for final goods, it stresses a problem which is rarely serious in the countries of the region. Final markets can often quite easily be created without recourse to BG, by import restrictions and, less easily, by export expansion.

On the other hand, although UG is correct in pointing to the scarcity of decision-taking in some countries,[4] it should not be contrasted, but it should be combined with the provision of more supplies. The contrast drawn by UG between scarcity of physical

---

[1] *Problems of Capital Formation in Underdeveloped Countries*, op. cit., pp. 30–1.

[2] 'Hirschman, on the other hand, might find it more difficult to support, by reference to the Burmese experience, his thesis that development strategy should be directed at maximizing investment (which he equates with development) decisions. Decision-making was indeed a critical factor in this experience. But the decisions which were most needed and most lacking were not investment decisions, but administrative, managerial and policy decisions.' Louis J. Walinsky, *Economic Development in Burma 1951–1960*, A Twentieth-Century Fund Study, New York, 1962, p. 593.

[3] *Strategy*, op. cit., p. 25.

[4] Though not in all: there is for example too much enterprise in Malaya.

resources and scarcity of decision-taking can be misleading. Those who stress resources say that decisions will be taken as soon as resources are available; those who stress decision-taking say that resources will flow freely as soon as adequate inducements to take decisions are provided. The former group of experts go out on missions and advocate high taxation in order to 'set resources free', the latter recommend low taxation in order to 'encourage enterprise'. Both views reflect misplaced aggregation and illegitimate isolation, two types of bias introduced by the careless use of Western concepts and models. No general formula will serve. The correct division often cuts across these categories. The question is what combination of resource policy, reform of attitudes (including 'incentives') and of legal, social and cultural institutions is necessary in a particular situation?

Moreover, the tendency of both BG and UG to underplay supply limitations diverts attention from the fact that planning must be directed as much at *restricting* supplies in certain directions as at *expanding* them in others. The policy package presupposes a choice of allocating limited supplies, i.e. supplies growing at a limited rate, and in response to certain stimuli, to the most important uses, combined with inducements to decisions of all kinds (not only investment decisions). These supply limitations are considerably less important in advanced industrial countries now and were less important in the early developing phase of many now advanced countries, like Sweden or the regions of recent settlement. These countries had almost unlimited access to capital at low interest rates, a reserve of skilled labour and plentiful natural resources. Again, certain underdeveloped regions in advanced countries (Southern Italy, the South of the USA) can draw on supplies but lack development decisions. The models developed in the BG *v.* UG controversy seem to have drawn on this kind of experience from 'ceilingless economies', which is relevant to South America but not to the entirely different problems of South Asia. The two important differences between, on the one hand, advanced countries now and in their development phase, and, on the other hand, the underdeveloped countries of South Asia are (1) that investments in advanced countries can more often be treated as marginal than in underdeveloped countries and (2) that advanced countries are and were high supply-elasticity economies with responses and institutions already adapted to economic growth.

13. The Questions Posed

Both doctrines have certain merits and certain faults. The trouble with advocating UG is that, for countries embarking on development, unbalance is inevitable, whether they want it or not, and governments and planners do not need the admonitions of theoreticians. All investment creates unbalances because of rigidities, indivisibilities, sluggishness of response both of supply and of demand in these low-elasticity economies and because of miscalculations.[1] There will be, in any case, plenty of difficulties in meeting many urgent requirements, whether of workers, technicians, managers, machines, semi-manufactured products, raw materials or power and transport facilities and in finding markets permitting full utilization of equipment. Market forces will be too weak or powerless to bring about the required adjustments and unless coordinated planning of much more than investment is carried out, the investment projects will turn out to be wasteful and will be abandoned.

In so far as unbalance does create desirable attitudes, the crucial question is not whether to create unbalance, but *what* is the *optimum* degree of unbalance, *where* to unbalance and *how much*, in order to accelerate growth; which are the 'growing points', where should the spearheads be thrust, on which slope would snowballs grow into avalanches? Although nobody *just* said 'create any odd unbalance', insufficient attention has been paid to its precise composition, direction and timing.[2]

---

[1] There is, indeed, a danger that planners turn necessity into a virtue, as the following euphemistic passage from the Second Indian Five Year Plan shows : 'There cannot be a complete balance between developments in each Five-year Plan ; to some extent, a measure of imbalance — seeming over-expansion in some lines and under-expansion in others — may facilitate more rapid and better-balanced development over a period. Considerations of this kind apply particularly to sectors like development of power, transport and basic industries where investments are by nature "lumpy".' *Second Five Year Plan*, 1956, Planning Commission, Government of India, p. 17.

[2] This accounts for remarks such as the following : 'To those not readily enchanted by the paradoxical, the Hirschman strategy may seem to resemble that incorporated in such statements as "The most efficient way to walk a tightrope is to advance, swaying precariously first to one side then to the other ", or "To teach your child to conduct himself safely in traffic, set him off to cross Times Square against the traffic light".' Louis J. Walinsky, *Economic Development in Burma 1951–1960*, op. cit., p. 594.

The second weakness of UG is that the theory concentrates on stimuli to *expansion*, and tends to neglect or minimize *resistances* caused by UG. UG argues that the active sectors pull the others with them, BG that the passive sectors drag the active ones back. While the former is relevant to South America, the latter is relevant to South Asia. It would, of course, be better, as Nurkse would have liked it, if *all* sectors were active, and the wish may have been father of the thought behind these models. But the problem is how to activate them. Activation measures must take the form both of positive inducements and of resistances to resistances. The UG model in the Hirschman version has the great merit, in comparison with many other models, of including attitudes and institutions, and in particular investment incentives, normally assumed fully adjusted to requirements, and of turning them from independent variables or constants into dependent variables. In particular Hirschman's discussion of forward and backward linkages is provocative and fruitful. It brings out the previously neglected effects of one investment on investment at earlier and later stages of production. But the doctrine underplays obstacles and resistances (also in attitudes) called into being by imbalance. Shortages create vested interests; they give rise to monopoly gains; people may get their fingers burnt by malinvestments and may get frightened by the growth of competition. The attitudes and institutions evolving through development will arouse opposition and hostility. Some of these resistances may be overcome only by state compulsion, but the governments of the 'soft states' are reluctant to use force and the threat of force and the reluctance to oppose vested interests will be strengthened by their apparently justified complaints. Once again, the absence of this type of reaction from the models is both appropriate for Western countries and is opportune to the planners in South Asia, but it introduces a systematic bias and neglects some of the most important issues.

Turning now to BG, we have seen that its main weakness is that it is concerned with the creation of complementary domestic markets as an inducement to invest, whereas markets in the countries of the region can usually be created by import restrictions, and, where possible, export expansion. This relates to final goods and principally to consumers' goods. As far as intermediate markets are concerned, Nurkse came out in favour of UG (vertical imbalance) in

his second Istanbul Lecture.[1] Social overhead investment provides
the conditions and inducements for consequential direct productive
investment. As for horizontal balance, he believed that the case
'rests on the need for a "balanced diet".'[2] But he later drew a
distinction between BG as a method and BG as an outcome or
objective.[3] What remains of the doctrine is the emphasis on the complementarity of markets for final goods as an ultimate objective
for investment incentives. But not only is absence of markets not
normally a serious obstacle to development; even where it is, it is
by no means the main obstacle and, in any case, balanced growth
cannot always remove it.

What is sound in BG is the stress on the investment package, on
the need for co-ordination, on the structure of an investment complex.
But investment is not the only component in this package: and there
is too much stress on the complementarity of final markets. What is
needed is a package of policy measures containing (*a*) complementary investments; (*b*) actions to reform attitudes and institutions, including the desire to invest, but also the ability and willingness to work (which may involve raising *consumption*), to organize
and manage and in particular to administer politically; (*c*) a carefully
thought-out time-table showing the sequence of the various measures
which would be determined by technological, political and sociological factors; (*d*) controls checking undesirable or less desirable
investments; and (*e*) policies designed to weaken or eliminate
obstacles and inhibitions to development, including resistances
induced by measures (*a*) to (*d*).

---

[1] R. Nurkse, *Equilibrium and Growth in the World Economy*, op. cit., pp.
259-78.

[2] ' The difficulty caused by the small size of the market relates to individual
investment incentives in any single line of production taken by itself. At
least in principle, the difficulty vanishes in the case of a more or less synchronized application of capital to a wide range of different industries. Here is an
escape from the deadlock ; here the result is an over-all enlargement of the
market. People working with more and better tools in a number of complementary projects become each other's customers. Most industries catering
for mass consumption are complementary in the sense that they provide a
market for, and thus support, each other. This basic complementarity stems,
in the last analysis, from the diversity of human wants. The case for " balanced
growth " rests on the need for a " balanced diet ".' *Problems of Capital Formation in Underdeveloped Countries*, op. cit., pp. 11f.

[3] *Equilibrium and Growth*, op. cit., p. 279.

14. Related Issues

The BG *v.* UG discussion is related to a wider and more fundamental dilemma: if it is stipulated that several things be attempted
(e.g., a series of mutually supporting investment projects, dispersal
over a wide region, encouragement of small-scale enterprise) either
each is so small in itself and in its effects that the total result is
negligible, or nothing is done at all. On the other hand, if efforts are
concentrated on a 'leading' sector or on a growing region or on a
large-scale project, absence of supporting projects may mean waste
or at best the further advance of an enclave.[1] Is it better to
achieve nothing because efforts are too widely dispersed or because

---

[1] J. K. Galbraith in a mimeographed and undated note on Pakistan's
Second Plan Outline, pp. 17ff., argues against ' the inclusion of all good things
in the Plan' and gives an example of the usefulness of concentration : ' In
the late eighteenth and early nineteenth centuries the accessible agricultural
area of the United States — that between the Appalachian Plateau
and the sea — was relatively small and there were occasional food shortages
in the sense that grain had to be imported from Europe. The solution was to
drive a canal to provide access to the abundant and rich lands of the Ohio
Valley. No other way of increasing production was so important ; it was
obviously worth while at this stage of development to concentrate on this
one thing alone. This in effect was done. After the Erie Canal was opened in
the eighteen-twenties food became abundant and cheap along the eastern
sea-board. Had a modern agricultural mission set about increasing food
production in the early nineteenth century, and in the light of modern technology and organization, it would have urged the establishment of experiment
stations, proposed an extension service, suggested the development and
adoption of new varieties of grain, advocated supervised credit, proposed more
attention to marketing services, and quite possibly have used the occasion
to stress the importance of starting work in home economics, farm management, rural health and rural sociology. The canal would have been only one
among all of these good ideas and would probably not have got built. And all
the rest being of far less immediate effect, the food imports would have continued. At a later stage it is worth while in a country such as the United States
to devote itself to ways by which production can be made more efficient.
But this is after the central opportunities are exploited. It is not a pattern
to be applied to countries where concentration on essentials is still the urgent
requirement.' See also his *Economic Development in Perspective*, Harvard
University Press, 1962, pp. 24, 31–2.

Galbraith's moral may not be applicable to South Asia. Even were there
similar big ventures to be undertaken, their spread effects would be unlike
those that followed historically in the U.S.A., where the government, at the
same time, did a number of other things, including some of those mentioned
by Galbraith.

concentration means sacrificing complementary measures? Should the butter be spread so thinly that it cannot be tasted or put on in a lump with the risk that it might drop off the bread altogether? Should all the eggs be put into one basket or distributed over many? Dissipation through dispersal or neglect through concentration? Less pessimistically: is it preferable to waste efforts by spreading them thinly or to neglect important areas in favour of development within a self-contained already more advanced region?

A priori considerations can be advanced on either side. On the one hand, economies of scale, indivisibilities, the need for a 'big push' and the presence of thresholds point to concentration. On the other hand, the necessity to change many things simultaneously and to co-ordinate action in various fields points to attack on a broad front. In practice the problem appears in such forms as: should the Indians spread their efforts to start community development and agricultural extension works over the 500,000 villages clamouring for them, thus running the risk that nothing will change, or should they concentrate on a few selected villages; should they rely on programmes raising yields while leaving aside numerous other desirable objectives, or should they combine these policies with others, directed at education, irrigation, public works, etc., each of which would have to be decimated?

The dilemma is made more complex because it contains three distinct choices: first the conflict between efficiency and other goals such as equity, justice, political strategy, preservation of communities and their way of life, etc.; secondly, the choices imposed by the requirements of efficiency; and thirdly the intertemporal solution of the conflicts between efficiency and other goals. Thus more redistribution towards the poor or backward regions may be possible in the longer run if strong emphasis is placed on efficiency, at the cost of sacrificing redistribution in the short run. To spread efforts widely merely for the sake of equality now, or because of political pressures, may mean less equality in the long run, whereas giving unto those who have may be the best way of lifting up those who have not.

The question turns on the nature of the spread effects which may be market-induced or policy-induced. It is permissible to let the centre grow at the expense of the periphery, if an efficient tax system can redistribute some of the benefits to the periphery. Such spreading of benefits may occur even without policy intervention if the centre demanded factors or products from the periphery, or supplied capital and enterprise to it. But the conditions for such automatic spread, viz. a high degree of mobility, competition and divisibility are not likely to be fulfilled. Not only may there be absence of spread effects or simply polarization within enclaves, but the presence of backwash effects would actually harm the periphery. Growth there may be retarded by the growth in the centre. Finally, the spread effects may be weakened or annulled by resistance effects. By these is meant the growth of anti-development forces induced by the process of growth itself. A policy of resistance to resistance effects must then accompany the development effort.

Such abstract categorizing yields no general formula which would solve the dilemma between concentration and dispersal. The circular interdependence of the relevant conditions will differ in different circumstances. Political facts, such as the demand to cover the whole Indian countryside with an agricultural extension service, cannot be evaded.

The notion of an Ideal Plan in which a set of objectives is contrasted with a realm of policies,[1] and the notion of Balanced Growth show certain affinities. In both cases there is a strict and permanent division between a set of ends and a set of 'neutral' means; 'efficiency' is served by adapting the means in an optimal fashion to the ends. But neither ends nor means nor 'other things', normally assumed constant, can be regarded as 'given'. Psychological, sociological, cultural and institutional limitations are just as real as physical limitations, though both types can be overcome by appropriate policies. The dichotomy between concentrate and disperse is also inspired by this type of model. In order to be able to take a decision, one would have to do the following things:

(1) muster evidence about consequences which may not be available or which may be extremely costly;

(2) know the objectives of policy and the solution of conflicts between objectives, which may not be known but open to exploration as a result of trial and error;

(3) reduce the complexity of objectives to a simple index which may be impossible;

[1] See Paul Streeten, 'Programmes and Prognoses' in Gunnar Myrdal, *Value in Social Theory*, Routledge & Kegan Paul, London, 1957.

(4) reach agreement between different social groups on the objectives of policy, whilst in fact there will be disagreement, compromise, persuasion or struggle;

(5) isolate a sphere of 'pure' policy which contains only neutral means, whereas in fact whole means-ends sequences may be valued, so that decisions are simply of the type: do this! or: do that!

Since none of these conditions is likely to be met, no general model can be used to decide, even in principle, let alone in any particular instance, on the correct answer. Each decision will have to be taken on its merits. By a process of learning, evidence will be accumulated, the ends will be clarified, the complexity possibly simplified, social divergence may be reduced and a growing area of 'neutral' means may be reclaimed from the initial morass of all-pervading valuation.

THE PACE OF DEVELOPMENT*

by R. F. Kahn

I

'To HIM who hath shall be given.' In its negative implication that sums up the basic problem which faces an underdeveloped country. Production relatively to population is severely limited by lack of physical resources and of skill. Although the standard of consumption is therefore low, there is only a small margin of production over the necessary minimum of consumption. And yet it is this margin which, apart from the use of foreign capital and of foreign aid, limits the amount of investment, and so limits the rate at which productivity and productive capacity can be increased as a result of development. It is a problem of the take-off, to use Professor Rostow's analogy.[1] If only the margin could be increased, production would grow faster and this would enable the margin to grow faster. In other words, any immediate effort will have a pronounced cumulative effect over future years and any immediate sacrifices are likely to be generously rewarded in the years to come. The trouble is that it is just at the early stages of development that an immediate sacrifice is so onerous. As has been recently stated in the report of a working party on development in Asia and the Far East, an acute and important conflict lies in 'the choices between immediate consumption and rapid growth based on high levels of investment. The major conflict for the countries of the ECAFE region is the conflict between present and future consumption — the problem of time preference.'[2]

This conflict arises, it is pointed out, 'because it is not possible for a country to use more than the total amount of resources available

* *The Challenge of Development*, Jerusalem, 1958. Reprinted with the permission of the Eliezer Kaplan School of Economics and Social Sciences of the Hebrew University, Jerusalem (Israel), and the author.

[1] W. W. Rostow, 'The Take-off Into Self-sustained Growth', *The Economic Journal*, March 1956, reprinted in Agarwala and Singh (eds.), *The Economics of Underdevelopment*, Oxford University Press, 1958, pp. 154–86.

[2] From the Report of the ECAFE Working Party of the Economic Commission for Asia and the Far East on Economic Development and Planning, *Economic Bulletin for Asia and the Far East*, November 1956, p. 3.

to it'.[1] This method of presentation is useful when applied to a country in which the available labour supply as well as all physical resources — natural resources and capital equipment — are fully utilized. For a country in which there is reasonably full employment, more labour can be applied to development only at the expense of applying less to the production of consumption goods. Here a higher rate of development means less production of consumption goods, and therefore less consumption. It is under conditions of full employment of labour that it is possible to apply the classical idea of accumulation as involving a sacrifice to the present generation, incurred for the sake of the future. And since the working population can then be treated as fairly homogeneous and since their consumption constitutes a large part of the total, it is not altogether unreasonable to regard decisions about rates of development as involving, at least in part, the problem of time preference on the part of the workers. For the same individual who suffers the sacrifice will secure the future benefit, or if he does not, his children will. This does not mean of course that other classes of the community, whose consumption is far from negligible, cannot, and should not, be called upon to pay heavier taxes and so share in the sacrifice involved in a higher rate of development, but the extent to which this is expedient and practicable depends on the social and political environment, and in particular on how far taxation of the wealthier classes has already been carried as a means of improving distribution of income independently of the rate of development.

This is the position in many developed countries today whose resources, including the labour force, are pretty fully utilized under the pressure of the various competing demands, including the demands originating from quite high rates of physical investment. And there are a number of countries or regions which would usually be described as underdeveloped in which there appears to be no important reservoir of surplus labour. For example, Professor Arthur Lewis's views about industrialization in Ghana are largely based on the fact that 'there is a shortage of labour in the Gold Coast which rapid industrialization would aggravate'.[2]

I want to confine myself to the more typical case of an underdeveloped country in which the labour force is very far from being

[1] Ibid.
[2] *Report on Industrialization and the Gold Coast*, Accra, 1953, p. 65.

completely utilized. This is the position in a large part of Asia. It is also of course the position in Israel. But at this point I must make it perfectly clear that my remarks are not directed at Israel. I do so with shame and regret. I do not pretend to have any detailed knowledge of any of the countries to which, in a very general way, my remarks might apply. One does, however, hear quite a lot about them. I wish that I could say the same about Israel so far as my part of the world is concerned. The result is that while I should hope that there will be some bearing on Israel's problems in what I have to say, I cannot pretend that it is directly prompted by them.

The main point which I want to make about the typical under-developed country, in which there is surplus labour, is that it is perhaps somewhat misleading to present the problem of forcing a high rate of development in terms of the sacrifice to 'the present generation as a whole', as it was put to the ECAFE Working Party by the Secretariat.[1] What is now involved is principally a redistribution of consumption between different classes of the community and not a reduction in the total. The sacrifice is confined to particular classes. They are important of course. But there is a danger of being too much concerned about 'substantial interference with the natural time-preference of the people as individuals'[2] and of forgetting that a high rate of development from the outset involves current benefit as much as current hardship, quite apart from the all-round benefit which gradually results from the improvement in the means of production. If we think too much of the time preference of those who make a temporary sacrifice we are apt to overlook the benefit to other classes.

The burden falls quite largely on those wage earners who would be fully employed anyhow; the benefit accrues quite largely to those who secure full employment in consequence of the high rate of development and to those who would otherwise have to support them. The factors introduced by the existence of peasant proprietors and of a surplus of rural population are fundamental to the problems of a typical underdeveloped country but they need not affect the main course of my argument at this stage, and for the time being

---

[1] From a working paper prepared by the Secretariat for the ECAFE Working Party, op. cit., p. 23.
[2] Ibid.

I will only allude to them and reserve more detailed consideration for later treatment.

I want to take as my basis a proposition which is so obvious that it seems sometimes to be overlooked. It is simply this. In principle there is no reason why under these conditions a higher rate of investment need necessitate a lower aggregate of consumption, as it would if labour were scarce. For this conclusion to be completely upheld it would be necessary to assume that no productive resources are used in common by the investment and the consumption sectors. On the face of it that may sound a rather wild assumption. One thinks at once of limited resources of foreign exchange, of raw materials produced at home such as steel, of transport and power facilities, and of particular kinds of skilled labour, as important scarcities which involve a conflict between the rate of economic development and the supply of consumption goods, in the sense that more of one necessitates less of the other — if the accumulated development of the past is taken as given. The qualifications thereby introduced to my basic proposition are not really fundamental. My case here rests on the enormous flexibility of a properly conceived development scheme — and to a minor extent on some limited possibilities of applying to the pattern of consumption the methods of Procrustes — by means of discriminatory taxation and some use of controls. If a given amount of foreign exchange is available for importing capital equipment, this does not mean that the character of the equipment is also given — spades might be imported rather than bulldozers. And in an underdeveloped country there are plenty of things to be done which can be done, if necessary, in a manner that does not seriously encroach on the services of scarce resources. To quote Professor Arthur Lewis: 'Roads, viaducts, irrigation channels and buildings can be created by human labour with hardly any capital to speak of — witness the Pyramids, or the marvellous railway tunnels built in the mid-nineteenth century almost with bare hands. Even in modern industrial countries constructional activity, which lends itself to hand labour, is as much as 50 or 60 per cent of gross fixed investment, so it is not difficult to think of labour creating capital without using any but the simplest tools.'[1] It seems

---

[1] A. Lewis, 'Economic Development with Unlimited Supplies of Labour', *Manchester School*, May 1954, p. 160, reprinted in Agarwala and Singh (eds.), *The Economics of Underdevelopment*, Oxford University Press, 1958, p. 421.

to me that one of the big failures in some of the underdeveloped countries lies in not exploiting on a greater scale traditional methods of construction which, although primitive, could add substantially to the accumulation of capital wealth by harnessing surplus manpower.

I want therefore to postulate that means are available for securing that development *could* take place, *in so far as it was thought desirable*, in such a way as to take full advantage of the profuse availability of general labour and to take fully into account the scarcity of other productive resources. At any moment of time the problem is then one of trying to secure a greater redistribution of consumption. For additional employment means that those who would otherwise have been unemployed or imperfectly employed would add to their consumption and that additional consumption would have to be at the expense principally of those who would be fully employed anyhow. And over any period of time the problem is one of trying to secure a more rapid growth in the production of consumption goods. In considering the possibilities of improvement, the basic questions to be asked about any development plan are these:

1. At any and each moment of time could the more privileged, including those who enjoy full employment anyhow, consume less, so that the available supply of consumption goods could be spread out more evenly, with the result that total employment could be greater, and the rate of development speeded up?

2. Could the technical character of the equipment and improvements in which the development is expressed be modified in such a way as to take fuller advantage of the fact that, in one sense, labour is a more or less free good?

3. Could development in the consumption sector be speeded up, so as to accelerate the growth of output of consumption goods — apart from any improvement secured under 2

(*a*) as a result of the gradual speeding up of the rate of development secured under 1?

(*b*) as a result of attributing rather more importance to aggregate consumption in the fairly near future and rather less importance to the build-up for the more distant future?

Such comments as, in my ignorance, I am venturing are comments on certain habits of mind into which, I believe, it is easy to drop. I do not suggest that any of the considerations which I am advancing are not familiar to those who have been concerned with these matters. I am not, I am afraid, claiming to say anything new. Indeed, I should prefer to feel that I was not stating anything, but was simply asking some questions, by way of reassurance. But if I am giving way to the temptation to make rash assertions, it is because I have the feeling that certain methods of presentation, which are not necessarily wrong in themselves, encourage habits of mind which are to some extent wrong, and result in the considerations which I am stressing, becoming to some degree a subject for not much more than lip service.

II

I want to spend some considerable time on my first question — that of the distribution of the available supply of consumption goods. There are at least three familiar methods of presenting the problem which is here involved. One is the method which I have already illustrated — that of a conflict between present and future consumption. I have already explained why that method lends itself to overlooking completely the fact of surplus labour. There is a further objection to it — the concept which it implicitly introduces of a homogeneous working class, each member of it enjoying much the same standard as other classes. Such consumption is quantitatively extremely important. It comprises the consumption not only of capitalists in the ordinary sense, few perhaps in number but often substantial in terms of aggregate income and consumption, but also of the poor but numerous peasant proprietors and small landlords. Quite apart from the question of securing a contribution from these classes, so as to divert more of the available consumption towards those who would otherwise be unemployed, there is the serious fact to be faced and dealt with that the consumption of these classes is actually enhanced by reason of a higher rate of development, which, so far from imposing a sacrifice, confers a benefit.

Neglect of the consumption of other classes is a tendency which arises equally from the other two familiar methods of presenting the problem of the redistribution of consumption which I am now coming on to, and I will not repeat the point. The second method which I want to mention involves the familiar idea that what limits investment is the excess of production over consumption in the consumption sector, because this has to provide the consumption of those employed in the investment sector.[1] This, of course, subject to various important qualifications, is perfectly correct as a statement. My objection to it is that it seems to make it natural, rather than highly unnatural, that the amount of labour which can be employed in any situation is strictly limited. It lends itself all too easily to calculations of the amount of employment which the system can stand. Of course, anybody who makes that sort of calculation realizes that the excess of production over consumption in the consumption sector, and the progressive development of that excess, depend on the success with which consumption is restrained as well as on the success with which production is expanded. But the formulation seems to me to encourage discussion in terms of aggregates and in terms of ratios, and the overwhelmingly fundamental question of the minimum consumption per head which can be tolerated for those who are fully employed seems to me to be overshadowed. Indeed, it is often extremely difficult to discover what is assumed about this.

This difficulty arises especially over the prospective influence of the carrying out of a development plan on the growth of consumption per head of those who are fully employed anyhow. For example, under the Indian Second Five Year Plan it is visualized that the rate of total consumption may increase by some 21 per cent and the long-term plan appears to provide for it to increase over the next ten years by something like 50 per cent.[2] If one makes due allowance for the prospective growth of population and of industrial employment, it would appear — though this is not, I think, stated — that a very considerable rise in the standard of living of those who are fully employed throughout is visualized. This may be politically desirable or necessary. If so the case is not presented — and above all it is not explained why it is politically desirable or necessary to achieve such a substantial improvement in the standard of living of those who are fortunate enough to enjoy full industrial employment.

[1] See, for example, M. H. Dobb, *Economie Appliquée*, 1954, No. 3, p. 303 (translated in his *On Economic Theory and Socialism*, p. 138) and 'Second Thoughts on Capital-Intensity of Investment', *Review of Economic Studies*, Vol. XXIV, No. 1, reprinted in the present volume, pp. 239-55. Mr. Dobb is careful to point out that he is presenting 'a very simplified two-industry model'.

[2] *Second Five Year Plan*, Government of India Planning Commission, 1956, p. 74 and chart facing p. 11.

It is expected that the carrying out of the Indian Second Five Year Plan will 'not have any significant impact on the carry-over of unemployment of the earlier period'[1] (although it will, relieve underemployment in agriculture and in village and small-scale industries)[2].

It is perfectly true that, with a growing population, the increase in the labour force over the five year period is expected to amount to ten million and that the addition to employment should keep pace with that, a result which, if achieved, will be an improvement on the First Five Year Plan, the execution of which failed to increase 'employment opportunities *pari passu* with the increase in labour force'.[3] In the disappointing character of the growth of employment in relation to the growth of population, development in India, both realized and prospective, suffers from the same characteristics as development in many other countries with growing population. This defect of development and of development programmes is widespread. The carrying out of the programme for Greece, with a less rapid growth of population than that of India, 'will leave a major part of the excess labour supply, roughly anticipated at about one million at the beginning of the period, unabsorbed in effective production by 1960'.[4] With an even less rapid growth of population, the four year plan for Italy is expected to leave unemployment at over one million, but this would represent halving the figure over the period of the plan and the Italian Ten Year Plan enjoys the distinction of aiming at the virtual elimination of surplus labour by 1964.[5]

It does seem *prima facie* that the need to allow a fairly rapid rise in the standard of living of the fully employed is not sufficiently questioned. The same growing volume of consumption, if spread out more evenly, would not only mean less human misery, because the growth of employment would be more rapid, but would actually mean a more rapid growth of development. A rise in the standard of living with any rise in productivity of the fully employed worker

[1] *Second Five Year Plan, A Draft Outline,* Government of India Planning Commission, 1956, p. 8.
[2] Indian *Second Five Year Plan,* p. 74.
[3] Ibid., p. 5.
[4] *Report of the Expert Group on the Economic Development of Southern Europe,* United Nations Economic Commission for Europe, 1956, p. 16.
[5] Ibid.

seems sometimes to be regarded as an economic law, rather than something acceptance of which puts a serious brake on economic development and prevents full advantage being taken of the availability of surplus labour.

I suspect that part of the trouble arises from the use of global investment coefficients, coupled with capital-output ratios, without a sufficiently detailed and specific enquiry into the underlying relationships. It sounds impressive when we read that in India the investment coefficient — the ratio of saving and net investment to the national income — is expected to rise from about 7 per cent in 1955–6 to about 11 per cent in 1960–1, to 14 per cent in 1965–6, and to 16 per cent in 1970–1. But the question is why the rise to the ultimate level of the coefficient is so slow. A more rapid rise could be achieved if it were possible more effectively and rapidly to harness surplus manpower, by diverting to those who would otherwise be unemployed and imperfectly employed more of the additional supplies of consumption goods. An important proviso, in so far as reliance is placed on private enterprise, is that by fiscal means the extra profits and agricultural incomes which are the result of high rates of development are prevented from absorbing more than a limited amount of the additional supplies of consumption goods.

Granted that proviso, the severity of which I do not wish to underestimate, my suggestion is that there is an undue readiness to regard the investment coefficient as simply part of the data. In India, we are told, the rate of economic development depends, apart from other considerations, on 'the proportion of the current income of the community devoted to capital formation'.[1] It seems to me to be as true, and perhaps more illuminating, to say that the proportion of the current income of the community devoted to capital formation depends on the rate of economic development. The fulfilment of a more ambitious programme would mean that consumption would grow even more rapidly, but that the consumption per head of those fully employed throughout would grow less rapidly, employment would grow more rapidly, and the growth of non-wage incomes — profits and agricultural incomes — would be more rapid. The scope of any such improvement is clearly subject to severe limitations.

[1] Indian *Second Five Year Plan*, op. cit., p. 7.

III

The temptation is, as I say, to take it too easily for granted that the amount of employment which the economy can stand must be severely limited. This is the reason, I suggest for the unadventurous spirit in which the question of rates of taxation is approached in many of the reports about development plans. It is astonishing how little space is devoted to the subject and how very unspecific and feeble are the remarks made about it in reports which on many other aspects of development are extremely specific and detailed.[1]

The Italian Four Year Plan and the Greek Economic Development Programme provide rather extreme examples of the kind of attitude which I have in mind. It is assumed that taxes will not be raised at all.[2] It is true that in both cases reliance is placed on a diminution of tax evasion. But in the main the substantial growth in government revenues shown in the plans is the result simply of the projected growth of national incomes. In the case of Italy it is actually estimated that government savings will increase proportionately less than national income.

While in all such various reports lip service is normally paid to the need for restraining consumption it is seldom realized with sufficient force that unless *rates* of taxation are progressively raised, or new taxes are introduced, consumption will grow with real income, and that the growth of government revenue based on pre-existing rates of tax does not represent any positive contribution to the problem. One might have thought that if the Italian and Greek Plans do not call for any revision of taxation policy, that is a very good reason for trying out more ambitious plans. The Pakistan First Five Year Plan involves an 'increase between the first year and the final year of the Plan period in the annual amount of public revenue available for development purposes' of 'about 13 per cent of the increase in the estimated gross national product'. It is stated that 'an increase of this magnitude appears to be quite within the

---

[1] In *The First Five Year Plan, 1955–60 (Draft),* issued by the Planning Board of the Government of Pakistan, Karachi, 1956, seven pages are, however, devoted to ' some suggestions in very broad terms about possible changes in taxation' (Vol. I, pp. 162–69).

[2] *Economic Development Programme for Italy,* United Nations Economic Commission for Europe, 1956, p. 111 ; *Report of the Expert Group on the Economic Development for Southern Europe,* op. cit., p. 22.

country's means '. But if this is so, why not try out a plan which the country could not quite so easily take in its stride? It is true that in the Pakistan Plan reliance is not placed entirely on 'the automatic result of expansion of production' but 'a series of positive measures will be needed to augment revenues'.[1] The Indian Second Five Year Plan aims at securing by means of additional taxation measures, including higher rates of tax, an addition to Central and State Government revenues which represents an addition of only 16 per cent to existing revenues.[2] One half of this addition is based on the recommendations of the Taxation Inquiry Commission and the other half was left to further investigation. I hope that I do not show lack of appreciation of the problems of increasing taxation in countries like India[3] and Pakistan. I certainly do not wish to support my case by undue emphasis on the facts that in the one country the ratio of tax revenues to national income is only $7\frac{1}{2}$ per cent,[4] and that it is rather less than that in the other.[5] But I do find it remarkable that the ratio of public to total saving visualized for the next five years is only 25 per cent in India[6] and 20 per cent in Pakistan.[7] This leaves 75 per cent and 80 per cent respectively to private savings.[8] These seem extravagantly high proportions for countries in which the great mass of the population live at standards of living which preclude personal saving. In the light of such figures the phrasing of the statement of the ECAFE Working Party that 'it is important that public revenues shall grow appreciably '[9] might, one feels, have been more robust without danger of exaggeration. Public revenues do in fact automatically grow more than 'appreciably' with the growth of national product. The point at issue relates to the tax rates and to the possibility of introducing new taxes.

---

[1] Pakistan — *The First Five Year Plan*, op. cit., p. 143.

[2] Indian *Second Five Year Plan*, op. cit., pp. 78, 91.

[3] For a study of the possibilities of collecting more revenue in India from personal and business taxes, see N. Kaldor, *Indian Tax Reform*, Ministry of Finance, New Delhi, 1956.

[4] Indian *Second Five Year Plan*, op. cit., p. 90.

[5] Pakistan — *The Five Year Plan*, op. cit., p. 161.

[6] Indian *Second Five Year Plan*, op. cit., pp. 77 *et seq*.

[7] Pakistan — *The First Five Year Plan*, op. cit., p. 17.

[8] External finance is planned to supplement total saving by 22 per cent of total saving in India and by 56 per cent in Pakistan.

[9] From the Report of the ECAFE Working Party, op. cit., p. 8.

Some misleading habits of thought perhaps prevent the attack on this problem from being as forceful as it might be. First of all there is the close association which one finds in some of these reports and documents between the fact of *public* investment and the need for *public* saving. In addition to covering all current expenditure out of current revenue, governments should, we are told, 'with the assumption of increasing direct responsibility for investment . . . also endeavour to finance a significant part of such investment by public saving'. In the light of this quotation from the Report of the ECAFE Working Party [1], it seems fortunate that in fact so much of the investment in these programmes *is* to be undertaken by public bodies. On the other hand, there may be some reluctance to exacerbate the opposition which is inevitable anyhow against the intrusion of the State into the field of enterprise by attaching to it a case for more drastic taxation.

The presentation of the Indian plan relates the need for public saving, and so for additional taxes, not only, on the one side, to the amount of public investment to be undertaken, but, on the other side of the account, to the amount of borrowing to be secured from the public.[2] It is thus made to appear as though borrowing and taxes are equally good ways of raising finance for the public authorities, provided that the borrowing is from the public and not from the banking and monetary system. Instead of the proper contrast being drawn between taxes and all forms of borrowing a most misleading contrast is drawn between taxes and borrowing from the public, on the one hand, and borrowing from the banking and monetary system — deficit finance — on the other hand. The case for additional tax revenue is much less impressive if it is derived purely from an estimated failure, which might turn out unduly pessimistic, to borrow enough funds from the public.[3] These defects of presentation are avoided by the Planning Board of Pakistan, which adds public and private investment together and balances

---

[1] Loc. cit.

[2] Indian *Second Five Year Plan*, op. cit., pp. 77 *et seq.*

[3] Even Mr. Kaldor accepts this line of approach and bases the need for additional taxation on this view, which would, he thinks ' be shared by most economists' that over the five-year period of the second Indian plan ' the amount of deficit expenditure which the economy can absorb is not likely to exceed . . . Rs 800 crores', as opposed to Rs 1,200 crores envisaged under the Plan (*Indian Tax Reform*, op. cit., p. 1).

the total against public and private saving taken together, neither borrowing nor deficit entering into the picture.[1] One hopes that this presentation will assist the Pakistan Government in resisting 'the over-riding pressure . . . for relief of one kind or another' which their Planning Board anticipates as soon as a surplus of current revenue over current expenditure is revealed.[2] In Greece, on the other hand, where public investment is to play a much smaller part, the complacent view towards taxation is no doubt associated with the statement that 'it is estimated that the funds required to finance the Public Investments in local currency will be readily available to the State'.[3]

I want to mention a further reason why the case for additional taxation appears to be put forward with lack of vigour. It is very much mixed up with the idea of securing a more equitable distribution of income and wealth. So long as this is confined to meaning an equitable distribution of the burden involved in a rapid growth of employment under an ambitious development programme, there is no need to cavil. Quite the contrary. Equity, so interpreted, would mean that the interests of these who would otherwise remain unemployed or imperfectly employed would come first in the scale of priority. The case for having public saving is based on considerations of equity in this sense. But this is not how it is interpreted. 'A reduction in inequalities has to proceed from both ends', we are told in connexion with the Indian plan. 'On the one hand, measures have to be taken to reduce excessive concentration of wealth and incomes at higher levels, and, on the other, incomes in general, and particularly at the lowest levels have to be raised.'[4] As to the excessive concentrations of wealth, we have been told by Mr Kaldor that without 'an efficient system of progressive taxation on the small minority of the well-to-do who in India number only about one per cent of the population . . . the rise in expenditure during the plan will inevitably increase the wealth of the richest classes disproportionately'.[5] It is about the ideal of raising incomes at the lowest levels that I am expressing doubt. Presumably this does not

[1] Pakistan — *The First Five Year Plan,* op. cit., p. 150.
[2] Ibid., p. 162.
[3] *The Greek Long-Term Programme of Economic Development,* United Nations Economic Commission for Europe, 1956, p. 44.
[4] Indian *Second Five Year Plan,* op. cit., p. 35.
[5] *Indian Tax Reform,* op. cit., p. 1.

refer exclusively to those who secure additional employment. In the minds of some people there may be the idea of a more equitable distribution of the existing burden of taxation, but the early stages of an ambitious development programme, designed to overcome the problem of the 'take-off' and to start the cumulative process of 'to him who hath shall be given', is the wrong time for *redistributing* the burden of taxation. Additional taxes should be aimed at increasing budget surpluses. This they cannot do if they are used for tax remissions. And if they are so conceived the adverse repercussions on private saving provide a very convenient argument for anybody who wants to obstruct, on classical lines, the attempt by such means to secure greater equality. To aim at a general transfer of income downward through the social scale is not helpful to economic development except in so far as it results from economic development. On the other hand, if the disparities which were causing concern were those which exist between those who are imperfectly employed and the rest of the community as a whole, including in heavy measure large numbers of workers as well as of peasants, the concern could usefully show itself in more ambitious development programmes, facilitated by ambitious taxes all round. I doubt whether these disparities were in mind when the Pakistan Planning Board wrote that 'existing levels of consumption are already austere for the vast mass of people, and it is neither desirable nor practicable to depress them any further. On the contrary, it is urgently necessary to raise them.'[1] There is a widespread tendency to regard the unemployed as outside the community with whose interests one is concerned. When one reads, in the same report, about 'the ideals of a free society', one is forced to wonder whether the neglect of unused productive power, combined with the misery which goes with that neglect, are purposively justified by reason of the enjoyment by the more fortunate majority of a higher standard of consumption than would be compatible with more rapid development.

Neglect, in so far as it is neglect, of the interests of the unemployed and imperfectly employed goes hand in hand with neglect of the question how in fact they live. The answer is of course that in a country which has no state scheme for their support they live on their relations. When an unemployed man is provided with work

[1] Pakistan — *The First Five Year Plan*, op. cit., p. 75.

or an imperfectly employed man moves into more effective employment, the rest of the family are relieved of the burden of supporting him. Their standard of living rises even if their real earnings do not rise and if their real earnings rise progressively through time their standard of living rises faster. This is, so to speak, an uncovenanted benefit, and if it is allowed to be fully realized the rate of capital accumulation is deprived of the progressive acceleration with which the gradual elimination of extreme poverty should be capable of cumulatively endowing it. The remedy is, in determining the future course of the rate of investment, to have regard to *standards of living* of the mass of the workers rather than of real earnings per head. But the trouble is that the burden of supporting the indigent is distributed between families, and between regions, in a far from uniform manner. If policy is based on the relief to the average or typical family, some families may suffer a progressively falling standard of living and for many families the improvement may appear inadequate. But the roughness of the justice therein involved is considerably less than the roughness of justice involved in some families being much poorer per head than others.

What I am really pleading for is a more purposive and conscious set of decisions about the desirable — in the sense of minimum necessary — growth of the standard of living of the fully employed wage-earners. That will then determine how far the pace of development can be gradually accelerated. An improvement in the rate of development, other things equal, means higher profits, and higher agricultural incomes, as well as lower real wage rates for those fully employed, than would prevail under the same conditions with a lower rate of development. This will mean higher consumption for the capitalists and the agriculturists, and this will be at the expense either of the improvement in the rate of development or of the real wage rates of those fully employed. And apart from the effect of higher capitalists' incomes on the distribution of consumption, they are likely to give rise to political objection and will tend towards a concentration of the private ownership of capital. That is the case for combining an ambitious development programme with a progressive programme for drastic taxation of profits and other incomes which benefit in real value from a high level of investment instead of, like real wage rates, being kept down. The profits accrue in increasing measure but if a considerable part is diverted into the surplus of state revenues over current expenditure, the additional saving which has to match the additional investment can take the form of public saving and does not necessitate the growth of private consumption which goes with a growth of personal saving.

On this line of argument it does not matter how large gross profits become because it is the size of profits net of tax, not of gross profits, against which objections arise. The argument is, however, subject to severe limitations. As taxation becomes more drastic, the temptation to evade it, and to avoid it, becomes bigger. The disincentive effects become more and more serious, and the political obstruction more and more obstinate.

Beyond a point it may be preferable to keep down the gross profit rather than to allow it to grow and rely on keeping down the net profit. The question is how this can be done without sacrificing economic development itself. The answer is by raising indirect taxation.[1] This too contributes to public saving. It enables a given rate of investment to be matched by a rate of saving of which a smaller amount is private saving, which means that it involves smaller profits. The prices received by the producers, net of additional indirect taxes, are depressed because consumers are provided with no additional purchasing power with which to pay the taxes.

The normal argument against greater reliance on indirect taxation, apart from taxes on luxuries, is that it falls on the poor and tends to be regressive. That is not inconsistent with its falling also on the producers — and keeping down profits. In general it will fall partly on the one and partly on the other. A further argument against additional indirect taxation then might be that a reduction of profit margins will mean loss of output — high-cost production will be cut out and physical resources used less intensively. These two arguments are not, however, independent. It all turns on the elasticities of supply. If these are very small, indirect taxes fall almost entirely on the producers and the question of loss of output scarcely arises. When I say that 'beyond a point' it may be preferable to keep down the gross profit, what I have in mind is the possibility that the pace of economic development may be sufficiently great for the pressure of demand to elicit almost the maximum output which the available natural resources and equipment are capable of yielding even though unlimited labour is available to work with them. If, and in so far as, that point has been reached, indirect taxes

---

[1] Cf. N. Kaldor. op. cit., p. 4.

can be used to supplement direct taxes — provided that they do not curtail profit margins to levels at which production begins to be seriously affected. The curtailment of profits will result in curtailment of capitalists' consumption and even if it operates at the expense of some loss of output of consumption goods, there will — if this loss is only small — still be a net gain of consumption goods available for increasing investment. (The situation here depicted is one in which, with a *given* rate of investment, the imposition of indirect taxes would cause prices paid by consumers to fall relatively to wages: more than the whole of the taxes would fall on profits.)

The decision as to which commodities could stand indirect taxes of this kind therefore turns not only on the elasticity of supply of the products of each type of physical capacity but on the extent to which curtailment of profits would result in a curtailment of the capitalists' demands for the products of the same type of capacity. Commodities which constitute the staple consumption of the poorer classes do not qualify unless their supply is highly inelastic.

Indeed, these somewhat paradoxical possibilities for the use, and for the effects, of indirect taxation are not inconsistent with the introduction of subsidies on the bare necessaries of life to help meet the shock resulting from any sudden inauguration of a bolder development plan. The point is that subsidies will succeed in keeping down prices against the pressure of a rise of demand only to the extent that the supply of the necessaries has some appreciable elasticity and only because additions to capitalists' incomes are not to any appreciable extent devoted to them. It is only under these circumstances that the use of such subsidies can be justified, and clearly the justification must be strong and the use restrained. Some of the foodstuffs which are important in the diet of the poor may in this way lend themselves to subsidies, provided that the response in the supply does not merely reflect substitution for other important crops. But if there is to be a sufficient elasticity of supply to justify a subsidy, it is almost certainly necessary that most of the consequent improvement in agricultural prices should be syphoned off by securing greater revenues from land taxes or the like. Otherwise, the result will be to increase the food consumption of the agricultural population — conceivably by more than the increase of production.

The elasticities of supply to which I refer here are elasticities of short period supply—within the limitation imposed by given amounts of physical resources — though in the case of food a year or so must be allowed for the full short-period adjustments to be made. It is, however, necessary for the argument that the imposition of indirect taxes, and the resulting curtailment of profits, should not prejudicially influence the manner in which new investment takes place in the production of the taxed commodities. The curtailment of profits should not go so far as to bring the desire to invest below what is required to absorb the physical resources which can be made available. Furthermore, reliance may have to be placed on profits for some of the finance needed to pay for the investment (though such reliance, if at all extensive, points to dangerous deficiencies in the financial system). In other words, some of the disincentives which result from heavy taxation of profits result also from the curtailment of net profits which is the effect of curtailment of gross profits; and when indirect taxation has been carried so far as to begin to have serious consequences of this kind, additions to it can no longer be justified as a form of taxation which avoids all the defects of heavy taxation of profits.

What is especially important is to ensure that investment is not directed to the less desirable ends, and in particular that additions to productive capacity are calculated to expand the production of the necessaries of life of the poorer classes. This will certainly not be achieved with any success except under some system of allocation and control, but so far as concerns the influence of indirect taxation, it will be of positive assistance if it falls with greater severity on the less essential commodities. The difficulty is, however, that for administrative reasons it will usually be necessary to confine indirect taxation to a limited number of classes of commodities and that a wide range of the less essential commodities and services will escape. This, it must be admitted, would add considerably to the weight which has to be placed on any system of allocation and control for avoiding waste of investible resources in private industry and trade.

There is one very important form of discrimination which is easily secured. One of the great problems in a rapidly developing economy is to prevent diversions from export to domestic markets. The imposition of a sufficient indirect tax, with exemption of exports, can secure for any commodity that the total rate of output and its division between export and domestic trade are unaffected by reason of a rise in the domestic demand.

The question, on which I have touched, of short-period elasticity of supply raises some issues of principle which I will mention in passing. I took as my basic proposition that it is possible to organize a higher rate of investment without thereby physically necessitating a lower aggregate of consumption, so that the economic problem is one of redistributing consumption rather than of enforcing a net overall reduction. But if there is some elasticity of supply, a higher rate of investment will, by raising demand, lead to a higher output of consumption goods and, therefore, a greater aggregate of consumption. The consumption of those who benefit will increase by more than the reduction of the consumption of those who suffer. My argument is then imbued with *a fortiori* force. Instead of dealing with a limiting case, to which Keynes may be thought by some to have little to contribute, we are now dealing with a case of Keynesian unemployment which differs from the conventional case only in the degree of the inelasticity of the supply curves. The only really acceptable reason for forgoing both the development and the additional output of consumption goods which a higher rate of investment would entail could be the unwillingness of those who are anyhow fully employed to accept a lower standard of living. That seems on the face of it a poor reason for failing to take maximum advantage of the physical possibilities for stepping up the production of consumption goods. What I have said so far can be regarded as a challenge to the wages system rather than to the operation of the profit motive. But if elasticity of supply is admitted, the challenge is widened and can be directed also at the system under which the volume of production depends on profits. An economic welfare theorist could devise a wonderful method of getting the systems to produce better results, under which the unemployed would bribe the employed to accept lower wages and both parties could then be better off with higher activity in both the investment and the consumption sectors. My suggestion of subsidies belongs, on the other hand, to the realm of practical politics, even though it is capable of useful application only in severe moderation.

The existence of appreciable elasticity of supply may mean that employment has not been carried to as high a level as the system is capable of 'standing', and that a higher rate of development would be perfectly feasible even without the introduction of special measures such as additional taxes. If the possibilities of production which exist even with the limits imposed by wage and profit systems, and by existing policies, are not being fully exploited, the immediate defect lies with the programme or with the execution of the pro- gramme. It may be premature to discuss the changes required to facilitate more rapid development if, up to a point, development could be speeded up without any important changes. Some authori- ties are inclined to take the view, about particular countries which are undergoing development, that the limiting factor is not at all the supply of consumption goods. It seems fairly clear that this was not the limiting factor during the period of the Indian First Five Year Plan. At the end of it 'prices . . . were lower by 13 per cent than when the plan started; in fact, they were slightly below the level on the eve of the Korean war'.[1] Foreign exchange reserves fell by less than was envisaged in the Plan. 'The severe fall, by about 10 per cent, in Indian food prices in 1954-5' which 'caused con- siderable distress in rural areas', is the reason why Dr Balogh, in discussing the Second Five Year Plan, welcomes the inclusion of labour-using public works; for the consequent increase in 'the income of the lowest wage earner' will 'increase demand for food grains, which are relatively abundant'.[2]

[1] Indian *Second Five Year Plan*, op. cit., p. 5. It is noteworthy that in a letter by Mr Eugene Black, Governor of the World Bank, to the Indian Finance Minister in the autumn of 1956 on the subject of the Second Five Year Plan, the record of the period of the First Plan is favourably contrasted with the prospects for the Second Plan unless the programme for the public sector is cut down.

[2] T. Balogh, 'India's Plan under Scrutiny', *The Banker*, July 1956. With his implicit criticism of the Plan for failing to take full advantage of existing resources, Dr Balogh combines the rather different criticism that 'investment in agriculture seems inadequate'. He is clearly thinking both of the possibility of speeding up the pace of development with existing agricultural resources and of the possibility of speeding up the growth of development by more rapid expansion of these resources. Similarly : 'The commodities that India needs most to prevent an increase in investment and income from leading to a monetary breakdown are the goods that are in heavy surplus in the United States—sugar, butter, cotton, wheat and rice.'

And elsewhere, in ' Problems of the Second Five Year Plan ', *Capital*, Calcutta, 20 December, 1956, Dr Balogh refers ' to the unusually long series of favou- rable monsoons, a recurrence of which over the second five year plan period can surely not be counted upon with any assurance '. The vagaries of the weather have, of course, to be reckoned with. The proposal of the Indian Planning Com- mission for the building up of buffer stocks is presumably put forward as something to be done in the event of exceptionally favourable weather rather

If Dr Balogh is right about this it means that the Plan, or its fulfilment, fails to comply with even the most conservative and unambitious criteria. As Mrs Joan Robinson has put it: 'If it is not fear of the unemployed eating too much when they are given work that prevents full employment from being the objective, there must be some other hidden snag which the planners are trying to steer past, and it would surely be best to find out what it is and seek for means to root it out'.[1] Dr Balogh tells us that in India, 'the two main bottlenecks are: first, organizing capacity, and, secondly, foreign exchange for essential (machinery) imports. It is not as if food imports at this juncture represented an important burden'.[2] And one is often told much the same about other countries too when one tries to find out what really are the factors which are limiting the rate of economic development.[3]

It certainly does seem to be a fact that investment is often held up by shortage of the foreign exchange required to pay for imports of equipment. The availability of foreign exchange must of course impose a decisive limitation on the maximum rate of development which can be carried out at any particular stage of the development process. This arises because imports supplement domestic production of consumption goods and because exports compete with consumption for the use of physical productive resources. In basing my argument on the hypothesis of a given total supply of consumption goods at any moment of time, I have implicitly been ruling out the possibility of improving on the planned rate of development at the expense of bigger imports and smaller exports of consumption

than at the expense of the rate of development calculated to absorb normal harvests (Indian *Second Five Year Plan*, op. cit., p. 39).

[1] Joan Robinson, ' Unemployment and the Second Plan', Supplement to *Capital*, Calcutta, 20 December, 1956.

[2] Balogh, ' Problems of the Second Five Year Plan', op. cit.

[3] Serious doubts as to the criteria which underlie development plans are raised by the following passage, relating to redistributive tax measures, from the Secretariat working paper prepared for the ECAFE Working Party : ' To the extent that a redistributive fiscal policy shifts purchasing power and real income from the rich to the poor, it tends to raise the effective demand for domestic products, reduce non-essential imports and provide greater inducement to invest in the domestic private sector. At the same time, redistributive finance, if applied too far in the form of high marginal tax rates, can impede the entrepreneurial effort and restrict further investment' (op. cit., p. 47).

goods. But this does not mean that the allowance of foreign exchange for imports of equipment should be allowed to dominate the rate of investment. If it does so it is because of failure to make sufficient allowance for the possibilities, referred to earlier in this paper, of importing equipment involving more capital-saving techniques and of carrying out part of the development by primitive methods requiring the use of very little capital per man employed. This brings into prominence Dr Balogh's other main bottleneck — organizing capacity. The fact that some techniques are less capital-intensive does not mean that a deviation towards them is easy to make. And, in general, it requires more organizing power, and not less, to cope with larger bodies of men endowed with smaller amounts of capital per head. But in a different sense the trouble is too *much* organization. There is, I feel, too premature a desire to ape the elaborate capitalistic processes of advanced industrial economies. There is also perhaps too much emphasis on the idea of balance in the development programme. The result is an unduly rigid relationship between the amount of foreign exchange available for importing the equipment and the amount of employment in the investment sector.

The shortage of organizing capacity is, of course, an extremely serious factor. This is not, however, a reason for unadventurous planning. In all countries development suffers from difficulties of organization. But the difficulties are faced more effectively where the targets are ambitious, and more effective steps will then be taken to improve and expand the available organizing capacity. It is important also that the system of allocation and control, required to prevent wasteful use of resources, should not be so elaborate and detailed as to frustrate the natural response to prosperity in socially constructive directions of the spirit of enterprise. Production will often be impeded by some rather simple physical bottlenecks which will yield fairly easily to treatment under the influence of 'natural forces', without involving heavy investment.

Poor organization, combined perhaps with the use of primitive methods of construction, does in a sense mean waste of resources. It means waste in a *real* sense if the resources in question are consumption goods which might be used to provide more useful alternative employment in the investment sector. It may also mean waste in a real sense if it involves squandering foreign exchange, in the purchase of equipment and in increasing the supply of

consumption goods, which might have been conserved and used to
better purpose later on when time allowed better organization to
be built up. But unlike foreign exchange the services of surplus
labour cannot be conserved. Failure to use them currently entails
carrying into the future nothing but human deterioration and de-
gradation, misery and unrest. The most that can be demanded is
that the value of the work carried out — with 'bare hands' or
however it may be — represents compensation from the social
point of view for the adverse effect on the standards of living of
those who would be fully employed anyhow, after allowance has
been made for the saving in cost of supporting indigent relations,
and after such allowance has been made as society, so to speak,
wishes to make for the consequent improvement in the standard
of living of those who secure the additional employment, and of
other classes of the community. My case certainly rests on there
being plenty of useful work to be done within the limits which I
have imposed — I am far from advocating public works undertaken
almost entirely for sake of the employment provided.

The case for driving the system rather harder than it appears
willing to go derives support from other considerations as well as
from difficulties of organization. The difficulties which stand in
the way of an adequate system of taxation are partly administrative
and partly political. Both kinds of difficulty are very powerful
when it is a matter of preparing proposals in cold blood — at a
time when the need arises purely from paper calculations about the
future and not from the pressure of present-day facts. Mr Kaldor
was invited to investigate 'the Indian Tax System in the light of
the revenue requirements of the Second Five Year Plan',[1] as actually
published. We shall discover fairly soon whether, under the pressure
of the execution of the Plan, Mr Kaldor's proposals, or their equivalent, are put into effect. What I suppose we shall never know is
whether, had the Plan been more ambitious, Mr Kaldor would have
felt able to formulate correspondingly more ambitious proposals.

The same considerations apply to the use of controls. It was only
when towards the end of 1956 the Indian foreign exchange reserves
started falling with unexpected rapidity that it had to be accepted
that a considerable amount of the less necessary imports could be
excluded. The Indian Planning Commission stresses the need

[1] N. Kaldor, op. cit., p. i.

for 'preparedness to adopt physical controls and allocations as necessary. . . . Controls on essential consumption cannot be ruled out in particular situations'. But it 'would be desirable on psychological as well as administrative grounds to avoid as far as possible control and rationing of the necessities of life',[1] and no doubt other controls as well.[2] But the way to reduce the risk of being forced to introduce additional controls is to exercise appropriate restraint in planning and execution. What one would really like to know is whether, in the secret minds of the planners, any ultimate resort to additional controls will vindicate the plans as adequately bold or condemn them for undue rashness.

I do not feel that, speaking in Israel today, there is need further to labour the point that the end plays a decisive part in determining the means.

In considering the possibilities of more rapid development I have been admitting that a sacrifice is involved — to a particular class of the community — and so far I have on the whole been at pains to confine the possible sacrifice to the forgoing of part of the year-by-year improvement in standards of living rather than to call at any point of time for an absolute fall in standards. It must, however, be admitted that the improvement on the development plan to be secured in this way will begin by being very small, and though it will increase cumulatively through time it may be a long time before it is at all considerable. The cumulative implication of 'To Him who hath shall be given' could be applied far more fruitfully if it was possible to face some small absolute fall in the immediate standard of living of the fully employed, resulting from a sudden jump in the rate of development. It is this, rather than the more modest attack confined to the rate of improvement, which involves the really serious political difficulties. They could be lessened by providing in the plan for a fairly rapid restoration to something rather better than the pre-existing standards, the rate of improvement

---

[1] Indian *Second Five Year Plan*, op. cit., p. 39.

[2] For a similar indication of reluctant apprehension, see the report of the ECAFE Working Party, op. cit., p. 12. The Pakistan Planning Board are naturally more unqualified on the issue. 'Extensive and rigorous controls on the use of resources . . . would be repugnant to the national ideals which have been enshrined in the Constitution recently adopted. . . . We must . . . give full consideration to the environment within which private enterprise can flourish.' (Pakistan — *The First Five Year Plan*, op. cit., p. 75.)

7

being severely restricted only after that has been achieved. It would be easier too politically if the rise of prices accompanying a sudden improvement in the rate of development could be associated with additional indirect taxation, so as to avoid a sudden increase in profits. This would have advantages from the economic point of view, subject to the considerations advanced earlier, and it would also help to allay apprehensions of a progressive rise of prices if the rise could, in people's minds, be attributed to extra taxes.

IV

I must deal very briefly with the third familiar method which I want to refer to of presenting the problem of the distribution of the available supply of consumption goods. It is the method which involves the use of that bewildering and misleading word 'inflation'. It is misleading because, as commonly used, it suggests that the weight of heavy demands on resources is dangerously onerous only in so far as monetary factors can be said to contribute to it.[1] Above all, it distracts attention from the part played by the wage bargain in fostering a progressive upward movement of prices. I will not here elaborate my views on the topic of deficit finance as we are, I believe, having a separate session on the monetary aspects of development. I will content myself now with saying that in my view the fundamental issue is not monetary but physical, as presented, for example, by the available supply of consumption goods and the question of their distribution. But I would not for a moment deny that a rapidly rising price level presents a serious obstacle to a country's development and that it is perfectly possible that as a result of trying to do too much a country may succeed in doing too little. Nor would I deny that, especially in underdeveloped countries, the speculative indulgence in hoarding of commodities and gold, and in wasteful forms of building, leads to misdirection of resources. These anti-social methods of holding private wealth call for strict controls and stringent penal measures. Their extent does also depend, among other things, on the general state of credit and on levels of

[1] For example : 'There is the danger that the amount of deficit finance proposed in the Second Plan will prove to be well beyond the capacity of the Indian economy to absorb without excessive price increases' — from the letter, already referred to, addressed to the Indian Finance Minister by the President of the World Bank.

rates of interest. This is a sense in which monetary policy is very important. But monetary policy must be conceived and developed in terms of the total stock of money in relation to other forms of private wealth, and some compromise has to be struck between the desire to promote socially constructive investment in the private sector and the desire to discourage anti-social methods of holding wealth. No assurance of correct monetary policy can be derived from matching the expansion of the monetary medium with the growth in the use of money for the purposes of day-to-day transactions.[1] This growth is a factor in determining the rate of investment which should be aimed at, because it requires restraint or consumption to build up the stock of money used for the purposes of day-to-day transactions. But the extent to which investment is financed by the monetary and banking systems will not determine whether the rate of investment is or is not dangerously high. The usual rule for the safe amount of deficit finance provides no assurance whatever that monetary policy starts off right and even if by some happy chance it starts right there is really very little assurance that it will be kept right by adherence to this rule.

This observation has perhaps more application to Israel than most of my paper. And in going on to my next point I have Israel especially in mind, and I will not shirk being blunt. The behaviour of money wages is the key to the behaviour of the price level in Israel, as in advanced industrial economies. In a country like India, on the other hand, the proportion of the working population which lives on wages is small. Even there, however, the wage system provides some sort of a base, small and uncertain though it may be, for the very large pyramid of the price structure, though obviously other important elements contribute to the danger that the system of prices will move progressively higher in an unsuccessful attempt to achieve stability. My main objection to the word inflation, in

[1] One is often told that a monetary theory which is applicable to advanced countries has no place in the underdeveloped countries. I have indicated in the text the importance in underdeveloped countries of anti-social forms of holding wealth. But on the main point of difference which is often stressed, the Pakistan Planning Board takes precisely the contrary view: ' Money is accumulated beyond transactions needs as one of the major methods of storing or holding wealth. In this respect, of course, the situation differs radically from that of highly-advanced industrial economies.' (Pakistan— *The First Five Year Plan*, op. cit., p. 155. It has been hinted earlier in the text that the usual mystique about deficit finance is avoided in this document.)

the sense in which it is commonly used, is that it seems to grant some partial absolution to the parties to the wage bargain. If only one was permitted to take the rather simple view that the vicious spiral was due to the unsuccessful attempt of wages to catch up prices, or something of that kind, and leave the quantity theory of money out of it, responsibility would be more clearly attached where it belongs. When labour is organized its leaders should be able to say to what extent their policy takes into account its full implications — in terms of a brake on economic development, of a drag on the growth of employment, and of postponement of the date at which surplus manpower will finally have been absorbed into full and effective employment and the benefits of capital accumulation can be more handsomely displayed in the form of rising standards of living as opposed to a rising volume of employment. If the carefully considered view of the representatives of organized labour is that the Government is trying, in the interests of absorbing immigrants into the economic life of the country and of its economic development generally, to impose too heavy a burden on those who are already well established in industrial employment, and if that view brooks no discussion or argument, one would have imagined that in a country like Israel there must be less heavy-handed and destructive methods of influencing the Government's policy than by operating through the wage bargain. I put it like that because I believe that a calm, scientific appraisal of the implications of a high rate of development will be conducted with a public spirit which is broader and more far-sighted than the public spirit which serves as a drag — an effective drag, but only up to a point — on wage movement. But, of course, it is quite essential that, for political and sociological reasons, as well as economic, the taxation of other classes should be severe, in application as well as intention. I have already mentioned the part which might be played by subsidizing some of the bare essentials of life. I need not expand on the futility of tying money wages to a cost of living index, but stabilization of an index based on the prices of a few bare necessities could serve a useful purpose.[1]

---

[1] It is worth noting that the last round of Swedish wage negotiations, which will result in very modest increases over the ensuing two years, has led to agreement that an escalator clause, which becomes effective if the cost of living rises by more than a certain critical amount, will not operate if the rise in the cost of living is attributable to special taxes imposed for anti-inflationary purposes.

Employers also need to be asked to exercise restraint in bidding up wages. This is not a very palatable view but I do not see how it can be avoided. It is especially important in countries in which there is no strong trade-union movement, and in which therefore the vicious spiral may result from the actions and attitudes of the employers as much as from those of the workers.

I am touching here on the tricky field of social psychology, and of the possible influences of education and propaganda in communities with which I am entirely unacquainted. All I will say is that I am not convinced that nothing could be achieved if the issues were presented on a straightforward and common-sense sort of basis. It is not merely the usual argument that wage increases defeat their own purpose. It is a question of securing some appreciation of the idea that wage increases retard economic development and that the benefits associated with development are not only those which lie in the future but also take the current form of less risk of unemployment and a smaller burden in supporting relations who are unemployed or imperfectly employed. It is particularly important in a country like India, where wage labour is a small proportion of the total, that this small tail should by every possible means be discouraged from wagging a very large dog.

V

Having dealt now, at rather considerable length, with three methods of presenting the problems involved in the distribution of the available supply of consumption goods, all of which I regard as misleading — though not necessarily as erroneous — I suppose that I should at least indicate a method which I would myself prefer. Granted the kind of economic system which rules in the countries which I have in mind, the problem, it seems to me, is best presented in terms of a vested interest on the part of a large majority of the population in a standard of living which, though low enough in all conscience, represents more than their share of the available supply of consumption goods, with the result that the minority have to live on a standard which is very much lower. The vested interest is partly the result of physical necessity. A man needs more food, and more clothes too, if he is doing hard work than if he is idle or doing only occasional light work. It is conceivable that, in particular countries at particular times, the total effective power of the whole labour force would be less if consumption was divided equally — just as shipwrecked sailors in a life-boat might be well advised to concentrate dwindling rations on those who man the oars, the rest being kept alive on a starvation basis. I doubt, however, whether the economic system could usually find full justification purely in terms of expediency. It is a system under which, to put it crudely and brutally, some must live on a starvation basis so as to enable those who are in effective and full employment to enjoy the higher standard which, for a mixture of reasons, they are able to maintain. The problem is how to secure that the starvation standard, which has to be the lot of some, is, progressively through time, the lot of as few as possible.

The problem is also to secure that it is the lot of those who are least able to make a useful social contribution by being in employment. This is the answer to those, like Dr Balogh, who argue that, in a country like India, 'a cut in private consumption expenditure', resulting from heavier taxation of the rich, 'will not . . . necessarily produce the desired results. A large part of this expenditure is devoted to servants or goods produced by handicraft. A non-discriminating cut in expenditure might, in fact, easily result in increased unemployment rather than increased investment.'[1] But if servants and craftsmen become unemployed it becomes possible to employ others instead who would otherwise have to remain unemployed. Granted that some have to starve, it is better that it should be the parasites of the rich rather than those capable of constructive work.

The solicitude which I appear to invite on behalf of the unemployed should not be allowed to suggest that I am urging the case for 'work for work's sake'. The case for taking advantage of the existence of surplus labour to increase output is not to be confused with any suggestion that greater employment should be secured at the expense of smaller output.

But the rejection of 'inferior' techniques does not rule out the possible adoption of more capital-saving methods, so as to secure a larger output, with the aid of the limited amount of capital that is available, by employing more labour. The natural bias against any deliberate encouragement of inefficient methods sometimes becomes a very wrong-headed bias in favour of highly capital-

---

[1] Balogh, ' India's Plan under Scrutiny ', op. cit.

intensive methods which are appropriate only to economies in which labour is scarce and dear. From this confusion there appears to have developed in some quarters a feeling of intellectual snobbery against taking into account the fact that labour is abundant. This is combined with the feeling that ' the most important single factor is promoting economic development ' being ' the community's readiness to develop and apply modern technology to processes of production '.[1] This entails using the same processes as are used in the most advanced countries.

There are of course great difficulties in the way of adjusting the application of modern technology, which has been developed in advanced countries, so as to take account of the relative scarcity of capital and abundance of labour in underdeveloped countries.[2] And of course imported plant is more likely in its character to be appropriate to the economic circumstance of the supplying country than of the importing country.

A more valid consideration arises with plant which is highly durable or which takes a long time to get into production. It is then necessary to consider to what extent during the life history of the plant labour is likely to become scarcer.[3] Hence the importance of finding an answer to a question put, in the context of the Indian Second Five Year Plan, by Mrs Joan Robinson : ' By the time the basic industries ', on the importance of building up which strong emphasis is laid, ' are ready to produce machinery, will the surplus of labour have been digested so that the time will be ripe to begin mechanizing industry and agriculture in earnest ? '[4]

The question of the right choice of technique is vast and baffling and I will confine myself to a few comments. First, the choice of technique in the production of consumption goods. This has become a familiar problem. Low wages in themselves ensure that under the influence of private enterprise relatively capital-saving techniques will be used — i.e. more capital-saving than would be used if wages were higher.[5] But the industrial wage is not so low as would be

---

[1] Indian *Second Five Year Plan*, op. cit., p. 6.

[2] Cf. *Analyses and Projections of Economic Development*, prepared by the Economic Commission for Latin America, New York, 1955, Vol. I, p. 8.

[3] On this, and the related issues, cf. *The Greek Long-Term Programme of Economic Development*, op. cit., p. 24.

[4] Joan Robinson, op. cit.

[5] But it is efficiency wages which matter and as against a relatively low wage per head has to be set any relatively low intrinsic efficiency of the labour.

necessary to reflect the fact that, in those countries of which I speak, labour is more or less a free good.[1] Does this mean that it would be desirable to deviate in the direction of even less capital-using techniques than will be adopted under private enterprise? Or, on the other hand, is it possible to rest on the idea that ' to the extent that the competitive market system is operating effectively, the need for any special policies for allocating resources among different purposes is obviated '?[2]

The usual answer is that private enterprise will promote the socially desirable technique provided that the social objective is to maximize the current rate of accumulation.[3] The reason is that the maximization of profit will maximize saving, including the contribution to public saving made by taxes on profits. This rule has in fact to be modified — even for operation on its own ground. It does not take into account the contribution to public saving made by indirect taxes. If the system of indirect taxation is such[4] that a substantial additional contribution is made to the revenue when more men are employed in producing additional consumption goods, this should be brought into account but is not brought into account by the calculations of private enterprise (which is influenced by the ruling rate of profit and not by the high rate of profit which would rule if indirect taxation were abolished but the rate of investment nevertheless maintained). Allowance also has to be made for the fact that a man who is provided with additional employment increases his consumption by less than the wage which he is now paid. In so far as the saving to his relations of the cost of maintaining him in unemployment, or in imperfect employment, becomes reflected in a higher rate of investment[5] (and a corresponding narrowing

---

[1] It is sometimes objected that in such countries the proper social cost of labour is the additional consumption which is required for physical reasons to enable a man to work efficiently, over and above what he has to keep alive on when he is out of work. This would be valid, however, only if no account were taken of this additional consumption in considering economic objectives. The normal procedure is based on the view — which seems justified — that a man derives satisfaction from the additional food which he can afford when he is in work, including that part of it without which he would be physically incapable of working.

[2] From the Report of the ECAFE Working Party, op. cit., p. 3.

[3] See, for example, M. H. Dobb, op. cit.

[4] In accordance with the argument advanced earlier in the text.

[5] As was urged earlier in the text.

of the gap between real wage rate and standard of living of those who were already in full employment), this again is something which is not allowed for in the calculations of private enterprise. Private enterprise, in its search for maximum profits, fails to make allowance for the existence of surplus labour except in so far as this is reflected in the wage rates which are paid, and for both the forgoing reasons this failure implies that it adopts a technique which, from the social point of view, is too capital-using even if the social objective is to maximize the current rate of accumulation, i.e. it would be desirable to use a technique requiring more labour and less capital for a given output.

The deviation in this direction called for by the two reasons which I have stated is limited. It would still be possible, by further deviation in this direction, to secure, for given current investment in the production of consumption goods, a more rapid growth of output and with it a more rapid growth of employment. The argument against this is that the more rapid growth in the fairly immediate future of output of consumption goods, of consumption, of national income, and of employment, would be at the expense of investment in the fairly immediate future, and therefore of consumption and income in the more distant future. To secure the objective of maximum rate of accumulation it is necessary to employ the available capital in a relatively inefficient manner, i.e. less productively than it would be employed if it were used with more labour. The reason can best be seen in terms of the function, as I have described it, of starvation in regulating the economic system. A more efficient use of capital would entail ' too ' rapid a diminution of the number of those who, unemployed or imperfectly employed, live on a starvation basis.

The question of the right social objective is of course crucial. Do we necessarily accept the view put forward by the ECAFE Working Party that ' the basic principle in economic development is the optimum use of resources, so as to maximize the rate of growth over time '?[1] Although the Indian Planning Commission refers to ' an attempt to work out the implications of the development effort

[1] Report of the ECAFE Working Party, *Economic Bulletin for Asia and the Far East*, op. cit., p. 3. The Working Party mentions as a conflict which does arise in practice that ' between such aims as the desire for full employment and maximum growth ' but this is not expressed in the form of a conflict between output at near and at distant dates.

in terms of factor allocations and product yields so as to maximize income and employment ',[1] and although they state that ' it is imperative that in a country with an abundant supply of man-power, labour-intensive modes of production should receive pre-ference all along the line ',[2] in the outcome it is difficult to infer to what extent the maximization of the rate of accumulation is not an overriding objective, in so far as the future course of the rate of accumulation depends on the pattern of current investment.

In advocating boldness in the planning of development, I have tried to throw doubt on the validity of the conventional idea of a conflict between the interests of the present and of the future. I have argued that, in a country with surplus labour a high rate of development need not involve such a conflict. The conflict is all in the present — between the interests of those who are fully em-ployed anyhow and those who could secure employment from a higher rate of development ; but in terms of the current rate of consumption regarded as an aggregate there need be no conflict. In this sense stepping up the rate of development can be of benefit in the present as well as in the future. When, however, it comes to the choice of technique for the production of consumption goods, and to the influence of that choice on the rate of development, there is a genuine conflict. It is conflict between the interests of the relatively near future and the interests of the relatively more distant future. These interests can be expressed in terms of income, and also of consumption, taken as aggregates ; while if full employ-ment can be assumed anyhow for the more distant future, there is a conflict between employment in the near future and standards of living in the distant future.

A choice of technique which sacrifices everything to the interests of the distant future is entirely without justification. It may seem feasible to ignore the simple political and psychological fact that people are more interested in benefits which they will enjoy early rather than late — and perhaps only vicariously enjoy through their children ; although neglect of this simple fact is impossible to reconcile with the respect which is paid, in the name of liberty and democracy, for the interests of those who are relatively fortu-nate in being fully employed anyhow as against the unfortunate

[1] Indian *Second Five Year Plan*, op. cit., p. 15.
[2] Ibid., p. 27.

who are unemployed or imperfectly employed. But what cannot be ignored is that an addition to consumption of given size means more when people are very poor than when they are less poor, and that the implication of development is that the people are gradually going to become less poor as time goes on. It seems reasonable to add that an addition to consumption of given size means more at a time when it accompanies extra employment than at a time when conditions of full employment have been achieved anyhow.

The real conflict, therefore, arises over the possibility of securing an addition to the consumption, and to the employment, of the present generation over the immediately coming years at the price of foregoing, in the more distant future, a large amount of consumption. How the appropriate rate of discount should be evaluated is a nice question. But it is clear that the right technique is a less capital-using one than the technique which is calculated to maximize the rate of accumulation.

What is here advocated is some sacrifice in this way of the rate of development for the sake of using capital more efficiently and for the sake of avoiding a nonsensical neglect of the interests of the near future as opposed to those of the distant future. This does not mean abandonment of the claim that rates of development are capable of being higher than in fact they are, as a result of greater restraint on consumption per head, or on the growth of consumption per head, of those who are fully employed anyhow and of the recipients of profits and agricultural incomes. What it means is that on the basis of the physical resources available at each moment of time, the highest possible rate of development should be achieved; but that the form in which physical resources are expanded with the passage of time should not be determined solely with an eye to securing maximum rates of development. In other words, there is a limit to the extent to which, for the sake of the rate of development, capital should be embodied in an inefficient form — by which I mean a form in which it results in a smaller output than it would be capable of if combined with more labour.

There is another aspect of the pattern of investment which also involves the same sort of conflict between consumption and employment in the near future and consumption in the distant future. But this time a bias towards consumption and employment in the near future is favourable, and not unfavourable, towards the rate of accumulation in the near future, though a higher rate of accumulation in the near future can be secured only at the expense of accumulation in the distant future, and ultimately of course of the accumulated stock of capital. These conflicts are involved in the choice between quick-yielding and slow-yielding forms of investment.[1]

It is frequently asked why far more of the available investible resources are not applied so as to secure quick results in the form of additional production of the goods which workers consume. In this way the over-riding bottleneck which limits investment could be more rapidly widened, and the growth of investment, as well as of consumption and employment, would be accelerated. In fact, it is usual to find that only a fraction of the total investment envisaged under a development plan is directed to agriculture. In the case of the Indian Second Five Year Plan, there was a last-minute decision of the National Development Council that 'it is imperative that the targets of agricultural production proposed in the Plan should be further improved upon'.[2]

On the other hand, the investment of resources in the build-up of, say, a steel industry, to be geared into a heavy machinery industry, and in the improvement of power and transport facilities, will ultimately, when the long periods of gestation have been completed, prove far more fruitful than the alternative quick-yielding investments — in terms of the consumption goods yielded. It may be well worth while making a sacrifice in the near future of some of the potential growth of consumption, and of employment, for the sake of much bigger gains in the more distant future.

This argument is a strong one and goes a long way. There is no clear-cut solution to the problem as to how far it should impose itself on the pattern of development. Essentially it is a question, once again, of the rate at which the more distant future is discounted (the concept of discounting the future being interpreted in the widest possible sense). The difficulty is that one does not know what rates of discount are implicit in any particular plan.

---

[1] The same sort of considerations are involved in dividing the available foreign exchange resources between the financing of imported equipment and financing of imported consumption goods (and raw materials required to make them) and of loss of exportable surpluses resulting from the stepping-up of domestic consumption.

[2] Indian *Second Five Year Plan*, op. cit., p. 3.

It so happens that very often long gestation periods go with high durability of the plant and equipment (which to a considerable extent is in such cases in the nature of constructions rather than ordinary machinery). This means that the more distant future, over which 'the much bigger gains' might be available, may be strung out very far indeed.

And of course long gestation periods and high durability mean that the techniques in question are highly capital-using. This brings one back to the question at what point, in relation to the distant horizons which the elaborate build-ups are aimed at, reasonably full employment is likely to be achieved. Part of the point of the question is, of course, that the allocation of investible resources to these slow-yielding capital-intensive forms of investment itself holds up the process of absorbing surplus manpower.

Despite the difficulties involved in the making of the relevant decisions, it is natural to ask what would be the economic implications of putting back in time, say by ten years, a part of the section of a plan which involves the long-term build-up. It would involve postponement — not by ten years but by something approaching ten years — of a part of the ultimate benefits, which in any case will not be fully realized for many years to come. Might not the postponement seem worth suffering for the sake of a more rapid absorption of surplus manpower and a more rapid growth *in the near future* of consumption — as well as of investment?

Whether that is so or not, the case which I have tried to indicate for securing bigger sacrifices — either absolute though temporary or at the expense of rates of improvement of standard — from the rest of the community, for the sake of drawing people more rapidly out of unemployment and imperfect employment, is strengthened if the whole of the resultant additional investment could be conceived as taking quick-yielding shape.

Before leaving this topic I would mention three further doubts. The first one arises over the extent to which under development plans the growth of consumption of basic necessities may be sacrificed for the sake of growth of consumption of less essential goods and services. This doubt gives rise to two separate questions. Is the benefit which development aims at insufficiently concentrated on the large majority of the community who are really poor? Secondly, is sufficient influence conceived as being exercised on the pattern of consumption of the poorer classes, in the form of discriminatory taxation and controls? It is natural enough with the growth of income that the demand for passenger travel, for the domestic use of electricity and for consumer capital goods should rapidly grow. But these particular demands involve high capital-output ratios and it would be well to contain them for a time.

My second doubt arises on the technique of planning. To secure internal consistency in a plan is not easy. But it is important (within limits). Is there, however, a danger that because a plan is internally consistent there will be a tendency to regard it as being necessarily a good plan?

My third doubt can also be expressed in the form of a question. Is there a danger that on the distant horizon, to which so much in these plans has to be aimed, it is a high rate of accumulation rather than a high rate of consumption which the build-up is designed to facilitate? Is there a danger of accumulation being regarded as an end in itself?

VI

Before I close I must include a sketchy elucidation of the implications of 'imperfect employment', as I have used the term, in my typical underdeveloped country. More important than total unemployment is underemployment, particularly in agriculture. But still more important is imperfect employment. This results from the overcrowding of workers into particular occupations, to such a degree that if some of them were diverted to other work the resulting loss of product would be small in relation to their own consumption. Imperfect employment, like underemployment, is particularly associated with agriculture, especially among peasant proprietors whose numbers are increasing rapidly. It is bound up with lack of alternative opportunities. But under a system in which each member of the family shares the fruit of the family's toil so long as he lives and works with them but ceases to receive his share if he leaves the family holding, the incentive to the individual to seek work elsewhere is unlikely to reflect the full economic benefit which the family, and society generally, would derive from his diversion to more productive work. The economic benefit is measured roughly by the excess of the wage in industry over the marginal product in agriculture, whereas the private incentive is measured roughly by the excess of the industrial wage over the agricultural average product. The agricultural marginal product under conditions of over-population tends to be very low indeed — it is sometimes described as zero or even negative.

The idea of imperfect employment can also be applied to those middleman activities which yield a smaller social than private gain. In so far as they are often conducted by uneconomically large family units, this then accentuates the imperfection. And some self-employment in service trades is also imperfect, in the same kind of sense.

In applying the foregoing analysis to a diversion of labour from agriculture to industry, allowance has to be made as a social cost for the loss of the marginal product in agriculture if it is at all appreciable, and to that extent the conclusions require qualification. The marginal product in the relevant sense should, however, be estimated after proper allowance has been made for the stimulating effect on agricultural efficiency of a withdrawal of surplus manpower — a factor which in itself will tend towards a low marginal product. Allowance also has to be made for the social cost involved in providing new dwellings and other services for immigrants into the towns.[1]

The standard of living among peasant proprietors tends for three separate reasons to benefit from a high rate of development; and where there is a landlord he will absorb some or most of this benefit. Firstly, there is the favourable effect of high and rising levels of income and expenditure on the terms on which food is exchanged for products of industry. Secondly, there is the favourable effect on agricultural efficiency of development in agriculture itself. And, thirdly, there is the effect of restraint, resulting from withdrawal of

[1] There must often be a strong case for small-scale industrialization in the rural districts, as well as for constructional activity based on the village, so that the labourer can continue to live as part of a peasant family, draw a share of the agricultural product and work for correspondingly low industrial wages, and be available for work at harvest time on the family holding.

Professor Arthur Lewis, who has been quoted earlier in the text on the shortage of labour in Ghana, points out elsewhere that 'in the Gold Coast, although there is an acute shortage of male labour, any industry which offered good employment to women would be besieged with applications', ('Economic Development with Unlimited Supplies of Labour', op. cit., p. 143, *The Economics of Underdevelopment*, p. 404) — surely a strong argument for dispersed industrialization.

labour into the towns, on the number of people who have to share the produce of any particular area of land.

To some extent a rise in rural standards of living is properly regarded as highly desirable, even though it operates at the expense of the growth of industrial employment (and at the expense therefore of the alleviation of rural overpopulation). The important thing is that any such rise should be purposive and not accidental, and that it should be limited to the minimum which appears essential. This is especially important because of the acute conflict between a rise in the rural standard of living and a rise in the standard of living of an unemployed worker who is drawn into employment — both being expressed in considerable measure in an increase in consumption of food. It is important also because any rise which has to be allowed in the rural standard of living necessitates an equivalent rise in the standard of living in the towns required to attract labour from the villages.[1]

The obvious mechanism to employ to restrain the rise in the rural standard of living is the land tax. It is of outstanding importance that the hesitation to increase land taxes, or even to restore their incidence in real terms to what it was, should be overcome.[2] As is stated by the ECAFE Working Party, 'the need for channelling a part of the increase in agricultural incomes to the exchequer can hardly be exaggerated'.[3] In India 'the land revenue at present . . . amounts to only 1 per cent of net product of agriculture'.[4] It remains to be seen whether anything will be done to increase it.

This of course raises in acute form the question of political feasibility which, in one form or another, is raised by nearly everything that I have said. The question to my mind is what is really meant by the 'democratic means and process' through which, according to the Indian Planning Commission, 'development . . . should be

---

[1] Cf. A. Lewis, ' Economic Development with Unlimited Supplies of Labour ', op. cit., p. 172.

[2] Cf. A. Lewis, ibid., p. 168. On p. 174 of this article Professor Lewis mentions that early experience of Japan, which is referred to also on p. 50 of the ECAFE working paper. (The three consecutive references to Professor Lewis's article above appear on pp. 431–4 of *The Economics of Underdevelopment*.)

[3] From the Report of the ECAFE Working Party, op. cit., p. 9. Cf. *Report of the Expert Group on the Economic Development of Southern Europe*, op. cit., p. 21.

[4] N. Kaldor, op. cit., p. 4.

achieved'.[1] Sometimes it is almost as though they are trying to tell you that nothing should be done which would not secure a clear majority on a referendum. Witness the following from the Report of the ECAFE Working Party: 'The problem of conflicts among objectives cannot be resolved by a bureaucratic decision in a democratic society. The people register their choices among different objectives . . . continuously in the market place, and at the ballot box and through various forums for the expression of public opinion. Where plans, programmes and budgets do not conform to popular decisions they are changed.'[2] Certainly the plans, programmes and budgets entailed in a bold development policy would on this basis receive inadequate public support, the minority who lack work being too small to carry the day. At the other end of the income scale the interests of an even smaller, though more vocal, minority do not seem to be overwhelmed through lack of voting power. 'If the gap between planned expenditure and resources is too great to be bridged otherwise than through such disastrous proposals, a better alternative is obviously to cut our plans down' was Mr C. Rajagopalachari's recent comment on the announcement of the new Indian taxes on wealth and expenditure.[3]

The fact is of course that it is not plans which are changed in accordance with popular decision but governments. No government can be expected to run a serious risk of being turned out as the result of introducing unpopular measures. Short of that, democratic governments are constantly putting through measures which would fail to secure a majority on a referendum. They do it partly through the instinct of self-preservation. Governments are judged not only by their failure to introduce unpopular measures but also by their failure to achieve results. If one is looking at all far ahead it is not timidity which appears to offer a safeguard against political upheaval.

---

[1] Indian *Second Five Year Plan*, op. cit., p. 24.
[2] From the Report of the ECAFE Working Party, op. cit., p. 3.
[3] *The Times*, London, 17 May 1957.

ACCELERATED INVESTMENT AS A FORCE IN ECONOMIC DEVELOPMENT*

by Howard S. Ellis

I

An increase in investment characterizes all economic development: indeed, aside from the rise of income *per capita*, it is probably the most central phenomenon. At first glance, therefore, it might be somewhat puzzling why theories which stress this factor should be in any way distinctive as theories of economic development.

In part the answer lies in relative emphasis. From the body of classical economics, one gathers the general impression that the mainspring of progress is the slow steady accretion of capital through individual saving, i.e., parsimony or frugality. Marx laid the primary emphasis upon the ' mode of production ', the organization of production; and Schumpeter, Spiethoff, and many subsequent writers have thought the innovating entrepreneur to be the *primum mobile* of economic growth or development. With Kuznets, who is indeed very loath to commit himself regarding causation, there seems to be a good deal of emphasis upon the increase of population, either internally or through immigration, and the possibility that it is a main independent variable. Other economists have stressed the gains in productivity, technical knowledge, and motivation springing from international trade and finance. And one must not fail to take account of theories which discover the most important impulses in non-economic factors — in political or social revolutions, ideologies, and the like. But there is a congeries of theories which — while not necessarily ignoring or denying the operation of one or all of these forces — lays the weight upon the *speed* of the investment process; indeed, in some cases this emphasis is almost exclusive. If

* *Quarterly Journal of Economics*, November 1958. Reprinted with the permission of the Harvard University Press, and the author. The author is obliged to the editors of *Revista Brasileira de Economica* for permission to publish in English an article originally appearing in Portuguese.

capital formation is rapid, other attributes of economic progress are practically certain to be realized; if capital formation is not *rapid*, economic development will be slight or fail to materialize altogether.

But, in addition to this emphasis, the theories I am considering have several characteristics which warrant their being grouped together. For one thing, these theories are generally strongly interventionist, at least so far as concerns the assumption of responsibility by the state for a greatly increased rate of saving, and — extending out from this basis according to the predilections of the individual writer — to more or less, and generally more, control (and sometimes operation) of the specific lines of investment and production. Secondly, these 'big push' theorists usually consider manufacture as inherently superior to primary production as a vehicle of development. These two characteristics are so general that I shall terminate the list with these alone for greater emphasis; but it would be tempting to point to the frequency also of an inflationary bias in writings of this sort, to autarkical leanings and to a fondness for general equilibrium planning as implied by linear or non-linear programming. But the interventionist and other features of these theories, upon which I shall want to comment later, are their overtones rather than their substance.

The substantive bases for an accelerated rate of investment through state intervention are principally three: a demographic argument, a line of reasoning involving the propensity to consume (or to save), and thirdly, conclusions reached from the technical discontinuities or 'lumpiness' of investment. Let me say clearly in advance that in no case do I reject the reasoning completely; but that in all cases I attach much greater weight than do the proponents of these theories to the limits of possible gain, to the risks and costs of the proposed line of action, and to the merits of alternative policies.

I turn first to the demographic argument for the big investment push, because here both the merits of the theory and its detractions are most conspicuous. The setting of the problem is an economy in which *per capita* incomes are low, capital is scarce and labour abundant, death rates have recently been lowered by modern methods of public health, and birth rates are high — a milieu highly inauspicious for economic development. In such a setting, the case for the *investment* attack has been most ably argued by Professors

Galenson and Leibenstein.[1] According to these writers, the only hope of eventually raising *per capita* incomes is temporarily to abandon the usual marginal productivity criterion for investment and in its place to maximize the 'marginal *per capita* reinvestment quotient', i.e., adopt techniques which 'lead ultimately to the maximum capital/labour ratio'. The reinvestment quotient should be maximized even if there is surplus labour in the economy because by definition, techniques of the sort appropriate to development are those which lead most speedily to the maximum of capital equipment per labourer and hence to maximum real wage rates.

One objection to this theory of development is that the ratio of capital to labour can *always* be raised and, short of some very remote limit, real wage rates can *always* be raised by more capital, so that the term for the application of the reinvestment quotient is indefinite. A second objection is that the theory ruthlessly sacrifices present gains in productive capacity to the furtherance of productive capacity. Galenson and Leibenstein are quite frank about this; indeed, it is partly their fear that any increase of *present* real wages will lead only to an increase of the birthrate that leads them to propose this policy. They are willing to accept even an increase of unemployment for the sake of techniques maximizing the ultimate ratio of capital to labour.

Now it is indeed quite possible that concern with unemployment may be excessive and may interfere with necessary reforms in agriculture and in industrial techniques.[2] 'In theory,' at least, additional unemployment caused by technological improvements can be absorbed, just as with the basic substratum of structural unemployment, by public works of a local, labour-intensive variety. But there are limits to the speed with which these projects can be planned and executed, and there are corresponding limits to the desirability of labour-saving techniques. Indeed, the employment of labour-saving, capital-intensive techniques in an economy with surplus or even cheap labour is an anomaly. The anomaly is basically

---

[1] Walter Galenson and Harvey Leibenstein, 'Investment Criteria, Productivity, and Economic Development', *Quarterly Journal of Economics*, LXIX, Aug. 1955, pp. 343–70, reprinted in the present volume pp. 182-212 ; see also Harvey Leibenstein, *Economic Backwardness and Economic Growth*, Wiley, New York, 1957, ch. 8.

[2] Ragnar Nurkse, 'Reflections upon India's Development Plan', *Quarterly Journal of Economics*, LXXXI (May 1957), 188–204.

that the government, in introducing these techniques, is discounting the future at a lower rate than the market.

I am not prepared to argue that this is never appropriate; indeed I would myself maintain that a good deal of the initiative for saving has to be taken by governments in the early stages of development through raising funds by taxation. But there are limits, outside the harshest totalitarian states, to this forcing of saving, first upon ordinary ethical considerations of human welfare and freedom, and secondly upon the pragmatic basis that the population may simply not tolerate an indefinite postponement of the fruits of progress. Thus the objection to Galenson's and Leibenstein's argument is partly a matter of degree; but it is also partly a matter of their cloaking under a phrase, 'the marginal reinvestment quotient', which has the air of an objective investment criterion, the purely arbitrary decision of authority to plough back productivity gains into plant and equipment for whatever period may be pleasing to that authority.

If their concern lest population increases absorb the gains of progress leads these authors to an intolerably stiff policy, the very opposite is probably the shortcoming of the doctrine proposed by John Stuart Mill and Frank W. Taussig. There are grains of a 'big push' thesis in this demographic theory also. If productivity could be thrust forward rapidly, it was argued, by whatever means, the immediate impact in raising real wages would give the population a taste for greater material comfort, which they would defend by reducing the size of their families. The trouble with this prescription, which might have worked and probably did work in times past, as, for example, in the industrialization of Japan, is that in the current scene the increase of population from lowered mortality rates is apt to eat up productivity gains before they can be transmitted into higher *levels* of living. This leaves the brunt of responsibility upon a rise of the *standard* of living, which, as Arthur Lewis has recently insisted, is a slow process.[1] But it is at least a process which has worked in the history of Western civilization, and has worked without compulsion upon the mass of humanity by the state.

Indeed, upon the assumption that a 'big push' of investment means only a temporary resort to compulsory limitation of consumption, what is ultimately to determine birthrates? Will the increase

[1] W. Arthur Lewis, *The Theory of Economic Growth*, London, 1955, p. 315.

of productive apparatus, such as Soviet Russia is now achieving through 'starving the present', result ultimately in higher wages or simply in more people? The answer lies, of course, in the ideals of the population regarding the family, monogamy, continence, and legitimacy, in literacy, sex education, the status of women and ethical and religious beliefs — in a vast complex of forces. Against these basic determinants, a period of accelerated investment for the sake of its demographic effects seems relatively short-lived and superficial.

II

Government-accelerated investment is sometimes justified as the key to economic development on the grounds of the attending behaviour of savings. I distinguish four types of this sort of theorizing; but the first, according to which the state may speed up development by enforcing a reinvestment of income continuously into capital goods, has already been considered sufficiently. This may be called a policy of explicit or openly avowed forced saving.

The second variety relies upon the concealed forced saving of inflation; and I need scarcely remark upon the large number of acquiescent friends or active advocates, even among the ranks of professional economists, that inflation seems to command. As a representative of this school of thinking one may take Professor W. Arthur Lewis of Manchester University, who holds that governments must choose between taxation and inflation in order to provide a necessary supplement to private voluntary saving, and that this choice is 'largely political'.[1] Inflations devoted to pure consumption or to the destruction of goods (e.g. war and armaments) become cumulatively worse by reducing the supply of goods relatively to money. 'Inflations for the purpose of creating useful capital are on the contrary self-destructive, since sooner or later they result in an increased supply of goods to the market.'[2]

Both parts of this proposition are completely indefensible. In the first place 'the *purpose* of creating useful capital goods' is generally poorly served by a 'big push' of state investment which exceeds tax income plus bond sales to private savers, i.e., by inflation. Inflation, as Schumpeter so eloquently sets forth in *The Theory*

[1] W. Arthur Lewis, op. cit., pp. 217 et seq.

[2] Ibid., p. 217 ; also p. 405.

of Economic Development biases the economic calculus by making estimates fallible and by making profitable, however well-motivated the original investments, all sorts of speculative activities through the multiplier or velocity-of-money effect. Lewis has himself dwelt upon some of these costs of inflation, including balance-of-payments deficits and the accompanying necessity of exchange controls, etc. The increased flow of goods *need* not be, and in all probability *will* not be, sufficient to prevent a continuous rise of prices as long as inflation 'for the purpose of creating useful capital goods' is pursued.

Indeed, the phrase 'sooner or later' applied by Lewis to the 'increased supply of goods to the market' reveals that, even aside from the various costs of inflation in inefficiency and the reduction of voluntary saving, inflationary financing of a given increment to investment is only non-cumulative if it is a 'once-over' performance. The yield of investment comes in slowly over the ensuing months or years and does indeed, if the investment is well conceived, give rise to an amount of deflation sufficient to offset the original investment (assuming with Lewis that it has been financed by inflationary means). But a repetition of inflationary increments to investment clearly produces cumulative inflation. I therefore take leave of the idea that a 'big push' automatically generates its own saving.

Quite a different line of thought is represented by those who believe that consumption lags in point of time behind variations of income because consumption is somewhat a matter of habit. Thus if income can be given a sudden forward thrust by a 'crash' investment programme, voluntary savings will for a while be a larger fraction of income, and will thus lay the ground for further advance.[1]

It is amusing to observe that the assumption that consumers do not keep pace with the rise of income is the direct opposite of the assumption made by those who argue that a sudden increase of income will, by raising the level of living, instil higher standards of living and thus reduce the birthrate. Both arguments for a big investment effort cannot be simultaneously valid. In view of the force of the 'demonstration effect' in the modern world and the tendency of welfare legislation and wage demands to equal or outstrip increases of productivity, I should not be hopeful of the

[1] This seems to be the type of discontinuity with respect to savings which Paul Rosenstein-Rodan has in mind ; cf. his 'Notes on the Theory of the " Big Push " ', in Ellis and Howard (eds.), *Economic Development for Latin America*, Macmillan & Co., London, 1961, pp. 57-66.

magnitude of savings to be achieved through a lag of consumption. But I should also be sceptical of the lowering of birthrates merely through a sudden increase of income, if other social and cultural factors remain unchanged.

The most sophisticated argument, linking an accelerated investment programme to increased savings, has been formulated by Gerald Alter, a member of the staff of the International Bank for Reconstruction and Development.[1] As the title of Alter's paper indicates, he is concerned with the capacity of a borrowing country to service its foreign debt. The model, constructed upon eight variables, shows 'that the likelihood of being able to service a larger volume of foreign capital is greater than the likelihood of servicing a smaller volume of capital inflow', a result which 'follows from the fact that very small increases in the required marginal savings ratio are associated with very large changes in *per capita* income'. Alter emphasizes the 'highly favourable savings effect which a "big push" makes possible'; and there seems to be no question that his model could be extended from the servicing of foreign debt to internally held public or private debt.

But the author himself clearly points out that the favourable outcome of accelerated investment is a possibility and not a certainty. Less favourable behaviour in the basic variables could reverse the outcome, as, for example, if the capital-output ratio should rise, the required amortization period for the debt should be shortened, population growth accelerated, or rates of interest on borrowed funds increased. The chance for achieving greater income by expanded investment is matched by greater risks. Thus Alter recognizes one of the 'facts of life' all too frequently ignored by proponents of massive investment programmes. Risk is a genuine economic cost, and its rational appraisal might easily account for the rejection of large-scale ventures in either the private or public spheres. Too great sensitivity to risk could indeed block progress; but this truth scarcely warrants the conclusion of a recent writer that 'Extra funds for investment should then be fearlessly extracted from the consumer and splashed about.'[2]

---

[1] Gerald M. Alter, 'The Servicing of Foreign Capital Inflows by Underdeveloped Countries', Round Table of the International Economic Association, Rio de Janeiro, August 1957, reprinted in the present volume pp. 508–31.

[2] P. Wiles, 'Growth *versus* Choice', *Economic Journal*, LXVI, June 1956, p. 254.

III

The chief basis upon which the 'big push' of investment has been justified, since its original enunciation by Paul Rosenstein-Rodan a decade and a half ago,[1] has been the possibility of realizing extensive external economies, and this ground is still a favourite with nearly all writers of this persuasion. But the great offset to the possibility that domestic development programmes should give rise to further external economies has been definitively set forth by Professor Viner: foreign trade makes available to the developing country the much more substantial economies realized upon world markets, independently of home investment.[2] This fact is now recognized by Professor Rosenstein.[3] But he fails to give overt recognition to the further fact adduced by Viner that the newly-developing countries nowadays are chiefly primary producers, and, as such, investment for exports and for marginal import substitutes, where external economies are presumably negligible, occupies a very large part of total investment. For this entire sector, the 'big push' loses its specific justification from external economies.

We are left then with that portion of production for the domestic market which does not substitute for imports. Still this can be a very substantial field, embracing purely local consumer goods production and most public utilities — transportation, communication, power, water and sewerage facilities, and the like. Even here, however, there are limits to potential external economies. Viner points out that certain investments — presumably in the case of fairly inelastic demand — are cost-reducing rather than output-expanding. Since external economies depend upon expansion of output in the initial industry, they become negligible for this category of investment. I should like to call attention to two further limitations of considerable significance. In the field of purely domestic goods, a large fraction will be personal services and very light industry (a

---

[1] P. N. Rosenstein-Rodan, 'Problems of Industrialization of Eastern and South-eastern Europe', *Economic Journal*, LIII, June–September 1943, reprinted in Agarwala and Singh (eds.), *The Economics of Underdevelopment*, Oxford University Press, 1958, pp. 245–55.

[2] Jacob Viner, 'Stability and Progress: the Poorer Countries' Problem', in Douglas Hague (ed.), *Stability and Progress in the World Economy*, Macmillan & Co., London, 1958, pp. 41–65.

[3] Rosenstein-Rodan, op. cit.

good deal of food and raiment production) in which the 'chunki-ness' of fixed investment is unimportant because fixed investment is itself a small fraction of costs. Since external economies are simply internal economies in adjacent industries, their significance is correspondingly small in these cases. It is furthermore worth re-membering that, in the case of public utilities, potential external economies do not pertain to the cost of the *equipment* of these industries if it can be more cheaply imported.

Taken together, all of these limitations need not entirely remove the possibility of external economies. But they are neither as uni-versal as often supposed nor, when they actually exist, as substan-tial. Furthermore and finally, though their existence does increase the productivity of the economy for given magnitudes of invest-ment, they do not constitute a reason for a *concentration of invest-ment in point of time* if — as would appear probable in any but the smallest countries — the 'chunkiness' of individual investments levels out to a fairly full utilization of capacities in the aggregate for all capital facilities together. This is a decidedly relevant consi-deration if 'accelerated investment' is taken, not as simply synony-mous with more investment continuously, but as a 'big push' followed by a lower rate.

IV

Beyond its substantive theoretical basis in the population, sav-ings, and external economies arguments, the doctrine of accelerated rates of investment has overtones for policy which its proponents, I am sure, would not be content to have ignored. One of these is the predilection for manufacturing over agricultural and other primary industries. In part this predilection may simply reflect a sentimental desire to see the country 'independent' of its neighbours, particular-ly the richer ones; but in part it may rest on rational arguments, such as the improvement in labour morale which is supposed to attend factory production, the cultural and demographic effects of large cities, which are supposed to be favourable to economic progress, and the risks of primary production from the fluctuations of world markets. On the other hand, agricultural and primary types of pro-duction have in their favour that they utilize the relatively abundant factors of land and labour and economize capital; that character-istically in the less developed countries they provide two-thirds or more of the national income; and that, by the same token, they supply the chief wherewithal for industrial imports and investment in general.

It would scarcely seem necessary at the present stage of the debate concerning economic development to say that the merits of investment in agriculture versus industry have to be settled according to the peculiarities of each country. By consequence, whatever merits may inhere in crash programmes of investment may just as well be associated with agriculture — irrigation, drainage, transportation facilities, reform of fragmented land-holdings, etc., — as with building industrial plants; in particular cases, indeed, more so.

Somewhat similar reflections would be germane to the penchant of the 'big push' economists for planning, state direction of investment, and extensive controls. Linear programming, for example, is essentially an information service, and the benefits of its information may just as well be made available to private as to public entrepreneurs. In and of itself, linear programming does not supply any rationale for accelerated investment. If it should appear desirable to supplement private voluntary savings by the fiscal arm of the state, the funds can be lent to private firms. The theoretical underpinning of accelerated investment programmes pertains to a *rate* of investment, and not necessarily to government controlled investment. Ordinary economic motivations of the individual and the firm are a powerful engine of economic progress. It would be regrettable if the economists of the free world created an impression to the contrary.

V

What, in conclusion, may be said of the general merits of the 'big push' philosophy of economic development? As a starting point for development some kind of impulse is, of course, necessary; a change from stagnation is not likely to come by almost imperceptible degrees. Economic historians and cultural anthropologists have pointed to various prime movers in economic change: to the roles of the foreign trader and foreign capital, to immigration and the transfer of techniques, to the process of technical innovation itself, to cultural change, and to political revolution. Among these, intensive programmes of state investment, as in the Japanese and Russian cases, should certainly take their place. But they are by no means the only or even the chief channel through which development can be achieved; and the demographic advantages, the capital accumulation, and the external economies to be expected from crash programmes of government investment can easily be over-rated.

A statistical summary of recent economic development throughout the world by John H. Adler reaches the important conclusion, among others, that 'a relatively low level of investment "pays off" well in the form of additional output '.[1] The author emphasizes this conclusion most sharply in connexion with India and Pakistan; but the chief reason for this conclusion, the prevailingly low capital-output ratio, is also characteristic of many other of the less developed countries of Asia and Latin America as his statistics reveal. Thus it appears that it is far from generally true that a massive injection of capital is a precondition of growth.

A general weakness of the 'big push' doctrine is that it frequently ignores the conditions for *evoking* the investment to which it ascribes such potency in the general picture of development, as well as neglecting the conditions under which investments, once made, can be fruitful. It is through the assumption of a *deus ex machina*, the state, which does all or most of the investing, that this theory is able to avoid the problems of securing not only the saving, but also the willingness to undergo risk, which is implied in investment. And it is only through a singular narrowness that the theory often implies that it tells the whole story of the successful operation of the economy, once the investment is made.

In point of fact, the conditions for the evoking of private investment and the conditions for the profitable use of capital are largely the same. I should place high upon this list the existence of stable and honest government, the absence of inflation, and the accessibility of the economy to the gains of foreign trade and commerce. But other factors, such as the improvement of general and technical education, the amelioration of agriculture (which bulks large in nearly all low-income countries), and progress along the family-limitation front would seem to be equally critical. Taken together, or in some cases even singly, we would seem to have identified a number of factors in economic progress which could outweigh a burst of state-engineered investment.

[1] John H. Adler, 'World Economic Growth — Retrospect and Prospects', *Review of Economics and Statistics*, XXXVIII, August 1956, p. 279; cf. also, p. 283.

Some food for thought concerning programmes of intensive investment would seem to be offered by certain points made recently by Simon Kuznets. His statistical and historical studies lead to the conclusion that 'current international differences in *per capita* income are congealed effects of past differences in the rate of growth of *per capita* income'. How far would it be necessary to go back into the history of the more advanced countries to reach levels comparable to the *per capita* incomes of the currently less developed countries? The answer is that we should have to go back about ten decades to reach the current income level of Latin America and about fifteen decades for that of Africa and Asia.[1] Thus, even at a very early stage in the industrialization of Western Europe, *per capita* incomes were probably as high as in Latin America today and certainly higher than in Asia and Africa. The economic development of the most advanced countries, at least, scarcely seems to be the result of crash programmes.

[1] Simon Kuznets, 'Quantitative Aspects of the Economic Growth of Nations', in *Economic Development and Cultural Change*, Vol. 5, October 1956; see especially pp. 23–5.

THE PLACE OF CAPITAL IN ECONOMIC PROGRESS*

by A. K. Cairncross

Capital occupies a position so dominant in the economic theory of production and distribution that it is natural to assume that it should occupy an equally important place in the theory of economic growth. In most of the recent writings of economists, whether they approach the subject historically (e.g. in an attempt to explain how the industrial revolution started) or analytically (e.g. in models of an expanding economy) or from the side of policy (e.g. in the hope of accelerating the development of backward countries), it is the process of capital accumulation that occupies the front of the stage. There is an unstated assumption that growth hinges on capital accumulation, and that additional capital would either provoke or facilitate a more rapid rate of economic development even in circumstances which no one would describe as involving a shortage of capital.

Yet there seems no reason to suppose that capital accumulation does by itself exercise so predominant an influence on economic development. In most industrialized communities the rate of capital accumulation out of savings is equal to about 10 per cent of income. If one were to assume that innovation came to a standstill and that additional investment could nevertheless yield an average return of 5 per cent, the consequential rate of increase in the national income would normally be no more than $\frac{1}{2}$ per cent per annum. We are told that the national income has in fact been rising in such communities at a rate of 2–3 per cent per annum. On this showing, capital accumulation could account for, at most, one-quarter of the recorded rate of economic 'progress'. Nor were things very different in the nineteenth century. In Britain, savings were a slightly higher proportion of income and the growth of income was rather slower

* A paper presented to the International Economic Association's Round Table on Economic Progress in August 1953, and published in L. H. Dupriez (ed.), *Economic Progress*, Louvain, 1955, and reprinted in the author's collection of essays : *Factors in Economic Development*, George Allen & Unwin, London, 1962. Reprinted by permission of the International Economic Association and the author.

116

— about 2 per cent per annum — so that capital accumulation made a larger direct contribution to the growth in income. The position was complicated, however, by population growth which cut the rate of increase in income per head to 1 per cent per annum, and diverted about half current savings into maintaining the stock of capital per head.

Even this way of putting things exaggerates the role of capital in economic development. For the yield on additional capital would rarely be as high as 5 per cent if there were not a discrepancy between the existing stock of capital and the stock appropriate to the existing state of technique. If innovation in the broadest sense of the term were at a standstill, accumulation would continue until the rate of interest fell to a point at which saving ceased. The sole object of accumulation in those circumstances would be to take advantage of the progressive cheapening of capital in order to introduce more roundabout methods of production, not to keep pace with current developments in technique. Ordinary observation suggests, however, that the scope for investment *in industry* to take advantage merely of lower rates of interest, once the long-term rate is below 5 per cent, is extremely limited, although there may be a good deal more scope in other directions where capital charges form an unusually high proportion of the final cost (e.g. in the erection of dwelling-houses, public buildings and the like).

The contribution of capital to economic progress is not, however, confined to the usufruct of additional capital assets, similar to those already in existence. It embraces three distinct processes. First, a greater abundance of capital permits the introduction of more roundabout methods of production or, to be more precise, of a more roundabout pattern of consumption. This covers the freer use of capital instruments in the production of a given product, the use of more durable instruments, and a change in the pattern of consumption in favour of goods and services with relatively high capital charges per unit cost. Secondly, the accumulation of capital is a normal feature of economic expansion, however originating. This is the process normally referred to as widening, as opposed to deepening, the structure of production. It may accompany industrialization, or any change in the balance between industries that makes additional demands on capital; or it may accompany an extension of the market associated with population growth, more favourable terms of trade, or the discovery of additional natural resources. Thirdly, additional capital may be required to allow technical progress to take place. It may either finance the discovery of what was not known before or more commonly, the adaptation of existing knowledge so as to allow of its commercial exploitation through some innovation in product, process or material.

Now of these three, the first is generally of subordinate importance; it is unusual for capital accumulation, unassisted by other factors, to bring about a rapid increase in income. The second, which also abstracts from any change in technology, accounts for nearly all the capital accumulation that has taken place in the past; forces making for rapid increase in income may be largely nullified unless they are reinforced by a parallel increase in capital. It is to the third, however, that one must usually look — at least in an advanced industrial country — for the main influences governing the rate of growth of real income per head. Whatever may have been true in the past, it is now technical innovation — the introduction of new and cheaper ways of doing things — that dominates economic progress. Whether technical innovation, in the sectors of the economy in which it occurs, makes large demands on capital is, however, very doubtful. Many innovations can be given effect to in the course of capital replacement out of depreciation allowances, which, in an expanding economy, may be fully as large as net savings. Others may actually reduce the stock of capital required. Existing buildings and existing machines can often be modified so as to allow most of the advantages of the new techniques to be gained. It is economic expansion, far more than technological change, that is costly in capital.

The direct, as distinct from the indirect, impact of technical change on capital requirements has been little studied as an empirical process. On the one hand, our knowledge of trends in the stock of industrial capital, whether in relation to employment or output, is extremely scanty; on the other, different types of technical change may have the most diverse effects on capital, from a net economy in the total stock to a very large increase in requirements per unit of output. Thus there seems neither enough statistical material on which to ground conclusions with any claim to validity nor any grounds for presuming that the predominant influence of technical change will lie in one direction rather than another. Most economists have been content to fall back on a study of the flow of gross investment rather than seek to reconcile estimates of the stock at fluctuating prices and rates of capitalization. Even in assembling the statistics relating to the flow of new capital they have preferred to deal in aggregates rather than analyse the broad changes in the pattern within the aggregate. It is practically impossible to trace the growth of capital in any individual industry or the divergence in rates of growth between sectors of the economy subject to rapid technical change and sectors where technical change has been slow or negligible.

The facts, so far as they go, suggest that capital and income do tend to increase at about the same rate. Both in Britain and the United States the ratio between the two has remained comparatively steady over the seventy or eighty years for which data with some claim to reliability exist, although there have been oscillations within that period. This relative constancy is obviously not inevitable and may, indeed, be entirely accidental. But there are also some general grounds for expecting that the ratio will be fairly stable or will change slowly.

In the first place, we are dealing with annual increments that are themselves small. If savings represent about 10 per cent of income and the stock of capital is equal to about four years' income, the rate of increase of capital will be $2\frac{1}{2}$ per cent per annum. The rate of increase of income in industrial countries is normally between 2 and 3 per cent. A marked divergence between the two rates can hardly occur so long as savings maintain some stability in relation to income and so long as productivity rises at what has come to be regarded as a normal pace. Even a divergence of 1 per cent per annum would be a long time in producing an unmistakable shift in the capital-income ratio, given the doubts that must necessarily surround estimates of the stock of capital in conditions of fluctuating price levels and rates of capitalization.

It happens, moreover, that compensatory influences have been at work over the past seventy or eighty years to keep the two rates together. In the early part of the period, population growth was much more rapid than in the later part, while technical progress was more rapid in the second part of the period than in the first. Thus initially the rate of increase of income was boosted by population growth and as this fell off, productivity gained momentum. Together, these influences tended to stabilize the rate of growth of income. On the other hand, there is little evidence, except in the inter-war period, of any really large reduction in the rate of capital accumulation. Savings before 1913 were probably somewhat in excess of 10 per cent of income — perhaps about 12½ per cent in the United Kingdom — and were a good deal lower between the wars; but they appear to have recovered since 1945 to not far short of the proportion that was normal in Victorian times.

Finally there are several important constituents of the stock of capital which one might reasonably expect to increase more or less *pari passu* with income and so help to stabilize the capital-income ratio. In the absence of a change in the rate of turnover of stocks and work in progress, for example, the total value of stocks should preserve a constant ratio to output and income. There is some evidence that this ratio has in fact stayed at about 40 per cent for a quarter, or even half, a century. It is easy to see that, in agriculture, the average should work out at about six months' output because of the importance of the annual crop which dwindles from twelve months' output to nil over the harvest year. In industry and commerce the ratio seems to be rather lower and to undergo little secular change.

A second example of some importance is provided by dwelling-houses. If one could assume that the proportion of income spent in rent and rates remained constant at, say, 10 per cent — and this was once a reasonable assumption — the stock of houses would bear a fixed relationship to the national income unless the number of years' purchase on house-property varied. Taking, say, fifteen years' purchase as a fair average, the stock of houses would work out at one-and-a-half years' income; and this, together with stocks and work in progress, would represent about half the capital stock of the community if the capital-income ratio were of the order of 4 : 1. Constancy in the rate of turnover of stocks and in the proportion of income spent on rent would thus exercise a strong damping influence on any tendency for the capital-income ratio to diverge from the previous norm.

It cannot, however, be assumed that the proportion of income spent in rent would remain constant in the absence of technical change since houses have themselves been subject to important innovations. The observed tendency towards constancy reflects a progressive improvement both in the number of rooms occupied per person and in the *type* of accommodation in use as income per head increases. Moreover, if rents are restricted, or the rate of interest alters, the argument advanced above is vitiated.

A third example is, or may be, public (non-industrial) property. This has, in some phases of world history, been the largest constituent of capital of all, whether one thinks of pyramids or cathedrals, medieval Florence or modern warfare. It is difficult, if not impossible, to reduce any of these to the economics of capital and income; the most important circumstance governing their finance appears to have been the ease with which the capital could be raised by charity, taxation or force. There is at least a presumption that the wealthier a country becomes, the more it will expend on public buildings; not perhaps, in exact proportion to the growth of the national income but at a rate that may not be very far out of accord.

Any force increasing income will almost inevitably, therefore, increase the demand for capital to a more or less corresponding degree in the form of stocks, houses and public buildings, whatever its impact on other sectors of the economy. On the other hand, there may be some types of capital (like the railway system) that need no increase; and if the bias of consumer expenditure is increasingly towards luxury goods and personal services at higher levels of income, this too will operate to lower the capital-income ratio as income per head rises, since luxuries and services normally make greater demands on labour than on capital per unit of expenditure. But it is unwise to lay too much stress on this point, both because the fact of a shift towards services is itself somewhat in doubt and because purchases of consumers' durable goods should, on a strict assessment, be reckoned as adding to the stock of capital.

If the capital-income ratio alters, therefore, it is likely to be because of a change in technique affecting the remainder of the national capital, after deducting houses, stocks and public property. This residue can be grouped under four headings: agriculture, public utilities, the extraction or manufacture of fuel and raw materials, and the processing industries. Of these the last is much the largest in point of employment in a country like Britain, since it includes most of the manufacturing industries of the country, notably the textile, engineering, and food, drink and tobacco trades. But in point of capital employed this group, even in Britain, comes after public utilities and raw materials and in most other countries ranks after agriculture. Thus if the capital-income ratio does alter appreciably it is generally to agriculture, raw materials, and public utilities that one must look for an explanation. Even in those groups there may be a quasi-automatic lift to the employment of capital, not because a larger stock per man is used but because the cost of the assets rises progressively with income per head, the building industry which constructs the bulk of the assets lagging behind in its rate of technical improvement.

If anything, one would expect some slight downward trend in the ratio of capital to income over the past century because the economic progress made in the second half of the nineteenth century made heavier demands on the savings of the period than does economic progress today. There was a rapidly growing population to be housed — and housing has been throughout the largest claim on new capital. There was a revolution in transport to be financed — and transport used more capital per man than any other industry. In 1914, for example, the British railways needed about £2,000 per man employed while cotton textiles, for example, needed only about £200 per man. Finally, there was the opening-up of new countries, largely with borrowed capital — by far the most important 'innovation' increasing real income all over the world. This meant the resettlement of entire communities in undeveloped areas, the building of the railway systems upon which the whole process of resettlement was pivoted and the construction of all the fixed capital needed to house and supply millions of immigrants. By 1913 Western Europe had poured as much capital into foreign countries as the national capital of the United Kingdom and the United Kingdom herself had about as much capital invested abroad as in the whole of her domestic industry and commerce.

The main impulse to capital accumulation over the years before 1913 came ultimately from the steam engine and the steamship. By 1913 that impulse had largely spent itself. In Britain, for example, perhaps one-fifth of current savings had gone into domestic railway-building in the sixties and seventies, and shipbuilding had taken another large slice. But after 1885 the annual absorption of new capital by the railways was only about a quarter of the amount that they needed in the twenty years before 1885. Elsewhere, and particularly in Canada, railway-building still headed the investment list, and shipping continued to grow with world trade. But by 1914 the major advantages of the revolution in transport had been exhausted and the world's stock of capital had, broadly speaking, been sufficiently enlarged to profit from it.

If now we move to the inter-war and post-war period, it is at once apparent that the requirements of transport have fallen into the background although still far from negligible because of the fresh revolution in road and air transport. A new public utility — electricity — has risen into prominence. But the most striking change has been in manufacturing industry, less in the processing industries (where mechanization has increased capital requirements) than in the group of industries that produces raw materials. Here, capital has been called in to redress the balance of raw material supply. Thus, aluminium, synthetic textiles, cement, chemicals, and even steel — all of which have risen in comparison with other materials like lead and zinc, cast iron, natural fibres, and stone — make extremely heavy demands on capital. A similar change has been at work in the supply of fuel and power: electricity and oil use more capital per unit of energy than coal and coke. At the same time, throughout manufacturing industry production methods have altered so as to provide the average worker with additional capital and generally also so as to involve the use of more capital per unit of output. This is most evident in agriculture and in factories using mass production techniques. Nevertheless, even now, this last element in the situation is not, in absolute terms, nearly as large in its demands on new capital as some of the others. In the years 1948–50 gross investment by the British engineering industries, excluding vehicles, averaged only £22 per worker, and by the clothing trades only £9 per worker; and some of this was in canteens and the like while a great part was merely in replacement of existing buildings and plant.

In the nineteenth century, therefore, the demand for capital was dominated partly by demographic factors — the growth and resettlement of population — and partly by the major innovation of the steam engine with all its repercussions on transport and on the distribution of population between and within countries. In the twentieth century neither demographic change nor any single outstanding innovation — except perhaps the use of electricity — exercises anything like the same influence. On the other hand, the pace of innovation has quickened and industrial requirements have assumed greater importance.

It is arguable, indeed, that, with the decline in the strain on savings caused by population growth, the absence of any large scale development of new countries and the corresponding shrinkage in foreign investment, technical innovation must come to play in the twentieth century the role that was played in the nineteenth

by the growth and resettlement of population. If it proves that
technical innovation does in fact require only a modest amount of
capital then there is an obvious danger of a repetition of the inter-
war experience of a prolonged maladjustment between current
habits of thrift and the openings for capital accumulation.

This is a possibility which does not affect all countries in the
same way. The position has been obscured by the war and its aftermath since one of the effects of the war was to cause a discontinuous
change in the capital-income ratio both because of the destruction
that took place and the arrears of maintenance and replacement
that accumulated. In a country like Britain, the loss of capital
was estimated at one-quarter while other assets in natural resources,
skill and so forth were left undepleted. So far as the loss fell on overseas assets, the capital-income ratio was unaffected since capital
and income disappeared together. But at home the pattern, both of
production and of consumption, has been distorted and the efforts
of producers and consumers to restore the previous pattern has
forced capital to a premium.

Whether a situation of this kind is or is not reflected in high
interest rates, the accumulation of capital acquires a special urgency.
There is a pronounced tendency to suck in foreign capital if it is
to be had and, because of the pressure on savings, a strong inflationary under-current. With capital accumulating at no more than
$2\frac{1}{2}$ per cent per annum it may obviously be a long time before the
capital deficiency is overtaken; and if national income recovers
quickly and innovation is at work the period may be still more
prolonged.

All this is familiar enough in terms of experience post World
War II. What may reasonably be asked is why experience post
World War I was so different. The answer no doubt differs from
country to country. But the two main points of difference are
probably the far greater damage and far larger arrears left by
World War II, and the higher capital charges that were in operation
after World War I. These higher capital charges were probably
responsible for more economy in the use of capital goods, notably
housing. In Great Britain, for example, efforts to deal with the
housing shortage had little effect until some five years after 1918
and this particular deficiency continued right on until 1939. The
pushing back of so large a slice of investment made room for other
items, many of them relatively small, of greater urgency in the

immediate post-war period. A third factor, of special importance in Britain, was the structural change after World War II in favour of the metal and engineering industries and the higher level of industrial activity in general. The rise in the British national income after World War I was largely attributable to an improvement in the terms of trade and did not involve a corresponding investment in home capital assets. But the rise after the World War II took place *in spite of* an adverse movement in the terms of trade, out of additional output, and involved heavy investment to relieve congestion and bottlenecks at various points in the economy.

At present, therefore, the emphasis is on capital as a limiting factor in development. But in the thirties — and even perhaps the twenties — the emphasis was very different. Technical development throughout the inter-war period was extremely rapid and productivity seems to have increased at a rate that is at least comparable with post-war experience. Yet net investment in manufacturing industry both in Britain and America was trifling; capital per man employed seems to have risen slightly but capital per unit of output undoubtedly fell. Capital accumulation was confined to a remarkable degree to housing and public utilities without any apparent inflection of the curve of productivity.

A second consideration, telling in the same direction, is the comparatively narrow base on which to build any large expansion in manufacturing capital. The capital employed in British manufacturing industry probably averages about £1,000 per head and, if so, the total is of the order of one-fifth of the national capital. Current investment measured gross forms a slightly higher proportion of total gross investment. No doubt it bears *indirectly* on all capital requirements and for that reason this consideration may be of limited force. But if technical innovation is to do in the next fifty years what steam and steel did fifty to a hundred years ago, the indirect reactions on capital requirements will have to be pretty vigorous.

To recapitulate the argument so far. Given that the national income is increasing, whether under the influence of technical progress, population growth, or some other factor, there is good reason to expect that additional capital will be required in some important sectors on a comparable scale. Habits of thrift — a phrase that must now be stretched to include not only the practices of corporations in adding to reserves but the propensities of Finance

Ministers — appear to admit of capital accumulation at a rate of about $2\frac{1}{2}$ per cent per annum, and this has in recent years been close to the rate of growth of income. Provided, therefore, that the capital requirements of industry — the main sector left out of account — are also increasing at this rate, the capital-income ratio will remain constant and the whole of the country's thrift will be effectively mobilized. There can be no guarantee, however, that industry's requirements will in fact mount at this rate, even in the long run. In the short run, for reasons that are familiar, the whole process of capital accumulation may be thrown out of gear.

Now the significant feature of this argument is that it hinges far more on the indirect than on the direct demand for capital. It assumes that technical progress operates largely in independence of capital accumulation and that capital is needed, not in order to allow innovations to be made but in order to consolidate the improvement in income that innovation brings about. Moreover, it implies that if, at any time, the process of innovation creates a bulge in the demand for capital, it should be possible to adapt the pattern of investment so as to accommodate the high-yielding requirements of industry by displacing part of the larger, but less remunerative, requirements of house-building, stock-building, and so forth.

It is hardly necessary to show that this implication may be mistaken. Public policy may maintain the demand for capital in the sectors capable of compression or the capital market may be so organized that industry is unable to draw capital from the sources that finance other forms of accumulation. But unless the bulge is a very large and consistent one it is doubtful whether innovation need suffer greatly.

The effect of technical progress is generally to widen the divergence between the actual stock of capital and the stock consistent with the full exploitation of current worker opportunities. Some part of the additional capital will be needed to finance the innovations in the sectors of the economy in which they arise ; some will be linked with the innovations directly, either because associated industries are offered a wider market or because social capital has to be provided in an area where it has become insufficient ; some will be linked indirectly, in the way already outlined, because the increased expenditure of consumers will give rise to a derived demand for capital. Now it is common to find that, particularly with a major advance in technique, the influence which it exerts on the scope for eventual capital accumulation is far more profound than its immediate impact on the current flow of capital formation. There is generally a chain reaction, strung out through time, one physical asset being wanted only after another has been created. Although the full consequences may be entirely foreseeable, development does not work up to its full momentum until a whole series of changes have occurred: an extension of capacity here, an application of the new technique there; a shift of location in one industry, a building up of new attitudes in another. The introduction of the steam engine, for example, brought into existence a large reservoir of projects that trickled out into capital formation all through the nineteenth century: the stock of capital appropriate to existing technique was far above the existing stock both because the steam engine was capable of wide application and because many industries that themselves made no use of it (such as bridge-building) were transformed in scale or (like agriculture and many pursuits ancillary to it) in location.

Moreover, because the chain reaction takes time and the innovation, is, *ex hypothesi*, a profitable one, the process is to a large extent self-financing. If there is a spate of such innovations, interest and profits are likely to show some response and a corresponding shift in the ratio of savings to income will ease the heavier burden of finance. It may happen, however, that the situation is not regulated in this way: interest rates may be sticky upwards as well as downwards. The probable outcome will then be a series of spurts in investment, followed by periods of indigestion. Excessively large bites, inadequate mastication, the selection of appetizing titbits rather than nourishing staples, and all the usual errors of judgment that attend a children's party may give rise to the familiar heavings that were known in the nineteenth century as the trade cycle. The Victorian period can be interpreted largely as a rush to overtake technique.

A variant of this situation is one in which there has been a considerable lag behind the known opportunities for the fruitful use of capital at existing rates of interest. A country may fail to make use of technical knowledge available elsewhere and suddenly become alive to the possibilities of applying that knowledge. At that stage its capital requirements will increase discontinuously and the additional capital which it requires before bumping up against the

limits of technical advance may be very large. It appears to be
this situation that is in the minds of those who assume that the
injection of additional capital into a country's economy will almost
automatically speed up its economic progress. Sometimes the argument is framed more specifically in terms of a shift of employment
from agriculture to industry, with a large net gain in productivity
from the shift, and the large capital investment needed to accomplish it operating as a brake.

This is a complex situation and it may exist in some underdeveloped countries. But it is by no means obvious that additional
capital, whether borrowed from abroad or accumulated through the
exertions of surplus labour in the countryside, would by itself suffice
to start off a cycle of industrialization. The problem is often one of
organization quite as much as of capital creation: of training man-
agements and men; of creating new attitudes towards industrial
employment; of taking advantage of innovations that need little
capital and using the resulting gains to finance investment elsewhere.

On the whole, there is a greater danger that the importance of
capital in relation to economic progress will be exaggerated than
that it will be underrated. How many successful firms, looking back
over their history, would single out difficulty of access to new capital
as the major obstacle, not to their growth, but to the adoption of
the most up-to-date technique ? How many countries in the van of
technical progress have found themselves obliged to borrow abroad?
It is where there has been a lag, where technical progress has been
too slow, that capital is called upon to put matters right. No doubt
where capital is plentiful, more risks can be taken and development
is speeded up, so that rapid development and rapid capital accumulation go together. But the most powerful influence governing
development, even now, is not the rate of interest or the abundance
of capital; and the most powerful influence governing capital accumulation, even now, is not technical progress.

INVESTMENT CRITERIA AND CAPITAL INTENSITY

INVESTMENT CRITERIA IN DEVELOPMENT PROGRAMMES*

by Alfred E. Kahn

Economists have in recent years given increasing thought to the conditions of economic development and progress. This resurgent interest has been stimulated in part by the practical necessity of setting out guideposts for governments engaged in programmes of reconstruction and development. The present comments evaluate three of the principles which have emerged from these speculations — three criteria for the selection of investment projects.

The major thesis of these comments is that the investment criteria under consideration are essentially erroneous, and sections I, II, and III seek to support this judgement. However, all have considerable usefulness as practical rules of thumb: first because their injunctions sometimes coincide with the economically sound principles, and second because, to the extent they err, they all err in stressing, and seeking to avoid, the omnipresent pitfalls which beset conscious efforts to force the pace of economic progress. Sections IV and V re-assess the rejected criteria in the light of these practical considerations. The conclusion (section VI) is less equivocal than it might be, mainly because the primary purpose of these comments is to demonstrate the error and harmful consequences of elevating practical rules of thumb to the rank of absolute principles.

I. THE CAPITAL-INTENSITY CRITERION

The first criterion is the capital intensity of alternative investments. The general rule is that nations engaged in reconstruction or development should economize in the use of scarce capital by concentrating on capital-light investments. The following statements by Norman S. Buchanan and J. J. Polak are typical:

* *Quarterly Journal of Economics*, February 1951. Reprinted with the permission of the Harvard University Press and the author. The author is indebted to Professors Edwin P. Reubens and Morris Mendelson and to James Ingram and John Dawson for their suggestions and searching criticisms.

If investment funds are limited, the wise policy, in the absence of special considerations, would be to undertake first those investments having a high value of annual product relative to the investment necessary to bring them into existence. [1] . . . Given the magnitude of the capital investment . . . it is desirable, from the point of view of foreign exchange, to maximize output and thus the rate of turnover; and also, given the possible output of a certain good . . . it is desirable to minimize the investment required in order to keep the cost of the service of the debt down.[2]

The rule which these authors have stated is incorrect. The correct criterion for obtaining the maximum return from limited resources is marginal productivity — or, from the point of view of society as a whole, social marginal productivity (SMP), taking into account the total net contribution of the marginal unit to national product, and not merely that portion of the contribution (or of its costs) which may accrue to the private investor. The SMP of capital is not correlated with the rate of turnover. The fact that in one industry (or one technique) a given investment is associated with an annual output of 20 per cent, and in another with an output amounting to 100 per cent, of the original outlay certainly does not signify, ordinarily, that the capital is less effectively used, or earns less, or is responsible for a smaller contribution to national production in the first than in the second. Ordinarily it means only that the ratio of capital to other resources employed is greater in the first.[3]

[1] Norman S. Buchanan, *International Investment and Domestic Welfare*, New York, 1945, p. 24 ; see also pp. 72, 106ff.

[2] J. J. Polak, 'Balance of Payments Problems of Countries Reconstructing with the Help of Foreign Loans', *Quarterly Journal of Economics*, February 1943, reprinted in Howard S. Ellis and Lloyd A. Metzler, ed., *Readings in the Theory of International Trade*, Philadelphia, 1949, p. 470.

[3] It might reflect merely a higher rate of capital consumption in the second project. Compare the following financial data for investments A and B, which differ only in that the equipment in A lasts only two years, in B ten years :

	A	B
Investment	$100,000	$100,000
Annual Data :		
Output	60,000	20,000
Depreciation	50,000	10,000
All other Costs	10,000	10,000
Capital Turnover	60 per cent	20 per cent

In a long range investment programme, in which real national capital must presumably be kept intact, there would appear to be no advantage in choosing the shorter over the longer-lived investment, since both yield the same annual output net of depreciation. However, see p. 146, below.

Of course, the relative abundance of different factors is a significant determinant of the SMP of each. Where capital is relatively scarce (compared with another area), its SMP will be higher and each investment will have to meet the more stringent test of a higher opportunity cost. In consequence, China will and should in general specialize in industries and use techniques requiring a lower capital: labour ratio than the United States. But this does not mean that in choosing between any two possible investments China must invariably select the one with the higher rate of capital turnover. Capital is not completely unavailable in China, hence infinitely expensive, nor labour in infinite supply, hence socially costless. Clearly, the capital-turnover criterion is useless in indicating at what point to stop substituting the plentiful factor for the scarce. The existence of a particular natural resource, specialized skills, particular climatic conditions, or the importance of a particular product or service may make the SMP of capital higher in a line which is more capital intensive than in another which is less so. The superiority of one technique over another, the inefficiencies of complete substitution of labour for capital, may dictate the heavier rather than the lighter use of the latter. The railway may use so much less labour than the ox-cart or the coolie that its construction may be imperative; reclamation of swamps may have a similar commanding superiority over an investment in swimming instructions for farm labourers or no investment at all — apart from a possibly higher capital turnover as well.

In some areas, within limits, the opportunity cost of labour may indeed be nil. This is obviously not the case in all of the countries engaged in reconstruction or development programmes to which Professor Buchanan would apply his criterion. However, in many there is concealed unemployment on the land, and one condition of a programme for increasing agricultural output is the removal of some of that surplus labour force. To the extent such labour is technically substitutable for capital (however wastefully by U.S. standards), the SMP of capital would be nil. Or, if a small investment (e.g., in initial transportation, housing, training, or simple tools) were required to tap this labour pool, SMP would be high for this minimum investment and nil for any larger, labour-saving expenditure. Beyond the critical point, hence, SMP would again accord with the Buchanan-Polak injunction to use as little capital as possible.[1]

Substitution of labour for capital is, however, seldom entirely costless. Labourers usually do have to be transported, trained, housed, and offered higher incomes to attract them and to keep them well enough to work. Rural labour, in many industries and countries, is incapable, without retraining, of substitution for capital because it lacks the skills which modern equipment frequently makes unnecessary.[2] Hence a substantial complementary investment relative to total output may be required. Moreover, to the extent of these costs of absorbing labour, substitution of capital for labour becomes possible and desirable; to what extent, only SMP of capital in each outlet, as compared with others, can determine.[3]

It is not surprising, therefore, that both Buchanan and Polak find their general principle often inapplicable in practice:

Yet after the war there would appear to be genuine obstacles to concentrating upon . . . investments where the degree of capital intensity is low. . . . The reconstruction of the war-damaged areas will . . . be a reconstruction of durable assets — buildings, utility

[1] See, e.g., Warren Wilhelm, 'Soviet Central Asia : Development of a Backward Area', *Foreign Policy Reports*, XXV, 1 February, 1950, pp. 225–6; Folke Hilgerdt, *Industrialization and Foreign Trade* (League of Nations Publications II, Economic and Financial, 1945. II.A. 10), pp. 36f., 49–53 ; H. Belshaw, 'Observations on Industrialization for Higher Incomes', *Economic Journal*, LVII, 1947, pp. 379–87; P. N. Rosenstein-Rodan, 'Problems of Industrialization of Eastern and South-eastern Europe', *Economic Journal*, LIII, 1943, pp. 202f., 210, reprinted in Agarwala and Singh (eds.), *The Economics of Underdevelopment*, Oxford University Press, 1958, pp. 245, 254f; K. Mandelbaum, *The Industrialization of Backward Areas*, Institute of Statistics, Monograph No. 2, Oxford, 1947, *passim* ; S. Kesava Iyengar, 'Industrialization and Agriculture in India Postwar Planning', *Economic Journal*, LIV, 1944, pp. 201f.

[2] It is also true, however, that where the labour force lacks the skills necessary to keep modern capital equipment operating efficiently, the SMP of capital will be low and substitution of capital for labour undesirable. The relative costs of remedying this or that deficiency of labour skill — the one which makes substitution of capital for labour economical, and the one which makes it uneconomical — will obviously vary, depending on the circumstances.

[3] Labour can suffer concealed unemployment in industry as well as in agriculture. The problem of underemployment on the land — each worker operating with ancient or no tools, little soil, and unproductive techniques — is not solved by employing labour equally inefficiently in manufacture. Mandelbaum, op. cit., pp. 8f.

plants, harbours, railways, docks, etc. These will have to be the things reconstructed. . . . But capital goods of this type are highly intensive: the annual yield is small in relation to their original cost.[1]

Industrialization, likewise, 'typically means bringing these capital intensive industries into existence'.[2] Both writers attempt to resolve this dilemma by authorizing exemptions from their general rule for such strategic bottleneck investments, however capital-intensive. In short, they must abandon their rule wherever it conflicts with the dictates of SMP.[3] They also argue at times as though the capital intensity criterion were primarily or solely applicable to programmes financed by foreign borrowing. But the means of financing are surely irrelevant. The problem is in all cases one of making the maximum use of limited resources; the ability of a country to meet service on its foreign debts depends (in the long run) on the imported capital being used in such a way as to make the maximum contribution (net of capital consumption) to national product.[4] SMP, not capital turnover, is the test of this.[5]

II. The Nature of the Product

A second criterion frequently encountered concerns the nature of the ultimate product: the general rule is that a sufficient portion of the investments must fall into what J. J. Polak has termed ' type I '— projects yielding additional export (or import-displacing) goods or services.[6] This rule provides insurance against balance-of-

[1] Buchanan, op. cit., p. 107 ; see also p. 72.

[2] Ibid., p. 76 ; see also Morris S. Rosenthal, 'Where is the Money Coming From?' *Bold New Program Series*, No. 8 (Public Affairs Institute, Washington, 1950), pp. 12–20.

[3] 'Transportation, communication and marketing facilities are perhaps the most productive form that real capital formation can initially assume in the low-income areas.' Norman S. Buchanan, 'Deliberate Industrialization for Higher Incomes', *Economic Journal*, LVI, 1946, p. 541. See also Mandelbaum, op. cit., pp. 63f.

[4] The parenthetical qualifications are introduced in accordance with the possibility discussed in note 3, above (p. 132).

[5] Of course, it may be desirable to produce certain *kinds* of goods rather than others. This brings us to the second, quite distinct, criterion, to which we now proceed. The first concerns only the capital : annual output ratio.

[6] Op. cit., pp. 468ff.

payments difficulties *after* the period of capital formation (we do
not deal here with the possible difficulties during the investment
process). There are two possible sources of such difficulties. The first
is the necessity for servicing any foreign obligations incurred in
financing the investment. We are concerned at this point only with
the second danger, and primarily with Professor Buchanan's version
thereof: 'After the investments have been completed, and the projects are in operation all yield income to the amount of the value
of their product. This income will consist of the distributive shares.
. . . Their expenditure by the recipients . . . will partially result
in an increased demand for foreign goods. . . . Thus it is that the
operation of the new industries will tend to increase imports. . . .'[1]

This balance-of-payments threat, it will be noted, is entirely
independent of the first. It develops out of the *operation* of successful
projects, whether or not originally financed by foreigners. And,
according to Professor Buchanan, it makes it necessary for countries
to hold within narrow limits those portions of their investment
programmes which will produce additional products for the home
market (type III), even though domestic savings be adequate to
finance the projects. Our contention is that these investments
'whose products by their very nature are not exportable'[2] involve
no such inherent threat to the balance of payments.

Our position may be summarized in three propositions: (1) It
is possible for investments to yield additional products for domestic
consumption, and to increase real national income, without increasing money income available for expenditure on (additional) imports;
(2) It is possible for such investments to yield additional money
as well as real income without increasing imports; (3) If it is *assumed*
that the conditions necessary for the outcomes above are absent, or
that only those investments are included in the dangerous type III
which do, *ex post*, increase national money income freely disposable
for the purchase of (additional) imports, the thesis is tautological:
the definition of type III necessarily implies a threat to the balance
of payments, but provides assistance in ascertaining, *ex ante*,
whether any given investment which is intended to increase, and

---

[1] *International Investment and Domestic Welfare*, p. 105.
[2] Ibid., p. 104 ; see also p. 102. As we shall see, Professor Buchanan's
definition of the dangerous 'type III' is not entirely clear.

which does indeed increase, the supply of products for the home market will turn out, *ex post*, to have fallen into this category. Yet Professor Buchanan implies very clearly, and erroneously, that all investments with this intention and consequence are almost certain to result in a weaker balance of trade.

In short, Professor Buchanan makes the apparently reasonable assumption of a marginal propensity to import greater than zero. Our argument reduces to the apparently surprising contention that this assumption is not reasonable.

(1) Real Income Increases, Money Income Stable

The factors responsible for the additional output may themselves consume it, without ever taking it to market. If better tools enable Chinese peasants to increase their production of food, they will undoubtedly first eat better. To the extent they do so, they consume their additional earnings, and have no reason to purchase more goods from others.[1]

The additional output, offered for sale, may force down the general price level, increasing real income without increasing the (money) distributive shares. There is no presumption here that imports will rise, despite the customary assumption that imports are a function of real income. On the contrary, lower domestic prices are likely to result in a reduction of imports. Such an investment may be said to fall really into what Buchanan and Polak term 'type II'— goods sold on the home market replacing other goods previously sold there — since its sales result in a reduction in the *money value* of sales of other products. This possible objection represents the first corroboration of our final proposition. Here is an investment which has had the effect of producing additional, unmistakably home market goods; its sales have occurred without reducing the physical quantity of other goods and services sold; its operations have therefore increased real national income. If it does *not* fall within Buchanan's interdicted group, the latter must be defined more narrowly than he defines it — so narrowly, indeed, as to be tautologous: 'industries which turn out, *ex post*, to have been

---

[1] Increased real national income may result in a redistribution of the pattern of expenditure of an unchanged total amount of disposable money income, but such a redistribution may just as well reduce as increase the volume of imports.

so financed that, by definition, they increase disposable national
money income and imports.'

(2) Money Income Increases to the extent of the Incremental Output

Even if MV increases sufficiently to sustain prices in the face of
the increased output, with the result that gross national money
income rises by the amount of the additional sales, there is still no
presumption that imports will be higher in the end. Assume, for
example, that the factors producing these goods — call them F —
are paid initially (and only initially) with the proceeds of a bank
loan, which provides the required expansion of M. The additional
purchasing power of F is not matched by equivalent reductions in
the earnings of other factors, and F may certainly be expected to
spend some of their added receipts on foreign goods, or on domestic
goods employing foreign raw materials.

However, F's continued receipt of an enhanced income is dependent on the sale of their (added) product to other income recipients — call them G. If the investment is undertaken by the government and its forthcoming services provided without charge, G
become not voluntary purchasers but taxpayers. In any case, *as
long as G* (or the government) *do not purchase the new products* (or
pay the additional taxes) *in an inflationary manner* (by reducing
their customary rate of savings, by borrowing or by activating idle
balances), F's expanded disposable money income must be matched
by an equivalent absorption of purchasing power from G, who must
be reducing their expenditures on other goods equivalently. Whether
the net effect of F's additional purchases (of imports, or other
domestic goods, produced, let us say, by H) and G's diversion of
purchases (to F products from imports or from H's goods) will be
higher or lower imports is indeterminate. There is no *a priori* presumption one way or another, despite the fact that national money
income is higher.[1] The marginal propensity to import may equally

---

[1] The fact that the new production may require foreign raw materials still
creates no presumption of a balance-of-payments problem, under present
assumptions. To the extent that part of the cost of the added goods consists of
imported raw materials, the sale of the added output entails a greater diversion
of G's purchases from H — whose products may equally require imported raw
materials — and from imports than F's income increases. The net effect
remains indeterminate.

well turn out negative or positive, depending on whose propensity is greater, F's or G's.[1]

The success of investments yielding additional goods or services for domestic consumption and the resultant increase in factoral returns, on the one hand, and increased national expenditure *for these goods* (by purchasers or taxpayers), on the other, are inevitably equivalent and mutually interdependent, under present assumptions. Were an amount of disposable money income equivalent to the incremental output not absorbed in purchasing these goods, it would not be earned — unless sales were financed in an inflationary manner. In short, the expansion of national *real* income *is* these added goods, and the increment to national *money* income takes them off the market. There can be no multiplier higher than unity, no superimposed rise in disposable money income available for expenditure on added imports — provided the purchasers have not altered the distribution of their (unchanged) incomes between spending and saving. (Actually the proviso need not be so stringent. As long as any reduction in G's savings is matched by enhanced savings on the part of F, there remains no probability of enhanced imports.)[2]

(3) The Tautology of the 'Type III' Criterion

There is some question whether the investment we have posited really conforms to Professor Buchanan's conception of type III. His classification of investments might hinge on their *initial* impact rather than on their ultimate outcome, type III being those which even at the outset involve no diversion of consumer (G) purchases

[1] Technically it is not G's marginal propensity to import which is relevant ; G's reduced imports result not from a diminution of income but from a redistribution of expenditure.

[2] An increase in GNP (gross national product) as a result of enhanced national productive capacity requires an increase in the average national propensity to spend, as Professor Domar has pointed out. The preceding discussion has fulfilled this requirement by implicitly attributing to F a marginal propensity to consume of unity. One might assume, equally, an absolute reduction in saving by G sufficient to offset any enhanced saving by F — or sufficient induced investment expenditure, or an absorption of incremental savings by taxes levied to finance the operation of the projects. The crucial point is that such an expansion in the average propensity to spend, sufficient only to absorb part or all of the expanded output, involves no possibility of a multiplied expansion of national income, and no probability of enhanced imports — in contrast with the probable consequences of an *autonomous* expansion in that propensity.

from other domestic goods or imports. By this standard, our example falls into type I or II. But type III investments, thus defined, can obviously not succeed except by violating the assumption to which we have thus far adhered — that planned national savings must not decline — and will indeed almost inevitably weaken the balance of payments. It does not follow from such a definition that investments which increase the flow of products for domestic consumption are dangerous, *per se*.

On the other hand, Professor Buchanan frequently appears to be defining his categories in terms of the ultimate balance of results — i.e., taking into account the effect of F's enhanced expenditures. In this case, type III investments are those which result ultimately in increased GNP (gross national product) through increased sales in the home market. But if this is his standard, he is wrong, as we have argued : such investments involve no probability of a positive marginal propensity to import and of balance-of-payments difficulties in the absence of an absolute reduction in national savings. We conclude, therefore, that Professor Buchanan's reasoning is either faulty or tautologous.

Clearly the proviso with respect to non-inflationary financing of type III sales is crucial. Hence Polak's definition of the investments meets this additional requirement : they are operations which yield 'goods sold on the home market in addition to those previously sold, and in excess of the increase in demand owing to the rise of incomes. For instance, investments may be made to produce durable consumer goods which are sold by an extension of consumer instalment credits. Or a municipality may invest money in public utilities or slum clearance projects, which it operates at a loss without covering this loss out of taxation.'[1] This proviso apparently escapes Buchanan, whose analysis of the danger of class III investments runs simply in terms of the nature of the product and its incremental character. The beast, then, is inflation, as Polak clearly states, not any particular form of investment or product.[2]

[1] Op. cit., p. 469.

[2] Ibid. Dr Polak is perhaps not without blame for the confusion about his type III. His three categories are not different investments 'associated with three types of product', as he says (p. 468). For this to be so, type III would have to embrace all goods sold on the home market in addition to those previously sold, as Professor Buchanan apparently thought it did. In fact, its distinguishing characteristic is not the type of product but the method of financing its sales.

The Advantages of Home-Market Industries

The advice to underdeveloped countries to shun investments, even if domestically financed, directed toward the production of additional goods and services for the home market, may be quite unfortunate. The marginal propensity to import is typically extremely high in backward economies, largely because of a meagre, undiversified domestic productive plant. Many observers have predicted that a decline in this propensity will follow the development of industries supplying additional consumption goods for the domestic market.[1] If it is necessary to reckon with the possibility that, in practice, the operation of new home market industries may perhaps induce dis-saving and hence additional imports, one must also recognize the probability that some of these products will supplant imports, on balance. A (net) MPI of zero is therefore not at all inconceivable, particularly if governments pursue prudent monetary policies.

Indeed, it is precisely because of their probable long-run effects on the propensity to import that there is much to be said in favour of such investments, particularly in overpopulated, backward economies. By reducing the (marginal) import leakage, they make possible a greater absorption of surplus labour into productive employment and hence a still greater increase of income than would otherwise result from given future investment expenditures.[2] Conversely, because before 1914 most international investment in truly primitive economies (i.e., outside of Western Europe, the United States, Canada, Argentina, Australia and perhaps India) went into the

[1] Such investments yield what Professor Eugene Staley has termed C-products : 'The increased consumption of these items in the newly developing countries would be exactly balanced by the increased production in the same group of countries. . . . It is worth pointing out that economic development is likely to increase domestic production and consumption even more than it increases international trade', *World Economic Development* (International Labour Office, Studies and Reports, Series B, No. 36, second edition, Montreal, 1945), p. 173.

Who can doubt that the higher income created by the fruition of an investment programme for providing the Indian peasant with more and better food, clothing, housing, medical care, and education will be absorbed in consuming these additional products and services? See Iyengar, op. cit., pp. 189–205 ; Mandelbaum, op. cit., p. 88 ; P. Ady, 'Colonial Industrialization and British Employment', *Review of Economic Studies*, XI (Winter, 1943), pp. 42–50.

[2] See P. Ady, loc. cit.

development of export industries, operating in more or less isolated segments of the debtor economies, it had a relatively small secondary effect on incomes and employment and contributed inadequately to economic development in those countries.[1]

An entirely specialized export operation, however rapidly expanding, has not ordinarily sufficed to set off and sustain the self-perpetuating, cumulative process of economic development. Professor Allyn A. Young perhaps intended no support for autarkic programmes when, developing the familiar thesis of Adam Smith concerning the relationship between the size of the market and technological progress, he emphasized the mutual interdependence of expanding output and expanding demand: 'The rate at which any one industry grows is conditioned by the rate at which other industries grow. . . .'[2] However it seems to be true that diversified home market industries, growing together and supplying each other with expanding markets, are essential components of the dynamics of technological progress.

III. DIRECT v. INDIRECT FOREIGN EXCHANGE REQUIREMENTS

The third criterion applies specifically to international lending: it is the general rule followed by the International Bank for Reconstruction and Development and the American Export-Import Bank to make loans covering only the direct foreign exchange requirements of specific development projects. The latter institution's loans are all tied. In the case of the former, the policy is dictated by Article IV of its charter.

The IBRD apparently considers (or at least until recently considered)[3] its policy economically sound. It did not take refuge in the mandate of its charter in justifying the following statement: 'Development is also hampered by the limited resources of domestic capital available in most underdeveloped countries.

---

[1] H. W. Singer, 'The Distribution of Gains Between Investing and Borrowing Countries', *American Economic Review, Supplement*, XL, May 1950, p. 475 ; see also Rosenthal, op. cit., pp. 35ff.

[2] 'Increasing Returns and Economic Progress', *Economic Journal*, XXXVIII, 1928, pp. 533f. ; see pp. 527–42 ; also P. N. Rosenstein-Rodan, op. cit., pp. 205f. (reprint p. 249).

[3] In its most recent report, it concedes 'considerable validity in principle' to the critiques of this policy. *Fifth Annual Report, 1949–1950*, Washington, 1950, p. 10.

'External expenditures are only a part, and usually a minor part, of the cost of the development project; the remainder must normally be derived from sources within the country concerned. The insufficiency of domestic capital for this purpose . . . '[1]

One is left with the definite impression that the Bank confused physical capital goods and their components with 'capital' or savings, and concluded from the fact that most of the former had to come from within the developing country that the latter did as well. Professor Buchanan has at certain times given evidence of the same confusion: 'A more important reason why only a small fraction of the total investment necessary for industrialization can come from abroad is to be found in the nature of the real capital needed.'[2]

In view of the mischief which such a misconception may do in retarding international investment for economic development, it seems desirable to underscore the simple error in this reasoning and in the policy which follows from it. The mere fact, which Professor Buchanan stresses continually, that much or most of the *physical* process of capital formation must take place on the spot, using domestic labour and materials, has nothing whatever to do with the profitability of such investments, the necessity for foreign financing, or the possibilities of repayment.[3] No greater tendency to default follows from the mere fact that the lending country in international investment — any more than the lending individual, in domestic investment — does not always supply capital *goods* but usually merely 'grubstakes' 'on-the-spot' construction. Lending is always a 'grub-stake' operation, the only determinant of whose success or failure is SMP (with the qualification for international as for interpersonal financing that a sufficient portion of the investment be designed to produce goods which can be sold to service the obligations). The only defensible additional criterion of whether or not resort to the IBRD is justified is the availability of local financing,

---

[1] *Fourth Annual Report, 1948–1949*, Washington, 1949, p. 9.

[2] Op. cit., *Economic Journal*, LVI, 1946, p. 549. See also his statement quoted on p. 148, below. Curiously, elsewhere he clearly avoids this error : *International Investment and Domestic Welfare*, pp. 18f., 96–100.

[3] See the present author's 'Palestine: A Problem in Economic Evaluation', *American Economic Review*, XXXIV, 1944, pp. 542f. ; Mandelbaum, op. cit., p. 84.

and that organization now shows signs of confining its investigations to these two tests.[1]

The issue is not whether such international agencies should make gifts under the guise of loans; the question is whether projects are to be granted or refused accommodation on 'economic' grounds extraneous to their productivity and possibilities of repayment.

Adherence to this criterion has interesting consequences. The kinds of investments which are basic to economic development, according to Professor Buchanan himself — transportation, power, etc. — are least likely to obtain foreign financing because they involve the heaviest on-the-spot expenditures. Conversely, debtor countries are thereby encouraged to push investment projects which require the maximum direct foreign exchange expenditure, regardless of whether they are the most productive.[2] Loans covering only direct foreign expenditure requirements are likely to accentuate rather than relieve the dollar shortage: to the extent that domestic savings are inadequate to cover the local expenditure costs, debtor countries must finance that portion of their investments in an inflationary manner, and the loans provide no foreign exchange to meet the resultant expanded demand for imports.[3] Thus these loans virtually necessitate an intensification, rather than make possible a relaxation, of exchange controls in the debtor countries, and make the minimum contribution to the restoration of multilateral trade.

[1] *Fifth Annual Report*, pp. 10f. However, the italicized qualification in the following statement would appear to indicate a continued adherence in principle to the earlier policy, exceptions being authorized only where they may be expected to be temporary :

'The Bank recognizes that a country may be in a position where its domestic savings are reasonably fully employed in productive investment and where the most advantageous kind of additional investment for it to make would be in ... projects ... which call principally for expenditure in domestic currency. *If this investment is likely to lead in a few years to a correspondingly higher level of domestic savings*, the provision of foreign exchange to finance the indirect ... requirements would serve *to tide the country over* the period of expansion without inflation. ... A loan for this purpose would generally be justifiable.' Ibid., p. 10 ; italics supplied.

[2] See the remarks of the U. K. delegate, Mr. Sidney Caine, before the U. N. Economic and Social Council (hereafter ECOSOC), Fifth Year, Tenth Session, 369th meeting, *Official Records*, 1 March, 1950, p. 198.

[3] Walter S. Salant, 'The Domestic Effect of Capital Export Under the Point Four Program', *American Economic Review*, *Supplement*, XL, May 1950, pp. 501f.

IV. Practical Value of the Rejected Criteria

The argument of the preceding sections is essentially negative, consisting of a criticism, primarily on theoretical grounds, of three widely accepted investment criteria. The criticism clearly implies a positive aspect: that the appropriate (alternative) criterion is SMP, with two provisos: (a) an avoidance of inflationary financing of any additional home market sales, and (b) a sufficient concentration on type I investments, to the extent (and only to the extent) that it has been necessary to resort to foreign financing. There is no reason to qualify these propositions, on principle. However, both are subject to considerable qualification when one enters the actual theatre of operations, where policy decisions must be made in the present on the basis of inevitably uncertain information about the future.[1]

Capital Intensity

Prediction of the outcome and consequences of prospective investments is an extremely hazardous undertaking. This is particularly true in primitive economies, where there are so many additional leaks, lags and frictions, so many uncertainties — with regard to the technical feasibility of projected undertakings, the availability of a sufficient and suitable labour force, reliability of supply of required materials and of transportation services, ability to sell the product. Estimates of SMP, based inevitably on experiences elsewhere, are very often likely to prove overoptimistic. Economic development is an organic process; it cannot be simply decreed by protective tariffs or ushered in by a heavy inflow of foreign capital. Where circumstances are not propitious, capital may be quickly dissipated.

These uncertainties beset the calculation of capital turnover as well as SMP. However, the later criterion is surely the *safer*. It avoids the particularly hazardous prediction of the indirect, social contributions of a given project, which may be used to justify the capital-heavy investment. Moreover, the heavier the utilization of capital in individual projects, the greater is the penalty for individual miscalculations — a wasted, largely unrecoverable expenditure of

---

[1] It seems desirable to acknowledge the particular contribution of Professor Edwin P. Reubens' criticisms to the formulation of this section.

resources: this is the familiar danger of keeping all one's eggs in one basket.

The more conservative procedure — general adherence to the capital-turnover criterion, with exceptions permitted only where the capital-intensive investment is clearly of a 'bottleneck' kind — is particularly desirable (a) where capital is relatively scarce and labour extremely plentiful and (b) where investment is financed in part by borrowing from abroad. With respect to the first circumstance (a), the rule of thumb of employing the minimum amount of capital necessary to absorb excess labour does indeed approximate the SMP criterion. It accords also with the lessons of anthropology: modest projects which employ relatively little capital and attempt, and require for their success, a minimal disruption of settled habits of thinking and living are more likely to succeed than those which involve a mass, frontal assault on non-western patterns of culture. (The force of these various precautionary observations obviously varies from area to area; it clearly applies far less to reconstruction programmes in Western Europe than to development programmes in Asia.) (b) Foreign capital must be attracted; it cannot be commanded. The consequences of a few major failures, by impairing the continued willingness of foreigners to lend or invest, may reach far beyond the projects directly concerned. Moreover, when the borrowers are governments, there arises the possibility of a continuing burden upon the economy as a whole, even though the particular projects thus financed fail.

There is an additional, practical advantage in a *prima facie* presumption in favour of the capital-light industry or technique. The rate of turnover of one investment may be higher than another because the first uses shorter-lived equipment.[1] Since all investment represents a gamble, and later technological developments may make earlier equipment obsolete, it would seem wise, should such a choice be available, where all else is equal, to select the method which returns the initial investment more quickly, provides greater liquidity, and hence offers an earlier opportunity to revise erroneous decisions in the light of subsequent developments.

It may not be most fruitful for lending countries to approach the problems of reconstruction and development in a conservative

---

[1] See note 3, p. 132.

fashion: several writers have argued convincingly to the contrary.[1] There is much to be said also for abandoning the popular fiction that debt must be paid back[2]— but such advice, again, must be directed at the creditor countries. Until the latter are willing to depart from traditional practices and attitudes (as has the United States, for example, in the ECA programme), borrowing countries must be cautious in attempting to make the most of what they have, and with such fixed obligations as they may have to incur, and to incur the minimum of such obligations to achieve any given result.

The Nature of the Product

Similar considerations may dictate caution in embarking on (type III) ventures which make no obvious contribution to the balance of payments. In any investment programme there resides the continuous threat of inflation. Investments may be undertaken in excess of voluntary domestic savings. Operation of the projects may similarly be financed in an inflationary fashion: (*a*) because of unforeseen lags, temporary or permanent, between payments to productive factors and sales of the forthcoming products; (*b*) because the increased availability of consumption goods may induce consumers, on balance, to dis-save; (*c*) because even though taxes cover the operating (and interest) costs, the taxes may so diminish saving — as, in all cases, to mean an almost certain increase in imports. Backward areas or reconstructing economies may in short choose a higher level of planned investment and consumption than can be supported in either the short or the long run without foreign aid.

Direct v. Indirect Foreign Exchange Requirements

The policy of the International Bank which we have criticized has, likewise, a practical rule-of-thumb validity. The direct foreign exchange requirements of an investment project are readily mea-

---

[1] See, e.g., H. W. Singer, 'Economic Progress in Underdeveloped Countries', *Social Research*, XVI, March 1949, pp. 1–11 ; FAO, 'Report on International Investment and Financing Facilities', (Fifth Session, FAO Conference, Washington, 21 November, 1949, C 49/16), pp. 13ff. ; P. Warburg, 'Bargain Basement Diplomacy', *Harper's*, CIC, November 1949, pp. 50–4 ; and Bruno Foa, 'America Picks up the Check', *Harper's*, CIC, July 1949, pp. 56–61.

[2] Seymour E. Harris, 'Foreign Aid and Our Economy', *Bold New Program Series*, No. 7, Public Affairs Institute, Washington, 1950, pp. 43f., 71.

sured, and represent an obvious justification for incurring the risks of foreign borrowing.[1] Capital goods are not directly consumed; the possibility of their dissipation is only indirect and long-run. The indirect requirement of foreign exchange to meet expanded demands for foreign consumption goods resulting from the shift of factors into domestic capital formation is less obvious, less certain, less readily measurable (it depends on whether or not there is actual or potential surplus capacity in the relevant domestic industries). To finance such needs gives the foreign lender less assurance of an efficient utilization of the funds and raises the danger of a direct dissipation of foreign exchange in enhanced consumption.[2] The customary restriction increases the incentive for developing countries to mobilize and make the fullest utilization of their own potential resources. Widespread rural underemployment and crude agricultural techniques in backward areas suggest the possibility of simultaneously shifting labour into construction projects and increasing food production, reducing the dependence on indirect foreign financing and enhancing the prospects of ultimate viability.[3]

V. The Hazards of International Financing

The case for conservatism in investment programmes is strengthened by a consideration of the probable dangers — for debtor and creditor alike — of future international investment. Professor Buchanan has raised the interesting question whether 'the process of capital accumulation with the help of foreign loans' may not be 'inevitably tenuous by its very nature':[4] 'One wonders if there is not something in the very nature of capital accumulation with the assistance of foreign borrowing, something more fundamental, which

[1] It is not a sufficient justification, of course; with sufficient domestic savings, a country can purchase whatever foreign goods it requires from the proceeds of its exports.

[2] See the remarks of Willard Thorp, in the U. N. ECOSOC, Fifth year, Tenth Session, 369th meeting, *Official Records*, 1 March 1950, pp. 190f. ; also Buchanan, *International Investment and Domestic Welfare*, pp. 99f.

[3] Wilhelm suggests that Soviet Central Asia was able to make substantial progress in industrialization in this manner without substantial recourse to foreign capital ; op. cit., pp. 218–28.

[4] *International Investment and Domestic Welfare*, p. 115 ; the succeeding quotations are from p. 116.

tends to make large-scale defaults highly probable.' He suggests tentatively that this more fundamental explanation is to be found in the fact that

real capital consists very largely of immovable structures and the fruits of construction; that these have to be made with home resources; and that, in general, the best that foreign lending can achieve is to 'grubstake' that undertaking. But there is no necessary guarantee that if one country grubstakes another on a sizeable scale that the results of the investment will yield net exports in sufficient volume to service the loans. That depends on the kinds of projects undertaken and their relative proportions in relation to the whole.

One might at the outset raise the question whether the financial record of foreign has, in fact, been worse than that of domestic investment — a question to which we do not have the answer.[1] Whatever the comparative record, one need have no hesitation in conceding that waves of foreign lending have indeed been succeeded with monotonous regularity by waves of default. It may be fruitful to inquire whether international investment does involve distinctive risks over and above those to which domestic investment is subject, to assess their importance in the future and their relevance to the issues here under consideration.

The Hazards Defined

There are two distinctive hazards of international investment. The first arises out of the differences in the alternative loci of capital formation. Investment in a developed, capital-rich economy is not the same thing as investment in an underdeveloped economy or one disrupted by war. The projects differ, and so do their prospects of success, purely in terms of domestic currency. The second hazard

---

[1] R. A. Lehfeldt found that in the years immediately preceding World War I, Britain's foreign investment earned a higher return than domestic, taking defaults into account. 'The Rate of Interest on British and Foreign Investments', *Journal of the Royal Statistical Society*, LXXVI, 1913, pp. 204f.; also A. K. Cairncross, 'Did Foreign Investment Pay?', *Review of Economic Studies*, III, 1935, pp. 73ff. However, Britain's experience in this generally prosperous period was probably not typical. Moreover, the fact that the risk premium was sufficient (but hardly more than sufficient), on those investments which succeeded, to compensate for those which failed, in itself appears in a negative way to support the general assumption that international investment is inherently more dangerous than domestic.

is the problem of transfer[1] which has in turn two separate components not ordinarily clearly distinguished.

The first is the monetary or 'macro' problem. The funds must be raised domestically — and they must be *really* raised; i.e., they may not be obtained in an inflationary fashion. Purchasing power in the debtor country must be reduced relative to that of the creditor.[2] This end is more likely to be achieved if the investment is successful — if revenue from sales or additional revenue from taxes are sufficient to make the required amount of currency automatically available for transfer. However, even such success is inadequate if it has been achieved in an inflated currency. Conversely, the necessary funds can be raised if there is a will to do so, even if the investment fails.

The second is the 'micro' problem: that of achieving the appropriate allocation or reallocation of resources. It is this difficulty which makes it necessary for countries to consider the *kinds* of products to be produced by projects financed with the aid of foreign capital. The reality of this problem would be denied or its importance minimized by those economists who argued, during the reparations controversy of the 1920s, that there was no transfer problem separate from that of raising the funds domestically, or who have argued in recent years, similarly, that the dollar shortage is attributable solely to 'pathological monetary conditions' in the dollar-short

---

[1] This is the sole distinguishing risk from the point of view of the country within which the investment is to occur. However, from the point of view of the potential capital exporter, prior to the danger that he may not be able to transfer his earnings if he invests abroad is the danger that there will be no earnings to transfer. This is not necessarily a greater risk on foreign than on domestic investment.

[2] This is the nature of the purchasing power shift required if the balance-of-payments problem is indeed one of transferring debt service. However (despite the frequent assumption to the contrary, arising out of the fairly general belief that it is changes in the capital balance which are ordinarily causal, with changes in trade balances ordinarily passive or induced) it is not necessarily the case that the country which has a payment to transfer has a weak balance of payments. The transfer of E.C.A. payments hardly requires relative deflation in the United States. Similarly, mounting British exports of capital were frequently associated in the nineteenth century with a strong balance of payments and improving terms of trade under the impact of rapidly increasing world-wide demand for British coal and capital goods. See the author's *Great Britain in the World Economy*, New York, 1946, pp. 4–8, 32–6, 150f.

countries : inflation and overvaluation of their currencies.[1] Following this view, all that is required for the successful service of international obligations — whether or not the investment has been successful (indeed, even if the obligation is sheer tribute, or if the balance-of-payments difficulties result from war-time destruction) — is the withholding of a sufficient volume of funds from the debtor country's income stream, in a non-inflationary manner; this automatically releases the required amount of additional goods for export. It would not be appropriate to examine this argument at length here. However, it clearly minimizes the difficulty of ascertaining, let alone following, the 'correct' monetary policy. And it ignores cr minimizes the rigidities and resistances, at home and abroad, to the required shifts of productive factors and alterations in the patterns of trade, which even correct monetary policies, however essential, cannot remove.

Summarizing, then, we have (1) the risk that the investment abroad will not prove successful in terms of the domestic currency of the borrowing country; (2) the macro-transfer risk — that the domestic currency of the borrowing country may in effect decline in value relative to that of the lender, after the loan has been made ; (3) the micro-transfer risk, which arises out of the imperfections of the market. Are there strong inherent reasons for international investment to fall prey to these distinctive pitfalls, apart from such possible and partial explanations as the greater imperfection of the international than the domestic capital market?[2]

The Risks of Developmental Investments

On the basis of section III, above, it seems possible to dismiss Professor Buchanan's answer to this question : that there is a danger

---

[1] See, e.g., Frank D. Graham, *The Theory of International Values*, Princeton, 1948, pp. 190–200, 274–83, 293–300.

[2] Although Professor Buchanan passes over such explanations in his quest for one 'more fundamental', it may be that these imperfections represent the fundamental defect of international compared with domestic investment. Its flow is apparently more subject to extreme and rapid changes because it is at one and the same time capable of earning much larger returns and more risky, hence more subject to changes in speculative anticipations. These speculative extremes perhaps encourage a greater number of bad loans in the boom and a more complete cessation of financing even good projects once the bubble is burst, and hence on both counts contribute to more widespread default.

11

simply because developmental investment consists primarily of on-the-spot expenditures. At the same time, a partial answer is certainly to be found in the fact that huge projects, requiring correspondingly large quantities of capital and supplying quasi-public services for the home market, must bulk large in these programmes.[1] Because of the size of the undertakings, because a substantial portion of their SMP is not directly appropriable by sale of their services,[2] and because of the pressure by impatient populations to proceed vigorously along these various fronts, governments will assume major entrepreneurial responsibilities in these areas, planning to finance subsequent operations in large measure out of taxes. Moreover, governments are likely to embark on large-scale investments of a welfare nature, which, similarly, represent a large drain on limited resources and provide services for the home market.[3]

Such investments may fall prey to each of the above-listed hazards of international investment.

(1) The private or social marginal productivity of capital thus employed may be less than interest costs, so that the foreign obli-

[1] It has often been pointed out that in many cases relatively small expenditures — for technical assistance, resource surveys, the provision of simple tools, for example — may yield substantial results. Many of these, however, serve only to lay the groundwork for heavy expenditures later. Technical assistance is not an alternative, but a necessary complement to large scale capital formation.

[2] For example, irrigation projects were undertaken by private enterprise in both the United States and Australia during the nineteenth century, but have since been carried on almost entirely by governments, and have seldom directly paid their way. The U. S. Reclamation Act of 1902 expressly relieves farmers of the burden of interest charges — a subsidy amounting to at least 40 per cent of the total cost of the projects. The inability of users to pay the full costs by no means proves that particular projects have failed to add sufficiently to national product (directly and indirectly) to cover the opportunity costs of the capital. John W. Haw and F. E. Schmitt, *Report on Federal Reclamation to the Secretary of the Interior*, 1 December 1934, Washington, 1935 ; D. R. Gadgil, *Economic Effects of Irrigation*, Gokhale Institute of Politics and Economics, 1948, esp. pp. 1–15, 172–5. See, however, note 2, p. 153.

[3] The boundary line between 'welfare' and 'productive' investments is not an easy one to draw. See Buchanan, *International Investment and Domestic Welfare*, pp. 104–5. Expenditures on housing, health, improved diets, education, research, like those on roads and port facilities are, within limits, a *sine qua non* of economic progress and of the success of other investments. See, for example, Myron Stearns, 'The Road that Food Built', *Harper's*, CC, June 1950, pp. 82–8.

gations impose a net drain on the economy. No investment is certain of success. Many of these are unusually uncertain, because of the very factors that make them necessary, and make it necessary for governments to undertake them: among these are (a) the very absence of the essential preconditions of economic progress — housing, transport, power, water systems, an established or readily cultivable domestic market, a literate, healthy, skilled labour force, susceptible to economic inducements, an indigenous entrepreneurial or trustworthy managerial class;[1] (b) the fact that many of those basic, quasi-public investments which must be undertaken have always defaulted in part, yet, defaulting, made their contributions to continued growth — like the American railroads, many of which never paid the people who financed them, yet whose cleared rights-of-way, roadbeds, tracks and locomotives remained to serve the country; (c) the elimination of the inhibiting scrutiny of the market in passing on and testing the results of various investments. Governments will have to justify many of their expenditures in terms of indirect and largely immeasurable economic benefits to society as a whole. Anxious for quick results, they are likely to err in the direction of over-optimism.[2] Stern economic requirements are not satisfied even by the certainty that particular expenditures of borrowed funds will yield great satisfaction, create jobs, increase productivity by some amount, or even save lives — unless the capital represents a gift.[3] The fact is that many of these programmes are

[1] See A. Bonné, 'Aspects of Economic Reconstruction in West and East', *International Affairs*, XXII, 1946, pp. 529f.

[2] There is a danger of failing to differentiate the gross benefits to localities and the net benefits, if any, to the economy as a whole, the real benefits and the purely monetary. An investment which raises land values, creates a larger market for the output of particular producers, increases the ability of an area initially to absorb but not necessarily continuously to support immigrants is not necessarily productive (perhaps a better adjective would be 'reproductive'), by economic standards.

[3] For example, had not most of the capital thus far invested in Jewish Palestine come in free, defaults would soon have halted the flow, and the enormously expanded Jewish population would have been physically incapable of supporting accustomed — or even reduced standards of living. See A. E. Kahn, op. cit., *American Economic Review*, XXXIV, 1944, pp. 538–60.

The gap between investments which are to some extent productive and those which are sufficiently productive to cover even relatively low interest charges unquestionably explains much of the current controversy over the International Bank's conservative lending policies, and recent proposals for either

essentially consumption expenditures: their possible indirect contributions to productive capacity are uncertain and long-range,
compared with their immediate drain on resources.

(2) The relationship between inflation and the transfer problem
brings out a delicate irony in the comparison of the records of domestic and international investment. The investment process is
itself inflationary; and secular inflation, as Keynes pointed out
many years ago, is a wonderful instrument for the euthanasia of
the rentier — silent and legal.[1] But the remedy is of no avail to a
debtor economy (unless its international obligations are fixed in its
own currency, in which case it has no transfer-problem). In short,
it is partly because foreign debtors do not have the same opportunities as domestic debtors for a creeping, semi-concealed, automatic
evasion of their obligations that they may be forced more often into
open default !

The macro-transfer problem is enhanced by the customary inclusion of repayment obligations in bond contracts. Even a successful investment, by SMP standards, may fail or create a transfer
problem because of the necessity of absorbing more purchasing power
from the economy than is added by the operation of the investment,
in order to pay back the principal.

Backward economies have typically been susceptible to inflationary tendencies, because of their underdeveloped saving habits
and institutions, weak governments and banking systems, high
marginal propensities to consume, and high rates of induced investment spending. Governmental commitments to better living standards and rapid development will probably strengthen the tendency
to attempt to live beyond their means and make the transfer problem
chronic.

(3) The quantity of additional exportable (or import-competing)
products forthcoming may prove inadequate to provide easily the

---

relaxing that agency's present requirements or supplementing it with another
international lending agency, empowered to make development grants or
loans at lower interest rates and longer maturities. See, e.g., Rosenthal,
op. cit., pp. 43, 46f., 52–7. The determination, *ex ante*, of the prospects of
such loans, and when they may cross the borderline between true loans and
partial gifts is beyond the competence of the present writer. See the FAO's
optimistic predictions, op. cit., pp. 5ff., 30f.; cf. IBRD, *Fourth Annual Report*,
p. 14.

[1] *Monetary Reform*, New York, 1924, pp. 11ff., 69–80.

additional foreign exchange required. The uncertain contribution to national productive capacity of public service investments is matched by the uncertainty of their contribution to the balance of payments. Foreign investment which expanded the capacity of debtor economies to supply food and raw materials for export may have made only an uncertain and inadequate contribution to economic development of backward areas,[1] but it minimized the micro-transfer problem. It is a basic dilemma of economic development that backward areas can make little progress without the aid of foreign loans, yet the kinds of investment required for development are frequently the least certain to make easy repayment possible.

Private international investments may be similarly misdirected and surely have been in the past. The comments above by no means support the thesis that private capital merely awaits 'a favourable climate' to assume the major role in international investment and economic development, and that *laissez faire* will create such a climate. The issue — like the issue between 'free enterprise' and 'planning' — is largely artificial.[2] However, when private investments fail, they default, and no balance of payments pressure results. Nor do such failures therefore threaten the viability of the capital-importing economy, except in so far as they discourage future capital imports. But the taxpayer does not enjoy limited liability. Government obligations continue as a claim on national output through tax receipts, which may or may not be high enough in real terms to eliminate the macro-transfer problem. There is a strong possibility that they will not be high enough in the new world economy, where

[1] Singer, op. cit., *American Economic Review*, XL, May 1950.

[2] Several investigators have reminded us that even in the nineteenth century, the 'golden age of *laissez faire*', a favourable climate required a substantial measure of government intervention. Henry C. Aubrey, 'Deliberate Industrialization', *Social Research*, XVI, 1949, pp. 158–82 ; Louis Hartz, *Economic Policy and Democratic Thought: Pennsylvania 1776–1860*, Cambridge, 1948. Also, such private investments as may be forthcoming may indeed be more successful in avoiding default, yet contribute inadequately to development, as Dr Singer argues has been true in the past. See also, on this issue, Rosenthal, op. cit., pp. 19f., 40–52 ; Thomas Balogh, 'Some Theoretical Problems of Postwar Foreign Investment Policy', *Oxford Economic Papers* No. 7, March 1945, pp. 93–110 ; reprinted in the present volume, pp. 473–91. Rosenstein-Rodan, op. cit. ; Yuan-Li Wu, 'A Note on the Postwar Industrialization of "Backward" Areas and Centralist Planning', *Economica*, n.s. XII, 1945, pp. 172–8 ; U. S. Council of the International Chamber of Commerce, *Intelligent International Investment*, New York, 1949.

governments do not accept the overriding obligation to pursue whatever monetary-fiscal policies are required for preserving balance-of-payments equilibrium without the need for exchange controls or depreciation.

VI. Conclusion

The hazards of international investment lend cogency to the investment criteria which we have earlier criticized. All are defective. Yet all lean in the direction of conservatism. Their value is that they are based on a realistic appraisal of the pitfalls of the process of economic development — the uncertainty that projects will succeed, the inflationary pressures, the danger of excessive recourse to foreign loans — and suggest precautions to minimize the wastes and resultant burdens.

However, there are limits to the desirability of adopting erroneous rules of thumb because they err on the side of safety; economists have long been taking accountants to task for precisely this policy. Taken as general principles, the various criteria discussed are wrong; frequently their implications are misleading, and the practical consequences of following them would be unfortunate. They discourage investments which may make an immense contribution to national productivity, or may materially improve living standards without necessarily threatening balance-of-payments stability or national viability.

The hazards of international investment present a challenge to intelligent planning; they do not dictate an unreasoning conservatism. The marginal productivity of capital in backward areas, particularly if capital is accompanied by technical assistance and investments are intelligently planned, is potentially immense. However, many projects essential to the realization of this potential are themselves difficult — politically and economically — to pay for. Successive over-optimism and default have been the traditional instruments for eliciting these investments and sloughing off the heavy resultant financial burdens. Intelligent planning in the future probably requires that creditor countries, assessing the benefits in broader terms than direct monetary yields and repayments, assume some of this burden consciously, extending loans carrying lower interest rates and longer maturities, and making outright gifts. Such a policy raises serious problems. The traditional criteria of the market place provided a neat and precise basis for allocating capital throughout the world. To the extent that lending and borrowing countries depart from those criteria, there ceases to prevail an objective and non-political standard for guiding the international flow of funds. However, the autonomous market always worked imperfectly. Investments have always turned out, in part, haphazardly distributed gifts, and their timing and distribution have always left much to be desired. The fruits of progress have always been unsatisfactorily distributed among the nations of the world (by political standards), and the political pressures to redress that balance cannot be ignored. The problem, then, is one of developing criteria to guide an international flow of gifts. Precedent is not lacking: ECA provides an instance of a system of international distribution according to need. The progressive income tax is another, on the domestic plane.

The devising of a system for the distribution of international grants-in-aid is essentially a political problem. However, the economist can bring to the task of directing investment an insistence on certain first economic principles, and can insist on rejection of those which are fallacious in theory and mischievous in effect. If the outcome of an improper application of the correct criteria for investment is likely to be some waste, default, and balance-of-payment difficulties (which have marked the economic record of all countries at all times), the result of ill-founded conservatism and a refusal to take calculated risks will surely be discouragingly slow progress, or no progress at all. Waste is part of the price of economic progress; an irrational refusal to pay the price means that nothing will be purchased.

THE APPLICATION OF INVESTMENT CRITERIA*

by Hollis B. Chenery

This paper is an attempt to bridge the gap between theory and practice in the analysis of investment in underdeveloped areas. Economic theory tells us that an efficient allocation of investment resources is achieved by equating the social marginal productivity of capital in its various uses. In developed countries, perfect competition provides a standard for judging such a distribution of resources without the necessity of measuring the marginal productivity save in exceptional cases.

In underdeveloped[1] areas, it is generally recognized[2] that both private value and private cost may deviate far from social value and social cost. In such cases perfect competition cannot even be used as a standard for many sectors of the economy; rather it is necessary to measure social productivity and to provide for some form of government intervention to achieve more or less efficient distribution of investment resources. This paper will be concerned with the practical possibility of measuring the social marginal product and of establishing a framework for making decisions based on such measurements.

* *Quarterly Journal of Economics*, February 1953. Reprinted with the permission of the Harvard University Press, and the author. He is indebted to Paul Clark, Donald McClelland, Kenneth Arrow and Alfred Kahn for helpful criticism of earlier drafts of this paper.

[1] There seems to be no precise definition of an underdeveloped area. I would accept A. N. McLeod's definition of 'a country or region with a relatively low ratio of capital and entrepreneurship to other factors of production but with reasonably good prospects that additional capital could be profitably invested', *American Economic Review*, June 1951, p. 411.

[2] See P. N. Rosenstein-Rodan, 'Problems of Industrialization in Eastern and South-Eastern Europe', *Economic Journal*, Vol. LIII, 1943, pp. 202–11, reprinted in Agarwala and Singh (eds.), *The Economics of Underdevelopment*, Oxford University Press, 1958; P. Baran, 'On the Political Economy of Backwardness', *The Manchester School*, January 1952, reprinted in Agarwala and Singh (eds.), *The Economics of Underdevelopment*, and J. H. Adler, 'The Fiscal and Monetary Implementation of Development Programmes', American Economic Association *Papers and Proceedings*, 1951, p. 592.

Most of the suggestions by economists for the planning of investment have assumed the framework of partial equilibrium analysis in which other things must be assumed to remain equal. As Kahn[1] has pointed out, such rules may be quite misleading when *ceteris paribus* conditions do not hold. One of the purposes of this paper is to determine whether the Social Marginal Productivity test can be approximated in practice by simple rules of thumb such as the balance-of-payments effect and capital intensity used by Buchanan,[2] Polak[3] and other writers. To do this the SMP must be formulated in terms of these factors and an examination must be made of investment choices in actual cases.

The approach used here is essentially an inductive one based on studies of investment programmes and problems in several countries with somewhat similar characteristics. To indicate the predominant types of investment problems and the relationships among the variables involved, the conditions of production and the institutional framework of investment are summarized first. In the second section a formula is developed for measuring the social productivity, and it is applied to two actual sets of investment choices. From this basis a re-examination is made of the usefulness of various rules of thumb in assessing investment programmes. Finally, a general method is sketched out for using data likely to be available in formulating investment programmes within the existing institutional framework.

I. STRUCTURAL FACTORS

The countries[4] on which this analysis is based are Greece, Turkey, Portugal and southern Italy.[5] They are similar in climate, natural

[1] Alfred Kahn, 'Investment Criteria in Development Programs', *Quarterly Journal of Economics*, February 1951, pp. 38–61, reprinted in the present volume, pp. 131–57.

[2] Norman S. Buchanan, *International Investment and Domestic Welfare*, New York, 1945, ch. 6.

[3] J. J. Polak, 'Balance of Payments Problems of Countries Reconstructing with the Help of Foreign Loans', *Quarterly Journal of Economics*, February 1943, pp. 208–40.

[4] The author has made field studies in these countries as part of his work for the Economic Co-operation Administration. The opinions expressed here are entirely his own, however.

[5] Southern Italy is comparable to the other Mediterranean countries, while northern Italy is considerably more industrialized. Only the former is considered here except when the data cannot be separated.

resources, and stage of economic development, as to some extent is the whole Mediterranean area. These characteristics make the possibilities for investment and further development in this area in some respects quite different from those in the Tropics or other underdeveloped areas. The applicability of the conclusions reached for these countries to other regions will be considered later.

Climate and natural resources provide similar limitations to investment in these four countries. The mild winters, limited rainfall, and hot, dry summers lead to specialization of agriculture for export and limit the production of some basic commodities. A considerable extension of agricultural output is possible through irrigation and land reclamation, which require large amounts of investment. Mineral resources are relatively limited, and there are few important opportunities for increasing exports through their exploitation except in Turkey. Agricultural products provide the bulk of exports.

The stage of economic development is quite comparable in these four areas. They have a *per capita* GNP of $150–200, less than half of that of the rest of western Europe but much higher than that in most of Asia and Africa. A considerable start has been made on industrialization, but transportation, power facilities, and skilled labour are still limiting factors. Except in Turkey, population pressure on existing resources is very great and has in the past been relieved by substantial emigration. Investment funds are scarce, as in all underdeveloped areas, and interest rates to private borrowers range from 10 per cent in Italy to 30 per cent in Greece.

In the four countries studied here, the Government directly influences over half of the total investment, either through direct participation or through granting of loans at low rates of interest. The ECA counterpart funds have increased the importance of the latter type of operations, particularly in Italy and Greece. The remaining investment resources are influenced in magnitude (through fiscal and credit policy) but only slightly in composition (mainly through control of imported equipment, which comprises about a quarter of total imports). Through both direct and indirect controls, the Governments have a decisive effect on the size and composition of total investment. None of the Governments mentioned has an adequate mechanism for assessing the economic impact of its investment operations, for setting up investment priorities, or for allocating investment resources among various fields.[1] There is therefore no investment 'programme' in the sense of an overall plan. There are rather programmes for agriculture, housing, public utilities, and many of the basic industries.

Estimates of the actual distribution of investment funds among the major fields are given in Table I below. It is notable that less than half of the total goes to commodity production. Less than 10 per cent is for types of production having low capital intensity, which are often recommended to underdeveloped countries. Producer services, which have the highest capital intensity, absorb more than a third of the total available funds, and much of the agricultural investment is in reclamation works, which have a very low rate of turnover. A major part of each investment programme is also in types of projects which will not improve the balance of payments. On the basis of even a cursory examination, therefore, it appears that either the investment programmes are badly directed or other criteria besides the capital intensity and balance of payments are needed.

TABLE I

INVESTMENT FIELDS[2]

(as per cent of total investment)

		Greece	Italy	Portugal	Turkey
A.	Primary Production				
	1. Agriculture.....	18	10	16	10
	2. Minerals........	2	2	?	11
B.	Industry..........	14	29	34	16
	Total Commodity Production......	34	41	50	37
C.	Producer Services..	35	34	38	38
	1. Power..........	(8)	(12)	(27)	(10)
	2. Transportation..	(27)	(22)	(11)	(28)
D.	Housing and Public Works..........	31	25	12[3]	25

[1] Source: 1949/50 submissions to OEEC and ECA estimates. Data refer to 1949 or 1950. All estimates are quite approximate.

[2] In Portugal no estimate is available for housing and it has been omitted. Portuguese data cover mainly the government investment programme.

[3] See, for example, *The Economy of Turkey*, International Bank for Reconstruction and Development, 1951, ch. IV.

II. Calculation of the Social Benefit of Individual Investments

The formulation of an optimum investment programme does not require an accurate measurement of the marginal productivity of each investment. It is sufficient to rank projects in order of their social value, determine the marginal project from the total funds available, and exclude all lower-ranking projects. In most under-developed areas the actual choice of investment alternatives is fairly limited. The rating system need only be detailed in the critical zone of marginal projects. The majority of investments will be clearly above or below this dividing line and can be accepted or rejected from fairly rough estimates. The method can be broken down into two or more steps, as shown below, to permit comparison first within one investment field and later among investment fields on the basis of the marginal projects in each.

In this section a formula will be developed to permit such a ranking of projects. It can be applied with greater or lesser accuracy according to the position of the investment sector in the priority scale.

The effect of an investment on a country's economy has several aspects or dimensions which are only commensurate under specified conditions. For example, any project will affect the national income, the balance of payments, and the distribution of income. So long as investment criteria are stated in *ceteris paribus* terms, the problem of comparable measurement of these diverse effects can be avoided. For practical use, however, these effects must be reduced to a common measure.

In the general case, we can take a welfare function containing an indefinite number of variables characteristic of a particular investment.

$$U = U\,(Y, B, D \ldots) \tag{1}$$

(all variables represent effects of a given investment)

Y = effect on national income,
B = total net[1] effect on balance of payments,
D = effect on distribution of incomes,
U = index of social welfare.

---

[1] Including multiplier effects and indirect imports for supplying industries. B may be divided between an investment effect, B_1, which is always negative, and an operating effect (B_2). The detailed calculation of these effects is analyzed in Section III.

The increment in U corresponding to a given increment in investment may be written:

$$\Delta U = \frac{\delta U}{\delta Y} \Delta Y + \frac{\delta U}{\delta B} \Delta B + \frac{\delta U}{\delta D} \Delta D + \cdots$$

Measuring U in national income units (with a given income distribution) and dividing through by $\frac{\delta U}{\delta Y} = 1$, this becomes:

$$\Delta U = \Delta Y + \frac{\delta Y}{\delta B} \Delta B + \frac{\delta Y}{\delta D} \Delta D \cdots \tag{2}$$

For simplicity, I shall ignore all variables except Y and B from now on,[1] although in particular cases it may be desirable to try to estimate D as well. I shall call ΔU the social marginal product[2] of a given investment. The marginal rate of substitution between Y and B will be called r. Equation (2) then becomes:

$$\text{SMP} = \Delta U = \Delta Y + r\Delta B. \tag{3}$$

The parameter r may be given various interpretations. Mathematically, it represents the amount of increase in national income which would be equivalent to an improvement of one unit in the balance of payments under specified conditions. Thus r measures the average overvaluation of the national currency at existing rates of exchange, taking into account the expected effect on imports and exports of the whole investment programme and also the balance-of-payments position at the beginning of the period. It may be thought of as a premium attached to foreign exchange earning or saving. If there is anticipated equilibrium in the balance of payments, $r = 0$.

---

[1] I have limited myself to the efficiency criterion for welfare increases only because of the availability of data rather than from unwillingness to make interpersonal comparisons. In countries suffering from structural unemployment, it would seem to me perfectly proper to introduce the differential effect of the investment on employment as a rough indication of D if this effect could be measured. The marginal rate of substitution between employment (without an increase in national income) and national income, $\frac{\delta Y}{\delta D}$ would certainly be positive, but any value assigned to it would represent a political and social judgment. In most underdeveloped countries, however, the equity criterion for welfare cannot be ignored.

[2] Kahn uses the term social marginal product for ΔY, but it seems desirable to include the balance-of-payments effect as well.

In underdeveloped countries in general, and particularly in those considered here, r may be expected to be appreciably greater than zero. Because of the structure of the economies as outlined above, there is little scope for reducing imports, whether by exchange depreciation or direct controls, without causing a larger decrease in GNP. As GNP increases, imports will increase at least in proportion, unless the investment is directed to import substitutes. Since the elasticities of supply for exports and of demand for imports are very low in the short run, an exchange depreciation which would make $r = 0$ is not usually desirable.[1] A better solution to the balance-of-payments problem is an investment programme which will produce equilibrium in the balance of payments.

In these circumstances, one limitation on the composition of investment is that it must lead to balance in the external receipts and payments over a specified period. Aside from relatively small decreases in non-essential imports, both reduced imports and increased exports require investment. The value of r should be selected which will satisfy this limitation through giving a sufficiently high value to foreign exchange earnings and savings.[2]

This method of introducing the balance-of-payments limitation has the advantage of making it possible to weigh the balance-of-payments effect against the effect of investment on GNP, which is essential in comparing actual investment projects. Similarly, the income distribution effect or other dimensions must be reduced to a common measure if they are to be included in the calculation.

We must now develop a measure of the term, ΔY, in equation (3) based on the type of data likely to be available for investment in underdeveloped areas. The effect on national income, ΔY, can be approximated by applying a set of corrections to the businessman's calculation of the annual rate of profit. (For single projects the difference between marginal and average productivity can usually be ignored). Beginning with the net private return over cost per unit of investment, corrections have to be made for the following factors to arrive at the net social return:

[1] Some 85 per cent of imports in these countries are producer goods, primarily raw materials. A reduction in these imports will reduce GNP by the amount of processing which they receive, which is several times the value of the imports. This is one factor in estimating r.

[2] Further discussion of the balance-of-payments premium will be found in Section III.

(a) *Tariffs, taxes and subsidies.* These must be eliminated in measuring the value of output. The effect of various means of protection may be removed by taking the social value of domestic production as equal to the cost of importing the same product.

(b) *External economies.* The value of goods and services to other producers[1] above the price at which they are sold must be taken into account in the case of transportation, utilities, and other items necessary to production. Where the chief use of the output is made by a small group of producers, as in a railroad spur to a new mining area, the external effects can best be measured by taking the investment in the railroad as part of the total investment in the project. For investment in services which are widely used, however, more approximate measures must suffice.

(c) *Unused resources.* When the investment will make possible the utilization of resources which would not otherwise be used (or used for less valuable purposes) only the social cost of utilizing the resources should be charged rather than the total rent or wages which a producer may pay. The cost to society of employing unemployed labour, for example, is only the increase in consumption which results. (If some of this increase in consumption can be supplied from other unused resources, that cost can be deducted.) If unemployment benefits are being paid, these can be deducted from the wage cost to get a rough measure of the social cost of labour.

On the basis of these elements, equation (3) can be expanded into the following formula for the social marginal product:

$$\text{SMP} = \frac{X + E - M_i}{K} - \frac{L + M_d + O}{K} + \frac{r}{K}(a B_1 + B_2)$$

$$= \underset{(a)}{\frac{V}{K}} - \underset{(b)}{\frac{C}{K}} + \underset{(c)}{\frac{Br}{K}} \quad (4)$$

where all variables (except B_1 and K) are annual flows:

SMP = average annual increment in national income (plus balance-of-payments equivalent) from the marginal unit of investment in a given productive use,

K = increment to capital (investment),

---

[1] Ignoring variations in consumer surplus as not being calculable in most cases.

X = increased market value of output (after allowance for subsidies and protection),

E = added value of output due to external economies,

M_i = cost of imported materials,

V = social value added domestically $= X + E - M_i$,

L = labour cost,

M_d = cost of domestic materials,

O = overhead cost (all other costs including replacement of capital),

C = total cost of domestic factors $= L + M_d + O$,

B = total balance of payments effect $= a B_1 + B_2$,

B_1 = effect of installation of investment on balance of payments,

a = combined amortization and interest rate on current borrowing,

B_2 = effect of operation on balance of payments.

The social product can be divided into three elements, as shown:

(*a*) Value added in the domestic economy per unit of investment.

(*b*) Total operating cost per unit of investment.

(*c*) Balance-of-payments premium per unit of investment.

Term (*a*) is the rate of capital turnover, corrected for imported inputs. The latter should be excluded in measuring the domestic resources utilized in conjunction with the capital goods added.

More complicated formulae can be elaborated, but this one utilizes all the data which can normally be obtained.

Equation (4) can be rewritten by combining terms (*a*) and (*b*) as follows:

$$\text{SMP} = \left(\frac{V}{K}\right) \left(\frac{V-C}{V}\right) + \frac{Br}{K} \tag{5}$$
$$\quad\;\; \text{(a)} \qquad \text{(d)} \qquad\;\; \text{(c)}$$

The SMP is thus the product of the percentage margin of social value over cost $\left(\dfrac{V-C}{V}\right)$ and the rate of capital turnover plus the balance-of-payments premium. This form of the equation shows that a decrease in the rate of capital turnover may be offset by a proportionate increase in the value margin and *vice versa*. The cost element (*d*) appears as a ratio to total value instead of to capital in this form of the equation; it is likely to be more constant and hence is more readily estimated in this form. The other two terms are unchanged.

Two examples of a calculation of the social productivity of investment are given in Tables II and III. In both cases the figures are merely illustrative of the type of results to be obtained because several approximations have been made. Current prices have been used, whereas the anticipated price over a period of years should be used.

TABLE II

SMP of Industrial Projects in Greece[1]

	(1) Lignite Mining Briquetting	(2) Nitrogenous Fertilizer	(3) Cement	(4) Phosphate Fertilizer	(5) Sulphuric Acid	(6) Glass	(7) Refractories	(8) Soda
Investment(K) (thousands of dollars)	23,350	17,000	6,750	2,450	1,450	2,800	650	3,500
(a) Capital Turnover $\left(\dfrac{V}{K}\right)$	·83	·67	·93	·74	·52	·86	1·16	·41
(b) Cost[2] Ratio $\left(\dfrac{C}{K}\right)$	− ·36	− ·29	− ·37	− ·37	− ·11	− ·43	− ·82	− ·27
(c) Balance-of-Payments Effect[3] $\left(\dfrac{Br}{K}\right)$	+ ·33	+ ·35	+ ·07	+ ·07	0	− ·04	− ·03	+ ·09
(d) Value Margin $\left(\dfrac{V-C}{V}\right)$	·56	·56	·60	·49	·79	·50	·29	·34
(e) SMP[4]	·80	·73	·63	·44	·41	·39	·31	·23

[1] Derived from data assembled by the ECA Mission to Greece.
[2] Omits overhead costs.
[3] Using $a = ·05$ in equation (4).
[4] SMP = (a) + (b) + (c) = (a) × (d) + (c).

TABLE III

SMP OF AGRICULTURAL PROJECTS IN SOUTHERN ITALY†

	Roads				Irrigation				Flood Protection			
	(1)	(2)	(3)	(4)	(5)	(6)	(7)	(8)	(9)	(10)	(11)	(12)
Investment (K) (millions of lire)	18	39	50	27	105	53	114	150	40	49	31	13
(a) Capital Turnover $\left(\dfrac{V}{K}\right)$	·25	·17	·14	·30	·96	·66	·75	·57	·77	·41	·32	·40
(d) Value Margin $\left(\dfrac{V-C}{V}\right)$	·6	·6	·6	·6	·2	·15	·2	·2	·2	·2	·2	·2
SMP = $(a) \times (d)$	·15	·10	·08	·18	·19	·10	·15	·11	·15	·08	·06	·08

†These examples were selected more or less at random from the files of the MSA Mission to Italy.

The first example is based on engineering estimates for various basic industrial plants in Greece. Because of the severe deficit in the Greek balance of payments when these projects were being considered, an illustrative value for r of $1\cdot0$ was used — i.e., the true value of foreign exchange to the economy over the planning period is assumed to be twice the existing exchange rate. Because of the importance of the balance-of-payments effect[1] it becomes the principal factor in the social productivity. Even if the value of r is reduced to $0\cdot2$, for example, the balance-of-payments effect changes significantly the conclusions drawn from the other elements alone. There is little relation between capital turnover and SMP, and the value margin is fairly constant.

The second example consists of sample evaluations of agricultural projects already under way in southern Italy. Here the balance-of-payments effects are fairly constant among projects and the value of r is low so that this term in the equation has been ignored. In these calculations a constant value margin based on cost studies for different types of production has been assumed for projects of the

---

[1] Only direct investment and operating effects are considered here. The elements which should theoretically be included are discussed in Section III.

same kind in the same area. Under these circumstances, the capital turnover becomes the determining factor in the social productivity, as in projects 5–12 for example.

III. INVESTMENT CRITERIA RE-EXAMINED

Investment criteria are usually stated in such terms as 'other things being equal, it is desirable to select investments having the highest rate of turnover on the capital invested'. As the previous examples have shown, such rules are of little value in practice unless the effect of the other factors can be estimated or one can identify the *ceteris paribus* situation. A study of the structural features outlined in Section I suggests the following bases for correlation among the various terms in the SMP:

(1) Sectors having a high positive value of $\frac{B}{K}$, the balance-of-payments effect, are found chiefly in agriculture and branches of industry which process domestic materials. A high value of the balance-of-payments effect is therefore frequently associated with a low rate of capital turnover because of the type of production involved.

(2) Some of the most valuable natural resources remaining to be exploited are water power, improvable land, and basic materials for chemical processes.[1] The high value margin is offset to some degree by low capital turnover, giving a negative correlation between terms (*a*) and (*b*) in equation (4).

(3) The advantages accruing to labour-intensive industries are offset in several sectors, such as heavy metal fabricating, by the high cost of imported raw materials and the diseconomies of small scale production.

(4) Differences in the rate of profit on imported commodities cause systematic variations in the margin of social value over cost. Many basic materials and chemicals, for example, are sold under monopolistic conditions. This fact increases the value of domestic investment to importing countries and offsets to some extent the high capital requirements in these sectors.

---

[1] In these sectors the difference between value and cost is high partly because the large-scale investment and advanced technology required have made their development slower.

It is clear from these considerations that negative correlations among the three factors are quite common. The possibility of using them separately in certain cases will now be examined. This review will serve as a convenient way of relating the present approach to the discussions by other authors of capital turnover and the balance-of-payments effect, the principal investment criteria which have been suggested.

(A) CAPITAL TURNOVER

Buchanan[1] and Polak[2] both emphasize the advantages of investments having a high turnover rate (or low capital intensity) and give the impression that this test will have wide applicability in choosing sectors for investment. The above factors suggest that when all sectors are taken together, there is if anything a negative correlation between capital turnover and SMP, because unused resources and the possibility of saving on imports or increasing exports occur predominantly in sectors having low capital turnover. The empirical evidence is equally strong. Capital-intensive investments are being stressed in all the investment programmes studied, and a review of these programmes does not suggest that a very great shift to less capital-intensive sectors would be desirable.

Kahn, in criticizing the conclusions of Buchanan and Polak, points out that 'The SMP of capital is not correlated with the rate of turnover.'[3] This statement is true when all sectors are taken together, but it does not rule out the use of the rate of turnover on a more selective basis. The turnover rate is particularly useful in choosing among projects within a given sector, as in the second example above. In these cases the balance-of-payments effect and margin of value over cost are likely to vary less, and the capital intensity can often be used alone in choosing among projects. Other examples are the selection of road transport over railroad investment, of diesel engines over railroad electrification, of less automatic spinning and weaving techniques in labour-cheap areas, etc. In such cases the problem is to choose among alternative techniques, locations, and factor combinations to perform similar economic functions; the economy of capital use is likely to be overriding.

---

[1] Buchanan, loc. cit.
[2] Polak, loc. cit.
[3] Op. cit., p. 39.

(B) Balance-of-Payments Effect

The balance of payments is one of the most widely used investment criteria. The main questions to investigate are: (1) whether the negative effect of investment on the balance of payments is of sufficient importance to warrant this emphasis, and (2) whether the balance-of-payments effect is often the deciding factor in determining investment priorities. The first question is particularly important, since well over half the total investment in the Mediterranean countries has no positive effect on the balance of payments. On this point, Kahn has sharply dissented from the conclusions of other authors that such investments must worsen the balance of payments.

To analyze the balance-of-payments effect, we may first distinguish between the effects during the investment period (B_1), which are always negative, and the operating effects (B_2). The main factors involved are:

Investment Effects (B_1)
   (1) Purchase of machinery and equipment abroad.
   (2) Multiplier effects of investment on income and imports.

Direct Operating Effects (B'_2)
   (3) Output of a commodity which increases exports or is a substitute for imports.
   (4) Imports (direct and indirect) for production of the given commodity.
   (5) Reduction of import requirements for production of commodities for which X is a substitute.

Indirect Operating Effects (B''_2)
   (6) Multiplier effect of inflationary financing of consumption.
   (7) Multiplier effect of change in export (import) surplus.

Of these, factor 3 is always positive. Factors 1, 2, 4, and 6 are always negative. Factors 5 and 7 may be either positive or negative.

Polak has suggested a classification of investments (which is used in slightly modified form by Buchanan) according to whether the operating effect is positive, neutral, or negative. Type I includes exports and substitutes for imports (factors 3 and 7), Type II replacements for goods presently consumed, and Type III home-market goods sold in excess of the increase in real incomes (factor 6). (Factor 4 is assumed constant for all types of investment and included with factors 6 and 7.)[1] His investment criterion is that the amount of investment in Type I sectors must be sufficient to offset the negative balance-of-payments effects of investments of Type III and of the investment phase of all types of project.

This statement of the balance-of-payments criterion is useful as a check on the whole programme, but is not a very operational approach when applied to individual projects. The division among categories is somewhat artificial because output of many commodities is likely to fall into several categories. Nor does the application of the test indicate what changes should be made in the programme in case it is not satisfied.

The use of the SMP formula will overcome these difficulties if a measure of $\frac{B}{K}$ can be obtained which will include all of these factors. They may be expressed algebraically as follows:

Investment Effects

$$\overset{(1)}{} \qquad \overset{(2)}{}$$
$$B_1 = -\,m_i\,K - mz\,(1 - m_i)\,K \qquad\qquad (6)$$

where

m_i = proportion of investment requiring imports (directly or indirectly),

m = ratio of increase in imports to increase in GNP (marginal propensity to import),

z = multiplier = $\dfrac{1}{m+s}$,

s = marginal propensity to save.

Direct Operating Effects

$$\overset{(3)}{} \qquad\quad \overset{(4)}{} \qquad\quad \overset{(5)}{}$$
$$B_2{}' = e\,(1 - \overline{m}_p)\,X - c\,\overline{m}_p\,X + g\,(\overline{m}'_p - \overline{m}_p)\,X \qquad (7)$$

where

e = fraction of output going to export or to reduction of imports (Type I),

---

[1] Polak, op. cit. Modifying this, Buchanan, op. cit., ch. 6, uses a broader definition of Type III because he apparently includes all investments not falling into categories I or II — i.e., those which increase output without improving the balance of payments. The latter definition seems more useful because it includes all possibilities. This broader definition of Type III reduces to Polak's when there is no source of increase in demand except the multiplier effect of the investment programme under consideration.

g = fraction of output replacing goods previously consumed (Type II),

c = fraction of output going to increase domestic use (Type III),

$(e + g + c = 1)$,

$\overline{m}_p$ = marginal ratio of producer imports (direct and indirect) to output for project in question,

$\overline{m}_p{}'$ = $\overline{m}_p$ for output which has been replaced by new production

Indirect Operating Effects

$$B_2{}'' = \overset{(6)}{-\; m\, z\, f}\, \overset{(7)}{(1 - \overline{m}_p)}\, X - m\, z\, B_2{}' \qquad (8)$$

where

f = fraction of output financed by inflationary means.

The expression for B is the total of these three components with the investment effects reduced to an annual basis:

$$B = a\, B_1 + B_2{}' + B_2{}'' \qquad (9)$$

where a = combined amortization and interest rate required on current borrowing.

The formula for the complete balance-of-payments effect of a given project[1] can then be written:

$$\frac{B}{K} = \left\{ \begin{array}{l} \overset{(1)}{-\,a\,m_i} \; \overset{(2)}{-\,a\,m\,z\,(1 - m_i)} \\[2mm] +\,\dfrac{X}{K}\left[\overset{(3)}{e\,u\,(1 - \overline{m}_p)} - \overset{(4)}{c\,u\,\overline{m}_p} + \overset{(5)}{g\,u\,(\overline{m}_p{}' - \overline{m}_p)} \atop \overset{\qquad\qquad(6)}{-\,m\,z\,f\,(1 - \overline{m}_p)} \right] \end{array} \right. \qquad (10)$$

where $u = (1 - m\,z\,) = \left(1 - \dfrac{m}{m + s}\right) = \left(\dfrac{s}{m + s}\right)$.

---

[1] The multiplier effect (2) is here attributed to the individual project because m_i varies among projects. For the economy as a whole, it is only increases in investments which have a multiplier effect. This formulation evaluates each project as a marginal project, but a correction must be introduced to make the effects additive.

In this form, the indirect and direct effects of factors 3, 4 and 5 are combined.

I have assumed that there are other factors operating in the economy to increase final demand apart from the investment programme under consideration (population growth, increases in exports, changes in tastes, etc.) and that therefore Type III investment is not necessarily limited to increased output of goods financed by inflationary means.[1] Dividing output between increased net consumption (c) and substitutes for goods already consumed in the economy (g) is almost impossible on a project by project basis, and therefore operationally it must be assumed that all output for which an associated reduction in some other type of consumption cannot be identified will result in a net increase in purchases in the economy as a whole. When this calculation has been made for all sectors of the economy, the total can be compared to an overall analysis of final demand. If the increase in consumption is overstated, a decrease in imports for other types of production can be introduced in calculating the value of r or applied proportionately to each project.

Equation (10) can be used to evaluate the effect of Type III investment — investment which results in a net increase in output of goods for domestic use. In the terminology used above, Type III is that portion of investment represented by output cX. For simplicity I will consider the pure case of Type III, in which $c = 1$ and e and g are zero. Kahn claims that aside from inflationary financing of output (term 6), the marginal propensity to import is likely to be zero in this case. For Type III investment not accompanied by inflationary financing, equation (10) reduces to the following form:

$$\frac{B}{K} = - a\left[m_i + m\,z\,(1 - m_i)\right] - \frac{X}{K}\overline{m}_p\ \left(\frac{s}{m + s}\right). \tag{11}$$

Kahn's argument amounts to saying that the last term (factor 4) is likely to be zero. This is only true if the marginal propensity to save (s) is zero or if the investment requires no operating imports $(\overline{m}_p)$. If the former is true, there will be no net increase in output without

[1] Polak limits himself to demand induced by the given investment programme and therefore $c = f$ in my terminology. Kahn, on the other hand, assumes that the operation of the given investment will somehow induce an equal increase in final demand ; this will only be true if the marginal propensity to consume is 1. See his footnote 1, p. 45, loc. cit. (present volume footnote 2, p. 139).

inflation, which is ruled out by the original hypothesis. The argument is only valid[1] where operating imports can be neglected.

I shall now try to evaluate the significance of the negative balance-of-payments effects of investments of Types II and III in the Mediterranean economies considered here. Considerably more than half of the total investment falls into these categories. The following values of the parameters in equation (10) have been estimated for southern Italy[2] and are probably sufficiently representative of the whole group:

$$m_i = \cdot 35,$$
$$m = \cdot 25,$$
$$s = \cdot 35,$$
$$z = 1 \cdot 66,$$
$$u = \cdot 583.$$

Inserting the parameters in equation (10) and assuming further that $\dfrac{X}{K} = 1 \cdot 0, f = 0, e = 0$, and $a = \cdot 10$ gives the following results:

$$
\begin{array}{cccc}
(1) & (2) & (4) & (5)
\end{array}
$$
$$\frac{B}{K} = - \cdot 035 - \cdot 027 - \cdot 583 \, c \, \overline{m_p} + \cdot 583 \, g \, (\overline{m_p}' - \overline{m_p}). \quad (12)$$

The average value of $\overline{m_p}$ may be taken at about $\cdot 20$.[3] For the average pure Type III project ($c = 1, g = 0$), equation (12) gives

[1] Kahn's argument in footnote 8, p. 44, (present volume footnote 1, p. 138) that the increase in operating imports will be offset by a decrease in imports for other types of production which will be replaced is inconsistent with his assumption of a net increase in production. Even when the new goods requires considerably less imports than the old, there will be a net increase in imports. Following Kahn's terminology, the income recipients from the new production (F) are now likely to be consuming the same goods as those previously consumed by the consumers (G) who have reduced their aggregate consumption to consume X. In effect, this means that total consumer imports and other producer imports are undisturbed, but that total imports will be increased by the direct and indirect import requirements of the new production.

[2] Based on Associazione per lo Sviluppo dell' Industria nel Mezzogiorno, *Economic Effects of an Investment Programme in Southern Italy*, Rome, 1951, ch. IV. The value of m_i determined in this study is $\cdot 425$ if southern Italy is taken as a separate region and $\cdot 129$ for Italy as a whole. The first case is more typical of the underdeveloped economies studied here.

[3] An accurate value of $\overline{m_p}$ would be obtainable by a solution to an input-output matrix, taking an increase in the output of one commodity or service and determining the total effect on imports.

a value of $\dfrac{B}{K} = - \cdot 18$ (or $- \cdot 15$ if term (2) is omitted). The range
of values for Type III commodity production may be from $- \cdot 07$ to
$- \cdot 30$. Only for investment consisting almost entirely of construction, such as housing and land reclamation, may factors (1) and (4) be
considered negligible. To the extent that these investments produce
substitutes for existing output, factor (5) may even be positive and
the whole balance-of-payments effect become zero.

It may be concluded that not more than a third of Type III
investment is free from a significant negative effect on the balance of
payments even if inflationary financing is avoided. This means that
the balance-of-payments premium rate will be significant even if the
balance of payments is in equilibrium at the start of the investment
programme.[1] The amount of Type III investment will be limited by
the positive effect attainable in Type I sectors. For pure Type I
investment, B/K comes out at about $+ \cdot 40$, using the same parameters. This suggests that the ratio of Type I to Type III must be at
least 1 to 3. Accurate results can be obtained only from individual
application of the SMP formula, however.[2]

Given the importance of the balance-of-payments term in Mediterranean countries, there remains the question of whether investment
projects can be so classified as to reduce variations in the other two
terms within groups of projects and make the balance of payments
the determining factor in estimating the SMP. Here the conclusion
is similar to that regarding capital turnover. Grouping by production
types and sub-types reduces variations in capital intensity and use
of domestic resources substantially. When projects have been subject

[1] This is true even when the total volume of investment is no greater than
in the previous year and hence term (2) is zero.

[2] The determination of the size of the investment programme also depends
to some extent on the balance-of-payments effect. So long as there is under-
utilized plant and labour, the increase in total demand resulting from investment can be satisfied in part from increased domestic production and in part
from increased imports. The balance of payments is therefore the ultimate
limitation on the size of the investment programme. The maximum desirable
size is determined by the point at which a net reduction in the sum of the terms
ΔY in equation (3) is required in order to achieve a balance in the external
accounts. This would result in a reduction in the total product of the whole
investment programme since in equilibrium the sum of the balance-of-payments terms is zero. This point may or may not be reached before labour is
fully employed.

to screening on the basis of private profitability, the variation in cost margin is also limited, so that the balance-of-payments effect often becomes the dominant factor when the value of r is high. (It was this selective process which led to the high correlation between balance-of-payments effect and the SMP in the Greek example.) The balance-of-payments effect can often bear the greatest weight in the preliminary ranking of projects within groups, therefore. It is not likely to be conclusive by itself, however, and may lead to serious waste of resources if improperly used.[1]

This testing of the balance-of-payments criterion leads me to a position closer to Buchanan and Polak than to Kahn. This is because there are relatively few investments which increase production for domestic use without at the same time increasing the requirement for producer imports. I agree with Kahn, however, that the balance-of-payments effect is of limited value as a *ceteris paribus* test.

(C) SOCIAL COST

The balance-of-payments and capital intensity terms have been suggested as separate tests of investment projects because they measure the economy of use of two of the most important scarce factors in an underdeveloped economy — capital and foreign exchange. The third term, which includes all other factors, is less likely to be useful as a rule of thumb because it is more difficult to calculate. Except for government projects, detailed cost data are usually lacking.

The social cost criterion can, however, be applied as a correction to the calculation of private profit. The usual problem facing government planners in a mixed economy is to choose among applicants for loan funds or foreign exchange permits. Assuming that all the projects meet the test of yielding to the investor the going rate of return on the capital invested, one can estimate the deviation of social cost from private cost in each case. The social profitability (term (d) in equation 5) is increased by the use of resources which are paid more than their social cost. Unemployed labour is the chief example. On the other hand, scarce resources such as electric power, transport facilities, and some raw materials often have a price less than their opportunity (or replacement) cost.

---

[1] Numerous examples of over emphasis on the balance-of-payments criterion can be found in the autarkic investment policies of pre-war Italy and Turkey.

The sum of these corrections, taken as the additional social profitability, is not often the dominant factor in the SMP equation.[1] It forms a useful correction to the results of applying the other two terms, however, and often serves to rule out uneconomic uses of scarce resources.

(D) OTHER TESTS

The three terms in the SMP formula provide the principal tests of individual investment projects. In addition, there are tests which apply only to the investment programme as a whole and which can only be used to make adjustments after a tentative programme has been formulated. The first of these is the net effect of the programme over time, both on GNP and on the balance of payments. The length of time before the investment yields results should be reflected in the discounting of future returns. The discount rate to be used in the calculations, however, depends on the proportion of long-term and short-term returns and may have to be revised after a tentative programme is formulated. The more returns are deferred into the future, the higher will be the premium on the balance-of-payments effect of Type I investments in the interim period. The discounting of future returns and the balance-of-payments premium together will reduce the average productivity of long-term projects and rule out all but the most profitable.

Regional balance is another test which can only be applied to the programme as a whole. The immobility of factors in an under-developed country makes balanced regional development of great importance because of the greater external economies which are obtained. The productivity of investment in transportation, power, and other services can only be determined after the investments in commodity production have been selected. The feasibility of the service investments, of course, affects the costs to be used in calculating the value of commodity production, and so successive approximations must be made. Good examples of this type of problem are the development of lignite deposits in Greece and hydro-electric resources in Turkey, where the whole regional development programme is needed to estimate the value of investment in the basic energy resources.

[1] Governments often act as if it were in subsidizing projects merely for their employment effect, however.

IV. Summary and Conclusions

The main purpose of this paper has been to seek a workable method of formulating and testing investment programmes in under-developed areas. The basic tool used is an approximation to the social marginal productivity which can be applied to individual comparisons among investment projects. The total effect of the programme is represented by parameters such as the rate of premium on foreign exchange savings and the rate of discount on future income. Both of these can be varied in successive approximations, if greater precision is needed.

Since data for economic analysis are particularly scanty in under-developed economies, one aim of the analysis has been to seek cases in which one or two of the terms in the formula would be determining. On the whole, this effort has met with only limited success. It is necessary to weigh all three terms to some extent. It has been shown that the use of any term in the SMP formula by itself may be misleading. There is not, however, complete indeterminacy in all cases. By classifying the projects according to production types and other known similarities, one can reach a close enough approximation to *ceteris paribus* conditions to enable one or two tests to do most of the work in intra-group comparisons. Priorities can thus be assigned within investment groups and detailed calculations made only to test out marginal projects in each group.

The planning process at present in operation in the countries studied consists of allocation of funds to various ministries and agencies in the annual budget and subsequent lending or direct investment by these authorities. The crucial step, and by far the most difficult, is the initial division of funds by general fields, which is at present done largely on a political basis.

The procedure suggested here would require a central co-ordinating agency to weigh the priority of the various fields based on the marginal projects in each group falling within the field. This comparison among different types of investments would require calculations using the whole SMP formula because *ceteris paribus* conditions would rarely occur. However imperfect this overall calculation, it would probably result in considerable improvements over the present piecemeal method, which does not take into consideration the overall effects of the various government programmes on the balance of payments, employment, the availability of capital to private sectors, etc.

Given a tentative allocation of funds by major fields, the separate investment tests are more useful in determining an order of priority among sectors and major projects. Their application would lead to the establishment of specific criteria for loan programmes and for public works programmes involving large numbers of projects. For example, an overall analysis of this type might lead to the conclusion that only land reclamation projects having a capital turnover greater than 0·5 should be financed[1] — other elements in the SMP formula being more or less constant in this sector. In the industrial field, a high value of the balance-of-payments effect might be a sufficient basis for granting a loan, since the test of private profitability would ensure minimum combined values of the other terms.

The examination of a number of investment programmes and the estimates behind them suggests that of the three terms in the SMP formula, the capital turnover is the one most often neglected and the one which leads to the most serious waste of resources.[2] The direct balance-of-payments effects are frequently overemphasized, while the indirect effects are usually ignored. Only in the case of labour is the difference between private and social cost recognized with any frequency. The bureaucratic process also tends to favour large projects over groups of small ones because they are more easily handled and show more tangible results. The net effect of these various biases is often to lead developing countries to try to follow the line of development of the older industrial areas rather than seeking a pattern more suited to their own resources. If properly applied, the SMP formula will indicate the direction in which an area's comparative advantage in international trade lies. Although it gives proper weight to saving on foreign exchange, it need not lead to autarky.

Although the above conclusions were based on an analysis of only one type of underdeveloped area, they would appear to be of general applicability, except for the particular conditions determining the balance-of-payments premium and the particular planning mechanism outlined.

---

[1] This type of criterion was actually used by the ECA in screening reclamation projects in Italy.

[2] An example of such a waste may often be railroad electrification, where a small saving in imports is achieved at the expense of a very low turnover rate. The SMP is therefore low.

The margin of error involved in calculations of this sort in under-developed countries may lead some readers to doubt the usefulness of the whole operation. In my opinion, however, the obstacles to the achievement of desirable results through free market forces are so great that they greatly reduce the social value of investment unless an attempt is made to offset them. The method used here is largely an effort to make such corrections for the difference between private and social profitability.

INVESTMENT CRITERIA, PRODUCTIVITY, AND ECONOMIC DEVELOPMENT*

by Walter Galenson and Harvey Leibenstein

I. A Suggested Criterion for Investment Allocation

In recent years there has been increased attention to the problem of establishing criteria for allocating investment in programmes for economic development. A general rule has emerged, from which practical policies are inferred. A. E. Kahn, in an article that appeared in 1951, set forth the 'rule of social marginal productivity' as a guide to investment, and deduced, among other things, that as a consequence of this 'rule', underdeveloped areas should choose industries and techniques requiring a lower capital : labour ratio than that prevailing in developed countries.[1] Hollis B. Chenery accepts the criterion of social marginal productivity, and attempts to demonstrate its application to a number of empirical situations.[2]

We propose in this paper to examine the conclusions that have been reached, and to suggest a line of reasoning that appears to us to be more in consonance with the peculiar problems raised by economic development. We do not intend to advance a complete model for investment allocation ; that would obviously be impossible within the confines of a brief paper. Our object is primarily to call attention to the shortcomings occasioned by the failure of economic theory in dealing with economic growth, to relax some of the assumptions that are relevant in treating static problems. We shall also indicate briefly some of the institutions and practices characteristic of backward areas which we believe must enter into the framework of a

* *Quarterly Journal of Economics*, August 1955. Reprinted with the permission of the Harvard University Press, and the authors. Several friends were kind enough to read an initial draft of this paper. The authors are grateful to them and especially to Professor Gottfried Haberler of Harvard University for many valuable suggestions. The responsibility for the paper itself remains, of course, entirely their own.

[1] Alfred E. Kahn, 'Investment Criteria in Development', *Quarterly Journal of Economics*, LXV, p. 38, reprinted in the present volume, pp. 131-57.

[2] Hollis B. Chenery, 'The Application of Investment Criteria', *Quarterly Journal of Economics*, LXVII, p. 76, reprinted in the present volume, pp.158-81.

theoretical formulation suitable as a guide for successful economic development.

Chenery voices the general proposition that 'Economic theory tells us that an efficient allocation of investment resources is achieved by equating the social marginal productivity of capital in its various uses.'[1] With this bald statement we can have no quarrel. However, it is open to the same general objection that Friedman raised with respect to Lerner's famous 'Rule': standing by itself, it provides no guide to policy.[2] The real question arises when one attempts to make precise the notion of 'efficient allocation' in this context.

In economic statics when we consider allocation of resources, we can attach a clear-cut test to the idea of efficiency. The test is the maximization of the value of the national product. That allocation which maximizes the value of national product is the efficient one — and equating marginal productivity in different uses is the rule for achieving such an allocation. But even here some ambiguity arises in the case of capital goods, and this may have something to do with the imperfect state in which capital theory finds itself. The difficulty arises because of the *ceteris paribus* assumption[3] necessary in comparative statics, e.g., we do not know of what value these capital goods will be to generations yet unborn. With respect to the production of consumer goods the situation appears to be fairly clear, since the valuation of the goods depends on their worth to the population in the current period, rendering the *ceteris paribus* assumption reasonable. But the valuation of capital goods depends on the value of the output stream generated by an increment of capital projected into the indefinite future. Apart from difficulties of predicting the output stream, there is also the problem of knowing what meaning to give to the *ceteris paribus* assumption in situations involving the indefinite future, as well as the practical consideration as to the value of the assumption under conditions in which technology, tastes, and population will most certainly change.

[1] Chenery, op. cit., p. 76, present volume p. 158.

[2] Milton Friedman, 'Lerner on the Economics of Control', *Journal of Political Economy*, October 1947, p. 405.

[3] i.e., tastes, size and composition of the population, the state of the arts and expectations remain the same. Or, another way of looking at it is that an 'efficient' allocation requires an accurate forecast of tastes, population, and the state of the arts in the future. See also Lionel Robbins, 'On a Certain Ambiguity in the Conception of Stationary Equilibrium', *Economic Journal*, June 1930, pp. 159-79, especially p. 168.

The question that immediately arises in applying conventional theory of problems of economic development is whether the goal of maximization of the national product necessarily leads to 'development'. Suppose that in every period 110 per cent of the GNP is consumed, would we then say that development is taking place even if in period after period the GNP is the maximum it could possibly be under the circumstances? As soon as we leave the theoretical world of statics, maximizing output is no longer a sufficient criterion, nor does 'efficiency' have the same meaning.

To get at the correct criterion, we must determine the appropriate goal of the economy during the process of development. Unfortunately, this cannot be done on the basis of economic analysis alone; a social welfare function of some sort is necessary. The goal must depend ultimately on values that come from outside economic analysis, and these are arbitrary to some extent. Nevertheless, a good case can be made for the proposition that the appropriate economic goal should be the maximization of *per capita* output, or *average* income, either over time, or at some time in the future.[1] This is hardly a startling position: it appears to be quite widely accepted. But it should be noted that maximizing *per capita* income is not at all the same as maximizing the national product once the *ceteris paribus* assumption is dropped.

For a closed economy, *per capita* income and *per capita* output are identical, but there may be considerable deviation between *per capita* output and the *per capita* level of consumption. If we are interested in alleviating the mass poverty that prevails in backward areas, then ultimately we must be interested in their *per capita* level of consumption. However, in the short run raising *per capita* output and raising *per capita* consumption may be antithetical, for the rate of capital accumulation will depend on the extent to which increases in output are not followed by equal increases in consumption. Thus, while the

---

[1] It should be noted that there are numerous and difficult problems involving the element of time that we do not consider in this paper. For example, the ordering of income magnitudes over time is a matter fraught with most important considerations of economic welfare ; and so is the precise future time at which it is desired to achieve maximum output. Unless the time path or the time horizon is given, there is no meaning to the concept of maximization in the future. As we shall see below, however, the time element is intimately related to specific variables, of which the rate of population change is perhaps the most important.

raising of *per capita* consumption levels may be, and perhaps must be an ultimate goal of development, if we concentrate on consumption as an immediate goal, it may be impossible of achievement as an ultimate goal. It is therefore *per capita* output that must be looked upon as an appropriate index of economic development.

We turn now to a consideration of the extent to which the practical corollaries which have been deduced from the social marginal productivity rule (SMP) focus on this goal. Although the literature is far from clear on this point it seems to us that three general corollaries of SMP have been advanced as valid policy guides. They are: (1) to maximize the current output: investment ratio; (2) to maximize the labour investment ratio; and (3) to maximize the export goods: investment ratio.

The discussion is often needlessly complicated by attempting to consider simultaneously development problems and balance-of-payments problems. Where investment funds or capital goods are obtained from abroad, a balance-of-payments problem *may* develop. The extent of the problem will depend, in part, on the allocation of the investment. But since the extent of the balance-of-payments problem will also depend on numerous other monetary conditions, both internal and external to the underdeveloped country, it is best, initially, to treat the two questions separately, and to leave the balance-of-payments problem for another occasion. We shall therefore omit corollary (3) in this paper, and consider only corollaries (1) and (2), and their relationship to the SMP criterion.

Kahn tells us that 'the SMP of capital is not correlated with the rate of turnover'.[1] The rate of turnover is of course the output: investment ratio. Yet later he concludes that '. . . general adherence to the capital-turnover criterion . . . is particularly desirable (*a*) where capital is relatively scarce and labour extremely plentiful. . . . With respect to the first circumstance (*a*), the rule of thumb of employing the minimum amount of capital necessary to absorb excess labour does indeed approximate the SMP criterion'.[2] But there is no clear-cut explanation why this should be the case. There are, however, good reasons to believe that the rate-of-turnover criterion is not likely to be consistent with the proper interpretation of SMP from the point of view of development.

[1] Kahn, op. cit., p. 39, present volume p. 132.
[2] Ibid., p. 51, present volume p. 146.

It is obvious that in computing social marginal productivity, we must consider the effect of an increment of capital on the output stream in the indefinite future, and not only on the magnitude of the output during the initial period. If the income stream is the same period after period, then the capital-turnover corollary would appear to favour, as Kahn correctly says in a footnote,[1] short-lived over long-lived capital. But if national capital is to be maintained, and the total effect on the income stream is to be considered, then the length of life of any individual capital good is an irrelevant consideration. If the income stream increases over time, then the application of the capital-turnover criterion *can* quite clearly result in the allocation of investment to uses that have a lower SMP than the alternatives. For example, between two alternatives, A and B, the following might be the case: Equipment in A lasts five years while in B it lasts ten years. Assume that in both cases the income streams over the life of the equipment is twice the investment cost. Clearly the rate of capital-turnover is twice as great for A as for B. But if replacements are made so that capital is maintained intact indefinitely, then with a rising output stream for B and a constant output stream for A it is certainly possible that the SMP for B would be larger than the SMP for A. Where industries of increasing returns with respect to scale are among the possible alternatives, it is likely that the capital-turnover criterion will result in the wrong choice. A constant or decreasing returns industry may have a higher capital

---

[1] The notion of short-lived *and* long-lived capital may need some amplification. For this purpose it may help if we reproduce the example given by Kahn (p. 39, present volume p. 132). 'Compare the following financial data for investments A and B, which differ only in that equipment in A lasts only two years, in B ten years :

Investment............	$100,000	$100,000
Annual Data :		
Output	60,000	20,000
Depreciation	50,000	10,000
All other costs	20,000	10,000
Capital Turnover	60 per cent	20 per cent

In a long range investment programme, in which real national capital must presumably be kept intact, there would appear to be no advantage in choosing the shorter- over the longer-lived investment, since both yield the same annual output net of depreciation.' However, as we will argue, there is an advantage in longer-lived investment because of the lower replacement cost in a growing economy.

turnover ratio than an alternative increasing returns industry, but the increasing returns industry may in the long run make a greater contribution to national product.

If SMP is to be interpreted in this context to take account of the addition to the income stream in the indefinite future (no matter how discounted), then we cannot assume, as a static interpretation of SMP would have us, that other things remain constant during this process; we must take into account the time pattern of possible changes as a consequence of the addition to capital. Thus, with respect to many investment alternatives, we have to account for such dynamic factors as the development of skills, the development of markets, overcoming production bottlenecks, etc., and the effect of these factors on the time pattern of output — circumstances under which the capital turnover rule is likely to come up with the wrong answer. In the short run, the capital turnover ratio could be highest in those endeavours that required few new skills, that depended on existing markets, and in which there were no production bottlenecks to overcome; but over the longer period it might be those investment alternatives that involved the learning of new ways of doing things that would make the greatest contribution to the social product.

We now turn to corollary (2), under which the labour/investment ratio is to be maximized. The extent to which labour can be absorbed in any economic process depends on the flexibility and adaptability of the other factors of production (i.e., capital). One can easily visualize situations in which the maximum labour absorption criterion would not maximize the addition to total output. Figure I illustrates such a situation. The investment in alternatives I and II

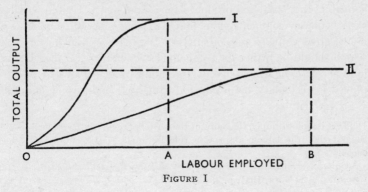

FIGURE I

are the same. The maximum absorption of labour in either case is up to the point where the marginal productivity of labour is zero, if we assume that the marginal productivity of labour on the land is zero. In Figure I, investment alternative I would absorb *less* labour but add more to total output than would investment alternative II. As a consequence alternative I rather than II is consistent with SMP. Nor is there any reason to believe that highly productive capital is necessarily related to rightly flexible and adaptable capital. Indeed, there is good reason to believe that quite the reverse is true. With respect to machinery it is likely that the more productive the machine, the more specialized it is, and as a consequence the less adaptable and flexible with respect to changes in other factors.

A second set of difficulties has to do with the time element. Corollary (2) does not tell us in any clear way when the labour is to be absorbed. If the labour employed as a result of the investment is the same period after period, then there is no problem, but suppose the time pattern of labour absorption varies from period to period, as it may with developing skills in the use of capital; then, of course, there is a problem similar to the one previously considered in our discussion of the capital turnover rule. We need not go through the difficulties involved on this point, since the analysis parallels that considered under the capital turnover rule. It would follow from such an analysis, even in those cases where over the initial life of the capital good, the labour absorption rule and SMP are consistent, that they need not be consistent in the long run when all the dynamic considerations are taken into account.

Corollary (2), if taken literally, would imply that labour displacing investment would almost never be accepted no matter how high its contribution to national product.[1] For example, the United Nations experts on development tell us that '. . . labour-saving technology is not of great value to an economy which is overpopulated. There the search should be rather for technologies which increase the yield of land per acre, or which enable large numbers of persons to be employed in secondary industries for a small expenditure of capital.'[2]

---

[1] This is not to imply that any of the writers previously mentioned would suggest that the labour absorption rule be applied apart from any other considerations.

[2] United Nations, *Measures for the Economic Development of Underdeveloped Countries*, New York, 1951, p. 7.

Investment in agricultural machinery would scarcely pass corollary (2), since it would increase the actual or disguised unemployment on the land. This is, of course, one of the implicit issues in the by now celebrated dispute between Professor Viner and his draftsman,[1] namely, that excess capacity is not an economic sin, but can be an economic virtue. Under conditions of decreasing costs the creation of excess capacity can lead to lower costs or greater output per unit of the variable factor regardless of what the fixed factor happens to be. Similarly, increasing the amount of excess labour by the introduction of labour displacing capital can result in a greater addition to output than the use of labour absorbing capital. In such a case corollaries (1) and (2) are also likely to be inconsistent with each other. The highest capital turnover rates may come about through the use of labour displacing rather than labour absorbing investment.

Finally, we may note that there is also a practical difficulty with the labour absorption rule. The extent to which the rule is useful depends on its greater ease of application than the general SMP criterion. Of what use is corollary (2), and what constitutes absorption, if the investment is to take place in an industry in which disguised unemployment exists? In order to measure the alternate points with respect to alternate investment possibilities the marginal productivity of labour in the industry (or sector) becomes zero. Surely, it would be difficult to show that this is any easier to measure than the SMP itself.[2]

It is a likely consequence of corollaries (1) and (2) that low labour productivity will be perpetuated. Wherever the SMP criterion or rules dictate the application of capital to agriculture, where there is likely to be a great deal of disguised unemployment, and where the potentialities for further population growth are usually very high, then it is highly probable that low labour productivity will be perpetuated. To begin with, the marginal productivity of labour on the land is likely to be extremely low. To the extent that investment increases productivity it will increase population and

---

[1] Jacob Viner, 'Cost Curves and Supply Curves', *Zeitschrift für Nationalökonomie*, 1933.

[2] See Wilbert E. Moore, *The Economic Demography of Eastern and Southern Europe*, ch. III, and Appendix II, for the difficulties involved in attempts to measure 'surplus' labour.

subsequently the labour force, and as a consequence *tend* to reduce average product to its former low level.[1]

The application of investment to capital-light industries such as handicrafts, corollary (1), is also likely to lead to the maintenance of low labour productivity. Since corollary (1) seeks to maximize output per unit of capital, it also implies, other things equal, using as much labour as possible with the existing capital.

We can summarize briefly why the practical corollaries that have been drawn from the SMP criterion are not appropriate for economic development. (1) The emphasis of these corollaries is on the productivity of capital, not on the productivity of labour. In the long run, given the inevitable population increases that accompany industrialization, it is quite possible to raise output per unit of capital without raising output per unit of labour (labour productivity) to any extent. But it is high labour productivity that makes possible high levels of living. Put differently, corollaries (1) and (2) may yield a maximum aggregate national product but not a maximum product *per capita*. The last two magnitudes can conceivably go in opposite directions. (2) The corollaries emphasize aggregate output and not the rate of investment, whereas it is precisely this rate that determines the extent of capital accumulation and as a consequence the capacity of the economy to produce goods and services in the future. The formal rules do not take into account what happens to the final product during any period, but it is just this that determines the rate of investment. (3) The rules enumerated above do not take into account changes in the factors other than capital. For example, no

---

[1] It may be argued that on ethical grounds, corollary (2) is sound in that it leads to lower mortality rates in agricultural areas. But this will only be a temporary gain that will be wiped out as soon as the consequent population increase reduces productivity *per capita* to its former level. Two sorts of welfare questions are involved. First, what sector should be favoured with the initial increase in productivity and income? Second, is it ethical to sacrifice a temporary gain in living standards in order to insure long-run permanent gains? These are very serious questions, and welfare questions so fundamental in significance can scarcely be dealt with in a footnote. However, it may be pertinent to point out that (1) there is almost universally a direct correlation between industrialization, broadly defined, and standards of living, and (2) there is probably no case of 'painless' industrialization on record, as any reader of *The Town Labourer* will recognize. Even in the United States, where an optimum situation for development prevailed, the immediate consequences were not always pleasant.

account is taken of the population growth that may be a consequence of investing in a certain manner and achieving a certain product mix. It is population and labour force growth that tend to reduce capital *per capita* and hence reduce output *per capita*. The crux of this argument is that the allocation of capital, the consequent allocation of the final product, and population growth are not independent factors.

If it be granted that the object of development is to attain a level of economic capacity which maximizes output *per capita* at a determined future time, then the correct criterion for allocating investment must be to choose for each unit of investment that alternative that will give each worker greater productive power than any other alternative. To achieve this result we must maximize (*a*) the amount of capital per worker, and (*b*) the quality of the labour force, i.e., its skill, knowledge, energy and adaptability.

Apart from the human factors, it is the capital:labour ratio that determines output *per capita*. From this point of view the criterion to be adopted is the one that leads ultimately to the maximum capital:labour ratio. The amount of capital per worker that is created in the long run depends on two broad factors: (1) the amount of investment year by year stemming from the product of the initial investment; and (2) the increase in the size of the labour force. We must therefore take into account the initial investment plus the sum of all subsequent reinvestments divided by the size of the labour force at the end of the stipulated time horizon.

The marginal principle applies here as it does elsewhere — but not marginal *productivity* in the usual sense. The criterion we suggest might be called the *marginal per capita reinvestment quotient*. The best allocation of investment resources is achieved by equating the marginal *per capita* reinvestment quotient of capital in its various alternative uses. The result of such a policy would be to maximize the *per capita* output potential at some future point in time.

To secure a clear notion of what is meant by the marginal *per capita* reinvestment quotient we must consider the basic factors involved in its determination. Briefly stated, the seven basic factors are as follows: (1) gross productivity per worker; (2) 'wage' goods consumed per worker; (3) replacement and repair of capital; (4) increments in output as a result of non-capital-using innovations, such as improvements in skills, health, energy, discipline, and malleability of the labour force; (5) declines in mortality; (6) declines in fertility; and (7) direction of reinvestment. The first six factors determine the *per capita* reinvestment available period after period, and the last one deals with its allocation.

The gross productivity per worker minus the consumption per worker determines the gross amount available for reinvestment per worker.[1] Deducting replacement and repairs per worker yields the net amount (per worker) available for reinvestment during any period. Over a succession of periods there may be increases in productivity that arise *not* out of additions to capital but rather because of increases in skill, organizational innovations, or improvement in health, energy, or discipline of the labour force that have to be taken into account. Capital per worker declines if the labour force grows at a more rapid rate than capital accumulates. But the rate of growth of the labour force will depend, for the most part, on the rates of mortality and fertility of the population, leaving aside the question of labour force participation.

It is a common experience in all underdeveloped areas that mortality declines at a faster rate and earlier than fertility as levels of consumption increase. Therefore, the greater the gap between output and consumption, the less the rate of population growth and the less the dilution of capital. The extent of fertility decline will also depend on the allocation of investment, since the type of investment that stimulates urbanization will create a more favourable environment for fertility decline than the type of investment that perpetuates the rural agricultural environment.

II. The Case for High Labour Productivity in Underdeveloped Areas

1. The Level of Labour Productivity in Underdeveloped Areas

We consider first such empirical data as are available with respect to the differences in labour productivity between developed and underdeveloped areas.

(*a*) An excellent statistical analysis has been made of the productivity of labour in underdeveloped areas relating to the cotton

---

[1] We abstract here from the very difficult problem of ensuring that this Ricardian 'surplus' is indeed reinvested, which involves either the creation of a Schumpeterian ideology among entrepreneurs, government control, or outright government investment. Which of these alternatives is adopted depends, of course, upon the specific institutional situation of the country undergoing development.

textile industry of five Latin-American countries — Brazil, Chile, Mexico, Ecuador, and Peru.[1] It was determined that for the so-called 'old' mills, which comprised 90 per cent of the entire industry in these countries, 'labour consumption per kilogramme of fabric (taking into account the process of spinning and weaving) is five times greater . . . than that which could be expected under the best conditions — within practical limits — of modernity of equipment, size, organization and administration'.[2] The standards against which labour inputs were measured were models, to which were attributed the 'best possible process and labour organization, and it was supposed that they would operate with the best efficiencies attainable without impairing the quality of the product'.[3] These standards were undoubtedly above the average efficiency of cotton mills in the United States, but since they were constructed by a U.S. engineering firm, it may be assumed that good U.S. practice served as a guide. It should also be noted that cotton textile manufacturing is one of the best developed and relatively most efficient industries in Latin America.

(b) The accompanying table purports to compare productivity in various Egyptian manufactures with that in the United States and Great Britain.

Industry	Output per Operative, in Pounds Sterling					
	United Kingdom, 1935		Egypt, 1937		United States, 1937	
	Net value of output	Index of output	Net value of output	Index of output	Net value of output	Index of output
Chemicals	617	100	69	11	1,145	186
Textiles	159	100	39	25	318	200
Clothing	168	100	61	36	356	212
Leather	237	100	45	19	417	176
Clay and stone	238	100	28	13	588	247
Paper	332	100	68	21	867	261
Food	487	100	82	17	760	156
All manufacturing	264	100	56	21	595	225

Source : Gamal Eldin Said, 'Productivity of Labour in Egyptian Industry', L'Egypte Contemporaine, Nos. 259–60, May–June, 1950.

[1] United Nations, Department of Economic Affairs, Labour Productivity of the Cotton Textile Industry in Five Latin American Countries, New York, 1951.
[2] Ibid., p. 5.
[3] Ibid., p. 127.

These figures indicate that for the years in question, productivity in Egyptian manufacturing as a whole was about 10 per cent of the U.S. level, though for the clothing industry, which is labour-intensive in the United States, the disparity was smaller.[1]

(c) Comparative productivity data for the Soviet Union in 1928, at the commencement of the industrialization programme, and the United States in 1939, are shown in the following table:

SOVIET PRODUCTIVITY IN 1928 AS A
PERCENTAGE OF U. S. PRODUCTIVITY IN 1939

Coal mining	20
Iron ore mining	11
Crude oil and gas extraction	24
Iron and steel	17
Cotton cloth	16
Shoes	38
Beet sugar	14
Manufacturing and mining	22

Source : Walter Galenson, 'Industrial Labour Productivity', in Abram Bergson (ed.), *Soviet Economic Growth*, Evanston, 1953, p. 190.

Soviet industry was considerably more advanced in 1928 than that of Egypt in 1937, and the difference is reflected in the comparative productivity data. Yet the Soviet 1928 level is seen to have been far below that of the United States, reflecting the great relative backwardness of the pre-planning Soviet economy.

(d) A comparison of manufacturing labour productivity in China (1936) and the United States (1935) yielded the conclusion that Chinese productivity was about 5 per cent of the U.S. level.

The difference is appalling. Yet this is not the whole picture. When the comparison is made between the output produced by an American worker and a Chinese handicraft worker, the result is almost unbelievable . . . one day's work of an American worker will be equivalent to fifty days' work of a Chinese handicraft worker. This

---

[1] Though the data appear to have been prepared carefully on the basis of censuses of manufacturing, they are subject to the limitation of more or less arbitrary exchange rates. The author converted at the rate of 97½ piastres to the pound sterling, which prevailed in 1944, adjusted for the decline in the internal purchasing power of the piastre from 1937 to 1944. The British and U. S. data were taken from L. Rostas, 'Industrial Production, Productivity and Distribution in Britain, Germany and United States', *Economic Journal*, April 1943.

low productivity is, of course, only partly due to the inefficiency of labour, and partly, perhaps mainly, due to the meagreness of capital investment.[1]

(e) Labour productivity in Ceylon *circa* 1950 is reported to have been from 20 to 30 per cent below the level prevailing in India.[2] So far as the authors are aware, there is not available a comparison of labour productivity in India and the United States, though observers are agreed that Indian productivity is low indeed.[3]

The foregoing data are not sufficiently homogeneous to support any precise generalization as to the level of industrial labour productivity that may be expected to obtain in an underdeveloped area. For one thing, there are likely to be sharp inter-industry variations. It is quite possible for single plants or industries within an industrially backward country to measure up to the levels of efficiency prevailing in advanced nations. However, the evidence that is available indicates that for manufacturing as a whole, a level of labour productivity above, say, 40 per cent of that of the United States is characteristic of a developed nation,[4] with substantially lower levels, perhaps 20 per cent and less, prevailing in underdeveloped areas. In other words, in a typically underdeveloped area, it will require at least five, and perhaps ten or even more workers to produce the same amount of goods as a single American worker.

2. *Labour Productivity and Capital Allocation*

From the policy interpretations of SMP that we have discussed above it would appear that India, for example, would be deviating from the prescribed course if in allocating capital to an industry, or to a process within an industry, it attempted to attain the U.S. (or British) labour productivity level unless such result were the unavoidable result of fixed technical coefficients, since the marginal product of the capital invested would undoubtedly be greater diluted

[1] Pao-San Ou and Foh-Shen Wang, 'Industrial Production and Employment in Pre-War China', *Economic Journal*, LVI, 433.

[2] International Bank for Reconstruction and Development (IBRD), *The Economic Development of Ceylon*, Baltimore, 1953, p. 523.

[3] See Wilbert E. Moore, *Industrialization and Labour*, Ithaca, 1951, p. 108.

[4] Just before World War II, Great Britain, Germany, Russia, Sweden, and Holland were said to be within a range of 40–50 per cent of the U. S. productivity level. L. Rostas, *Comparative Productivity in British and American Industry*, Cambridge, 1948, p. 40.

than concentrated.[1] Labour productivity should presumably rise at a relatively slow rate as capital trickles into the defiles marked by marginal productivity.

In fact, actual development programmes have often run counter to these prescriptions. In the case of a group of Mediterranean countries, the major share of recent investment of industrial capital has gone into high capital-intensity producer services.[2] A similar allocation of capital in Mexico caused some disquiet to an apparently orthodox-minded International Bank mission.[3] A disproportionately large share of Soviet capital resources have been diverted into capital-intensive heavy industry rather than into more labour-intensive light industry, and into capital-intensive processes within industry.[4]

Some arguments in favour of the goal that we have advanced, i.e., maximization of the capital : labour ratio through application of the criterion of the marginal *per capita* reinvestment quotient, and against the practical corollaries of SMP follow :

(*a*) It may be well to dispose first of the popular argument that allocation of investment to labour-intensive industry is a social

[1] We assume that there is a direct correlation between capital intensity and labour productivity. This proposition cannot be proved on the basis of data presently available. It has been asserted of Europe that 'there is a close relationship between horse-power per head and output per head '. United Nations, *Economic Bulletin for Europe*, Vol. 3, No. 1, p. 24. However, Rostas found 'no correlation between horse-power per unit of output and output per worker, i.e., industries where horse-power per unit of output is higher in the United States are not identical with industries where United States output per worker is also relatively high'. L. Rostas, op. cit., p. 54. We should judge that the relationship between capital intensity and labour productivity is closer at lower than at higher states in industrial development, i.e., that the capital factor plays a more important role as a determinant of productivity where there is little capital than where industry is already heavily capitalized.

[2] Chenery, op. cit., p. 76.

[3] The mission noted in its report : 'In Mexico, the principal capital goods industries require a much higher investment of capital per unit of value added and per worker employed than the major consumer goods industries. It is this factor which makes the orientation of industrial investment toward capital goods industries a matter of especial concern in a country where capital resources are scarce and the potential market for capital goods smaller than for consumer-goods.' IBRD, *The Economic Development of Mexico* Baltimore, 1953, p. 65.

[4] See Norman M. Kaplan, 'Capital Formation and Allocation', in Abram Bergson, op. cit., p. 37, and the comments of Alexander Erlich, ibid., pp. 92–7.

desideratum where surplus population exists. For the very short run, it is incontrovertible that the maximum number of persons can be put to work with the minimum amount of capital investment if the capital is simple in form and widespread in its distribution. For example, the WPA programme in the United States, the purpose of which was employment regardless of output, represented a logical application of this principle. In the longer run, however, there is considerable doubt of the general validity of the proposition.

The point may best be illustrated by a simple model. Let us assume that a product can be manufactured under alternative combinations of labour and machinery, e.g., with an automatic machine requiring little labour or with a semiautomatic machine requiring more labour. For any year, the employment provided by any combination of men and machines, can be represented by the following equation:[1]

(1)
$$E_{t+1} = E_1 \left(1 + \frac{p - ew}{c} \right)^t$$

1. The variables may be defined as follows:
   I = total investment in any period
   P = gross value added in any period
   W = total real compensation of labour in any period
   w = real wage rate
   N = number of machines
   p = output per machine, i.e., $P = Np$
   E = total employment
   e = number of workers per machine, i.e., $E = eN$
   c = cost per machine
   v = wage cost per machine, i.e., $v = ew$

It is assumed that $I = P - W$, i.e., that the total amount invested in any period is the difference between total gross value added and the real compensation of labour. Then:

(1.1) $I = P - Ew$
(1.2) $I = Np - Ew$
(1.3) $I = Np - eNw = N(p - ew)$
(1.4) $c\Delta N = N(p - ew)$

$$\Delta N = \frac{N(p - ew)}{c}$$

(1.5) $\dfrac{\Delta E}{e} = \dfrac{N(p - ew)}{c}$, from the relationship $\Delta E = e\Delta N$

(1.6) $\Delta E = \dfrac{eN(p - ew)}{c}$

(1.7) $\Delta E = \dfrac{E(p - ew)}{c}$, and substituting $v = ew$,

(1.8) $\Delta E = \dfrac{E(p - v)}{c}$

This yields the basic equation: $\Delta E_t = E_t \left(\dfrac{p - v}{c}\right)$

(2.1) $E_{t+1} = E_t + \Delta E_t = E_t \left(1 + \dfrac{p - v}{c}\right)$

(2.2) $\dfrac{E_{t+1}}{E_t} = 1 + \dfrac{p - v}{c}$ for all t

(2.3) $E_t = E_1 \dfrac{E_2 E_3}{E_1 E_2} \cdots \dfrac{E_{t-1} E_{t-1} E_t}{E_{t-2} E_{t-2} E_{t-1}}$

(2.4) $E_t = E_1 \left(1 + \dfrac{p - v}{c}\right)^{t-1}$

This may be rewritten

(2.5) $E_{t+1} = E_1 \left(1 + \dfrac{p - v}{c}\right)^{t}$, and in our original symbols

(2.6) $E_{t+1} = E_1 \left(1 + \dfrac{p - ew}{c}\right)^{t-1}$

where E_{t+1} represents employment in the $t + 1$ year, E_1 employment in the initial year, p the output per machine, e the number of
workers per machine, w the wage rate, and c the cost per machine.
If E_1, p, and e are assumed to be parameters, then the value of
E_{t+1} will depend upon the relationship of c and w.

Essentially, all this formula does is to state formally a simple
notion that can be grasped intuitively: that the larger the portion of
the output of an industry, or a society, which is reinvested rather
than consumed, the more rapid will be the process of capital accumulation, and *pari passu*, the growth of employment opportunities in
industry. Conversely, the greater the share of output that is consumed, the slower will be the rate of expansion of capital and
employment.

The following data for the Indian textile industry *circa* 1943, may be used to illustrate the application of the formula:[1]

	Capital investment per worker (rupees)	Value added per worker (rupees)	Annual earnings per worker (rupees)
1. Power machinery, large scale..	1200	650	80
2. Power machinery, small scale..	300	200	80
3. Automatic loom, cottage industry..................	90	80	80
4. Hand loom, cottage industry..	35	45	80

So, for example, if we apply the data for a small scale power loom to formula (1), we have, for year $t + 1 = 5$, the following:[2]

$$E_5 = 4 \left(1 + \frac{200 - (1)(80)}{300} \right) + 15 \cdot 3$$

Similarly, the formula may be applied to the above data for other types of mills, and for other time periods, the results being as follows:

HYPOTHETICAL EMPLOYMENT PROVIDED BY INITIAL
INVESTMENT OF RS 1200 IN VARIOUS TYPES OF COTTON
TEXTILE MACHINERY

Year (t + 1)	Modern mill, large scale	Power loom, small scale	Automatic loom, cottage industry	Hand loom, cottage industry
5	5	15	13	35
10	34	83	13	35
15	242	444	13	35
20	1,718	2,390	13	35
25	12,200	12,860	13	35

[1] The source of the capital and value added data is *The Eastern Economist*, 23 July, 1943, p. 340. The figure of 80 rupees used in the illustration was purely hypothetical, chosen for purposes of illustration. In fact, annual earnings in the non-cottage sector of the Indian textile industry were considerably higher in 1943, varying from 204 rupees in Bihar to 832 rupees in Bombay. A. N. Agarwala, *Indian Labour Problems*, Allahabad, 1947, pp. 49f. However, the capital data in the example may well refer to an earlier year, and since there was a severe wartime inflation, a realistic wage figure is difficult to determine. Moreover, the wage should be differentiated among the various sectors of the industry.

[2] In applying this formula, it is assumed that total investment in each case is 1200 rupees, so that in the case of the small scale power loom, an initial investment of 1200 rupees would make $E_1 = 4$. In each case e is taken to equal one, and therefore p is equal to the value added per worker.

It is assumed in the above example that the total product, less labour cost, is reinvested each year. No allowance is made for capital replacement, although this could be accomplished by reducing the product available for reinvestment by a depreciation factor, thus slowing up the process of capital accumulation. As we shall see, however, it may be quite appropriate to disregard the depreciation factor in an economic development model of this character.

It is clear from the above example that the wage rate (w) is the critical variable; that the amount of employment provided in any future year by a unit of investment depends largely upon the wage deduction from the product of industry. If, for example, an annual wage of 150 rather than 80 rupees had been used,[1] employment provided by the large-scale modern mill would have been 24 in ten years, as against only 16 in the small scale power mills. The higher the real wage level, the greater is the advantage in terms of potential employment accruing from the use of capital-intensive machinery.[2]

(b) Failure to introduce capital-intensive techniques at the outset of the industrialization process may create insurmountable institutional barriers to modernization. This is true particularly in democratic communities, where labour : capital coefficients cannot be altered by fiat. The case of Cuba is very much in point :

Cuban industrial development has been greatly retarded by labour's resistance to new machinery, modern methods, or virtually anything that will increase the efficiency of production . . . When improved methods or machinery are introduced into a factory with permission of the workers, it is generally under the stipulation that the same number of workers be employed as were used under the older, inefficient methods. The workers also commonly see to it that the new equipment turns out no more products than the old.[3]

In neighbouring Puerto Rico, 'the legislative branch of the Insular governments, which is highly responsive to the representations of the electorate, has shown considerable interest in creating and protecting job opportunities, although these sometimes involve makework practices for a class of firms which might otherwise be

---

[1] See *supra*, n. 2, p. 199.

[2] Thus in Surinam, where wages are relatively high, it was suggested that 'the development of the country must rather be in the direction of relatively high capitalized production, where the productivity of the workers can be great enough to justify their level of wages '. IBRD, *Surinam*, Baltimore, 1952, p. 26.

[3] IBRD, *Report on Cuba*, Washington, 1951, pp. 143f.

unnecessary'.[1] Low productivity in Mexican textile manufacturing was attributed in large measure to 'present contract legislation for the industry, which stipulates the number of workers to be employed in relation to the capacity of the mills, and establishes an inflexible basis for the proportion between production and wages'.[2]

In all of these countries it was observed that newly established factories had considerable latitude in determining their labour capital ratios; it was in the older, established plants that the problem was acute. This suggests that the failure to adopt the correct criterion at the very outset of a development programme may render infinitely more difficult the attainment of high output per worker, which must be the eventual goal of a development programme.

(c) Industrialization almost inevitably means urbanization, and urbanization entails charges upon the production surplus available for capital accumulation. In some countries, e.g., Turkey, an industrial labour force must be recruited from the farm and brought to the city, entailing a considerable investment in such urban facilities as housing, sanitation, water and canteens. But even where large cities with surplus manpower already exist, as in India or China, the social costs involved in bringing newly recruited industrial workers up to a minimum efficiency level may be very considerable. The Colombo Plan, for example, allocated 18 per cent of projected capital investment to 'social capital', compared with only 10 per cent to 'industry and mining'.[3] In the case of Egypt, it has been pointed out that many workers are living below the subsistence level, in completely inadequate houses, leading to chronic undernourishment, and high disease rates, which in turn result in a high rate of absenteeism and low productivity. Where an efficient labour force is to be maintained, the social capital costs may be very high. Such costs are often neglected when the criterion of SMP, and particularly its accompanying corollaries, are advocated.

The establishment of the highest initial productivity of labour will minimize urbanization cost by bringing into the industrial labour force a minimum of workers. One may question the wisdom

[1] Simon Rottenberg, 'Labour Cost in the Puerto Rican Economy', *Revista Juridica of the University of Puerto Rico*, Vol. XX, No. 2, Nov.-Dec. 1950, p. 59.

[2] *Labour Productivity of the Cotton Textile Industry in Five Latin American Countries*, op. cit., p. 84.

[3] Chiang Hsieh, 'Underemployment in Asia', *International Labour Review*, July 1952, p. 32.

of *minimizing* the transfer of manpower from agricultural employment to industrial and urban pursuits, but the optimal transfer rate would probably be significantly lower than the maximum rate of labour absorption. The establishment of a high initial productivity of labour, following our criterion for allocating capital, will yield a lower ratio of urbanization cost to output per worker than under the orthodox criterion, and thus contribute to maximizing the rate of capital formation.

(*d*) Too little attention has been paid to the *pattern* of industry which will facilitate, or, indeed, make possible, industrial development. It is not a matter of indifference whether capital is allocated, say, to the manufacture of iron and steel, or to the manufacture of textiles. Development mission recommendations are all too prone to assume that funds invested in light industries based, for example, on local raw materials, will in some unexplained manner lead eventually to economic development.

Properly speaking, neither the criterion of SMP in its orthodox interpretation nor our SMP criterion will lead automatically to the establishment of an industrial pattern which will maximize industrial development. This is a subject as yet largely unexplored, and it can probably best be tackled in terms of a model investment grid, based upon the specific conditions of each underdeveloped area. However, the above-cited corollaries of SMP are likely to lead in a direction other than industrialization, for the average productivity of capital tends to be greatest in light industries, where a considerable amount of labour may be used, and least in heavy industries, where the substitutability of labour for capital is less.[1] Conversely, our criterion of maximizing the capital : labour ratio tends to favour those industries which are essential to the development of modern industry.

(*e*) As we have pointed out, the usual prescriptions for capital allocation favour short-lived over long-lived capital goods. From the

[1] This is an empirical statement for which factual proof is largely lacking. However, 1947 U. S. Census of Manufactures data indicated that capital investment per worker in American industry clearly tended to be greater in the heavy capital goods industries than in the light consumer goods industries. For example, capital investment per worker in the industrial chemicals industry was $15,868 ; in iron and steel, $7,309 ; in machinery (excluding electrical), $6,993 ; compared with $4,673 per worker in textile mill products $2,954 in apparel ; $3,376 in leather and its products. There were exceptions to the rule, such as canning and preserving, with $10,036 invested per worker, but in general the data appear to support the statement in the text.

point of view of our suggested criterion a strong case can be made for the obverse rule; viz., that there are considerable advantages to be gained from longer-lived rather than shorter-lived capital goods. Domar has demonstrated that under conditions of growth, replacement: gross investment ratios can be considerably lower for longer-lived than for shorter-lived capital goods.[1]

At the outset it should be made clear that it is replacement and not depreciation that is the significant variable for purposes of development. Depreciation cost, as usually conceived, is an accounting matter,[2] and is not directly connected with the productive power of a capital good at any point in time. Thus, for our purposes the important variable is not net investment, as usually defined, but gross investment less replacement cost. (For ease in communication we shall refer to gross investment less replacement as GIR.)

Initially there are three advantages to longer-lived capital under conditions of capital growth. (1) The longer the life of the capital, the longer the period of time during which no replacements have to be made, and hence the greater the available output per man during this period than with capital of a shorter life. (2) Out of a greater output per man there is the possibility of greater reinvestment per man. (3) With greater output and reinvestment per man there is a greater chance of overcoming the critical minimum effort[3] hurdle than otherwise.

If the capital stock is to be maintained intact, then eventually replacements must be made. But even after the advantage of the early no-replacement period has passed, there is still an advantage in a capital stock that is on the average longer-lived than shorter-lived under conditions of growth. This is because the longer the average life of the capital, the smaller is the proportion of gross investment needed for replacement, and therefore the larger is the GIR period after period. For example, suppose that the rate of gross investment growth is 5 per cent per year, then, according to Domar's

---

[1] E. D. Domar, 'Depreciation, Replacement and Growth', *Economic Journal*, LXIII, March 1953, pp. 1–32.

[2] Strictly speaking, physical depreciation interpreted as user cost is an economic variable that does have to be accounted for. In order not to complicate the argument we assume that user cost is an insignificant portion of accounting depreciation. In any event, user cost is a short-run cost consideration since it varies with output.

[3] See below, p. 207, for a discussion of this term.

figures,[1] if the average length of life of capital is four years, the ratio of replacement to gross investment will be 82 per cent per year; if the average length of life of capital is ten years the replacement : gross investment ratio drops to 61 per cent; and if the average length of life of capital is thirty years, the replacement : gross investment ratio drops as low as 22 per cent. Clearly, the greater the life span of investment goods, other things equal, the greater the possibility for economic growth.

3. Population Growth and Development

(a) To a considerable extent our arguments in the previous sections were based on the notion that there is a dependent relationship between the allocation of investment, the consequent allocation of the labour force, and the growth and quality of the population. Although this is hardly a novel idea it is customary for economists to argue as though these were independent matters.[2] Solutions that may appear to be appropriate in instances where the population problem is disregarded often cease to be appropriate when it is recognized that the population aspect is an integral and inseparable part of the problem. Although we cannot go into detail at this juncture, we shall indicate something of the nature and significance of this point.

In considering the population factor there are three things about which we can be fairly certain on the basis of past experience : (1) that economic development, if it takes place, will be accompanied by rapid population growth; (2) that the only way to reduce population growth is to reduce the birth rate; and (3) that declines in birth rates, if they take place, will follow rather than precede declines in death rates. This implies that in order to avoid the Malthusian dilemma, and at some point to achieve a slackening of population growth, it is necessary to create an environment that is conducive to a reduction in birth rates. From past evidence it would appear that the urban, industrially and commercially developing sectors rather than the rural agricultural areas provide the environment conducive to falling birth rates.

---

[1] Domar, op. cit., p. 8.

[2] For example, Professor Viner, in observing that population increases will tend to worsen a country's terms of trade, argues that '. . . this will apply equally, as a tendency, to countries whether they are predominantly agricultural or predominantly industrial, and the appropriate remedy in either case would be to check the rate of population growth '. (Viner, op. cit., p. 142.)

Reference to the vital statistics of most underdeveloped areas suggests that economic development will be accompanied by rapid population growth. On the average the underdeveloped countries of the world are increasing their population at a rate of 1·4 per cent per year.[1] Improved nutrition and public health measures that often accompany economic development can reduce death rates so that the average rate of growth may rise to 2 or 2·5 per cent per year. The last rate will yield an increase in population for the underdeveloped two-thirds of the world of some two *billion* people by 1984. So much for the magnitude of the problem.

The reasons behind the other assertions have been investigated and long studied by demographers and ably summarized by Professor Notestein:

The more rapid response of mortality than of fertility to the forces of modernization is probably inevitable. The reduction of mortality is a universally acceptable goal and faces no substantial social obstacles. But the reduction of fertility requires a shift in social goals from those directed toward the survival of the group to those directed toward the welfare and development of the individual. This change, both of goals and of the social equipment by which they are achieved, is at best a slow process. As a result, the period of modernization is virtually certain to yield rapid population increase.[2]

On the factors that were and are responsible for the eventual reduction in birth rates Notestein writes that they

... center around the growing individualism and rising levels of popular aspiration developed in urban industrial living. With the growth of huge and mobile city populations, the individual came to depend less and less on the status of his family for his place among his fellows. The station to which he was born gave place to his accomplishments and possessions as the measure of his importance. Meanwhile, the family lost many of its functions to the factory, the school, and commercial enterprises. All these developments made large families a progressively difficult and expensive undertaking; expensive and difficult for a population increasingly freed from older taboos and increasingly willing to solve its problems rather than to

[1] This generalization is based upon a study of the United Nations, *Demographic Yearbook*, 1953.
[2] Frank W. Notestein, 'Population — The Long View', in Theodore W. Schultz (ed.), *Food for the World*, pp. 40f.

accept them. In short, under the impact of urban life, the social aim of perpetuating the family gave way progressively to that of promoting the health, education, and material welfare of the individual child; family limitation became widespread; and the end of the period of growth came in sight.[1]

If Notestein's view is correct, and it is certainly true for the past, then the allocation of investment funds can be important in determining the point at which the rate of population growth declines. Certainly, investment in agricultural-rural pursuits will have much less effect (if not a negative effect) in fostering fertility declines than the creation of an urban industrial-commercial environment where the factors mentioned by Notestein can take root, grow, spread, and have their effect on the birth rate.

At first blush there may appear to be an apparent contradiction between the point just made and our previous recognition of the problem of the social cost of transferring workers from agriculture to urban pursuits. We cannot suggest that on the one hand, city-ward migration should be reduced in order to minimize the social costs of urbanization, and at the same time that rural-urban migration be maximized in order to facilitate the reduction of fertility rates. But this is only an apparent dilemma. Both the fertility effect and the social transfer costs effect must be taken into account and balanced against one another in terms of their combined effect on the eventual capital: labour ratio. These two factors are not entirely antithetical, for it is rising standards of living as a consequence of increasing wages and productivity in the urban environment that creates the proper atmosphere for fertility decline. If wages in the new industries are permitted to decline through the substitution of labour for capital, this will not only reduce the rate of reinvestment but also diminish the creation of those social conditions that lead to the economic and social mobility conducive to fertility decline. Thus, an optimum rate of urbanization should not be confused with the short-run maximum rate; it is rather the highest rate consistent with the maintenance of increasing wages and productivity under general social conditions conducive to fertility decline.

There is another viewpoint from which the two factors are not contradictory. The net social transfer cost is the opportunity foregone of adding to the stock of producers goods. But that part of the

[1] Ibid., p. 41.

social transfer cost that aids in fertility reduction makes an indirect contribution toward increasing the capital : labour ratio. Thus, expenditures on educational facilities, birth control clinics, or other facilities that change attitudes or dispense information conducive to fertility decline contribute toward increasing capital per worker in the future. Much more can be said on this aspect of our problem but we would certainly go beyond the bounds of this paper if we attempted to derive a theory of the optimal rate of urbanization.

Our interest in the possibility of achieving varying rates of population growth as a result of different investment patterns arises out of the consequences of varying rates of population growth on the *per capita* output potential. First, population growth reduces the capital: labour ratio and as a consequence reduces the *per capita* output potential. Second, population growth, through its adverse effect on *per capita* output and savings, tends to reduce the rate of reinvestment as a consequence of any initial investment. Thus, the lower the rate of population growth, or the earlier the decline in the rate of population growth sets in, the greater the *per capita* reinvestment quotient. In sum, the allocation of investment will affect not only total output but also the distribution of the labour force, the growth of the urban sector of the community, the social and cultural conditions under which people live, and the consequent attitudes towards early marriage, family size, and the resultant population growth. Therefore, the allocation that maximizes current output may be quite different from the allocation that maximizes the ultimate capital: labour ratio or the ultimate output potential per man.

(*b*) If an underdeveloped country is to develop successfully, it is necessary for that country to make a large initial effort to increase output and to do so very early in the development attempt. If the initial or early effort does not reach a critical minimum, then it is likely that the country will revert back to its former underdeveloped stage. The reasons for the need of an initial or early minimum effort follow:

(1) The potential growth of population makes it necessary to have initially a sufficiently large increase in capital, which induces successive increases in capital, so that it is not possible for the population increases to reduce the average amount of capital per worker.

(2) A minimum effort is necessary in order to create the economic environment where external economies are possible. For example,

railroads, communication systems, and irrigation works all may require large-scale initial efforts.

(3) The initial effort must be sufficient to raise incomes per head so that savings can be achieved, to continue the rate of capital accumulation. For once the rate of capital accumulation declines, there is always the challenge of population increases reducing the amount of capital per head.[1]

The critical minimum investment necessary will depend, in part, on the allocation of the investment funds. The SMP corollary allocation may or may not minimize the critical minimum investment necessary, while the allocation under our criterion, which directly takes into account the population factor, will tend to maximize the chances of overcoming the critical minimum. For that allocation that yields a lower rate of population growth, or leads to an earlier decline in the rate of population growth, reduces the critical minimum investment necessary, other things equal.

We may note that the critical minimum effort thesis implies the desirability of rapid capital accumulation early in the process of development not only in order to overcome the population hurdle, but also because there may be a connexion between the tempo of change, the rate of urbanization, and the creation of an environment conducive to the lowering of the birth rate. This last point, while not an established fact, would appear to be a reasonable speculation since growing individualism, economic and social mobility, loosening of family function, and lesser dependence on family status and traditional values generally go hand in hand with a quickening economic tempo.

4. *Some Obstacles to High Labour Productivity in Backward Areas*

The determination of a correct general criterion for capital allocation is not tantamount to its application. It may well be that environmental and institutional factors dictate extensive modifica-

---

[1] For an elaboration of this idea see H. Leibenstein, *A Theory of Economic-Demographic Development*, Princeton University Press, 1954, ch. IV and V. H. W. Singer appears to suggest the same idea, in somewhat different words, when he argues that the underdeveloped economies are faced with a series of interlocking vicious circles that only an able, significant, and sustained effort can break. 'Economic Progress in Underdeveloped Countries', *Social Research*, March 1949, pp. 5ff.

tions in practice.[1] For example, even if it were determined that an indigenous iron and steel industry was basic to rapid development, the lack of iron ore and fuel might prevent its establishment. There may be a hundred reasons why a high initial level of labour productivity is impossible of achievement.[2]

It is our belief that the criterion of the marginal *per capita* reinvestment quotient and the corollary of a high capital : labour ratio are appropriate general guides in programmes for economic development. In this section we shall consider some of the factors which stand in the way of the indicated solution for allocating available investment resources.

(*a*) The surplus of manpower, and the consequently low wage level, that characterize the major underdeveloped areas of the world, are serious stumbling blocks in the path of economic growth. The surplus may be hidden in the form of underemployment in agriculture, where the marginal productivity of labour must often approach zero; or it may be all too evident in the form of chronic urban unemployment. In extreme cases, low quality labour may be virtually a free good; in Ecuador, for example, it was estimated that a cotton mill could have ten times as many workers as an American mill without any difference in the relation of the labour cost to the value of the finished product.[3] 'Because of keen competition in the employment market, the levels of wages earned in these occupations are kept extremely low, and because of low wages the management has little incentive to raise its standards of efficiency.'[4] In such situations the employment of as large a number of workers as possible appears not only to make good economic common sense, but to be socially desirable as well.

One possible solution under these circumstances is to alter conditions to conform with our criterion by making labour scarce artificially. This can be done in a number of ways: by legislation establishing relatively high minimum wages and working conditions;[5] by

---

[1] Also moral or religious considerations may require modifications of the criterion.

[2] See Wilbert E. Moore, op. cit., ch. V.

[3] *Labour Productivity in the Cotton Textile Industry in Five Latin-American Countries*, op. cit., p. 67.

[4] Chiang Hsieh, 'Underemployment in Asia', *International Labour Review*, June 1952, p. 703.

[5] It is quite true that higher wages by themselves reduce the amount of production available for reinvestment. The point is that higher wages, by

direct governmental control of manpower; or, in the case of state industry, by imposing high labour productivity targets upon management. None of these prescriptions is an easy one to follow. The islands of favoured employment will have to be protected by the government in some manner, for individual entrepreneurs will find it difficult to resist the constant temptation of cheap labour. Yet there is ample precedent for such a policy; one may cite the oil refineries in the Near East, where foreign management polices the barriers, and a modern Egyptian textile mill where native entrepreneurial policy is effective in this regard.[1]

(b) The shortage of skilled labour is almost invariably cited as an obstacle to high productivity,[2] and undoubtedly it is. Yet there is reason to believe that the difficulties in this respect are exaggerated. Looking to the Russian industrialization experience, it was necessary to train for the semi-skilled trades millions of raw farm-hands within the space of a few years. During the First Five Year Plan the Soviet industrial labour force roughly doubled in size. Of the 12·5 million new workers who entered industry for the first time between 1928 and 1932, 8·5 million had been peasants.[3] The training they received was certainly not thorough; most of it was done directly on the job. True vocational schools were virtually non-existent. Yet though the process was wasteful, it sufficed, and permitted the Russians to take greater pains with subsequent generations of labour inductees. The training of technical personnel was a longer-range problem, and here the cadres of well-trained pre-Soviet engineers were of great importance. By 1940, however, technical schools were turning out large numbers of qualified engineers and technicians.

restricting the use of manpower, may lead to a lower *total* wage bill, depending upon the elasticity of the demand for labour and the absolute magnitudes involved. Furthermore, by developing a socio-economic setting in which we can overcome the institutional barriers to rising productivity we can get a larger surplus for reinvestment.

[1] Gamal Eldin Said, op. cit., p. 506.

[2] e.g. : 'Even more serious, there will in all likelihood be severe shortages of skilled labour for jobs which require technical knowledge, or which involve the exercise of organization or supervisory talent.' IBRD, *Surinam*, p. 89. 'Other difficulties may well emerge in the supply of foremen, skilled and semi-skilled workers.' IBRD, *The Economic Development of Iraq*, p. 83. '. . . the acute shortage of trained personnel . . . is one of the main obstacles to rapid progress.' IBRD, *The Economic Development of Ceylon*, p. 55.

[3] Solomon Schwarz, *Labour in the Soviet Union*, New York, 1951, pp. 9, 31f.

(c) Under contemporary conditions of economic development in the democratic countries, a strong labour movement is likely to arise at the inception of industrialization, rather than at a fairly advanced stage as in the past. Moreover, the unionism of backward areas is apt to be radical in its orientation, in view of poor labour conditions and the impatience of workers with the seeming inability of the method of collective bargaining to secure for them immediate betterment. There is therefore ever present the danger that resources will be diverted from investment to consumption, that the seeds of industrial development will not be permitted to mature.

High productivity, with its implication of fewer and better paid workers, will tend to mitigate the upsurge of labour protest, to moderate the extremism of the labour movement, and to provide a climate of worker opinion favourable to technological change.[1] This is by no means a complete answer to what will undoubtedly be one of the crucial problems in industrialization, but at least it can be said that the high productivity solution appears to provide the labour conditions which are most propitious for success.

III. Conclusion

We have endeavoured to show in the foregoing pages that the criterion of allocating investment on the basis of the marginal productivity of each unit of capital invested is not suitable for contemporary underdeveloped areas because of the invalidity of what we have termed the *ceteris paribus* assumption. When the facts of rapid population growth, political instability, and institutional obstacles to technological change, all of which are generally typical of underdeveloped areas today, are taken into account, it becomes clear that time is of the essence in developmental programmes. The process of development must be sufficiently rapid to satisfy the swiftly burgeoning aspirations of people suddenly released from a Malthusian world and endowed with political power. The alternative is the constant encroachment of consumption upon the national product; falling rather than rising *per capita* incomes as a consequence of explosive population growth; and eventual chaos as the

---

[1] We assume that the low productivity solution will yield such small results in terms of higher standards for the larger number of workers affected as to have little mollifying effect upon the degree of labour protest.

mass organizations called into being by industrialization in 'width', rather than in 'depth', are forced to exploit their power by pressure from below.

Our thesis, baldly, is that successful economic development under present conditions, particularly in the face of gross backwardness, hinges largely upon the introduction of modern technology upon as large a scale as possible. Professor Gerschenkron has pointed out that in the past,

> To the extent that industrialization took place, it was largely by application of the most modern and efficient techniques that backward countries could hope to achieve success, particularly if their industrialization proceeded in the face of competition from the advanced country. . . . This seems to explain the tendency on the part of backward countries to concentrate at a relatively early point in their industrialization on promotion of such branches of industrial activities in which recent technological progress has been particularly rapid. . . . In viewing the economic history of Europe in the nineteenth century, the impression is very strong that only when industrial development could commence on a large scale did the tension between the pre-industrialization conditions and the benefit that may be expected from industrialization became sufficiently strong to overcome the existing obstacles and to liberate the forces that made for industrial progress.[1]

This applies with even greater force to twentieth-century Asia and Africa, with their far greater relative and absolute backwardness. These areas can best hope to see the completion of successful programmes of economic development within the reasonable future, and (what is critical) under the auspices of political democracy, if in allocating available capital resources, the twin desiderata of up-to-date equipment and relatively high initial capital/labour ratios are kept to the fore.

Alexander Gerschenkron, 'Economic Backwardness in Historical Perspective', in Bert F. Hoselitz (ed.), *The Progress of Underdeveloped Areas*. Chicago, 1952, pp. 7ff.

SOME NOTES ON THE CHOICE OF CAPITAL INTENSITY IN DEVELOPMENT PLANNING*

by Amartya Kumar Sen

I

Considerable attention has been paid in recent years to the problem of choosing between alternative techniques of production that are open to an underdeveloped economy. The object of this paper is to discuss the basic issues involved in the choice. We shall start by examining the various criteria that have so far been suggested. In the light of the criticisms of these, an alternative suggestion will be put forward. In the second section the problem will be discussed in terms of some simple models, partly to clarify the differences between these criteria, and also to study how factors like the cost of labour or the foreign trade situation influence the choice. In this paper we shall concentrate on the problem of choice of techniques for the consumer goods sector only.

The criteria for choosing between techniques of production for an underdeveloped economy that have so far been explicitly put forward can, I think, be classified into three groups. We shall examine them one by one, at the end of which an alternative suggestion will be put forward as a fourth criterion.

A. THE RATE-OF-TURNOVER CRITERION

Professor J. J. Polak, while discussing the investment criteria of countries reconstructing after the war, suggested that investment for development should be chosen according to the rate of turnover, i.e.,

* *Quarterly Journal of Economics*, November 1957. Reprinted by permission of Harvard University Press and the author.

The author is indebted to Mrs Joan Robinson and Mr Maurice Dobb for comments and suggestions on an earlier draft of this paper. This is a slightly altered version of a paper for which the writer was awarded the Stevenson Prize of Cambridge University for 1956.

213

the ratio of output to capital.[1] Along with a few other considerations, like the exporting possibility of the goods produced, a high output to capital ratio was made the basis for selection. The same suggestion was put forward also by Professor Norman S. Buchanan. 'If investment funds are limited, the wise policy, in the absence of special considerations, would be to undertake first those investments having a high value of annual product relative to the investment necessary to bring them into existence.'[2]

That this criterion is very imperfect as a general guide to policy is not difficult to realize. For one thing, a high rate of turnover may be associated with a high rate of depreciation and the rate of *net* output may not necessarily be high. But this difficulty can be avoided to some extent by stating the criterion in terms of the *net* rate of turnover, which is how it is actually put in most cases. The main defect of the theory is that it ignores the cost of employing labour in operating the capital. When the cost of employing labour in an economy is zero, a very good case can be made for the criterion of maximum addition to net output from a given amount of capital investment. If, on the other hand, employment of labour involves some cost to society, we have to take that into account.[3]

B. THE 'SOCIAL MARGINAL PRODUCTIVITY' CRITERION

From what we have said in the last paragraph it is just one step to arrive at the social marginal productivity criterion as put forward by Professor A. E. Kahn.[4] It is suggested that from the addition to output due to the investment, the alternative output sacrificed as a result of drawing factors of production from other fields into this one has to be subtracted. Thus the factors are valued at their social

---

[1] 'Balance of Payments Problems of Countries Reconstructing with the Help of Foreign Loans', *Quarterly Journal of Economics*, February 1943, p. 208. Reprinted in *Readings in the Theory of International Trade*, American Economic Association, 1949.

[2] *International Investment and Domestic Welfare*, New York, 1945, p. 24.

[3] See A. E. Kahn, 'Investment Criteria in Development Programs', reprinted in the present volume, pp. 131f.

[4] Op. cit. See also H. B. Chenery, 'The Application of Investment Criteria', reprinted in the present volume, p. 158.

opportunity cost, i.e., at what they could have produced in other fields had they not been drawn into the investment under examination. This criterion would lead to a different result from that of the rate-of-turnover approach, so long as the social opportunity cost of labour is positive. When, however, there is large-scale unemployment, the opportunity cost of labour is nil, and thus labour becomes according to this approach costless. Ignoring factors other than labour, now there is no need for any subtraction and we find Kahn arguing that in this case the Polak-Buchanan criterion is 'particularly desirable'.[1] Thus in an economy of this sort Kahn recommends the technique with the least capital coefficient, i.e., with the maximum rate of turnover.

Professor W. A. Lewis also puts forward a similar view when discussing the question. 'Special care', he argues, 'has to be taken in those countries which have a large surplus of unskilled labour, for in such circumstances money wages will not reflect the real social cost of using labour. In these circumstances capital is not productive if it is used to do what labour could do equally well; given the level of wages such investments may be highly profitable to capitalists, but they are unprofitable to the community as a whole since they add to unemployment but not to output.'[2] 'It is then [when there is surplus labour] arguable that the real cost of using labour in cottage industry is zero, whereas factory production uses scarce capital and supervisory skills.'[3]

In assessing this criterion, I think, we have to start by asking what it is that we are trying to achieve. If we are trying to maximize immediate output, labour should be valued according to its social opportunity cost and the above criterion seems quite appropriate. If, however, we are interested in the future as well, we have to look at the *rate of growth* of income governed by the accumulation of capital. And there is no reason to believe that the maximum rate of output would also give us the maximum rate of excess of production over current consumption, when employment is a variable. Here even if the alternative social product is nil, the cost of labour will be positive, given by the increase in consumption due to extra

[1] Op. cit., p. 51. See also p. 40.
[2] *The Theory of Economic Growth*, London and Homewood, Illinois, 1955, p. 386.
[3] Op. cit., p. 140.

employment.[1] Thus the social marginal productivity criterion is all right if we are not interested in the future at all. But if we take a long term point of view, the criterion need no longer be valid.[2]

C. The Reinvestment Criterion

W. Galenson and H. Leibenstein christened their criterion as that of 'marginal *per capita* reinvestment quotient'.[3] For clarification of what it means, we may quote the authors:

To secure a clear notion of what is meant by the marginal *per capita* reinvestment quotient we must consider the basic factors involved in its determination. Briefly stated, the seven basic factors are as follows: (1) gross productivity per worker; (2) 'wage' goods consumed per worker; (3) replacement and repair of capital; (4) increments in output as a result of non-capital using innovations such as improvements in skill, health, energy, discipline and malleability of the labour force; (5) declines in mortality; (6) declines in fertility; and (7) direction of reinvestment.[4]

[1] Chenery, op. cit., seems to confuse this point. His theory is basically a variant of the SMP criterion with a 'welfare function' involving 'effect on national income' (along with effects on balance of payments and income distribution). Now, when one is interested in the total national income for the period, one should value labour at its opportunity cost. Instead he values labour (equations 4 and 5) at the 'increase in consumption' (pp. 82f., present volume pp. 165f.). 'The effect on national income, ΔY, can be approximated by applying a set of corrections to the businessman's calculation of the annual *rate of profit*' (p. 82, present volume pp.165f., italics mine). This appears to me to be a confusion between the rate of surplus and the rate of income flow. There is no reason why |in national income measurement the increase in the consumption of the wage earners should not be included. The concept of the social opportunity cost is legitimate for the calculation of total output but not for the calculation of the rate of growth of output; the concept of the gap between marginal production and marginal consumption is legitimate for the latter, but not for the former. To avoid confusion, the distinction has to be appreciated.

[2] The criticism of Walter Galenson and Harvey Leibenstein ('Investment Criteria, Productivity and Economic Development', reprinted in the present volume, pp.190f.) also boils down to this point about the valuation of labour though this may not be quite obvious.

[3] Op. cit., p. 351, present volume pp. 191f. For a neat presentation of a basically similar criterion and also for an interesting study of various other aspects of the problem of choice of capital-intensity, see M. H. Dobb, 'Second Thoughts on Capital Intensity', reprinted in the present volume, pp. 239–55.

[4] Op. cit., p. 352, present volume pp. 141f.

Galenson and Leibenstein provide the criterion with somewhat more manageable dimensions when they discuss the growth of employment. It is clear that what the authors are interested in, briefly stated, is the flow of net investment that is created by a unit of investment today. From the formula on page 357 (present volume p. 197) the rate of reinvestment is found to be equated to

$$r = \frac{p - ew}{c},$$

where p = output (presumably *net* output) per machine;

      e = the number of workers per machine;

      w = real wage rate;

      c = cost per machine.

This actually turns out to be not much different from the capitalist's rate-of-profit criterion. This coincidence is easy to explain. If the whole of the profit is reinvested[1] and the whole of the wages consumed, the rate of profit and the rate of reinvestment must come to the same thing.

Professor K. N. Raj of the Delhi School of Economics puts forward a similar criterion.[2] But since he considers specifically the case of a change from cottage industrial to factory production, he draws our attention to the necessity of subsidizing those who become jobless due to technological change. Thus he regards the cost of maintaining the new unemployed as part of the total costs. This makes his criterion less favourable to more mechanized production than the Galenson-Leibenstein criterion.[3] This criterion is applicable, given

---

[1] Galenson and Leibenstein do make this assumption. 'We abstract here from the very difficult problem of ensuring that this Ricardian "surplus" is indeed reinvested . . .' (op. cit., p. 352, n. 6, present volume, p. 192 n.).

[2] 'Small Scale Industries — Problem of Technological Change', Special Article, *The Economic Weekly* (India), 7 and 14 April, 1956. This point is discussed also by Hans Neisser, 'Investment Criteria, Productivity, and Economic Development : Comment', *Quarterly Journal of Economics*, November 1956, p. 644, and by Galenson and Leibenstein in their 'Reply', ibid.

[3] As the dole paid to the unemployed is increased relative to the wage rate, Raj's criterion approaches that of the rate of turnover. In the limiting case where the dole is equal to the wage rate, the two criteria coincide. The labourer gets the same income whether he is employed or not, and the technique that maximizes production also maximizes surplus. Raj also assumes that the rural cottage-industrial wage rate is lower than the urban wage rate. This also makes his criterion more favourable to less mechanized production.

its value judgement, to the case where less mechanized production is being *replaced* by more mechanized production. It would, however, be very difficult to apply when we are contemplating *initiation* of production and wondering whether to make it more or less capital-intensive. In those cases, I think, it would be nearly impossible to separate out, from the pool of the jobless people, those who would have been employed had a less mechanized production technique been chosen.

The essence of the reinvestment criterion (whether the unemployed people are paid doles or not) lies in its use of the rate of growth formula associated with the names of Harrod and Domar. The reinvestment formula can be transformed into the growth economics terminology without much difficulty.

$$r = \frac{p - ew}{c} = \left(\frac{p}{c}\right)\left(1 - \frac{ew}{p}\right) = \frac{s}{a},$$

where $\qquad a =$ capital coefficient $= \dfrac{c}{p}$

and $\qquad s =$ savings ratio $= \dfrac{p - ew}{p}$,

assuming that the whole of wages is consumed and the whole of the rest reinvested. Thus the maximization of r results in the maximization of the rate of growth.

The Galenson-Leibenstein criterion is based on a number of simplifying assumptions, e.g., the techniques have the same gestation lag, the whole of the surplus is reinvested, and so on. These, however, do not constitute any basic limitation of the theory as in actual calculations they could be taken care of. Some questions can, however, be raised about the fundamental validity of the Galenson-Leibenstein criterion.

First, it is assumed in the criterion that the total amount of investment that one can make in the initial period, is fixed irrespective of the technique chosen. Only with this assumption can one say that the technique which gives us the maximum rate of investible surplus per unit of capital investment will give us the maximum rate of growth. That the assumption need not be valid can be realized very easily if we take cases with different propensities to consume of the factors contributing to the respective investments. If, in the case of investment A, the owners of factors of production consume half of what they get, an investment of $100 will mean an addition to the effective demand for consumer goods of $50 in the next round. If in the case of investment B, the factor owners consume whatever they get, the same amount of investment will lead to an additional effective demand for consumer goods of $100 in the next round. Thus given the real resources available in the economy, we may be in a position to have a larger initial capital investment if we chose technique A rather than B. It is therefore possible that even if technique B gives a higher rate of investible surplus *per unit of capital investment*, it may not give us a higher rate of growth.

The practical importance of this criticism depends, of course, upon the actual size of the difference in the propensities to consume. This difference will vary from case to case, but in some cases it may be quite important, as technological change often implies the replacement of a number of unskilled labourers by some skilled workers with lower propensities to consume. Also the producers of different co-operating factors of production may have different spending habits.

Secondly, the same problem may arise in a different garb in connexion with international trade. Galenson and Leibenstein do not distinguish between the costs of buying foreign goods and those incurred in the home economy. When one technique has a higher import-content than another and when extra foreign aid is not specially available when the first is chosen, the balance of payments problem introduced by the adoption of the first technique has to be taken into account. I think the best way of measuring the additional cost of higher import-content is to value the import at its export-equivalent. That is, we have to see how much more exports we have to ship abroad to meet the additional imports. Thus if technique A has no import-content and technique B involves imports worth $100 in addition to expenditures made at home, and if to meet the foreign currency requirement of $100 we have to export $150 (at home prices), by subsidization or other methods, we should add $150 and not merely $100 to home costs in the latter case.[1]

This is a consideration of great practical relevance for very many choices of techniques. Thanks to the lack of a sector producing modern capital goods in an underdeveloped economy, the difference

---

[1] If there is scope for cutting down other imports to finance this and if that rather than expansion of exports is the method chosen, we have to examine its social cost.

between the import-content of factory production and that of cottage industrial production is simply enormous, and choice between the two is very often the basic question in investment allocation in an underdeveloped economy. The Galenson-Leibenstein approach neglects this aspect of the problem altogether.

Thirdly, the Galenson-Leibenstein criterion neglects the fact that present income may be more valuable to society than future income. While the social marginal productivity criterion pins its attention on the present, the rate-of-reinvestment criterion goes to the other extreme. A higher rate of reinvestment may mean a higher rate of growth of income and thus may promise higher income some time in the future, but that in itself is no reason for choosing that technique. If we value present income more than future income, we may prefer to have a lower rate of growth and a higher rate of immediate income. This preference for the present need not arise from 'irrational telescopic psychology', but, for example, may be due to the very rational consideration that our present income being less than our future income, the value of additional income to us is much more at the present moment. This problem of time preference leads to a number of complexities which we shall encounter when we try to put forward an alternative criterion; but that a complete neglect of the problem is illegitimate seems clear. The SMP and the reinvestment criteria represent the two extreme positions on this time question.[1]

D. The Time Series Criterion

In the light of our criticism of the reinvestment criterion we can put forward an alternative suggestion. When confronted with the choice between various techniques, we start by finding out our 'best

[1] Since this paper was written, two articles on capital-intensity have come out in *Quarterly Journal of Economics*, February 1957, namely by Otto Eckstein, 'Investment Criteria for Economic Development and the Theory of Intertemporal Welfare Economics', p. 56, and by Francis M. Bator, 'On Capital Productivity, Input Allocation and Growth', p. 86. It is particularly necessary to refer to Professor Bator's article, as he denies the importance of the problem of choice over time involved in the question, on which we have put so much emphasis. In fact Bator's model leads him to conclude (p. 99) that there is 'no conflict' between maximizing the present output and maximizing the growth rate. This conclusion is the result of his assumption that 'the rate of saving is independent of the (as if) market imputed distribution of income' (p. 98). This, of course, amounts to assuming away the problem itself.

guess' of the time series of real income flows corresponding to each technique. This is done by applying the rate of reinvestment with corrections due to the variability of the volume of investment as we choose one technique rather than another. The variability, as we have shown earlier, may arise from things like different spending habits of the factors of production and varying import-content of investments employing different techniques. If $\left(\dfrac{r_1}{r_2}\right)$ is the ratio of reinvestment with technique 1 and technique 2 respectively and if $\left(\dfrac{m_1}{m_2}\right)$ is the ratio of the volumes of investment that can be undertaken when we choose the respective techniques, technique 1 will lead to a higher or a lower rate of growth depending on whether $m_1 r_1 >$ or $< m_2 r_2$. This way the two time series of real income flows are obtained.[1] In deriving the two time series one has to remember that there need not be constant returns to scale, as normally assumed, and the relative factor prices may also change with the scale of production, as factors need not be in equally elastic supply.

After getting the two time series of income flows we have to apply the relevant rates of time discount, and even if $m_1 r_1 > m_2 r_2$, we need not necessarily choose technique 1. The time discount is necessary, it appears to me, because of at least two reasons[2]: (a) the diminishing marginal social utility of income with the rising income level,[3] and (b) the uncertainty of the future. If marginal social utility of income falls quickly and becomes negligible as income rises beyond a certain level, it is possible that a higher rate of

---

[1] Actually due to the interdependence of economic activities a better way of looking at the problem may be in terms of alternative combinations of fixed-capital-stock and current-input-flow matrices. A more capital-intensive technique involves raising some items of the former matrix to reduce some items of the latter.

[2] The much-discussed 'telescopic psychology' does not appear to me to be strong ground for time-discount in planning problems. We are interested not in the value to today's men of the satisfaction of the men of tomorrow, but in the value of the satisfaction of tomorrow's men themselves. So the 'optical illusion' need not be taken very seriously.

[3] We are assuming cardinality and interpersonal comparability of utility. This is, as three decades of criticism has made abundantly clear, not quite correct. However, even if we use more sophisticated social welfare functions, the fact that we value income less when we have more of it must, it appears to me, be taken into account.

growth of income may not give us a higher sum of total social satisfaction. Again beyond a point it becomes very difficult to apply all these rational calculations, as it is too difficult to foresee what is going to happen. Thanks to the imperfection of our knowledge, it is not possible to work out all the results of today's actions, for all time to come. We may choose a high degree of capital intensity and sacrifice some amount of present income for expected future benefit; but a technically advanced war, for example, may settle all problems before that future arrives. Thus in addition to the utility function with the assumption of perfect certainty, we need a valuation of uncertainty discount for a rigorous solution of the problem.

In applying our criterion to actual choices of capital intensity such a rigorous solution is not possible as we cannot get the required utility and uncertainty functions. A less satisfactory but more workable method is to fix the period of time we are going to take into account and see whether the loss of immediate output incurred by choosing the more capital-intensive technique is more than compensated by the extra output from it later, before the period of consideration is over. We may actually conceive of a 'period of recovery' (T) defined[1] as the period of time in which the total output (the sum of yearly flows) with the more capital-intensive technique, is just equal to that with the less intensive technique.[2] Figure I illustrates the period of recovery. The H and L curves give the two time series of consumption flows with the respective techniques. OT represents the period of recovery, as the surplus-area for the more capital-intensive technique (BCC') is exactly equal to its deficit-area $(BA\hat{A})$.

The period we are ready to take into account is U (given by our judgements). When $U < T$, technique L is preferable; when $U > T$,

[1] It is actually more meaningful to define the period in terms of the recovery of the *consumer* goods output rather than in terms of that of *income* as such. In the following models, in fact, we do define it in terms of the consumer goods output.

[2] This is similar to the Soviet 'period of recoupment' but not the same. We are looking at the problem from the point of view of alternative output flows with given investment possibilities; the period of recoupment refers to the alternative costs to produce a given flow of output.

The importance of the period to be taken into account in technological choices is emphasized also by K. N. Raj, 'Application of Investment Criteria in the Choice between Projects', *Indian Economic Review*, August 1956.

technique H should be chosen; the point of indifference is given by $U = T$. If we assume $U = 1$, we get the rate-of-turnover criterion; being interested in the first period only, the technique with the higher rate of immediate output is preferred. If we assume $U = \infty$, we get the rate-of-reinvestment criterion; being equally interested in all time to come, a higher *rate* of growth is all we want.

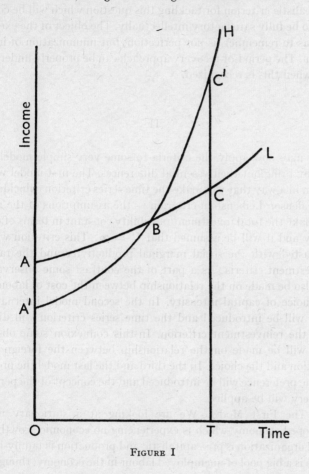

FIGURE I

The defect of this approach lies in its arbitrariness. We have to assume that up to the end of the period U, each unit of income is equally valuable and there is no preference over time. But beyond that point no income is of any value at all. This brings in the time factor rather suddenly and with extreme severity.[1] But such arbitrariness is difficult to avoid due to the very nature of the problem, and the approach of the period of recovery may have considerable operational value. In any case by choosing non-extreme values of U it can be made less arbitrary than the approach of the SMP criterion or that of the criterion of reinvestment. It is impossible to arrive at a realistic criterion for tackling this question which will be considered to be fully satisfactory intellectually. The object of the exercise, one has to remember, is not perfection, but minimization of imperfection. The period-of-recovery approach can be properly understood only when this is recognized.

II

We may now apply the criteria to some very simple models and thereby bring out their essential differences. The first model will be chosen in a way that will make the time series criterion coincide with the Galenson-Leibenstein criterion — the assumptions of the model will make the total investment possibility constant in terms of direct outlay and it will be assumed that $U = \infty$. This criterion will be contrasted with the social marginal productivity and the rate-of-reinvestment criteria. As a part of the contrast some observations will also be made on the relationship between the cost of labour and the choice of capital intensity. In the second model international trade will be introduced and the time series criterion will diverge from the reinvestment criterion. In this connexion some observations will be made on the relationship between the foreign trade situation and the choice. In the third and the last model the problem of time preference will be introduced and the concept of the period of recovery will be applied.

(*i*) The First Model. We are looking at a stationary underdeveloped economy which is experiencing no economic growth. The social organization is pre-capitalistic and production is family-based. There is a big pool of unemployed labour in the economy, though due to the social organization, the unemployment may be 'disguised'.

---

[1] This is more illegitimate for the ' diminishing marginal utility ' part of time preference as it is a function of income and not of time as such. The uncertainty factor, however, is more definitely a function of time.

The government is contemplating the initiation of economic development with some public investment. It has decided against using the method of 'forced savings' through inflation and it will invest only to the extent that a technical surplus of production over current consumption is already available. Thus if the subsistence economy provides no surplus at all and if there is no foreign help, the economy is obviously in the grip of complete stagnation.[1] Let us assume that the government has managed to realize some surplus through taxation or other means, and that the problem is in what form to invest it.

The economy consists of two sectors — the 'backward' subsistence sector and the 'advanced' sector under construction. We refer to them as sectors B and A respectively. Labour supply to sector A, we assume, is perfectly elastic in the relevant range due to immigration from sector B.[2]

Sector A can be subdivided into two departments — I and II, the former producing capital goods and the latter corn, which we take as a 'composite commodity' to avoid the index number problem.[3] For analytical convenience all factors other than labour and capital will be ignored. We assume further that all the techniques have the same gestation lag, that a capital good once created lasts forever (i.e., there is no depreciation), that the real wage rate per labour-hour is the same for all the techniques and is constant over time, and that the whole of the wages bill is consumed and that the whole of the surplus over wages is reinvested. In this particular model we also assume that capital goods are produced by labour alone and that the economy is closed. We shall deal with a choice between two techniques — H and L; the former has a higher capital intensity, defined as the number of labourers employed in department I to produce enough capital goods to employ one labourer in department II. We use the following notations for technique L.

---

[1] Compare this problem with that of Marx's 'Primitive Accumulation'.

[2] For a discussion of the reasons for using this type of 'classical' supply curve of labour, see W. A. Lewis, 'Economic Development with Unlimited Supply of Labour', *Manchester School*, May 1954, p. 139, reprinted in Agarwala and Singh (eds.), *The Economics of Underdevelopment*, Bombay, Oxford University Press, 1958, pp. 400f.

[3] See Joan Robinson, 'The Production Function and the Theory of Capital', *Review of Economic Studies*, XXI (1953–4), p. 85. See also *idem*, *The Accumulation of Capital* London, Macmillan and Co., 1956, pp. 64f.

$\underline{w}$ = real wage rate per period in the production of corn;
$\overline{w}$ = real wage rate per period in the capital goods sector;
a = 'capital intensity' as defined above;
P_c = labour productivity in corn production in department II of sector A;
L_i = labour employed in department I;
L_c = labour employed in department II;
C = total corn produced in sector A;
W_c = total wages bill in department II of sector A;
and N = the surplus of corn production over the wages bill $(C - W_c)$, in department II.

In the case of technique H we use primed notations. Numerical suffixes refer to the relevant time periods.

As temporary assumptions we have $w = w'$ and $\overline{w} = \overline{w}'$. We know that $a < a'$. Obviously P_c must be less than P'_c; otherwise there would be little reason to take the more capital-intensive technique seriously.

Let us start with a surplus S of corn extracted from sector B to make the initiation of Sector A possible. We assume that wage earners in department II are paid out of their production.

$$L_i = \frac{S}{\overline{w}} \quad L_c = \frac{S}{\overline{w}a} \quad C = \frac{SP_c}{\overline{w}a}.$$

Similarly
$$C' = \frac{SP_c'}{\overline{w}a'}$$

If we are interested only in the total product for the first period, our choice would depend on whether

$$\frac{P_c'}{a} > , = \text{ or } < \frac{P_c}{a}. \tag{1}$$

This is the rate-of-turnover criterion.[1]

Production in future years will depend not merely on the flow of output from the initial investment, but also on that from additional investments undertaken with the surplus product. So if we are

[1] The social marginal productivity criterion coincides with this, as unemployed labour is available in the economy.

interested in the maximum rate of growth of output, the relevant consideration is the rate of surplus.

$$N_1 = C_{1'} - W_{c1} = \frac{S}{w} \cdot \frac{P_c - w}{a} \cdot$$

$$N_1' = C_1' - W_{c1}' = \frac{S}{w} \cdot \frac{P_{c'} - w}{a'} \cdot$$

We should choose H or L or be indifferent between them depending on whether

$$\frac{P_{c'} - w}{a'} > , < \text{ or } = \frac{P_c - w}{a} \text{ respectively.} \tag{2}$$

This is the rate-of-reinvestment criterion.

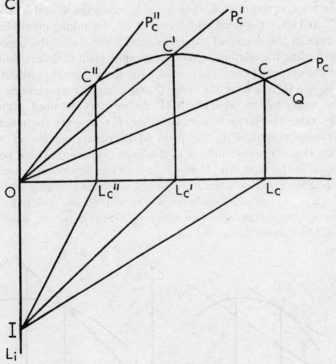

FIGURE II

All this can be represented in diagrammatic form without much difficulty. In Figure II there are three axes — the south representing employment in department I, the east employment in department II and the north the corn output of the latter department. OI is the amount of labour that can be employed with the available corn surplus at the prevailing wage rate. Employment in department II depends on the degree of capital intensity chosen, it being defined as the number of labourers that have to be employed in department I to produce enough capital goods for employing one man in department II. Three degrees of capital intensity are used in the figure, represented in the increasing order by the tangent of the angles OL_cI, $OL_{c'}I$ and $OL_{c''}I$ respectively. The employment created as a result of this investment is OL_c, $OL_{c'}$ and $OL_{c''}$ respectively. With increasing capital intensity, the product per unit of labour in department II rises, represented respectively by the tangents of the angles P_cOL_c, $P_{c'}OL_c$ and $P_{c''}OL_c$. Thus the corn output when the first technique is chosen is CL_c, when the second is chosen $C'L_{c'}$ and when the third is preferred $C''L_{c''}$. By taking infinitesimal changes in the degree of capital intensity, we derive the curve Q representing the relationship between employment in department II and the output of corn, governed by the technological possibilities. In Figure III, we have the curve Q and a line W_c representing the total wages bill in department II. As we have assumed a given wage rate, the latter is a straight-line. E represents the point of maximum output. P is the point of maximum surplus of corn production over consumption, as the slope of curve Q at that point is equal to the wage rate. If we adopt the rate-of-turnover criterion, or the SMP criterion when unemployed labour is available without affecting production elsewhere, we should choose point E. If, however, we adopt the rate-of-reinvestment criterion, point P should be chosen.

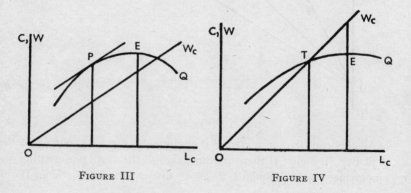

FIGURE III   FIGURE IV

An interesting possibility is represented by point E lying below the wage-line, as in Figure IV. This means that the maximization of output would involve negative surplus.[1] Point T gives maximum output consistent with the condition that output covers the wages bill ($P_c = w$). It is thus possible that full application of the SMP criterion or the rate-of-turnover criterion may involve capital contraction rather than accumulation.

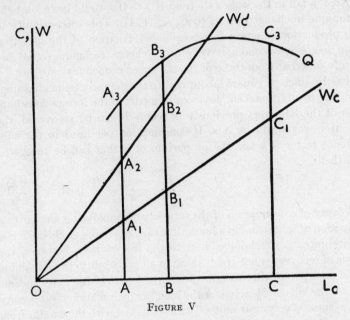

FIGURE V

In Figure V, it is illustrated that a rise in the wage rate makes it more profitable to choose a more capital-intensive technique. When the wage-line moves up from W_c to $W_{c'}$, the point of maximum surplus becomes A rather than B, as $B_2B_3 < A_2A_3$, although $B_1B_3 > A_1A_3$.[2] This follows also from relation (2), as a technique

---

[1] I am indebted to Joan Robinson for drawing my attention to this possibility.

[2] If, however, lower productivity (with the same technique) tends to go with lower wages, this effect will to that extent be countered. See M. H. Dobb, 'A Note on the Degree of Capital Intensity of Investments in Underdeveloped Countries', *Economie Appliquée*, VII (1954); reprinted in his *On Economic Theory and Socialism* (London, 1955), p. 148. Also see *idem*, 'Second Thoughts on Capital Intensity of Investment', reprinted in the present volume, pp. 239–55.

with a higher rate of surplus per labourer $(P_c - w)$ is relatively less affected by a rise in the wage rate.[1]

From this it does not follow, however, that a lower wage economy should necessarily choose a lower degree of capital intensity. In fact, the scope of variation of capital intensity may be very limited, and it may well be that, of the available techniques, the same is best for most wages. In Figure V, if A and C were the only techniques that existed, a fall in the wage rate from $W_{c'}$ to W_c would have kept the technique unchanged at A, $(C_1 C_3 < A_1 A_3)$. This discontinuity in the production function is a possible explanation of the fact that even low wage economies very often choose techniques that are hardly different from those of the advanced economies.

Lastly, since we equate labour cost to the net increase in consumption due to additional employment, if a part of the former consumption of the labourers previously in sector B can be recovered, the effective wages will be less. If consumption per head in the subsistence sector is k and the proportion of it that can be recovered is q then

$$N_1 = \frac{S}{w} \cdot \frac{P_c - w + kq}{a} = \frac{S}{w} \cdot \frac{P_c - w(1 - f)}{a} \text{, putting } f = \frac{kq}{w}.$$

Recovery of consumption of the formerly unemployed is similar to a reduction of wages and in a borderline case can make us choose a less capital-intensive technique. Left to the free market, however, the scope of recovery is not great, since, in all probability, the remaining rural population will consume nearly the whole of the extra income left by the villagers leaving for the town, as their marginal propensity to consume is very near unity. Taxation linked with the exodus from the rural area, or some system of 'compulsory delivery', may, however, achieve this end. This shows the dependence of technological choice on the fiscal policy in operation in the economy.[2]

[1] See in this connexion, Joan Robinson, 'The Production Function and the Theory of Capital', op. cit. Also see *idem*, *The Accumulation of Capital*, op. cit., ch. 10.

[2] This point, among others, is discussed in the Indian context in my note on 'Labour Cost and Economic Growth', *Economic Weekly* (India), 29 September 1956. It was followed by some controversy on this question, among others in the October and November issues of the *Weekly*, which may be interesting, especially to those who are fond of polemical writings. A controversy on an identical point seems to have taken place in *Quarterly Journal of Economics*, November 1956. See Hans Neisser, op. cit., and Galenson and Leibenstein, 'Reply', op. cit.

Before we move over to the next model, we may summarize the observations we have made on the connexions between labour-cost and technological choice. (1) Even if there is a lot of unemployment in an economy and the social opportunity cost of using labour is nil, it will be a mistake, if we are interested in the rate of growth of the economy, to treat labour as costless and to substitute capital by labour whenever possible. (2) If the rate of growth is our criterion, lower wages should influence our choice in favour of lower capital intensity, though in many cases, due to the discontinuity of the production function, this point is of only academic interest. (3) The higher the amount of former consumption of the newly employed people that can be recovered through taxation, or compulsory delivery, or other means, the lower should be the capital intensity chosen, given a continuous production function.

(*ii*) The Second Model. Let us now release the assumption that machinery can be produced by labour alone, which means we also have to give up the assumption of the economy being closed, as an economy which is just starting to develop has to import some machinery (at least to make other machinery) to be in a position to exploit modern technology rather than re-enact the whole drama of industrial revolution from beginning to end step by step. It is assumed that while machinery for technique L can be produced by labour alone, that for technique H needs capital goods imported from abroad. This contrast agrees roughly with that between cottage industrial and factory production which all underdeveloped countries face. For a large number of processes, like spinning, weaving, oil-pressing, rice-pounding, this contrast is very sharp — cottage industrial production involves the use of very simple tools that can be easily produced and factory production involves much more sophisticated machinery that has to be imported from the industrially advanced countries. The choice between the two is very often one of the most controversial problems of development planning. For the sake of simplicity let us also assume that while the machines to make consumer goods last forever, machines to make machines wear away in a year.

Let us assume that in the case of technique H the value of machinery needed per person employed in department I at the initial foreign price is given by d. We assume, to start with, that such machines are in perfectly elastic supply. In the absence of foreign loans or aid, this foreign exchange has to be earned by exports. We assume that a part of the corn surplus is sent abroad and sold at a constant price g per unit. Thus to employ one man in department I (technique H) we need $\left(\bar{w} + \dfrac{d}{g} \right)$ amount of corn. This gives us a surplus-flow of $\left(\dfrac{P_c' - w}{a'} \right)$ amount of corn. If, on the other hand, we employed $\left(\bar{w} + \dfrac{d}{g} \right)$ amount of corn in department I with technique L, the surplus would have been

$$ N = \left(\bar{w} + \frac{d}{g} \right) \cdot \frac{1}{\bar{w}} \cdot \frac{P_c - w}{a} = \left(1 + \frac{d}{g\bar{w}} \right) \cdot \frac{P_c - w}{a} . $$

Therefore, assuming the same gestation lag for both the techniques, technique H is more, or less, surplus-yielding than technique L or equally so, according as

$$ \frac{P_c' - w}{a'} > , < \text{ or } = \frac{P_c - w}{a} \left(1 + \frac{d}{g\bar{w}} \right) . \tag{3} $$

When corn is not in perfectly elastic demand and foreign machinery is not in perfectly elastic supply, the condition naturally is more stringent. When η is the relevant arc elasticity of foreign demand for corn and e the relevant arc elasticity of supply of foreign machinery,[1] the condition to be satisfied becomes:

$$ \frac{P_{c'} - w}{a'} > , < \text{ or } = \frac{P_c - w}{a} \left[1 + \frac{d \left(1 + \dfrac{1}{e} \right)}{\bar{w}g \left(1 - \dfrac{1}{\eta} \right)} \right] . \tag{4} $$

[1] The use of the concept of elasticity here is a bit illegitimate, as in our model there is no trade prior to this transaction. In reality, however, we are likely to start with some trade and in actual cases the effect on other transactions has to be taken into account. In order to cope with both sorts of situations without making our formulae too complicated, the definition of arc elasticity we resort to is :

$$ \left(\frac{\text{change in quantity}}{\text{final quantity}} \Big/ \frac{\text{change in price}}{\text{original world market price}} \right) $$

When we start from a no-trade position, change in quantity is equal to final quantity, and the value of the elasticity reduces to the ratio of the other two terms.

A few conclusions follow from this. (1) The higher these elasticities, *ceteris paribus*, the higher should be the degree of capital intensity chosen, assuming that higher capital intensity in an underdeveloped economy goes with larger import-content because of the lack of a capital goods sector in the economy.

(2) Also the relevant elasticities are likely to be smaller when the volume of transactions are larger. As a result there is a sort of 'diminishing returns' with increased production employing the technique. Thus even if the more mechanized production is preferable up to a certain point, beyond that it may become less economic. Thus a development plan may involve both the more mechanized and the less mechanized techniques for the production of the same commodities.

(3) This also makes it desirable, given the values, for the state to intervene in the technical decisions taken by the private sector. The private entrepreneur may take into account the rise in the price of foreign machinery but not the increase in the quantity of exports necessary to pay for one unit of imports.

(4) The dependence of the choice of technology on the trade elasticities leads to an interesting possibility of asymmetry. Even if it is profitable not to *import* foreign machinery and to apply the less mechanized technique L, it does not follow that if these advanced machines were given to the country, the right course for it would be to export them and to use the proceeds for production with less mechanized techniques.

Let η_1 be the relevant arc elasticity of foreign demand for machinery and e_1 the relevant arc elasticity of foreign supply of corn. If a machine is sold abroad, the earning of foreign exchange is $d\left(1-\dfrac{1}{\eta_1}\right)$

With that the amount of corn that can be imported is given by $\dfrac{d\left(1-\dfrac{1}{\eta_1}\right)}{g\left(1+\dfrac{1}{e_1}\right)}$. Thus instead of employing the machine (technique H) in

the country and getting a surplus flow $\dfrac{P_c{}'-\bar{w}}{a'}$, if $\left[\bar{w}+\dfrac{d\left(1-\dfrac{1}{\eta_1}\right)}{g\left(1+\dfrac{1}{e_1}\right)}\right]$

amount of corn is employed in department I for technique L, the surplus-flow we get is:

$$\bar{N} = \left[\bar{w} + \frac{d\left(1 - \frac{1}{\eta_1}\right)}{g\left(1 + \frac{1}{e_1}\right)} \right] \frac{P_c - w}{a} \cdot \frac{1}{\bar{w}} \cdot$$

We should prefer technique H, or technique L, or be indifferent, according as:

$$\frac{P_c' - w}{a'} > , < \text{ or } = \frac{P_c - w}{a} \left[\bar{w} + \frac{d\left(1 - \frac{1}{\eta_1}\right)}{g\left(1 + \frac{1}{e_1}\right)} \right] \cdot \frac{1}{\bar{w}} \cdot \quad (5)$$

Thus there is a range within which it would be economic to *use* technique H-machinery if one has any, but not to *import* any if one has none. From relations (4) and (5), we get the condition as:

$$\frac{P_c - w}{a}\left[1 + \frac{d\left(1 + \frac{1}{e}\right)}{\bar{w}g\left(1 - \frac{1}{\eta}\right)}\right] > \frac{P_c' - w}{a'} > \frac{P_c - w}{a}\left[1 + \frac{d\left(1 - \frac{1}{\eta_1}\right)}{\bar{w}g\left(1 + \frac{1}{e_1}\right)}\right]. \quad (6)$$

The width of the range within which the value of $\dfrac{P_c' - w}{a'}$ must lie is given by

$$R = N - \bar{N}$$

$$= \frac{P_c - w}{a} \cdot \frac{d}{\bar{w}g}\left[\frac{\left(1 + \frac{1}{e}\right)}{\left(1 - \frac{1}{\eta}\right)} - \frac{\left(1 - \frac{1}{\eta_1}\right)}{\left(1 + \frac{1}{e_1}\right)} \right]$$

$$= \frac{P_c - w}{a} \cdot \frac{d}{\bar{w}g} \cdot \alpha, \text{ putting } \alpha \text{ for the expression within brackets.}$$

The lower these elasticities the higher is the value of α and the larger is the range R. If for example, $e = e_1 = \eta = \eta_1 = 2$, the value of $\alpha = 2 \cdot 67$. If on the other hand, $e = e_1 = \eta = \eta_1 = 3$, the value of $\alpha = 1 \cdot 5$. The limiting case is where $e = e_1 = \eta = \eta_1 = \infty$ when $\alpha = 0$ and the range does not exist, $R = 0$. On the other extreme, if $\eta = \eta_1 = 1$, the range is infinite and any value of $\dfrac{P_c' - w}{c'}$ would satisfy the asymmetry.

This is likely to be a very important practical consideration for actual decision-making as (*a*) the trade elasticities are often quite low and (*b*) the import-content of factory investment, given by

$$\left[\frac{d}{g}\bigg/\left(\frac{-}{w}+\frac{d}{g}\right)\right],$$ is often quite high compared with cottage industrial

production of the same goods involving practically no imports.[1] This may be a case for the Indian planning policy of (i) building up a capital goods sector to produce machinery for *domestic use* in the future, and (ii) the production of consumer goods as much as possible by cottage industrial methods for the time being, which has led to a not inconsiderable amount of discussion on 'inconsistency' in public policy.[2]

This aspect of the problem has unfortunately been neglected in most of the discussions on the question. For example, the otherwise excellent report on *Processes and Problems of Industrialization in Underdeveloped Countries* published by the United Nations has possibly the wrong end of the stick altogether when, referring to the temporary control of factory-consumer goods industries in India to help the cottage industries, it declares: 'Such a damping down of production is *obviously* not in the interest of rapid industrialization: it is part of the price paid for easing transition from manual to mechanical production and for preventing the sudden dissolution of the ancient industrial organization. . . .'[3] On the contrary, it is possible that such a temporary damping down of factory consumer-goods production may indeed help us to have the most rapid industrialization that the economy can achieve, by supplying consumer goods with the help of primitive techniques until the growing factory industries in

---

[1] When the possibility of importing consumer goods is included, even cottage industrial production may, however, have some indirect import-content arising out of its income effect.

[2] Whether this was *actually* the consideration which prompted the Government of India to take recourse to this asymmetrical policy, it is difficult to say, as the government has not yet bothered to tell us what criterion it adopts in choosing between techniques. Also, one must remember, that the above argument can be valid only as far as the government control of the creation of *new* output capacity is concerned. This provides no argument for the restriction of factory output *below capacity*.

[3] United Nations, 1955, ch. 3, p. 49, italics mine.

the economy begin to supply the machinery needed for factory production.

(*iii*) The Third Model. In this model we release the assumption of an absolute preference for a higher rate of growth and use the concept of 'recovery' discussed earlier. We employ the notation of the previous models and, to keep the illustration simple, go back to the assumptions of a closed economy and of machinery being produced by labour alone.

Let us assume that while the less capital-intensive technique (L) offers a higher rate of turnover, it offers a lower rate of investible net surplus, i.e., while $\dfrac{P_c'}{a'} < \dfrac{P_c}{a}$, $\dfrac{P_c' - w}{a'} > \dfrac{P_c - w}{a}$. Let Y_0 be the output of sector B (the subsistence sector) which remains unchanged in spite of the exodus of population from it to the 'advanced' sector.[1] Let S be the amount of corn surplus extracted from sector B every year from year zero. With technique L, consumer goods output in the first period is $\left(Y_0 + \dfrac{SP_c}{\overline{w}a} \right)$. In the second period we get in addition an output of $\dfrac{SP_c(P_c - w)}{(\overline{w}a)^2}$ from the capital stock created by the surplus (sector A) of the first period, and an output of $\dfrac{SP_c}{\overline{w}a}$ from the same year's extraction of S amount of corn from sector B. Thus the time series of real consumption flows, when technique L is chosen, is given by:

$$Y_1 = Y_0 + \frac{S}{\overline{w}} \cdot \frac{P_c}{a}$$

$$Y_2 = Y_0 + \frac{S}{\overline{w}} \cdot \frac{P_c}{a} \left[1 + \left(1 + \frac{P_c - w}{a\overline{w}} \right) \right]$$

---

[1] Our model is based on a number of simplifying assumptions like those of unlimited supply of labour force from the unemployment pool of the subsistence sector, absence of depreciation, unchanging technical knowledge and so on, which are clearly unrealistic. But as the model is for illustrative purpose only, this does not really matter. When, however, we try to apply this approach to actual problems, these complications have to be introduced.

$$Y_3 = Y_0 + \frac{S}{\overline{w}} \cdot \frac{P_c}{a} \left[1 + \left(1 + \frac{P_c - w}{a\overline{w}} \right) + \left(1 + \frac{P_c - w}{a\overline{w}} \right)^2 \right]$$

.

.

.

$$Y_n = Y_0 + \frac{S}{\overline{w}} \cdot \frac{P_c}{a} \left[1 + \left(1 + \frac{P_c - w}{a\overline{w}} \right) + \left(1 + \frac{P_c - w}{a\overline{w}} \right)^2 + \right.$$
$$\left. \ldots\ldots\ldots + \left(1 + \frac{P_c - w}{a\overline{w}} \right)^{n-1} \right]$$

$$= Y_0 + \frac{S}{\overline{w}} \cdot \frac{P_c}{a} \cdot \frac{\left(1 + \dfrac{P_c - w}{a\overline{w}} \right)^n - 1}{\dfrac{P_c - w}{a\overline{w}}}$$

$$= Y_0 + S \cdot P_c \cdot \frac{\left(1 + \dfrac{P_c - w}{a\overline{w}} \right)^n - 1}{P_c - w}$$

The sum of the series up to t th year is given by

$$\sum_{n=1}^{n=t} Y_n = tY_0 + \sum_{n=1}^{n=t} SP_c \frac{\left(1 + \dfrac{P_c - w}{a\overline{w}} \right)^n - 1}{(P_c - w)}.$$

This gives us the *total* consumption of the nation over t years, when technique L is chosen. Similarly, when technique H is chosen, the same is given by $\sum_{n=1}^{n=t} Y_n' = tY_0 + \sum_{n=1}^{n=t} SP_c' \dfrac{\left(1 + \dfrac{P_c' - w}{a'\overline{w}} \right)^n - 1}{(P_c' - w)}.$

The difference between the two sums can be expressed as

$$D_t = S \cdot \frac{P_c'}{P_c' - w} \cdot \sum_{n=1}^{n=t} \left[\left(1 + \frac{P_c' - w}{a'\overline{w}} \right)^n - 1 \right]$$
$$- S \cdot \frac{P_c}{P_c - w} \cdot \sum_{n=1}^{n=t} \left[\left(1 + \frac{P_c - w}{a\overline{w}} \right)^n - 1 \right].$$

The least value of t that makes $D_t \geqslant 0$, is the 'period of recovery', T. If T is shorter than the period we are going to take into account, U, technique H is preferable. If it is longer, technique L is to be chosen.

If we put $U = t = 1$, D_t reduces to $\dfrac{S}{w} \left(\dfrac{P_c'}{a'} - \dfrac{P_c}{a} \right)$. This is

negative and we choose technique L. If, on the other hand, we put

$U = t = \infty$, D_t must be positive as $\dfrac{P_c' - w}{a'} > \dfrac{P_c - w}{a}$; thus

technique H is chosen. The first represents, in our model, the rate-of-turnover and the SMP criteria and the second the rate-of-reinvestment criterion. In the last analysis these criteria are found to be the limiting cases of a more general approach.

SECOND THOUGHTS ON CAPITAL INTENSITY OF INVESTMENT*

by Maurice Dobb

I

The term capital intensity has been traditionally taken to mean the ratio of capital to labour. Labour may be measured in terms of quantity of labour (e.g., in man-hours) over a certain period such as a year, or alternatively in terms of the wage-bill over a certain period. Capital may be taken as including both fixed and circulating capital (which involves an awkward double-counting element by including the fund devoted to purchasing labour — unless this is deliberately excluded as it is from Marx's 'constant capital' and hence from his 'organic composition' ratio); or alternatively capital may be confined to fixed capital, which has certain obvious advantages. When we generalize the notion from a particular industry (or even a particular piece of homogeneous equipment) to the economy as a whole, the well-known difficulties about valuing capital inevitably enter, and may affect the resulting ratio even when one is concerned with differences or changes in an ordinal sense. For those schools of thought that treat capital as reducible essentially to time, the quantity of capital is expressed as some 'period of production' or 'investment period'.[1] Mr Kaldor has stated that the nature of capital as a collection of heterogeneous objects makes 'the ratio between capital and labour ... not so immediately obvious as, say, the ratio between factor A and factor B, where both these factors are viewed as a collection of physically homogeneous units. In fact, there is no absolute, or unique, measure of this ratio. But one can conceive several "indices" which give an "ordinal" measurement of it'.[2] He goes on to suggest that 'such an index is the ratio between "initial cost" and "annual cost" involved in the production of a certain stream of output.' 'The relation between

* *Review of Economic Studies*, 1956-7. Reprinted with the permission of the *Review of Economic Studies*, and the author.

[1] Cf. Martin Hill in *Economic Journal*, December 1933, pp. 601 and 609; C. H. P. Gifford, ibid., p. 617; F. A. Hayek, *Pure Theory of Capital*, pp. 73, 83.

[2] 'Capital Intensity and the Trade Cycle', *Economica*, February 1939, p. 42.

initial outlay and annual outlay can be regarded as a measure of the proportion in which "capital" and "other factors" are combined in a particular productive unit, i.e., of its "capital intensity" of production. . . . Increasing the degree of (normal) capital intensity thus implies the installation of superior equipment with a greater labour-saving capacity.'[1]

This ratio is not the same (nor need it change in the same way) as the capital : output ratio on which attention has recently been focussed (and in terms of which capital-intensity is sometimes measured, if not defined).[2] How the latter moves relatively to the former will depend on the change in labour productivity resulting from any change in technique. If, however (although, only if), one makes the somewhat drastic assumption of changes in technical methods proceeding within a framework of 'given technical knowledge', one can conclude (on the basis of 'diminishing returns' to the use of more capital with a given quantity of labour) that the two ratios will tend to move in the same direction. (Otherwise, if labour productivity were to rise in greater proportion than the capital : labour ratio, the capital : output ratio would, of course, *fall* when the other ratio rose.) In comparing different lines and forms of investment there is no reason at all (as we shall see) for associating a difference in the one ratio with a like difference in the other.[3]

It is easy enough to visualize the technical reality implied in such a capital : labour ratio, even if the translation of the technical picture into economic terms (of social cost or of value) involves

[1] Ibid., pp. 43f. Elsewhere Mr Kaldor says : 'Where the investment period is a definable concept, it provides a good index to the degree of capital intensity' ; and again, 'fundamentally both these concepts [investment period and degree of capital intensity] attempt to do no more than to measure the quantity of capital by measuring the ratio of the stock of capital goods to other factors'. (*Econometrica*, April 1938, pp. 169f.)

[2] e.g., Professor Hawtrey identified his 'deepening' with 'an increase in the amount of capital employed for each unit of output', (*Capital and Employment*, 1937, p. 36).

[3] For examples of the fallacy involved in confusing the two ratios see citations given by A. E. Kahn in *Quarterly Journal of Economics*, February 1951, pp. 39f, reprinted in the present volume, pp. 132f ; also further comments on the same point by W. Galenson and H. Leibenstein in *Quarterly Journal of Economics*, August 1955, pp. 346f, 351, reprinted in the present volume pp. 185f, 190f respectively.

difficulties; and one can, of course, apply the notion both to production as a whole, with its existing stock of technical equipment and productive methods, and to the technical forms which *new* investment assumes. For questions of investment policy it will be the latter that will have the greater interest. What is less clear is whether this ratio is also connected with the 'depth' of the capital structure in the sense of its distribution between final stages of production close to the consumer and 'earlier' stages concerned with intermediate, or producers', goods — or more shortly, its distribution between consumer-goods industries and capital-goods industries. Analogy with the 'time structure of production' and the 'investment period' (with its notion of 'stages' in a 'vertical division of labour ')[1] suggests that this is another facet of the same relation; and in discussions of investment policy and economic development (e.g., in underdeveloped countries), it has been quite commonly taken for granted that to devote a high proportion of investment to the capital-goods industries is a sign of high capital-intensity of investment and is governed by the same principles as the choice of highly labour-saving technical forms.[2] If we view the matter in investment-period terms, it seems evident that labour employed in erecting a steel plant is more distant from any resulting increase of final (consumers') output than labour devoted to making or erecting looms.

Under stationary conditions with no net investment 'capital structure' in the one sense will be, it is true, an index of capital-intensity in the more usual (technical) sense (given a constant replacement-rate of equipment): indeed 'depth' in the former, however measured, will be a necessary equilibrium condition of a high ratio of the latter. But as soon as we depart from stationary conditions and have new investment in the picture, this no longer follows, and we have no right to identify the two notions, whether we are speaking of the 'depth' of the capital structure as a whole or of its rate of change as a result of the distribution of new invest-

---

[1] Cf. Hayek, op. cit., pp. 73f; also R. G. Hawtrey's 'generations of instruments', *Capital and Employment*, pp. 21f.

[2] One reason for this supposition may be that a low interest rate has been regarded as an encouragement both to labour-saving technique and to a high rate of investment, both of which tend to encourage a high rate of expansion of the capital-goods industries.

ment. We shall see that there is at least one very important difference
between them.

II

In discussion during recent years of the appropriate criteria for
investment policy in underdeveloped countries it was at first taken
for granted that the maximizing theorems usually employed in
static analysis (with *given* resources and given wants) were applicable. It is now coming to be recognized that such theorems are
in fact not applicable to conditions of development, at least without
substantial qualification, even when the marginal productivities in
terms of which these theorems are framed are defined as *social* net
products. Instead of an equalization of marginal social net products,
two recent writers have spoken of a 'marginal *per capita* reinvestment quotient' as a criterion.[1] But even when discussion has
turned in the direction of specifically dynamic criteria, there would
seem still to be room for clearer definition of what it is that should
be maximized. As we shall try to show, one may arrive at very
different conclusions according to the way in which one's policy-
objectives are defined. Moreover, it is not only a matter of defining
policy-objectives: one's very analysis of the problem will be dependent on the view one takes of the factors that determine investment
in an economic system at any given point of time.

In a very simplified two-industry model used elsewhere by the
present writer[2] the crucial investment determinant was taken to be
the supply of wage-goods, or subsistence, available to those employed
in the capital-goods industry; this being dependent in turn on the
difference between production and consumption (wages) in the
wage-goods industry (agriculture, producing corn). Writing L_c for
the labour in the wage-goods industry (which was assumed to be
determined by the existing stock and type of capital equipment
available to that industry),[3] P_c for the productivity per worker in

[1] W. Galenson and H. Leibenstein, loc. cit., p. 351, present volume p. 191:
this quotient should be equalized 'in its various alternative uses '; with the
result of maximizing 'the *per capita* output potential at some future point in
time '.

[2] In *Economie Appliquée*, 1954, No. 3, reprinted in his *On Economic Theory
and Socialism*, p. 138.

[3] The actual assumption was that of fixed coefficients for any given type
of capital equipment : e.g., one tractor, one tractor-driver, whatever the
power of the tractor might be.

the given period and w for the real wage per worker, potential investment, measured by the amount of employment in the capital-goods industry (L_i), was governed by $\dfrac{L_c\,(P_c - w)}{w}$. While the rate of investment was always subject to this constraint (given the level of w)[1], investment policy had a choice between different types of capital goods (e.g., types of tractors), costing different amounts of labour to manufacture but yielding different levels of labour productivity (P_c) when put to use in the consumer-goods industry[2].

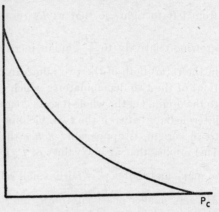

Writing P_i as productivity per worker in the capital-goods industry in terms of product units (e.g., tractors), the alternatives open to investment policy can be represented by a curve showing the relationship between a falling P_i and a rising P_c as the form of investment becomes more capital-intensive. It is to be noted that P_i is here taken as an index of capital intensity, since a rise in it is associated with the use of more expensive capital goods (e.g., tractors) with a given amount of labour in the consumer-goods industry.

The fall of the curve from left to right depends on the assumption of a rising cost in labour of more capital-intensive capital goods. There could be various relationships, however, between the changes in P_i and P_c. On the one hand, these might be so related that a proportional rise in P_i involved a proportional fall in P_c; in which

---

[1] A crucial assumption of this model was that the supply of labour to industry was perfectly elastic (owing, e.g., to large rural over-population), so that there was no constraint on investment *other* than the available surplus of wage-goods.

[2] P_c may be regarded simply as productivity per worker, say, per annum (and w analogously as the annual real wage per worker) on the assumption that capital goods once created are eternal, or alternatively as productivity per worker net of amortization of the machine if the latter is assumed to have a determinate length of life.

case our curve would be a rectangular hyperbola. This would imply that δP_i (which is, of course, of minus sign) gets *smaller* relatively to δP_c as P_c rises — in other words, that it gets progressively easier without limit to raise P_c further as capital intensity rises. This does not seem a very realistic assumption to make in a *given* state of technical knowledge; and seems to run counter to the conventional assumption of 'diminishing returns' to labour applied to increasing the capital intensity of capital goods. On the other hand, δP_i could not be growing relatively to δP_c as one moved from left to right, so that as P_c rose the value of $\dfrac{\delta P_i}{P_i}$ would be growing relatively to $\dfrac{\delta P_c}{P_c}$ at an increasing rate owing to changes in the ratios both of the two numerators and (in an opposite direction) of the two denominators; which would yield a curve concave to the origin. On the whole it seems reasonable to assume a situation intermediate between the two, yielding a curve that, while convex to the origin, is appreciably *flatter* than a rectangular hyperbola. This implies that at low values of P_c capital goods are very cheap to make and that $\dfrac{\delta P_i}{P_i}$ is fairly small relatively to $\dfrac{\delta P_c}{P_c}$. As P_c rises, δP_i gets smaller relatively to δP_c but not in a very marked degree; so that at high values of P_c (i.e., towards the right half of the curve) $\dfrac{\delta P_i}{P_i}$ (which will be of minus sign) will be large relatively to $\dfrac{\delta P_c}{P_c}$, and there will be an absolute limit to the possible rising of P_c.

From the curve of this first diagram can be derived the following relationship between the combined productivity of labour in both sectors of industry and the productivity of labour in the consumer-goods sector as capital intensity of investment changes. The former

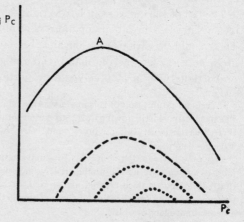

quantity, the ordinate of our second diagram, can be regarded as a measure of the ultimate productivity (in terms of final output of consumer goods at a later date) of labour employed in making capital goods for the consumer goods industry. The curve of the relationship between this quantity and changes in capital intensity as measured by P_c derives its peaked shape from the assumptions stated in the last paragraph about the curve of our first diagram.[1]

What is the correct position on this curve to choose?

About points on the left-hand slope it would seem that there could be no doubt or dispute. Is there not clearly gain and no loss in moving up-hill to the summit (marked A) which represents the maximum value of P_iP_c, and hence the most advantageous use of labour in the capital-goods industry? Until this point is reached, the rise of productivity from rising capital intensity more than offsets the rise in cost of making the capital goods in question.[2] Since at A the labour employed in the capital-goods industry achieves its maximum effect in adding to the final output of consumer goods, this might seem to be unquestionably the correct position for investment policy to choose.

An answer cannot, however, be given to this question until we have first postulated the objective of investment policy; and the policy objectives may be various. In the first place this may be to maximize employment in the near future; in which case it is by no means clear that one should follow the curve to its summit at A. Since employment in the capital-goods industry is at any time fixed (given w) for the reasons we have given, employment in the

---

[1] The values of P_iP_c, as measured along the ordinate of the second diagram, represent successive rectangles under the curve of the first diagram. If, therefore, the latter curve were a rectangular hyperbola, the curve of the second diagram would be a horizontal straight line. It is our assumption that the curve of the first diagram is *flatter* than a rectangular hyperbola (and *a fortiori* if it is concave to the origin) which gives the curve of the second diagram its peaked shape ; the condition for the latter reaching the maximum value of P_iP_c at A being that $\dfrac{\delta P_c}{P_c} \bigg/ \dfrac{-\delta P_i}{P_i} = -1$ and that

$\delta \left(\dfrac{P_i}{P_c} \dfrac{\delta P_c}{\delta P_i} \right)$ is negative.

[2] It is to be noted that this curve has *not* the same properties as the curve which is sometimes used to relate capital intensity (expressed as a ratio of capital to labour) to average productivity of labour. In the latter case total output (with a *given* amount of capital) is *not* rising up to the summit of the curve (since employment is falling).

consumer-goods industry (assuming this to depend on the amount and type of equipment available to it) will be maximized by choosing to invest in very cheap equipment — in other words, one will choose a position as far as possible to the left of A, with a low P_c but a high P_i. If, however, one is seeking to maximize the value of the national income in the present, one will then choose the summit of the curve at A. It may be noted incidentally that at this point the capital: output ratio will be minimized (though *not* the capital: labour ratio). But if, *per contra*, the aim is to bring about the maximum rate of increase of investment (in other words, the maximum acceleration of the rate of growth of the economy as a whole), then one will go beyond A down the *right-hand* slope. One will do so because, although total production will be smaller than if one had stopped at A, the labour-saving effect of higher capital intensity in the wage-goods industry (i.e., the rise of P_c *per se*) will cause the *surplus* of wage-goods to continue to rise as one moves down the right-hand slope beyond A. This surplus will be maximized (given L_i) when P_i $(P_c - w)$ is maximized; and the degree of capital intensity where this is so will represent a higher value of P_c than that at which $P_i P_c$ is maximized.

How far down the right-hand slope beyond A this new point will be evidently depends upon the level of w.[1] The higher is this level, the more important is the w-saving effect of higher capital intensity (or, the smaller is the quantity $\dfrac{P_c - w}{P_c}$, the larger will be the proportionate change in it from any given change in P_c). This can be represented by introducing into our previous diagram a series of curves indicating the relationship of P_c, not to $P_i P_c$, but to P_i $(P_c - w)$. One will then have from left to right a series of curves for different values of w; these curves having their peaks at higher values of P_c than the peak of the main curve (i.e., their peaks will be to the *right* of A, and successively further to the right the higher is the value of w).

This dependence of the optimum degree of capital intensity upon the level of wages, although it was implicit in the writer's article that has been mentioned, should no doubt have been made more

---

[1] And also, if w moves over time with changes in P_c (i.e., if policy provides for some rise in the standard of life with rising labour productivity in the wage-goods industry), upon the nature of this relationship between changing w and changing P_c.

explicit.[1] Once it has been granted, does not the traditional view that choice of capital-intensity should be governed by factor proportions re-enter by the backdoor? It is true that on certain assumptions this is the case. But before one hastens to conclude that a low-wage country must always choose a lower degree of capital intensity of investment, it should be noted that what is relevant here is wages as a ratio to labour productivity (i.e., w/P_c in our notation); and only if this ratio is lower in underdeveloped than in developed countries will the traditional corollary hold.

The relevant comparison here is, of course, the ratio of wages to productivity with any given technique, and not the ratio actually prevailing in the countries under comparison, since the latter will be influenced by the techniques adopted in the two countries, which may be themselves the resultant of the prevailing wage : productivity ratios for given techniques (or for the range of possible techniques). If one adopts the assumption that labour productivity depends exclusively on the technical equipment with which labour works (or the proportions in which factors are combined in production) and that labour is the same factor of production (in the sense of having the same intrinsic capabilities) in all countries, then it can easily be shown that higher capital intensity is appropriate to a country with a high (absolute) wage-level than is appropriate to a country of lower wages. This may be referred to, perhaps, as the Samuelsonian case (since the train of argument involved is analogous to that used by Professor Samuelson in propounding a well-known proposition about international factor-price equalization). If one holds, *per contra*, that labour productivity is dependent to any considerable degree upon the level of wages, and will be high or low under any given technique according as the wages and the standard of life are high or low, the Samuelsonian corollary need no longer apply. For any given technique (or the whole range of alternative techniques) it is possible that the wage : productivity ratio may be the same in a country where labour is cheap as in a country where labour is dear. The view that differences of diet and standards of life are associated with different intrinsic efficiencies was, of course, the basis of the century-old 'economy of high wages'

[1] While it was mentioned on p. 310 of the article (p. 147 of the book), it should have been explicitly mentioned five pages earlier (pp. 305 and 143 respectively) where it was implicit, but no more, in a footnote that attempted to define the optimum degree of capital-intensity if surplus is to be maximized.

principle, which during the past century has accumulated a large amount of evidence in its own support. It is possible that growing automation, relegating labour to the role of a mere supervisor of machines, is reducing the importance of this association today. But with traditional techniques, at least, it looks as though the association of high productivity both with high capital intensity and high wages may be at least as much because high wages are a necessary condition (from the subsistence angle) for maintaining the high work intensities that advanced techniques involve as because the adoption of advanced techniques is prompted by the dearness of labour. At any rate the association between these three variables is evidently a complex one of mutual, rather than simple one-way, determination.

Another assumption implicit in the 'Samuelsonian case' is that the existence of a surplus of labour (in the shape of actual or 'disguised' unemployment) will cause the wage-level of those in employment to fall to the level of the potential productivity of the marginal unit of this labour reserve (which may be very close to zero if one is referring to the rural surplus population working primitively at some margin of village occupations). Only then will the corollary that a relatively abundant population necessitates labour-intensive forms of investment apply, since only then will the size of the labour reserve be directly relevant to the wage level in industry and hence to the choice of industrial technique. It is commonly the case, however, in predominantly agrarian countries that industrial wages are substantially higher than wages in rural employments; this differential being often of the order of magnitude of 2 : 1 or even more. Whether this difference is to be explained by the kind of consideration mentioned in the last paragraph or by imperfect mobility between village and town or by some combination of both is a question into which we need hardly enter here.[1] But clearly it is the former wage-level that is relevant to any decision about investment forms in factory industry and not the purely 'notional wage' of the rural unemployed (what point can there be in maximizing a purely notional surplus?).

---

[1] Cf. on this some remarks of Professor W. A. Lewis in 'Economic Development with Unlimited Supplies of Labour', *The Manchester School*, May 1954, p. 150, reprinted in Agarwala and Singh (eds.), *The Economics of Underdevelopment*, Oxford University Press, 1958, pp. 411f.

If one's policy is to maximize employment in the present or near future, then of course the right answer may be to put no investment at all into factory industry, and instead to equip every surplus hand in the village with a spade or a hoe (or at least a trowel). Yet again, if town and village are to be treated as two separate sectors of the economy, having different *kinds* of labour with different wage levels, then, even though maximizing employment is not one's exclusive aim, it may be right to adopt different and apparently contradictory technical forms in the two sectors, as does the Indian Second Five Year Plan which combines ambitious investment in modern steel plants with considerable investments in cottage industry.

To put the whole issue of rival policy objectives in perspective, one should perhaps add this in parenthesis. It is as well to remember that a course of increasing total investment at the maximum possible rate may do more within the not-so-distant future to absorb any reserve army of rural unemployed into employment (as Soviet experience shows; employment having there increased to between 4 and 5 times what it was 25 to 30 years ago) than the minimum-capital-intensive use of the existing investment potential (at the expense of its growth-rate) can do in the near future. In other words, maximizing investment potential and maximizing employment may only be in conflict as policy objectives within a fairly narrow time horizon; and discussion of such matters might be less at cross-purposes if the participants were careful to indicate the time-dimension to which their maximizing propositions referred.

III

In many types of constructional work (rail- and road- and canal-making or building are obvious examples) the higher cost of a more complex project (a lower P_i in our notation) may express itself in the use of a larger quantity of labour and resources at any one time or in the use of a smaller amount of labour over a longer period of time. In the former case the choice of the more complex project will involve a reduction in the number of parallel and competing projects that can be undertaken at any time (with a given total investment potential). In the latter case there need be no reduction in the number of parallel projects *started* together; but there must obviously be a reduction in the number of such projects that can be *completed* during any stretch of time (say, a quinquennium or a decade), compared with what could have been if simpler and less costly ones had been chosen instead. Accordingly, nothing is gained (indeed something may be lost) by adopting the second alternative instead of the first; and it is immaterial whether one conceives of extra cost in terms of extra labour (in the sense of the input of a larger proportion of a *given* investment potential per unit of time) or in terms of extra time.

There may well be certain types of capital goods or constructional projects, however, that require a certain minimum period for their completion, or at least can only be completed more quickly than this by incurring certain additional costs, so that a production period of a minimum length represents the least-cost method.[1] In so far as this is so, there will be two distinct ways in which future productivity can be increased: by investing more labour initially or by using more time in the sense of lengthening the period between the start and the completion of an investment project. We could represent the latter by adding a third dimension to our previous diagram. From any point on the curve in the second diagram it would be possible to travel backwards in that dimension (with an eastward inclination) and uphill; each such movement representing a move to a higher P_c *without* any fall in P_i (since more time and not more labour is in this case the price of the higher P_c). As one moves

[1] The reason for this, if it is not some technical constant such as the maturing period of a wine or the cooling period of a metal, must presumably be some bottleneck factor in the existing equipment of the capital-goods industries, causing 'short-period diminishing returns'. Such bottleneck difficulties will be relative to the demand on the capital-goods industries (or of special sectors of them) at any one time; and one way of reducing this demand will be to extend the period of construction of the various projects. Extensions of this period will progressively ease the pressure on bottlenecks, *ceteris paribus*, and hence progressively involve an economy; so that a picture of falling cost with lengthening of period may be a truer one than that of a minimum period. But it is important to bear in mind that, where bottleneck easing is the reason for the economy, the degree of economy associated with any degree of lengthening of the period cannot be postulated independently of the total number (and character) of the investment projects in train; and in so far as it is *only* a matter of pressure on bottlenecks, the same result could be achieved by reducing the total number of projects started at one time and finishing them more quickly, without any sacrifice of the number of completions over a series of years (from a social standpoint mere dragging out of the production period could have no advantage *per se*).

backwards and uphill, the slope of the hill will become progressively less steep (if we adopt an analogous 'diminishing returns' assumption about the effect on productivity of successive 'lengthening').

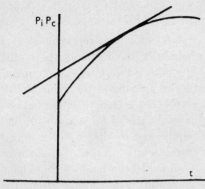

It might at first seem as though there could be no reasonable limit to this movement uphill until the summit of the time-hill was reached, by analogy with the movement uphill to A in the other (west-east) dimension in our second diagram. This, however, is not so, since lengthening the period before investment can bear fruit forfeits the advantage of having fruit available wherewith to augment the investment-potential at an *earlier date*. Hence, if one's aim is to maximize investment and/or output at some future date (or a series of dates), one may be losing on the swings of delay what one gains on the roundabouts of raised productivity. Buying higher productivity with successive lengthenings of the period will accordingly be confronted at some point with an offsetting disadvantage; the magnitude of this disadvantage depending upon the size of what has elsewhere been termed[1] the 'compounding effect' of reinvesting the earlier-accruing (though smaller) surplus from 'shorter methods'. This 'compounding effect', which consists of the capacity of any given investment to produce an increment of the investment potential within any given period, can be depicted in familiar fashion as a line rising at a certain angle from the time-axis (projected negatively) of our diagram. Its point of tangency with the slope of our 'hill' will then define the optimum degree of movement up the time-slope of the hill.[2] The ratio of wages to productivity (w/P_c) will again

---

[1] *Economie Appliquée*, 1954, No. 3, p. 309 (p. 146 of book).

[2] If we write $\frac{\delta s}{\delta t}$ as the compounding effect per unit of time, the point of tangency between line and curve will be where $\frac{\delta s}{\delta t} = \frac{\delta P_c P_i}{\delta t}$. For lower values of P_c lower on the slope $\frac{\delta s}{\delta t}$ will be smaller, and the slope of our line accordingly 'flatter'. As P_c rises with movement up the slope the line will become 'steeper' until its tangency with the slope halts further movement up the slope.

appear as a determinant of the angle of this ascending line, and hence of its point of tangency with the hill-slope; so that the result will depend on this ratio as it did in our previous case (the point of tangency coming earlier on the hill-slope, *ceteris paribus*, the lower the level of w relative to P_c).[1]

Hitherto we have taken no account of capital replacement as a demand upon the capital-goods industries (having implicitly treated capital goods once created as eternal — subject to current maintenance which could be allowed for in arriving at the value of P_c). Another form of what might be considered as 'lengthening', but one associated with a *fall* of P_c and possibly also of P_t, is a substitution of more for less durable capital equipment yielding a lower annual output (with or without lower current costs of operation) but over a longer physical life. In terms of our model this might seem to have nothing to commend it. Its compensating advantage (from the standpoint of growth) is that in future years it would enhance the share of the gross-investment potential available for net investment by reducing the replacement demand on the capital-goods industries (provided of course that this effect of greater durability was not offset by its greater cost). Clearly, however, such a change has nothing essentially to do with a change of capital intensity in the sense in which we have been discussing it.

IV

We have suggested above[2] that a leading, if not the main, reason why an extension of the period over which investment projects are stretched may increase productivity is the existence of bottlenecks in the conditions of supply of capital goods. To the extent that this is so, attention is shifted towards productive capacity in the capital-goods industry (e.g., steel-making capacity or machine-toolmaking capacity) as the determinant of investment and hence of the rate of economic growth. The model to which we have referred hitherto

---

[1] The optimum point can therefore be defined quite simply by measuring on the ordinate a length to represent the level of wages and from the point on the ordinate so reached drawing a tangent to the curve. The slope of this line will then represent the highest possible value of $\dfrac{\delta s}{\delta t}$.

[2] p. 224, fn. 1.

would then need appropriate adaptation to make fixed capital in this sector of industry the crucial investment determinant (instead of the supply of wage-goods).

If we were to adapt our model accordingly, we should have to assume that, in some sense or other, wage-goods were in perfectly elastic supply to the capital goods industry. The crucial decision would now consist, no longer of a choice between capital goods of different efficiencies for the consumer goods industries, but of a choice between making capital goods for consumer goods industries and making capital goods for expanding the capacity of the capital goods industry itself — making tractors or making machine-tools for making tractors. It would then follow that the larger the proportion of current investment devoted to the latter, the more rapid the rate of growth of the investment-potential of the economy; and that such investment has a growth-inducing capacity of a higher order than that of investment devoted to enlarging productive capacity for making consumer goods[1] (which in a planned economy would be equivalent, of course, to a decision to raise w by a given amount).

If we thus focus attention upon the decision concerning this crucial proportion, it becomes clear that there is no reason to suppose that a change in this proportion will change productivity, as we assumed in our previous model to be the result of changing the technical type of capital good that went into production. Nor does there seem to be any place in our re-adapted model for the 'diminishing returns' assumption of our previous one (on which the special shape of the curve of our diagram, rising to a peak and then falling, depended). Hence, if we were to relate changes in this crucial proportion to changes in output at any given future date, this relationship

---

[1] Indeed, whereas investment in building, say, a textile mill has a once-for-all effect in enlarging final (consumers') output when the mill goes into production, investment in a steel plant, by increasing the annual rate at which new textile mills, etc., can be built in the future, has an effect on the future *growth rate* of final output.

There will clearly be a certain distribution of investment between the two sectors that will maintain the growth rate of national income constant. A distribution of investment more favourable than this to the consumption-goods sector will cause the growth rate of the national income to decline and conversely. (Cf. the writer's 'Some Questions on Economic Growth', *Indian Journal of Economics*, July 1955, p. 8.)

when graphically expressed should be a linear one. There is accordingly no reason why the ratio of wages to productivity should play any part in determining this type of decision as it did with the previous one. Conditions of relative factor-supply can have nothing to do with the decision, which will be exclusively concerned with the rate at which it is thought desirable that output should grow.

It may be noted that in the case we are now considering any conflict between the policy aims of maximizing employment and maximizing the growth rate disappears, since (except to the extent that the techniques in use in capital goods industries are *per se* less labour using than those in consumer goods industries) whatever augments the investment potential will also augment employment both in the near and in the distant future.

In practice, however, it is unlikely that wage-goods will be in elastic supply; and accordingly in any actual situation one will need to take account of *both* types of investment determinant — the supply of wage-goods and the amount of capital equipment in the capital goods industry — if in different degrees in different circumstances. This will mean that in any actual situation a ceiling will be placed on the proportion of investment that can be devoted to the capital-goods sector by the need to provide an additional supply of consumer goods to cater for the increase in employment (and hence in the wage-bill) that any enlargement of productive capacity in the capital goods sector must involve. Here again in setting this ceiling (and in defining the maximum possible growth rate of the economy) both the capital intensity of investment and the level of wages will enter as determining factors: i.e., this ceiling will be higher, the higher is the capital intensity of investment in the capital-goods sector and the higher the ratio of productivity to wages relatively to the degree of capital intensity in the consumer-goods sector.

The *proportionate* expansion in the supply of consumer goods required by a given expansion of employment will of course be unaffected by whether the existing wage level is high or low. But the absolute size of the requisite increase, and hence the demand made for this purpose upon any given investment total, will be dependent on the level of wages. Thus a low-wage country might seem to demand a smaller slice of investment for consumer-goods industries, and hence to have a higher potential growth rate, were it not that the existing relative size of the capital goods industry in low-wage countries is likely to be equivalently small. This consideration indicates that the capacity for growth may be cumulative; since as a proportion of total investment the minimum requisite investment in consumer-goods industries (with a given wage level) will be smaller the larger is the relative size of the capital-goods industries; and as the latter grow, the larger the proportion of their output than can be devoted (if need be) to their own further enlargement.

INVESTMENT CRITERIA AND
THEIR APPLICATION*

(With particular reference to choice of projects and project designs)

by K. N. Raj

In framing a programme of development, there are a large number
of decisions about investment which have to be taken. There is,
in the first place, the decision about the rate of investment — how
high or low it should be. Secondly, there is the decision about the
distribution of investment between different categories — how much
should be allocated to industries, to agriculture, to social services,
etc. Then come the decisions about the location of investment, the
projects to be chosen within each category of investment, the
designs most preferable among the possible alternative designs for
a particular project, and the related problem of techniques.

The rate of investment and its distribution have both very important economic implications, but the decisive considerations in
fixing them are in the main social and political. Economic reasoning
can indicate the conditions and the relative rates of growth under
alternative assumptions, but cannot by itself offer criteria for choice
between alternative patterns of economic development; it is precisely such alternative patterns that are involved in the decisions
about the overall rate and distribution of investment. In the same
category of decisions may also be included, to some extent, those
which involve making a choice between the development of one
region and another.

But once these decisions have been taken, and the allocations have
been made for different types of investment and different regions,
the problem would remain of choosing between various projects
and project designs. The question that is posed in investment
decisions of this limited character would be typically something
like this: given the investment allocation, say, for the development
of irrigation, and alternative technical and locational possibilities,
how are alternative projects and project designs to be ranked and

* *Some Economic Aspects of the Bhakra-Nangal Project*, Asia Publishing
House, Bombay, 1960, pp. 15–34. Reprinted with the permission of the
Delhi School of Economics, University of Delhi, and the author.

some selected in preference to others? We shall have in mind here, primarily, investments which are meant to build up the 'overheads' of economic development.

If the choice of a project or project design is linked up with the development of a particular region, which is desired for one reason or another, it introduces a non-economic consideration and, as indicated earlier, economic reasoning and criteria alone cannot determine the choice. But even here, it may be useful to apply them and make an assessment of the economic cost, in the short run, of promoting the development of one region and fore-going in the process the exploitation of the possibilities elsewhere. More important is that, even if there is no choice in the matter of allocation due to considerations of regional development, a choice does often exist between alternative project designs, the social cost of some of which may be greater without correspondingly larger social returns. Certain project designs, for instance, may involve heavy initial investment, while other designs permit the phasing of the investment expenditure over a longer period and, at the same time, do not make any significant difference to the output for a period of years. To ignore altogether the economic considerations involved in alternative project designs, because the location is determined by non-economic value judgements, would be to place a premium on ventures that are unnecessarily capital-consuming; it would, indirectly, encourage wastage and bad planning of all kinds in the name of these larger values.

In other words, given the rate of investment and its broad allocation between different categories — in determining both of which various non-economic values and objectives are likely to be the decisive considerations — the scope and need for applying economic reasoning and criteria are greater the wider the range of technically feasible alternatives within each category.

This does not mean that the economic reasoning and criteria, to be applied to the type of investment decisions indicated, can be formulated independently of the social values and objectives on which the investment programme as a whole is based. Indeed, without them, it will be impossible to give any specific content to the concept of social economic value as distinct from private economic value. But it does mean that, given the larger social values and objectives already adopted in the process of choosing between alternative patterns of economic development, the modes of reasoning familiar in economic analysis can furnish a set of criteria which are logically consistent with these, and also some ideas as to how they may be applied to problems presented by the fact that different technical alternatives have different economic implications.

From the economic point of view the differences between alternative projects and project designs within given categories can be considered under four heads: (i) differences in the volume and type of the labour required for construction, (ii) differences in the volume and the type of equipment and materials required for construction, (iii) differences in the period involved in the construction, and in the life of the project, and (iv) differences in the volume of output consequent on the investment. The question is, on what basis a social valuation of the costs and returns involved in these differences can be attempted so as to be able to choose one alternative to another. In analysing below the problems of valuation involved, we shall take social cost to mean the 'opportunity cost' from the social point of view incurred by the use of scarce resources, and social returns to mean the additions to the output of the community as a whole.

SOCIAL COST OF EMPLOYMENT OF UNUTILIZED LABOUR

Let us first consider the problem of valuing the social cost of labour. It is usual to assume that there are large reserves of unemployed labour in underdeveloped economies. To the extent that such reserves exist, their utilization in investment projects does not obviously involve any reduction in output elsewhere, and it would be correct to say that it has no social cost, since society as a whole does not have to forgo anything in the process. It would follow that projects whose construction requires more labour are not more costly from the social point of view than those which require less; indeed, if the use of more labour helps to save other scarce resources in construction, the former would be preferable to the latter.

This line of reasoning may, however, be disputed on two grounds. Firstly, it can be argued that while surplus labour undoubtedly exists, in the sense that the aggregate output in such economies is likely to remain unaffected by a withdrawal of part of the labour available in the existing productive units, this labour is not always available for employment elsewhere, such as in investment projects.

What is implied here is that, though the productivity of a large part of the working population may in effect be zero, the supply price of labour is likely to be quite high (relatively to its marginal productivity) even in these economies. This becomes significant from the economic point of view if we concede the second line of argument, usually advanced alongside, that more employment also means more consumption on the part of those directly or indirectly involved, and that this additional consumption constitutes a social cost. On this line of reasoning, therefore, the lower the wage elasticity of the supply of labour, and the higher the propensity to consume out of additions to income, the larger is the social cost of employing additional labour in underdeveloped economies.

But the proposition that the additional consumption by those directly or indirectly benefiting from increased employment constitutes in itself a social cost cannot be accepted without qualification. It is true that if the aggregate output and, therefore, the total amount available for consumption remain the same as before, increased consumption on the part of some will necessarily mean that less is available for others. But however much this may appear as a cost to the latter, there is no reason whatever, from the economic point of view, to regard it as a cost to the society as a whole. In fact, in so far as the same volume of output as before is used to sustain a higher rate of investment, which in due course would increase output, it can be legitimately argued that a positive economic gain accrues to the society as a result of the redistribution.

The additional consumption can, however, be regarded as a social cost under two conditions: (a) if the reduction caused in the amount available to others for consumption leads either to a fall in their output or indirectly, after a time, to a curtailment of the surpluses marketed by them; and (b) if the pressure on available domestic supplies makes it necessary to draw upon scarce foreign exchange resources for supplementing them.

Both these possibilities figure very prominently among the considerations which are taken into account before arriving at decisions on the overall rate of investment under any given set conditions. It is common knowledge that increased incomes generated by higher rates of investment may lead to a scramble for resources; also, that the pressures created may, by their repercussions within the economy and on its foreign exchange position, impose a cost which the society is not in a position to bear. Consequently, the rate and the pattern of investment are usually so determined and arranged, at least in conception, as to prevent serious repercussions on either the stimulus to produce and exchange or on the foreign exchange position.

It does not, of course, follow that once the decisions on the overall rate and pattern of investment have been taken, the impact of the additional consumption demands generated by investment in a particular project can be disregarded. But it can be legitimately said that the larger decisions concerning the rate and the pattern of investment imply already certain assumptions regarding the likely effect of the investment on demand, the extent to which this demand can be suppressed without adverse consequences on output and investment, and the foreign exchange leakages that may be caused despite the planned increases in domestic supply. These assumptions could therefore provide certain norms in terms of which, at the next stage, the social cost of employing labour in alternative projects and project designs might be assessed and compared.

Thus, for instance, if the planned increase in the rate of investment is not large, and other factors like the method of financing this investment, the marginal propensity of the income recipients to consume, and the capital : output ratios are such that the additional demand created can be expected to be met by the anticipated increases in domestic supply, both the possibilities mentioned earlier, which would require us to impute a social cost to the employment of labour, would not arise. On the other hand, if these are such as to leave a large gap between the demand created and the supplies available and this gap needs to be covered in part by additional imports (or reduction of exports), a social cost must be imputed to the employment of labour.

We must also recognize that, even if the increases in domestic supply are adequate to meet the additional demand created, the investment required to produce these increases in supply may impinge on resources which have alternative uses from the social point of view. To the extent that this is true, the net additions to consumption on account of the employment of labour must still be regarded as having a social cost. Part of these net additions to consumption may be met by resources which have no immediate alternative uses (as, for instance, by neglected little patches of land in kitchen gardens being used to produce more vegetables), but it would be difficult to judge in each case which of the resources required have alternative uses and which have not. From a practical point of view, therefore, it may be better to treat the entire additions to consumption as a social cost in the first instance and revalue this cost later according to our assessment of how far they are met by resources which have no alternative uses, how far by drafts on foreign exchange, and how far by domestic resources which have alternative uses.

Given the proportion of the additional consumption which might involve drafts on foreign exchange, there is the question of how the social cost corresponding to this expenditure can be estimated. Following the above reasoning, it will be obvious that the cost must be reckoned as higher the greater the premium that needs to be placed on foreign exchange within the assumptions of the investment programme. If a high rate of investment, requiring imports of capital goods, is sought to be sustained without the assistance of foreign loans (or grants), the premium placed on foreign exchange will tend to be greater than otherwise. The actual premium will depend upon the elasticities of demand and supply of exports. The estimation of the appropriate premium may have to be based on rough assessments, but the essential point to note here is that the same amount of leakage in terms of foreign exchange may imply higher social cost under one set of conditions than in another.

It is only in these relative terms that the social cost of employing labour can be defined and concretized. For the social cost of the use of any particular resource depends, by the very nature of the concept, on the values applicable from the point of view of the society as a whole; these values are embodied partly in the premises underlying certain policy decisions taken by the society (or rather, its representatives) within a planned economy. The actual computation of social cost with reference to these premises will undoubtedly present many difficulties, and may have to be based on rough and ready methods, but if the analytical basis is clear it becomes easier to weigh the various considerations involved in each procedural issue and to judge what kind of assumptions and approximations one may proceed with in quantitative estimation.

Social Cost of Materials and of Machinery and Equipment

The same reasoning as is applied to the evaluation of the social cost of employing labour can also be applied to the evaluation of the social cost of materials, and of machinery and equipment, used for construction. There are certain types of materials such as stones, sand, gravel, earth, etc., which may be available in such abundance in certain areas that their use for new constructions does not require diversion from other lines of production. In these cases, the only social cost involved would be that, if any, on account of the labour which needs to be employed for digging them up and for processing them into a form in which they can be used; since these would already have been taken into account in computing the social cost of employment of labour, no further adjustment is really called for. But there are also materials which are scarce and have alternative uses within an investment programme, such as cement, steel, etc. The social cost of these must be regarded as at least equal to the cost to the agency undertaking the investment, but it may be more to the extent that their use involves a draft on foreign exchange. As in regard to the leakage in foreign exchange on account of employment of labour, the social cost must be reckoned here as higher the greater the premium that needs to be placed on foreign exchange within the assumptions of the investment programme.

In the earlier stages of economic development (and sometimes even later), machinery and equipment (not to mention various materials) have usually to be imported from abroad. If there is pressure on foreign exchange — as there is bound to be when the rate of investment is being raised — the social cost of using machinery and equipment in construction is therefore necessarily higher than the private accounting cost. To the extent that this is so, and the social cost of employing labour is reckoned to be lower than the private accounting cost, the case for using labour in substitution for machinery wherever possible, and the extent to which it would be desirable to do so, will be obvious.

While, however, the effect of making these adjustments will be to concretize and throw into sharper relief the case for preferring projects and project designs involving the use of more labour and less machinery, there are two qualifying considerations. One is that, on the reasoning we have adopted, the margins of difference between private and social cost, whether in the case of labour or of machinery, would depend on some of the premises underlying the investment programme taken as a whole. If an increase in the rate of investment is contemplated without a planned increase in the output of consumption goods for which demand would rise, and there are at the same time no physical controls, the foreign exchange leakage on account of the employment of labour may well be greater than the social cost of using labour-substituting machinery. In other words, preference for projects and project designs involving the use of more labour and less machinery can be established through economic reasoning only subject to certain other conditions being satisfied in regard to the investment programme taken as a whole.

Secondly, the scope for substitution of labour for machinery is limited, frequently, for technical reasons. Thus, for instance, in the construction of dams and canals, particularly in excavation work for foundations (when underwater excavation is involved), tunnelling operations in rock, blasting below water, etc., a certain degree of mechanization is unavoidable. Also, where the height of the dams, and the pressures they are designed to withstand, are considerable, the specification requirements of such projects would make it essential to use modern machinery to a very considerable extent.[1]

One of the technical factors usually regarded as weighting the scale in favour of machinery is the time element involved in construction. 'A two-yard excavator with about ten men can do a job in a day which the same number of men would take a month to do.' If rigid time schedules for different stages of work are involved, for reasons such as those imposed by monsoons, this economy in time will be obviously a decisive consideration in favour of machinery. However, there are important qualifications to be noticed. The first — to which pointed attention has been drawn in a Report submitted to the Government of India — is that, if the large amount of time usually consumed in planning for equipment and awaiting deliveries, as well as the frequency of breakdowns in machinery, are taken into account, the time factor does not always work to the advantage of machinery. Also, 'if jobs are started well in advance, and time schedules are relaxed where it is reasonably possible to do so, it should be possible to avoid the necessity of rush-schedules on many jobs and thus bring them within the scope of manual labour'.[2] Secondly, even if the time involved in the use of manpower is greater, it does not necessarily follow that time-saving methods of mechanization must be adopted. From the technical point of view, there are often two or more alternative courses

---

[1] *Report of the Construction Plant and Machinery Committee*, Ministry of Irrigation and Power, Government of India, 1954. See particularly chapter XV on 'Manual Labour versus Machinery'.

[2] Ibid.

possible, and whether the more time-consuming or the less time-consuming method is to be adopted depends on the cost to be imputed to time from the economic point of view. We shall consider presently this question of the social cost of time.

Though technical considerations in some cases leave no choice in the matter of construction methods, the case often made out for the use of machinery in preference to labour is not based on such technical considerations but on estimates of cost which either ignore altogether the difference between private accounting costs and social costs, or assume implicitly that, on the conditions and assumptions underlying the investment programme, the difference between the two is negligible. Since this is a matter of some importance, we shall give below an instance of such reasoning from the same Report to which reference has been made above.

In work involving the transport of earth, there is a choice between at least four alternative methods in India. The first is the use of donkeys — which can be employed conveniently when the lead is not more than about one quarter of a mile; secondly, it is possible to use bullock carts, which can be employed conveniently for leads up to a mile; thirdly, there is motor-truck transport, which is regarded by engineers as 'cheaper in initial cost' but 'more costly on running expenses'; and lastly, there is the modern earth-moving equipment, technically the most advanced of all. Taking the last two alternatives, the facts broadly are that the capital cost of trucks required to carry a specified amount of earth would be only about half of the capital cost of a fleet of earth-moving machinery required to do the same work; but the labour needed in the former case — for excavation, loading and unloading, compacting and watering, and for driving and maintaining the trucks — will be about fifteen times as high (though undoubtedly a larger proportion of this need be only unskilled labour). On the conventional basis of cost valuation, the unit rate per 1,000 cubic feet of laid bank has been found to be, therefore, about 20 per cent higher in the case of the motor-truck technique. What is more, the unit rate falls progressively in the case of the technique employing earth-moving machinery as the machinery is utilized for a longer period of its life, while the unit rate in the former case remains almost steady.[1] It has been concluded from this that, though a high degree

[1] Ibid., Appendix 5.1.

of utilization of the equipment, as well as continuity of construction, are essential for securing lower costs, 'for jobs involving large quantities of earthwork spread over the life-time of the equipment, machinery work would be much cheaper than manual work.'

Now it should be obvious that, given certain conditions and assumptions concerning the investment programme as a whole, it would be appropriate in an underdeveloped economy to impute a lower cost to the employment of unskilled labour and a higher cost to the employment of imported machinery, equipment and materials than will be normally done on the conventions of private cost accounting. If even minor adjustments are made along these lines, it is doubtful whether the technique involving earth-moving machinery will have the comparative economic advantage which has been claimed for it. Indeed, if we extend the analysis further to the other alternative techniques, it may be found that the economic advantage lies with techniques using even more unskilled labour and even less imported equipment.

It is no doubt true that the employment of labour on a large scale in limited areas may present serious organizational difficulties and that, on practical considerations, it may still be necessary to have a degree of mechanization above the optimum indicated on theoretical reasoning. But, this apart, the problem of choice of techniques in construction has to be looked at, all the time, from the point of view of social cost, rather than of private accounting cost as is now the general practice. Moreover, as indicated earlier, it is important to remember in judging the economic case for the use of machinery, the large capital cost that has to be incurred by way of spare parts for machinery and the cost and frequency of breakdowns. It has been found, for instance, in India, that the cost of the spare parts held against machinery used in irrigation and power projects amounts to about 15 to 20 per cent of the capital cost of the latter, that only 52 per cent of the available plant hours is being utilized due to sickness of equipment, and that 'until the technical skill of operation, maintenance, and repairs improves, it is uneconomical to prolong the life'.[1]

---

[1] Ibid., ch. VII and IX. The judgement that 'it is uneconomical to prolong the life' is based apparently on an estimate of private costs and, to that extent, needs qualification.

EVALUATION OF THE TIME ELEMENT IN INVESTMENT

We come next to the question of the social cost of time. The time factor is relevant to the choice between alternative projects and project designs in two ways. In the first place, there are differences in the period required for construction, and correspondingly there are also differences in the time that elapses before the products become available. In other words, the periods of gestation may differ. Secondly, the durability of some constructions may be greater than that of others; or, to put it in another way, the rates of physical depreciation may differ. The question now is on what basis we can impute a social value of time, by applying which we can choose between projects involving different periods of time both in the matter of gestation and of durability.

If we adhere to our definition of social cost as the opportunity cost to the society arising from the use of scarce resources, the total social cost involved in gestation is obviously the value of the output that could alternatively be realized in the meanwhile with the same resources. Given our initial approach, the investment allocations as between different lines of investment must, however, be taken as given, which means that increases in output that might be realized over any period by shifting investment into other lines are ruled out of consideration. It becomes then a question of examining the alternative possibilities within the same line of investment and of valuing, over time, different streams of output.

If the rate of output in the case of projects with shorter gestation periods is higher, there is of course no problem, for they are then always preferable to projects with longer gestation periods. But the difficulty arises because the rate of output realizable through projects with short gestation periods is, in many cases, lower than in the case of those with longer gestation periods. One has then to balance the advantage of a higher rate of output realizable through the latter against the disadvantage of having to forgo the output which could be realized through the former, even if at a lower rate, in the intervening period. Obviously, the longer the period over which the value of the different streams of output is estimated and compared, and the smaller the discount for time in the evaluation of the output realizable later the more preferable will projects with longer gestation periods (and higher rates of output) tend to become.

There are thus three distinct considerations involved in making a choice between different projects or project designs, in any given line of investment, with reference to their period of gestation. First is the maximum rate of output realizable through the alternative which has the shortest gestation period. Once this is ascertained from among the various alternatives open, it can be expressed as so much per annum per unit of investment, and it would represent in effect the output that would have to be forgone each year in choosing an alternative with a longer gestation period.

The second is the appropriate rate of discount on account of time preference. It is commonly assumed (as we have noted earlier) that, in the case of individuals, the same volume of output (or income) is usually valued less in the future than in the present, and that this requires a certain rate of discounting for time in decisions concerning streams of output (or income) over a period. Even if this is so in the case of individuals, there is little justification in applying such a discount for time in decisions made by, and affecting, a whole society. Society is a continuing entity, and there is, therefore, no reason why it should necessarily prefer present to future satisfaction. All one can say is that, at any particular moment, the mental vision of a society, even taken as a whole, may not extend in time beyond a point. This suggests not the desirability of a uniform rate of discount for time but rather the practical necessity of confining all calculations about future streams of output, and balancing of costs against returns, to a finite period in which such calculations will be meaningful. This — the time horizon of planning — therefore, is the third consideration involved. Each planning authority has, consciously or otherwise, such a time horizon, and it should not be difficult to express it in terms of years extending into the future.

Given the rate of output realizable per annum through the alternative with the shortest gestation period, the rate of discount on account of time preference (which, on the above reasoning, might be taken as zero), and the time horizon of planning, it should be possible to estimate the total output which, at the minimum, must be realized within the same time horizon by alternatives with longer gestation periods, in order to become preferable. If the rate of discount on account of time preference is taken as zero, the maximum rate of output realizable per annum, through the alternative with the shortest gestation period, would in effect be the social cost of time, and it would perform, in our calculations, the same function as the rate of interest used by private entrepreneurs in assessing the current value of future output realizable through alternative investments. The time horizon merely sets a limit to the series of annuities which have to be calculated in the case of each alternative.[1] It goes without saying that, if the durability of the asset created by any of these alternatives is shorter than the assumed time horizon, the annuities to be taken into account will also be correspondingly fewer in number.

There are two further considerations, however, which are relevant in this context. Firstly, the stream of output available through each alternative is valuable not only in itself but for the further increase in investible surpluses it makes possible. A project with a short gestation period increases the volume of potential investible surpluses at an earlier date, and strictly speaking, therefore, one should take into account its own stream of output as well as the additional stream created by the additional investment. It may prove difficult to make a quantitative estimate of the latter over time, but obviously it should not be ignored for that reason. It will also be seen that, even if account is taken of this only in a qualitative and rough-and-ready kind of way, this is a consideration which will weight the scales in favour of the quicker maturing projects.

Secondly, on the assumption with which we started — that the total investment allocation for the particular line of investment over a certain period is given, as also presumably some targets of output to be reached in the future — the choice actually open, as between alternatives with different gestation periods, may be much narrower than might appear from calculations on the lines indicated above. In fact, if the initial investment allocation has been made with reference to the capital and time required in a particular technique for yielding the desired increases in output, there can be no freedom at all in this matter within this period.

In practice, the investment allocations and output targets are not fixed with reference to one particular technique even in the short period. It is recognized, when making the investment allocations, that while increases in output might be realized more quickly

---

[1] A solution, with some resemblance to the one suggested here, can be found in P. Mstislavsky's 'Some Questions of the Effectiveness of Capital Investment in the Soviet Economy', *Voprosy Ekonomiki*, 6/1949, as reported in *Soviet Studies*, vol. I, no. 4, pp. 363–76. See also comment by Nien-ching Yao in *Soviet Studies*, vol. II, no. 3, pp. 296–300.

through projects with short gestation periods, more substantial increases in output could often be realized through projects with longer gestation periods; the proposed targets of output over time (which, in a sense, reflects the time preference of planners in that line) are, therefore, more economically realized by a combination of projects with different gestation periods rather than by relying on only one kind.

Moreover, for periods longer than the immediately foreseeable future (say, extending beyond five to ten years), the investment allocation and the output targets, in particular lines, are seldom *both* fixed rigidly in advance; at best only one of them is indicated dimensionally as a guide to perspective planning.

If this is the case, there is obviously scope for choice between projects with different gestation periods, within a certain range. It poses then, at the operational level, the problem of deciding within the limits set, which of the alternative projects or project designs with different gestation periods are more preferable than others, or in other words, how they might be ranked in order of preference. The method outlined for the purpose earlier is admittedly a compromise, and hence open to certain theoretical objections. But on the other hand, this is a field in which a completely satisfactory solution seems almost impossible. The method suggested may, therefore, be of some use in dealing with the practical necessity of having to choose between projects of different gestation periods within a long-term programme of development.

The problems presented by the time factor are, however, further complicated if we bring into the picture the aspect introduced by the durability of investments. We may be confronted with two projects, both of which can be completed within the same period of time; but one costs twice as much as the other, and though its output is not correspondingly larger, it is expected to be several times more durable than the other. On what basis then are we to choose between them?

The direct effect of durability is on current costs via the rates of depreciation. A project which is less durable has a higher rate of depreciation per annum, and to that extent a larger deduction must be made from its gross output to arrive at the net addition per annum on account of the project. The question, therefore, comes down to how we should estimate the rate of depreciation.

The usual custom in private accounting is to divide the total cost of a capital equipment, as on completion, by the number of years it is expected to be in use. Thus if the total cost is 100, and the life of the equipment is twenty years, the rate of depreciation would be taken as 5 per cent.

But the changes in the value of a capital equipment, and therefore also the cost of its depreciation, are not the same to the society as a whole as it might seem useful to reckon from the point of view of private accounting. The value of a capital equipment to a community depends, in the ultimate analysis, on what it can produce relatively to the input of labour involved, and if therefore, as a result of increase in labour productivity, the same capital equipment can be produced at less cost at a later stage, the value of the equipment installed earlier will, in effect, depreciate in terms of its output. The opposite will be the case when productivity of labour is falling.[1]

An even more important consideration, weighting the scales in favour of projects with less durability, is that, though a project which is less durable may have a higher rate of physical depreciation, the amortization quotas of the early years may not actually be required for replacement. These quotas, therefore, represent further investible surplus during the period, and the increase in output accruing from the investment of this surplus may more than cover the resources required for the replacement of the depreciated capital stock at a later stage. This means that, even if the net output of two schemes is the same after allowing for the different rate of depreciation, there might be a case for preferring the scheme with the larger gross output, i.e., the one with the shorter life.

These various considerations introduced by the time factor in investments can conceivably be given a definite operational meaning if each choice presents itself separately, such as longer periods of gestation against higher yield, or higher capital cost against lower rate of depreciation. But when they present themselves all together, it becomes necessary to evaluate various factors against each other, and this can perhaps be done only in some arbitrary way.

ESTIMATION OF THE SOCIAL PRODUCT

Lastly, we come to the problem of valuation of the product. As was pointed out at the outset there are special reasons why, in

[1] See S. G. Strumilin, ' The Time Factor in Capital Investment Projects ', *International Economic Papers*, No. 1.

underdeveloped economies, there is likely to be considerable divergence between the private and the social product. This divergence is apt to be great particularly in the case of investments which build up the ' overheads ' of economic expansion and growth. It would seem therefore, that some way of assessing the social product of investments must be found in order to be able to choose between the alternatives open at any moment.

This problem of estimation of the social product is, however, beset with many conceptual and practical difficulties. These arise from the difficulty of defining and tracing the external economies to which are ultimately attributable the divergences between the private and the social product, and also from the complicated character of the processes which are set in motion by investments of the kind we have in mind here.

External economies could accrue in a variety of ways as the result of an investment. In the first place, even at the construction stage, an investment, merely by increasing the demand for certain factors of production and products, may make possible larger output from existing units of production. This can be expected, for instance, when the existence of large surpluses of labour comes in the way of efficient production and a draining away of part of this surplus is itself sufficient to increase productivity. Where output also is below capacity on account of the smallness of markets or other imperfections, the increase in demand created by an investment may stimulate increased output. Secondly, apart from the effect on output via the additional demand at the stage of construction, an investment may, on completion, help to increase productivity in existing units by improving the supply of factors required by them or by making possible new combinations of factors which increase their productivity. Such gains in output will, in turn, increase real income and, therefore, the demand for the products of other units which may have excess capacity and are in a position to supply more. Thus every increase in output tends to widen the market for output in general, and opens out possibilities of increasing output still more through drawing in unutilized labour, making worth while further division of labour, as well as in other ways. Through both their supply and demand effects, an investment at one point can thus increase output at other points in the system, and we have to take all of them into account in estimating the social product of the particular investment.

The expansion of output induced by an investment is, however, a very complex process in practice, and the exact sequences and time-lags are not always easy to establish. The case is perhaps simplest where unutilized capacity and complementary factors of production exist and where, therefore, a mere increase in demand can be expected to increase output. But these conditions are usually satisfied only to a limited extent in underdeveloped economies, and so our concern has to be mainly with cases where investment assists increases in output by actually increasing the supply of certain factors of production.

Very often, even when the market conditions are favourable for increasing output, expansion is not feasible without further investment in the enterprises concerned. Indeed, one of the purposes of 'overhead' investments is primarily to create conditions in which other supplementary investments can be undertaken. This means that, though the economies created by the initial investment provides an inducement to these other investments, the divergences between the private and the social product of the initial investment will begin to show only to the extent that the supplementary investments are actually undertaken to exploit these economies.

This raises a serious difficulty. If we are concerned with an economy in which new investments are constantly taking place, and the scale and pattern of the investments are affected by their profitability, we cannot obviously ignore, in estimating the social product of an investment, the increases in output accruing from investments whose profitability it has increased. At the same time, it is clear that unless the initial investment creates by itself the additional capital required for these supplementary investments, the output accruing from these cannot be legitimately treated as the social product of the former. Moreover, even if we were to do so, given the interdependence of investments over space and time, and its corollary that one investment usually leads to another, how far is one to go on pursuing the effects of an investment in order to estimate its social product?

The only way of overcoming this difficulty, it would appear, is by not allowing ourselves to be drawn into the question of how far the initial investment provides by itself the additional capital required for the subsequent induced investments, but to confine our attention to a specific time period and region, determined by the perspective of the whole investment programme; take into account the magnitude and the distribution of the investment which, within the assumptions of the programme, appear likely to take place; lump together the initial 'overhead' investment with the investments which could be regarded as induced by it; and relate the total of this to the total of the expected increases in output from them.

This is obviously not a very satisfactory solution, but the assumptions implicit in this approach are not entirely arbitrary. For it will be clear that the additions to investible resources created over a period cannot be attributed to any one investment but depend on the investment programme over the period taken as a whole, the capital coefficients, the decisions regarding the plough-back of increases in output, etc. Moreover, if, as we have assumed from the beginning, the rate and pattern of investment over the relevant period are already given, it should be possible, even if only very roughly, to assess how much of the further investments required to exploit the economies offered by an 'overhead' investment will in fact be forthcoming during the period, and how much would be the consequent increases in output.

The reliability of such estimates will depend to a large extent on the investments available to the planning authority for ensuring that the rate and pattern of the actual investments undertaken conform to its own planned design, as well as on various other factors affecting organizational efficiency. Obviously there are distinct limitations in regard to both these in systems where, even when the programme is visualized as a whole, the direct execution of the plans by the state and its agencies is confined to a few selected spheres. But this only means that, in estimating the social product attributable to 'overhead' investments, we must recognize that the basis on which the initial investment decisions are taken is necessarily less firm than in systems in which the follow-up measures can be forecast and realized with greater certainty. In other words, it is not a case against attempting to make the best judgement possible under the conditions, but merely a limitation, in attempting the forecasts, which arises from the basic social and political premises underlying planning in the given system.

To a large extent, the accuracy with which we can assess the magnitude and pattern of the investments to follow over a long period is not likely to make much difference to our problem, since what we are concerned with here is the choice between alternative

projects and project designs within the same categories of investment. Whatever assumptions are made for estimating the social
product of one project or project design will also, therefore, hold
good in estimating the social products of others, except to the
extent that difference in location might require changing some of
these assumptions.

On the reasoning above, it will be obvious that we can also ignore
the increases in output that may be realized merely as a result of
the increases in demand generated by the investment. For such
increases in demand are traceable to unutilized capacity in existence, and given the overall rate of investment there is not likely to
be much difference between the increase in output stimulated by
investment in one project and the increase stimulated by investment in another.

Having decided what should and should not be included in estimating and comparing the social products of alternative investment
projects, the question arises how they should be valued. In the light
of what we have said earlier about the social cost of expenditures
involving foreign exchange leakage, it will be obvious that increases
in output which save foreign exchange should be valued higher
than those which do not. The savings may arise either because they
help to increase exports or because they help to replace imports.
The way in which a particular increase in output stimulates exports
or replaces imports may, of course, be difficult to trace, and to that
extent a measure of arbitrariness is perhaps inescapable, but the
case for revaluing output on this basis cannot itself be doubted.

Before we close this analysis, a word may be said about the
assumptions on which the comparative values of the social products
of alternative projects and project designs are relevant to the initial
investment decisions. It is clear that once we lay down social returns
as a basis of choice, we are concerned necessarily with the relationship between the social cost of an investment and the value of its
social product. Estimates of the social product will have to be based
on some assumptions about supplementary investments. But should
the *direct* product of the primary investment be actually smaller
than estimated, the project on which this investment is made will
not necessarily remain as preferable as before even if, by changes
in the supplementary investments, the estimated increase in the
social product can be realized. It is easy, for instance, to slip into

the reasoning that, though the area irrigated by an irrigation project or the amount of water proposed to be made available turns out to be smaller than estimated, it could be made up by greater use of fertilizers or by some other new techniques of production and that the project, therefore, remains as preferable as before. It is particularly easy to adopt this line of reasoning and pay inadequate attention to the direct increases in output, when the techniques to be used for exploiting the economies offered by the investment and the follow-up investments, are not clearly specified at the outset. Needless to say, when the assumptions regarding these are changed, the entire terms of reference, on the basis of which one project or project design is preferred to another, are also changed.

It will be obvious, therefore, that even while the value of the social product is important as a basis of choice, the emphasis on this cannot be at the expense of attention to be given simultaneously to the estimates of the direct output of the investments concerned.

INVESTMENT DECISIONS

SOME OBSERVATIONS ON THE CAPITAL:OUTPUT RATIO*

by **W. B. Reddaway**

The object of this short paper is to discuss the usefulness of 'the overall marginal capital : output ratio' as a tool of analysis. In particular it considers the usefulness of

(*a*) constructing models which assume a fixed value of this ratio (and then, for example, vary the amount of investment);

(*b*) commenting on a draft plan by saying that it is implying a value of this ratio which experience in some other period, or some other country, shows to be unrealistic, when the Plan has in fact been prepared without any assumption about it, by working from sectors.

It was in fact a comment of this type — made about the paper by the Perspective Planning Division entitled *Certain Dimensional Hypotheses Concerning the Third Five Year Plan*[1] — which led me to produce in an informal document the analysis given in this paper ; this is now being published with only a minimum of tidying-up and without doing the hard work needed to produce a formal article. Since it has been traditional for India's Plans to compute a marginal (or incremental) capital : output ratio and to discuss it at some length, the topic is of some interest.

DEFINITIONS

It is not necessary for the purpose of this note to consider in great detail which of the many possible definitions of 'capital' and 'output' (and hence of the marginal capital : output ratio) is really best. I shall follow what seems to be the traditional Indian practice, which I understand as follows:

* (With particular reference to India's Third Five Year Plan). *Indian Economic Review*, February 1960. Reprinted by permission of the *Indian Economic Review*, and the author.

[1] This is a paper prepared in 1959 by the Perspective Planning Division of the Planning Commission as a first step in the formulation of the Third Five Year Plan.

Whole Economy. On the *capital* side, one takes investment during the period of (say) five years, measured *net* of the amount needed for renewals done in that period (rather than net of depreciation). On the *output* side one takes the increase in the net national output (or income) between the year before the Plan period and the last year of the Plan. All measurements must, of course, be made at the same price level.

One Sector. To obtain a corresponding ratio for each sector, the main point is that, on the output side, one must work with a figure which is 'net' not only of depreciation, but also of inputs purchased from other industries.

A 'sector' may be defined in whatever way is found convenient, but the definition must be the same for output and investment. An example will show the kind of problems which arise.

Thus, in the case of agriculture, it is probably wise to include the 'industry' of supplying irrigation water in the agricultural sector: this decision enables one to include the investment in irrigation with the sector which it is meant to benefit, and to avoid having to value the 'output' of water, because it is not sold outside the sector.

On the other hand, it is probably best to leave the industry of producing artificial fertilizers in the manufacturing sector, even though the investment in it is also designed to raise agricultural output. The reasons are various: thus it is rather strange to think of an enormous chemical factory as being part of 'agriculture'; the fertilizers may be used to replace imports (or exported) rather than to raise agricultural output; and one is interested in the fertilizer industry as a separate industry, or as part of chemicals. Consequently the impact of the new fertilizer plants on agriculture is shown as the purchase of a new *input*, and — we hope — an increase in output which more than covers the cost. In this case there is extra net output in agriculture with no extra capital, apart from a little working capital.

With a number of projects — notably power and transport — we clearly cannot group them with the sector which they are destined to 'serve' because they serve almost the whole economy. We must treat them as industries or sectors on their own, with their own capital:output ratio (a very high one). The size of this ratio is vitally affected by the price policy followed in selling their output.

ANALYSIS AT SECTOR LEVEL

It is obvious that anything connected with a capital : output ratio should first be considered at sector level. All types of capital : output relationship vary greatly from one sector to another, so that figures for the whole economy are affected by the changing composition of output and investment.

Let me then start by saying how I would *like* to be able to analyse the past and think about the future for a single sector — though still ignoring a good few difficulties. We may not have all the information, but it is wise to be clear about what one ought to find out or guess.

Output. Within each sector, I would then like to see the increase in output between two dates divided into these components.

(i) Increase due to better methods applied to old plant, involving little or no net capital expenditure (called P for progress).

(ii) Changes due to fuller (or lower) utilization of old plant, as a reflection of changes in demand (called D).

(iii) Changes due to introducing of double-shifts, etc. (S).

(iv) Changes due to better weather (W).

(v) Changes of the kind for which a certain relationship between capital and output may reasonably be assumed as 'given' by technical factors[1] — at least if we assume a fixed number of shifts, fairly full utilization, and no shortage of labour; the bringing into use of new steel-mills is a good example. If the capital cost of these is x and the capital : output ratio in a new mill is r, then the increase in annual output $= x/r$.

Investment. Investment in the period will consist of x, plus any capital expenditure designed to save labour without increasing output (M for 'modernization') and plus (or minus) an adjustment for the difference between expenditure on construction in the period and completion[2] (L for 'lag').

[1] In some sectors (e.g. services) this assumption may not really be legitimate even for expansion based on new establishments; the increase in output requires increased capital, but the ratio is only 'fixed' within very wide limits. Moreover even in industry there is liable to be a markedly lower capital : output ratio for *extensions* of existing factories than for completely new units. However, these complications are ignored here, so as not to exaggerate the case against the simple use of capital : output ratios.

[2] For a fuller discussion of this last item, see my article 'The Importance of Time Lags for Economic Planning' in the Annual Number of *The Economic Weekly*, January 1960.

Observed Capital : Output Ratio. If we work from historical statistics (or from figures for future years included in a plan) the traditional marginal capital : output ratio for a sector is then equal to

$$\frac{x + M + L}{\dfrac{x}{r} + P + D + S + W}$$

Under what circumstances are we justified in assuming that this ratio — even at sector level — is approximately fixed, in the way which is usually assumed in models? And can we assume that it will have much the same value in different countries, or in different periods?

The simplest way of securing this fixity would be to assume that M, L, P, D, S and W were all bound to be small relatively to the first term of the numerator or denominator, so that the ratio would be approximately equal to r. This is, I think, what most people who argue as though the capital : output ratio were a given fact tend to do: they think of it as a technical relationship applicable to a new plant.

Alternatively, we may be able to say that one or more of the factors will not prevent the ratio from being fairly *stable* — though no longer equal to r — if it is always about the same proportion of the first term (and of course always has the same sign); thus in a steadily developing sector, the lag (L) may always raise the capital : output ratio by about (say) 5–10 per cent. This means, however, that for model-building we cannot analyse what happens if we want the sector to show a violent spurt, unless we say that this will change the supposedly fixed ratio.

In a general way it may be satisfactory to assume little or no change in shift-working (S) or in the effect of demand on utilization (D) or in the influence of the weather (W) provided that — in taking historical cases — the years chosen for comparison make this plausible. Moreover if we take a moderately long period — say five years — the influence of these factors becomes *relatively* less important compared with growth, though the Indian experience of favourable monsoons at the end of the First Plan showed how careful one must be to distinguish permanent from temporary factors.

In looking to the future, it may also be right to assess the effects of S conservatively, even if the Government's policy is to press for

multiple shifts; and similarly there is likely to be under-utilization
of capacity in *some* industries in the final year as well as in the first,
so that ignoring changes in it may be right for the aggregate, even
though the plans for particular sectors must take account of initial
under-utilization where it exists.

With rather less confidence, one might say that in underdeveloped
economies M can be treated as *relatively* small and always positive —
though in advanced countries this is not the case, as the work done
by the Department of Applied Economics at Cambridge has shown
for the U.K.[1]

The real trouble, at sector level, comes from P. There are sometimes large opportunities for raising output by methods which
involve negligible amounts of additional capital — but sometimes
these opportunities are relatively small. Variations between countries
are likely to be large, both in the opportunities and the extent to
which they are utilized, and the same is true as between periods
in one country. In such cases, relating the increase in output to the
capital investment seems to me to be of little value, because the
main reason for rising output will be the introduction of better
methods, whilst there will be *some* extra output due essentially
to new capital (e.g. major irrigation works). One cannot judge from
the capital : output ratio shown in a plan whether the output assumed is too optimistic or too pessimistic.

As a corollary to the above, it is extremely misleading to assume
that the capital : output ratio for the period is independent of the
amount of investment: a moderate increase in output can be
obtained with very little investment, by relying on P, but a bigger
increase will require capital expenditure on new plant, etc. Consequently the capital : output ratio in the period is a sharply increasing function of the amount of investment, not a constant. Moreover,
a further reason for this is that if this period's investment is raised,
the proportion going into unfinished projects usually grows.

Sector Level : Summary. To sum up, at the sector level the observed
marginal capital : output ratio is only elastically related to r — the
real 'causal' parameter which tells you how much additional
capital you need to get 1 unit increase in annual output at the
margin, if that capital (plus the required labour to work it) is

[1] See, W. B. Reddaway and A. D. Smith, 'Progress in British Manufacturing
Industries in the Period 1948–54', *Economic Journal*, March 1960.

the only force at work to produce it. Because P is positive, the observed figure may be far lower than the 'causal' one; but in cases where new facilities take a long time to construct and a great deal of construction is started in the period, the observed figure may be well above r because of L.

At the sector level, I would myself always like to prepare (or criticize) a Plan for a country with surplus labour by starting from the increase in output desired for that sector, thinking about the amounts which might reasonably be expected from P, D and S, and then assessing the additional capital needed for the rest by reference to data on r from new factories or major expansions; this gives x, and additions are needed for L (which may be substantial) and for M. The observed 'marginal capital : output ratio' for other periods or countries offers a tempting short-cut, but it would only be a very crude guide unless one had solid reasons for thinking that the 'adjustments' would have similar effects — and for this it is almost essential that the annual percentage increase in output should be broadly similar, since otherwise the proportion of extra output contributed by P is most unlikely to be the same. (The alternative 'justification'— to assume that P is small in both countries — is, in my view, very dangerous.)

The Economy as a Whole

As a matter of arithmetic, the overall capital : output ratio is the average of the sectorial ones, weighted by the output increases. As the sectorial ratios vary enormously, the assumption of a constant overall capital : output ratio depends on the weights being approximately fixed.

This particular assumption needs to be justified, but it does not bother me as much as it used to do, since I realized that the weights are the *output increases*, and not the amount of investment. The sectors with exceptionally high capital : output ratios — housing, power, railways — seldom account for much of the increase in net output, so that the weight attached to these ratios is in any case small (under 10 per cent of the total); as a result, the overall ratio is normally fairly close to those of industry and agriculture. If one were considering a Plan which proposed to get *twice* the usual proportion of the output increases from housing, etc. the capital : output ratio would be raised substantially (the weight of these sectors being increased from say 7 to 14 per cent); but this would mean that these sectors took a truly enormous proportion of the investment, so that such a Plan is unlikely in an underdeveloped country. We clearly cannot *reduce* the weight from 7 per cent to anything like zero, so that the extent to which the overall ratio can be reduced by changes in composition is also limited.

Consequently, whilst the logical case for assuming that the overall ratio 'must' be of a certain size is even weaker than with sectorial ratios, it is the limitations of the latter assumption which seem likely to be the more crucial in practice.[1] If one were presented with a 'Plan' that only specified the total investment and the increase in national income, it might be of *some* value to compute the implied capital : output ratio and compare it with other experience; but without much more data, one's conclusions could only be of the most tentative kind.

In judging the plausibility of a Plan from this limited information, it might seem reasonable to assume that the incremental capital : output ratio would normally be lower for a slow rate of income growth, for the two reasons which we noted at the sector level : 'progress' can contribute a big proportion of the extra output with only a trifling contribution from capital, and capital expenditure is likely to be little bigger than completions — i.e. L is small — when capital expenditure is increasing little. However, there is a counter-factor which may be important, particularly if population is increasing: some projects with a high capital : output ratio are almost 'overhead' in character (e.g. housing or Government building) and so may constitute a bigger proportion of a 'small Plan' than of one designed to secure a big rise in income. This composition effect may offset the ones operating at sector level.[2]

Technique for Examining a Plan

As a rule, however, one is given more data than is implied above. If one is given sector figures for output at the beginning and end of the period, and for investment, then one can do two things:

[1] Of course hypothetical models might assume a very much higher emphasis on housing and/or public utilities.

[2] For model-building the plausibility of taking the capital : output ratio as constant (rather than an increasing function of the amount of investment) needs also to be considered against the probability of changes in the composition of investment. Thus increased investment might mean a bigger propor-

(*a*) First one can consider whether the figures for each sector seem plausible in the light of experience elsewhere and of any explanations given about expected 'progress' etc.; the crude capital : output ratio implied may be of some help, but its plausibility must be considered in the light of the points made above. Personally I find it more helpful to try to think whether the increase in output seems plausible in view of *all* factors (of which the investment figure may or may not be the most important). For this purpose it always seems helpful to compute the *percentage* increase in output which is assumed, because it is likely to be easiest to consider P as giving a certain *percentage rise per year*.

(*b*) One can also consider whether the proportions of output increase (or of investment) assumed for the various sectors seem plausible — with special attention to the capital-intensive sectors.

Personally I do not think that there is then much virtue in 'summing the thing up' by computing an overall capital : output ratio and commenting on that. But if one *does* assert that the implied ratio is too low, one must, as a matter of arithmetic, be asserting one or both of the following:

(*a*) The implied sectorial ratios are too low.

(*b*) The composition of the Plan has too little expansion in the capital-intensive industries.

Since these are quite distinct points, and no judgement can be passed on the overall ratio without investigating the assumed composition, any assertion about the former being too low should state on which ground(s) it is based.

The Third Plan. The paper *Certain Dimensional Hypotheses* did not give *exactly* what one would like for the above kind of criticism, particularly if one wanted mainly to work from capital : output ratios, because the investment and output figures do not adopt exactly the same classification. However, one can broadly line up the investment and output figures as shown in Table I. Moreover, the paper gave a good deal of supporting information about agriculture (the crucial sector) in the text, to show what factors were expected to produce the rise in output.

It does not, therefore, seem right to say boldly that the assumed increase in output is too big 'because the capital : output ratio ought

tion in utilities — at least for a country in the early stages of development — but a smaller proportion in housing; these effects might be off-setting, but one cannot really generalize.

to be 3 instead of $2 \cdot 2$'. That may be one's personal intuition, and may induce one to start on an investigation, but it should be supported by something more concrete, e.g.

'I do not believe that the rise of agricultural output can be as big as 29 per cent in five years since better methods never produce such rapid results'; or

'The capital : output ratio shown for mining and manufacturing is actually lower than in countries X, Y, Z, whereas with such a rapid expansion it is almost certain to be higher, because progress in existing plants can contribute proportionately little, completions are bound to be well below expenditure, and the plants are bound to have exceptionally great teething troubles'; or

'It will be difficult to prevent more construction of houses, which will mean that less capital is available for sectors where it would have a bigger effect on output.'

Unless one is prepared to say things of this kind, I do not see that one can legitimately have a view about the overall ratio; *if* one is prepared to say them, it seems much more useful to do so.

For my own part I would hesitate to do more than put tentative questions, which would not necessarily be couched in terms of capital : output ratios. 'Do you really think that better methods in agriculture will produce such rapid results? Will you *both* have so much fertilizer available in the time *and* induce the peasants to use it?' 'Have you allowed enough for the teething troubles of new industrial plants, as well as the period of construction?' 'Is it not likely that *both* investment *and* the increase in output will be lower, through administrative delays, difficulties over sites, etc.?'

This sort of approach seems to me to get down to examining the real reasons why output will rise, which are not confined to the increase in the capital supply. In an underdeveloped country this is certainly a major factor, and one need not perhaps bring the quantity of *labour* available into the picture (which would be a key item in the U.K.). But discussions about the capital : output ratio, and assumptions made about it by model-builders, seem in danger of diverting attention from other factors.

TABLE I

NET INVESTMENT AND INCREASE IN OUTPUT IN THE THIRD
FIVE YEAR PLAN, AS GIVEN IN THE PAPER ON 'CERTAIN
DIMENSIONAL HYPOTHESES'

Net Investment in 5 years		Increase in net output comparing 1965 with 1960			Incremental capital: output ratio
Item given in CDH	Rs. crores	Item given in CDH	Rs. crores	% of 1960	
I *Agriculture, etc.*					
Agriculture	800				
Irrigation	700				
Total	1,500	Agriculture	1,700	29	0·9
II *Mining and Manufacturing*					
Mining and Oil	300				
Power	700				
Basic Industries	1,000				
Organized Industries	1,000				
Total	3,000	Mining and Manufacturing	1,150	85	2·6
Small-scale Industries	300	Small Industries and Construction	300	27	1·0
III *Railways and Communications*					
Transport and Communications	1,300	Railways and Communications	200	57	6·5
IV *Housing*					
Housing	1,800	Rentals	100	20	18·0
V *Other Services*					
Schools, Hospitals, etc.	600	Government Administration	200	36	
Roads	400				
Other construction	400	Professions and Services	200	27	
Addition to stock	700	Trade and Commerce	650	33	
	2,100		1,050	32	2·0*
GRAND TOTAL	10,000		4,500	36	2·2

* This figure is not really meaningful, as the data are not comparable.

INVESTMENT POLICIES AND 'DUALISM' IN UNDERDEVELOPED COUNTRIES*

by Albert O. Hirschman

Economists have not shown much interest in the tensions and conflicts that accompany economic development. Not unlike the Marxist who shrugs off revolutions as 'birthpangs' of a new society, the economist has tended to consider social and cultural disruptions in underdeveloped countries as the inevitable by-product of growth. But just as the nature and course of a revolution profoundly affects the society that it brings forth, so is the course of a country's development intimately conditioned by the manifold tensions which it experiences during its struggle to break away from economic stagnation. Failure to include these conflicts in the empirical basis of our analytic structures may mean the loss of important insights. For instance, we persist in attempts to view the developmental process as a self-generating and self-sufficient activity moving along a smooth exponential path, when any observer of the reality of underdeveloped countries is fully aware of the ever-present dangers of abortive development and of the important ways in which progress and backwardness clash and interact.

This article is an attempt to build some of these interactions into the analysis of development. Its first two sections deal with the conflicting claims and uneven growth of different regions within an underdeveloped, but developing economy. After describing the principal methods of governments in coping with situations of this kind, we pass to consider economic problems of a country that has become split into a developed and an underdeveloped region. The last two sections deal with some structural consequences of the close cohabitation of progress and backwardness within the same country, first for the type of industrialization and then for the kind of

* *The American Economic Review*, September 1957. Reprinted with the permission of the American Economic Association, and the author. The author is indebted to Henry J. Bruton, William Fellner, and David Granick for helpful comments on an earlier draft. The theme of this article has been further elaborated by the author in his book, *The Strategy of Economic Development*, Yale University Press, 1958.

industrial organization that are promoted and are likely to prove most effective in this particular environment.

I. The Regional Distribution of Public Investment

The regional distribution of public investment is the resultant of powerful forces acting on the policy-makers of underdeveloped countries.[1] Three principal patterns may be distinguished: dispersal, concentration on growing areas, and attempts to promote the development of backward areas.

In contrast to widespread impressions, the most pervasive tendency of governments of underdeveloped countries in making their investment decisions is not so much the obsession with one dam or one steel mill, as the dispersal of funds among a large number of small projects scattered widely over the national territory.

While this pattern is *dominant* only in countries where dynamic economic growth has not yet taken hold,[2] it can be said to exert a steady pull in practically all underdeveloped countries. The most obvious reason is that public investment decisions are easily the most political ones among the economic policy decisions taken by governments. Whether to build a road here rather than there, whether to construct a power plant that is to supply towns A, B, and C, rather than D, E, and F, these are questions that have decisive local political impact.

Thus, as all governments regardless of their democratic character desire and need support from all sections of the country, the temptation is strong to scatter the investment effort far and wide. Disconnected roads are built at many points, small diesel power plants and aqueducts are installed in many towns without adequate provision for their maintenance; even low-cost housing programmes which should obviously concentrate on relieving critical shortages and on slum clearance in the big cities, are often similarly dispersed.

More fundamentally, the tendency toward wide dispersal of investment funds may be due to the fact that some traditional societies

[1] For an attempt to account for economic policies of underdeveloped countries in other fields, see my 'Economic Policy of Underdeveloped Countries', *Economic Development and Cultural Change*, July 1957.

[2] See Benjamin Higgins, 'Development Planning and the Economic Calculus', *Social Research*, Spring 1956, XXXII, pp. 35–56.

can conceive economic progress only as a force that ought to affect equally all members and sections of the community. Such societies are therefore unprepared and unwilling to make the choices about priorities that are the essence of development programmes. Experience with community development projects has shown that the belief or suspicion, however mistaken, that a project will lead to individual enrichment, may easily spell its failure.[1] Similarly, within the setting of a country, the feeling may be widespread that there is something wrong with even temporarily preferred treatment for some regions, a feeling that it might be politically dangerous not to take into account.

Finally, the dispersal pattern can be explained by certain shortages usually affecting underdeveloped countries. The elaboration of the many small projects into which public investment is typically split up when this pattern is dominant, requires comparatively little engineering and planning talent, whereas the larger projects in electric power, transportation or basic industry require far more such talent than is usually available to the government. This is why entirely too much has been made of the argument that development is held back, not by the scarcity of funds, but by a scarcity of 'bankable', i.e., well-conceived and engineered, projects. The question which should come first, the project or the funds, is really of the chicken-egg variety. Obviously funds can be spent only on clearly defined projects. But without definite expectations that funds — from domestic or foreign sources — will be forthcoming, the considerable cost of engineering and economic studies and the administrative effort required to gather the necessary staff and to obtain the assistance of foreign consultants will most likely not be undertaken. The promise of foreign funds — provided the studies prove the project feasible and worth while — is particularly important if this effort is to be made, as a large project usually results in one region obtaining for the time being a substantial advantage over all others. This is an investment decision which the local government may find it difficult and imprudent to make unless it

---

[1] For a good example, see A. R. Holmberg, 'The Wells That Failed: An Attempt to Establish a Stable Water Supply in Viru Valley, Peru', in *Human Problems and Technological Change*, E. H. Spicer, ed., New York, 1952, pp. 113–23; also P. S. Taylor, 'Can We Export the "New Rural Society"?', *Rural Sociology*, March 1954, XIX, pp. 13–20.

has the feeling — and the excuse vis-à-vis the other regions — that international development capital is not to be had at all on other terms.

Moreover, the study and preparation of a large-scale project implies in itself — especially in countries where there is the rhetorical tradition of confusing the word with the deed, and the announcement of plans with their realization — a commitment to the region which is going to be principally benefited. Governments are therefore reluctant to start such studies unless they feel reasonably sure that they will be able to 'deliver'. Unless they have assurances in this regard, they would be politically much better off to let sleeping projects lie.

The International Bank for Reconstruction and Development has often defended itself against charges of insufficient lending by the argument that there were not enough 'bankable' projects available.[1] But in fact the Bank frequently has acted in accordance with the point of view just outlined, i.e., it has helped in the preparation of such projects by virtually committing itself in advance to the financing of their foreign exchange costs, including even the cost of the preliminary engineering surveys.

In this way the availability of international development capital may make for a shift from dispersal of public investment towards concentration on a few key projects. The 'demonstration effect' of similar projects undertaken in other countries also works in this direction.[2] But the most important force opposing the tendency toward excessive dispersal of public investment is the growth pattern characteristic of rapidly developing countries. Development often

---

[1] Statements to this effect can be found in several of the Bank's annual reports; e.g.: 'Perhaps the most striking single lesson which the Bank has learned in the course of its operations is how limited is the capacity of the underdeveloped countries to absorb capital quickly for really productive purposes. . . . The Bank's experience to date indicates that the Bank now has or can readily acquire sufficient resources to help finance all the sound productive projects in its member countries that will be ready for financing in the next few years, that can appropriately be financed through repayable foreign loans and that cannot attract private capital.' *Fourth Annual Report, 1948-9*, pp. 8, 13.

[2] The demonstration effect is perhaps more important in raising the propensity to invest of public authorities than in increasing the propensity to consume of the public. The latter relation is stressed by R. Nurkse, *Problems of Capital Formation in Underdeveloped Countries*, Oxford, 1953, pp. 57f.

begins with the sudden, vigorous and nearly spontaneous growth of one or a few regions or urban centres resulting in serious shortages of electric power and water supply, as well as in housing and transportation bottlenecks. Thus, urgent demands for several types of capital-intensive public investments appear and must be given the highest priority whether or not they correspond to the government's sense of distributive justice and to its pattern of regional political preference. The public investment in overhead capital in turn makes possible further growth in industry and trade of the favoured areas and this growth requires further large allocations of public investment to them.

Determined as it is by the volume of private investment and the general rise in income in the developing areas, public investment clearly plays here an 'induced' role, and investment choices are often remarkably and unexpectedly obvious.[1] It is not always easy, however, to have these obvious choices adopted, partly because of the continuing desire of governments to revert to the policy of scatter, and partly because a new pressure soon makes itself felt, namely to accelerate development in the areas that have fallen behind.

A situation in which the bulk of public investment is continuously being sucked into the comparatively developed portions of the national territory cannot in the long run be considered satisfactory by governments, because of compelling equity considerations. In fact, the attempt to change drastically the distribution of public investment in favour of the country's poorer sections generally comes at a point that seems premature to the foreign observer or adviser for the simple reason that the more rapidly advancing sections do not strike *him* as so outstandingly prosperous. It is, however, quite understandable that the attempt should be made long before these sections have come anywhere near fully developing their potential. Moreover, the poorer sections of the country, where careers in industry and trade are not promising, often produce, for this very reason, a majority of the country's successful politicians and thereby acquire weighty spokesmen in the councils of government.

Whatever the correct timing, the channelling of large-scale capital expenditures towards the underprivileged areas of the country

[1] Cf. my 'Economics and Investment Planning — Reflections Based on Experience in Colombia' in *Investment Criteria and Economic Growth*, M. F. Millikan (ed.), M.I.T., Cambridge, (Mass.), 1955, pp. 35–54.

contains the danger of misguided and excessive investment — a danger which is always more present in a region that has not yet experienced real development than where spontaneous growth has already staked out fairly well the areas in which public investments are urgently required.

It is possible that the transition from the second pattern — concentration of public investment on spontaneously growing areas — to the third — attempt to ignite development in the heretofore stagnant areas through 'autonomous' public investment — is facilitated by certain peculiar properties of public investment. Usually the second phase results not in a mere shift from scatter to concentration of a given investment total, but in a considerable enlargement of the total amount of funds required for public investment. These funds are secured through the introduction of new and higher taxes or through other *permanent* revenue-raising devices.

On the other hand, it is probably reasonable to assume that the need for the investment of public funds in the country's spontaneously growing areas is particularly heavy in the initial stages of development, as basic utilities are created and rapidly expanded. After development has proceeded for some time, the need for public investment in relation to private investment tends to decline and in any event an increased portion of public investment can be financed out of earnings of previous investments. This kind of change in the mix of public investment with private investment is implicit in the term 'social *overhead* capital' often used to designate the kind of investments which are primarily financed by public funds.

As the taxation and other measures which have financed the original spurt in public investment continue to yield revenue, some funds may thus become, if not unemployed, at least less compellingly employed than previously. This is likely to be immediately sensed by the officials responsible for apportioning public investment and provides an excellent opportunity to those among them who would want to change its geographic composition in favour of the less developed sections.

II. DIVERGENT DEVELOPMENT OF DIFFERENT REGIONS

On probability grounds alone, economic growth is unlikely to start everywhere at the same time and to proceed everywhere at the same speed within an economy. Once some areas and sectors have pulled ahead of others, they assert a powerful attraction not only for the simple reason that nothing succeeds like success, but also because external economies are coming into being at these 'growing points'. There can be little doubt that an economy, in the process of lifting itself to higher income levels, must first develop within itself some such regional centres of economic strength. Inter-regional inequality of growth is therefore an inevitable concomitant of growth itself.

To simplify our exposition, we shall call 'North' the region or regions of the country which are experiencing growth and 'South' those that have fallen behind. This terminology is suggested by the fact that a large number of backward areas appear to be located in the South of the countries to which they belong. The term 'South' as used here does not include *un*developed — i.e., largely unsettled — areas.

After the first spurts of growth in the North, it is no longer obvious what course development will take. Normally one might expect that little by little the higher incomes in the North will trickle down to the Southerners, either as a result of purchases and investments by the North in the South, or because of migration of Southerners to the North. But there are important ins-tances of countries where the initial advance of a region has resulted in a North-South split which has shown considerable durability. Under what conditions is such a lasting split likely to emerge?

In the first place, it must be noted that the initial advance of the North, instead of spilling over to the South, may affect it adversely. If the North industrializes, some Southern handicraft industries may become depressed as a result of competition, and real incomes in the South may also fall as Northern manufactures, produced behind newly erected tariff walls, replace similar goods previously imported from abroad at lower prices. Moreover, the economic expansion of the North may attract only the more enterprising young men from the South as well as whatever capital is generated there.

Nevertheless, if the North specializes in manufactures and relies on the South for primary products, this sequence cannot continue for long. In view of the low supply-elasticity characteristic of the South, the increasing demand for foodstuffs and materials in the developing

North will turn the terms of trade sharply against the latter.[1] In this way, either the advance of the North is going to be halted by rising labour and material costs, or the South is eventually going to be spurred into becoming an efficient producer — in both cases, the gap between the two regions is likely to be narrowed or closed.

But what if the North possesses within itself a large and productive agricultural area or is able, as a result of expanding exports, to supply its needs in primary products from abroad? Under such circumstances, it is easy to see that the South could indeed remain in the backwater of subsistence agriculture, almost entirely cut off from any beneficial effects of economic progress in the North while it would remain exposed to the already noted adverse effect of factor mobility on its own manpower and capital resources.

Under these conditions — which are or were fairly typical of such backward regions as Brazil's Nordeste, Colombia's Oriente, and Italy's Mezzogiorno — the split of the country into a progressive and a depressed area could persist for a long time. Economic, as distinct from the already noted political, pressures to remedy the situation will arise only at a relatively late stage, usually when the expansion of Northern industries begins to be seriously hampered by the insufficient size of the home market or when balance-of-payments difficulties make the country realize that it would save foreign exchange by an improved use of Southern resources. Whenever such economic arguments can be combined with the already noted political forces working in the same direction, a determined effort to pull the South out of its stagnation is likely to be made.

The preceding analysis gives us a hint as to the kind of investment which is likely to yield the best results in the South. With the considerable advance of the North in manufacturing, the best chance for the South to break into the pattern of self-sufficient growth of the North lies probably in a major effort to improve its agriculture so as to become a supplier of agricultural raw materials and foodstuffs

---

[1] This situation has been fully analysed by H. G. Johnson for the case in which a developing industrial country trades with a stagnant agricultural country; see his 'Economic Expansion and International Trade', *The Manchester School*, May 1955, XXIII, pp. 96–101. Cf. also W. A. Lewis, 'Economic Development with Unlimited Supplies of Labour', *The Manchester School*, May 1954, XXII, p. 173, reprinted in Agarwala and Singh (eds.), *The Economics of Underdevelopment*, Oxford University Press, 1958, p. 443.

for the North. Agricultural resettlement, irrigation and drainage schemes, and the establishment of extension services are likely to be of particular importance in this endeavour to move away from subsistence agriculture. Other investments in North-South integration, e.g., in education and in essential transportation links, are also likely to be highly beneficial.

On the other hand, large-scale investment in social overhead capital such as electric-power facilities, modern highway networks, and urban redevelopment may be ineffective in promoting economic growth in the South. Such investments should by all means be undertaken when there exists a reasonable degree of confidence that entrepreneurial initiative will manifest itself as soon as the resulting facilities become available. But in view of the long stagnation of the South, such confidence can hardly be justified. When development is not actually underway large-scale investments in overhead facilities are essentially equivalent to the use of monetary policy in a depression: the availability of power and transportation facilities is of a purely permissive nature but it cannot by itself set development in motion, just as the availability of excess reserves at low interest rates to prospective borrowers does not of itself insure economic expansion at the bottom of a depression. The nature of public works spending in a stagnating underdeveloped area is thus fundamentally different from its role during a depression in an industrial country. The equivalent of the latter in an underdeveloped country is agricultural development or the outright establishment of state-owned industries, provided of course that their technical and economic feasibility has been studied and provision is made to administer them with some competence. In this sense, the Paz de Rio steel mill in Colombia's backward Oriente will probably turn out to be, in spite of initial difficulties and setbacks, an effective development move compared with any programme to provide such an area with plentiful public utilities whose capacity might go begging for years.

III. Economic Consequences of 'Dualism' for Industrial Development

The North-South split is nothing but a special aspect of the often noted 'dual' character of underdeveloped countries where the hypermodern exists side by side with the traditional, not only in techniques of production and distribution, but also in attitudes and in ways of living and of doing business.

Probably one of the principal economic characteristics of these countries and more generally of any country where industrial development is incipient and spotty, is the existence of two distinct wage levels, one applicable to the industrial sector and the other to the non-industrial and pre-industrial sectors which comprise most of trade and other services (except banks and insurance companies) as well as handicraft and small-scale industry.

With mobility far from perfect, the dual wage level reflects different marginal productivities of labour in the modern and pre-industrial sectors of the economy, but it is also explained by social security and minimum wage legislation which is usually enforced and enforceable only in the larger industrial units, by the high cost of living (particularly of housing) in the growing industrial cities and by persistent preferences for the traditional and more independent pursuits in agriculture, small trade and small industry.

While labour is cheaper in the underdeveloped sector of the economy, capital is typically more expensive, also for a variety of reasons: access to the banks is difficult and interest charges are much higher, machinery, equipment and tools are bought at retail rather than imported directly from the foreign manufacturer at important savings, etc.

To illustrate what happens to industrial development in countries under these conditions, a familiar diagrammatic technique may be employed.[1] The terms 'North' and 'South' will now not necessarily refer to geographically distinct areas, but to the industrial and pre-industrial sectors of the economy which may be, and in fact often are, closely intermingled.

In Figure 1 the ordinate measures capital and the abscissa physical units of labour input. We assume two distinct wage and capital cost-levels and therefore the expenditures corresponding to identical labour and capital inputs differ from North to South. For the

[1] For recent applications to related problems, of R. S. Eckaus, 'Factor Proportions in Underdeveloped Areas', *American Economic Review*, September 1955, XLV, pp. 539–65, reprinted in Agarwala and Singh (eds.), *The Economics of Underdevelopment*, Oxford University Press, 1958, pp. 348–78, and Yale Brozen, 'Entrepreneurship and Technological Change', in *Economic Development — Principles and Patterns*, H. F. Williamson and J. A. Buttrick (eds.), Englewood Cliffs, N. J., 1954, pp. 236–41.

purpose of the argument, it is supposed that one homogeneous good is to be produced and that two processes are available, the industrial one which is comparatively capital-intensive and necessarily uses 'expensive' labour and 'cheap' capital, with the expansion path *OA*, and the labour-intensive pre-industrial process which uses 'cheap' labour and 'expensive' capital and is shown by the expansion path *OB*. We shall now draw a constant-expenditure line for different combinations of labour and capital reflecting the dualistic situation we are describing. Let *DC* be such a line for the industrial process used in the North, and let labour in the North be twice as expensive as its southern counterpart, while capital costs are, say, two-thirds of what they are in the South. Then we derive a corresponding constant-expenditure line *RE* for the pre-industrial process by making *CE* equal to *OC* and *OR* equal to twice the length of *RD*.

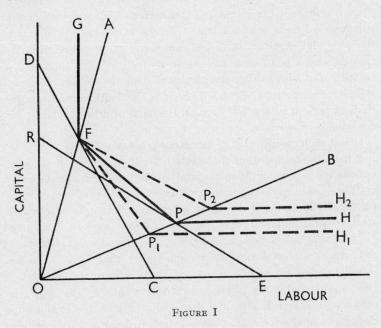

FIGURE I

On these assumptions, any combination of labour and capital shown by points on lines *DC* and *RE* require the same expenditure, it being understood that line *DC* refers to Northern and line *RE* to Southern conditions. If the industrial process is used, it is possible to produce with this expenditure the quantity of output corresponding to OF and the same expenditure yields the output corresponding to OP in case the pre-industrial process is used. Now, if production OF happens to be equal to production OP, in other words if the constant-product line is represented by $GFPH$, it is a matter of indifference whether the commodity in question is produced by the one or the other process. If, on the other hand, the constant-product line going through F is correctly shown by GFP_1H_1, the pre-industrial process is less expensive and will be adopted. On the other hand, if the constant product line is GFP_2H_2, then the labour-intensive process is more expensive for the same output than the industrial process and the latter will be used.

Of course, the neatness with which the diagram shows under what conditions the industrial process can or cannot compete with the pre-industrial one is blurred in the real world. As the Southern wage is ordinarily implicit and as Southerners will take considerable squeezing of their earnings before they actually stop production, the potential investor in modern industrial processes is not confronted with a point such as P against which he must successfully compete, but with a range of such points along the OB line. He must therefore be sure that he can out-compete the South not only on the basis of present prices, but even on the basis of prices that may be considerably lower.

Under such conditions, the industrial processes that have least to fear from the competition of the South are those which are entirely outside the technological and capital capabilities of the local handicraft and small workshop industries. These are the processes characteristic, for instance, of chemicals, petroleum refining, basic iron and steel, cement, pulp and paper, but also of many 'modern' consumer goods, from radios and light bulbs to toothpaste and aspirin.

There is a second type of manufacturing that is liable to be introduced in countries characterized by dualism in the cost structure, namely industries turning out products similar to those of the pre-industrial sector, but producing them with such superior efficiency and productivity that they are able to crush any competition from the old industries. The classical example here is, of course, the textile industry, particularly spinning.

Finally, we come to the industries where dualism is vindicated. Here the appearance of modern industrial methods is seriously handicapped by the possibility of competition from independent, small-scale producers. Examples that come to mind are the manufacture of furniture, shoes, apparel, bricks, ceramics, cigars (as opposed to cigarettes), baskets (holding back the development of modern forms of wrapping, bagging and packaging), as well as large parts of the food-processing and construction industries. Most services, in particular retailing, also are in this category. In truck and bus transportation, the dual wage situation and the relatively small size of the needed capital investment make for organization along traditional small-business lines in preference to modern large-scale operations, and consequently the service provided has a distinctly pre-industrial flavour in spite of the modern equipment used.

In all these sectors which jointly form a fairly substantial part of any economy, the advantages of modern industrial methods apparently are not decisive enough to overcome the traditional or small-scale way of doing things. The use of machinery is unable to offset the advantages of using Southern labour or would do so only at levels of output that are beyond the capacity of absorption of the economy.

The phenomenon which we have described may be an aspect of the factor proportions problem that has been overlooked. Much attention has been given by economists — though not much yet by engineers — to the question of adapting modern technology to countries where labour is cheap and plentiful and where the introduction of certain labour-saving (as opposed to capital-saving or product-improving) innovations may not be justified. While the search for evidence of such adaptation apparently has been somewhat disappointing, it would be wrong to conclude that differences in factor endowments and costs relative to those of industrial countries are not exerting profound effects on the pattern of development in underdeveloped countries. But these differences are perhaps more importantly reflected in the outright *absence* of modern methods from a number of branches of commerce and industry, than in the always difficult transformation of technical processes in those branches into which modern industry is moving.[1]

[1] See, however, David Granick, 'Economic Development and Productivity Analysis: The Case of Soviet Metalworking', *Quarterly Journal of Economics*, May 1957, LXXI, pp. 205–33, for interesting evidence on the use of labour-intensive methods, principally in auxiliary operations such as materials handling, inspection and repair.

The absence of something is always a little hard to notice and this may explain why the one stressed here has not received the attention it deserves. Nevertheless, it is the partial character of industrial penetration into underdeveloped countries which is behind the pervasive impression of 'dualism', i.e., the feeling that the economic structure is a rather incongruous mixture of the new and the old — airplane and mule, oil refinery and basket weaving, gleaming modern office buildings and unsanitary food markets, etc. Whether or not they are geographically separate, these two sectors simply appear to co-exist, each with its own standards of workmanship, efficiency, bargaining and human relations in general.

It has recently been contended that underdeveloped countries should give priority in their investment programmes to capital-intensive industries with a highly advanced and complicated technology. By drawing on historical evidence, Gerschenkron has eloquently argued that only by establishing such industries will a country be able to generate the momentum it needs to break the fetters of the past,[1] while Galenson and Leibenstein have advocated this course on the ground that capital-intensive industries make for high profits and therefore for high re-investible savings.[2]

Whatever the intrinsic merits of these somewhat paradoxical views, they are perhaps not needed to explain and defend the preference for capital-intensive lines of production which many industrializing countries have exhibited. Viewed in the light of our analysis, this preference can be justified on quite orthodox grounds even for a capital-poor and labour-rich economy. It would probably be wasteful for such an economy to invest its scarce capital resources in duplicating lines of production that are already being carried on, even though inefficiently. A better use for capital would almost certainly be in the establishment of new-product industries. But in such industries capital-output ratios are likely to be typically high whereas they tend to be comparatively low in industries that would produce goods and services similar to those turned out by existing small-scale operators.

[1] Alexander Gerschenkron, 'Economic Backwardness in Historical Perspective', in *The Progress of Underdeveloped Areas*, B. F. Hoselitz (ed.), Chicago, 1952, pp. 3–29.

[2] This is their principal thesis as exposed in 'Investment Criteria, Productivity, and Economic Development', *Quarterly Journal of Economics*, August 1955, LXIX, pp. 343–70, reprinted in the present volume pp. 182-212.

In other words, the most efficient use of capital in underdeveloped countries is not in capital-intensive industries *qua* capital-intensive; it is in industries that open new product horizons for the economy and these industries are likely to be more capital-intensive than others with which the country can dispense for the time being because the needs served by them are satisfied by existing handicraft and cottage industries. Therefore, what looks like a puzzling preference for capital intensity on the part of capital-poor countries in effect turns out to be the incidental result of a perfectly common-sense way of *husbanding* capital.

With respect to this pattern of industrialization, today's underdeveloped countries enjoy a definite advantage over nations where modern manufacturing first developed. In the latter nations, as is well known, the industrial revolution introduced fundamental technological innovations into iron, textile and pottery manufacturing, with immediate adverse impacts on the well-diversified handicraft and small-scale industries that had previously supplied these products.[1] In today's underdeveloped countries, on the other hand industrial progress can concentrate on a wide range of useful and desirable products that are entirely new to the economy. As a result, the traditional handicraft and cottage industries are given a valuable respite which can be utilized to improve the efficiency of their operations and the quality of their output.

It must be understood that if this opportunity is not taken advantage of, industrial methods will eventually infringe upon the handicraft sector. As the economy grows in size, industrial methods will reveal themselves superior to the pre-industrial ones in more and more areas in spite of the dual-wage situation. But the absence of sharp competition by modern industry during the first stages of development should make it possible to save a strong handicraft and small workshop tradition where it exists. It is well known that small and inexpensive additions of capital equipment, made available at easy credit terms, and combined with technical education and co-operative marketing, may considerably improve the performance of these industries.[2] By providing them with a new margin of

---

[1] Cf., e.g., J. L. and B. Hammond, *The Rise of Modern Industry*, London, 1937, Pt. II.

[2] Cf. H. G. Aubrey, 'Small Industry in Economic Development', *Social Research*, September 1951, XVIII, pp. 269–312. For encouraging evidence

protection against encroachment by big industry, successful efforts
in this direction would also make it possible progressively to reduce
the wage gap. Clearly, this is a more promising approach than the
always futile attempt to freeze existing situations through legislative
action. For many countries, this approach also seems wiser, and may
be even more efficient in setting the stage for unified development
than a policy of letting 'nature take its course', i.e., passive re-
signation to the squeeze of many old trades and skills which so
unreasonably refuse to die.

In conclusion: Dualism brings with it no doubt many social and
psychological stresses, but it has some compensating advantages
and represents in a way an attempt by the economy of an underdeveloped country to make the best of its resources during a transi-
tional phase. While countries may be anxious to put this phase
behind them, they ought to realize that in doing so they must not
necessarily follow the path of those nations that industrialized in
an earlier period.

IV. TECHNOLOGY AS AN AID TO MANAGEMENT IN THE MODERN SECTOR

The preceding section has shown that the type of industrial
development which takes place under conditions of dualism in
today's underdeveloped countries holds out special opportunities of
survival for small-scale industry. At the same time this survival and
staying-power of the older, labour-intensive production and distribution methods are likely to influence the organization of the
modern sector in several ways.

In a society where dualism prevails, operators in the modern
sector will feel that they are manning an output where they are
always in danger of being contaminated by the old and in many
respects so much more pleasant ways of working and doing business.
Examples of such contamination are frequent: the pasteurizing
plant whose milk one is strongly recommended to boil thoroughly
before drinking; the first-class hotel that three months after a
triumphant opening, has become third-rate; the 'supermarket'
which slowly takes on again the familiar aspects of the much decried

from Indonesia, see K. Nagaraja Rao, 'Small Scale Industry and Economic
Development in Indonesia', *Economic Development and Cultural Change*,
January 1956, IV, pp. 159–70.

open-air affairs. To avoid such deterioration, modern industry will often feel that it has to maintain a fighting position and is likely to consider any modification of advanced technology in the labour-intensive direction as infiltration of the enemy.

This attitude may spring from a correct instinct. The advisability of adopting more labour-intensive processes is usually evaluated on the assumption that work and quality standards will not deteriorate. But for a number of reasons, the validity of this assumption is highly doubtful in underdeveloped countries.

The impact on labour efficiency of machine-paced as opposed to operator-paced operations first comes to mind here. It is certainly true that an untrained labour force is likely to perform incomparably better in machine-paced operations, not so much because of a tendency toward slacking when the machine does not compel the work, as because machine-paced operations provide for steadiness of pace and regular brief rest periods which the inexperienced self-paced worker has difficulty in observing.[1]

In addition, modern machinery and equipment have a more subtle influence in *inducing* efficiency at all levels of labour and management. With better and more modern machinery, all personnel experience a feeling of obligation to live up to the performance of the equipment just as better highways induce improved driving habits and modern sanitary facilities better habits of personal cleanliness and hygiene.

A closely related point is that the most modern, i.e., the most capital-intensive, plants are at a considerable advantage in competing for that scarce article, namely the trained engineer and the skilled workman. The poor workman always complains about his tools, as the saying goes; but, conversely, the poorly equipped factories are always the ones that complain about their workers, and probably with good reason.

But the most important function of modern technology is as an aid to management in the performance of new, unfamiliar and

---

[1] Cf. U. S. Department of Labour, *Hours of Work and Output*, Bulletin No. 917, Washington, 1947. This bulletin reports on the differential effect on workers' productivity of increases in daily work-hours during wartime. One of its conclusions is (p. 11) : 'Where the workpace is controlled by the machine, thus affording the operator some brief rest periods while waiting for the machine to perform its operation, the increase in output is more nearly proportional to the increase in hours [than in operator-paced operations].'

perhaps somewhat uncongenial tasks. Cooperation in large organizations meets with special difficulties in underdeveloped countries.[1] By predetermining to a considerable extent what is to be done, where and at what point of time, the machines and the mechanical or chemical processes they perform reduce these difficulties immeasurably in comparison with a situation where work schedules depend exclusively on the convergence and co-ordination of many human wills and actions. The latter situation is characteristic of most administrative processes and this circumstance helps to explain why the performance of the political and administrative process is so defective in most underdeveloped countries, while achievements in large-scale manufacturing are often quite creditable. That industrial technology can be considered as an aid to management is also confirmed by the observation, frequently made in these countries, that efficiency is far higher in the plant- than in the office-operations of industrial firms.[2]

The productivity effects of technology have been so spectacular that this efficiency-enhancing property has gone largely unnoticed. Ever since Adam Smith, it has been realized that the division of labour induces mechanical inventions. But the inverse relationship also deserves to be stressed. The technical processes carried out by machinery provide factory operations with a basic structure and rhythm which in effect deal out functions and determine sequences. If it is correct, as Chester Barnard has said, that 'processes of decision . . . are largely techniques for narrowing choice',[3] then the use of modern technology in manufacturing is one of the most powerful of such techniques.

---

[1] The nature of these difficulties is discussed in my *The Strategy of Economic Development*, Yale University Press, New Haven, 1958, ch. I.

[2] United Nations, *Labour Productivity of the Cotton Textile Industry in Five Latin American Countries*, New York, 1951, *passim*.

[3] C. I. Barnard, *The Functions of the Executive*, Cambridge (Mass.), 1938, p. 14. Note also the following description of assembly problems in M. E. Salveson, 'On a Quantitative Method in Production Planning and Scheduling', *Econometrica*, October 1952, XX, p. 562: 'In an assembled commodity, if there are n component parts there will be theoretically $n!$ different sequences in which the parts can be assembled together. . . . In any real situation, it would be prohibitive to enumerate all of these different sequences and select the one which is optimum. . . . Instead an engineering type of analysis is used to select some one sequence of assembly according to which the assembly methods and tooling are laid out.'

The degree to which modern technology facilitates coordination, varies from one industry to another. In some industries, the technology consists of a basic process around which work falls into place almost naturally; examples are smelting, petroleum refining, cement, brewing and many others. In other industries, such as construction and much of metal working, as well as in most service industries, not only is individual work largely operator- rather than machine-paced, but work in general is not patterned around one or several key technical processes. As a result, sequences are far less rigidly compelled, it is impossible to identify any one process as central, and tasks are typically defined in terms of their *direct* contribution to the achievement of the goal — the final product — rather than in terms of the roles performed in different phases of the production process. In these 'product-centered' industries technology makes therefore much less of a contribution to the co-ordination of efforts unless it succeeds, by organizing 'flow', in imitating the conditions prevailing in the 'process-centered' industries. Thus, the efficiency-enhancing and co-ordination-promoting property of modern technology tends to be much more pronounced in process-centered than in product-centered industries.[1]

It is possible to classify a plant (or industry) into one or the other category by asking the question whether it has a definite capacity.[2] If a positive answer can be given, as is the case with a blast furnace, a refinery, or a brewery, we have a process-centered situation: with a certain equipment, it ought to be possible to produce so many tons or gallons per day. In the product-centered industries, on the other hand, it is not possible to make this kind of statement: there is no such thing as a set capacity of a construction firm or of a repair shop. This test illuminates another aspect of the manner in which technology in process-centered industries acts as an aid to management: the rated capacity of the plant provides managers with a performance goal and an objective criterion of failure or success, provided demand is adequate. This is a very

---

[1] In the product-centered industries, the well-known human drive to complete a task once it has been started, helps to some extent in stimulating work performances; but this effect is clearly much weaker than that deriving from technology in process-centered industries.

[2] This test was suggested to me by Alan S. Manne.

valuable mechanism in underdeveloped countries where competition is often not a sufficiently strong spur to good performance.[1]

We conclude that there are various ways in which capital enhances the efficiency of management and therefore of labour[2] and that this *stimulating* function of capital is of particular importance in underdeveloped countries where modern manufacturing is surrounded on all sides by a pre-industrial society with its own work habits and without experience in co-ordinating and directing large-scale organization.

That there exists a strong social need for this stimulating function is suggested by the fact that, in the absence of modern technology, it is frequently performed in co-operative work by other devices, such as singing.[3] A particularly striking example of the elaborate way in which the function is performed in a primitive society is given by Raymond Firth in his description of the role of ritual in canoe-building and net-making in Tikopia.[4] He shows in minute detail how 'certain types of ritual make for conformity of the work to a time-schedule and so help to safeguard the task from miscalculation and inertia'. The ritual acts not only as a 'unifying factor for the assembly of labour' and as a 'general stimulus to the productive process', but also as a specific guide in the course of this process

[1] In the paper cited in footnote on p. 293, I pointed out that underdeveloped countries experience particular difficulties in insuring effective maintenance of equipment and machinery and that they therefore are likely to do comparatively well in industries or technologies where maintenance is virtually compelled by technical characteristics, as is the case when non-maintenance carries extremely stiff penalties. For example, the descending order of performance of air lines, railroads and highways in these countries seemed to be explainable by the decreasing degree of compulsion to maintain them that is characteristic of these three modes of transportation in the order cited. This point can now be seen to be a special illustration of the inter-action between techniques and work performance which must be kept in mind in development planning.

[2] The close relationship between organizational and managerial skills on the one hand, and labour productivity on the other, has been shown by Frederick Harbison, 'Entrepreneurial Organization as a Factor in Economic Development', *Quarterly Journal of Economics*, August 1956, LXX, pp. 364–79.

[3] Georges Friedmann, *Industrial Society*, Glencoe, 1955, pp. 157–9, and sources there cited. Cf. also C. J. Erasmus, 'Cultural Structure and Process: The Occurrence and Disappearance of Reciprocal Farm Labour', *Southwestern Journal of Anthropology*, Winter 1956, XII, p. 452.

[4] Raymond Firth, *Primitive Polynesian Economy*, London, 1939.

since 'the traditional sequence of rites of necessity involves a corresponding sequence of technical operations'.[1]

Finally, Firth shows that 'with similar environmental, technical and social conditions, work of this kind (i.e., work involving co-operation in large-scale activities) is performed with less regularity, secures a smaller labour force and is integrated less effectively where it is not accompanied by such ritual'. His conclusion is that the extra degree of capital intensity implicit in the time-consuming performance of ritual is fully justified since without it output would substantially decrease and deteriorate.[2]

The parallel is complete with the special stimulating role which modern technology performs and which because of difficulties in co-operation and the inexperience in management is particularly needed in underdeveloped countries. Here also some additional capital-intensity may sometimes be well worth while if it 'safeguards the task from miscalculation and inertia' and prevents decay.

It may well be therefore that production functions are not the same for developed and underdeveloped countries even though the underlying technological possibilities are identical. The marginal rate of substitution of labour for capital is larger in underdeveloped countries as, with the loss in managerial and labour efficiency consequent upon the adoption of less capital-intensive methods, more labour is needed than in developed countries to make up for a given decrease in capital.

Using again the usual diagram, with labour and capital measured respectively along the abscissa and the ordinate, the constant-product curves for a given output of any good may be expected to coincide for industrial and underdeveloped countries only along their most capital-intensive segments. Thereafter the curves will follow different paths, with the isoquant of the underdeveloped country— curve AB in Figure 2 — lying somewhat to the right of the isoquant AC that applies in the industrial country. Only the latter is a genuine technical possibilities curve.

With this situation, it becomes immediately evident that identical relative factor prices in both countries should result in the adoption of more capital-intensive processes in the underdeveloped country

[1] Ibid., pp. 183, 179, 125 and 181.
[2] Ibid., pp. 182–4.

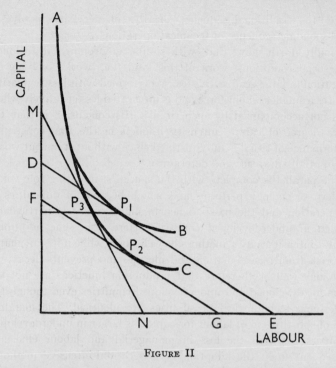

FIGURE II

than in the industrial one.[1] This is shown by comparing the points
of tangency P_1 and P_2 of the two parallel lines DE and FG. Conversely and more realistically, if we assume that relative factor
prices are less favourable to labour in the underdeveloped country,
this does not necessarily mean that it should adopt less capital-
intensive techniques than the industrial country. For instance, line
MN reflects a higher ratio of labour costs to capital costs than line
DE and yet, at their points of tangency P_3 and P_1 with the isoquants
to which they belong, both ratios result in the same capital requirements.

Care should be taken not to read more into the preceding argument
than it can bear. As stated at the outset, it applies only to the
problem of appropriate factor proportions *within* the industrialized
sector of the economy, not to the division between the industrial
and pre-industrial sectors, which was considered in Section III.

[1] Capital intensity is here understood to be measured by the capital : output,
rather than by the capital : labour, ratio.

Secondly, with the low wage rates prevailing in some under-developed countries there remains the possibility that the limited choices which modern technology has to offer, are *all* too capital-intensive, even after taking into account the factors here discussed.

Thirdly, the argument has stressed above all the role of modern technology in determining the key production processes and in providing management with a guide to the basic breakdown of functions and sequences. There remains much room for labour-intensive operations on the periphery once they are fitted into the requirements of the central process. This applies, for instance, to materials-handling and internal transportation where, according to most observers, the variability in capital intensity from one country to another is greatest.[1]

Thus, our findings strengthen only moderately the case of the 'capital-intensivists' in the current controversy about appropriate factor proportions in underdeveloped countries. Any practical usefulness our analysis can claim may rather lie in the investment criterion it contains. For if it is correct, then industrial planners in underdeveloped countries should see to it that the industries and techniques that are introduced are preferably those that induce minimum standards of performance on the part of labour and management. To disregard this criterion might not result so much in additional labour requirements to make up for the loss of efficiency (this might rather be considered an advantage by the planner concerned with under-employment) as in speedy deterioration in the quality of output. Such deterioration could have a seriously demoralizing influence on the whole industrialization programme.

There will of course be industries which do not rate highly from the point of view of our criterion, but whose establishment is nevertheless necessary or desirable on balance for a number of other reasons; repair facilities for machinery and vehicles are an example. It will nevertheless be useful to be aware of the special handicaps under which firms engaging in such activities are likely to operate, so that their management, personnel, and techniques may be selected with the appropriate safeguards.

Naturally, before any such practical applications, an empirical verification of our hypothesis should be undertaken. This might not

---

[1] Cf. Granick, op. cit., and Seymour Melman, *Dynamic Factors in Industrial Productivity*, New York, 1956, ch. III.

be too difficult. If we are correct, labour productivity differentials between an underdeveloped and an industrial country should be much larger in certain industries (e.g., metal fabricating) than in certain others (e.g., cement) even when essentially similar techniques are used in both countries.[1]

CONCLUDING COMMENTS

This article has focussed on a phenomenon that occurs constantly in the process of economic growth, namely the uneven course of progress of different industries and geographical areas within a country. It has been shown that the resulting split of a developing nation into advanced and traditional sectors may be of considerable width and duration and that this split may in turn affect the nature of subsequent development. Tentative suggestions have been derived from the analysis for economic development policy in such matters as public investment in an underdeveloped country's own backward area, the role of small industry, and the type of technology appropriate for the modern sector of the economy.

Only passing mention was made of the social and political consequences of uneven development. However, serious dangers for a country's peaceful and democratic evolution are implicit in the numerous conflicts that are certain to arise from the cleavage

---

[1] It occurs to me that Leontief's celebrated findings about the comparatively high labour content of U. S. exports could be considered corroborative evidence (see his 'Factor Proportions and the Structure of American Trade: Further Theoretical and Empirical Analysis', *Review of Economics and Statistics*, November 1956, XXXVIII, pp. 386–407, and literature there cited). Conversely, Section IV of this paper provides an explanation of Leontief's statistics, related to the one he has proposed himself. I have suggested that it may be easier for underdeveloped countries to approach the efficiency standards of the advanced industrial nations in capital-intensive, process-centered, than in labour-intensive, product-centered industries. Therefore, as world-wide industrialization progresses, the comparative advantage of the advanced industrial countries may come to lie increasingly with certain types of labour-intensive goods and services. This can best be illustrated by a fanciful hypothesis. Let us imagine that certain labour-intensive services such as maintenance of roads, buildings and machinery, or the issuing of official permits, or the handling of personnel relations, could become objects of international trade at moderate transport costs. I have no doubt that in this eventuality the older industrial nations would specialize in the export of these services, quite possibly importing steel and cement in exchange.

between 'North' and 'South' and from the prolonged coexistence of modern industry with many traditional forms of production and distribution. On this score also, some value may attach to a more intimate understanding of the nature of these conflicts, of their probable course and possible resolution.

INDUSTRIAL INVESTMENT DECISIONS:
A COMPARATIVE ANALYSIS*

by Henry G. Aubrey

I

In presenting this paper to an audience of historians I find myself in a painfully ambiguous position. I am not qualified to talk to you as a historian; therefore what I am going to say will lack the richness of empirical detail that usually characterizes historical papers. On the other hand, in order to qualify as 'comparative analysis' this paper ought to have a firm theoretical foundation for its analysis, and accepted standards of reference for its comparisons. Unfortunately, the development economists are still at the beginning of their difficult attempts to isolate the factors that make for economic development, and the complex inter-action of these factors has so far eluded systematic analysis and presentation.

My purpose in pointing to this unsatisfactory state of affairs is apologetic rather than critical. Evidently this paper cannot fully live up to what the title seems to promise. It will now be also understood why I shall raise issues when I might have been expected to present conclusions. I honestly feel that the best I can do is to discuss certain hypotheses regarding the factors that influence industrial-investment decisions in developing countries; to present some observations that seem to bear witness to the plausibility of these assumptions; and to arouse the interest of historians in continued discussion and in the kind of search for further historical evidence that I am unfortunately unable to provide to the desirable extent.

What kind of historical research appears to hold most promise from a developmental angle? There is hardly a volume on economic development that does not relate the experience of Western industrialization. However, few authors openly suggest that developing countries today need to duplicate that earlier course. Yet the implication lingers that this historical experience is relevant.

* *The Journal of Economic History*, December 1955. Reprinted with the permission of *The Journal of Economic History*, and the author. The author is a staff member of the Research Department of the Federal Reserve Bank of New York. His views, however, do not necessarily represent those of the Bank.

On the other hand, one might well favour the presumption that future developments are likely to differ from the past. A fundamental change of policies, methods, and pace has taken place. Except in periods of national emergency, Western industrialization was largely left to proceed in an unhurried manner, free from planning or direction from above. This is not the typical course today. Developing countries now want to move fast to keep up, perhaps even catch up, with those more advanced. This attitude is reflected in a policy of deliberate acceleration of economic growth. Under such pressure, with planning as an instrument of policy, and public investment as an instrument of implementation, one might expect that the relative weight of development measures, probably the very sequence of events, will significantly diverge from past patterns.

Why, then, seek enlightenment in history? There are some lessons to be learned from historical comparison. Even though one suspects that overall 'stages' and 'patterns' cannot be as easily determined or generalized as we have sometimes fondly hoped, there are some fundamental relationships that can serve as a safe point of departure.

One of the most important growth relationships is that which links an increase of output with a rise of investment or an increase of productivity, or both. The flow of investment, domestic and foreign, has therefore become the focus of a significant part of our development literature. It also constitutes the topic of this paper. A great deal of discussion has proceeded on a general level. A high propensity to invest in Western countries was associated with 'rationality', with social, religious, or other cultural traits, and thereby, it seemed, moved beyond the boundaries of economic argument. Whether intended or not, this approach seems to imply that non-Western people lack the prerequisites for massive investment, unless and until they somehow acquire similar characteristics.

I cannot help sensing something faintly sanctimonious in the presumption that 'rationality' goes with our Western attitudes, while less advanced people mostly obey tradition and sentiment. I would certainly not deny the strength of such non-economic factors. Yet, as an economist I refuse to believe that, in less developed countries, business men who prove to have a very shrewd perception of profit opportunities, are swayed by non-economic factors to quite the extent that has come to be accepted by many economists and historians. Could it be that we misinterpret their motives?

In order to experiment in this direction I am proposing a slight change of approach. I shall assume that investment preferences, including those termed 'traditional', are rational and can therefore be explained in terms of the two chief considerations that enter into all investment decisions: profit and risk. Undoubtedly there are other factors, but I should prefer to assign them a residual role; in other words, I would first search for economic motivations of investment behaviour before I concede that the limits of economic analysis have been reached, as they eventually must be.

This slight, and by no means revolutionary, change of emphasis makes for a more detailed scrutiny of the component elements of investment decisions. We have first to determine the individual factors a business man wants to explore. Then only can we comprehend why the economic conditions in underdeveloped countries make for decisions that frequently seem undesirable from the developmental point of view. The method of comparison, historical, institutional, and perhaps also socio-cultural, becomes again meaningful if we thus attempt to dissect the process of decision-making. While it is difficult to understand, describe, and compare general patterns, it is feasible to deal in this manner with concrete factors and magnitudes, and hence with the considerations and expectations to which they give rise in the prospective investor's mind. The present paper is an attempt to apply this method, first generally, and then specifically to industrial investment in the subcontinent of India and Pakistan. It is hoped that the discussants will be willing to bring their varied experiences in other regions to bear on this problem.

II

The literature on economic development is replete with references to lack of entrepreneurial initiative in underdeveloped countries. Individuals and institutions alike, observers say, prefer traditional activities to new ventures. Since industry is, by definition, rather new in these countries, the preferences run strongly to commerce, real estate, and money transactions. These activities, it is argued, are not 'productive' like industry. Moreover, speculative types of transactions, for example, in real estate or commodities, are usually favoured over 'solid' long-term enterprise, like manufacturing.

These observers perhaps describe the symptoms of the trouble correctly, but their diagnosis is erroneous. True, business men in underdeveloped countries are not sufficiently guided by growth considerations in their investment decisions. It is, however, hardly constructive to assume that they are blind or act irrationally. On the contrary, they are shrewd followers of the profit motive. The relevant question therefore appears to be: Why do these business men consider it more profitable to invest in the so-called traditional pursuits, in preference to industry? What are the factors that shape their investment preferences? How could these preferences be made to conform to the investment requirements of growing economies?

The last item deserves scrutiny before we enter into the analysis of prevailing entrepreneurial motivations. We might first inquire what the role of entrepreneurship ought to be under contemporary conditions, a normative, not an analytical, question. At this point, it is customary to take recourse to Schumpeter, but in discussing development today this may be misleading.[1] The less developed countries are not in need of 'innovators' as much as of 'imitators', people who apply the techniques already developed elsewhere. This does not seem to require the exceptional personal qualities of the 'Schumpeterian' entrepreneur. Nor is it, perhaps, essential that the entire cultural-intellectual climate of the country be first re-oriented in a direction that reproduces some favourable historic constellation in the West — if there really ever was without question anything so definite.

I do not mean to make light of the relevance of what is somewhat vaguely termed the 'climate of entrepreneurship'. Probably its most effective ingredient is the example set by a significant number of business men successfully engaged in certain activities, particularly in manufacturing industry. But are these the Schumpeterian pioneers or their imitators? It is a peculiar twist of the Schumpeterian concept that the glory belongs to the pioneer; yet it is the imitation on a massive scale by his lowly followers that transforms the pioneer's forward step into a magnitude of economic relevance.[2]

---

[1] See also H. W. Singer, 'Obstacles to Economic Development', *Social Research*, XX, Spring 1953, pp. 19ff.

[2] In underdeveloped countries, moreover, the imitation and adaptation of foreign techniques is, in a way, also a pioneering step, as daring as innovation under more advanced conditions.

To imitate what was initiated elsewhere requires knowledge of a very specific sort. Under backward conditions the absence of essential elements of information, skill, and experience is, however, quite pronounced. It is therefore desirable to concentrate on such specifics in preference to the elusive concept of 'climate'. This will be done in the following section.

III

Since I have dealt with this topic before, an apology is due to readers of another paper[1] for using my earlier findings for a working hypothesis. It rests on the assumption that among business men, or prospective business men, profit motivation is the most forceful determinant. True, considerations of status, prestige, etc., may also be important but the pool of chiefly profit-oriented business men is large enough even in underdeveloped countries to invite investigation of their investment preferences without attempting to explain why other persons stay away from business altogether.

Before a business man invests in a new venture, he will attempt to weigh his profit prospects against the risk of incurring losses. To do so requires information in many specific directions. The factors that determine his future profit are the size of the market for his product and the share of the market he can conquer, the selling price, his cost of production, including the cost of capital, selling expenses, and other overhead expenditure, and not overlooking reserves for bad debts and other contingencies.

The extent of information available on these items, to be discussed shortly, will shape the prospective investor's profit expectations. However, even if objectively complete information were available this would not make for a state of subjective certainty because the investor will also have to weigh the possibility that all

---

[1] 'Investment Decisions in Underdeveloped Countries', in *Capital Formation and Economic Growth*, a conference volume of the National Bureau of Economic Research, Princeton, 1955. Since that paper was drafted there appeared an article on the subject by Martin Shubik, 'Information, Risk, Ignorance and Indeterminancy', *Quarterly Journal of Economics*, LXVIII, November 1954. See also B. S. Keirstead, *An Essay in the Theory of Profits and Income Distribution*, Oxford, 1953, and W. T. Easterbrook, 'Uncertainty and Economic Change', *The Journal of Economic History*, XIV, No. 4, 1954, pp. 346–60.

or some of the information cannot be safely projected into the future. The degree of such 'predictability' of profits and risks, in turn, depends on objective and subjective factors related to the time horizon.

Rather than continue this discussion in general terms, I propose to take up a few of the items that enter into rational profit and loss appraisals in order to demonstrate the low state of information in underdeveloped countries compared with intelligence available elsewhere. One of the most crucial items is the *volume of sales* as determined by the size of the market and the competitive situation. To appraise the market for specific commodities is quite difficult because detailed statistics are usually lacking. In industrial countries, moreover, a prospective investor has other reference material, such as trade literature and market surveys; he can obtain the advice of trade associations or hire the services of skilled and experienced advisers. Such facilities are lacking in most underdeveloped countries and the prospective investor has to make the best guess he can about the magnitude of demand. To estimate future trends, cyclical, or growth of demand, may well exceed the ability of most traders, no matter how experienced.

Where the prospective market is very limited, the investor is apt to consider the entry too risky unless he is given some assurances that he will not have to share it with uncertain numbers of competitors. He attempts therefore to obtain, and often is granted by governments, security against the entry by others. At the least, he is customarily accorded protection against competitive foreign products through tariffs, import restrictions, and other devices. This, incidentally, reassures the prospective industrialists not only about the volume of future sales, but also regarding the *sales price*, another important determinant of his venture's profitability. Such measures will lessen his uncertainty and this, it will be recalled, is the relevant aspect for our purpose.

As a next step, a decision has to be taken about the *size of plant* and the *suitable technology*. In this respect smallness of the market may keep the plant from reaching the most economical size. The size of plants tends to be smaller in underdeveloped countries. Moreover, reversed factor costs, cheap labour, and high cost of capital, may call for a technology that differs from that employed in individual countries. Recognition of such an ambiguity introduces an additional element of uncertainty into investment decisions: if it is not safe to

imitate advanced industrial techniques, what is the alternative?
Where else can a more appropriate technology be found? Will the
prospective investor have to become a 'pioneer' after all?[1] His
dilemma is intensified by the fact that he lacks the advanced technical services that are locally available in industrial countries. If he
has to secure experts from abroad, the difficulty of selection also
makes for uncertainty, and the high cost adds to the risk.

Investors in underdeveloped countries are also at a comparative
disadvantage in estimating their *capital requirements*. Since most
equipment has to be imported, capital needs are inflated by the cost
of transportation over great distances. Moreover, the absence of
basic facilities often compels new industries to build their own power
plant, transportation links, and repair shops; they also have to keep
larger stocks of repair parts and raw materials than would be
required in a more highly developed industrial and commercial
framework. Furthermore, the correct estimation of all these requirements calls in turn for more technical knowledge and familiarity
with sources of supply than is usually available locally. Under-
estimation is dangerous because additional capital is hard to secure
owing to the wariness of commercial banks toward new ventures.
Over-capitalization, however, is expensive because the cost of capital
is very high in most underdeveloped countries. Either way, uncertainty results and the risk is increased on that score.

The *supply of labour* is another critical factor. As a rule, there is no
shortage of unskilled labour but a very crucial one of skills on all
levels. In contrast to advanced countries, there is no pool to draw on
and most new enterprises have to train their workers, foremen, and
even technicians and managers from scratch. This is expensive and,
what is more, the actual cost is difficult to estimate in advance.
Worse yet, productivity cannot be estimated with any degree of
confidence. Many factors, including social and cultural characteristics, make for generally low productivity of labour, and this inevitably lowers the productivity of capital as well. Hence, advanced
types of equipment often produce in underdeveloped countries less
per unit of investment than anticipated. The risk of over-estimation
is very real in this field.

Cost calculations are also affected by uncertainties regarding the
availability and cost of raw materials and all kinds of supplies that

---

[1] This corresponds to Schumpeter's 'adaptive innovation'.

have to be brought in over great distances. Even where it seems possible to calculate the cost within tolerable limits, the degree of certainty diminishes rapidly as one looks into the future, since supply and international prices are beyond the control of any individual developing country.

The *time horizon* is of particular interest in this respect. As we have seen, it is difficult enough to obtain currently relevant information in many respects — and there are more items than I have discussed here. Moreover, the future significance of such limited information diminishes rapidly as we envisage longer time spans. In part, this is due to objective factors because the economic and political stability of underdeveloped countries is often in doubt. Their prosperity suffers from cyclical fluctuations abroad; this affects the size of the market and the price level. The foreign exchange position of such countries is usually extremely vulnerable; this affects the availability of imported raw materials and other supplies and, in the case of devaluation, also prices and markets. Furthermore, governments are often unstable, administrative arbitrariness is rife, and investors consequently lack a healthy sense of continuity and security.

This deficiency of confidence in the future might help explain the 'flightiness' of *investment preferences* in underdeveloped countries. If investors shun long-term involvement and prefer rapid turnover it may well be because a 'quick dollar' is also a safe dollar. Commercial transactions are wound up in short order; if necessary, they can be liquidated in time to 'get out from under', or at least rapidly adapted to changing conditions. One might object that preference for real estate investment does not fit this explanation. However, real estate finds a ready market among individuals who seek a stable store of wealth in times of trouble, a hedge against inflation, or rapid appreciation of value. This type of investment thus also offers the safety that is found in liquidity. Industrial capital, by contrast, is invariably tied down for unpredictably long periods, and this illiquidity breeds risks.

Hence, what is considered safe investment in Western countries may not necessarily appear secure under different conditions. Knowledge and information, as we saw, offer only a slim foundation for investors' expectations. The extent to which we can supplement such scant information by intuitive judgement resting on familiarity depends on the breadth of our *experience*. Ability to appraise the degree of uncertainty that is inherent in the time element comes more easily to a person who is familiar with past developments of comparable relevance. Traditional pursuits which rest on a broad base of experience therefore appear safer than new ventures.

New industries by definition lack a comparable background of experience. Therefore they are viewed as even more hazardous than objective factors of uncertainty make them appear. From this point of view one understands why industrial investment, especially in untried directions, should be regarded as a gamble — much more so than what we consider speculative activities; for the professional speculator makes his investment decisions not once, but many times over, and he can fall back on a vast background of experience in comparable transactions. Industrial ventures, by contrast, are started infrequently during an individual's lifetime, or only a single time.

To sum up our working hypothesis: investment preferences reflect the expectations of investors regarding probable profits and possible losses. These expectations will be partly shaped by the amount of information that can be secured about various components of cost calculations. In addition, the degree of certainty that such current calculations can safely be projected into the future will have to be taken into consideration. A foreshortened time horizon causes expected profits to be discounted, and the possibility of losses to be over-rated. The state of information in the industrial field is low in underdeveloped countries. The extent to which it can be at least partially supplemented by intuitive judgement depends on the individual entrepreneur's background of experience. If his past activities can be related to essential characteristics of the proposed industrial venture, he will more easily discount the risks and do justice to the opportunities.

IV

An application of this hypothesis to the analysis of entrepreneurial initiative will now be attempted. Past discussions have centered on speculation why entrepreneurial initiative appears to be lagging in underdeveloped countries. My analysis makes for a different approach that leads up to the inverse question why, despite the difficulties confronting decision-making, there actually is as much entrepreneurial initiative as we can observe. In some instances the 'climate' has changed within a surprisingly short time span.

Certainly Mexico, after the revolution and the radical reforms of the 'thirties, did not seem to offer a particularly promising climate to the private investor; yet the pace and the breadth of entrepreneurial initiative during the decade following World War II is truly astonishing. Similar developments can be observed in other Latin American countries. In particular, the interest of middle-class investors frequently awakens faster than current beliefs in the strength of traditional investment preferences would seem to take into account.[1]

Such a rapid expansion of the entrepreneurial base is quite consistent with our hypothesis. Once new enterprises have been successfully established, the 'newness' and related risk are steeply reduced. Conversely, observable success provides a foundation of experience on which later entrants can draw in their search for vital information. However, in addition to explaining the progressive broadening of entrepreneurial initiative we ought to trace this development all the way back to its origin. How did the earliest enterprises come to be established? Who were the entrepreneurs who set the course?

In this direction important and successful research has been undertaken which I need not refer to in a meeting that includes distinguished students of entrepreneurial history. However, most of these studies refer to industrially advanced countries — for obvious reasons the most tempting objects of investigation. On the other hand, if we believe that the early history of industrialization need not fully repeat itself, the study of less remote beginnings gains in interest. Unfortunately the material is usually not well organized, if at all available, and it is not surprising that this field has so far not attracted many historians. I submit, however, that it may be more rewarding than expected; the results, moreover, are of great importance to those who wrestle with the vital question of where developing countries can hope to turn for entrepreneurship.

Country studies provide material for further research, but they do not often contain all the requisite details. If I am going to offer some observations on entrepreneurship in India and Pakistan this is only incidentally due to a recent four-month mission to that subcontinent.

---

[1] See, for instance, the experience in establishing the first closed-end investment company in Venezuela when 1,400 stockholders nearly doubled the initial subscription goal. — Robert Bottome, *Journal of Commerce*, 17 June, 1955.

A fair amount of information is drawn from recent descriptive and historical studies of business communities in India.[1]

A person imbued with the lagging-entrepreneurship school of thought might be surprised to learn that India's major industries owe their origin chiefly to native initiative, not to the British overlords. Textiles, steel, cement, sugar — in all these industries the first successful plants of significant size were established by Indians, with British capital usually entering in relatively short order. How did this come about and who were these native entrepreneurs who truly 'pioneered' these industries in the subcontinent?

These industrial leaders all have their roots in certain narrowly defined business groups. Parsis and Gujeratis were most in evidence initially, with Muslims and Jews in less prominent positions. Marwaris entered somewhat later and have been gaining in importance over the last several decades. Offhand one might well question the justification of placing emphasis on groups rather than individuals. However, for one thing, the structure of Indian society actually makes for a division in groupings or 'communities' that are rather sharply distinguished by origin, religion, or other characteristics. Such groups tend to intermarry and to keep close, if not exclusive, social and business contacts. This cohesion seems to impart to these groups certain common traits, including occupational patterns.

One might well recognize this structural phenomenon without, however, necessarily accepting what seems to follow. Perhaps under the influence of widely shared sociological and anthropological

[1] D. R. Gadgil, *Notes on the Rise of Business Communities in India*, Institute of Pacific Relations, April 1951 (mimeographed); Helen B. Lamb, 'The Indian Business Communities and the Evolution of an Industrialist Class', *Pacific Affairs*, XXVIII, June 1955, and 'Development of Modern Business Communities in India', in *Labor, Management and Economic Growth*, Proceedings of a Conference on Human Resources and Labor Relations in Underdeveloped Countries, Ithaca, 1954 (mimeographed). General sources consulted include D. H. Buchanan, *The Development of Capitalistic Enterprise in India*, The Macmillan Co., New York, 1934, and S. M. Rutnagar, *Bombay Industries : The Cotton Mills*, Bombay, 1927. I am indebted to George B. Baldwin and Andrew Brimmer for letting me read several unpublished papers prepared by them at the Center for International Studies, Massachusetts Institute of Technology; to Morris D. Morris of the University of Washington for material on India prepared by him; and to Robert I. Crane for the loan of several papers prepared under his supervision at the University of Chicago. I am grateful to Mr I. Khurshid, Librarian of the Planning Board, Government of Pakistan, for valuable information and stimulation.

concepts, some observers assume that the economic behaviour of members of such communities is chiefly determined by traits that can be attributed to group characteristics like national origin, religious precepts or prohibitions, caste traditions, or simply the 'otherness' of minorities. Thus, much is occasionally made of the fact that the Parsis are of foreign origin and were never integrated in the Hindu caste system. On the other hand, the Parsis immigrated about a thousand years ago and their customs differ no more from those of the rest of the population than those of countless 'natives' differ among themselves. Many Gujeratis belong to the Jain religion, and their preference for trading has been related to the fact that they could not go into agriculture because their religion forbids the killing of any animate being, such as insects. I am not qualified to judge the occupational impact of this factor but it hardly explains satisfactorily a pioneering proclivity in industry, with which we are here concerned.

Similarly, religion and traditions were held responsible for the fact that the Muslims in India did not play so prominent a role in industrialization as the Hindus. Yet, today in Pakistan there is a veritable flowering of industrial entrepreneurship among the Muslims who, after partition, proceeded to establish private industry on an unprecedented scale. Have the character traits of these people changed in such short order? Would it not be more realistic to assume that the changed economic environment is responsible for this spurt of activity?

This new entrepreneurial element in Pakistan shares one characteristic with the aforementioned Hindu communities: most industrialists belong to specific groups such as Kutchis, Khojas (Ismaelis), Bhoras, etc., that have long been specializing in trade. It is interesting to note, too, that the geographical origin of these Hindu and Muslim groups is virtually identical: the Bombay-Gujerat-Kutch area, the oldest and most important trading region of India. Incidentally, some Muslims in these groups were early converts from Hinduism; they have, moreover, the same historic-economic background as their Hindu counterparts who belong to the traditional trader and money-lender castes.[1]

---

[1] This is also true for the Marwaris who originated in Rajputana (now Rajasthan), the desert region west of Bombay, whence their activities spread not only west but also east to Calcutta where they became prominent in trade and banking, later also in industry.

Other similarities could be mentioned in a more speculative vein. Judging by outsiders' descriptions of Kutchis in Pakistan and their counterparts in India, the same sharp perception of opportunities and hard drive toward profit goals characterize both groups. One might even wonder about the significance of the fact that the Parsis in India and the Khojas (Ismaelis) and Bhoras in Pakistan are small groups with a strong sense of cohesion among themselves and business orientations that transgress borders. It ·may also be worth mentioning that the Ismaelis are adherents of the Aga Khan who counsels the faithful from abroad and is not above occasionally including sound business advice in his periodic messages.

In line with the hypothesis I presented before, I would prefer to assign a residual role to such factors. The most outstanding similarity between the Muslim and Hindu groups that became prominent leaders in industry is, undoubtedly, their background as traders. I propose to show that this background of general experience, and the specific information it affords to prospective industrialists, might well have been important factors in industrial-investment decisions, though they cannot remove uncertainty altogether. Let us once more take up the elements discussed in the preceding section, beginning with the size of the market.

A trader is better placed than an outsider if he plans to manufacture commodities he has previously only sold. The Parsis and Gujeratis, for instance, have long been connected with the processing and exporting of cotton, and with the import and trade of textiles. It stands to reason that a wide experience in trading or in financing such trade provides a most useful background of experience that helps a prospective industrialist to find his bearings, correctly assess the market, and anticipate the prices at which he could expect to sell. Moreover, he can achieve some security by hitching his own interest to that of the nation. Where governments want to promote national industrial development they are usually willing to attract and assist newcomers by concessions and inducements designed to guarantee a safe market at profitable prices. An experienced trader knows what he wants and he is well placed to appraise what he gets.

The procurement of capital is not so great a problem to traders as it might well be to outsiders. As a rule they have amassed some wealth through their commercial activities, and as members of similar-minded groups they can hope for additional funds from relatives and friends. Moreover, when the time comes for importing the capital goods required for the establishment of new industries the importer-trader benefits from his international associations. He knows Western ways; he can obtain information, locate reliable sources of supply, and secure technical advice and specialized personnel. For instance, it has been said that the Parsis found it easy to establish proper connexions because they had long been close to the British as their agents in foreign trade and, generally, as a link between them and less international-minded Indians.

Broad commercial experience clearly helps in many ways that affect the soundness of cost calculations. Even though manufacturing has its own characteristics, the amount of information needed by a merchant is much smaller than what a commercially less experienced person would have to find out. The businessman also commands resources and skill that outsiders usually lack.

The merchant does not, by any means, specialize only in short-term transactions. He, too, has to take chances and, especially in foreign trade, he needs to think ahead and plan at least for the intermediate term.[1] Thus, while industrial investment covers a longer time span than trade, this extension of the time-horizon makes fewer demands on a trader with experience and vision than on other newcomers to industry.

It is, of course, well known that traders have played a prominent role in industrialization. The preceding discussion, however, helps to show that the traders' ability to use capital derived from pre-industrial activities is only one factor, and perhaps not the most important one. Furthermore, the approach selected by me affords an economic outlook on phenomena that used to be explained exclusively in non-economic terms, for example the fact that 'alien' traders are frequently in the forefront of industrialization: Greeks, Syrians, Armenians, and Jews in Egypt; refugees from Asia Minor, in Greece; French ('Barcelonetas') in Mexico; Italians in Brazil; Lebanese and Syrians ('Turcos') all over Latin America.[2]

[1] See also Bert F. Hoselitz, 'Entrepreneurship and Economic Growth', *American Journal of Economics and Sociology*, XII, October 1952, p. 99.

[2] See Charles Issawi, *The Entrepreneur Class in the Middle East*, paper prepared for the Conference on the Near East of the Social Science Research Council, 1952 (mimeographed); George Wythe, *Industry in Latin America*, New York, 1949, *passim*.

It is tempting to view this phenomenon from a nationality angle, as it has in fact been done. I would rather attempt to explain it by the business background of these people. As immigrants they tended to establish themselves in trade, the field they knew best, and one from which they were less likely to be barred than from pursuits traditionally reserved for well-entrenched natives. Their perception of opportunities, sharpened by the newcomers' ambition, caused such persons to look in new directions, such as manufacturing. They knew their markets, they had kinsmen and friends in foreign parts, and hence they did not lack information and counsel. What might have seemed a gamble to others, may well have looked like an obvious opportunity to the more cosmopolitan-minded.

The emphasis on traders as industrial entrepreneurs should not blind us to the fact that different backgrounds are not altogether lacking. In the history of Western industrialization craftsmen have often taken the lead. This is much less likely to be repeated in under-developed countries today where the craftsmen tend to be tradition-bound and are frequently economically depressed beyond rehabili-tation. Middle-class elements, government employees, and profes-sional people sometimes shift to industry as happened in Egypt.[1] A similar trend seems to shape up in Pakistan as well. However, recruits from these strata are less likely to act as pioneers in industry than to follow the profitable lead of others. This is a necessary function indeed, and very important for broader development; but it is less significant in the early stages with which we are mostly concerned in this paper.

I should not like to close this section without referring to the stimulus imparted to entrepreneurial initiative by wars or other emergency situations. Wars usually reduce the availability of imports and encourage substitution by domestic manufactures. This opportunity assures prospective industrialists of good prices and of a secure market free from foreign competition. We know from our analysis that this is an important consideration for invest-ment decisions. Historically, external troubles have long been known to promote industrialization.[2] The effects of World War II can be

---

[1] See A. A. I. El-Gritly, 'The Structure of Modern Industry in Egypt', L'Égypte Contemporaine, 1947, pp. 374ff.

[2] See, among others, Henry G. Aubrey, 'Deliberate Industrialization', Social Research, June 1949, pp. 180ff.

observed in many countries in Latin America and elsewhere.[1] Regions that served as arsenals for a theatre of war were exposed to a particularly strong demand for military and civilian goods. This development has been quite pronounced, for instance, in Egypt and India.

The impact and the aftermath of partition were responsible for unusual opportunities in Pakistan. Business enterprises abandoned by fleeing Hindus were available to newcomers, including Muslim refugees from India. The demand for goods was nearly unlimited, since the new State began its existence virtually without any modern industry. Thus the prospects for new enterprises were favourable, while an unprecedented degree of social mobility provided a reservoir of eager initiative. Moreover, investment funds were not lacking, some brought along by refugees, others accumulated during the war and postwar periods. I know instances of illiterate persons who started out in the 'transportation business' with a couple of donkeys carrying sand and stone, and progressed to build up a sizeable construction business. Others began as small contractors for the army and now own machine shops and a variety of other commercial and industrial enterprises.

Undoubtedly a shortage of goods that promises secure markets, good prices, and high profits offers an effective incentive for industrialization. For instance, within a few years private capital established a modern textile industry in Pakistan large enough to satisfy the domestic market — in fact, already too large for the present level of demand. Chronic exchange shortages, resulting in import restrictions, constitute another perennial stimulus in Pakistan and elsewhere. Clearly, safe markets and related elastic expectations emerge again as potent factors in industrial-investment decisions.

V

The preceding review suggests that the limits of economic analysis in the discussion of entrepreneurial behaviour have not been reached. While I do not deny the strength of non-economically motivated

[1] See H. Mendershausen, 'The Pattern of Overseas Economic Development in World War II; Its Significance for the Present', *Economia Internazionale*, August 1951, pp. 10ff.

attitudes, I feel that the economist ought to give precedence to the search for underlying *economic* determinants of such apparently non-economic motivation. This cannot be done unless suitable hypotheses are first developed. In the field of investment preferences I have suggested the breaking-down of the rationale of investment decisions into its component elements; in other words, to analyse the factual information available to a prospective investor, its relevance for the future, and the profit-and-loss expectations that arise from such considerations.

A cursory review intimates that we ought not to be content with explaining the strength of traditional preferences in underdeveloped countries in terms of their conservative, static character alone. We can find economic reasons for this attitude that are related to the greater degree of certainty with which the prospects of traditional ventures can be appraised, compared with long-term industrial investment. If my analysis of these factors in this and in my earlier paper is found sufficiently suggestive to warrant further investigation, it seems to open a rather wide field for comparative analysis. Historical material regarding the origin of industrial enterprises might be reviewed and special research undertaken to investigate the information on which investment decisions might be based. If intuition is substituted for imperfect information, the rationale of such judgements is equally interesting, since seemingly irrational thinking still rests on a verifiable image of reality.

For the economist the purpose of such research is not psychological insight but the formulation of policy. Persons interested in greater investment activity ought to know the obstacles, not in vague terms of 'investment climates', but in specific directions that are amenable to remedial action. If concrete information is lacking, we can outline the requirements and suggest how the data can be secured and made available to investors. If lack of confidence is at fault, we can attempt to formulate realistic policies designed to restore it. Insecurity can be attacked by legal and institutional measures, even though the political and administrative shortcomings may be beyond immediate redress. The time horizon can be lengthened by safeguards and guaranties that promise to lessen the most intractable risks. Such policies, however, depend on a prior factual analysis of the relative weight of the various factors. In the past we have had to rely on a generalized conception of what the investor's needs were supposed to be. Moreover, the investor's case was all too frequently presented in a manner that was coloured by the writer's own idiosyncrasies and that abounded in *clichés* and stereotypes. No matter how difficult the task, it is time for historical and comparative analysis to tackle the problem in a more thoughtful and judicious manner.

DEFICIT FINANCING AND INFLATION

DEFICIT FINANCING OF PUBLIC CAPITAL FORMATION*

(with special reference to the inflationary process in under-developed countries)

by H. W. Singer

The purpose of this note is extremely modest. It merely attempts (Section I) to list some of the general inter-relations which determine the effects of financing government capital formation by deficit, and (Section II) to mention some of the considerations that have more special validity in underdeveloped countries. In this way, it is hoped to clarify some concepts and provide a basis for discussion. It should be made clear that the note is limited to a discussion of deficit financing for productive public investment only.

I

GENERAL INTER-RELATIONS AND EFFECTS

The problems of definition and measurement of deficit financing are many and confusing. Apart from the obvious need of first defining the scope of 'government' and of 'capital expenditure', there are different justifiable measures of the public deficit, each of them of specific significance and specific application to different purposes. Definitions can be adjudged bad only where they are inappropriate — or not the most useful ones — in relation to the specific purpose of a particular discussion or analysis.

For the purposes of an introductory discussion here, it may be best to fix attention firmly on the allocation of real resources. We may start out with 'unborrowed' private domestic savings, i.e. the excess of private domestic incomes — personal and corporate —

* *Social and Economic Studies*, September 1958. Reprinted with the permission of the Institute of Social and Economic Research, Jamaica, and the author. The author gratefully acknowledges valuable comments on an earlier draft of this note from his colleague, Mrs. O. B. Forrest.

over private consumption of goods and services. It should be noted that we have excluded from available private savings any part which may — by borrowing — have been placed at the disposal of the government by loan prior to the public capital formation here considered. These 'unborrowed' private savings are available to be used for three purposes: (a) financing private capital formation; (b) financing an export surplus[1] or (c) 'deficit' financing of public capital-formation. The concept of deficit financing most suitable to this particular approach must be the excess of public capital formation over and above any surplus[2] of 'genuine' government revenue left after covering other (non-capital) government expenditure, due adjustment being made for transfer items and cash balances. 'Genuine' government revenue is defined as government revenue which represents a real transfer of a claim to resources prior to, and independently from, the process of public investment. Revenue does not cease to be 'genuine' because its real incidence is on savings rather than consumption, or because it involves a future commitment to repay the provider of the revenue.

The purpose of this definition is to throw light on the disposition of the real resources not claimed by the owners of the 'available', i.e. unborrowed, private savings. Thus defined, an increase in the government deficit — whether due to an increase in public capital formation or a reduction in 'genuine' government revenue or an increase in other public consumption of goods and services — forms an additional claim against the 'available' private savings. This additional claim will be accommodated either by *making room for it*, through separate (autonomous) adjustments, whether a reduction of other claims or an increase of available private savings, or else it will have to be *squeezed in* and cause (induce) adjustments in the other claims or in the available savings. Prominent among the mechanisms which induce such adjustments when the claims are squeezed in are inflationary pressures exercised by the increased deficit.

We can now say that an increased government deficit will be inflationary to the extent that no room is made for it by one or the other of the following changes (or of course a combination of these):

---

[1] Which may, of course, be negative — in this case it is the import surplus which finances, and the above sentence should be turned around.

[2] This may also be a negative figure.

(a) a voluntary reduction of private consumption (increased propensity to save), without an increase in private capital formation or in the export surplus;

(b) a voluntary reduction of private capital formation, without an increase in private consumption;

(c) an increase in private incomes without an increase in private consumption or private capital formation;

(d) a foreseen or pre-arranged reduction in the export surplus, or increase in import surplus, e.g. if foreign exchange reserves can be drawn down, or if increased foreign grants, loans or credits are known or assumed to be available, or if income from foreign investments is anticipated to increase.

While the absence of such adjustments produces inflationary pressures, the presence of such adjustments is not sufficient to ensure the absence of inflationary pressure. It is clear that problems may arise concerning the mobility of resources released by the reduction in private consumption, and their transformation into the resources required for the increase in public capital formation. Resource immobility may be a separate cause of inflationary pressure, even if 'room is made' and the deficit is matched in the aggregate analysis. This is further discussed in section II.

An increase in public capital formation will not be inflationary — at least in the aggregative sense — if it is accompanied by a corresponding reduction in other government consumption of goods and services or a corresponding increase in genuine government revenue — or a suitable combination of the two. In this case, there is in fact no deficit financing on the definition used here, i,e. no additional claims on available savings, and no reduction of available savings if other things are assumed to remain equal. Discussion on the inflationary impact of an increased government budget, even when balanced, has served to emphasize, however, that other things are not likely to remain equal. One can hardly neglect the incidence of increased taxation and genuine borrowing on private savings.

But this complication applies also to the adjustments mentioned under (a), (b), (c) and (d) above, which imply an assumption of other things remaining equal. In the actual economic process, the aggregates mentioned here, i.e. private consumption — private savings — private capital formation — import surplus — foreign investment — public capital formation — other public consumption of goods and services — public revenue, form an interdependent system. Changes in any one item are highly likely to produce changes in the others. There are obviously numerous possible situations and chains of events following upon a change in any one of these interdependent quantities, such as public capital formation, and their analysis could become extremely complex. The great range of possible situations also offers scope to a great variety of different policies capable of influencing the events flowing from a change in one of these quantities, such as public capital formation, and hence bearing upon the nature and extent of inflationary pressure.

What happens if these adjustments to 'make room' are not made, or if their effect is cancelled out by their impact on the interdependent system? It is clear that in an *ex-post* sense, a deficit-financed attempt to increase public capital formation *must* always be financed by consequential changes in the other aggregates, or else the attempted increase in capital formation could not in fact take place. Where the government increases public capital formation, and where other things remain equal, in the end there *must* be a reduction of private consumption or of private investment or a deficit on the current balance of payments or a reduction in current government expenditure or an increase in government revenue. And in the end the sum total of these changes must be equal to the increased public capital formation.

The important difference is that where room is made for the additional claims on available savings by the prior or simultaneous autonomous adjustments described, the increased deficit will not have an inflationary impact. Where adjustments are induced by squeezing in the additional claims, these adjustments are almost certainly[1] the result of an inflationary impact of the government deficit, even though this impact may be repressed or concealed, and even though the final — as distinct from the immediate — impact need not necessarily be inflationary.

But there are three facts which rob these propositions derived from elementary static inter-relations of much of their usefulness:

[1] The exception is where we can attribute an immediate, i.e. simultaneous, increase in total output directly to the increased public capital formation; in that case even the immediate impact need not be inflationary. The exception is obviously more important for the long-term than for the immediate impact, although even during the period of capital formation it is conceivable that the anticipated effects of public investment formation will increase the total available supplies of consumption goods.

(*a*) The inflationary impact of a deficit incurred for public capital formation is not just a mechanism of adjustment, of 'squeezing in' the additional claims on available resources. It has other repercussions of its own which may affect the immediate situation as well as the long-range objectives of public policy; (*b*) The changes in the other aggregates — autonomous or induced — which will 'finance' the deficit one way or another are changes *in the relative sense only*; (*c*) The increased public capital formation is in fact intended to change the other national income items and their relations, so that it is hardly consistent to assume constancy of these other factors. Something more should be said about these three complicating factors.

First, the inflationary impact has a life of its own. The nature of the interdependence of public capital formation, and of the deficit incurred to finance it, with the other economic aggregates is such that the extent of the inflationary expansion required to complete the process of squeezing in and produce the final *ex-post* 'finance' of the government deficit may be large; or it may not be easily predictable; or it may contain in itself strong cumulative elements, particularly when different social groups attempt to shift the incidence of the required adjustments; or it may itself have strong repercussions on the aggregates involved, e.g. affect the productivity of the economy, or the productivity of the capital formation which takes place. The adjustment mechanism will affect the distribution of incomes and thus affect the underlying aggregates and propensities. In fact, it is in the redistribution of income towards profits and the consequent increase in savings (or perhaps in the built-in high marginal rate of taxation which results from progressive tax rates combined with fixed monetary income ranges), that most analysts see the main way in which the inflationary mechanism brings itself to an end, and results in a new equilibrium of available savings and total demand for savings. But these self-adjusting forces may be weakened in their operation (especially in inflation-alert economies), or they may even be overwhelmed by opposite, cumulative forces. At any rate, the inflationary process created by government deficits — quite apart from its function of providing finance for the increased deficit — may have most important effects of its own which may nullify, or more than nullify, any hoped-for benefits from increased public capital formation. We cannot disregard these other effects of the mechanism by which an increase in the deficit 'finances itself'. Inflationary pressure is a mechanism of providing 'induced backing' for public investment — but it is also a great deal more than that.

Second, a government deficit is only one of many elements which determine the total of inflationary or deflationary pressures. The preceding analysis tells us only whether increased public capital formation financed by deficits will have inflationary effects or not, compared with the situation *as it would be otherwise*. It is quite possible that in the absence of increased deficit financed public capital formation the general economic situation would have been deflationary, e.g. because of a decline of private investment or an increase in private savings, or a drop in export incomes not compensated by a reduction in imports, or because of abundant crops or an increase in the productivity of labour, or an increased demand for money perhaps due to a shrinkage in the subsistence sector and an expansion of the monetary sector of the economy. Or, indeed, for many other possible reasons. In this case the above analysis remains formally correct. But deficit-financed public capital formation will then be inflationary only in a relative sense, namely in that it compensates for a deflationary trend. It will be reflationary rather than inflationary.[1]

On the other hand, the trend, even without the increased deficit-financed public capital formation, may already be inflationary, perhaps as a result of similar previous deficits. Since we are interested in the absolute impact of government deficits we must take into account the prevalence of inflationary or deflationary trends in the economy apart from public capital formation financed by deficits. It is at this point that the existence of unemployed resources becomes important. It also follows that once a government deficit has created an inflationary situation, the question of whether or not to continue an original deficit becomes entirely different from the question of the original justification for the deficit. Hence the analysis, in any case complex because of the mutual interdependence of all the factors involved and because of the non-neutral effects

[1] This is especially so, if 'deficit-financing' occurs after the collapse of a previous export boom, within the framework of a compensatory budget policy under which surpluses built up during the export boom are gradually used up. Such surpluses can include both budgetary reserve funds and foreign exchange reserve funds.

of the adjustment mechanism itself, will become even more complex when the situation in the absence of a deficit, or increased deficit, can be assumed to be stable.

Third, there is the effect of the public investment itself. As has been pointed out in a different context, if, during the period of deficit-financed public capital formation, output shows an increase so large that additional private savings out of increased incomes equal the additional public capital formation, the effect of the deficit will be reflationary rather than inflationary. If this increase in output can be directly connected with the public capital formation, then the impact of the latter could be justly described as non-inflationary. Such a connexion is natural to assume in the longer run. Public investment may directly produce output, or more likely it may induce additional output by making private capital more productive or by raising the productivity of labour generally. But all these effects will normally follow only with a time lag upon the period of actual capital formation. Furthermore, quite apart from this time lag, the observed marginal output : capital ratio, except in periods of recovery from depression, is not normally more than 40–50 per cent; and this includes the increases in output not causally associated with increased capital formation. If we assume that half the actually observed increase in output can be attributed to investment as such, the 'causative' output : capital ratio would be, say, 25 per cent. This means that it would take four years before the increased output equals the deficit incurred; and even if all additional income arising from the additional output were immediately saved or taxed away in the first round, it would take four years for the supply of savings to catch up with the increased demand for them. In the meantime, of course, the adjustment mechanism set in motion by the deficit as well as expenditure out of increased incomes (since in practice not all the increased income will be saved or taxed) would have transformed the original situation, and other determinants of the economic situation would also be changed beyond recognition.

Where there are unemployed resources to begin with, the 'causative' output : capital ratio may of course be higher than 25 per cent and the increase in output required to provide the additional savings necessary for restoring equilibrium could be achieved correspondingly more quickly. But even under the most favourable assumptions, it is unlikely that the increased savings out of additional output *per se* will come along in sufficient time to overtake the effects of the inflationary mechanism. Instead, we must put our hopes either in deflationary policies during the period of capital formation or else in self-equilibrating tendencies of the inflationary mechanism itself.

The special justification of deficit financing for public capital formation where there are unemployed resources would normally have to be on different grounds: The opportunity cost of the additional public investment will be less, and hence its social productivity higher, if the resources used would otherwise be unemployed. The restoration of equilibrium will then be at a higher level of production — and probably a lower level of prices — than otherwise. With unemployed resources present, one buys more additional output with each unit of deficit finance — hence the price is more likely to be worth paying, and the resulting inflationary pressure more likely to be amenable to compensatory action or to remain within the safety limits beyond which cumulative forces are released.

II

SOME SPECIAL FACTORS IN UNDERDEVELOPED COUNTRIES

Some special factors may now be briefly listed which determine the effects of deficit-financed public capital formation in underdeveloped countries, within the context of the general analysis presented under I above.

The situation is superficially similar to that of developed countries in a depression, in that in many underdeveloped countries a supply of unutilized labour can be assumed to exist at the going wage rates in the 'modernized' sector of the economy. It is admitted that unemployment of labour may take different forms — it may be disguised rather than open, or it may be concealed by the economic and social structure of agriculture and handicrafts — but one may assume an over-supply of labour, in the sense that a potential working force for expanded production is in existence, and that its present marginal productivity is nil or very close to nil. There may indeed also be unutilized reserves of raw materials and even of fixed capital equipment, although certainly not to the same extent as in an industrial economy in underemployment equilibrium, or in depression. But as against this superficial similarity, there is the important difference that the more productive employment of this unemployed or underemployed labour force is obstructed by something more than a shortage of effective demand.

The difficulty of transforming latent resources into actual output in underdeveloped countries is more deeply rooted. Different analysts have differed about what these other root causes are — and indeed they may be different as between different underdeveloped countries. Lack of entrepreneurship or technical knowledge, the lack of an adequate framework of public services, lack of incentives for increased effort, ignorance, lack of a market or credit organization, lack of communications, immobility of resources, absence of adequate economic institutions have all been cited with different degrees of emphasis. A common factor of all these cited obstacles is that they relate to deficiencies of effective supply rather than of effective demand.

In so far as a lack of essential public services and of communications is among these obstacles, public capital formation assumes particular importance in creating the preconditions for an expansion of output, and this may add to the importance of public investment, financed, if necessary, by deficits. Again, however, the analogy with the case for public investment and compensatory public finance in more developed countries during periods of depression is more superficial than real. The purpose of the public expenditure is different in the two cases. In the depression case, it is to increase incomes and create the demand and price incentives for resumed production; the greater the multiplier the greater the effect. The public capital formation is justified by its monetary and secondary effects. That is why it might even consist of building pyramids or burying gold or bank notes in disused coal mines. In underdeveloped countries, public investment could be economically justified only for its impact on productivity, for lowering cost curves and increasing the elasticity of supply curves — not for raising demand curves. Hence, the monetary income effects of deficits incurred to finance public investment are not the main purpose, but an unintended by-product. If output cannot be expanded under the impact of rising demand, the case for deficit-financed public investment is obviously greatly weakened. It is, in fact, reduced to an argument of *pis aller*, or of political or administrative expediency. The expansion of public services is essential — and better ways of doing this may be barred for political or administrative reasons. The income effects of a deficit will normally be at best a helpful accessory. The redistribution of income in favour of profits, as well as the broadening of demand, may possibly serve to assist in the movement towards the main objective, e.g. by adding a further inducement to private investors to take advantage of the opportunities presented by lower cost as a result of the provision of better public services. But the lowering of real cost curves remains the chief objective.

Marginal rates of savings and taxation in underdeveloped countries are often — but not necessarily or universally — very low. This can be attributed to the low level of incomes, the nature of tax systems, the difficulties of effective tax administration, the lack of savings institutions and facilities, a high propensity to consume even in the face of a redistribution of incomes towards profits, etc. Whatever the reasons, the multiplier must in underdeveloped countries often be assumed to be quite high. To this should be added that often there are no surplus foreign exchange reserves so that the capacity to run an import surplus is small, while the marginal propensity to import may be high. Where foreign exchange, and especially accretions of foreign exchange, are largely reserved for producers' goods, and there is little or no home production of these producers' goods — both being the case in many underdeveloped countries — the availability of imports becomes a determinant of investment. Thus an increase in the import surplus may be in fact associated with inflationary pressures.[1]

The marginal rate of savings or taxation may be particularly low where the increase in incomes associated with the act of deficit-financed public investment will accrue partly in kind. For instance where previously unemployed or underemployed farmers are drawn

---

[1] This does not invalidate the general analysis presented in Section I. If the increased level of investment were carried out without the larger import surplus, the situation would be even more inflationary than it actually is. But the point here is that the attempt to step up investment would not and could not have been made without the availability of more imported capital goods. In this sense we can say that an increased import surplus will *de facto* increase rather than diminish inflationary pressures, since the increased investment based on it requires also domestic resources and raises domestic incomes.

from the countryside as a result of deficit-financed public works or construction of urban public utilities, the real *per capita* income of those remaining on the land is increased. But this increase may take the form, not of higher money incomes through additional sales, but of increased consumption in kind. Since the persons drawn from the countryside will in their turn also have a high propensity to consume, and specifically also to consume food, the multiplier may become *pro tanto* very high, and the inflationary gap may express itself sharply in terms of food shortages.

Thus, while the multiplier is likely to be high in underdeveloped countries, the response of supplies to price increases and pressure of demand is likely to be small. Where the factors reducing productivity or lowering elasticity of supply are simultaneously tackled, there may, of course, be an expansion of supplies hand in hand with the deficit-financed public investment; alternatively the public investment may itself be specifically directed towards removing some of the obstacles.[1] In the first case the combined result need not be inflationary; in the second case, while the immediate effects would be inflationary, the longer-term effects would be beneficial, and the inflation would be self-correcting after a time if it is not allowed to become cumulative in the earlier stages. Productive public investment directed towards reducing obstacles to increased supply in the more immediate future, or simultaneously with an attack on these obstacles by other means, provide the classical case in defence of deficit financing.

Added to low productivity and to low elasticity of supply when confronted with increased demand, there is a third related, yet distinct characteristic. This is resource immobility, i.e. a low capacity of shifting resources from one use to another, or from one sector to another. While resource immobility obviously contributes to inelasticity of supply, the distinction is of analytic and practical value. Super-imposed upon the difficulty of increasing supplies of given sectors from the resources already committed to it, there is the further difficulty of augmenting the resources committed to one sector by reducing the resources committed to another. In a developed, especially an industrial, economy with a large stock of capital, resource mobility is to some extent provided by the depreciation of

---

[1] This latter possibility is limited by the fact that not all the obstacles holding back supply can be affected by public investment.

capital. This continuously sets free resources in one branch which are then available for use elsewhere. In a growing economy, resource mobility is facilitated by the fact that it is easier to change the allocation of new resources than to change the distribution of resources already committed; it is easier to have differential rates of growth in different sectors of the economy than to have some absolutely declining. An underdeveloped country has neither much capital to depreciate nor a large volume of fresh resources from growth. Fundamentally, however, the greater ability to shift resources observed in more developed economies must be treated as a concomitant of technical progress, technical ability and a high level of skill and training in the population. That is to say, the same forces which are fundamental to a high level of income are also fundamental to resource mobility. The two tend to go hand in hand.

Resource immobility has an important implication. To set free resources to the extent of, say, 5 per cent of national income in order to augment investment by that amount, it is not sufficient that the same amount of resources should be taken away from consumption or private investment or current public expenditure. This is a necessary, but not sufficient, condition. If the resources set free by the reduction in consumption or other expenditure can not be transformed into the resources required for additional investment, the sacrifice will *pro tanto* have been made in vain. It is not difficult to conceive of situations where an increase in investment by 5 per cent of national income may involve curtailments in other directions of perhaps 8 or 10 per cent of national income. This situation has some resemblance to the multiplier effect involved in curtailing domestic incomes in order to achieve certain required reductions in total import demand.

The comparative immobility of resources between sectors in underdeveloped countries, combined with a greater inelasticity of supply within each sector, has consequences which can be expressed in various ways. First, in underdeveloped countries global pressure of demand on resources is more dangerous and more liable to lead to inflation; hence, to maintain stability, underdeveloped countries may have to forgo, at least partially, the use of one of the instruments which might otherwise be conducive to economic growth. Second, in underdeveloped countries measures to increase the mobility of resources as between sectors are a pre-condition for raising the degree of pressure of total demand on resources, since a pressure of total demand will inevitably require adjustments in the allocation of resources between sectors. Third, in the underdeveloped countries the burden of adjustment which will be thrown on imports will tend to be correspondingly greater; the difficulties of achieving an expanded balance of supplies from domestic production lead to an increased need to add to supplies, especially in the bottleneck sectors, through imports from outside.

This last point perhaps deserves special emphasis. One of the means of overcoming the difficulties created by resource immobility and inelasticities of supply is by utilizing export proceeds, foreign exchange reserves of foreign credits. Such foreign exchange resources, normally, are freely available for supplementing supplies wherever they are particularly short, and offer an escape from the limitations of resource immobility. This alone would give export promotion a high priority in many actual situations in underdeveloped countries. Added to this there is the fact that export promotion also offers an escape from the limitations set by the narrowness of domestic markets. For these reasons, export promotion, where possible, appears to be the natural answer to some of the fundamental dilemmas of economic development.

Within limits, the effects of export promotion can also be achieved by import substitution. But only within limits: import substitution will itself require investment with an import content; hence it may add to the immediate problems even where it holds prospects of a long-run solution. Secondly, import substitution may adversely affect exports. Thirdly, it may result in uneconomic industries. On the other hand, import substitution avoids the marketing difficulties and some of the risks of export promotion. And the resources set free by import substitution would also normally be freely available as between different uses. Export promotion, and import substitution, will often offer the only immediately possible solutions to some of the problems posed by resource immobility.

As has been indicated above,[1] in underdeveloped countries, with their fluctuating export proceeds, foreign exchange reserves may be accumulated during export booms, for use in subsequent periods of export slumps, in which deficit-financed public capital formation could then be non-inflationary. This procedure, however, presupposes a capacity for self-denial and restraint during periods of export

[1] See p. 344.

booms. It also presupposes political stability, and a government which resists the temptation to snatch quick advantages during its own term of office. Where impatience — popular or governmental — is great, and where the need for progress is pressing, such self-denial is not easy. Furthermore, in any given export boom it is not easy to be sure that it is only a temporary situation. Nevertheless, the policies of governments and statutory marketing boards, as well as the existence of currency linkages which introduce an element of automatic stabilization, have in fact opened up opportunities for compensatory policies of this kind. There remains the problem of making certain that such 'temporary' or 'compensatory' phases of deficit financing are in fact kept on a temporary or compensatory basis, i.e., terminated at the proper time. (This difficulty is akin to the difficulty of terminating protection given to infant industries.) In both cases, there is the ever-present danger that 'nothing is so lasting as the provisional'.

While underdeveloped countries are at a disadvantage, generally speaking, in respect of adjustment of supplies to intensified demand, they are perhaps at an advantage as regards the danger of a cost inflation, or wage-price spiral. It is difficult to be dogmatic about this. The bargaining position of non-agricultural labour, and especially of skilled labour, in underdeveloped countries is some-times very strong. But by and large, especially where unemployment and underemployment prevail and where there is pressure of popu-lation on land and on developed resources, the general picture is that temporary inflationary pressures are less likely to set off wage-price spirals. This must not be confused with the possibility that industrial wage rates in underdeveloped countries may be higher than would be best in the light of the resource endowment of these countries, and of the low marginal productivity of labour in alternative occupations, especially agriculture and handicrafts. Wage rates can be structurally too high, without being very sensitive to moderate increases in prices induced by deficit-financed capital formation. To the extent that this is true, in fact, cuts in real wages induced by rising prices may help *pro tanto* to correct the structural 'excess' of industrial wages, judged in relation to economic growth requirements. But this would be a dangerous approach, unless the policy-makers can be certain of the point at which the wage-price spiral begins to operate.

If a combination of high multipliers, low elasticities of supply and resource immobility is typical of underdeveloped countries, it follows that deficit financing of public investment is particularly dangerous, at least until these three characteristics have been modified prior to, or simultaneously with, the deficit-financed expenditure. These warnings could be fortified by reference to other characteristics of underdeveloped countries. Where habits of monetary exchange and use of monetary institutions are still in their infancy and have to be carefully nursed, it may be especially dangerous to have the value of money depreciate. Where the discipline of reconciling ambitions with limited resources has to be developed, the requirement of a balanced budget should not be easily abandoned. Where shifts to profits may easily result in increased speculation, high-level consumption or capital flight, the mechanism of inflation loses much of its purpose. Where administrative controls are particularly difficult, inflation may more easily get out of hand. This is indeed a formidable array of warning signals to those thinking of applying the technique of deficit financing in underdeveloped countries, even as the counterpart of productive public investment. The warnings look serious enough to cause acute apprehension in regard to deficit-finance proposals in most, or nearly all, actual combinations of circumstances that are likely to be encountered in underdeveloped countries.

But there remains the exceptional combination of circumstances. There remains the case where perhaps there is a special opportunity to increase production of food and other consumer goods conspicuously and rapidly with the aid of public works, and bridge the interval by drawing on a previously accumulated surplus of foreign exchange. There is perhaps the case of the underdeveloped country with very high marginal rates of savings or taxation. There is the case of underlying deflationary tendencies offering scope for public deficits.

There is, finally, the case where better alternatives to deficit financing, such as increased taxation, are politically or administratively impossible, or where its broader economic effects are especially harmful, and where yet some forms of productive public investment are an absolute precondition of economic progress, and where economic progress in turn is an absolute precondition for political and social stability. But even where deficit financing leads to increased capital formation the dangers of deficit financing must still be weighed against the dangers of economic stagnation or deterioration; and it is often far from clear that the non-existence of better alternatives should be accepted as a genuine premise of debate.

Where the need for public investment over and above what present revenues permit is so crucial and imperative, it is difficult to see why the effort to overcome the obstacles obstructing the use of less dangerous methods of financing could not also be made. A determination to achieve the end would seem to presuppose a determination to make possible the best means. So that even if the discussion is restricted, as it is in this paper, to the financing of productive investment, it would appear that the circumstances justifying deficit financing as a deliberate choice would be rather special and the justified doses closely circumscribed.

THE EFFECT OF INFLATION ON ECONOMIC DEVELOPMENT[*]

by Graeme S. Dorrance

I. INTRODUCTION

The problem

In many of the less highly developed countries, incomes are not rising as rapidly as the desires of the community. In these countries, personal savings are low, so that only limited resources are released for the expansion of the community's capital. At the same time, the tax systems provide only enough revenue to meet part of the community's desires for government services, with very small surpluses available to finance development. Under these circumstances, inflation may appear to be an easy method of providing finance to expand investment and hence to be an easy way of obtaining capital for a more rapid expansion of output. If a government can persuade the central bank to create money to finance a development programme, or if the banking system freely makes loans to private investors for the finance of physical investment, the problem of expanding the community's real assets may appear to be easily solvable. Consequently, it is sometimes argued that 'a case could be made for making inflation an instrument of (development) policy, rather than the control of inflation an object of policy'.[1]

There is no doubt that, on occasion, a monetary expansion somewhat greater than the current increase in real output will introduce an element of flexibility in an economy, and lead to some 'forced saving' releasing resources for development. However, there are strict limits to the amount of development which may be fostered in this way. Admittedly, the available simple evidence on the relation between inflation and growth is difficult to interpret. The difficulty is

[*] *International Monetary Fund Staff Papers*, March 1963. Reprinted by permission of the *Staff Papers* and the author. This is a revised version of a paper prepared for presentation to the Conference on Inflation and Growth in Rio de Janeiro, 3–11 January, 1963.

[1] H. J. Bruton, *Inflation in a Growing Economy* (Annual Lectures by Visiting Professor of Monetary Economics, 1960–1, University of Bombay, Bombay) p. 57; parentheses added.

common in analyses of the effects of pervasive influences, like the degree of inflation, on phenomena which are also subject to other, complex, forces.

Table 1 presents summary data gathered from three sources. This evidence varies from the inconclusive simple comparison of average rates of growth for the years 1954–60[1] as derived from the UN national account statistics, to the rather more persuasive conclusions

TABLE 1. RELATIONSHIP OF RATES OF INFLATION TO ECONOMIC GROWTH
IN RECENT YEARS†

	Annual Rates of Growth Per Capita (*per cent*)		
	Stable countries	Mild inflation countries	Strong inflation countries
Sample based on UN data	2	2	2
ECLA sample	3	—	2
U Tun Wai samples, based on *per capita* national income			
Unadjusted	6	2	3
Adjusted for terms of trade	4	1	1
per capita social product	4	3	—

† For description of stable, mild inflation, and strong inflation countries, and for statement of countries and periods covered, see Appendix, p. 385.
For sources of data, see Tables 11, 12, and 13 (pp. 386–8).

obtained from a recording of the data relating to specific periods of rather constant price change identified by U Tun Wai.[2] The rates of growth in the simpler comparisons are based on one observation per country; hence each observation reflects not only the effect of inflation but also the effects of the available natural resources and their stage of exploitation, and the general political atmosphere and other influences, such as the general social attitudes, in each country. The separation of shorter periods for individual countries when different rates of price increase prevailed, based on Tun Wai's observations, tends to strengthen the influence of the rate of inflation, as distinct from other forces, in the last three comparisons in Table 1. These

[1] To be more precise: 1954–60 in most cases, in some cases shorter periods within that time span.
[2] ' The Relation Between Inflation and Economic Development: A Statistical Inductive Study ', *Staff Papers*, Vol. VII (1959–60), pp. 302–17.

latter data suggest that in the postwar years the less highly developed countries have, on the average, enjoyed annual increases in *per capita* output of approximately 4 per cent during those periods when they maintained monetary stability. During periods of mild inflation the increase in output in these countries was only half as great. During periods of strong inflation, the increases in output tended to be even smaller.[1]

It is true that individual units of investment financed by bank credit are likely to be created even in inflationary conditions. It is not the immediate products of monetary expansion which are in question; rather it is the overall effect on progress which deserves consideration. An expansion of the monetary system's assets involves an equal expansion of its liabilities. Unless members of the community are willing to increase the real value of their money balances by an amount equal to the increase in bank credit, and thereby indirectly to provide finance for the new investment, either prices will rise, or imports will be so encouraged and exports discouraged that there will be a fall in the community's capital held in the form of exchange reserves, i.e., a disinvestment in reserves offsetting the newly financed domestic investment. If prices rise, the real value of any increase in money holdings will be eroded. This fall in the real value of money may be considered as a tax on money holders. Inflationary policies, or policies which lead a government to be weak in resisting inflationary pressures, may be assessed by criteria similar to those used in assessing alternative taxation proposals.

The efficiency of any tax is largely dependent on the degree to which it cannot be evaded. The degree to which a tax 'cannot be evaded' is, in turn, largely a function of the degree to which it does not lead to incentives encouraging evasion. A mild inflation may well encourage little, or no, evasion of the 'inflation tax'. On the other hand, a strong inflation, and frequently a mild one also, will lead to

---

[1] It should be recognized that these conclusions are more positive than the conclusions in some other studies. The difference between the conclusions in Table 1 and those of other studies may be explained by the fact that the data in Table 1 cover a fairly large number of countries where the rate of inflation is high, whereas the data used by most other authors are dominated by relatively low rates of inflation. For example, of the more than 100 annual rates of price change analysed by Bhatia ('Inflation, Deflation, and Economic Development', *Staff Papers*, Vol. VIII, 1960–1, pp. 101–14), only 14 were larger than 5 per cent, and only 3 of these were in excess of 10 per cent.

community reactions which have effects similar to those of widespread tax evasion.

A development policy may have wider aims than the encouragement of a high level of investment. It may be directed to the encouragement of types of investment different from those which would emerge in an economy in which all economic decisions are made by individual economic units acting without positive inducements by the government. If an attempt be made to foster development through an 'inflation tax', the types of economic incentive induced by inflation are also relevant to its effectiveness. A strong inflation creates distortions in the economy, which may be regarded as comparable to the undesirable incentives induced by unsatisfactory forms of taxation.

It must be recognized that rapid economic development, by evoking supply shortages in certain specific fields, frequently leads to increases in the prices of certain commodities. The number of these may be fairly large. Under these circumstances, some rise in the average level of prices may frequently be an unavoidable companion of economic progress. This observation does not, however, lead to the conclusion that inflation aids development, or that its control should not have a high priority among the targets for economic policy.

The Significance of Expected Price Increases

The monetary system operates on the assumption that money serves as a satisfactory medium of exchange, *numéraire*, standard for debt repayment, and store of value. If prices are stable or rising imperceptibly, money will be accepted by the community for all these purposes. If prices rise markedly, individuals and businesses will cease to hold money for the latter two of these four purposes. If prices are not expected to remain stable, the economic adjustments attempted by the community will be different from those which will be attempted when price stability is expected.[1] In some respects, the problem facing the analyst is the comparison of these different adjustments.

[1] It must be recognized that the degree of price change required to influence expectations is not only rather indeterminate in any particular case, but will depend to a considerable extent on the degree of price stability in earlier years; even so, it will differ from country to country, and between countries with similar monetary experiences.

The Effect of Inflation on The Desire for Liquidity [1]

Inflation has two effects on the desire for liquidity, which are related to the two basic reasons why individuals and businesses wish to hold liquid assets — the speculative and precautionary motives. Inflation increases the value of effective liquidity, thereby raising the community's desire for it, but it makes the most generally accepted store of liquidity — money and financial assets denominated in money — unacceptable sources of protection. This strengthening of the community's wish for liquidity and weakening of the usefulness of the traditional store of liquidity will exert their greatest influence on the types of investment undertaken during periods of inflation, but they will also work to reduce the total flow of resources available for investment.

If an inflation were expected to proceed at a uniform rate, it might have little effect on the community's desire for liquidity. In practice, the rate of any inflation is unpredictable, and the variations in this rate are likely to become more pronounced as the average rate of inflation increases. In a stable economy, price movements are reasonably predictable. In an inflationary economy, if the current rate of price rise is 20 per cent a year, the rate next year may almost equally well be approximately 10 per cent or over 40 per cent.[2] This uncertainty regarding the future course of prices creates an incentive for liquidity. With the future uncertain, the probability of unpredictable investment opportunities arising, or business difficulties occurring, is increased. Hence the desire to hold liquid assets for speculative and precautionary purposes is strengthened.

However, during an inflation money and financial assets denominated in money cannot be depended on as stores of liquidity, since

---

[1] This section, and Part III below, are based largely on A. S. Shaalan, 'The Impact of Inflation on the Composition of Private Domestic Investment', *Staff Papers*, Vol. IX (1962), pp. 243–63.

[2] See, for examples, the data in Table 23, p. 396. (The Appendix, pp. 385–401, contains Tables 11–29.) For a discussion of the effect of uncertainty regarding the rate of inflation on the structure of interest rates, leading to higher rates for long-term deposits than for short-term ones, and higher rates for short than for long loans, see C. D. Campbell and C. S. Ahn, ' Kyes and Mujins — Financial Intermediaries in South Korea', *Economic Development and Cultural Change*, Chicago October 1962, pp. 64–5.

they decline in real value as prices rise.[1] They even fail to provide acceptable liquidity to bridge the gap between transactions, because the intervals between cash receipts and disbursements may be long enough for prices to rise appreciably. In these conditions, attempts will be made to acquire assets whose value is expected to rise in the interval before the investment opportunity or other occasion for disbursement arises. This flight into non-monetary assets is the source of many of the distortions which accompany an inflation, and is a partial cause of the decrease in the flow of resources to investment.

Inflation is not the only problem of development

The control of inflation is only one of the problems facing a government wishing to encourage rapid economic development. The fight against illiteracy, the reform of bureaucratic practices, the building of basic sanitary facilities for the eradication of endemic diseases, the substitution of competitive for monopolistic trade practices, the encouragement of a widespread spirit of entrepreneurship, and the creation of an adequate amount of social capital, may be important pre-requisites for rapid growth. However, attacks on these problems are likely to be more feasible in an atmosphere of financial stability : a rapid inflation will make the failure of such attacks much more likely.

II. The Flow of Resources for Development

Acceleration of development, or the maintenance of a high rate of economic progress, calls for encouragement of the flow of resources to development uses and their utilization in the most productive directions. These resources can come only from that part of total domestic output which is not consumed, or from foreign borrowing. Hence, a development policy may be judged by its influence on output, the rate of saving, the decisions of foreign lenders, and the uses to which the total flow of investment funds are put. The future level of output will be, in large part, determined by current and foreign borrowing, and by the productivity of the investments financed from these sources.

[1] Presumably, this is what Keynes had in mind when he stated that ' money itself loses the attribute of liquidity if its future supply is expected to undergo sharp changes '. (*The General Theory of Employment, Interest and Money*, New York, 1936, p. 241, n.1.)

DOMESTIC SAVING

Amount

General observations. In all countries, a considerable part of the community's saving takes the form of the accumulation of financial assets. In most poor countries, money forms the major part of the community's financial assets. Even in wealthy countries, financial assets denominated in money (money itself, savings deposits, insurance policies, bonds, etc.) absorb a large part of the community's saving. The willingness of individuals and businesses to hold an expanded quantity of money, or financial claims denominated in money terms, is influenced by their expectations regarding the future price levels. If prices are expected to rise markedly, holders of money will try to limit any increase in the money value of their holdings, or may even attempt to dispose of them. Evidence of community reaction to inflation is provided in Table 2. Historically, the ratio of money to income in all but the wealthiest countries has tended to rise, but in recent years this ratio, on the whole, has declined in countries where inflation has prevailed. The simpler comparison of the value, in terms of constant prices, of the increases in money leads to similar conclusions. In countries which have gone through fairly extended periods of strong inflation, the volume of savings accumulated in the form of money and quasi-money has been quite small, whereas in the more stable countries these accumulations have been substantial. In Argentina and Bolivia the real value of money holdings has even declined. It should be remembered that this latter comparison is limited to changes in the value of these holdings. It does not take account of any changes in the real value of transactions which these holdings are required to finance.

Saving in the form of money accumulation is only one part of saving through the acquisition of financial claims. A large part of money accumulation is involuntary. Other holdings of financial assets are voluntary. These latter holdings are likely to rise less (or fall more) than those of money if prices are expected to rise. The experience of Argentina and Brazil, outlined in Table 26, may be taken as typical. Between 1950 and 1961 the money holdings of Argentine residents rose almost ten-fold. However, the increase in quasi-money was only seven-fold and holdings of government debt remained constant over the period. While Argentine residents increased their money holdings by more than 800 per cent (which

TABLE 2. COMPARISON OF RATES OF INFLATION AND OF INCREASES IN
MONEY AND QUASI-MONEY†

(*in per cent*)

Countries	Average Annual Rates of Change in Recent Years in Ratio of Money to Income	Average Increases from 1948 to 1961 in Real Value of Holdings of	
		Money	Money and quasi-money
Stable countries	—	79	103
Mild inflation countries	−2	100	138
Strong inflation countries	−3	19	11

† See Tables 16 and 17 (pp. 391–2).

in fact represented a decline of 25 per cent in the real value of these assets), the wider group of financial assets rose by only 685 per cent, representing a decline of more than 40 per cent in their real value.[1] In Brazil, where money holdings have, until recently, tended to increase slightly in real value, all financial assets, taken together, have, until the last few months, been remarkably stable in real value. The decline in the value of financial assets other than money has offset any saving forced by monetary action.

It is true that this argument says nothing more than that one element of saving will be reduced. Yet, it is the element of saving most widely accessible to non-property owners in less highly developed countries. Individuals who forgo money savings will undoubtedly divert some of their saving to other forms. However, consumption is also a rival for expenditure, if saving in the form of accumulation of assets denominated in terms of money is unattractive. Consequently, a communal shift away from holdings of financial assets is almost certain to be associated with a decline in total saving.

Personal saving. In part, the decline in saving may be explained by the changes in income distribution which are likely to accompany a strong inflation. In the early stages of a mild inflation, the belief that prices will not rise markedly may well lead wage earners to accept nearly constant money payments, and pension plans which

[1] An examination of some unpublished data on insurance in Argentina indicates that the increase in all financial assets was less than 650 per cent.

promise fixed money payments. Consequently, in the early stages of a mild inflation, there may be a shift in income distribution from the relatively low-income wage earning and pension groups, who have a low propensity to save, to the relatively wealthy profit recipients, who are likely to have a higher propensity to save.

Once wage earners realize that the real value of fixed money earnings is likely to decline, they will press for higher wages or for sliding scale adjustments which will ensure, at least, the maintenance of the real value of their earnings. At the same time, employers, with rising money profits, will be willing to compete for workers by agreeing to higher wage payments. Similarly, prospective pensioners will not be satisfied with retirement programmes which relate benefits to past money incomes. Pressures will be exerted for the adoption of plans with escalator clauses. Governments, acting on the basis of humanitarian motives, will accede to these pressures. As a result, pension programmes will be developed which, in effect, relate pension payments to the cost of living, the level of minimum wages, or some similar escalating provision. This process will result in a shift in income distribution from the wealthy back to the less wealthy, with a consequent decline in saving.

Whether these forces will be sufficient to make the final distribution of income more or less favourable to the relatively poor is probably impossible to determine. Table 27 suggests that, if reasonably long periods are taken, the degree of inflation has relatively little influence on real wage rates. Similarly, the data in Table 28 suggest that the shift in the distribution of income may be quite small, with perhaps a slight increase in the share going to wage earners in periods of inflation.

At the same time, inflation will be associated with a qualitative redistribution of profits. Every rapid inflation provides an opportunity for fortunate speculators, and their ostentatious consumption gives an impression of a radical shift in the community's income distribution. However, these groups are not likely to be large savers relative to their incomes. The *nouveaux riches* are likely to be more typical of this group than the frugal entrepreneurs who reinvest profits to build industrial empires.

Business saving. The pressures which depress personal savings will have a similar influence on business saving. In addition, strong inflation will bring forth two specific pressures encouraging businesses to distribute, rather than to reinvest, current earnings.

The strengthening of the desire for liquidity which results from inflation will discourage long-term investment. As a result, shareholders will press company managers to distribute profits.

Moreover, as shown below, in their search for liquidity and profitable investment, residents of countries where there is inflation are likely to shift from domestic to foreign investment. Shareholders in companies, being among the wealthy and more sophisticated members of the community, are persons who have the knowledge of, and effective access to, foreign investment. For this reason also, they are likely to put pressure on company managers to pay dividends rather than to retain earnings, so that the proceeds of these payments may be transferred abroad.

Comparative statistics on company practices are very scanty, to say the least. One, admittedly unsatisfactory, comparison is given in Table 19. Statistics on the activities of corporations controlled by U.S. residents, but operating in other countries, identify the data, by country, for only a relatively few countries. In the years 1957–60, the records relating to those less industrialized countries where prices were stable indicate that companies operating in these areas tended to reinvest half their disposable earnings. Similar companies operating in countries where prices were rising tended to reinvest only half as much.[1]

Government saving. If saving by the private sector is inhibited by inflation, it is possible that the shortfall might be made up by government saving. The data in Table 3 indicate the reverse. However, this relationship reflects primarily the attempts of some governments to finance investment by budget deficits. That is, in effect some countries have made inflation an instrument of development policy rather than making the control of inflation an object of policy.

There is one important factor which will tend to increase government expenditure and lead to budget deficits. Even though a worker realizes that his wages are increased, he strongly resents a rise in his rent or in the prices of bread or beans, and particularly resents any increase in public utility prices. In an attempt to forestall some

---

[1] A similar conclusion is obtained if the data relating to Venezuela (where investment in crude oil production is of a technological form which is not amenable to expansion through reinvestment of earnings) and to Brazil and Indonesia (where restrictions on capital repatriation led to forced reinvestment of earnings by foreign companies) are excluded from the comparison.

of the undesirable effects of inflation, the government may attempt
to restrain the rise in prices of consumer goods. Farmers and other
producers will expect, and will provide supplies only if they receive

TABLE 3. RELATIONSHIP OF RATES OF INFLATION TO BUDGET DEFICITS,
SELECTED YEARS†

Countries	Average Budget Deficits as Percentages of Gross National Product
Stable countries	2
Mild inflation countries	2
Strong inflation countries	5

† See Table 18 (p. 393).

the benefits of, rising prices. If the price of one commodity is controlled while other prices are rising, the demand for the price-
controlled commodity will increase. If the supply of a commodity is
to be encouraged, its price must rise relative to other prices. Hence,
government restraint of price increases will only be possible if the
production of the price-controlled goods is subsidized. The cost of
these subsidies may well absorb substantial amounts of government
expenditure. For example, the persistent deficits of government-
owned public utilities, resulting from rising costs and opposition to
rate and fare increases, are a common characteristic of government
accounts in countries experiencing a strong inflation.

This is exemplified by the fiscal problems of the Government of
Ceylon. In the past few years, factors which might lead to rapidly
rising prices have been present in that country. The Government has
striven to restrain these pressures, largely by using subsidies to sup-
press the effects of inflation, and has met with considerable success.
Because of the country's high propensity to import (even though
subject to controls, imports are equal to approximately 40 per cent of
Gross National Product and imported goods account for over 40 per
cent of consumer expenditure), the domestic price level is determined predominantly by foreign prices. The evidence of inflation has
appeared primarily in a 60 per cent reduction in the country's
foreign exchange reserves in the five years ending in 1962. Government revenue rose (Table 4), partly as a result of increased tax rates
and new taxes, but government expenditure increased more rapidly

in the six years ending in 1960 (the latest period for which data are available). Consequently, the Government's cash accounts changed from a position of near balance to a deficit equal to approximately 7 per cent of Gross National Product. If the Government had been able to avoid the expenditures made to restrain the inflation, its

TABLE 4. CEYLON: PRICES AND GOVERNMENT FINANCE, 1955–60

	1955	1956	1957	1958	1959	1960
Pre-subsidy cost of living index	100	103	104	106	109	107
Effect of subsidy [1]	1	4	3	3	5	5
Subsidized index	99	99	101	103	104	102
	(million rupees)					
Government revenue [2]	1,185	1,280	1,271	1,293	1,349	1,413
Government expenditure	1,068	1,322	1,507	1,554	1,774	1,863
Other than capital investment and inflation transfers [3]	563	670	831	713	895	948
Capital investment	357	431	396	499	493	496
Inflation transfers	148	221	280	342	386	419
Surplus or deficit (−)	117	−42	−236	−261	−425	−450
Excluding capital investment and inflation transfers	622	610	440	580	454	465
Excluding inflation transfers	265	179	44	81	−39	−31

SOURCE: Central Bank of Ceylon, *Annual Report for the Year 1961.*
[1] Food subsidies as per cent of personal consumption.
[2] Revenue plus grants under Colombo Plan and from other sources.
[3] Food subsidies and losses of railway and electricity departments.

excess of current revenue over current expenditure would have provided surpluses to finance its investment expenditure in the fiscal years 1955–8, and the 1959 and 1960 deficits would have been small.

The decision to provide food subsidies and to cover the operating losses of the railways and electricity departments induced inflationary deficits in the years 1956 to 1960. Even with the investment programme, there would have been inflation-repressing surpluses in the early years.

Purchase of Foreign Assets

In an inflationary economy, foreign financial assets serve to protect liquidity. In so far as they are claims denominated in money terms, they provide the same quality of protection that domestic financial assets provide in a stable environment. In so far as the expectation of price increases has, as a concomitant, an expectation of exchange depreciation, domestic claims will be expected to decline in real value, whereas foreign claims will not. Consequently, it may be expected that inflation will lead to an increase in the community's desires to hold foreign assets, and that savings will be diverted from the purchase of domestic assets to the purchase of foreign assets. Any expectation that the exchange rate will depreciate to a greater degree than domestic prices rise will strengthen the desire for foreign assets.[1]

Comprehensive statistics on the acquisition of foreign assets by residents of countries experiencing inflation are not available. A number of estimates of the total amounts involved have been made, but they can be no more than guesses. The few available statistics are depressing. In the five years ending in 1961, private residents of Latin America, other than banks, increased their investments in the United States by approximately one billion dollars.[2] The summary in Table 5 of data on the acquisition of short-term foreign assets by

TABLE 5. MEXICO : AVERAGE NET PURCHASES OF SHORT-TERM FOREIGN ASSETS BY RESIDENTS, 1951–60[1]

(in millions of U.S. dollars)

Years of	Average Net Purchases
Monetary stability	—
Mild inflation	8
Strong inflation	12

[1] Based on data in Table 20 (p. 394).

[1] See Part IV for a discussion of this point.

[2] Derived from *Survey of Current Business* and *International Financial Statistics*.

residents of Mexico provides an example of the relation between these capital movements and the rate of inflation. Indeed, 'a particularly unfortunate feature of the international financial scene in the last decade has been the large flow of private capital from those less developed countries which have tolerated inflation to countries, frequently wealthy, which have maintained monetary stability'.[1]

Purchase of Financial Assets

Even if inflation did no more than lead to a shift in the flow of saving from the accumulation of financial assets to the purchase of other types of assets, this would involve a decline in the 'quality' of saving. It may be argued that, if all domestic capital markets were perfectly linked, if the different availabilities of capital in each market were reflected solely in the different rates of interest prevailing, and if these rates reflected only the liquidity and risk elements in the capital transactions, financial transactions might be considered to reflect purely economic forces. If these conditions prevailed, each economic unit desiring to invest would have to compete with all the others desiring to invest, and this competition would be based on the relative returns to be earned in different activities and the relative costs of borrowing from different sources. Under these conditions, investment should be channelled to the most productive uses. It must be admitted that these perfect conditions do not prevail in any market, and that the capital markets of all the less highly developed countries tend to be more inflexible than the markets of the more highly developed countries. Yet, anything which encourages the flow of savings to the financial markets may be expected to increase the economic desirability of the resulting investment which the community's saving makes possible. Anything which limits the flow of savings to financial markets, or reduces the opportunity for self-investors to acquire financial assets, may be expected to limit the influence of economic criteria on investment decisions.

FOREIGN CAPITAL

Amount

In addition to the release of domestic resources through saving, just discussed, resources for development may be obtained by

---

[1] International Monetary Fund, *Annual Report, 1962*, p. 44.

borrowing abroad. But just as an outward flow of capital is encouraged by an inflation (above, pp. 363–4), so an inflow in the form of portfolio investment is discouraged by inflation.

A major part of private international capital transfers arises from equity investment by non-residents. This flow is largely in the form of direct investment by experienced entrepreneurs interested in establishing types of production not previously undertaken in the developing economies. This is frequently one of the major sources of capital for the productive diversification of staple-exporting economies. The volume of this investment is largely a function of its expected return. Inflation may be expected to raise the money return on investment. If the exchange rate could be expected to depreciate at the same rate that prices increased, inflation would tend to have a neutral effect on prospective non-resident purchasers of domestic equity investments. However, as will be indicated below, the exchange depreciation is likely to be more severe than the increase in prices induced by inflation. Hence, the net return to non-resident equity investors in inflating economies may be expected to deteriorate. Therefore, the flow of equity capital to inflating economies will probably be lessened.

There is one very positive impediment to non-resident investment induced by inflation. It will be indicated that one of the effects of inflation is a deterioration of the foreign balance and that this induces the government to take protective action. One of these acts may be the restriction of payments to non-residents. Payments on capital account to non-residents are prime candidates for such restrictions. At the first sign of inflation in a country, non-residents will fear that restrictions of this kind will be imposed and will refrain from investing there. They may even attempt to repatriate previous investments in anticipation of such restrictions. This type of reaction probably accounts for the disparate movements of international capital indicated in Table 6. This shows that net private direct investment in less highly developed countries by residents of the country with the largest capital exports increased at a rate 20 per cent faster than the comparable increase in investment in a group of mild inflation countries during the eleven years ending in 1961. The comparable increase in a group of countries where prices were rising rapidly was equivalent to only a little more than the reinvestment of earnings at a rate equivalent to 4 per cent of the capital invested.

(in per cent)

Countries	Average Increases
Stable countries	214
Mild inflation countries	177
Strong inflation countries	55

† See Table 21 (p. 394).

Protection of Foreign Investors

It was suggested earlier that development policies are designed to make the flow of resources for investment greater than they would be in the absence of such policies. Since in the absence of government intervention, inflation is likely to have a depressing effect on the flow of foreign capital to a developing economy, it is likely to make a government more willing to protect foreign lenders. If this protection is to be effective, it is almost inevitable that it must err, if it errs at all, on the side of being excessive. That is, inflation may lead to the adoption of policies which give better terms to foreign lenders than they could command under stable conditions.[1]

The degree of uncertainty created by inflation may be greater in the opinion of foreign than of domestic investors. Not only is the uncertainty regarding the real domestic value of future earnings increased by inflation, but uncertainty regarding the future course of exchange rates is created and there is also the fear of exchange restrictions. To allay these fears, the government of an inflation-ridden economy may be pushed to borrow directly from abroad or to guarantee the repatriation of private loans raised abroad. However, development must, almost inevitably, include risky investment. No matter how astute investors may be, some investments will be unprofitable. If such investments have been financed through private channels, the process of bankruptcy will lead to a sharing of the cost

---

[1] This statement is not contradicted by the policies of certain governments restricting foreign investment in certain fields (e.g., exploration for petroleum). These policies may be adopted for specific national purposes, and the inflationary or non-inflationary climate is irrelevant. Within the constraints set by such policies, inflation is likely to increase the pressures on these same governments to take positive steps to increase the inflow of non-resident capital.

of any unsuccessful investment between borrowers and lenders. If they have been financed by government borrowing, or with a government guarantee, the full cost of investment, which in restrospect will be seen to have been unwise, will be borne by residents of the borrowing country.[1]

Changes in Relative Prices

The distortion of the price structure created by inflation is likely indirectly to discourage saving and encourage consumption. In most non-industrial countries, investment has a high import component. The excessive exchange depreciation induced by inflation, and the protective import substitution policies likely to be adopted by the authorities, frequently lead to relatively large increases in the prices of investment goods. The experience in nine Latin American countries, summarized in Table 7, suggests that one unit of consumption expenditure forgone in a stable country would permit the use of 15 per cent more investment, in real terms, than in the mild inflation countries, and almost 40 per cent more than the average for the strong inflation countries. This rise in the relative price of investment

TABLE 7. RELATIVE PRICES OF INVESTMENT GOODS, SELECTED LATIN
AMERICAN COUNTRIES, 1960†

(average for all countries = 100)

Countries	At Free Market Exchange Rates	At Parity Rates
Stable country	86	82
Mild inflation countries	100	95
Strong inflation countries	120	114

† See Table 22 (p. 395).

[1] These comments should not be taken as a generalized condemnation of government borrowing, or of inter-government capital transactions. Under many circumstances, they serve highly useful purposes. Many forms of investment, which are appropriate for foreign financing (e.g., a part of social investment in roads, water, and sanitation works), can only be handled by the government or its agencies. Many of the sources of capital in the modern world are governments or inter-government agencies (International Bank for Reconstruction and Development, Inter-American Development Bank, etc.) which may be expected to make only loans with government guarantees.

goods decreases the money rate of return on investment, and consequently on saving, with a resultant discouragement of investment and encouragement of consumption.[1]

Conclusion

This analysis, which appears to be supported by the available statistics, suggests that inflation is likely to evoke forces which both diminish the resources available for development and reduce the true effectiveness of those funds which continue to flow to investment. Saving is likely to be lower than under stable monetary conditions, and to take forms which lead to a lessening of the adaptability of the economy and to a lessening of the force of economic criteria in the choice of final investment. The inflow of foreign capital is likely to be reduced, and the terms on which it comes to the country are likely to become more stringent with regard to its eventual repayment.

III. The Direction of Investment

Inventory Investment

The effect of inflation on the desire for liquidity has already been discussed. If money, and financial assets denominated in money, cease to provide satisfactorily protected liquidity, other sources of this protection will be sought. The accumulation of saleable inventories is one means of obtaining realizable assets whose real value is likely to be maintained in the face of rising prices. Consequently, inflation may be expected to encourage investors to forgo the purchase of financial assets which could have financed long-term physical investment and to accumulate inventories directly. As a result, the available resources will be devoted to inventory stockpiling rather than to long-term investment.

Moreover, in addition to the disadvantages of illiquidity attached to long-term fixed investment, there is an element of uncertainty. In an environment of unstable prices and rising costs, the long gestation period involved in fixed investment means that its eventual cost is indeterminate, and hence the possibility of financing the total-

---

[1] For a more complete discussion of this point, as related to one country, see R. Hayn, 'Capital Formation and Argentina's Price-Cost Structure', *Review of Economics and Statistics*, August 1962.

outlay may be questionable. As a result, it may prove impossible to complete projects.

There are strict limits to the changes which may be made in the structure of a given stock of physical assets. Most of these changes must result from the channelling of currently accruing resources into the most desired form of asset. As the changes desired may well be large in relation to total annual investment, it may be expected that a large part of this total may be devoted to inventory investment, until the structure of the community's stock of physical assets is changed. Subsequently, the flow of investment resources will be divided between inventory accumulation and fixed asset formation, in the ratio which the community wishes to maintain between these components of its stock of physical assets. Hence, in a brief period of inflation, or in the early stages of a longer inflation, a marked

TABLE 8. RELATIONSHIP OF INFLATION TO VARIABILITY OF INVENTORY INVESTMENT, SELECTED COUNTRIES, SELECTED YEARS†

Countries	Rate of Inflation		Inventory Investment as Percentage of Gross Domestic Investment	
	Annual average (*per cent*)	Standard deviation	Annual average value	Standard deviation
Stable countries				
Philippines	1	4	15	6
Ecuador	2	4	16	3
Mild inflation countries				
Colombia	7	6	9	12
Mexico	7	9	14	9
Peru	8	3	11	3
Strong inflation countries				
Brazil	19	8	10	9
Chile	38	24	3	13

† See Table 23 (p. 396).

diversion of investment resources toward the accumulation of inventories may be expected. In the later stages of a prolonged inflation, the ratio of inventory investment to fixed investment may be expected to be somewhat higher than it was prior to the inflation, but it should be less than in the early stages of inflation.

Table 8 indicates that, in two relatively stable countries, the inventory component of gross domestic investment has been relatively stable. There is some indication that in one of these, Ecuador, the ratio of inventory accumulation to total investment has been slightly correlated with the rate of inflation. In two mild inflation countries where the rate of inflation has varied (Colombia and Mexico), there is clear evidence of correlation between the rate of inflation and shifts in the stocking of inventories. In two strong inflation countries (Brazil and Chile), the rate of inventory investment has varied markedly. In Brazil, when the rate of inflation rose, inventories were increased sharply. Thereafter, even though inflation might be rapid, the rate of inventory investment reverted to a more normal level; when the rate of inflation was reduced, there was a temporary decline in the rate of inventory investment. In Chile, similar effects appear to have followed after a lag.[1]

HOUSING

The implication of the above analysis is that inflation encourages excessive investment in inventories, which is a form of short-term investment, and at least temporarily discourages long-term investment in fixed assets. Nevertheless, it is frequently suggested that an inflationary economy is characterized by excessive investment in luxury housing — a form of long-term investment. However, this paradox is apparent rather than real. Encouraged to acquire physical rather than fixed-money assets, savers must find some asset which satisfies their demand. One of the physical assets most easily acquired by individuals is residential property. Hence, inflation may be expected to encourage the demand for houses, either for occupation or for rent. In many of the inflation-ridden economies, governments are prone to control money rents. Hence, the return on rental housing is prevented from rising in step with the increase in the level of prices. The outcome is that savers are encouraged to buy houses for self-occupancy and discouraged from investing in rental property.

Data on the distribution of expenditure between housing and other forms of investment are scarce, and data on investment in houses for owner-occupancy are practically non-existent. The indirect indi-

---

[1] See Table 23, as well as Table 8, for the basis for these observations.

cation of the effect of inflation on the demand for building materials, presented in Table 29, is consistent with an argument that inflation leads to a rise in the relative demand for buildings, as distinct from other forms of investment. While these data are consistent with the arguments presented here, they should be used with caution because the demand for building materials is more subject to the distorting effects of inflation than is the demand for most other products. The prices of all investment goods tend to rise more during inflation than the general level of prices. Stocks of building materials (other than cement) are prime targets for inventory investment, as they tend to be durable (bricks, pipe, tile, etc.), their cost of storage (on the sites of incomplete buildings) is relatively low, and they may be financed from a variety of sources (e.g., both by bank loans for working capital and by construction mortgages).

BUSINESS FIXED ASSETS

The pressures exerted by inflation on the allocation of investment funds to the purchase of different types of fixed asset may be separated into those which may be termed 'fundamental forces', and those which reflect the adjustment of individual economic units to the 'inflation restraining' actions of the government.

Requirements for investment in fixed assets differ markedly between industries. Some activities (e.g., railroad transport) require long-lived equipment, whereas others (e.g., highway transport) require much shorter-lived equipment. It may be taken that the most appropriate combination of investment in different activities will result from the interplay of competing demands by investors looking for the most profitable investments (adjusted to take advantage of subsidies and taxes where these are considered desirable for social reasons). However, some of these investments involve long-term commitments and hence will be influenced by the community's expectations. If investors believe that the prospective economic parameters will be similar to those presently existing, or if they can reasonably expect that changes in these parameters will be orderly, they can have a firm basis for their decisions. Technological factors will then be the primary determinants for the distribution of investment. If investors expect rapid change in basic economic relations, they will be hesitant to commit themselves for long periods. If capital investments may be amortized quickly, an investor has more frequent opportunities to review his decisions. The expectation of

rising prices will therefore be likely to bias investment decisions
toward the purchase of fixed assets with relatively short lives. For
these reasons, an inflationary economy may be expected to evolve
along lines where long-term industrial and social investment is
discouraged, and where resources flow more readily to those fields in
which returns may be achieved most quickly. Such an economy may
be expected to become one where railway transport deteriorates,
while trucks have their useful lives curtailed bouncing roughly on
pot-holed roads.

As suggested earlier, inflation brings forth two reactions by
governments:

(1) The impetus to imports calls for protection of reserves, which
may involve active encouragement of import-substituting activity
and exchange restrictions.

(2) The reactions of the community to increases in the cost of
living are likely to force the government to institute price controls
over 'the basic necessities of life'.

An active policy of encouraging import substitution may involve
protection of domestic production from foreign competition. This
protection may be given by administrative restrictions, tariffs, or
excessive currency depreciation. It is possible that the rapid development of import-substituting production may entail nothing more
than an acceleration of part of the overall development process.
It is also possible that it will lead to the encouragement of activity
which, in the absence of protection, would remain unproductive
almost permanently in the face of foreign competition.

Some indication of the extent of desirable diversification which has
been achieved in recent years may be obtained by comparing the
export data for individual countries. If a country is able to diversify
its export sales, there are grounds for believing that it has been able
to expand the production of goods other than its staple exports, and
that this expansion has been in the fields where it enjoys some degree
of comparative advantage. If it does not achieve diversification of
export sales, there are grounds for believing that it has lost some of
its comparative advantages, and that any diversification of production which has been achieved has involved the expansion of output
in those fields where its costs are high by international standards.
Table 9 summarizes the changes in the volume of exports between
1953–4 and 1958–9 in two groups of countries. In both groups, the
volume of staple exports (major exports) expanded. However, in the

TABLE 9. PERCENTAGE INCREASES, 1953-4 TO 1958-9, IN VOLUME OF
MAJOR AND MINOR EXPORTS, SELECTED COUNTRIES†

Countries	Major Exports	Minor Exports
Stable countries	18	39
Strong inflation countries	10	—

† See Table 24 (p. 397).

stable countries the volume of other exports (minor exports)
expanded more rapidly than exports generally, providing some
evidence that these countries achieved some economically desirable
diversification of production. In the strong inflation countries the
volume of minor exports was unchanged during these years. Whereas
the minor exports accounted for approximately one-tenth more of
the total in the stable countries, this proportion fell by approximately one-sixth in the strong inflation countries.

To protect exchange reserves from the erosion induced by
inflation, many countries have resorted to exchange restrictions.
Many restrictive systems have been based on multiple exchange
rates, which have the adverse qualities to which attention has
frequently been drawn.[1] They frequently provide minimum
exchange depreciation for certain basic export products. This prefer-
ential treatment adds to the structural distortions of the economy,
discussed earlier. The favourable rates provided for the import of
essential commodities serve to discourage domestic production and
encourage activities (usually the production of non-essential goods)
which are given the greatest degree of protection. Often these are not
the most appropriate uses for the country's resources. For example,
the exchange rate system of Indonesia at the end of 1961[2] could be
described as a government production plan, designed to penalize
the production of rice and to divert domestic resources from investment to personal consumption, particularly of luxury items.

Investment decisions made by private entrepreneurs are primarily
influenced by the expected profitability of investment. The relative
profitability of investment in any activity is a function of the prices

[1] e.g., International Monetary Fund, 'Decision on Multiple Currency
Practices', Annual Report, 1957, pp. 161-2.

[2] See International Monetary Fund, Thirteenth Annual Report on Exchange
Restrictions, 1962, pp. 174-5.

of final output rendered possible by the investment compared with the prices of final outputs which could be achieved by alternative investment. Governments frequently attempt to restrain inflation by imposing controls on the prices of the basic necessities of life, or of community services. Under these circumstances, the general rise in other prices is equivalent to a relative fall in the prices of the basic necessities or services. If price controls are not accompanied by subsidies to the producers of the price-controlled goods and services, investment in the production of basic necessities and community services will become relatively unprofitable and will be discouraged. Consequently, if the consumer is protected, as he frequently is, from the evils of inflation, the result may well be to divert investment, so that he is deprived of access to potential supplies of basic necessities and community services.

This aspect of inflation is seen most frequently in the public utility field. Many public utilities are natural monopolies. Hence, their prices are frequently subject to control by regulatory bodies. This control, with the almost inevitable legalism involved in its administration, is likely to create a lag in the rise of public utility prices behind other prices. Moreover, the regulatory process makes this field a prime candidate for price control to restrain increases in cost of living indices. Hence, inflation will almost inevitably lead to a diversion of investment from public utilities. As a result, the recurrent power shortages, which are one of the aspects of life in an inflationary economy, are easily comprehensible.

Conclusion

These arguments, which are supported by observation, suggest that inflation is likely to evoke forces which divert the resources available for domestic investment to an excessive accumulation of inventories and the building of houses for occupancy by the relatively wealthy, rather than to the construction of productive facilities or the provision of housing for the major part of the community. Of the productive facilities actually built, a bias develops toward investment in relatively short-lived projects, and the attraction of truly low-cost production tends to be weakened, while resources are diverted from the production of basic necessities and investment goods to the production of consumption goods, particularly luxury commodities.

IV. THE BALANCE OF PAYMENTS

The frequency with which inflating countries have had to resort to the International Monetary Fund for assistance, together with the relatively small volume of continuing drawings by non-inflating countries, provides clear evidence of the relation between strong inflation and balance-of-payments difficulties. These difficulties arise because strong inflations encourage capital flight, strengthen import demands, and reduce export supplies. They make large exchange rate depreciations necessary. The attempts to limit exchange pressures often lead to the imposition of restrictions which have distorting effects on the structure of investment and production.

IMPORTS

When there is a generalized excess demand for goods it will quickly become evident as a demand for purchases from the most readily available elastic source, i.e., from foreigners. Hence, one of the first effects of inflation will be a rise in imports. In the early stages, the effect of expanding demand on the price level may be dampened by the ability of the community to import. With a small rise in domestic prices, foreign supplies become relatively cheaper and the pressing demand from the domestic economy will be diverted to the larger world economy. This diversion will limit the demands impinging directly on the domestic economy and will restrict the immediate effects of inflationary pressures on domestic prices.[1]

In many countries, the impact of inflation on imports is repressed by trade controls, so that the level of imports is determined, not by relative prices, but by administrative decision. However, the trade controls and the exchange depreciation in inflating countries provide clear evidence of the payments difficulties of these countries.

EXPORTS [2]

Just as inflation may be expected to encourage imports, it may be expected to discourage exports. Rising domestic demand will impinge on those export goods which are suitable for domestic consumption, and will divert them from export to domestic sales or

---

[1] See, for example, the discussion of Ceylon, pp. 361–3 above.

[2] This section is based largely on Gertrud Lovasy, 'Inflation and Exports in Primary Producing Countries', *Staff Papers*, Vol. IX (1962), pp. 37–69.

stockpiles.[1] Of course, in many cases, this diversion will be limited. An economy with only a few basic export products is not likely to increase its consumption of these products sufficiently to affect markedly the supply available for sale to foreigners. Even a doubling of domestic consumption of Brazilian coffee or Malayan rubber would lead to relatively small percentage declines in the supplies of these goods on world markets. However, it is easy to overstate this argument. All export production involves the use of some generalized resources. In any economy, excessive demand will impinge on these generalized resources, and bid them away from the production of export goods. This may be a somewhat longer-run effect, and is likely to be an influence leading to a structural distortion of the economy rather than to immediate short-term balance-of-payments difficulties. However, it is not merely coincidental that the volume of exports made available by Argentina, Bolivia, Brazil, Chile, and Haiti declined during the half-century between 1913 and 1958, and that these countries have experienced almost continuous inflationary pressures since World War I.

In the period 1953 to 1959, the export experience of the three groups of raw material exporting countries differed markedly, as indicated in Table 10. These differences do not reflect varying market

TABLE 10. AVERAGE CHANGES, 1953 TO 1959, IN DOMESTIC PRICES, EXPORT PRICES AND VOLUME, AND EXCHANGE RATES, SELECTED COUNTRIES †

(in per cent)

Countries	Cost of Living	Export Prices	Export Volume	Exchange Rates
Stable countries	9	− 5	24	—
Mild inflation countries	43	−10	19	64
Strong inflation countries	400	−16	6	700

† See Table 25 (p. 398).

conditions, as the grouping bears no relation to the export products of these countries. Exporters of coffee, cotton, non-ferrous metals,

[1] One aspect of this problem is exemplified by the following quotation from a report on the decline in the marketable supply of sisal: 'Brazilian growers are simply retaining their stocks as a hedge against inflation' (*The Statist,* 2 November, 1962, p. 328).

and rubber are in all three groups; of cereals, meat, and wool in the stable and strong inflation groups, and of fish and sugar in the stable and mild inflation groups. Consequently, it is not surprising that the average change in the world market prices (i.e., export price indices in terms of U.S. dollars) have moved in the same direction and by approximately the same amount for each group of countries. While the volume of exports of the stable countries rose by one-quarter, and of the mild inflation countries by one-fifth, the increase for the strong inflation countries was less than one-sixteenth. The pressures of inflation led to a domestic absorption of resources in those countries where domestic prices were rising, preventing them from participating in the expansion of world demand for their products.[1]

THE EXCHANGE RATE

The incentives to capital exports and the discouragement of capital imports, caused by inflation, have been discussed above. These influences augment the balance-of-payments difficulties on current account so that, unless action is taken, an inflating economy's international reserves are soon dissipated. The action which is needed may take the form of restrictions on imports or on capital payments, or it may include exchange depreciation. If inflation is continued, it is practically inevitable that the exchange rate must depreciate.

Moreover, if imports are not restricted, the eventual exchange depreciation is likely to be greater than the rise in domestic prices. The excess demand caused by inflation will meet supply inelasticities. The spillover of demand into the foreign market and the reduction of exports, consequent on inflation, can only be offset by a greater rise in the domestic equivalent of foreign prices than of purely domestic prices. As shown by the comparison in Table 10, the depreciation of the exchange rate in mild inflation countries exceeded the rise in domestic prices in the period 1953–9 by almost 15 per cent on the average. In the strong inflation countries this excess averaged 75 per cent.[2]

---

[1] Given the decline in average export prices, there was a rise in the volume of demand, but not necessarily a rise in the demand schedules for the products of these countries.

[2] If allowance is made for the fact that world prices rose by approximately 10 per cent during this period, and that hence a 10 per cent rise in domestic prices would have been consistent with exchange stability, these percentages become 25 and 80, respectively.

While there is ample evidence to support the view that the exchange rate will depreciate by more than the increase in domestic prices, it does not follow that this is a smooth progress. Most governments attempt, either consciously or unconsciously, to maintain confidence in the value of money. One of the quickest ways to destroy this confidence is to allow the exchange rate to depreciate. Therefore, it may be expected that the government will attempt to maintain the rate, for a period at least. Six examples of the pegging of exchange rates, at one time or another, are provided in Chart 1. Periods when the rate was pegged despite pressures toward depreciation are indicated by stability of the exchange rate (light) lines coinciding with decline in the price (heavy) lines. Such pegging action has two repercussions. First, as the domestic currency prices of exports and imports are maintained, the pressures of inflation are given full play; if the rate were allowed to depreciate, the depreciation would mitigate or even offset the balance of payments effects of inflation. Second, with exchange depreciation clearly forecast by the rise in prices, the inducements to capital flight discussed above, are strengthened.

V. STABILIZATION PROBLEMS

THE DIFFICULTY OF STABILIZATION

It is often alleged that, even though inflation may be undesirable, a cure by means of a stabilization programme may be worse than the disease of inflation. Those who favour monetary reform are accused of placing a higher value on price stability than on economic growth. If the analysis presented in this paper is valid, an economy experiencing inflation must be one where development is proceeding less rapidly than it would if the economy were stable, all other conditions being similar. It does not follow, however, that a change in the climate will immediately ease an inflating economy's difficulties. In particular, it does not follow that a stabilization programme will bring an immediate increase in output.

The desirable reshuffling of the economy, resulting from stabilization, may lead directly to a temporary decline in the demand for physical investment. There is an inevitable lag between the decision to create physical capital and the actual consumption of resources in capital production. On the other hand, investment already in progress may be abandoned rather quickly. One of the effects of

CHART 1. SELECTED COUNTRIES: EXCHANGE RATES AND PURCHASING
POWER OF MONEY, FIRST QUARTER 1851–SECOND QUARTER 1962
(*As percentages of 1951 averages*)

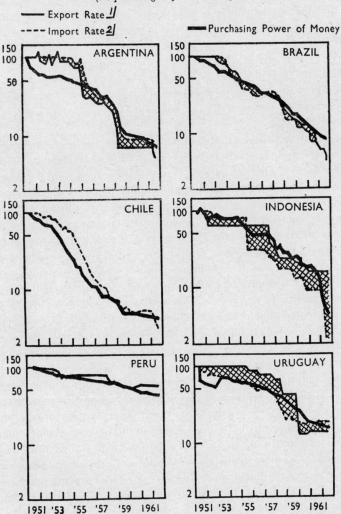

¹ For Argentina and Indonesia, implicit export rate ; Brazil, implicit export
rate excluding coffee; Peru, principal exchange rate, which does not differ
markedly from the implicit export rate and the implicit import rate; Uruguay,
principal export rate.

² For Argentina, Brazil, and Chile, implicit import rate; Indonesia, ' other '
import rate ; Uruguay, free rate.

inflation is the encouragement of industries which would be uneconomic in a non-inflationary world. Stabilization may bring a
quick cut-off in the development of these industries, leading to a
decline in the demand for investment resources. While a stable
environment will make alternative industries appear to be profitable fields for investment, it takes some time for entrepreneurs to
convert their investment desires into consumption of resources.
Hence, the period immediately after the start of a stabilization
programme may well be marked by a lag in the consumption of
investment resources, with a consequent decline in the production
of capital goods.

It might be thought that, as inflation is a situation of generalized
excess demand for goods and services, a reduction in demand might
do no more than eliminate the excess. But the situation which
develops in an inflation is that the supply of goods and services,
which necessarily cannot be less than effective expenditure, includes
types of commodities and services for which demand will exist only so
long as inflation continues. The reduction of this demand caused by
the cessation of inflation, and its replacement by expenditure
appropriate to stable conditions, involves a corresponding readjustment of supply. It would be utopian to expect that all phases
of this readjustment process would be closely synchronized. There
are particular difficulties in the smooth adjustment of investment
expenditures, which follow from the effects of inflation discussed
above. In the first place, inflation induces an accumulation of
inventories in excess of those which would have been built up in
stable conditions. Necessarily, therefore, the cessation of inflation
will lead to disinvestment in inventories, reversing this part of the
flow of demand. Secondly, investment in industries during the
inflation is likely to have been directed to those enjoying a high
degree of protection. In so far as the exchange rate is unified or
changed to a more realistic one, or in so far as stabilization by
strengthening the balance of payments (e.g., by reducing purchases
of imports for addition to inventories), enables exchange restrictions
to be eased, the protection afforded these industries will be dimi-
nished, and their attractiveness for investment will decline. Thirdly,
the increasing attractiveness of physical assets during an inflation
may be expected to lead also to a rise in the demand for owner-
occupied housing. Once stabilization is under way, the existing
supply of this type of housing, together with the rising demand for

financial assets, can be expected to lead to a reduction of investment of this kind. And even if stabilization and the easing of rent control make rental housing a desirable form of investment, it takes time to convert desires to invest into orders for bricks and mortar.

Thus the flow of resources evoked by an inflation will be not only in excess of, but also partially inappropriate to, the flow of demand in stabilized conditions. The severity of the consequential adjustment problems, and the time required to solve them, will depend, in part at least, on the degree to which the economic system has been distorted. This degree of distortion will in turn depend largely on the duration and rate of the inflation which is being brought to an end. When the inflation has not been too severe, and in its current bout has lasted no more than about two years, as in Peru at the time of the adoption of its 1959 stabilization programme, the problem is not too serious. When inflation has been rampant for decades, as in Argentina by 1958, the problem will have become very serious.

It should be emphasized that the depressive influences discussed above are temporary, rather than fundamental. After a relatively short period, they should evaporate. If the stabilization programme is effective, the period of uncertainty must pass, and a new set of expectations should enable investors to make plans for future capital creation, with a consequent rise in their demands for resources. The decline in investment arising from the lag between the end of development of protected industries and the expansion of more economic (from a long-range view) alternative investment, is by definition a temporary cut-back in investment. Likewise, by definition, disinvestment in inventories must also be temporary. The general adjustment which should accompany stabilization (including the elimination of controls, such as ceilings on rents) may be expected to revive the demand for investment in rental housing to replace the decline in the demand for owner-occupied residences. The general flight from real assets to financial assets, which is one of the healthy signs of stabilization even though it may exert depressing effects on investment, should also be temporary. After a short period of adjustment, individual economic units may be expected to desire additions to their stocks of both physical and financial assets. At the same time, the capital flight resulting from inflation should stop. The switch in the flow of saving from foreign to domestic investment, and the repatriation of earlier accumulations of foreign assets, will lead to an increase in the demand for domestic resources.[1]

A government which decides to eliminate the distortions created by inflation will be faced with a host of problems while the economy is readjusting to a condition of monetary equilibrium. There is no doubt that the difficulties facing the community will be dependent on the imagination exercised by the government. A stabilization programme which relies on monetary instruments alone will involve more stresses in the economy than one which includes fiscal and broader economic improvement measures as well. If a stabilization programme can be quickly associated with measures for the development of previously neglected facilities (e.g., the rehabilitation of obsolescent railway systems and the development of public utilities), the stresses will be eased. Foreign assistance (e.g., drawings on the International Monetary Fund to make more rapid elimination of exchange restrictions possible, and loans from the International Bank for Reconstruction and Development to facilitate the redeployment of resources for development) will make the elimination of distortions in production easier. However, no cleaning-up process is pleasant. Stabilizing an inflating economy is one of the least pleasant of the operations facing a responsible government.

THE CASE FOR FIRM ACTION

If an abrupt ending of an inflation is likely to bring a temporary decline in output, is not some alternative possible? Might not a tapering-off policy be adopted? Might not the rate of inflation be brought to an end slowly? The answer to these questions is that a gradual approach is fraught with more danger than sudden stabilization.

Among the real damages done by inflation is the distortion created in the economy. There is need to reorient the system. Drastic changes must be made in the community's expectations. These changes are not likely to occur if the community believes that the government may be lukewarm in its attack on inflation. If individuals see little change in the economic climate, they will be under

---

[1] For a discussion of one example of the change in direction of international capital movements, see the reference to this aspect of the changes in Spain following the adoption of a stabilization programme in 1959, in International Monetary Fund, *Annual Report, 1962*, p. 49.

very few effective pressures to change their views. The fundamental changes which are required will not take place.[1]

The persistence of expectations as to the movements of prices is a particular problem to be faced in introducing a stabilization programme. In the early stages of an inflation, individuals may continue to believe that prices will soon stop increasing. But once inflation is established, they will expect prices to go on rising; and even if they believe that the inflation has been halted, and that prices will be stabilized, they will not expect stabilization to take place immediately. Moreover, they will always be conscious of the possibility that the programme may fail. Even, therefore, when money and financial assets begin once more to appear attractive, the acquisition of such assets may be deterred by a lingering fear that they may again decline in real value. By contrast, the continued holding of inventories offers protection, even if the programme succeeds, against any loss except that of the potential income from financial investments; and the holder of foreign financial assets risks the loss only of the possibly excessive returns on domestic financial assets over the return on foreign ones. If the programme fails, such holders stand to gain much more. Thus, to enable a stabilization programme to succeed, it is above all necessary for the government to convince the community that the value of money will henceforth be maintained.

In short, an attempt to slow down an inflation will take a long time to be effective and its final result will be uncertain. The restrictions on credit necessary to bring some stabilization will deter

---

[1] The following is an assessment of the effect of these fundamental changes in one case:

'Now that the initial steps to stabilize the Spanish economy have been so successful the key to further progress seems to lie in the lowering of the import tariff and the abolition of the remaining import quotas. Spanish industry may be said to have grown up in the past 25 years in a hot-house atmosphere of complete freedom from foreign competition, and until imports began to be freed three years ago there had been no incentive or necessity to produce better goods at lower prices.

'But the limited measure of foreign competition to which it has already been subjected, together with free access to raw materials, has worked wonders. (In all fairness it should be said that during all that period Spanish manufacturers had to make do with substitute or makeshift materials in erratic supply, often smuggled in and sold at exorbitant prices.) Competition among manufacturers has made its appearance and quality has improved out of recognition.' (*The Times*, London, 23 November 1962, p. 19).

borrowers from investing, but the inflation-induced distortions of the economy are likely to persist. The continued rise in prices (even though it be slower than before) will deter the accumulation of financial assets and continue to act as a brake on the flow of resources to investment. Unless the authorities are firm in their attack, the atmosphere of financial stability necessary to induce a revival of output to levels higher than those which would have prevailed under inflation will not emerge.

VI. CONCLUSION

This review of the relation between inflation and economic development leads to the conclusion that the control of inflation should be one of the major objects of economic policy in a developing economy. It is true that, *per se*, rapid economic development is likely to provoke inflationary pressures. Therefore, one of the problems calling for high priority on the part of the authorities in a rapidly developing economy is the restraint of inflation.

Inflation diminishes the volume of resources available for domestic investment. Community saving is reduced, and a considerable part of this saving is channelled to foreign rather than domestic investment, while the flow of capital from abroad is discouraged. A substantial part of the reduced flow of resources for domestic investment is diverted to uses which are not of the highest social priority. The accumulation of large inventories is encouraged. The diversion of savings from the capital markets, where investment decisions are more subject to longer-term economic criteria, is exemplified by the diversion of investment from productive uses for the entire community to the building of owner-occupied housing for the relatively wealthy few. The apparent profitability of certain short-lived investments leads to distortions in the productive structure which make the economy less adaptable. Balance-of-payments difficulties are symptoms of the underlying stresses. To reduce the foreign deficits, the authorities are almost forced to resort to controls, which in most cases protect uneconomic production. Political pressures lead to further restrictions which, in the last analysis, create further distortions. Economic activity becomes steadily more distorted.

However, if the economic system has been allowed to get out of hand, the authorities must decide to stabilize, or not to stabilize. There is no doubt that the process of stabilization is difficult, but difficult or not, it is a prerequisite to rapid economic growth.

APPENDIX

'Selected Countries'

The term, 'Selected Countries', in the tables presented in this Appendix refers to all the less highly developed countries for which the relevant data are available in the sources. South Africa is not included, however, because its dual social structure makes statistical averages difficult to interpret, nor are the countries of the Eastern bloc. In several tables, Finland and Greece are included. The tables do not include other countries in Western Europe nor, of course, the United States and Canada.

'Selected Years'

In the tables compiled for this study, an attempt has been made to use series extending from 1948 to 1961. Many of the data, however, are not available for the full period. In these cases all the available data have been used, and the tables are stated to refer to 'selected years'. In many of the tables where annual averages are used, the time periods are not the same for all countries. Where tables are derived from other sources, no attempt has been made to alter the time periods covered by the original authors.

Classification of Countries

Countries are classified as stable, if the percentage increase in the cost of living index is less than 5 per cent a year for the period covered. If the rate of increase is 10 per cent or more, they are classified as being subject to strong inflation. The intermediate countries are considered to be subject to mild inflation. These boundary criteria should not be considered as separating clearly definable situations. Rather, they are arbitrary limits intended to identify rather different situations. They may be considered to be on the high side; in part they have been adopted because some price increases have been almost universal in the post-war period.

Ordering of Countries

Within each group, countries are arranged by the degree of inflation experienced, with the country experiencing the lowest rate of inflation placed at the top of the table, and the country with the highest rate at the bottom.

Weighting of averages

Where averages are given for groups of countries they are un-weighted averages, unless it is stated otherwise (e.g., when the value of exports is relevant to a comparison of changes in exports).

TABLE 11. INFLATION AND ECONOMIC DEVELOPMENT, SELECTED COUNTRIES, SELECTED YEARS[1]

(in per cent)

Countries	Rate of Inflation[2]	Rate of Growth Per Capita[3]
Stable countries[4]	2	2
Philippines	—	3
Ceylon	1	—
Pakistan	1	—
Guatemala	1	2
Syria	1	−2
Burma	2	4
Malaya	2	—
India	2	1
Ecuador	2	2
Venezuela	2	5
Honduras	3	—
El Salvador	4	2
Mild inflation countries[4]	7	2
Thailand	5	1
Iceland	7	2
Colombia	8	2
Peru	9	1
Strong inflation countries[4]	35	2
Brazil	20	2
Indonesia	22	3
Paraguay	32	3
Chile	33	—
Korea	66	1

SOURCES: Based on data in United Nations, *Yearbook of National Accounts Statistics, 1961*, and International Monetary Fund, *International Financial Statistics*, hereafter referred to as *IFS*.

[1] Generally 1954–60; see p. 385 for description of 'Selected Years'.

[2] Average annual increase in cost of living index.

[3] Average annual increase in real gross domestic product per capita.

[4] See p. 385 for the basis of these classifications.

TABLE 12. INFLATION AND ECONOMIC DEVELOPMENT, SELECTED
LATIN AMERICAN COUNTRIES, 1955–9

(in per cent)

Countries	Rate of Inflation[1]	Change in *per capita* Product[2]
Stable countries	1	11
Guatemala	—	16
Ecuador	—	4
El Salvador	1	4
Venezuela	2	21
Mild inflation countries	8	2
Mexico	8	88
Colombia	8	1
Peru	8	−3
Strong inflation countries	35	8
Brazil	23	21
Argentina	39	−6
Chile	43	3

SOURCES: Based on data in Economic Commission for Latin America,
Economic Survey of Latin America, 1959 (E/CN.12/541), p. 57, and *IFS*.

[1] Average annual increase in cost of living index.

[2] Change from 1955 to 1959 in index of gross domestic product *per capita*.

TABLE 13. INFLATION AND ECONOMIC DEVELOPMENT[1]

(in per cent per annum, compounded)

Countries	Period	Rate of Inflation[2]	Rate of Growth *per capita*[3]
	Selected Periods of Relative Stability		
Puerto Rico	1947–50	−4	10
Lebanon	1948–54	−2	4
Philippines	1947–54	−1	4
Panama	1948–52	−1	2
Cuba	1947–54	—	—
Egypt	1950–3	—	−5
Ceylon	1951–4	—	—
Dominican Republic	1950–5	1	4
Venezuela	1949–53	1	4
India	1948–53	1	1
Ceylon	1947–51	2	9
Turkey	1948–54	3	6
Brazil	1947–50	4	7
Guatemala	1946–54	4	2
Ecuador	1950–4	4	2
Argentina	1952–4	4	6
Northern Rhodesia	1946–53	5[4]	23
Colombia	1951–5	5[4]	6
Average[5]		2	6
(Average, excluding Northern Rhodesia)		(1)	(4)
	Selected Periods of Mild Inflation		
Pakistan	1950–3	5	−3
Japan	1951–4	6	3
Honduras	1946–52	6	2
Puerto Rico	1950–3	6	2
Kenya	1947–54	6	4
Southern Rhodesia	1947–53	7	5
British Guiana	1948–51	7	1
Mexico	1947–54	8	2
Average[5]		6	2
	Selected Periods of Strong Inflation		
Peru	1948–53	10	6
Thailand	1950–3	13	−1
Brazil	1950–3	17	−1
Chile	1946–52	22	1
Israel	1950–4	29	5
Paraguay	1950–4	84	5
Average[5]		29	3

SOURCE: U Tun Wai, 'The Relation Between Inflation and Economic Development', *Staff Papers*, Vol. VII (1959–60), Table 1, pp. 303–4.

(See foot of p. 389 for notes to this Table.)

TABLE 14. INFLATION AND ECONOMIC DEVELOPMENT

(*in per cent per annum, compounded*)

Countries	Period	Rate of Inflation[1]	Rate of Growth *per capita*[2]
	Selected Periods of Relative Stability		
Philippines	1947–54	−1	4
Panama	1948–52	−1	2
Dominican Republic	1950–4	1	6
India	1948–53	1	1
Venezuela	1949–53	1	3
Turkey	1948–54	3	6
Brazil	1947–50	4	5
Colombia	1951–5	5	4
Average		1	4
	Selected Periods of Mild Inflation		
Pakistan	1950–3	5	−3
Japan	1951–4	6	2
Southern Rhodesia	1947–53	7	4
Mexico	1950–4	7	—
Average		6	1
	Selected Periods of Strong Inflation		
Colombia	1948–51	14	—
Brazil	1950–3	17	−1
Israel	1950–4	29	5
Average		20	1

SOURCE: U Tun Wai, op. cit., p. 305.

[1] Average annual increase in cost of living index.

[2] Average annual increase in *per capita* national income, deflated by cost of living index and adjusted for changes in the terms of trade.

[1] This covers all the cases in Tun Wai's table for the years after the end of World War II hostilities, except for those affected by rebellions or immediate postwar reconstruction.

[2] Average annual increase in cost of living index.

[3] Average annual increase in per capita national income deflated by cost of living index.

[4] Between 4·5 and 5·0.

[5] Weighted by number of observations for each country.

TABLE 15. INFLATION AND ECONOMIC DEVELOPMENT

(in per cent per annum, compounded)

Countries	Period	Rate of Inflation[1]	Rate of Growth *per capita*[2]
	Selected Periods of Price Stability		
Ceylon	1951–4	−1	1
India	1948–53	1	1
Japan	1951–4	3	6
Honduras	1946–52	4	3
Turkey	1948–54	4	4
Brazil	1947–50	5[3]	7
Average		3	4
	Selected Periods of Mild Inflation		
Mexico	1947–50	5	3
Guatemala	1946–54	5	2
Argentina	1952–4	7	2
Ceylon	1947–51	7	5
Average		6	3
	Selected Periods of Strong Inflation		
Brazil	1950–3	12	2
Chile	1946–52	22	1
Argentina	1948–52	27	−4
Average		21	—

SOURCE: U Tun Wai, op. cit., p. 306.

[1] Average annual increase in weighted averages of sector prices.

[2] Average annual increase in social product, deflated by the sector price index and adjusted for changes in the terms of trade.

[3] Figure in source is 4·9.

TABLE 16. AVERAGE ANNUAL RATES OF CHANGE IN RATIO OF MONEY TO
INCOME, SELECTED COUNTRIES, SELECTED YEARS[1]

(*in per cent*)

Countries	Change	Countries	Change
STABLE COUNTRIES	—	MILD INFLATION COUNTRIES	—2
Very wealthy countries	—3	*Wealthy countries*	—4
United States	—3	New Zealand	—3
Canada	—3	Australia	—4
Switzerland	—1		
Wealthy countries	—2	*Average countries*	—1
Sweden	—2	France	3
Belgium	—2	Norway	—4
United Kingdom	—2	Finland	—3
Denmark	—4		
Average countries	—3	*Poor country*	
Venezuela	—	Colombia	2
Netherlands	—5		
Poor countries	2	*Very poor countries*	—1
Austria	—	Mexico	—1
Cuba ·	1	Peru	—2
Italy	3		
Lebanon	6		
Very poor countries	2	STRONG INFLATION COUNTRIES	—3
Greece	6		
Portugal	1		
Japan	1	*Poor countries*	—5
Dominican Republic	3	Israel	—8
Guatemala	1	Argentina	—3
Ecuador	—	Chile	—3
Honduras	—2		
United Arab Republic	—2	*Very poor countries*	
Ceylon	2	Brazil	—
Thailand	1	Paraguay	—1
Pakistan	4		
India	—1		
Burma	6		

SOURCES: Based on data in *IFS* and United Nations, *Monthly Bulletin of Statistics*.

[1] See p. 385 for description of 'Selected Years'.

Because the ratio of money to income tends to be declining in the very wealthy and wealthy countries, and rising in the poor and very poor countries, this table incorporates a dual classification, by wealth and by rates of inflation. The classification by wealth is based on United Nations, *Per Capita National Income in Fifty-five Countries, 1952–4*. Countries estimated to have had, at that time, average *per capita* incomes equivalent to more than US$1,000 are classified as very wealthy countries; those with per capita incomes in the $750–1,000 range, as wealthy; in the $500–750 range, as average; in the $250–500 range, as poor; and below $250, as very poor. Countries within each group are arranged by descending order of *per capita* income.

TABLE 17. RELATION BETWEEN CHANGES IN REAL VALUE OF MONEY HOLDINGS AND CHANGES IN COST OF LIVING, SELECTED COUNTRIES, 1948–61

(in per cent)

Countries	Average Annual Increase in Cost of Living	Change in Real Value of Holdings of[1]	
		Money	Money and quasi-money
Stable countries	2	79	103
Dominican Republic	—	216	165
Philippines	0·5	77	139
Ceylon	1	84	109
Burma	1	162	178
Ecuador	2	124	156
Guatemala	2	50	85
Venezuela	2	108	176
Portugal	2	65	83
India	2	13	47
Pakistan	2	81	99
Honduras	2	25	49
Costa Rica	3	72	101
Ireland	3	14	9
El Salvador	3	41	89
New Zealand	4	16	16
Thailand	4	125	158
Nicaragua	4	73	88
Mild inflation countries	7	100	138
Iran	5	61	..
Mexico	7	97	102
Turkey	7	131	187
Colombia	8	141	158
Peru	8	69	104
Strong inflation countries	27	19	11
Brazil	19	114	72
Argentina	29	−31	−40
Chile	33	8	41
Bolivia	56	−17	−26

SOURCE : Based on data in *IFS*.

[1] Given by $\frac{M}{L} - 100$, where M is the 1961 index (base, 1948 = 100) of money (or money plus quasi-money) and L is the 1961 index (base, 1948 = 100) of cost of living.

TABLE 18. CENTRAL GOVERNMENT AVERAGE ANNUAL SURPLUSES OR
DEFICITS (−) AS PERCENTAGES OF GROSS NATIONAL PRODUCT, SELECTED
COUNTRIES, SELECTED YEARS[1]

Countries	Percentages
Stable countries	−2
Burma	−4
Panama	−1
‘Ceylon	−3
Ecuador	−1
Pakistan	−4
Venezuela	1
Honduras	—
Israel	−5
Australia	1
New Zealand	−3
Mild inflation countries	−2
India	−5
Peru	−1
Mexico	—
Colombia	—
Strong inflation countries	−5
Korea	−8
Chile	−2

SOURCE: Based on data in *IFS*.
[1] See p. 385 for description of 'Selected Years'.

TABLE 19. FOREIGN COMPANIES CONTROLLED BY U.S. RESIDENTS: PER CENT
OF EARNINGS RETAINED, SELECTED COUNTRIES, 1957–60

Countries	Percentages
Stable countries	49[1]
Dominican Republic	19
Panama	72
Guatemala	−48
Honduras	47
Australia	60
Philippines	46
Japan	54
New Zealand	23
India	64
Mild inflation countries	18[1]
Venezuela	12
Mexico	22
Colombia	58
Strong inflation countries	33[1]
Peru	16
Chile	14
Brazil	52
Indonesia	47
Argentina	46

SOURCE: Based on data in *Survey of Current Business*.
[1] Weighted by value of direct investments at end of 1957.

TABLE : 20. MEXICO : PRICE CHANGES AND NET PURCHASES OF SHORT-
TERM FOREIGN ASSETS, 1951–60

Year	Change in Cost of Living Index[1] (per cent)	Net Purchases of Short-Term Foreign Assets by Mexican Residents (million U.S. dollars)
1951	19	9
1952	—	21
1953	10	2
1954	13	44
1955	17	−23
1956	−2	−13
1957	13	17
1958	9	27
1959	—	−9
1960	8	−4

SOURCES : Based on data in *IFS* and International Monetary Fund, *Balance of Payments Yearbooks*.
[1] Year-end comparisons.

TABLE 21. CHANGES IN VALUE OF U.S. PRIVATE DIRECT INVESTMENT IN
SELECTED COUNTRIES, 1950–61
(*in per cent*)

Countries	Changes in Value
Stable countries[1]	214[2]
Panama	700
Dominican Republic	−1
Philippines	195
Guatemala	19
India	397
Venezuela	204
Honduras	53
New Zealand	52
Australia	373
Mild inflation countries[1]	177[3]
Colombia	120
Mexico	98
Peru	201
Strong inflation countries[1]	55[4]
Uruguay	−11
Argentina	78
Brazil	55
Indonesia	153
Chile	34

SOURCES : Based on data in *Survey of Current Business*, August 1962, p. 22.
[1] Averages for groups are changes in total value of investments in the countries in the group.
[2] Excluding Panama : 197. Excluding Panama and Venezuela : 188.
[3] Excluding Peru : 110.
[4] Excluding Indonesia : 54.

TABLE 22. COMPARISON OF PRICE RELATIVES OF INVESTMENT AND
CONSUMPTION GOODS, SELECTED LATIN AMERICAN COUNTRIES, 1960[1]

Countries	At Free Market Exchange Rates	At Parity Rates[2]
Stable country		
Ecuador	86	82
Mild inflation countries	100	95
Colombia	92	87
Mexico	95	91
Peru	114	107
Strong inflation countries	120	114
Uruguay	117	110
Brazil	116	110
Argentina	164	157
Paraguay	108	105
Chile	93	88

SOURCES: Economic Commission for Latin America, *Comparative Prices and the Purchasing Power of Currencies in Selected Latin American Countries* (E/CN.12/589), pp. 43, 47.

[1] The figures for each country represent the cost of an assortment of investment goods expressed as a percentage of the cost of an assortment of consumption goods. The respective assortments are the same for each country; and, on the average for the nine countries, the cost of the assortment of investment goods is equal to that of the assortment of consumption goods.

[2] As computed in source.

TABLE 23. RATE OF INFLATION AND INVENTORY INVESTMENT, 1950–60

(based on data in current prices)

Year	Philippines		Ecuador		Colombia		Mexico		Peru		Brazil		Chile	
	A¹	B²	A¹	B²	A¹	B²	A¹	B²	A¹	B²	A¹	B²,³	A¹	B²
1950	··	··	··	17	··	··	··	··	11	15	7	−3	··	··
1951	9	14	11	17	··	··	··	··	10	16	5	10	22	6
1952	−6	14	2	12	··	··	15	—	7	9	22	25	21	−9
1953	−4	18	1	26	8	−9	−2	−3	9	7	22	15	25	37
1954	−1	28	3	18	9	−1	5	29	5	10	18	19	77	−20
1955	−1	26	2	17	−1	—	16	20	5	9	19	8	74	−2
1956	2	12	−5	14	6	7	5	18	5	7	22	8	58	21
1957	2	16	2	16	15	34	5	17	8	9	20	15	25	−7
1958	3	10	—	17	14	16	11	17	13	11	16	—	27	−3
1959	−1	9	—	11	7	12	3	17	··	16	37	··	38	5
1960	5	4	2	15	4	13	6	14	··	··	··	··	12	5
Average	1	15	2	16	7	9	7	14	8	11	19	10	38	3

SOURCES: Based on data in United Nations, *Yearbook of National Accounts Statistics* and *Statistics of National Income and Expenditure : IFS.*

¹ Rate of inflation, i.e., percentage change in annual average of cost of living index.

² Inventory investment as percentage of gross domestic investment.

³ Excluding stockpiling of coffee and cotton by the government.

TABLE 24. VOLUME OF MAJOR AND MINOR EXPORTS, SELECTED
COUNTRIES, 1958–9

(1953–4 = 100)

Countries	Major Exports[1]	Minor Exports
Stable countries[2]	118	139
Malaya	107	153
Philippines	110	181
Central American Republics[3]	126	181
India	102	120
Ghana	100	138
Australia	131	135
Sudan	175	114
New Zealand	121	124
Strong inflation countries[2]	110	100
Turkey	93	79
Uruguay	67	57
Argentina	125	104
Brazil	115	112
Indonesia	92	84
Chile	128	116
Bolivia	66	70

SOURCES: Based on data in Gertrud Lovasy, 'Inflation and Exports in
Primary Producing Countries', *Staff Papers*, Vol. IX (1962), pp. 65, 66.

[1] The major exports for each country are identified in the source.

[2] Averages are weighted by 1959 export values.

[3] Costa Rica, El Salvador, Guatemala, and Nicaragua.

TABLE 25. DOMESTIC PRICES, EXPORT PRICES AND VOLUMES, AND
EXCHANGE RATES, SELECTED COUNTRIES

Countries	Cost of Living, 1959[1] (1953 = 100)	Export Prices, 1959[2] (1953 = 100)	Export Volume, 1958–5[3] (1953–4 =100)	Exchange Rates, 1959[4] (1953 = 100)
Stable countries[5]	109	95	124	100[6]
Malaya	92	131	126	100
Dominican Republic	102	92	115	100
Ecuador	102	94	150	100
Ceylon	104	107	104	100
Philippines	104	94	132	100
Guatemala	105	76	127	100
Portugal	107	96	127	100
El Salvador	107	74	162	100
Ghana	112	116	106	100
Costa Rica	113	84	120	101
India	115	100	111	100
Sudan	115	90	149	100
Australia	116	74	132	100
Nicaragua	116	82	164	100
Ireland	117	104	111	100
New Zealand	124	98	124	100
Mild inflation countries[5]	143	90	119	164
Thailand	119	86	114	116
Iceland	130	105	123	..
Finland	130	95	132	139
China (Taiwan)	150	85	136	208
Spain	150	92	108	152
Peru	152	91	143	164
Mexico	154	..	127	145
Colombia	162	80	95	273
Strong inflation countries[5]	500	84	106	800
Turkey	217	88[7]	86	..
Paraguay	240	95[7]	110	400
Uruguay	244	70	65	..
Indonesia	311	105	90	500[7]
Brazil	325	64	114	600
Argentina	464	75	116	1,000
Chile	1,040	..	125	1,350
Bolivia	2,990	92	67	6,250

[1] Based on data in *IFS*.

[2] Based on U.S. dollar price indices in *IFS*.

[3] Based on data in G. Lovasy, op. cit.

[4] For countries with multiple currency systems, the degree of exchange depreciation was computed by dividing the change in the domestic currency value of imports, recorded in *IFS*, by the recorded change in the U.S. dollar value of imports.

[5] Averages are weighted by 1959 export values.

[6] Changes in fluctuating rates within the limits of the Articles of Agreement of the International Monetary Fund have been ignored.

[7] Estimate.

TABLE 26. HOLDINGS OF SOME FINANCIAL ASSETS BY PRIVATE SECTOR, 1950–62

| End of Year | Brazil (billions of cruzeiros) | | | | | | Argentina (billions of pesos) | | |
	Money	Quasi-money	Government securities	Life insurance[1]	Total Current value	Total 1951 value[2]	Money	Quasi-money	Government debt
1950	..	..	..	..	...	...	22	11	3
1951	91	20	8	8	127	127	27	11	1
1952	104	21	8	10	143	117	30	12	2
1953	124	22	8	11	165	111	38	15	3
1954	151	25	8	13	197	112	44	18	3
1955	178	24	8	14	224	107	52	20	4
1956	217	25	7	17	266	104	60	29	2
1957	291	29	6	19	345	112	68	30	1
1958	353	33	8	25	419	118	99	41	1
1959	501	39	11	28	579	119	142	45	1
1960	692	57	12	32	793	121	179	60	3
1961	1,042	67	..	..	...	130[3]	205	75	3
1962[4]	1,368	73	..	..	...	75[3]	...	..	..

SOURCES: Brazil — from *IFS*. Argentina — money and quasi-money, from *IFS*: government debt prior to 1957, estimates by the author; subsequently, from Banco Central de la República Argentina, *Boletín Estadístico*.

[1] Total assets of life insurance companies.
[2] Current value divided by cost of living index (base, 1951 = 100).
[3] Estimate.
[4] September.

TABLE 27. AVERAGE ANNUAL CHANGES IN REAL WAGES,[1] SELECTED
COUNTRIES, SELECTED YEARS[2]

(*in per cent*)

Countries	Change
Stable countries	2
Viet-Nam	1
Australia	1
Burma	1
Philippines	2
Ceylon	4
United Arab Republic	5
Honduras	−3
India	2
Costa Rica	3
Pakistan	—
New Zealand	1
Guatemala	3
Mild inflation countries	2
Finland	3
Mexico	2
Strong inflation countries	1
Peru	2
Brazil	1
Argentina	−1

SOURCES: Based on data in *IFS*.

[1] Average annual change in money wage rates divided by average annual
change in cost of living index.

[2] See p. 385 for description of 'Selected Years'.

TABLE 28. CHANGES IN COST OF LIVING AND IN SHARE OF WAGES AND SALARIES[1] IN NET DOMESTIC PRODUCT

Countries	Average Annual Increase in Cost of Living Index,[2] 1950–7	Change from 1950 to 1957 in Percentage Share of Wages and Salaries in Net Domestic Product[3]
Stable countries	2	−1
Ceylon	1	−4
Costa Rica	2	−1
Canada	3	1
Mild inflation countries	7	—
New Zealand	6	1
Colombia	6	1
Finland	7	—
Australia	8	−3
Strong inflation country		
Brazil	18	2

[1] Including income of unincorporated enterprises (e.g., farmers) as part of wages and salaries.

[2] Calculated from *IFS*.

[3] From E. H. Phelps Brown and M. H. Browne, 'Distribution and Productivity Under Inflation, 1947–57', *Economic Journal*, December 1960, p. 732.

TABLE 29. COMPARISON OF INDICES OF GENERAL WHOLESALE PRICES
AND OF PRICES OF BUILDING MATERIALS, SELECTED COUNTRIES, 1959

(1953 = 100)

Countries	General Wholesale Prices (1)	Building Material Prices (2)	Col. 2 ÷ Col. 1 (3)
Stable countries	107	105	99
United Arab Republic	117	109	93
Guatemala	102	107	105
Venezuela	104	98	94
Thailand	115	103	90
Iraq	106	107	101
Syria	101	104	103
Lebanon	102	108	106
Mild inflation countries	157	175	113
Iran	123	168	137
Spain	149	155	104
Mexico	143	161	113
Colombia	187	203	109
Peru	181	187	103
Strong inflation countries	470	478	102
Excluding Paraguay	*528*	*573*	*114*
Paraguay	297	193	65
Turkey	227	278	122
Brazil	305	354	116
Chile	1,053	1,086	103

SOURCES: Columns 1 and 2 are from A. S. Shaalan, 'Impact of Inflation on
the Composition of Private Domestic Investment', *Staff Papers*, Vol. IX
(1962), Table 5, p. 259.

ROLE OF FISCAL POLICY

FISCAL POLICY IN A DEVELOPING COUNTRY*

by **John H. Adler**

I. INTRODUCTION

The bibliographical note appended to the last chapter in W. A. Lewis' *The Theory of Economic Growth* ends with the following sentence: 'There is regrettably very little theoretical discussion of the fiscal problems of underdeveloped countries.'[1] There is ample reason for this deficiency, which has not disappeared since Lewis' book was first published. The fiscal system and the fiscal policy of any country reflect its citizens' general economic views and aspirations, which it may have in common with other countries, or may be peculiar to it; but they also are the result of the country's social and cultural institutions, its resource endowment, the structure of its economy, the distribution of income, and the seat of political power, in a configuration which is inevitably unique. Any general discussion of fiscal problems is thus bound to be of limited usefulness since right below the surface of the broadest generalizations lurks a multitude of specific exceptions to the general rules. Nevertheless, some principles of fiscal policy which are pertinent to low-income countries endeavouring to advance economically at a faster pace than in the past may be derived from observation and speculation.

This paper deals with various aspects of fiscal policy under four headings. After a note on empirical evidence some general principles of government finance relevant to developing countries are presented.

* From K. Berrill (ed.), *Economic Development with Special Reference to East Asia*, Macmillan & Co., London, 1964. Printed with the permission of the International Economic Association, and the author. A Spanish translation of this paper also appeared in the Bulletin of the Centro de Estudios Monetarios Latino-Americanos.

The views expressed in this paper are those of the author and not necessarily those of the International Bank for Reconstruction and Development. The assistance of Dr. H. H. H. Eschenberg in the preparation of the statistical tables is gratefully acknowledged.

[1] W. A. Lewis, *The Theory of Economic Growth*, George Allen and Unwin, London, 1955, p. 419.

The next two sections discuss the revenue structure, and comment on the financing of public capital expenditure, while the last part deals with the role of deficit financing of government expenditures in low-income countries.

II. NOTE ON EMPERICAL EVIDENCE

Any attempt to present fiscal data of a number of countries on a uniform basis runs into conceptual and statistical difficulties which can be overcome only at great expense of time and effort.[1] And even the most perfect international comparison does not prove very much, since what may be the best possible fiscal arrangement for one country may be an unworkable scheme for another. Moreover there is a difference between the observed pattern of revenue and expenditure and what might be conceived, on the basis of some criteria, as the most desirable pattern. The data themselves do not reveal anything about the reasons for the difference between the observed and the desirable.

Nevertheless, the fiscal data which have been assembled in the appended tables permit some general observations about the major characteristics of the fiscal structure of low-income countries, as compared to those of advanced countries, the differences in coverage, classification, etc., of the data notwithstanding.

LEVEL OF REVENUE AND EXPENDITURE

The ratios of public revenue and public expenditure to the gross national product are substantially higher in advanced than in low-income countries. There are of course wide variations among the countries shown within the two categories of 'low-income' and 'high-income' countries in Table 1; the variations are commented on below. But in spite of the differences from country to country and the limited comparability of the data it is obviously significant that the unweighted average of the ratios of revenue to GNP for all low-income countries amounts to 14·7 per cent while that for high-income countries is 22·0 per cent. The corresponding average

[1] Cf. A. M. Martin and W. A. Lewis, 'Patterns of Public Revenue and Expenditure', in *The Manchester School of Economic and Social Studies* Vol. XXIV, September 1956, pp. 203–44.

ratios for expenditure are 16·1 per cent and 22·3 per cent. The averages include revenue and expenditure of state and local authorities only for those countries for which they are separately shown in the table. Since state and local expenditures are by and large more significant in high-income countries than in low-income countries, a more complete coverage of revenue and expenditure of authorities other than the central government would probably result in an even wider difference.[1]

An explanation for the differences in the ratios of public revenue and expenditure to GNP must be sought both on the revenue and expenditure side. As to revenue, it is quite clear that in the low-income countries the scope for taxation is smaller than in advanced countries; later on we shall have more to say on this. On the expenditure side, the difference is only in part accounted for by defence expenditures which are considerably larger in advanced than in low-income countries (Table 1). But with the exception of those of the United States, they do not exceed 7 per cent of GNP in the advanced countries compared with an average of 2·9 per cent for low-income countries.[2] There is also considerable evidence suggesting that a part of the difference in public expenditure in low-income and high-income countries not accounted for by defence outlays is due to transfer expenditures, mainly for welfare purposes. The large amounts of transfer payments included in the public expenditures of high-income countries are a reflection of the high income of these countries; they are something which less-developed countries have to forgo as much as possible, and can forgo, because the social arrangements of family ties, community relations, etc. are such that the need for public welfare expenditures is smaller.

But even if transfer payments and defence expenditures account for a significant part of the difference between the ratios of govern-

---

[1] One factor however may result in an understatement of the ratio of revenue to GNP in less-developed countries, particularly in Latin America. Exchange profits resulting from lower exchange rates applicable to exports, or certain kinds of exports, compared with rates applicable for imports, are generally not shown as government revenue since they usually accrue to central banks. To the extent to which these profits are transferred by the central bank to the government and used to finance public expenditures, they are very much like an export tax and therefore should be included in revenue.

[2] Which because of the inclusion of Burma, Egypt, Iraq, and Israel has probably an upward bias.

ment revenue and expenditure to GNP in advanced and less-developed countries, it may well be argued that government expenditure in low-income countries is too small and that attempts should be made to increase it. The argument rests on the proposition that the unit cost of government is likely to be higher in low-income than in advanced countries for a wide variety of government services. For example, in a country in which the literacy rate is low, a person qualified as a school teacher or government clerk is bound to command a higher pay relative to the average income than in advanced countries — even if by the standards of high-income countries the salaries of teachers and clerks in low-income countries appear to be ridiculously low. The unit cost is also likely to be higher for other kinds of expenditure — e.g. the cost of uniforms for military and police personnel, equipment for hospitals, government offices, workshops of technical service, etc. cost more or less the same in low-income and high-income countries and therefore require a relatively higher outlay in low-income countries.

Three conclusions may be drawn from these observations. First, the need for additional public revenue in low-income countries is not necessarily a reflection of the need for economic development expenditure but is due in part also to the higher unit cost of public expenditure. Second, because of that and because of the limitations on the ability to raise revenue every effort should be made to avoid 'frills' in public expenditures. Third, although the governments of many low-income countries are constantly under pressure to expand the scope of its activities, the high unit cost of functions which only public authorities can perform, such as the maintenance of law and order, the provision of educational facilities, public health, and sanitation, are strong reasons to limit the scope of government operation.

A comparison of the revenue and expenditure of low-income with those of high-income countries inevitably leads to the question what constitutes the 'proper' level of government revenue. Some experts have pointed out that the increase in the share of government revenue and expenditure and national production is a fairly recent development and that in countries in which the share of government in the national product is low, it is still appreciably higher than the ratios of government revenue to national income which prevailed a hundred years ago in countries which are now

advanced.[1] But it seems quite inadmissible to conclude therefrom
that low-income countries nowadays should get along, or, at any
rate, should attempt to get along with a level of revenue comparable
to that of the United Kingdom or the United States a hundred years
ago. To the contrary, it may well be argued that government
expenditure is inadequate in countries in which the ratio of government revenue and expenditure is less than 10 per cent of GNP,
and the optimum ratio of revenue to GNP for low-income countries
may be substantially above that figure, notwithstanding the limitations on the organizational and administrative ability of the governments of many low-income countries to make effective use of fiscal
resources.

Revenue and Foreign Investment

The figures shown in the appended tables indicate clearly that,
from a fiscal point of view, countries which are able to attract
foreign investment in large-scale enterprises stand to derive considerable fiscal benefits from it. The share of government revenue in the
national product of countries with large oil investment (Iraq,
Venezuela), foreign-owned mining operations (Chile, Peru) and
foreign investment in agriculture (Ceylon, Costa Rica, Guatemala,
Panama) is substantially higher than in most other low-income
countries. The ratio of tax revenue to income of these companies is
a multiple of the national average; therefore the burden of taxation
on all other income is correspondingly smaller. Thus, from a fiscal
point of view, foreign investment is to the host country's advantage,
except for the not too likely event that it necessitates government
expenditures which would not be required if there were no foreign
investment.

Limitations of Direct Taxation

One difference between the revenues of low-income and high-
income countries which is clearly revealed by the figures shown in
Table 2 is the significantly lower proportion of total revenue derived
from direct taxes in the low-income countries. The reason for the
lesser reliance on direct taxes in low-income countries is the fact
that direct taxes in general and personal income taxes in particular

[1] A. R. Prest and I. G. Steward, *The National Income of Nigeria*, Colonial
Research Studies No. 11, H. M. Stationery Office, London, 1953, p. 83.

are *par excellence* suitable for countries with a fairly high level of economic advancement; more will be said on this subject in Part IV of this paper. The lesser role played by direct taxes in low-income countries would become even clearer if the imposts on foreign enterprises could be shown separately.

TAXATION OF FOREIGN TRADE

The limited use of direct taxes in low-income countries is offset to a considerable extent by heavy reliance on exports and imports as a tax basis. The low-income countries shown in Table 2 derive almost 30 per cent of their total revenue from taxes on exports and imports, while in advanced countries the comparable figure is 11·5 per cent.[1] A number of public finance experts have expressed misgivings about the use of taxes on exports and imports as a major instrument of taxation. Actually a fairly good case can be made for the extensive use of both export and import taxes.[2]

PATTERN OF PUBLIC EXPENDITURE

While it appears possible to obtain some general impressions from a comparison of the revenue data of a number of countries with low and with high incomes, comparison of the expenditure pattern does not lead to useful generalizations.[3] To some extent the apparent lack of significant similarities and systematic dissimilarities in the pattern of expenditures is due to the vagueness and limited comparability of statistical classifications. But even if these limitations of information could be eliminated, it seems likely that the expenditure pattern would reflect differences in resource endowment, the structure of the economy, social institutions, etc. which could not readily be taken into account in a comparative study of public expenditure. Therefore it seems preferable to confine the discussion of expenditures to some general observations on capital expenditure which do not imply an even approximate similarity of the overall expenditure structure.[4]

---

[1] If exchange rate profits and other measures used in lieu of export and import taxes were included, the share of these taxes in total revenue would be even larger.

[2] Cf. Part IV, below.

[3] Cf., however, A. M. Martin and W. A. Lewis, op. cit.

[4] Cf. Part V, below.

III. Some Principles of Public Finance

Challenge of Basic Principles

Some of the basic ideas which, in the last fifty years, had been evolved as 'principles of public finance' have in recent years been questioned with increasing frequency, and challenged as to their general validity. This process of reappraisal of what was considered a generally accepted body of ideas was the logical consequence of the introduction (or, more exactly, re-introduction) of dynamic consider-ations into economic thinking. Three propositions in particular have been seriously challenged and, as a result, undergone considerable modification; or, to put it more cautiously, their general validity has been challenged with some success.[1]

The first principle is that the only equitable form of taxation is a tax, or a system of taxes, which is at least moderately, but prefer-ably steeply, progressive. This principle, the fiscal application of the concept of the diminishing marginal utility of income, has been challenged on the ground that the growth of an economy requires a certain rate of capital formation and that at least private capital formation depends largely on the concentration of resources in the hands of a limited number of economic units in the system. A related argument against a progressive system of taxation is the contention that progressive taxation has serious disincentive effects on produc-tive effort in general, and entrepreneurial willingness to take risks in particular.

True, the proponents of progressive taxation always were aware of the limits which the requirements of capital formation and economic incentives impose on the principle of progressiveness. But the renewed emphasis on capital formation as one of the basic determinants of the rate of economic growth has presumably weak-ened the case for a progressive tax structure, or at least thrown some doubt on the general applicability of progressive taxation to all countries in all conditions.

---

[1] The principles enumerated and discussed in the next few paragraphs are stated in their simplest form and without proper qualifications. It is realized that some of the modifications which are emphasized in the discussion were always present in the minds, and sometimes also in the writings, of the expo-nents of the principles. But the impact of these modifications on policy certainly has become greater in recent years and therefore the distinction made here between the 'original' principles and their recent modifications may be justified.

The second proposition which has been underlying most discussions of government finance was the at least tacit assertion that all 'normal' government expenditures were exhaustive in the sense that they did not produce any benefits comparable to the benefits which could be derived from private expenditures of the same amounts, either for consumption or investment. Only in the case of capital expenditure for self-liquidating projects was it admitted that a return for the economy as a whole could be expected.[1] The result of this way of looking at public expenditure was that it became an objective of public policy to keep government expenditure to a minimum; the smaller the share of government in the national product, the better for the economy.

The desirability of keeping government expenditure to a minimum at all times has been challenged on two grounds. In the first place, it has been argued that under some conditions the economy stands to benefit from an increase in public expenditures. For instance, even such 'wasteful' outlays as those for the maintenance of law and order or for public buildings may have a favourable effect on the efficiency of the economy as a whole and enhance total output.

But even if in a particular period a certain government outlay does not produce any measurable benefits it still may be preferable for the economy as a whole to incur the expenditure if it will yield benefits in the future.[2] For instance, outlays on primary education may be completely 'wasteful' in the sense that they do not immediately contribute to the efficiency of the economy, or in any other way enhance its growth, but the advantages of a literate labour force and, more generally, of a literate electorate may assert themselves in the long run and thus bring about a situation in which the advantages of increased outlays become greater than the disadvantages of an increased tax burden.

The third basic proposition of public finance which has been completely modified in the last 25 years is the stipulation that all expenditures other than those for self-liquidating projects must be paid for by current receipts, except in unusual circumstances such

---

[1] The distinction between self-liquidating capital expenditures on the one hand, and all other public expenditures on the other, was the basis of the principle that the former should be financed 'below the line' through loans rather than taxation.

[2] In order to make the flow of benefits in the future comparable with its present cost it must of course be properly discounted.

as war or a natural disaster. The sanctity of the balanced budget has been challenged by what may be termed the Keynesian principles of public finance. They suggest that within the limits imposed by balance-of-payments considerations the government has the task of maintaining a level of economic activity close to full employment, and impose upon the government the obligation to supplement by public outlays in excess of public revenues the expenditures of the private sector wherever the latter are inadequate. The logical corollary of this Keynesian concept of deficit financing is of course the accumulation of Treasury surpluses and the retirement of the public debt to the banking system, whenever total outlays of the private sector threaten to exceed the supply of goods and services.

There is no need in the context of this paper to comment at length on the Keynesian policy prescriptions and on their complex relations with monetary policy. It is worthy of note, however, that of the three challenges to classical principles of public finance the third has received in low-income countries a great deal more attention than the first two although, as will be argued below, it is much less relevant for underdeveloped countries than the first two.

The Burden of Taxation and the Benefits of Expenditure: The Production Principle of Public Finance

The discussion of the 'classical' principles of public finance and their recent modifications form an essential background against which the key issues of fiscal policy of low-income countries can be sketched. The fiscal dilemma of less-developed countries can be presented in its most general form as follows: Taxes on consumption cannot be increased because the average level of consumption is so low that even a temporary further lowering of consumption levels is socially and politically unbearable. Taxes on savings, through the imposition of progressive taxes affecting primarily the income of the well-to-do, are undesirable because they may lead to a decrease in the rate of private, and perhaps of total, capital formation. Therefore total tax revenue cannot be increased.

A resolution of this dilemma can be attempted on two grounds. In countries in which *per capita* income is rising it may be sufficient to increase taxes only to such an extent as to limit the *growth* of *per capita* consumption. If a tax increase does not adversely affect the rate of private capital formation and if the additional revenue is used to enhance the rate of economic growth, the economy as a whole benefits. The size of the tax increase is, of course, limited by the amount by which *per capita* income grows. It must be zero in countries in which the growth of aggregate income does not exceed population growth. Moreover, increased taxes on consumption are difficult in countries in which income growth is concentrated in one sector, or a group of sectors, while income stagnates in the rest of the economy. In that case an increase in taxation aiming at a curtailment of overall consumption growth inevitably implies an absolute curtailment of consumption in some parts of the economy and may therefore become socially and politically unacceptable.

The argument for an increase in taxation can be greatly strengthened, however, by bringing into it the increase in public expenditure which is associated with the tax increase, if the additional public expenditure results in benefits greater than, or at least equal to, the burden of the additional tax, and if the incidence of the additional tax can be matched to the greatest extent possible by the incidence of additional benefits.

The relation between the burden of additional taxes and the benefits of additional public expenditures is not just a convenient piece of abstract reasoning but is likely to be of considerable practical significance. An increase in taxation of, say, agricultural production may be expected to affect adversely the level of agricultural output. However, the disincentive effect of increased taxes may be offset, or more than offset, by the stimulating effects of public expenditure on, say, farm-to-market roads which lower the cost of transport and thus leave the agricultural producer better off.

In the preceding example the incidence of increased taxes and that of increased benefits is on the same sector of the economy. The justification of an increase in taxes and a corresponding increase in expenditures becomes more uncertain, if the incidence of the tax and that of the benefits is on different groups or sectors in the economy. But the basic principle, that an increase in taxation is justified as long as the favourable effects on output (and indirectly on material well-being) of increased public services exceed the adverse effects of the tax increase, is the same.

The practical conclusion for the public finances of low-income countries to be drawn from these considerations is, that the limit of public expenditure does not only depend on the ability of the public authorities to obtain revenue without curtailing consumption of low-income groups and without adversely affecting private capital formation, but on the 'productivity' of public expenditure in terms of increased productive efficiency and improved economic organization.

This 'productivity' of additional public expenditure in turn depends to a considerable extent on the efficiency with which services are produced. The question of the efficiency in providing public services will be further explored in the next section; only one point needs stressing here. The dilemma, besetting many low-income tax countries, that on the one hand production in all sectors of the economy suffers through the lack of education of the working population, while on the other hand government does not have the means of providing such essential services as a modicum of general and technical education, or public health and medical facilities, disappears, if the benefits of such services, which only government can adequately provide, are properly appraised against the economic cost of additional taxes.

However, if the over-riding objective of economic policy of a low-income country is to obtain a high rate of growth of *per capita* production and income, it must also be realized that some types of public services are more conducive to increased output than others. Social welfare expenditures, for the aged, the sick, the destitute, though good and desirable on humanitarian grounds, and undoubtedly providing important benefits to the immediate beneficiaries, do not contribute to productive efficiency, and do not provide incentives to production, while the taxes, necessary to finance them, have inevitably some adverse effects on production. Therefore, low-income countries are well advised to resist the tendency of emulating, on grounds of social justice, the scope of social welfare expenditures which has in recent years characterized the public expenditure pattern of advanced countries.

In more general terms, in the light of the growth objectives of low-income countries, a consideration of the incidence of the tax burden and of the benefits of public expenditure leads to what might be called the Production Principle of public finance, which may be stated as follows: An increase in public expenditure is justified, as long as the stimulating effects of additional expenditure on productive effort, including capital formation, exceed the disincentive effects of additional taxes. The principle is based in part on the assumption that the most important factor enhancing the material welfare of the economy and its constituent units is the growth of

total economic production;[1] it is a substitute for the static principle
that because of the declining marginal utility of money an increase
in welfare can be most readily achieved through a more even distribution of income, including the redistribution of income through
the fiscal system.

THE REDISTRIBUTION OF INCOME THROUGH THE FISCAL SYSTEM

·It is clear that there is a close connexion between the objective
of production growth and capital formation. Since in low-income
countries the level of private capital formation is generally determined by the income accruing to the uppermost income groups,
particularly the small class of entrepreneurs, a redistribution of
income through the fiscal system in favour of lower-income groups
and at the expense of the high-income groups runs counter to the
production principle of public finance, because such a redistribution
affects adversely the rate of private savings and private investment,
and thus conflict with the growth objective. A certain degree of
redistribution of income through the fiscal system is unavoidable,
because, as indicated above, for social and humanitarian reasons a
part of government expenditures has to be devoted to providing
services which primarily benefit the lowest-income groups without
significantly affecting their contribution to total production. But,
aside from that, there is no reason why the pattern of public expenditures in low-income countries should be such as to result in a
redistribution of income. To the contrary: if the pattern of government expenditures is designed to support the objective of production
growth, it inevitably brings a large share of benefits to the entrepreneurial class. The progressive incidence of benefits — particularly of expenditures for social overhead capital but also of
current 'development' expenditures — is likely to offset partially,
or completely, the progressive incidence of the tax system.

Thus the incidence of the benefits of public expenditures may
justify some degree of progressiveness in the tax structure. But
because of the importance of private capital formation in the growth
process, it appears desirable to keep the degree of progressiveness
moderate.

[1] 'Economic' implies that the composition corresponds to the desires of
the community at the prevailing system of price relations, or at some other
price relations which, for some reason, are considered more desirable than
those prevailing.

LIMITS OF PUBLIC EXPENDITURE: DEEPENING *v.* WIDENING OF
PUBLIC OPERATIONS

The production principle of public finance not only determines
the optimum level of public revenue and expenditure, but also has
a direct bearing on their composition. Economists, concerned with
the purely economic aspect of development, frequently overlook
that it is not only the level of production which is underdeveloped,
but that in many low-income countries administrative organization,
technical competence, managerial knowledge, etc. are also underdeveloped, both in the public and in the private sector. Many low-
income countries have no roads, or bad roads, because the government has no funds to build them, but often also because it has
failed to develop an effective system of building and properly
maintaining them. Educational facilities are inadequate because
teacher-training is inadequate; little attention is given to adopting
the school curriculum to the country's specific needs. The financial
administration of public enterprise is deficient, because not enough
persons have been trained in accounting and book-keeping; the
goods and services which they provide are deficient because
production techniques, quality controls, etc. are deficient.

The efficiency with which government services are provided is, of
course, an important factor determining their unit cost, or, conversely, given an amount of public revenue to finance public services,
the efficiency with which the services are provided determines their
volume and their quality.

The low level of productive efficiency is not confined to the public
sector but exists in the private sector as well. However, it is an
essential characteristic of the working of a competitive system of
enterprise, that in time inefficiency is self-correcting; the most
inefficient productive units are eliminated by price and quality
competition within the country or from abroad. But this mechanism
does not operate over a wide range of public services which are
produced by the government only, and which are not sold and not
subject to the market test. It is therefore of paramount importance
for the government to strive constantly to improve the efficiency of
its operations and, if necessary, seek foreign assistance for this
purpose.[1] In order to attain improved efficiency, it is desirable for

[1] The fiscal section of the Secretariat of the U.N. has in recent years provided effective technical assistance for the improvement of the fiscal administration, and the U.N. Technical Assistance Administration has helped in

the government to confine its range of activities to the provision of such services as cannot be, or are not likely to be, provided by the private sector. Government can contribute most to the growth of the economy by extending its operations in depth, not by widening the scope of its activities.

This conclusion runs counter to the contention that the government of a low-income country must make itself responsible for providing such goods and services which private enterprise is unable or unwilling to provide at a particular time, because the private sector either lacks the necessary technical knowledge and organizational ability, or because it lacks the capital resources necessary for those undertakings for which large-scale operations and, therefore, heavy initial capital outlays are essential (e.g. steel mills). The argument for the government to take on the task of producing goods and services which private enterprises are unable or unwilling to produce, because they lack technical competence, is based on the assumption that somehow government can acquire the missing competence more readily than a private firm.

Except in the most exceptional circumstances, which are hard to conceive, this assumption appears unwarranted. In most cases it is likely to be more efficient if the public authorities assist in bringing the missing technological experience from abroad to co-operate with private producers, and to provide such tax incentives and, if necessary, subsidies to private enterprise to overcome the reluctance to take risks in a hitherto untried line of production.

If private initiative for the production of some important goods and services, or for the exploitation of some natural resources is not forthcoming, because the initial capital requirements are beyond the limits available to a private firm, then it may be preferable for the government to lend assistance through the provision of funds (e.g. through a development bank supported by the Treasury), or a guarantee, than to enter the field itself as an entrepreneur.

There may be exceptions to this 'rule of reluctance' for the government to expand the scope of its operations into pursuits which can be left to the private sector. These exceptions may be particularly important in the field of public utilities where the argument that competition cures and prevents inefficiency does not

improving administrative machinery in general. The bilateral provision of technical assistance has also made important contributions to improving the efficiency of public administration in low-income countries.

apply because of the monopolistic or quasi-monopolistic attributes
of utilities. But even in that case it must be realized that the
losses of public undertaking are not a necessary cost of economic
development, but that they are likely to be detrimental to the
development process.[1]

IV. REVENUE STRUCTURE FOR ECONOMIC GROWTH

On the basis of what has been said in the preceding sections it is
possible to develop some general notions about the most desirable
characteristics of the revenue structure of low-income countries,
and to indicate what role should be assigned to various taxes. The
tax structure must of course reflect the structure of the economy,
its pattern of production and income distribution. But despite the
wide variations in institutions, endowment, and economic structure
among low-income countries some meaningful general observations
pertaining to the major types of taxes can be made.

INCOME TAXES

The role of income taxes, particularly of taxes based on global
personal income, is necessarily more limited in low-income countries
than in advanced countries. In the first place, the main advantage
of personal income taxes, i.e. that they make a high degree of
progressivity possible, is, as has been argued before, much less
important in low-income countries than in high-income countries.
In the second place, as has been pointed out in an excellent paper
by R. Goode, the effective administration of an income tax, covering
a wide range of income and a large number of payers, is exceedingly
difficult in low-income countries.[2] An income tax can be used as a
mass tax only if a large share of total income is paid out as salaries
and wages, if a large proportion of income is recorded in some form,
if the population is literate, and so on; these conditions are rarely
fulfilled in low-income countries. Conversely, an income tax is a
poor instrument of taxation for agricultural producers and shop
keepers, who account for a large share of total income in many
low-income countries.

[1] Cf. Part V, below.
[2] 'Reconstruction of Foreign Tax Systems,' in National Tax Association,
Proceedings of Forty-Fourth Annual Conference, 1951, pp. 212–22.

Nevertheless, there is a place for income taxes in the revenue structure of low-income countries. The conditions making income taxes effective, are likely to prevail in the highest-income brackets. For them some degree of progressiveness appears desirable, or, because of the benefits which they derive from government services, at least not objectionable;[1] in the absence of some progressive taxes at the highest-income levels, the incidence of total taxation may even become regressive, a clearly undesirable situation.

In a number of low-income countries, particularly in Latin America, attempts have been made to expand the scope of taxes on income through the imposition of flat rate taxes on salaries and wages, dividends, interest, rents, etc. The difficulty with such schedular taxes is that they are bound to lead to a shifting from the income recipient to the source of income (e.g. from the wage earner to the enterprise employing him) and thus becomes a tax on production. In general, it is probably to a low-income country's advantage to concentrate on improving the administration of income taxes affecting a limited number of tax payers before embarking on the much more difficult task of broadening the tax base and increasing the number of persons subject to the tax.[2]

REAL PROPERTY AND LAND TAXES

There is a good deal of evidence that suggests that real property and land taxes have been neglected as revenue sources in many

---

[1] The partial substitution of an expenditure tax and a net worth tax for the personal income tax, which were advocated by N. Kaldor in *Indian Tax Reform*, Report of a Survey, Ministry of Finance, New Delhi, 1956; and *An Expenditure Tax*, George Allen and Unwin, London, 1955, and which have been introduced in India and Ceylon, is an attempt to meet the main objection to taxation of high incomes at highly progressive rates, i.e. its adverse effects on private savings. It would go beyond the intended scope of this paper to comment on these fiscal innovations, and the criticisms levied against them.

[2] Because of the technical complexity of the subject no attempt is made here to discuss the role of corporate or company income taxes, or, more generally, of business income taxes, in the revenue structure of low-income countries. This role depends on the importance of large-scale business enterprise, particularly of foreign-owned companies, in the economy. As a general rule, taxes on net business income are preferable to taxes on gross income, or other substitute taxes, such as export taxes, because the latter are likely to lead to certain distortions in the pattern of production and in financial arrangements.

low-income countries.[1] The most important reasons for it are: (a) the political influence of landowners and owners of urban property; (b) the erosion of the tax base through inflation and the failure to correct the excessively low valuation bases through higher rates; and (c) the difficulty of making property assessments and keeping them up-to-date.

This neglect is the more regrettable since real property taxes are in some respects superior to taxes on income. Since the tax liability of the property owner is based on the value of the property, and not on the income derived from it, the tax does not vary with income and does not have the same disincentive effect as income taxes, and particularly high income taxes, have on productive efforts. It has even been suggested that property taxes be used as a means of insuring the efficient use of the property, either by imposing higher rates on property that is left uncultivated,[2] or by using the value of the property in its most efficient use as a basis for the tax assessment, with the value of the improvements not included in the valuation.[3] But except in unusual circumstances serious objections on grounds of equity may be raised against the method of 'unimproved valuation'.

It is frequently charged that property taxes are essentially undesirable because they are almost inevitably proportional. In the case of low-income countries this deficiency — if it is one — can be overcome by exempting from the tax property below a certain value. The exemption can be devised in such a way as to spare small peasant holdings. This would also make the administration of the tax much easier.

The other shortcoming of property taxation, i.e. the difficulty of surveying and valuing property, should not be an unsurmountable obstacle. Recent technological advances of aerial photography make cadastral surveys much less expensive and much less time-

---

[1] Cf. Martin and Lewis, op. cit., pp. 224–5; H. Wald, *The Taxation of Agricultural Land in Underdeveloped Economies*, Harvard University Press, 1959, *passim*.

[2] *The Basis of a Development Programme for Colombia*, Report of a Mission of the International Bank for Reconstruction and Development, Washington, D. C., 1950, p. 262.

[3] This method of assessing the 'unimproved' value of property was recently introduced, on an experimental basis, in Jamaica, following the example of Australia.

consuming. The uniformity of land use and crop patterns in low-income countries also helps to simplify valuation.

Consumption Taxes

Because of the restricted role of income and related direct taxes, and the impossibility of obtaining more than a limited amount of revenue from property taxes, a large part of the government revenue of low-income countries must inevitably consist of taxes on consumption. The disadvantage of consumption taxes, particularly of those falling on commodities and services with a high-income elasticity, is their disincentive effect on productive effort. But, on balance, this disincentive effect is likely to be smaller than in the case of income taxes, which, as has been pointed out, have the additional disadvantage of also affecting private savings.

Moreover, the traditional objection against consumption taxes, i.e. that their incidence is likely to be regressive, does not apply to low-income countries. The report of the Indian Taxation Inquiry Commission, and other studies concerned with the tax structure of low-income countries[1] have found that the incidence of consumption taxes is moderately progressive over a fairly wide range of income groups. This is due to the differences in consumption patterns at various income levels. At the lowest level, which prevails mainly in backward rural areas, a high proportion of consumption is consumption of subsistence production which inevitably escapes taxation. With rising income levels, encountered in more advanced rural areas and among urban dwellers, a growing proportion of consumption consists of purchased goods other than staple goods. While for reasons of equity the latter remain untaxed, the former can be taxed through excise levies or import duties.

Import duties are bound to be important in the taxation of consumption because in low-income countries the income elasticity of demand for imports is high, and the collection of revenue is particularly easy in the case of imports. The imposition of high duties on 'non-essential' imports may have the undesirable side effect of according protection to the domestic production of the same

[1] Cf. H. C. Wallich and J. H. Adler, *Public Finance in a Developing Country—El Salvador, a Case Study*, Harvard University Press, 1951, p. 132. J. H. Adler, E. R. Schlesinger, E. O. Olson, *Public Finance and Development in Guatemala*, Stanford University Press, 1952, p. 138.

non-essentials, but this can be easily avoided by matching the duty by a domestic excise tax.[1]

For reasons of administrative ease it is usually advisable to devise excise duties on domestic products in such a way as to collect them, like import duties, on the narrowest point in the flow of the taxed commodities. This means that the best place to tax manufactured goods is at the plant, and agricultural products at the processing stage (e.g. cotton at the gin, oil seeds at the oil presses). Sales taxes imposed at the retail stages and turnover taxes, on the other hand, are virtually ruled out in low-income countries because of the absence of sales records and cash registers.

It is impossible to indicate in general terms which commodities should be subjected to consumption taxes and which should remain untaxed. Only two broadly applicable rules may be mentioned. One is that the coverage of consumption taxes should be fairly wide because the narrower the range of coverage, the greater the avoidability. For reasons of equity, and, in the case of countries with a significant proportion of subsistence agriculture, for reasons of administrative ease as well, staple goods should not be taxed. But it would be bad practice to confine consumption taxes to 'luxuries' and 'non-essentials'.

The second rule, which is in part a restatement of the first, is that the best revenue yield will come from commodities with a high income and a low price elasticity of demand. The combination of high income and low price elasticities explains the very sharp increases in the yield of liquor and tobacco taxes in low-income countries, particularly in Latin America, in the post-war period.

Export Taxes

One of the most significant differences between the revenue structure of high-income and low-income countries is the virtually complete absence of export taxes in the former, and their frequency and importance in the latter. Export taxes are a source of large revenues in low-income countries because they are easy to collect and because they frequently constitute a downward extension of income taxes which could not be accomplished by any other method.

---

[1] This is not to say that protection of domestic production is always undesirable; this is obviously not the case. But it may be useful to distinguish rather clearly between revenue and protection objectives of import duties.

They are a particularly useful tax device in countries where production for export is carried on by a large number of agricultural producers.[1]

Export taxes have two disadvantages. First, they add to the instability of revenues because export proceeds, which form the tax basis, are likely to fluctuate more than total income. This volatility of yield which characterizes also import duties — they vary with the level of imports which in turn depends on the level of export earnings — is no over-riding argument against the use of export taxes; but, as will be explained in the last section, it requires a fair degree of fiscal discipline to offset it.

The second drawback is more serious. Export taxes have a disincentive effect on export production, and may result in a shift of productive effort from export commodities to production for the home market. The strength of the disincentive effects depends on the responsiveness of the producers to economic incentives (and disincentives) and on the availability and attractiveness of alternatives to export production, including the alternative of a decline in productive effort.

The high degree of responsiveness to discriminatory treatment explains for example the decline in export production of Argentina in the first ten years after World War II, while the limited response, and the absence of alternative production opportunities explain, at least in part, the continued growth of export production of Nigeria in the face of exceedingly heavy export taxes and related levies on export producers.[2]

The possibility of adverse effects on the balance of payments must be taken into account in the designing of export taxes. The

[1] E.g. Ghana, Nigeria, British West Africa, Burma, several Central American countries. Profits of monopolistic marketing boards, though originally devised for purposes of income equalization, may be considered as akin to export taxes. Exchange rates discriminating against certain exports (e.g. the coffee rates in Brazil), or exchange taxes imposed on certain exports (e.g. the recently introduced *retenciones* of Argentina) fulfil the same function. Cf. E. R. Schlesinger, *Multiple Exchange Rates and Economic Development*, Princeton University Press, 1952, particularly p. 20.

[2] For a more extensive treatment of export taxes, cf. J. H. Adler, 'The Economic Development of Nigeria: Comment', in *The Journal of Political Economy*, Vol. 44, October 1956, pp. 425–34 and P. T. Bauer, 'Reply', ibid., pp. 435–41. The 'Comment' was in response to an article by P. T. Bauer 'The Economic Development of Nigeria' in *The Journal of Political Economy*, Vol. 43, October 1955, pp. 398–411.

most effective way of doing this is to devise a sliding scale of rates which vary more than proportionately with export prices. An incidental, but exceedingly useful, effect of sliding rates is the dampening of fluctuations of receipts of the export producers.

In a number of low-income countries export duties have been used instead of, or in addition to, taxes on the income of large-scale enterprises producing export commodities. The case for the use of export taxes in these circumstances is much weaker than in the case of an export sector consisting of a large number of small-scale producers. If exports are produced by large-scale enterprises it may be preferable to rely on direct taxes.[1]

V. Financing Capital Expenditure

The most important reason why in many low-income countries public revenues fall short of the level which would conform to the production principle of public finance, is the large amounts of revenue required to finance capital expenditures. The need to finance capital expenditures arises for several reasons. First, although inefficiency and administrative difficulties impose limitations on the desirable level of public expenditures, there remains a volume of public capital expenditure which is an essential pre-requisite for economic growth. Second, even if for reasons of efficiency it is inadvisable for the government to proceed with certain investments, the government may have to provide financial resources if an undertaking is to be owned and operated in the private sector.[2] And third, the volume of private savings which can be channelled through the sale of government securities into the public sector is in most low-income countries small, sometimes because the total volume of transferable savings is small, and sometimes because inflationary price movements, or the fear of such movements, prevent the establishment of a market for government securities.

The resources of the government of low-income countries are frequently supplemented by grants and loans from abroad. But

---

[1] Cf. R. Goode, op. cit. pp. 217–20.

[2] E.g. the financing of private industrial enterprises through development banks which are government-owned, or which obtain financial resources from the government; the provision of credit facilities for agriculture.

grant funds for economic development expenditures can take care
only of a small fraction of the public capital expenditures, and loans
are often limited to the cost of the import content of capital expenditures. Moreover, the debt service burden of foreign loans on the
balance of payments also restricts the amount of foreign loans that
a government can prudently incur. Therefore, at least a part, and
in most low-income countries a major part, of capital expenditures
must be financed through tax receipts.

FULL-COST PRICING

The problem of finding financial resources to pay for the expansion
of economic overhead facilities can be greatly alleviated by
systematically applying the principle of full-cost pricing to state
enterprises.[1] As used here, the term full-cost pricing means that the
prices charged for the goods and services sold by state enterprises
must yield receipts large enough to cover operating costs, the cost of
replacing capital (depreciation charges at replacement cost) and a
reasonable return on the capital. Depreciation reserves and capital
returns together will in most instances go a long way toward meeting
the cost of modernization and expansion so that the claims on the
Treasury (and perhaps on borrowings from abroad) for these
purposes can be kept to reasonable amounts.

The principle of full-cost pricing should be applied not only to
public enterprises which are revenue producing (e.g., railroads,
power companies, ports), but also to economic overhead facilities
which provide free services (e.g., roads). In the case of the latter,
the revenue which is attributable to the public facilities should be
large enough to pay for them; for example, gasoline taxes, motor
vehicle licence fees and other taxes attributable to motor transportation, taken together, should yield enough revenue to pay for
the average annual cost of the highway system. In some instances
it may be difficult to determine accurately the increase in revenue
which is attributable to the services provided by public facilities;
multi-purpose projects in particular, providing a variety of benefits
and giving rise to some cost other than capital and operating cost
proper, are likely to have revenue consequences which are difficult
to assess.

[1] E. M. Bernstein and I. G. Patel, 'Inflation in Relation to Economic
Development' in IMF *Staff Papers*, Vol. 2, No. 3, November 1951, p. 393.

REVENUE FEED-BACK

But leaving aside these difficulties, which are theoretical-conceptual as well as statistical,[1] it is clear that in low-income countries the capital projects with the higher direct or indirect revenue yields are preferable to those with lower yields, the presumption being that the level of the revenues accruing to the public enterprise or the government is more or less proportionate to the net social yield of any given project. But even if the social yield of a project A with a low revenue 'feed-back' may be somewhat higher than of a project B with a high revenue 'feed-back', project B may still be preferable to project A if the revenue is conceived of as available for further public capital expenditure — or, more generally, for further expenditures enhancing economic advancement — while a large part of the social yield of project A does not accrue to the government and only leads to an increase of private consumption.

It is quite conceivable and even likely that exceptions to the general rule of maximum revenue 'feed-back' (which may be thought of as supplementing the principle of full-cost pricing, particularly for the selection of new projects) will occur and will have to be allowed for. But it should be clear that the principle runs counter to the view, frequently held in low-income countries, that low-priced public services, especially the provision of cheap public power, are a pre-requisite of economic development. The view implies that the external economies which accrue to the users of public services at economic prices do not offer enough inducement to private producers, and should therefore be extended further so as to 'externalize' a larger part of the social return.[2] Related to this position is the suggestion, implied in the concept of the 'big push', that in low-income countries social-overhead facilities should be built ahead of demand, in order to have the greatest possible growth stimulating effect.[3]

If 'building ahead of demand' means that the appraisal of a public investment project should take account of the growth of

[1] Cf. P. O. Steiner, 'Choosing Among Alternative Public Investments', in *American Economic Review*, Vol. 49, No. 5, December 1959, pp. 893–916.

[2] A. O. Hirschman has used the term 'internalize' to describe the opposite process. *The Strategy of Economic Development*, Yale University Press, 1958, p. 57.

[3] Cf. R. Nurkse 'Comments' on paper by P. N. Rosenstein-Rodan presented to Round Table of the I.E.A., Rio de Janeiro, 1957, pp. 4f.

demand in the immediate future, rather than the present level of demand, nobody can seriously question the proposition. But if it means that economic-overhead facilities should be provided even if their discounted future returns to the government fall short of their total cost, including discounted future cost, then again a subsidization scheme, which conflicts with the rule of maximum revenue feed-back, is implied.

The difference between the 'big push' strategy, and the position taken here may be conveniently stated in these terms: the 'big push' strategy stresses the importance of ample economic overhead facilities as indispensable for economic advancement, but is not concerned with the fiscal problem which it implies; the position taken here, while accepting the indispensability of adequate economic overhead facilities, stresses the importance of assuring a *continuous* flow of fiscal resources into the financing of economic overheads. In other words, it is based on the belief that it is more important to assure an *economic* supply of power, transportation, etc., at an *adequate* price than to provide economic overhead services at a subsidized price, but run the risk that an adequate supply cannot be sustained.

VI. DEFICIT FINANCING

So far the exposition has proceeded almost entirely on the assumption that total government revenue equals total expenditure; only in connexion with the financing of capital expenditures was the possibility mentioned that the tax revenue may be supplemented by borrowing internally or from abroad.

There is no need to labour the proposition that an increase in aggregate expenditure — presumably by an excess of government expenditure over receipts — in order to increase the volume of effective demand is not a policy prescription applicable to low-income countries. This is so because the constellation of under-utilized resources does not permit an immediate response to an increased level of total demand; the response is likely to be slow and sluggish.[1] Instead of pursuing this argument further it may be more useful to indicate the conditions determining the extent to

[1] J. H. Adler, 'Deficit Spending and Supply Elasticities', in *Indian Journal of Economics*, Vol. 3, No. 144, July 1955, pp. 17f.

which the governments of low-income countries can incur public expenditures in excess of public revenue.

Two methods of deficit financing may be mentioned as not likely to cause inflationary pressures although they result in an increase in the money supply and aggregate expenditure. Some increase in the money supply is necessary in order to meet the liquidity needs of a growing economy. The increased liquidity can be provided in part by deficit financing, i.e. the purchase of securities by the banking system from the government. But in most instances it would be inappropriate for the government to pre-empt the entire increase because such a policy may impede the functioning of the private sector, even if the increase in government expenditure leads to an increase of bank deposits and makes a secondary credit expansion possible.

Another possibility for the government to increase the money supply through a budget deficit exists in low-income countries where a part of the economy is not completely monetized. In such a country it is likely that each year another segment of the subsistence sector, where little or no money is used, becomes 'converted' to holding money. If this happens the government can again through a cash deficit claim a share of the permissible increase in the money supply.

But aside from these two limited possibilities, governments of low-income countries can incur a deficit only when the deficit does not lead to an increase in the money supply. The money supply will not increase (*a*) if the private sector purchases securities from the public sector; (*b*) if government securities are sold abroad, or resources are obtained from abroad through grants; (*c*) if an increase of bank credit to the public sector is offset by a decrease of bank credit to the private sector; and (*d*) if the sales proceeds of government securities to the banking system are used to purchase goods from abroad.

Possibilities (*a*) and (*b*) have already been mentioned in the preceding section; it has also been indicated that the total flow of funds from these sources is in most countries likely to be limited.[1] Case (*c*) is of interest as an alternative to 'pure' deficit financing.

[1] There are of course exceptions to the proposition that non-inflationary borrowing of funds by government from the private sector is small in low-income countries. The most important exception is India where the Government can count on a steady flow of private savings becoming available to

If in a low-income country it is considered essential that public expenditure be increased beyond ordinary revenue (and receipts from domestic and foreign borrowing), then it is preferable to attempt to determine the impact on the private sector of the government's increased claim on resources beforehand by curtailing the volume of financial resources available to the private sector than by letting the price increases, caused by the increased money supply, determine the impact. In other words, if resources are to be 'squeezed' from the private sector for the benefit of the public sector, it is better to have the squeeze accomplished by credit policy than by the mechanism of price inflation.

It is clear, however, that this method of transferring resources to the government also cannot be used indiscriminately since, if relied upon for any prolonged period, it is bound to affect adversely the functioning of the private sector.

The last possibility of deficit financing — the sale of government securities to the banking system and the use of the proceeds to purchase goods abroad — is under certain conditions of some practical significance. If the central bank of a low-income country holds foreign exchange reserves in excess of 'normal' needs, and the government can make effective use of them, for example for the purchase of capital equipment, it does not have to purchase the foreign exchange, but can borrow it. The central bank increases its holdings of government securities at the expense of foreign securities and there is no increase in the money supply and aggregate domestic expenditures.

A type of deficit financing somewhat akin to case (*d*) is sound policy in a low-income country with a revenue system which depends to a large extent on taxes on exports and imports. The export proceeds of such a country are bound to show wide fluctuations, reflecting price changes and, in the case of agricultural commodities, changes in the size of crops. The level of export proceeds also determines the volume and value of imports. The changes in the value of exports and imports in turn cause wide variations in the yield of taxes on exports and imports. The extent of the variations depends on the characteristics of the taxes, whether they are based on the

the public sector. In recent years, foreign grants have also been an important source of financing expenditures, either directly, or indirectly, through the creation of 'counterpart' funds.

volume or the value of the trade, and whether the rates are proportional or progressive with respect to the value.

In practice it is impossible to vary the rate of government expenditure at short notice in order to keep it in line with total revenue. Even if it were possible, it would be undesirable to do so, particularly since the main cuts and increases would have to fall on capital expenditures because a large proportion of recurrent expenditure consists of salary payments which cannot be reduced or increased at will. Therefore it is unavoidable that cash surpluses accumulate and are followed by cash deficits, if the rate of expenditures remains more or less constant.

There is a good deal to be said for this sort of cyclical sequence of surpluses and deficits because it dampens the impact of export booms and recessions on the economy. But in order that this policy be truly cyclical, it is essential that the expansion of government expenditures be controlled while export earnings and tax yields are high, that surpluses be allowed to accumulate, and that the accumulation of fiscal surpluses be matched by an increase in foreign exchange reserves. If this is done, the incurring of a cash deficit subsequently will not strain the economy too much. If the deficit is not to raise domestic prices unduly, a substantial portion of the income generated by it must be allowed to 'leak out' through increased imports. Clearly, if foreign exchange reserves are not accumulated in times of high export earnings, the scope for such 'leakage' will be limited and the impact of deficit financing on domestic prices will be more than is needed to keep the domestic productive resources fully employed.

Unfortunately, this apparently simple prescription of letting both 'windfall' revenues and foreign exchange reserves accumulate during an export boom is not easy to carry out. Governments of low-income countries, constantly under pressure to increase expenditures, find it difficult to restrain expenditures, or to enter into new expenditure commitments when export earnings and revenues increase. They may find it even more difficult to interfere with the liberal use of foreign exchange (for imports and other payments) by the private sector when exchange reserves are rising. One method of exercising fiscal and monetary discipline in such circumstances is to sterilize the cash surplus by allocating it to a 'revenue equalization reserve', to hold this reserve in foreign exchange, and to make use of it only when revenues decline below their 'normal' level.

But even if account is taken of all these possibilities the fact remains that in low-income countries the range of non-inflationary deficit financing is narrowly circumscribed. It is therefore of paramount importance for low-income countries to conduct their fiscal operations in such a way as to assure a flow of tax revenue large enough to meet the essential requirements of public services, and to make the best possible use of fiscal resources by practising efficiency and economy in their application. If this is done, fiscal operations can make an important contribution to economic growth.

TABLE 1: SHARE OF GOVERNMENT FINANCE IN THE NATIONAL PRODUCT[a]

Low-Income Countries	Fiscal Years Ending	Revenue as % of GNP	Total Expenditure as % of GNP	Defence Expenditure as % of GNP
		(Average of period)		
Africa				
Egypt	1954–6	21·06	21·12	5·50
Ghana	1952–8[b]	12·21	14·46	...
Asia				
Burma	1954–7	20·09	23·11	7·77
Ceylon	1954–7	20·23	21·20	0·60
India[b]	1956–8	A 7·32	A 11·66	2·15
		B 5·60	B 9·20	—
Iraq	1953–7	31·42	25·71	5·40
Israel	1954–9[b]	20·13	29·61	4·86
Japan	1954–8	13·28	13·17	1·94
Philippines	1954–8[d]	9·35	10·35	1·77
Latin America				
Argentina	1953–8[d]	9·58	13·14	2·91
Brazil	1953–8[d]	A 8·78	A 10·29	2·81
		B 5·71[e]	B 6·51[e]	—
Chile	1953–8[c]	13·03	13·96	2·77
Colombia	1953–7[c]	9·85	10·35	2·30
Costa Rica	1953–7	12·68	12·09	0·57
Ecuador	1952–7[c]	9·97	10·66	2·29
Guatemala	1953–7	13·47	14·87	1·32
Honduras	1952–7	8·59	9·47	1·22
Mexico	1953–7	8·82	9·91	0·65
Panama	1953–6	16·63	18·33	...
Peru	1953–6	13·86	14·48	2·78
Venezuela	1954–8[d]	18·91	16·31	1·45
Europe				
Greece	1952–7[c]	16·01	19·39	6·36
Spain	1952–7[c]	12·48	12·45	3·06
Turkey	1954–8[c]	12·74	14·44	4·17
AVERAGE — *All Low-Income Countries*		14·66	16·09	2·94
High-Income Countries				
North America				
Canada	1953–8[d]	15·75	16·01	6·05
United States	1954–7	A 16·53	A 16·64	10·92
		B 8·07	B 8·77	—

(*Table continued on p. 434*)

TABLE 1.—(*Contd.*) : SHARE OF GOVERNMENT FINANCE IN THE NATIONAL
PRODUCT[a]

High-Income Countries	Fiscal Years Ending	Revenue as % of GNP	Total Expenditure as % of GNP	Defence Expenditure as % of GNP
		(Average of period)		
Europe				
Australia	1953–8[b]	26·78	27·15	1·05
Belgium	1953–7	17·51	20·88	3·85
Denmark	1954–9[b]	17·03	17·47	3·03
Finland	1954–7	24·63	25·30	1·66
France	1953–7	19·81	21·61	6·78
Germany (F.R.)	1954–9	A 14·41	A 14·39	3·86
		B 14·90	B 11·97	—
Italy	1953–8[b]	17·05	19·61	3·40
Netherlands	1954–8	21·44	22·30	5·31
Norway	1953–8[b]	19·34	18·35	4·15
Sweden	1954–8[b]	21·62	22·75	4·73
Switzerland	1954–7	A 8·20	A 7·33	2·66
		B 7·01	B 6·55	—
United Kingdom	1954–9	26·25	27·32	7·19
Oceania				
Australia	1954–8	A 20·29	A 17·44	3·48
		B 8·00	B 12·78	—
New Zealand	1953–8	26·64	22·41	2·73
AVERAGE — *All High-Income Countries*		21·95	22·31	4·43

[a] Gross national product of same period, or nearest calendar year.
[b] 1958 revised budget estimate.
[c] National income instead of GNP.
[d] 1957, 1958 revised budget estimate.
[e] Includes governmental transfer payments.
A. Central Government.
B. State and local government.
. . . not available ; — not applicable.
Source :   U.N., *Public Finance* (New York, 1959). See notes to Tables for
         definition of terms and coverage.
         I.M.F., *International Financial Statistics*, February 1960.
         U.N., *Yearbook of National Accounts Statistics*, 1958.

TABLE 2. COMPOSITION OF PUBLIC REVENUE

| Low-Income Countries | Fiscal Year Ending | % of Total Revenue | | | Other Revenue |
| | | Direct Taxes | Indirect Taxes | | |
			Total	Customs Duties[a]	
Africa					
Egypt	1954–9	18·82	43·24	. . .	37·93
Ghana	1952–8[b]	11·47	66·27	64·7	20·76
Asia					
Burma	1954–9	27·33	45·39	27·4	27·28
Ceylon	1954–9	23·42	66·46	54·5	11·15
India	1956–7	A 21·96	53·28	29·1	26·00
		B 17·83	—	—	82·19
Iraq	1953–8	7·29	25·09	18·4	67·63
Israel	1954–9[b]	37·15	48·67	22·3	14·18
Japan	1954–9	47·80	32·71	3·2	19·51
Philippines	1954–9[c]	38·79	46·40	30·2	14·81
Latin America					
Argentina	1953–8[c]	35·1	36·8	2·5[d]	28·1
Brazil	1953–7[c]	A 37·7	51·6	. . .	10·7
		B 60·7	19·8	—	19·5
Chile	1953–8[c]	36·9	52·3	17·1	10·8
Colombia	1953–8	46·4	42·4	31·4	11·1
Costa Rica	1953–8	17·63	72·23	58·9	10·14
Ecuador	1952–7	13·1	78·6	43·1	8·3
Guatemala	1953–7	7·90	81·25	51·5	10·85
Honduras	1952–7	17·26	76·74	51·6	5·89
Mexico	1953–8	27·10	56·8	28·6	16·1
Panama	1953–8	22·0	47·4	25·4	30·6
Peru	1953–8	23·4	59·7	32·0	16·9
Venezuela	1953–8[c]	26·9	27·6	13·4	45·5
Europe					
Greece	1952–7	17·4	54·2	21·3	28·4
Spain	1952–7	45·8	48·5	4·9	5·7
Turkey	1954–9	59·1	29·3	7·6	11·6
AVERAGE (Central Governments Only)		27·8	51·8	29·05	20·4
High-Income Countries					
North America					
Canada	1954–9[b]	57·0	36·9	10·3	6·1
United States	1954–8	A 80·8	15·0	. . .	4·2
		B 69·4	30·7	—	—

(*Table continued on p. 436*)

TABLE 2.—(Contd.) : COMPOSITION OF PUBLIC REVENUE

| High-Income Countries | Fiscal Year Ending | % of Total Revenue | | | Other Revenue |
| | | Direct Taxes | Indirect Taxes | | |
			Total	Customs Duties[a]	
Europe					
Austria	1953–8[b]	44·10	43·92	4·7	11·98
Belgium	1953–8	41·95	20·12	6·6	37·92
Denmark	1953–8[b]	43·6	48·8	. . .	7·6
Finland	1954–8	22·6	52·5	13·2	24·9
France	1953–8	25·5	68·4	2·1	6·2
Germany					
(F.R.)	1953–8	A 40·0	53·6	. . .	7·8
		B 92·0	5·9	—	2·1
Italy	1953–8[b]	20·5	53·8	21·9	25·6
Netherlands	1954–8	56·5	43·5	10·0	—
Norway	1953–8[b]	29·6	60·0	7·4	10·4
Sweden	1954–9[b]	48·3	37·8	. . .	13·9
Switzerland	1954–9	25·4	58·5	28·0	16·1
United Kingdom	1954–8	49·5	41·7	. . .	8·8
Oceania					
Australia	1953–8	61·79	35·81	8·2	2·29
New Zealand	1953–8	61·17	31·31	14·1	7·51
AVERAGE (Central Governments Only)		44·3	43·9	11·5	12·8

[a] Mainly export taxes and import duties.

[b] 1958 revised budget estimate.

[c] 1957, 1958 revised budget estimate.

[d] 1954–7 only.

A. Central Government.

B. Local government.

. . . not available; — applicable.

Source : U.N., *Public Finance* (New York, 1959). See notes to Tables for definition of terms and coverage.

　　　I.M.F., *International Financial Statistics*, February 1960.

　　　U.N., *Yearbook of National Accounts Statistics*, 1958.

Note : Total may not add because of rounding.

FISCAL MEASURES AND CAPITAL ACCUMULATION*

by **A. R. Prest**

INTRODUCTION

The object of this paper is to survey some of the fiscal measures by which the authorities can influence the level of investment in underdeveloped countries. To reduce the area sufficiently to make the perimeter visible we shall not attempt to discuss a large number of related issues, highly important as they may be. We shall assume that, on some basis or other, the authorities have decided that a certain aggregate rate of investment in an economy is desirable; that they also have views about the way in which this total should be split between different sectors and different regions of the country; and that, furthermore, they believe that the private sector would not by itself aim at, or at any rate succeed in reaching, these objectives if the government simply stood by as a sort of neutralist observer. We shall not investigate the basis for any such objectives — whether it is derived from a mathematical model of development, political bargaining, hunch or conspiracy is, for the purpose of this paper, immaterial. We shall limit ourselves very largely to the technical questions of the relative merits of the different fiscal measures which can be used to further these objectives. Nor shall we discuss, except *en passant*, the complementary measures whether political, social or economic which may be needed if investment incentives are to be successful or fruitful. This does not for one second mean that we underestimate the importance of building up labour skills or training management and the like. Quite the contrary: but we shall not be primarily concerned with such issues here.

---

* This paper has been specially written for this volume but draws heavily on previous ones, especially the author's *Public Finance in Underdeveloped Countries*, Weidenfeld & Nicolson, London, 1962, 'The Expenditure Tax and Economic Development' in *Public Sector and Economic Development*, Instituto de Estudios Fiscales, Ministerio de Hacienda, Madrid, 1963, 'Corporate Income Taxation in Latin America', paper presented at O.A.S. — E.C.C.A. — I.B.D. Conference, Santiago, December 1962, and 'Taxes, Subsidies & Investment Incentives', paper presented at O.E.C.D. Conference, Athens, December 1963.

One other important preliminary issue must now be tackled. The level of investment can always be increased by extending the size of the public sector, relatively to that of the private sector, and then instructing the managers of the various state enterprises to expand capital formation in various specified ways, any necessary finance coming from the government's general revenue or its internal or foreign borrowing. We shall rule out this kind of approach from our survey here by assuming a more or less given size ratio for the two sectors. Given this background, we shall then concentrate primarily on fiscal incentives to the private sector of the economy. This in turn implies that the private sector is assumed sufficiently important for its investment achievements to be an important contribution to the overall level of capital formation in a country.

It will be convenient to discuss the stimuli to the private sector under two headings: incentives to private investment and incentives to private saving. Having dealt with the private sector in this way, we shall then have a little to say about investment policy in the public sector.

FISCAL INCENTIVES TO PRIVATE INVESTMENT

In this section, we shall review the incentives in common use,[1] discuss their relative merits in theory, look at the practical experience of some countries in using these techniques and finally ask what lessons can be drawn for the future.

Accelerated depreciation — first introduced in the form of initial allowances, in the U.K. Budget of 1945 — has become a well-known and widely used government device for promoting private investment. Essentially, the taxpayer is allowed to postpone some tax liabilities into the future and therefore benefits by the compound interest on this postponement. Sometimes these concessions are described as a temporary interest free loan but this is misleading: 'temporary' may be a very short or very long period depending on the rate of growth of a firm's capital stock, 'interest free' means

---

[1] This restriction means that we shall not discuss some tax measures which have some theoretical merits but are not commonly found, e.g., the substitution of capital taxes for income taxes as a means of increasing the attractiveness of risky investment outlets. (In fact, this particular proposal has recently been criticised on theoretical grounds. Cf. C. S. Shoup 'Taxation in a Low-Income Developing Country', *Public Sector and Economic Development*, op. cit).

entirely different things to a big national corporation and a small local workshop and a 'loan' would be indistinguishable from a gift if a firm never earned sufficient profits to repay it. Although calculation of the precise benefit received by any individual firm is complicated in detail there can be no disputing that there are two general elements in it: one is that it increases the liquid resources of a firm at the time, or shortly after the time, it makes any investment and the other is that it reduces the riskiness of investment. Both these propositions are well-known and well-documented[1] and so it is not necessary to discuss them further here.

Accelerated depreciation can be amplified and extended in various ways. One is to allow firms to write off the costs of capital equipment in any way they please, a system which operated in Sweden at one time and which has been introduced in respect of new plant and machinery in manufacturing industry in certain designated areas in the U.K. in 1963. This may give rise in fact to the same time distribution of capital allowances as would occur with a prescribed system of depreciation but whether it does or not (and unless a prescribed system were very generous, the chances are that it would not) the freedom of companies etc. to choose their own time-pattern for depreciation for tax purposes, instead of having one imposed on them, makes this system different in principle. Another way in which accelerated depreciation may be extended is by a system of subsidies on investment, for example, the investment allowances of the U.K. or the investment credits of the U.S.[2] In this case, it is not so much a matter of postponing tax liabilities on any particular investment as one of receiving a subsidy as well as the ordinary depreciation allowances. Comparison of the relative inducements to investment offered by the subsidy method will be more advantageous to firms. And in fact it is not difficult to show that, in a wide range of possible cases, the revenue loss over the whole life of a piece of capital equipment is likely to be less with investment subsidies than with accelerated depreciation, given the same degree of investment incentive in both cases.

[1] See, e.g., R. A. Musgrave, *Theory of Public Finance*, pp. 343f.

[2] The main difference between these two systems is that in the U.K. the allowance is a deduction in computing taxable profits whereas in the U.S. it is a credit against the tax bill. If companies pay different rates of tax (e.g., a lower rate for small firms) the U.S. system differentiates in favour of the lower rate payers whereas the U.K. system is neutral between them.

A different form of relief from income tax is to be found in the case of tax holidays, or relief from tax from the profits of a (new) venture for some specified period. This technique has been used in a number of underdeveloped countries during the post-war period. Tax relief of this sort can be thought of as being equivalent to a permanent reduction (as distinct from temporary abolition) of the rate of tax on profits. Viewed in this light, it can be seen to have risk-reducing and liquidity-increasing effects — but the size of these effects now depends on the level of profits rather than the level of investment, the relevant determinant in the accelerated depreciation case.

Indirect taxes and subsidies can be manipulated in a variety of different ways — such as cancellation of import duties or sales taxes on raw materials and capital equipment used at home, duties on imports, subsidies related to turnover or to factor inputs, relief from export taxes and so on. Choice between these different methods will largely depend on whether the aim is to expand output for export as well as for home sales, administrative considerations and so on.

It would be a lengthy, tedious and unnecessary grind to compare all the relative merits and demerits of these various techniques for influencing private investment. But some of the more important points must be made all the same.

If we compare the relative effects of the tax holiday and investment subsidy (or accelerated depreciation) methods, there are three major points of contrast. The first is one we have already touched on — that the basis of tax relief is entirely different in the two cases, being based on the level of profits in one case and the level of investment in the other. This means that the distribution of any given amount of tax relief between firms cannot be expected to follow the same pattern in the two cases, with, for example, firms with high rates of return on fixed capital or high ratios of working to fixed capital benefitting relatively more in the tax holiday case.

The second point is that accelerated depreciation and investment subsidies markedly cheapen the cost of capital equipment relatively to that of labour. We must therefore expect to find that both industries and firms which are relatively capital-intensive will benefit more from these methods than from the usual tax holiday arrangement.

Thirdly, financial relief which depends on the amount of investment is more amenable to government control than is a tax holiday on profits, both because investment can be more easily controlled than profits and because this type of incentive can usually be withdrawn more quickly, if need be.

One comparison between accelerated depreciation and investment subsidies centres on the relative benefits to long-lived and short-lived capital equipment. It is easy to see that accelerated depreciation is of relatively greater benefit to long-lived than short-lived equipment, in that the present value of tax deferment is greater in the former case.[1] Whether investment subsidies confer relatively greater benefits on short-lived than on long-lived investments is a matter for some argument. But whatever the answer on this point, there can be no question that if accelerated depreciation and investment subsidies confer the same benefits on equipment of average length of life, the former will be relatively more beneficial to long-lived and the latter to short-lived equipment.

Another point is one we have already touched on — that investment subsidies incurring the same revenue loss as accelerated depreciation are likely to give greater investment incentives. Yet another is the accounting point that the time pattern of depreciation is unaffected by investment subsidies.

The various techniques for manipulating indirect taxes and subsidies can be made to give any degree of protection one wants to domestic industry, although it would be foolhardy to think that our knowledge of the system is always sufficiently deep to avoid consequences one does not want. Two points should be made about this type of intervention. First, although some of the stimulus to investment is direct in character (e.g., relieving imports of capital goods of customs duty) some is indirect (e.g., via subsidization of domestic output of consumer goods) and some may simply be a substitution of domestic for foreign capital goods (e.g., subsidization of domestic output of capital goods). Second, there is the well-known and time-honoured difficulty of removing concessions of this kind once they are embedded in peoples' consciousness, even though the original justification may have long disappeared.

So far we have not allowed for the fact that some of the beneficiaries of investment incentive devices may be foreign companies.

[1] Cf. J. Black 'Investment Allowances, Initial Allowances and Cheap Loans as Means of Encouraging Investment', *Review of Economic Studies*, 1959–60, for a full discussion of this point.

If so, we encounter the well-known difficulty that tax reliefs, whether of the tax holiday or accelerated depreciation variety may run to waste in the sense that Double Taxation Relief treaties operate in such a way that a lower tax bill in the country of operation means a higher tax bill at home. In such cases, tax concessions by the government of one country simply result in a present to the government of another country. This need not always be so: one exception is when some or all of an overseas operating company's profits are free from home taxation, another is when 'tax-sparing' arrangements (whereby the home country agrees to reduce domestic tax liabilities *pari passu* with special tax concessions in the operating country) and another is when tax concessions are of the indirect kind (e.g., subsidies on output) so that the foreign firm retains part of the benefit. Despite these escape routes, the dangers of tax concessions for investment purposes running to waste always exist in the case of expatriate firms.

We have now covered some of the more important issues of general principle. What light is shed by practical experience on these matters? It would be completely beyond the resources of a single investigator to conduct a comprehensive survey of the practical workings of these techniques in recent years and so we must content ourselves with examining the record of a few countries. As a consequence, we run the risk of a biased sample, but that cannot be helped.

Evidence relating to a small number of underdeveloped countries has been gathered together in a recent publication.[1] On the whole, this does not suggest that investment incentive devices have had much effect in increasing the level of investment. The effects were most marked in Puerto Rico, but in neither Mexico nor the Philippines was the evidence such that one could judge that investment had been appreciably greater as a result of the concessions — though in the nature of the case it is extremely hard to reach firm conclusions on this point one way or the other.

Another source of information is the *Draft Second Five Year Plan 1964-8* for Trinidad and Tobago.[2] A distinction is made there

---

[1] J. Heller and K. M. Kauffman, *Tax Incentives for Industry in Less Developed Countries*, Harvard Law School (International Programme in Taxation), Cambridge, Mass., 1963.

[2] Government Printer, Trinidad, 1963, pp. 109 and 218.

between, on the one hand, income tax holidays, unlimited carry-forward of losses, accelerated depreciation and import duty concessions etc. for new industries and, on the other hand, initial allowances to existing industries. The general conclusion is that the former had been more successful than the latter in stimulating investment, and indeed the rates of initial allowance were halved in the 1963 Budget. Two features of the newly established pioneer industries were their capital intensive nature and their heavy dependence on foreign capital.

As an example of an area at an intermediate stage of development, we can take the Italian South. In the period between 1947 and 1957 a variety of devices for encouraging private investment was tried, the most important of the financial and monetary incentives being: exemption for ten years from taxation on business profits from new investments, exemption from indirect taxes, relief on transport costs, creation of new credit institutions and government procurement (20 per cent of government expenditure had to be in the South). Since 1957, additional measures have been brought into operation: some tax exemption for retained earnings used for plant replacement or extension, some local tax exemption, capital grants for small plant modernization, cheap credit for periods up to fifteen years, provision of government built factories.

In the nature of things, it is impossible to say precisely how much these concessions contributed to the development of the Italian South for these years. The very fact that the concessions had to be reorganized and increased in 1957 implies that they had not been uniformly successful before that date. Nevertheless the general impression one gains from the literature on this subject (e.g., in 1960, a firm capable of earning a 6–9 per cent return on capital before tax in the North would have earned 12–15 per cent in the South) is that these various measures have been reasonably influential.[1]

Evidence is now beginning to accumulate about the effects of investment incentives in more advanced countries, especially under the auspices of the current National Bureau of Economic Research — Brookings Institution investigation into these matters. If one takes the case of Britain there seems to be some evidence, though by no

[1] Cf. V. Lutz, *Italy: A Study in Economic Development*, Oxford University Press, London, 1962; also, G. Ackley and L. Dini, ' Tax and Credit Aids to Industrial Development in Southern Italy ', *Banca Nazionale del Lavoro*, Quarterly Review, December 1959.

means conclusive, that initial allowances and investment allowances have played an important part in influencing investment decisions.[1] But, of course, it can always be argued that these measures would not necessarily meet with the same response in underdeveloped countries.

The time has now come to point to some lessons for the future. The first is the need to keep incentives as simple as possible. This proposition can be defended on several grounds: the lack of detailed knowledge of the working of many of these economies and hence the probability of waste if intervention is too ambitious, the scarcity of resources available to government to administer complicated schemes, the failure of the private sector to understand complex schemes, and so on. What happens when governments try to be too clever is well illustrated by the impossible complications of corporate income tax law in some countries. Specific illustrations of this general principle can be found in the operation of investment incentives and in the treatment of retained earnings. There have been various attempts to confine investment relief to net investment thereby excluding replacement from tax concessions. But this is something which some of the most developed countries have been unable to do; the legislation on these lines in the U.S.A. in 1961 ran into such serious trouble that it had to be abandoned and the authorities in the U.K. have never been persuaded that it would be workable. Another example is the practice of taxing retained earnings at a lower rate when used to buy capital equipment (e.g., Italian South, and some Latin American countries). This confuses two separate issues, the encouragement to saving and the encouragement to investment, and implies either that capital investment financed from market funds is somehow inferior to that financed from retained earnings or that retained earnings lent to other firms (or the government) are inferior to retained earnings used internally on plant expenditure. Neither of these propositions strikes one as valid under all circumstances.

Closely allied to the need for simplicity comes that of certainty. We all live in an uncertain world and our ability to predict the

[1] Cf. R. M. Bird, 'Depreciation Allowances in the U.K.', *National Tax Journal*, March 1963; A. S. Mackintosh, *The Development of Firms*, Cambridge University Press, Cambridge, 1963, especially Ch. IX; also E. Balopoulos *An Econometric Study of the Public Sector in the U.K.* (unpublished Ph.D. dissertation, University of Manchester).

future is extremely limited — perhaps more so than some economists are willing to admit. But there is no case whatever for multiplying uncertainties by frequent and arbitrary changes in tax laws. If the main purpose of investment incentives is to raise the long term level of investment rather than offset cyclical downturns — and this clearly is the case in underdeveloped countries, and perhaps in the majority of developed countries too — the emphasis should be on the stability of these tax arrangements, rather than their variability.[1] No doubt, this throws a greater burden of short term adjustment on consumption and the public sector, but that is one of the prices which may have to be paid in pursuing any policy of high *and* stable investment.

It should be noted that these two arguments — simplicity and certainty — are connected. It is precisely when the authorities enact very complicated tax legislation, attempting many types of differentiation between industries, regions etc. that frequent changes in the legislation may be found necessary. So pursuance of both policies together may be expected to yield a particularly rich harvest.

Another general point is the treatment of inventories. Investment incentives are almost always concentrated on fixed investment. This may indeed have repercussions on stock holding in so far as, for example, better communications reduce the minimum necessary ratio of stocks to output. But incentives to improved methods of stock control and the like — it must be noted that whilst one may want to *increase* the ratio of fixed capital to output, the aim with stocks may well be to *decrease* the ratio — should clearly have a place in tax incentive legislation.

Finally, there is something to be said about the treatment of foreign enterprises. First, it is reasonable to expect that tax concessions to expatriate companies should benefit the company and not its home government. So one must expect to see further developments of the kinds mentioned on pp. 441f.[2] Secondly, the point is sometimes made that concessions to foreign companies are pointless in that the total amount of investment by foreign companies in

---

[1] For criticism of Greek legislation in this respect of. A. G. Papandreou, *Strategy for Greek Economic Development*, Athens, 1962, p. 103.

[2] Some countries now try to frame their incentive legislation in such a way that concessions are only available to those foreign companies whose governments do not share in the proceeds.

underdeveloped countries is more or less fixed: therefore the only
net effect of tax incentives, for all underdeveloped countries taken
together, is to make a present to these foreign companies.[1] This is a
large issue which obviously needs detailed discussion. But, at the
risk of superficiality, it does seem worth saying two things: first,
that the evidence that foreign investment is a fixed quantum is so
thin as to be invisible and, second, that all underdeveloped countries
cannot be treated as a homogeneous unit — there may well be
reasons why one country should offer more favourable concessions
than another for one type of investment and yet be less favourable
to another type.

FISCAL INCENTIVES TO PRIVATE SAVING

Before embarking on a discussion of the ways in which the fiscal
system can be arranged so as to stimulate private saving, relatively
to consumption, we must say something about the inter-relationship
between this side of fiscal policy and that relating to private investment. The first general proposition is that if there is an increase in
private investment and if (a) there are few slack domestic resources
available and (b) foreign loans or aid are not available, or not sufficiently available and (c) it is either undesirable or impossible to
provide finance from government sources either by cutting down
government spending on goods and services or by raising more tax
revenue, then it will be necessary to stimulate private saving if
inflationary pressures are to be avoided. This is a straightforward,
standard piece of economic reasoning and need not detain us. What
should be stressed, however, is that private decisions to save and
to invest are by no means completely independent of one another in
the countries which concern us here. This point can be illustrated
from opposite ends of the spectrum: on the one hand, the small-scale
entrepreneur may have very limited access to any sources of finance
other than his own and on the other, direct investment by foreign
firms will often be accompanied by the complete provision of funds
from their base countries. In cases such as these, it is not very
meaningful to distinguish between investment and savings incentives: the decisions to save and to invest go hand in hand and if the
government is successful in stimulating one half of the joint decision,

[1] It is accepted, of course, that there may be some redistribution of total
foreign investments between different underdeveloped countries.

it will succeed in the other half too. This does not mean that policy can be confined solely to the investment side or to the savings side; it may well be that influences from both sides are necessary to get the combined machinery going. All it does mean is that it is artificial to treat the two sides as operating independently of one another.

There is another, and different, sense in which policy must take account of inter-relationships. If private investment increases, then (on the assumptions listed above) it will be necessary to stimulate private saving if inflationary dangers are to be avoided. On the other hand, the level of private investment depends, in part at least, on the level of known current and expected future consumption. If private saving is stimulated the reduction in current consumption may be such as to cut the ground from under the feet of the investment decision takers. When this point is taken into account, it can be seen that the judgement of the right degree of stimulation to be given to private saving calls for a very delicate balancing of possibilities — neither so much that investment is cut back nor so little that strong inflationary forces are unleashed.

With these complications in mind, we shall now examine some of the technicalities of fiscal stimulation of private saving. It will be convenient to divide the analysis so that we look first at devices for encouraging total saving and, second, at devices for diverting saving into particular channels. In both cases, we shall assume that the government aims at keeping the same level of total revenue and so any substitution of one tax for another has to satisfy this constraint.

Fiscal stimulation of private saving must in some way or other involve relatively favourable treatment of those elements with high marginal propensities to save. In principle, one can analyse the various possibilities in two ways — by looking at the objects of the differentiation (e.g., high personal incomes as against low ones) or by looking at the techniques (consumption taxes versus income taxes). We shall ourselves follow the latter approach and deal in turn with taxes on persons, taxes on companies and changes in the relative importance of the two.

There are many ways in which taxes on persons can in principle be used to stimulate saving. First, one can use personal income tax for this purpose, the most obvious example being an income tax which is proportional or very slightly progressive. Compared with the highly progressive form one usually finds this would give advantages to rich people, who are usually thought of as being high savers. This proposition is a very dubious one however. First, it is common in the underdeveloped parts of the world to draw attention to the luxury consumption of the rich classes. Statistical evidence on these matters is, not surprisingly, scarce; but in a sense this does not matter. If the rich have a high average propensity to consume, tax benefits are unlikely to stimulate saving much; and even if they have not, the very fact that they are popularly supposed to have rules out this solution from practical politics in the world as it is today.

Another standard recipe in the personal tax field is to change the relative weight of taxation on consumption and saving. This can be done in a variety of ways: the replacement of income tax by an expenditure tax, (i.e. a tax on income less saving), the replacement of income tax by direct taxes (e.g., retail sales taxes), the exemption of interest from income tax and so on. Analytically, these suggestions all reduce to a common form: that of increasing the rate of return on saving relatively to that on consumption. As I have examined the arguments for the expenditure tax variant of these devices at length elsewhere [1] it would be superfluous to go into all the details again here. Although any such tax substitution must tend to work in the desired direction, it would be unwise to expect very much in the way of quantitative effects for at least three reasons. First, there are the obvious administrative limitations in underdeveloped countries. India and Ceylon have both imposed expenditure taxes in recent years but only on very small fractions of the population — and India has in fact abandoned even this experiment. Of course, partial taxes on consumption (e.g., on imported durables) can be imposed all right; but the encouragement to saving argument is weaker, the more partial the consumption taxes are. Second, the precise extent to which these taxes turn the net margin of advantage in favour of saving is a complicated matter; but it seems safe to say that the conditions under which the change is really substantial are stringent and somewhat unlikely to be satisfied in practice. Third, all these arguments rest on the assumption that saving responds positively to an increase in the effective rate of return; and the evidence for such a proposition is more conspicuous by its absence than its presence.

[1] 'The Expenditure Tax and Economic Development', op. cit.

Although the 'substitution' effects of this sort of tax change are likely to be small, it must be remembered that there are also 'income effects' to take into account — in the sense that switches from income taxes to spendings taxes are likely to confer relative benefits on upper-income groups and any other high savers. To get a complete picture of the result, we must therefore repeat the analysis applicable to changing the progressiveness of income taxes. This, too, as we have seen, is not absolutely clear cut, but it may nevertheless be true that this is the more likely way of generating additional savings from tax changes of the type we are now considering. Finally, it should be remembered that there are all sorts of ways in which actual tax systems differentiate against saving to a greater degree than is implied in a system of proportional or even progressive income taxation, in that there are taxes on wealth, heavier rates of tax on unearned than on earned income etc. So even if it is felt that the savings advantages of wholesale switching from income taxes to spendings taxes are insufficient to justify the change, there may still be a case for scrutinizing the savings disincentives embodied in many tax systems, as we actually find them.

The usual way in which corporate income taxation is levied so as to encourage saving is to give special relief to retained earnings, for example, the differential profits tax which prevailed in the U.K. from 1947 to 1958. There are all sorts of complications in systems of this sort, some of them undesirable (e.g., the advantages conferred on old timers over newcomers to an industry) but it would seem likely all the same that this is a method of encouraging saving. For even if one takes the extremist line that all corporate taxes are passed forward, the substitution of a differential corporate tax for a straight one will confer advantages on those firms ploughing back large proportions of their profits. Consequently, one would expect their prices to rise relatively less and so their importance to increase in the long run.[1]

Finally, it may be possible to boost savings by changing the relative importance of taxes on companies and individuals. Exact prescription is impossible in view of the very differing relations between corporate and personal income taxes which prevail in different countries, but if, whether as a result of the existing tax

---

[1] It can, however, be argued that some of these tendencies are offset by wealth-effects, e.g., if share prices rise as undistributed profits are increased, there may be increases in consumption.

arrangements or otherwise, corporations are disposed to save a larger fraction of the marginal £ of income than individuals, a redistribution of the tax burden between the two can obviously stimulate saving.

We now pass to the fiscal stimuli needed to push savings into particular channels. The kind of argument which one frequently meets is that saving takes the wrong forms in underdeveloped countries — that it is frequently oriented in 'unproductive' directions such as the acquisition of land or precious metals or currency hoarding rather than 'productive' forms such as loans to industry. Some of these arguments are simply fallacious: the stock of land in a country is fixed and therefore savings cannot be absorbed in that way for a country taken as a whole. The same may also be true of precious metals, though the argument in that case is less conclusive in that extra demand may conceivably lead to more domestic production in some cases or to more imports from abroad in others. As for the hoarding kind of argument, there are two broad classes of remedy available to the authorities. One is to attempt to improve the working of the various capital markets in a country. This may be partly a question of general government encouragement, provision of information, legal arrangements and so on. But there is also scope for fiscal policy, for example, the arrangement of taxes on issues and transfers of securities or specific exemption of income from tax in the case of those securities deemed to need encouragement. Such encouragement may, of course, take the form of removing discriminatory taxes which have been imposed on previous occasions. The second class of remedy open to the authorities is to tailor the supply of assets to meet the public's preferences, for example, if the public wishes to add to its assets in cash form, the government can create more credit and use this as the basis for financing private enterprise. Similarly, if the public is prepared to buy government, though not industrial, securities, the necessary financial resources can be made available to those firm wanting to expand their stock of capital equipment out of the proceeds of an issue of government stock.

It would clearly be rash to generalize about these two types of remedy: the need for them and the scope for them will obviously differ from country to country. But there is one general difference which must be noted. Active tailoring of government securities to fit market conditions does amount to the replacement of private by public enterprise in one sector of the economy[1] and so, if this point is thought to be important, it might sway one in the direction of the alternative type of policy. But, it must be added, in the rudimentary state of capital markets which one finds in many underdeveloped countries, the problem is likely to be more one of discouraging the possible emergence of private activity in this field rather than superseding what one finds at present.

One important aspect of government policy in the area is the treatment of domestic savings which flow abroad. The number of occasions on which such outflows can be justified from a social point of view are very limited. For even when the individual owner in the underdeveloped country gains thereby — and, of course, the reason for capital outflows is often political uncertainty and related considerations, rather than economic returns — the likelihood is that the addition to total income in the underdeveloped country is less than it would have been if the capital had been deployed domestically. Policy to give effect to these considerations has to be many sided and cannot just be fiscal in character. But in so far as fiscal weapons do come into these matters, the moral is likely to be that one has to adjust tax rates on investment income at home to keep net returns at least as high as those which can be earned on investment abroad, after taking into account liability to foreign as well as domestic tax.

Public Investment and Public Saving

Although we have concentrated in this paper on incentives to private investment and private saving, it would be quite wrong to conclude without recognizing the importance of public investment even in economies where the public sector is relatively small. Even if one wearies a little of the vague parrot cries about infrastructure, social overhead capital and so on, it is simply not realistic to expect that private investment incentives will be successful unless public investment programmes in roads, harbours, airfields and public utilities generally, not to mention education and health, are also carefully organized and co-ordinated. Unless this is so, one is bound to find that less private investment is started or that projects are abandoned before completion or that even when completed they turn

[1] Cf. Milton Friedman, *A Programme for Monetary Stability*, Fordham University Press, New York, 1960, p. 62.

out to be unsuccessful because the necessary complementary services or supplies are not available. In the last resort investment is a whole and if there is both a public and a private sector it is no good concentrating on one sector at the expense of the other, either in the sense of letting one expand much faster than the other or in that of devoting much more effort and thought to one than the other.

The choice between different investment projects in the public sector — the assessment of benefits and costs and the relative merits of the present value test and the internal rate of return test — must be regarded as outside the scope of this paper.[1] So must the still larger issues of the choice between current and capital expenditures in the public sector and *a fortiori* that of the overall size of the public sector. It is sufficient for our purposes to draw attention to the presence and the importance of these different issues. Finally, there are the myriad problems of execution, management and control of investment projects (e.g., such important issues as charges for public utilities) once they have passed the planning stage. But detailed attention to this would open up many aspects of public administration, which we have neither space nor competence to deal with.

The very last issue is that of public saving. A series of budget surpluses may be a prime requirement of development policy aiming at a high level of total investment. This means that, leaving aside the possibility of cuts in government current expenditure, general tax receipts have to be expanded by some means or other. This in turn opens up all the wider issues of the effects of higher tax rates on incentives to private investment, saving and effort. If we take private saving as an example, this means that the relevant question now is 'How can tax receipts be expanded whilst minimizing the reduction in private saving?'— and not the question we dealt with earlier, i.e. 'How can the tax structure be rearranged so that we increase private saving whilst maintaining tax revenue unchanged?' The answers to the two questions will often be on similar lines (e.g., changing the relative importance of consumption taxes and income taxes) but, on the other hand, some techniques such as the introduction of social security schemes, which more or less

---

[1] Cf. Earl R. Rolph, 'The Growth of the Public Sector and Economic Development' in *Public Sector and Economic Development*, op. cit., for a succinct account of these matters.

automatically yield an excess of revenue over expenditure,[1] come more into the limelight at this point. This is also the point at which one has to consider the merits of compulsory saving schemes on the lines proposed in Ghana and British Guiana in recent years, for example, how far they discriminate between different classes of the community, how far they result in lower personal consumption and how far in lower personal saving (or at any rate lower personal saving available in the home country), as well as the broader political issues.

There is no need to stress that acceptable solutions to such conundra are hard to find. This, at least, is a feature which really is common to all underdeveloped countries.

[1] This characteristic holds even after the building up stage has been passed in those cases where population is rising rapidly or where *per capita* contributions rise faster than outpayments per beneficiary, due to rising money incomes.

TAXATION OF AGRICULTURE IN DEVELOPING ECONOMIES*

by Haskell P. Wald

The revenue needs of underdeveloped countries seeking to accelerate their economic growth are overwhelmingly large, considering the low taxable capacity and other formidable obstacles to tax collection there. These countries, therefore, must find practical means of tapping virtually every revenue source possible, with the particular aim of mobilizing additional savings to finance a higher rate of capital formation. But they must also be constantly on guard against tax policies which, by pushing segments of the population deeper into poverty or by blunting desirable economic incentives, would thwart a sustained economic expansion. For these compelling reasons, rational tax planning, as opposed to outright expediency or blind acceptance of traditional fiscal measures, deserves a high place on the agenda of government in developing economies.

For the economist, the starting point of rational tax planning is a ranking of broad categories of private and public expenditures for current and investment purposes according to a scale of national priorities. On the basis of such an ordering of priorities, informed judgements can be made regarding the amount and location of relatively low-priority purchasing power (i.e., tax-paying capacity) which might be diverted with economic advantage from private hands to the government. The end-purpose of the taxing-spending process, as the economist conceives it, is the improvement of the

* This paper is mainly a restatement of ideas and policy principles presented in the author's book, *Taxation of Agricultural Land in Underdeveloped Economies*, Harvard University Press, Cambridge, Mass., 1959, and in the *Papers and Proceedings of the Conference on Agricultural Taxation and Economic Development*, International Programme in Taxation, Harvard Law School Cambridge, Mass., 1954, edited by the author. Extensive bibliographical references are contained in those two volumes and are not repeated here. A Spanish translation of the paper appeared in *El Trimestre Economico*, April-June, 1961.

The views expressed in this paper are those of the author and should not be regarded as representing the views of any organization with which he is or has been associated.

overall allocation and use of a country's productive resources.[1] Taxes, except when they are paid out of funds which would otherwise remain idle, release resources from private use, while government spending captures resources for government purposes. By channelling resources from low-priority to higher-priority needs as shown by the expenditure rankings, the taxing-spending process is able to promote economic welfare and, if properly planned, economic development as well. Ideally, only the least necessary private expenditures should be curtailed by taxation, and government expenditures always should be arranged to yield the maximum total benefit to the community.

This paper analyses in a general framework, without concentration on any particular countries, the tax-paying capacity of the agricultural sector and the means of tapping that capacity for government purposes. Sectoral fiscal studies, while useful to tax planning in all countries, are a prime requirement in developing economies. This is so because such studies are needed to complement economic development planning, which is necessarily organized along sectoral lines. Indeed, the major intersectoral and intrasectoral resource transfers needed to accelerate development must be effected principally through fiscal instruments as the best way to avoid a disruptive inflation.

It is unnecessary to belabour the fundamental importance of the distinction between the agricultural and non-agricultural sectors in development and tax planning. The two sectors obviously require separate consideration in view of the sharp contrast between them as regards not only their economic characteristics, but also their structural, institutional, cultural, and even demographic features. As might be expected, this sectoral differentiation permeates the tax laws of all countries with agricultural sectors of any importance.

In the first section below, the economist's conception of the taxing-spending process as a whole is applied to the special problem of setting revenue goals for agriculture in developing economies. Next, the present methods of taxing agriculture in these economies are reviewed. The concluding section suggests improvements in these methods which may enable them to serve more effectively as instruments of development financing.

[1] Public officials responsible for tax policy must of course adopt a broader concept of the taxing-spending process than the one defined above, in order to allow for political and social objectives.

The Agricultural Sector's Tax-paying Capacity

Tax-paying capacity is inherently difficult to measure. One reason, as already indicated, is that it depends upon the purposes of government spending. Capacity may not exist for financing low-priority spending — simply because the funds might serve higher-priority needs if left in private hands — and yet may be ample for highly essential government programmes. Indeed, tax-paying capacity may even be found in what is generally considered to be private subsistence spending, provided the funds are necessary to finance vital public services (for example, health and sanitation) and provided less essential private spending is beyond the reach of the government's taxing arm. Secondly, measurement is difficult because of the subjective element in decisions on the relative essentiality of private and government spending and on the respective advantages of current consumption and investment. These decisions must be responsive to preferences expressed in voting instead of in the market place. Is it more essential to improve diets or to build schools? To improve private housing or to build better roads? Faced with such questions, public officials can always take refuge in a strictly pragmatic approach, by raising taxes until practical administrative or political limits are reached, or until seriously adverse economic repercussions are noticeable. Such an approach might succeed, but the economist will not be satisfied without attempting a more analytical testing.

Quantitative Aspects

To ascertain the tax-paying capacity of the agricultural sector, various kinds of information must be correlated and interpreted in the context of a development plan. It is too much to expect definitive quantitative answers, but to calculate even crude indices of capacity, particularly if such calculations help to clarify conceptual issues, would advance tax planning in most countries.

At the most elementary statistical level, there are data on the size of the agricultural population. In the underdeveloped countries, with a few exceptions, the bulk of the population — perhaps between 60 per cent and 75 per cent — is in the agricultural sector. The direct relevance of that type of factual information to questions of tax-paying capacity is limited to a *per capita* tax, which is of course impractical except at a very low rate, but population statistics form the basis for further deductions.

Income statistics, preferably by broad income classes within each economic sector, are the chief data for elucidating questions of tax-paying capacity. Agriculture's share of total national income generally is far less than proportionate to its population in under-developed countries. According to widely accepted estimates, average *per capita* income (cash and non-cash) in agriculture typically is between one-fourth and one-third of the non-agricultural average. These income ratios, when combined with the preceding population ratios, yield a range of 30 per cent to 50 per cent, representing the proportion of agricultural income to total national income in underdeveloped countries generally.[1] The upper part of this range is probably applicable to many of the very poor countries. Agriculture's share of total income is an appropriate standard to use in tax planning whenever the policy aim is to have total direct and indirect taxes roughly proportionate to income in each sector of the economy.

On the basis of the meagre information available on the sources of tax receipts by economic sectors, the proportion of the total existing tax load allocable to agriculture generally appears to be considerably below the range of 30 per cent to 50 per cent corresponding to its income share in most underdeveloped countries. This does not necessarily mean, however, that agriculture is being under-taxed relative to other sectors, because these countries may not be aiming at proportional taxation. In fact, the appeal of the latter goal as a tax ideal would seem to be small, except in the uncommon case of a country where the income inequalities among the population are small. The most convincing theoretical argument favouring proportionality acknowledges the desirability of a tax-free minimum income for everyone, thus recognizing the absence of tax-paying capacity at the bottom of the income scale, and it limits proportional taxation to incomes in excess of that minimum. With the latter limitation, the overall pattern of taxation would depart sharply from a proportional distribution based on each person's total income.

Because the usual disparity between *per capita* incomes in agriculture and industry is in the order of one-to-three or one-to-four, agriculture's share of total national income certainly must overstate

---

[1] Few countries would need to rely on the rough estimating procedure illustrated above, because most of them have their own national income statistics indicating agriculture's share.

its relative tax-paying capacity. To correct the overstatement, either a minimum individual exemption can be allowed in estimating tax-paying capacity, as suggested above, or else a gradually rising ratio or tax-paying capacity to income can be postulated. If the first approach is followed, the minimum exemption, which should be set in relation to the marginal essentiality of government spending and the availability of other revenue sources, need not be calculated on a *per capita* basis, but it can differentiate between adults and children, in recognition of the fact that family living costs do not increase proportionally with family size. Moreover, it would seem appropriate to assume a lower scale of exemptions for agriculture than for other sectors, because the minimum living requirements in many basic categories — food, clothing, transportation, recreation, etc., — are lower in agricultural communities than elsewhere. Under the second approach, the rate of progressivity selected as the target should accord not only with an acceptable standard of equity among tax-payers, but also with the need to avoid harmful economic effects. It should be observed that both methods imply at least a moderately progressive overall tax structure as the aim of policy.

It would be a frivolous exercise, in a general discussion of this sort, to make hypothetical calculations to illustrate the application of the preceding suggestions, because the standards that would be favoured in different countries are impossible to anticipate. In all likelihood, even a very poor country which attempted the calculations would find that it could hardly afford to ignore the tax-paying capacity of its agricultural sector, even if that capacity were only a small fraction of the sector's proportionate income share. To claim that the manifestly low incomes which typify the agricultural sectors of underdeveloped countries leave no margin of tax-paying capacity may be intuitively appealing, but it does not seem to accord with a realistic assessment of priorities. Those who make that argument may be ignoring the invariably skewed distribution of income within agriculture; or else they may be assigning a lower priority to government programmes, and in particular to public investment which would lead to higher agricultural output, than appears consistent with the requirements of most of these countries.

Generally speaking, the fiscal restrictions on government spending in most underdeveloped countries are not due to the total exhaustion of their tax-paying capacity as defined by economists, but instead to the formidable practical difficulties of absorbing the available capacity. Pockets of untapped tax-paying capacity probably exist in all these countries and in every economic sector. The instances of over-taxation, when closely examined, can usually be ascribed to improper selection of tax instruments, inefficient planning of the government's budget, or poor administration, rather than to an inordinately heavy overall tax load.

Definitional Aspects

The most widely accepted and satisfactory basis for the allocation of taxes among individuals is net income, which provides a comprehensive measure of a person's economic well-being. The definition most appropriate to this usage is the total value of a person's consumption during a given period, increased or decreased by the change in his net wealth. The ownership of wealth (tangible and intangible) has usefulness of its own in measuring tax-paying capacity, but chiefly as a means of compensating for observed deficiencies in the net income criterion rather than as a general standard.

In income tax legislation, the tax base is often restricted to income that is realized by the individual through market transactions, thus exempting the value of goods and services produced and consumed (or invested) by the same household. The latter exemption may be an administrative necessity for income taxes, but it is inappropriate when income is being used to measure economic well-being. In the predominantly subsistence agricultural economies of underdeveloped countries, perhaps two-fifths or more of the sector's income may represent home-produced food alone. Inclusive of the imputed value of owner-occupied dwellings, fuel gathered by the household, and improvements by owners on their property, the non-monetary proportion of agricultural incomes is substantially higher. In the non-agricultural sector, on the other hand, the non-monetary proportion is quite small.[1]

If tax-paying capacity is to be determined on the basis of monetary and non-monetary income combined, the tax base should also be equally inclusive. As shown in a later section, a land tax is readily

[1] *The Taxation Inquiry Commission, 1953-4,* Government of India, presented estimates showing that 45 per cent of total consumer expenditure in the rural sector (against 10 per cent in the urban sector), was outside the monetized sector of the economy in India. The percentage declines with increasing expenditure levels.

adaptable to a broad concept of income — much more readily, in fact, than an income tax. Other taxes that might be imposed directly or indirectly on the agricultural sector — such as sales taxes, marketing taxes, and export levies — are necessarily restricted in their impact to market transactions.

In view of the desirability of protecting the living standards of the lowest income groups to the fullest possible extent, one might ask whether tax-paying capacity in the agricultural sector might be gauged with reasonable accuracy by the amount of cash income alone and without regard to non-cash income. Clearly, farmers growing basic food crops will reserve enough of their production for their families' needs before selling produce in the market; moreover, farmers growing other crops will frequently set aside some land for a family garden. These cases suggest a possible parallel between the exemption of non-cash income and personal exemptions allowed by net income taxes.

For the mass of farmers in many countries, no serious injustice may be involved in the use of a cash income standard in determining tax-paying capacity. That approach cannot be given a blanket endorsement, however, for several reasons. The non-monetary sector of agriculture cannot always be closely identified with a subsistence existence. Sumptuous living can in fact be supported largely on a non-monetary basis, with food consumed lavishly, textiles woven and sewn at home, and servants and other help paid in kind. Moreover, food may be available in excess of consumption requirements and yet never reach markets because of a lack of economic incentives (which may be weakened by taxation) or because of poor marketing facilities. Finally, in those sections of a country where agricultural production is market-oriented, farmers may choose to specialize in cash crops and purchase grain and other basic goods in the market place. Such farmers require substantial cash income merely for subsistence needs. In all cases in which non-monetary income is unequally distributed among the population, its exclusion from the tax base would involve a departure from the appropriate standard for measuring tax-paying capacity.

Dynamic Aspects

Perhaps the most promising aspect of agricultural taxation in underdeveloped economies lies in its dynamic aspects. The late Professor Nurkse argued this point forcefully, in connexion with his thesis that the incremental savings ratio is a crucial determinant of growth. In densely-populated countries, where ' disguised unemployment ' in agriculture is substantial and represents a potential source of economic saving which is running to waste, the government should seek to withdraw funds from agriculture to match the withdrawal of idle manpower as workers are shifted to industry. A substantial amount of tax financing of development is thus possible under these circumstances without reducing the *per capita* income of the remaining population in agriculture. In sparsely settled countries, on the other hand, an improvement in agriculture through technological changes may be a prerequisite for increased capital formation throughout the economy. The incremental capital-output ratio may be lower in agriculture and the returns may come more quickly than in industry. Unless part of the increased agricultural income is siphoned off by taxation and used for additional investment, a sustained, rapid pace of development will be difficult to achieve.

These arguments favour flexible revenue instruments and adaptation of the tax structure to changing needs. They stress the importance of substantial tax absorption of increases in income as the development programme bears fruit, in order to permit non-inflationary financing of a growing investment budget. They single out increments of income, particularly in the agricultural sector where manpower is likely to be released, as a source of above-average tax-paying capacity. Finally, they draw attention to the opportunities for incentive applications of taxes in order to encourage the needed shifts of resources.

AVAILABLE FISCAL INSTRUMENTS

A more varied selection of fiscal instruments is available in the agricultural than in the industrial sector. This is indeed fortunate because the conventional tax instruments, such as general or selective sales taxes and income taxes, are of limited effectiveness in the agricultural sector. Sales taxes are blocked from wide usage there, in view of the importance of non-monetary transactions. A broadly-based income tax would encounter not only that obstacle but also the lack of farmers' records of income and expenses, the generally low educational level of the agricultural population, and the impossibility of adapting the withholding method of tax collection to agricultural incomes.

On the other hand, some characteristics of the farm sector facilitate tax collection. Most important, because the bulk of the sector's income is derived from working the land, extensive use of presumptive tax assessments is possible. In addition, the large importance of staple grains and other crops that are easily collected, measured, and stored simplifies the valuation of output and also permits payments in kind as an alternative to payments in cash. Finally, where agricultural exports are large, they may be conveniently taxed when they are ready to be shipped out of the country or through the instrument of government marketing boards.

Out of necessity, the underdeveloped countries have fashioned an incredibly wide assortment of revenue-raising instruments applicable to agriculture. Some of these serve important non-fiscal purposes; among the more obvious examples are Burma's rice marketing board and the compulsory sales of grains and other products at below-market prices to the government in Taiwan, Mainland China, and several countries of the Middle East. Another group of instruments comprises export levies and multiple-exchange rate systems, which frequently produce large revenues derived from the internal agricultural sector. Generally less significant as absorbers of agricultural incomes are sales taxes, income taxes, capitation taxes, and various kinds of fiscal monopolies.

In most underdeveloped countries, however, some form of levy tied to the ownership or use of land is the mainstay of their agricultural tax system. This type of tax, deeply rooted in fiscal experience almost everywhere in the world, is known by various names: land tax, land revenue, land income tax, property tax, tithe, and gross produce tax. A marketing tax imposed in lieu of a direct tax on agricultural land should also be included in this group. Although this group of taxes has declined in revenue importance since World War II, except perhaps in countries where in-kind tax collections are made, the increased attention now focused upon agriculture's role in economic development has stimulated efforts to rebuild their fiscal productiveness.

This prominent family of taxes on land has had too anomalous a growth — with little evidence of a process of natural selection leading to improved forms — to permit a clear-cut classification of the many different types for analytical purposes. At the risk of oversimplification, the following description groups them into three major categories, depending on whether the taxes are assessed according to (1) land area, (2) a rental value concept of land value, or (3) an income concept.

Taxes assessed on the basis of land area are the most rudimentary of land taxes in structure and administration. The tax may be levied at a uniform rate according to land area or at a graduated rate according to the economic classification of the land. The latter method, followed in Jordan, for example, provides a crude blending of a simple area approach with a more advanced assessment according to the economic value of land.

The second category, consisting of taxes assessed according to a rental value concept, has the distinction of conceptual kinship with a celebrated doctrine, the Ricardian theory of economic rent. Very few countries, however, follow the much-publicized examples of Australia and New Zealand in taxing only 'site value', which might be said to correspond to Ricardo's concept of value due to 'the original and indestructible powers of the soil'. There are two basic types of rental value land taxes. Under the older taxes, the leading example being the 'land revenue' in India and Pakistan, rental value is generally expressed as an amount purportedly equivalent to the annual value of the use of the land; under the newer ones, which include the property taxes common in Latin America, the assessed capital value is the tax base. If the value of land were determined exclusively by economic forces operating in an active and openly competitive land market, these alternative measures of land value would be reciprocally related, as principal is to interest. In actual operation, however, the two methods yield different results, not simply because the quantitative expression of the tax base is almost always a figment of the assessors rather than a realistic value, but also for other fundamental reasons.

Because of the variety of prevailing rental arrangements and the notorious imperfections of rental markets for agricultural land, actual rents paid are of limited usefulness in assessing taxes according to annual rental value. Among the better taxes, the general approach is to start from an estimate of the income-producing capacity of each class of land, following presumably standardized land classification and assessment procedures, and then separate out the portion representing rental value. Many appraisal formulas are tied to a fictional concept of a cultivator of average skill, who employs standard amounts of seed, fertilizer, and other production requisites.

Each field need not be rated in detail, but its rental value may be fixed in relation to that of a standard producing unit.

The assessment practices are decidedly more lax for capital value than for annual rental value taxes. The information on the selling prices of land is not at all reliable, because the sales each year are relatively few in comparison with the number of fields to be appraised, and selling prices very often do not reflect true market valuations. Many countries with the capital-value type of tax have not had land surveys, not to mention scientific soil mapping and productivity surveys. Some of them continue to rely on self-assessment by landowners.

The selling price of land, except when it is influenced by subjective factors such as the prestige of land ownership, tends to reflect the discounted value of the *anticipated* rental value of land in its *optimum* economic use. In contrast, annual rental value is more likely to be determined with reference to *current* rather than anticipated income and with reference to *present* use even though a different land use might be more profitable. These differences can cause a striking disparity between the results of the two methods of assessment when applied to idle land bordering on an expanding urban area or to an agricultural area experiencing rapid economic development. Divergences between the two assessment methods can also result because of differences between the treatment of improvements on the land.

The third major category of land taxes employs an income concept to measure the tax base. Many of these taxes are similar in outward form to those already described, but they differ because of their more inclusive tax base. The income concept covers not only rental value (i.e., income attributable to the properties of the land) but also the return to labour and producers' capital.

Like the rental value concept, the income concept as applied in land taxation is susceptible of different interpretations. The secular tithe is assessed against the gross harvest or gross income. It does not depend upon a land survey or land register because it is assessed by inspectors who visit the farms regularly at harvest time. Other forms of land taxes based on gross yield or gross income are assessed according to the rated productivity of land and do not vary with each year's actual harvest. Only a few land taxes are assessed against net income, and a presumptive value, as opposed to ascertained net income, is always used. Finally, there are the taxes on marketed produce, such as the '*istihlak*' introduced in Iraq and Syria to replace their former land taxes. These are collected when produce is brought to the market for processing or sale to distributors, consumers, or exporters.

This list does not exhaust the different types of land taxes. Some countries have had special taxes on increases in land value, and special assessments, or ' betterment levies ', are sometimes levied to finance specific public improvements which yield localized benefits to land values. Absentee landowners may be subject to penalty taxation on their land holdings. Special taxes are also imposed on unimproved land in countries seeking to curb land speculation. Forests, mines, and oil and gas resources obviously require special treatment in land taxation.

A Suggested Approach to More Effective Agricultural Taxation

In its basic design, a plan for more effective agricultural taxation should provide for: (1) a means of mass taxation which would raise large amounts from a broad segment of the agricultural population without imposing excessive burdens on particular groups; (2) a more exclusive tax applying to the wealthier recipients of agricultural income; (3) one or more taxes designed to tap windfall incomes arising out of fluctuations in export prices or out of domestic developments; and (4) special tax provisions for regulatory purposes.

Non-fiscal Applications

Examining this programme in reverse order, it may be noted that many countries have grafted regulatory or incentive provisions onto their land taxes. This is not in itself proof of the value of these provisions as instruments of policy, but at least it indicates the existence of numerous opportunities for non-fiscal applications. Mention has already been made of special taxes on idle land and on absentee ownership. Conversely, tax concessions might be granted to those crops which a country is aiming to encourage or to land improvement activities such as land reclamation, irrigation, and soil conservation.

On the whole, the chief danger is not that governments will ignore these non-fiscal applications, but rather that they will employ them without prudent discretion and restraint. The tax instrument may be less appropriate to use than outright subsidy payments or direct controls over production and distribution. If a revenue loss is involved, it may be more than the country can reasonably afford. Tax penalties or concessions may undermine the equity of the tax system. If precedents are established which force the government to extend favourable tax treatment to more and more groups, the tax load will be shifted more onto persons who may not have the capacity to carry it, while the intended incentive effects of the favourable tax treatment would tend to be destroyed as additional classes of tax-payers become eligible for such treatment.

Selective Taxation of High Incomes

The second and third parts of the overall plan outlined above can be implemented in a few countries by the extension of a global or schedular income tax to the agricultural sector. Because such a tax preferably should be based on ascertained net income as shown by tax-payers' accounting records, its immediate application may necessarily be limited to very wealthy landlords and managers in plantation economies, for example, and to such corporate enterprises as exist in agriculture. High marginal tax rates should be used cautiously, however, because they run the risk of damaging investment incentives and reducing the flow of private savings into investment. Troublesome problems of administration may be involved in this proposed extension of income taxes, yet tax planning should take account of the expected growth of a country's administrative capacity to undertake more advanced methods of taxation and to bear the heavier cost of these methods as further economic progress is made.

In addition, a judicious use of export levies might succeed in absorbing windfall gains arising out of fluctuating prices in world markets. Even in export economies, however, export taxation and land taxation have more important complementary than substitutional relationships with each other. Export taxes have been a flourishing revenue source in the post-war period, but they are not always sensitive to basic equity requirements and they sometimes impair a country's ability to export.

Reform of Land Taxation

Most governments in underdeveloped countries are likely to attach considerable importance to the fact that land taxes can be applied broadly to all of agriculture and thus have a comparatively large revenue potential. Moreover, these taxes provide a means of breaking through the tax collection barriers of a substantial non-monetized sector, widespread illiteracy, and low living standards. Land taxes also offer significant practical advantages because the land (or its produce) stands as security for the tax, the liable tax-payers usually are easily identified, and almost all countries can draw on their previous experience with these taxes to fashion a more effective levy to meet present-day needs. Finally, a strengthened land tax could afford desirable support to local government, which might brace a country's political health.

The existing land taxes, almost without exception, have major defects as instruments of development financing. Many Latin American countries, for example, do not even have satisfactory land maps and their records of land ownership and field boundaries are inaccurate and incomplete. Such conditions not only prevent equitable tax assessments and more productive tax yields, but they also are an impediment to improvement of many important phases of land administration (e.g., controlling tenancy conditions, surveying land use, planning agrarian reforms) and to the establishment of a system of land-based credit.

The scope for improvement of the basic tools of assessment probably is considerable in almost every underdeveloped country. Another urgently needed reform to bring the taxes in line with modern requirements is to make the tax yield more responsive to price and production changes. Such responsiveness is generally absent because of the long interval between assessment periods and because of a disinclination to make frequent changes in tax rates. Of course, assessments that are not kept current can also be a source of flagrant inequities among tax-payers. The superficially plausible notion that rate changes can be used to compensate for assessment values that are behind the times ignores the fact that the impact of inflation or development on land values and income is not likely to be spread evenly over the agricultural sector. The assessments must first be equalized.

It was the depreciation of land tax revenues in the world-wide inflation after World War II that did most to expose the disadvantages of revenue inflexibility.[1] In addition, there is a growing recogni-

---

[1] Taxes on marketed produce and tithe-like levies vary automatically with changes in production and prices. In-kind collections provide flexibility with respect to price changes but not necessarily with respect to fluctuations in production.

tion of the potential contribution of flexible taxes to economic stability and also of the desirability of diverting part of the increase in income generated by economic development to the financing of new investment.

What is needed is a scheme of annual revisions by means of an easily applied formula. Although precise adjustments would be impractical, reasonably satisfactory results could be obtained by employing price and production indices measuring average changes for the principal commodities in different agricultural regions. To avoid too frequent revisions of the tax, small changes in the relevant indices could be passed over. A plan of this sort would still permit above-average returns on individual farms to go tax free and below-average returns to be relatively over-taxed (i.e., the marginal tax rate, practically speaking, would be zero for the individual farmer). This structural feature of most existing land taxes offers maximum incentive for the adoption of better techniques of cultivation.

It should also be possible to purge the land tax of its *in rem* characteristics. This could be done if the tax assessments allowed for the tax-payer's personal circumstances. The minimum exemption — which is necessary for strictly administrative reasons if not for others — might be varied according to the number of the tax-payers' dependents, and allowances might also be provided for other factors affecting tax-paying capacity, such as loan obligations and losses due to catastrophes. Tax assessments should be aggregated for all land parcels belonging to each individual. An instance of recognition of the tax-payer's personal circumstances is the granting of tax concessions to new landowners in countries that have had a land reform.

Rationalization of the Land Tax Base

The remaining problem area of land taxation is one in which satisfactory solutions may prove hardest to reach within the limits set by administrative and institutional factors. Apart from improvements in the methods of assessment, the tax base itself must be reformed in concept, to bring it in closer conformity to individual tax-paying capacity.

The ideal plan requires ratings according to presumptive net income. To achieve this, two types of soil classifications are necessary: (1) in terms of inherent soil characteristics (i.e., scientific soil mapping to determine the 'soil profile'); and (2) in terms of economic use capabilities, as determined by potential water supply, climate, exposure to sunshine, topography, availability of farm implements, etc. Each delineated land area should be assigned a rating in accordance with its potential net income under average growing conditions and proper management, with appropriate allowances for distance from trading centres and other market factors. The use of yardstick farms, as found in parts of Central Europe, can be a valuable aid in such a rating process.

The above approach is suggested as a target on which the underdeveloped countries, particularly those in which the typical farmer is an owner-cultivator, should set their sights, provided the preconditions for heavy reliance upon land taxation are present. The requirements for its successful implementation in all its phases are doubtless prohibitive for many countries; it is certainly not within the early reach of countries which have not had previous experience with cadastral surveys.

Countries which find that the plan just outlined is on too grand a scale for them to adopt should turn their attention to alternative methods which might serve as stepping-stones towards the ideal plan. Ratings based on 'normal' gross yield have the advantage of simplicity, although they do not obviate the need for accurate land records and at least a rudimentary land classification system which could be used in conjunction with unit yield tables. If the tax were based on a varying fraction of the rated gross produce — in order to allow for estimated differences in the income earning potential of different fields after production and marketing costs — the result would be in keeping with the principle of taxing according to presumptive net income. It would not be a major undertaking for countries having land taxes assessed according to annual rental value to convert to the standard here proposed, because they may already possess much of the necessary information on soil classification and production expenses. On the other hand, countries which rely primarily on information on the selling price of land, or on self-assessment by landowners, must put their major initial effort into land mapping and land classification surveys in order to obtain a more realistic estimate of market value. Perhaps they would do better if they shifted to a classified-rate area tax. This would involve a simplified classification of land by easily recognizable criteria bearing on productivity and location, with a graduated tax rate schedule to reflect in a crude way the relative net income potential of each standard class of land. Such a system would assure far better results than are possible with the loosely administered property taxes in many countries.

Marketing taxes may be the only feasible means of collecting large revenues from agriculture in countries where farming regions have not been surveyed and where there are no established ownership and tenure rights in land. Such taxes, however, tend to discourage the movement of produce to the cities and they may be damaging to agricultural output because of their effects on marginal producers.

Conclusion

This paper has discussed how a properly conceived and applied system of agricultural taxation offers a promising solution to some pressing fiscal problems of countries in early stages of economic development. It has emphasized these countries' needs for fiscal instruments that are equitable and harmonize with acceleration of economic growth. The list of available fiscal instruments in the agricultural sector is a long one. Although land taxes often present strategic advantages over other methods of raising revenue, they have lost ground in recent years because of their structural rigidities and a general neglect of their potentialities. Specific suggestions have been outlined to bring land taxes into step with modern principles of taxation, as a prelude to making these taxes more productive of revenue and more efficient as instruments of economic policy.

Experience teaches that reforms of the type discussed are a laborious and painstaking task requiring the effort and skill of imaginative technicians and policy makers who are completely conversant with the economic and institutional setting in their respective countries and are able to judge the size of the administrative burden that can be successfully managed. No two countries can follow exactly the same path, but all can profit from the experience of others.

FOREIGN FINANCE AND AID

SOME THEORETICAL PROBLEMS OF POST-WAR FOREIGN INVESTMENT POLICY*

by T. Balogh

The importance of a successful solution of the problem of foreign investment for post-war reconstruction is obvious. It must form part of any comprehensive attempt to ensure full employment on an international scale, which at the same time would diminish the gross and politically dangerous discrepancy between the amounts of productive equipment available per head of the population in the fully industrialized, on the one hand, and in the underdeveloped countries on the other. The difference in real income between these areas would thereby be mitigated.

1. The general problem of foreign lending in its bearing on international agreements aiming at the maintenance of full employment has been investigated by the Oxford Institute of Statistics.[1] Mr. Knapp,[2] in an interesting and valuable contribution, has applied the modern theory of employment to the problem of the mechanism of international capital movements to test the validity of the traditional theories. The present paper has more restricted aims. We shall attempt to apply certain principles which have come to be generally accepted to the field of foreign investment where older misconceptions still threaten to influence the policy of the great Powers.

A. We shall inquire whether the freedom of private capital movements can be expected to lead to optimum distribution of resources. This problem will be dealt with under two headings. We shall first determine whether discrepancies between the gross and net private return do not vitiate the traditional view. Secondly, we shall bear in mind that the classical theory is based on the assumptions (*a*) that full employment is maintained; (*b*) that the rate of accumulation is governed solely by the decisions of individuals; (*c*) that the structure

---

* *Oxford Economic Papers*, March 1945. Reprinted with the permission of the Oxford University Press, and the author.

[1] 'New Plans for International Trade', Supplement No. 5, *The Bulletin of the Institute of Statistics, 1943*; *The Economics of Full Employment, 1944.*
[2] *The Review of Economic Studies*, 1943.

and quantity of capital equipment, as well as the skill of the population is a given datum (i.e. independent of the employment and investment policy of the government). Whenever these (implicit) assumptions are not fulfilled the 'classical' conclusions are falsified.

B. We shall try to show that capital autarky does not necessarily involve intolerable sacrifices of the standard of life of poorer countries, provided an appropriate policy with regard to the distribution of national income is pursued.

2. The first approximation to a theory of foreign investment is simple. The yield of capital investment, it is said, is — as any other price — the index of its scarcity. Capitalists try to invest in areas and outlets where the return is highest, and it is taken for granted that, if this condition is fulfilled, the real productivity of capital will also be at its maximum. Therefore, it is argued, interference with the free flow of capital would not only hinder economic progress in backward areas, but the rich countries would also be acting against their own interests, since such interference would mean that they would have to be content with a smaller return on their investment.

Even during the period of continuous upward trend — which cyclical fluctuations interrupted only temporarily — of the nineteenth and beginning of the twentieth century, when internal and international political risks were limited and the economic system of the world was homogeneously individualistic (though at very varied stages of economic maturity), this picture was far from being accurate.

The process of foreign investment was not, as orthodox theory would have it, a gradual equalization of returns on capital in a static system, operating through contrary movements of prices (and incomes) in the lending and borrowing countries. It operated even then through dynamically determined waves of investment opportunities resulting in an increase of investment at the (lending) centre and the (borrowing) peripheries. The opening-up of new areas through foreign investment intensified the booms and shortened the depressions and thus co-determined the upward trend of the period. But this stimulated and did not retard progress in the lending countries.

The relative backwardness, moreover, of over-populated but underdeveloped countries tended to be stabilized by this free interplay of economic forces.[1] The *relative* advantages gained by the industrial countries were cumulative. Attention was focused on the case of the opening up of under-populated and potentially rich areas.

3. The present state of affairs, at any rate, is essentially different. In international economic matters, we are confronted with an almost complete disintegration of the world economy. The opposing belligerent camps are more or less hermetically sealed against one another. Even between Allied nations, the blockade, counter-blockade, and shortage of the means of transport has reduced inter-communication to a minimum, strictly regulated on the basis of military necessity. During the enforced autarky — which has necessarily induced far-reaching changes of the productive structure not merely of the belligerents, but also of the neutrals — the former had to mobilize their economic system for war and this resulted in further structural alterations which renders the re-integration of their economic structure into a united world economic system more difficult.[2] Technical progress has been very rapid throughout this period, but was necessarily extremely uneven geographically.

The present rise and development of autarkic units contrasts sharply with the interdependence of economic progress before the last war, in spite of the fact that industrial and agricultural protectionism has become sharp in many parts of the world after 1880.

Given these changes — however regrettable their cause — the reversal of the trend can only come gradually and will, probably, even if enlightened policies are followed, not lead to the position which would have come about if the double interruption of international economic development had not taken place. Technical progress enforced by the blockades has produced 'Ersatz' materials which have come to stay on their own right. Marketing connexions and creditor-debtor connexions have been broken and liquidated. Their re-establishment will be difficult and may prove costly. The

[1] Internationalism of the *laissez-faire* type therefore, was always a questionable policy for these territories. They were kept in economic dependence, not by brute force as the European countries under Hitler's new order, but by the 'rules of the game', which, though historically established by force, became, in due course of time, elevated to the status of 'the rule of the law'.

[2] These autarkic units began to form, not in 1939, but at least as early as 1929. In certain areas, such as Central Europe, the centrifugal development away from international interdependence has been uninterrupted since 1914.

spread of depression consequent upon the bankruptcy of producers who become inefficient as trade reopens internationally might be avoided by appropriate full employment policies. The resistance of these producers even against their elimination might be overcome by some measure of compensation. Their influence would be broken by full employment policies which would reduce the support of labour for protective measures: because of the less specific character of labour, it can easily find alternative remunerative occupation, provided that full employment demand is maintained. Nevertheless the international division of labour will in all probability be narrower. The 'natural' relative advantages will be less because of the rise of 'substitute' products; the increasing importance of technique in determining productivity; and finally because, intimate business connexions once broken, the natural inertia (i.e. imperfections) of markets work against the old, and in favour of new, suppliers.

4. Technical progress has had a further and equally important consequence. In the last century, industrialization and the intensification of agriculture depended on the extent of the supply of entrepreneurial ability and capacity to invest as well as of highly skilled labour. This limited the area and the rate of potential industrialization in many parts of the world, where, unlike England and the United States, the income distribution favoured classes who were incapable of productive enterprise or unwilling to engage in it. There was no alternative to private enterprise, however inefficient, as practical experience of the working of a different system was lacking and administrative capacity was not available for large-scale public enterprise in the countries which needed it most. In many countries outside the Anglo-Saxon world, the State, nevertheless, made itself responsible, however inefficiently, for certain basic public services, e.g., transport and industries necessary for national defence.

At present, the pace of industrial progress in poorer areas depends primarily on the systematic large-scale application of up-to-date knowledge through the establishment by the State of a few mass-production units managed by a small number of technical experts and utilizing a labour force which can be easily trained even in primitive areas to the required semi-skilled standard. The raising of the standard of life depends therefore on the conscious and co-ordinated planning of industrial development by public agencies (for the risk and the initial cost of establishing such units can hardly be borne by private investors), and not on the chance of possessing energetic entrepreneurial social classes. We cannot, for these reasons, accept without analysis the traditional views on foreign investment as a guide for post-war reconstruction policy.

A. PRIVATE INVESTMENT AND PROGRESS

1. THE FREEDOM OF CAPITAL MOVEMENTS

5. Entrepreneurs who have a free choice between different investment opportunities in different national areas will act on the basis of *pure net return*. This must be sharply distinguished from the *gross overall return*, i.e. the observable return of the investment on the basis of the market price of the asset and the income stream it yields. The gross overall return includes (*a*) the risk premium, (*b*) direct taxation falling on the income stream which is payable after the (nominal) income has materialized. We shall call pure gross return the yield which remains after the deduction of the risk premium but before paying tax. Thus we have three yields: (*a*) gross overall, (*b*) pure gross, and (*c*) pure net. In the case of foreign investment the problem of double taxation complicates the matter and stands in the way of the equalization of pure gross returns internationally, as entrepreneurs can escape double taxation by not investing abroad. To this extent the foreign direct tax acts as a duty on capital import.

The classical theory assumes that pure net returns (which are taken to be equal to pure gross returns) depend on relative capital intensity of production and tend to be equalized by competition.

In the past thirty or forty years, however, the internal rigidity of the economic system increased substantially. Competition, moreover, became more imperfect. In consequence the return from investment can no longer be regarded as an index of the scarcity and productivity of capital; it is influenced much more by the degree of monopoly in industry. Economic and social policy which prevents monopolistic exploitation and/or attempts the redistribution of the national income consciously in favour of the poorer classes (e.g., by control of prices)[1] or controls the rate of interest will reduce the gross overall return on capital as contrasted with areas where such regulation does not obtain.

---

[1] Possibly as a measure facilitating the maintenance of full employment, cf. Institute of Statistics, op. cit.

The investors' behaviour depends not simply on the overall return, but also the riskiness of the investment. If such measures safeguard full employment they will reduce the objective riskiness of investment. It is unlikely, however, that the fall in the risk premium in respect to areas which follow progressive policies will offset the enforced decline of overall return. The reason for this is not far to seek. The confidence of private investors, rightly or wrongly, is not usually heightened by progressive social policies. Indeed, if capitalists fear political changes thought to be inimical to their interests, even a high gross overall return on capital will not tempt them to invest. The risk premium rises. Pure gross return falls. The same applies to policies (such as, e.g., full employment policy pursued through deficit spending) which would leave gross overall returns unchanged or even increase them. An outward flow of capital might set in which might, in the end, defeat the attempted progressive economic policies.

6. Nor is this all. It is not the pure gross, but the pure net return on capital (net of taxation) which determines the actions of the investor who has not committed himself. The difference between these yields varies widely in different parts of the world. In sharp contrast with the past state of affairs, direct taxation of income now reduces net returns very substantially below gross. The reduction will be heaviest in the most progressive economic systems. If private investors were permitted to equalize net returns internationally, the pressure on progressive economic systems would be overwhelming.

We conclude, therefore, that private net return on capital after taxation does not provide a valid index of its scarcity or productivity. Hence the freedom of capital movements will not necessarily lead to an optimum social distribution of capital between countries. Countries which wish to pursue progressive economic policies are, on all counts, not merely justified in maintaining the strictest control over capital movements, but are forced to do so.[1]

---

[1] In the United States, with its vast liquid reserves, a control over the export of capital might not be a *conditio sine qua non* of progressive economic policy. In Europe, including Britain, it certainly is an essential measure and will remain so in any future which it seems fruitful to contemplate. The attempt of the Blum Government to prevent sabotage of its radical internal policy by frightened investors through the export of their capital was defeated by appealing to the 'liberty' of the individual.

2. FOREIGN INVESTMENT AND PRIVATE PROFIT EXPECTATIONS

7. The second axiom of classical theory is that maximization of world output would automatically be brought about by private enterprise on the basis of profit expectations. This belief is based on the assumption that the current return on private capital investment — or rather the even less perfect criterion of current expectation by fallible investors of the total private return on present investment over a long period — provides a sufficient index of the desirability of the international capital investment from the point of view both of the lending, and of the borrowing country.

This view presupposes that social and private net returns are proportionate if not identical in the short and in the long run. It therefore presupposes that private investors foresee all adjustments which have to be made and developments which occur in the lending and in the borrowing country as a result of the invest-ment. It assumes that the consequences of the lending and of the servicing and repayment[1] of the loans are either known or if not known are irrelevant from the point of view of the *communities concerned*.

But private investors cannot, in the nature of things, form an opinion about the indirect effects of their decisions. We shall there-fore discuss some of the most important cases in which total social and expected private net returns might be expected to differ signi-ficantly from one another.[2]

(i) *Current and future private yields* on capital investment might differ considerably. The flow of foreign investment does not in real life take place in an equilibrium situation of full employment. If that were the case, new capital investment would increase the capital equipment per head and result in a gradual fall of the yield. Wages would increase and labour would be transferred from less to more productive uses. This process would gradually equalize the marginal efficiencies of capital in different countries.

In actual fact additional private investment tends, in a position of less than full employment, to increase the yield of capital and

---

[1] i.e. more than the average difference between social and private returns, cf. R. F. Kahn, 'Optimum Output', *Economic Journal*, 1934.

[2] Cf., e.g., M. Kalecki, *Review of Economic Studies*, February 1937; and N. Kaldor, *Economic Journal*, 1938.

start an upward spiral. This spiral is simultaneous or nearly simultaneous in both the lending and the borrowing countries. It will stimulate investment both in the borrowing and in the lending country, thus providing its own justification for the duration of the boom. Whether and in what direction gold movements will take place will depend on the magnitude of the multipliers and the income and price elasticities of demand and supply in the borrowing and lending countries respectively.[1]

(ii) *Current and future private returns* might differ substantially, especially in *new industries*. This is one aspect of the difference between (current) private and (future) social cost, the aspect which concerns the private investor. The general case will be discussed below under (iv). In this context we need to mention merely that differences of this type, described by Marshall, will arise when the increase in the scale of production decreases cost either for individual firms within the industry which is expanding or in other industries which supply the materials and services. The risk of starting industry on a sufficiently large scale, however, is prohibitive unless the programme of industrial expansion is consciously planned and co-ordinated [cf. below (iv)]. The classic 'infant industry' argument, which covers these cases, applies to a far greater range of industries than generally supposed. Indeed, if correctly interpreted, it can be applied to the (underdeveloped) economic system as a whole. In many cases tariff protection might equalize the difference and thus resolve the contradiction between private unprofitability and public desirability. It would seem, however, more efficient to direct investment activity by the grant of a subsidy (*a*) because the budgetary charge which thus becomes necessary renders the burden visible and it can be properly allocated, and (*b*) because the subsidized industry is more amenable to public control, and therefore steps can be taken more easily to safeguard efficiency and prevent protection from giving rise to an increased degree of monopoly in the protected industry and thus either to monopoly profits or the continuance of inefficiency. As we shall see below, however, the most important cases of constructive planning cannot easily be accomplished by

[1] The German import of capital in the period 1924-8 provides a good example for the case in point. Its abrupt end when the speculative boom in the U.S. suddenly raised the private expectation of profit in that country is equally illustrative of the problem under discussion.

relying entirely on private enterprise however modified by public intervention and assistance.[1]

(iii) The most important of the divergencies which have to be taken into account is that which may arise between *current social* and *current private* cost. A special aspect of this case has been dealt with under (i). The most important cause of this is the underemployment of an economic system. If there is unemployment the social cost of additional production (for home and foreign markets) is obviously less than the net private cost of the additional output to the employer increasing his scale of operations. The community must directly or indirectly maintain the unemployed. Their capacity to work if kept in idleness over a prolonged period of time will, moreover, deteriorate, thus further increasing and extending the incidence in time of the social loss. It might be argued, therefore, that the State could justifiably stimulate exports or home production competing with imports. Attempts to attain full employment by increasing the foreign balance by increasing exports — by depreciation or export subsidies — would be to create balance-of-payment problems abroad and are likely to be countered by the foreign countries which are affected. The lasting favourable results of such a policy are likely to be negligible. The harm done by retaliation is likely to be considerable. The policy of stimulating export surpluses would, moreover, also tend to limit the increase of the real income consequent on the increase of employment, partly because it would divert productive effort into directions in which the country has no natural advantage, partly because the forcing of exports would tend to turn the terms of trade against the country.[2] A country suffering from unemployment as a result of a slump abroad would, however, be justified in protecting its balance of payments if it at the same time takes steps to increase home demand and thus regains full

---

[1] Most *laissez-faire* attacks on protective policies assume implicitly that the State will rely entirely on the price mechanism to bring about the desired change and would not use direct controls. This explains the identification of protection with the support of inefficiency and monopoly.

[2] Similar 'over-export' takes place if labour in the industries affected by unemployment accepts exceptionally low wages. The export subsidy is then borne by the workers. Tariff protection (and most forms of control of imports) has the relative advantage of turning the terms of trade in favour of the protectionist country.

employment. Without protection its balance of payments would worsen.[1]

It would, however, be open for a strong country suffering from unemployment to stimulate its business activity by granting long-term loans on favourable terms on condition that those loans are spent exclusively on its products. In contrast to the method just described, this policy is not open to the objection that it depresses business activity elsewhere. Nor would it necessarily worsen the terms of trade of the lender as it would create additional demand abroad for its products. Indeed, under favourable circumstances, e.g., if the loan gave rise to a general expansion of activity and given a high income elasticity of demand for imports in the borrowing country the loan might turn the terms of trade in favour of the lending country. This tendency would be strengthened if the investment increased the productivity in industries which supply the lender with primary products. But if the lender itself is not merely a mature industrial country but also a large-scale producer of primary commodities even the fact that the loan is used for the purpose of industrialization need not have the normal effect (as in the case of purely industrial lending countries) of tending to worsen the terms of trade of the lender. In any case the 'automatic' effect of an increased demand in the borrowing countries on the terms of trade could be increased (and, if unfavourable, consciously altered) if the loans were used to bring about more intimate connexions between the lending and the borrowing country and thus to increase the imperfections of the markets of the borrowing country in favour of the industries of the lending country. This, in fact, would happen if the management, running, and servicing of the new capital installations financed by the foreign loan created in the borrowing country a special demand for the skilled man-power of the lender or if the commercial and other connexions established would ease the difficulties of export.[2] The impact effect of these foreign loans on the

[1] Or rather to restore the balance to its previous state if the slump abroad had the impact effect of worsening it (cf. Oxford University Institute of Statistics, op. cit.).

[2] These imperfections should be distinguished from a decrease in the cost of export due to increasing turnover and the increasing perfection of the knowledge of the borrower's market by the lender (and vice versa) which will turn the terms of trade against the lender without decreasing his real income. 'Tied' loans enforce imperfection in favour of the lender.

lending countries' economic system will depend on a number of factors. If the lending country suffered from unemployment an additional investment would increase employment and consumption. Hence its social cost would be negative, whether the investment was home or foreign.[1] If the increase in effective demand was entirely due to foreign investment this would not increase domestic capital intensity as much as would home investment,[2] though, in contrast to the continuation of unemployment, it would not, of course, retard it. Thus foreign investment may retard the relative improvement of the share of wages in the national income. Total national real income, however, would increase more than it would have done through an exclusively home investment because of the relative improvement in the terms of trade. If the increase in employment would otherwise have increased the difficulties of balancing current international payments, e.g., because the foreign elasticity of demand was very low, this relative improvement might be important if not essential.[3] This might well be the case if other countries pursued a

---

[1] If it were fully employed the consequence would be similar. Then the choice would be between a policy which either decreases the rate of increase in home durable assets or increases the ratio between investment and consumption. Cf., however, M. Kalecki's article, ibid.

[2] If the alternative to foreign investment consisted of 'pure', i.e. unremunerative, public works, the choice is between the 'communal' enjoyment of the works created and the increase in real income.

[3] The income distribution in the lending country would be different if the latter alternative were followed. It can be shown by the technique evolved by Mr. Kaldor (*Economic Journal*, 1938) that the lending policy under favourable circumstances yields better reserves all round. It would in all probability be preferred by the entrepreneurial classes in the lending country and this for two reasons: (1) It would not necessitate deficit spending or interference with internal income distribution; (2) Even non-productive foreign investments could, in the short run, be expected to be less immediately competitive with existing home productive capacity than the stimulus to home investment, and, if necessary, it could easily be prevented from becoming so by appropriate policies (duties, quotas, etc.). Even if the foreign loans are State granted or State guaranteed there are rational grounds for their being preferred. The increase in the National Debt is balanced by an acquisition of a foreign asset. The foreign investment is the alternative to home public works; it is easier to be hopeful about its eventual repayment than to face an inevitable increase in the 'burden of the National Debt'.

The discrimination implied in this method of export finance against countries unable to grant loans is mitigated by the fact that it is likely to result in a net increase of world employment. In this respect it is similar to clearing agree-

forward foreign investment policy. Otherwise the choice between
home and foreign investment will depend on political considerations,
including home social policy pursued (e.g., the possibility of distribut-
ing the improvement in the national real income fairly).[1] In the long
run the lending country must adapt itself to having a demand for
imports greater than originally corresponding to full employment,
so as to permit the servicing of its foreign investments without
deflation or default.

The consequence of this policy to an industrial country, which
was unable to compete in lending with a more fortunate rival, and
thus unable also to maintain its own markets and connexions,
might be serious.[2] Its terms of trade would, in all likelihood, deteriorate. The industrialization of backward or primary producing areas
would tend to decrease the supply of primary products, partly
because the absolute volume of supply may fall as a result of the
transfer of productive factors from primary to secondary or tertiary
industries,[3] and partly because the increase in the standard of life
in the backward areas will increase their demand for primary products in competition with the mature industrial countries. The
import prices of the industrial country will tend to rise. If the industrial country does not create new demands for its services and
producers' goods, and the market for these is very imperfect,
depending on the grant of loans, its export prices may fall
seriously. The consequent worsening of the terms of trade might
prejudice its material progress.

ments, concluded with respect to 'additional export '. The present tendency
to discriminate between 'discrimination' practicable for an *export surplus*
country by way of *loans*, and that which can be applied by an *import surplus*
country through *commercial agreements* might be sound propaganda from the
point of view of the former. It certainly has no scientific basis. Cf., op. cit.

[1] The phenomenal increase in British foreign investments in the nineteenth
century, despite heavy losses suffered as a result of over-speculation and
frauds, simultaneously with an increase in the standard of life of a rapidly
growing population could in all probability be attributed to some such development. Given an efficient organization the United States could parallel the
British example in this century on a vastly greater scale.

[2] This problem is discussed in greater detail by the present author in an
article on 'Retaliation' (*Review of Economic Studies*, 1944).

[3] This effect need not exert itself in the case of over-populated areas. Cf.
A. J. Brown (*Industrialization and Trade*, Royal Institute of International
Affairs, 1943).

(iv) Finally we must consider some cases in which the *current private* and *future social* returns differ significantly.[1] The future social return must be interpreted as embracing gains accruing to the community (direct and indirect) through the changes made possible by the new development. Investment of this type will be desirable from the long-run point of view of the community as a whole, though no private entrepreneur could undertake it at his own risk because the return directly accruing to him would be insufficient to cover the cost incurred and the risks borne (or, vice versa).

a. The planned creation of new industries would lessen the risk borne by each part of an industrialization plan if it were attempted singly by individual entrepreneurs. The latter could, therefore, not undertake investments except if tempted by exorbitant rates of profit or interest to cover their risks. The publicly financed and coherently planned industrialization, however, would eliminate the risk of the new undertaking being unable to find profitable markets, by concomitantly and generally raising the purchasing power of a country or a region as a whole.[2] Thus government agencies in the lending and in the borrowing country, by co-operating with one another, could, even without financial loss, promote an investment programme at much lower rates of return than would be acceptable to single investors financing individual ventures abroad. The further reduction in the lenders' risks and thus a fall in the gross rate of interest or return (i.e. the burden on the borrower) would accrue from the fact that public agencies need not take into account the liquidity of the assets acquired in the course of the investment programme. Public agencies could always obtain finance. The private investor, on the contrary, would encounter the additional risk of not being able, in emergencies, to liquidate his asset.

b. The cost structure of any single investor (excluding the cost of bearing risk dealt with above) is not independent of general economic progress. It will be affected — increased or decreased — by the rise of other industries, the development of transport and other

---

[1] From a purely logical point of view this category embraces the previous groups. In this context we shall only discuss the cases which do not fall easily into the narrower classes already analysed.

[2] On this and related points cf. the interesting article by P. N. Rosenstein-Rodan (*Economic Journal*, 1943), reprinted in Agarwala and Singh, *The Economies of Underdevelopment*, Oxford University Press, 1958, pp. 245–55.

communication facilities (cf. above). The skilling of man-power is especially a cost which no single entrepreneur can incur, as the benefit does not necessarily accrue to him unless the movement of labour is restricted. The same applies to the cost of transport, which decreases with increasing turnover. The competitive position is thereby cumulatively strengthened. The cost of providing such facilities must be borne by the community as a whole. Government agencies by their taxation policy could effectively impute general costs, and recover windfall capital gains accruing in the system as a whole, and thus not merely regulate economic incentive, but also safeguard a satisfactory distribution of the national income. Without adequate central planning, and control over the execution of development plans, monetary instability, speculative excesses, and a misdirection of productive resources might result from that competitive scramble for man-power and supplies, which occurs regularly in booms, with consequent losses to the community.

c. Industries which depend for efficiency on mass-production methods are unlikely to be started in small economic areas. The establishment of such industries depends on large amounts of capital equipment. They are subject to very high risk, as in a small economic area their internal market in an unplanned system is uncertain, and their possible outlets by export at least precarious, on account of the potential retaliatory measures abroad. Foreign investors will, moreover, be apprehensive that the governments in those areas will intervene against the establishment of one or a few large-scale concerns even if the country could support them, not merely because of the threat of monopolistic exploitation once the foreign-owned large-scale concerns eliminated the small and inefficient native producers, but also because the process of elimination will inevitably result in distress to the small producers and cause political agitation. It is, therefore, improbable that private enterprise will lead to the establishment of optimum scale units of production in smaller national economies. Publicly owned, or publicly guaranteed and controlled industry, whose markets are assured by the general industrialization plans and the consequent increase in consuming power, would make possible far more rapid economic progress in many areas of the world than would reliance on private initiative. The waste of productive opportunities could be ended without having to fear monopoly exploitation and the dissipation of (at least part of) the gain in excess capacity.

We might conclude that in view of the existence of significant differences between the social and private returns on capital investment, unregulated foreign investment could not secure optimum production and maximum progress, either in the backward areas or in the lending countries. The difference between 'objective' (social) and 'subjective' (private) risk is considerable enough to prevent a substantial and, in certain circumstances, overwhelming, portion of investment programmes which would be technically practicable and economically profitable under a planned system of industrial development. Returns which are substantial enough to tempt foreign investors would be so high as to reduce substantially, if not nullify, the benefit of the development concerned to the borrowing country.[1] If these developments are financed by means of fixed interest loans contracted in periods of expansion, which seemingly justified the commitments, the position of the debtor might be seriously worsened as a result of the borrowing.

The most important task of foreign investment in future will be to aid in the industrialization of backward areas. To accomplish this task, however, industrialization must be planned and executed through the co-operation and initiative of the governments of the lending and borrowing countries in some suitable way, through an International Investment Board.

This conclusion is considerably strengthened if the problem of repayment is envisaged. The fact that this problem did not arise in the nineteenth century and did not form part of the classical discussion of the subject was due to a fortunate coincidence of economic development in the west of Europe and overseas. Foreign investment in that period was mainly undertaken to open up empty overseas areas for primary production. Repayment proceeded smoothly except in the case of palpable frauds and speculation, because at the same time the population of the creditor countries increased rapidly and with it the demand for the commodities the production of which they had financed. If effective demand in the lending countries in the long run is not increased to a level

---

[1] The portion of the national output of some colonies taken in the shape of profits of private companies operating in those areas, amounts to a more considerable part of the output than the rate of current saving even in the richest areas.

corresponding to over-full employment,[1] a stable position cannot be maintained. Foreign investment can only solve the problem of surplus in the balance of payments in the medium long run. In the shorter period deflationary crises in the lending countries could be prevented from spreading and thus causing international complications and general bankruptcy by appropriate currency agreements.[2] Without such agreements on home and international economic policy the 'capacity to pay' of a country cannot be guaranteed however 'sound' the purpose for which the foreign loan or investment was at the time of lending.

B. FOREIGN INVESTMENTS AND PRIVATE CAPITAL

8. It is largely assumed in discussing problems of international reconstruction that capital development, within each country and internationally, depends entirely on voluntary saving. If this were immutable, poorer areas could hardly hope to achieve an ordered industrialization programme without the help of richer countries. In addition a rapid industrialization would seem to require the continuance of a considerable inequality of income, for in those areas the working classes cannot save. Even so, they could not under all circumstances rely on the wealthy saving and investing a sufficient portion of their disproportionately high incomes. Indeed, it might not be possible even in richer, mature countries affected by the war, e.g., Britain and France, to pursue at one and the same time physical and social reconstruction on this basis.

Physical reconstruction in those circumstances would depend on the encouragement of entrepreneurs, i.e. on increasing the inequality of income. But an increase in the income of the richer classes might (while increasing saving) also increase the demand for foreign goods and services the procuring of which will be especially difficult in the

---

[1] i.e. to a level of demand' which in a closed economic system would lead to inflation, in an open economic system to an import surplus. This could be done, for example, by a systematic reduction of working hours while maintaining wages if the terms of trade cannot be turned in favour of the paying country.

[2] Cf. *Oxford Institute of Statistics Bulletin Supplement*, No. 5, 'New Plans for International Trade', and also the author's article on the Central European Transfer Crisis, *International Affairs*, 1932.

post-war period.[1] Social reforms, on the other hand, would increase the incomes of the poor and consumption in general and so encroach upon the volume of practicable investment. The dilemma cannot be solved by exclusive reliance on private initiative.

Fortunately the assumption that the rate of investment depends on the rate of voluntary saving (at full employment) is incorrect and the conclusion therefore invalid. If would be possible to render economic progress independent of the voluntary decisions of individuals by financing investment out of communal or enforced savings. Investment finance institutions could be established by using revenue obtained from progressive direct taxation, and/or private savings, enforced by a strict control of consumption, and could be canalized for the purpose of domestic and foreign investment controlled by an Investment Board.[2]

A simple re-distribution of income might have little effect in mitigating poverty.[3] The proposed method of tackling the problem, however, opens wholly new prospects. Economic and social progress would no longer be alternatives tending to be mutually exclusive. At least partial capital autarky can be established by government investment policy without hardship in poor areas.[4]

---

[1] E.g. foreign travel. The South American millionaires were notorious absentees in Europe and spent there a considerable portion of their income, which, had it been to increase capital equipment at home by purchasing foreign machinery, would have considerably accelerated economic progress. The position was similar in Central Europe.

[2] In India, for example, it would be possible by these methods to increase investment to as high a rate as 15 per cent of the national income, i.e. to a rate substantially higher than that of Britain before this war without impinging on the standard of life of the lower-income classes. This saving is in addition to the huge credit balances India has accumulated during the war which could be used to obtain additional capital goods.

[3] Though its indirect effects in maintaining effective demand might be considerable; with this aspect of the matter we are not concerned in this context. Estimates such as those by Mr. Colin Clark (*The Conditions of Economic Progress*) which have been recently used to show the Utopian character of hopes for rapid economic progress, are based on the assumption that capital accumulation is exclusively financed by voluntary savings. They have no relevance to economies in which industrialization and investment are planned, such as the U.S.S.R., Nazi Germany, and war-time Britain.

[4] The Government, of course, need not restrict its finance to public, but could also stimulate private enterprise by its investment funds. The suffering of the people of the U.S.S.R. was due not so much to capital autarky but partly to the sudden worsening of the terms of trade of the U.S.S.R. with the outside world due to deflation, to economic nationalism, partly to the social

The maintenance of full employment and the abolition of disguised unemployment would represent a far greater gain than the help received by backward areas through foreign loans for their capital development in the pre-1939 period, a large part of which was, moreover, wasted. If measures are taken, moreover, to enforce efficiency in production and prevent the investment being dissipated in imperfectly competing excess capacity, the cumulative increase in productivity, even in poorer areas, would establish a firm basis for a rapid advance in the standard of life.

International agreements which would make possible the international maintenance of full employment by using any deficiency in effective demand in the mature countries to further the development of the underdeveloped areas would be welcome. But, in view of the foregoing they must safeguard the independence of the debtor to pursue internal policies which it deems desirable. The basic programme of industrialization must be domestically financed. If, in addition, the aid of mature countries can be secured it would hasten reconstruction while aiding the lending countries in the management of their economic affairs. If such satisfactory and equitable international solutions should prove impracticable, poorer countries — especially if they establish close co-operation with one another and so make possible a wide regional division of labour — need not despair of the future even in the absence of foreign loans from mature countries.

C. CONCLUSIONS

Our considerations indicate that, in order to secure optimum progress:

(1) Most countries must maintain rigid control over foreign payments if we wish to pursue progressive economic policies.[1]

revolution carried out concomitantly, and finally to the forced pace of industrialization due to the justified fear of outside military attack.

[1] This conclusion has been accepted by the more thoughtful of American official experts (*The United States in the World Economy*, p. 20): 'In times of business expansion in the United States and economic or political difficulties abroad, foreigners tended to shift funds to the United States in heavy volume, although largely into speculative stocks and other impermanent forms. International capital movements of this nature fulfilled little or no useful function. Unless brought under control in the future, such movements might readily nullify efforts along other lines to attain greater stability in international transactions and would decrease the amount of dollars available to foreigners for purchases of American goods and services.'

(2) No reliance can be placed on private profit expectations as a guide and criterion for international investment [1] — international investment must be planned and undertaken by some international agency in conjunction with an international currency agreement.

(3) Failing such agreement and the establishment of an international Investment Board, poorer countries can rely on communal saving by way of taxation or rationing, plus investment control for their planned and speedy economic development without having to enforce intolerable hardship on the poorer classes of their population. Exchange controls will give them all powers necessary to prevent the increased taxation or restraint on their entrepreneurial classes from exerting a deterrent effect on capital investment. The gains which can be derived from planned investment and maintenance of full employment are, in all probability, far greater than any advantage which could be derived from the aid of unstable mature countries unwilling to enter into satisfactory international agreements. [2]

---

[1] 'The fundamental requirement is that investment programmes be formulated on a comprehensive and long-range basis and executed at a reasonably regular rate and in a manner that will both strengthen the economic and social structure of the borrowing country and provide reasonable returns and adequate safeguards to the investor. The responsibility for developing such programmes will doubtless be borne chiefly by the governments concerned, and much of the capital may have to be provided through official agencies. Certainly the methods of foreign-bond flotation employed in the 'twenties would be both unacceptable to the individual investor and undesirable in the interest of international stability.' (*The United States in the World Economy*, p. 19).

[2] The present paper was written for a private conference organized by Nuffield College, Oxford, on the International Aspects of Full Employment in September 1943. In the meantime the United Nations Monetary and Financial Conference (held at Bretton Woods 1–22 July, 1944, Final Act, Cmd. 6546) published its proposals for solving the post-war international currency and investment problem. The proposals for the establishment of an 'International Bank for Reconstruction and Development' undoubtedly represent an important advance on the attempts undertaken in the inter-war period to develop international investment. But they fail to recognize the lessons of the past. They hope to ensure the 'soundness' of international loans by arbitrary provisions, which will sharply limit the effective lending power of the new institution. Only the finance of individual 'projects' is contemplated instead of the planned re-development of whole areas. The proposals thus neglect those vital considerations which were discussed in Part A (2) of this paper. The effective contribution which the proposed Bank can render to the solution of the problem of ensuring international stability and increasing the speed of development of poorer areas should not therefore be overestimated.

INTERNATIONAL INVESTMENT TODAY IN THE LIGHT OF NINETEENTH-CENTURY EXPERIENCE*

by **Ragnar Nurkse**

To many Americans today the problem of international investment is doubtless a source of perplexity and even of some irrita-
tion. Ever since the last World War great expectations have been
placed on the export of private American capital as a means of
bridging the dollar gap as well as financing world economic development. In reality, private foreign investment throughout the period
since 1945 has fluctuated at a low level and without any sign at
all of an upward trend.[1] This is most disappointing. We suspect
that the export of capital from Great Britain was one reason why
the international economy of the Victorian era did not know of a
chronic sterling shortage. We recognize, above all, that foreign investment was associated during that era with a tremendous spurt
in world production and trade. There is in America a feeling of
nostalgia for the nineteenth-century environment that made this
flow of capital possible. The question is: why can we not re-create
that environment?

The answer, I submit, must start from the fact that the circumstances in which overseas investment, and more especially
British investment, went on in the nineteenth century (which I
take to have ended in 1914) were in some ways quite exceptional.
To realize this is of more than historical interest. So long as the
peculiar features of that experience are not fully appreciated,
memories of wonders worked by foreign investment in the past
can only lead to false hopes and frustration.

Recent researches have made it possible to estimate approximately
the percentage share of her national income that Britain used to

* *The Economic Journal*, December 1954. Reprinted with the permission of
the Royal Economic Society, and the author. A paper prepared for discussion
at the Conference of the Association of University Teachers of Economics at
Sheffield on 2 January, 1954. The author's thanks are due to Mr. David Butt
and Sir Donald MacDougall for a number of valuable and helpful comments.
[1] Cf. *Federal Reserve Bulletin*, October 1953, pp. 1039–42.

lend abroad. Occasionally one finds the same proportions being applied to the present American national income as an indication of what the United States could or should do. Over the fifty years that preceded the outbreak of the first World War, it seems that Great Britain invested overseas an amount equal to about 4 per cent of her national income. In the later part of the period (1905–13) the ratio was as high as 7 per cent. If the United States today were to devote similar percentage portions of her national income to the same purposes, she would be exporting funds to the tune of $12 billion or, if we apply the higher percentage, some $20 billion each year. These figures are almost absurdly large and tend to confirm the view that there was something unique about Britain's foreign investment.

It was unique in that the greater part of it — roughly two-thirds — went to the so-called 'regions of recent settlement': the spacious, fertile and virtually empty plains of Canada, the United States, Argentina, Australia and other 'new' countries in the world's temperate latitudes. It was unique in that it went to these places together with a great migration of about 60 million people,[1] including many trained and enterprising persons, from the British Isles as well as Continental Europe. The conditions that made this flow of private capital possible do not exist to any great extent today, and probably cannot be re-created.

It was in the newly settled regions, which received two-thirds of the capital exports and practically all the emigrants, that nineteenth-century international investment scored its greatest triumphs. The remaining third of British capital exported (or more accurately a quarter, since some went to Continental Europe) was employed in a different type of area, where its achievements were much more dubious: tropical or sub-tropical regions inhabited, often densely, by native populations endowed in some cases with ancient civilizations of their own. The areas that formed a minor field for overseas investment before 1914 are the major problem today: the truly backward economies, containing now about two-thirds of the world's population. The empty and newly settled regions, from which international investment derived its brilliant general record and reputation, are today, in *per capita* income, among the most prosperous countries in the world.

---

[1] This is a gross figure; some of the migrants returned.

Labour and capital are complementary factors of production, and exert a profound attraction on each other. The movement of labour to the new regions attracted capital to the same places at the same time. And the other way round: the flow of capital stimulated the migration of people to these places. To some extent, it is true, the parallel movements of capital and labour might plausibly be interpreted as two separate effects of a common cause; namely, of the opening-up of the vast reserves of land and other natural resources. But the complementary nature of the labour and capital movements, based on the complementarity of the two factors, is equally plain. Any barrier to the transfer of one would have reduced the flow of the other. Labour and capital moved along side by side, supporting each other.[1]

In the twentieth century the situation is totally different. The capital exports from the United States can be viewed rather as a *substitute* for the movement of people. Capital and labour are still complementary, and still basically attract one another. But as things now are, restricting the movement of labour in one direction increases the need, if not the incentive, for capital to move in the opposite direction. Cheap labour, instead of being allowed to come to the United States to work with American capital there, is to some extent supplied with American capital abroad (supplied by the American Government as in the years since 1945, if not by private profit-seeking investors, as in the 1920's). The underlying pressure — not necessarily the profit motive, but what we might call the global social pressure — is very strong for more capital to move out from the United States to work with the cheap labour in the world's backward economies. But notice that in this situation, in sharp contrast to the predominant nineteenth-century pattern, capital is being urged to go out to work with people that have not grown up in a capital-minded milieu, and may not be culturally prepared for the use of western equipment, methods and techniques.

With this situation in mind, we can perceive what I think is the basic rationale of the present American emphasis on direct

[1] It is interesting to observe that the parallel nature of the two factor movements shows itself also, according to Professor A. K. Cairncross (*Home and Foreign Investment, 1870–1913*, Cambridge, 1953, p. 209), in the close agreement with which capital exports and emigration from Britain varied from decade to decade between 1870 and 1910.

business investment as a means of financing economic development. The advantages rightly attributed to it are, first, that it
goes out with American enterprise, tied up with American 'know-
how', and, secondly, that it is likely to be productively used, not
swallowed up — directly or indirectly — by immediate consumption
in the receiving country. Since, however, in the low-income areas
the domestic market is small, this type of investment tends inevitably in such areas to concentrate on extractive industries —
mines, plantations, oil wells — producing raw materials for export
mainly to the advanced countries. This is, in effect, the so-called
'colonial' pattern of foreign investment, of which American oil
operations abroad are now an outstanding example. It has its
drawbacks as well as its virtues. But, in any event, the stress laid —
even in the original Point Four programme — on direct investments
in economically backward countries should not, in my opinion, be
dismissed as merely a product of conservative business ideology; it
reflects in part an essential difference in the present-day environment
of international investment as compared with the nineteenth century.

In the aggregate flow of capital in the nineteenth century, the
'colonial' type of venture played a minor role. Looking at Britain's
foreign investment portfolio in 1913, we find that, of an estimated
total of about £3,700 million outstanding at that time in nominal
value, 30 per cent was in loans to governments, as much as 40
per cent in railway securities and some 5 per cent in other public
utilities, so that no less than three-quarters of the total was in public
or public-utility investments. The rest includes banking, insurance
and manufacturing companies, as well as investments directly in
raw-material extraction. The total should be increased by making
some allowance (say, £300 million) for private holdings and parti-
cipations not represented by securities listed on the London Stock
Exchange; but that would make little difference to the proportions
indicated. It is therefore far from correct to assume, as is sometimes
done, that the 'colonial' form of enterprise in the extraction of
mineral and plantation products for the creditor country was the
typical pattern of foreign investment. To call it the 'traditional'
pattern might be justified in view of its history in earlier centuries.
But in the nineteenth century its total amount was comparatively
small; and what little there was of it appears to have been concentrated, as one would expect, in colonial and predominantly
tropical areas.

To the new countries, by contrast, capital moved chiefly through the medium of securities carrying a fixed return (i.e., bonds and preference shares) issued by public authorities and public-utility undertakings. To these countries, it appears, capital could safely be sent in the form of relatively untied funds, with a good chance that it would remain capital there, because the people in these places, having come from Europe themselves, knew what to do with capital and how to handle it. Cultural adaptation was no problem.

These countries — the 'regions of recent settlement' that absorbed the bulk of British overseas investment — were offshoots of European civilization.[1] For Britain, or at any rate for Europe as a whole, investment in these areas was essentially a process of capital widening rather than deepening. Indeed, when Britain sent capital out to work with Swedes, Poles, Germans and Italians emigrating overseas, she may have done so at the expense of the deepening which her own economy is said to have needed in the period just before the first World War. But international investment in the nineteenth century was, of course, unplanned, and was determined by private rather than national advantages. French and German activities in Eastern Europe and the Near East were an exception in this respect. As Professor Viner has remarked, 'the French loans to Russia . . . bore a close resemblance to the programme of military aid to Western Europe which we are now embarking on.'[2]

Great Britain's national advantage, apart from the return flow of interest and dividends, seemed to be handsomely served through cheaper food and raw materials, though this benefit was shared by other importing countries that had made no corresponding investments and, besides, as we now realize, was derived in part

---

[1] The precise composition of this group may give rise to some debate, though essentially the line is clear. It takes in Canada, the United States, Australia, New Zealand and South Africa. In South America it certainly includes Argentina and Uruguay, rich farm and grazing lands in temperate latitudes settled predominantly by recent immigration from Europe. I would perhaps include also the southern tip of Brazil, to which the same description largely applies, and in which most of Brazil's productive capacity, including immigration as well as foreign capital, has been concentrated since the middle of the nineteenth century.

[2] 'America's Aims and the Progress of Underdeveloped Countries', in B. F. Hoselitz (ed.), *The Progress of Underdeveloped Areas*, Chicago, 1952, p. 184.

from *Raubwirtschaft,* through soil depletion and erosion in some of the rich new plains (for example, in the virgin grasslands of the Mississippi valley).

Production of primary commodities for export to the industrial creditor countries is characteristic of the 'colonial' pattern of direct investment in economically backward areas. In the regions of recent settlement foreign investment can also be said to have been induced essentially by the raw-material needs of the industrial centres — especially by Great Britain's demand for the wheat, wool, meat and dairy products, which she decided not to try to produce for herself, and which these temperate regions were particularly well suited to produce. The capital that came into these regions did not, however, enter into primary production itself, but was employed above all in building up the costly framework of public services, including especially transport, which laid the basis for domestic industrial development, as well as for the production of raw commodities for export. These areas are now, and have been for some time, predominantly industrial,[1] a fact entirely compatible with the large or even preponderant share of primary products in their export trade.

Nineteenth-century foreign investment centred on the railway — that 'great instrument of improvement', in Lord Dalhousie's phrase. If account is taken not only of railway securities but also of the use to which many government loans were put, it seems that well over half of Britain's external investment before 1914 went into railway construction. The great bulk of this was in the newly settled countries. The Indian railways, though an important individual item, accounted for less than one-tenth of the total of overseas railway securities held by British investors in 1914. The United States and the Argentine alone accounted for more than half of that total. In the new countries the railway was important as a means of migration. The great pioneer lines — first in the United States, later in the Argentine and elsewhere — were deliberately planned and built *in advance* of current traffic needs; they themselves created the settlement and economic growth that eventually led to a full demand for their services.

Although individual promoters sometimes played the most conspicuous part, the railways in the new countries were built,

[1] See F. Hilgerdt, *Industrialization and Foreign Trade,* League of Nations, 1945, pp. 26, 39 and *passim.*

as a rule, if not directly by governments, at any rate with extensive government assistance in the form of land grants, subsidies and guaranteed returns to the investors. In view of this fact, one can safely say that the bulk of international investment in the nineteenth century depended on government action in the borrowing countries. In French and German capital exports, some of which also went to the new world, the proportion of government loans and other public investments was even higher than in the British case.

It is true that the transport revolution, to which the cheapening of British food imports (especially in the years 1880–1900) was largely due, was a matter of steamships as well as railways. While railway construction overseas was a major object of international financing, British shipbuilding counted almost entirely as part of British home investment. Since ship and railway building had much the same effects on international trade and the terms of trade, the distinction between home and foreign investment appears in this case somewhat arbitrary. In the internal economic expansion of the new countries, however, the railways had, of course, a very special part to play, rather different from that of the ships. And so we hear, for example, that 'in the Argentine, the railway is like a magic talisman: for wherever it goes it entirely transforms the economic and productive conditions of the country.'[1]

Overseas railway investment became predominant from about 1870 onwards. But this does not mean that the earlier part of the century can be ignored. While the total of foreign investment was much smaller then, so was everything else. We should note that by 1870 Britain's overseas assets had already grown to about the same order of magnitude as her annual national income. Capital imports were a prominent feature in the economic history of the United States for many years before the Civil War.

---

[1] A. B. Martinez and M. Lewandowski, *The Argentine in the Twentieth Century*, London, 1911, p. 108. A statement such as this applies to a type of region with the particular physical and human characteristics already noted. It would not apply in the same way to a country like India, where, for reasons that cannot be entered into, the railway 'did not give rise to a flood of satellite innovations' and 'destroyed more employment opportunities (e.g., in traditional village industries) than it opened up' (L. H. Jenks, 'British Experience with Foreign Investments', *Journal of Economic History*, 1944, Supplement, p. 75).

It is clear that the main flow of capital in the nineteenth century was not to the neediest countries with their 'teeming millions', which were indeed neglected, but to sparsely peopled areas where conditions for rapid growth along familiar western lines were exceptionally favourable. If we were to look round for similar opportunities in the twentieth century, I do not know where we should find them if not in the further development of the same regions of recent settlement; or else perhaps in Siberia — a vast area reputedly rich in natural resources, which may be longing for an injection of skilled labour from Europe and capital from the United States.

Once the main facts about the nineteenth-century capital flow are set out in something like their true proportions,[1] it is curious to see how little they fit in with some preconceived notions that have been widely current. Bernard Shaw, for example, in Act I of *The Apple Cart*, made one of his characters talk about England sending her 'capital abroad to places where poverty and hardship still exist: in other words, where labour is cheap. We live in comfort on the imported profits of that capital'. Consider, more seriously, the summary which Mrs. Joan Robinson gives (in *The Rate of Interest and Other Essays*, 1952, pp. 157–8) of the views of Rosa Luxemburg:

> The capitalist nations are surrounded by primitive economies, each insulated from the others like a nut within its shell, waiting to be cracked. The capitalists break open a primitive economy and enter into trade with it, whether by enticing its inhabitants with

[1] I have thought it superfluous to give detailed references to the well-known sources, such as the works of C. K. Hobson, L. H. Jenks, H. Feis and the Royal Institute of International Affairs. Among recent essays and articles that I have found useful, the following should be mentioned: N. S. Buchanan, 'International Finance', *Survey of Contemporary Economics* (vol. II, ed. by B. F. Haley, 1952); P. Hartland, 'Private Enterprise and International Capital', *Canadian Journal of Economics and Political Science*, February 1953; Sir Arthur Salter, 'Foreign Investment', *Essays in International Finance*, Princeton University Press, February 1951; Brinley Thomas, 'Migration and the Rhythm of Economic Growth, 1830–1913', *The Manchester School*, September 1951; L. H. Jenks, 'Railroads as an Economic Force in American Development', *Enterprise and Secular Change* (ed. by F. C. Lane and J. C. Riemersma, 1953); H. S. Ferns, 'The Establishment of the British Investment in Argentina', *Inter-American Economic Affairs*, Autumn 1951; J. F. Rippy, 'British Investments in Latin America, End of 1913', ibid.; A. H. Imlah, 'British Balance of Payments and Export of Capital, 1816–1913', *Economic History Review*, 1952 (vol. V, No. 2).

commodities they have never seen before, by political cunning or by brute force. Now exports to the primitives provide an outlet for the product of the last batch of capital goods created at home. After a little while another nut is broken, a use for more capital is thereby found, and so on, as long as the supply of untouched primitive economies lasts. . . . When the stock of unbroken nuts is exhausted, the capitalist system collapses for want of markets.

This is one variant of neo-Marxist doctrine and, like others, it neglects some crucial facts. No pre-existing markets were conquered in the new countries. Markets were *created* there by labour, enterprise and capital all drawn from Europe. In the industrially primitive countries markets were and have remained unattractive because of mass poverty. Why is it, for example, that in the 1920's Canada, Australia and New Zealand, with already quite highly developed industries of their own and with a combined population of only 17·4 millions, imported twice as much manufactured goods as India with her 340 million people?[1]

The American public also, perhaps because it lives in one of the new countries itself, does not always appreciate the peculiar nature of the nineteenth-century investment experience. Some of us are too apt to forget — or to take for granted — all that went with it and to assume, from that experience, a 'simple equivalence of the pace of capital transfer and the pace of development'.[2] Keynes in 1922 made a remark that is worth recalling: 'The practice of foreign investment, as we know it now, is a very modern contrivance, a very unstable one, and only suited to peculiar circumstances.'[3] He cautioned against extending it by simple analogy to a different set of circumstances. Private foreign lending in the 1920's can be viewed in part as a backwash of the great momentum which it had gathered before 1914. Was it because in Central Europe foreign investment was applied to a situation to which it was unsuited that it came to grief there? It might perhaps have worked; Hitler did not give it a chance. Yet the fact is that it did not work.

Will it work, and if so, how will it work, in the 'underdeveloped' areas of which we hear so much today? The preceding remarks have all been leading up to this question. My purpose here is to

[1] F. Hilgerdt, op. cit., p. 84.

[2] Honor Croome, 'The Dilemma of Development', in *New Commonwealth*, 9 November, 1953, p. 487.

[3] *A Revision of the Treaty*, p. 161.

present the question, against the background of past experience, rather than try to answer it. In the time that remains I will only hazard a few brief comments on three general topics: direct business investment, public-utility investment and governmental grants.

The assumption I am making here — that it is the low-income areas that constitute the main problem of international investment in the mid-twentieth century — may be challenged as arbitrary and not entirely justified. The most profitable opportunities may still be in the 'regions of recent settlement'. But having regard to their high income levels, these fortunate regions can, in the present discussion, be left_to provide, by and large, for their own development needs.

For reasons mentioned earlier, direct investments by American business firms — usually financed from corporate reserves rather than security issues on the capital market — are thought to be particularly well suited to the economically backward countries. But they have their shortcomings also. In the life of an industrially primitive community they are apt to create not only a dual economy[1] but also a dual society, in which conditions for the diffusion of western technology may actually be the reverse of favourable. Foreign business investment is not always a happy form of encounter between different civilizations. Besides, if techniques are to be of wide and permanent use, they must be adapted to local conditions. The methods of giant corporations, whose foreign operations are sometimes only a side-show, are often too standardized to favour such adaptation. And so the local economy may not get much help from the example they give; the example is often inapplicable. Let us remember that the Japanese acquired industrial techniques very effectively before they began to receive any substantial foreign business investments. Also the technical assistance programmes now in operation remind us that there are other ways of spreading technical knowledge.

As a rule, when foreign business enterprise is attracted to economically backward areas, it is mainly for the production of raw materials for export markets, for the simple reason that the domestic market in such areas, even if protected by import restrictions, is

---

[1] Cf. H. W. Singer, 'The Distribution of Gains between Investing and Borrowing Countries', *American Economic Review, Papers and Proceedings*, May 1950.

generally too poor to afford any strong inducement to invest.[1] The natural result is a 'colonial' investment pattern, open to the familiar criticisms that it tends to promote lopsided rather than 'balanced' growth, and that it makes for instability due to high dependence on foreign demand for one or two staple products. If this type of direct investment is to take place in any considerable volume, it presupposes a long-run prospect of rapidly expanding demand in the industrial centres for the raw materials which it seeks to provide. Despite the forecasts of the Paley Report, there is no firm assurance of such an expansion except for certain minerals. Governmental purchase agreements alone cannot give this assurance in the absence of favourable basic demand conditions. A temporary stimulus might be got from the removal of United States tariff protection on primary products (such as sugar, copper, wool), but little can be hoped for in this direction.

In the last few years one of the chief economic obstacles to a greater flow of business funds to low-income countries has been the high level of business profits obtainable at home, from developing American natural resources and catering to the American mass market. Conditions may change. It is not inconceivable that business investment abroad might greatly increase in the future and that it might bring substantial benefits to the poorer countries. Yet, on the whole, it seems unlikely that direct investment alone can become anything like an adequate source of international finance for economic development. It played, as we saw, a minor

---

[1] From the latest comprehensive figures for American direct investments (*Survey of Current Business*, December 1952), it can be seen that of the total invested in Canada and Western Europe at the end of 1950, 23 per cent was in extractive industries, as much as 60 per cent in manufacturing and trade, 6 per cent in public utilities and 11 per cent in miscellaneous activities, including cinemas and other entertainments. Of the investments outstanding on the same date in all other countries, which with a few exceptions are economically backward, 60 per cent was in extractive industries, mostly petroleum and mining, with 20 per cent, 17 per cent and 3 per cent respectively in the other groups. This pattern is by no means new. We know that in 1929 only one-fifth of total American direct investment was in manufacturing, and 84 per cent of this was in Western Europe, Canada, Australia and New Zealand. 'Only to a very small extent, therefore, did American direct investments enter into manufacturing for the domestic market in underdeveloped countries.' (United Nations, *International Capital Movements in the Inter-War Period*, 1949, p. 32.)

part in the nineteenth century. Can we rely on it to play a major part today? I doubt it.

What is most urgently needed today is a revival of the public or public-utility type of international investment that used to dominate the scene. The International Bank has hardly begun to fill the gap left by the disappearance of this type of private foreign lending. If the past cannot be reproduced, it is all the more imperative to devise a new pattern suited to present needs and conditions. Critics have wondered how much of nineteenth-century foreign investment would have survived the tests and rules laid down by the International Bank. The Bank, being dependent on the private capital market for most of its loanable funds, inevitably reflects to some extent the attitudes of the private investor. And the private American investor is still waiting for a change in the weather, and remains unimpressed by statistics showing that only 15 per cent of the dollar bonds (not counting direct investments) floated in the 1920's by underdeveloped countries — that is, aside from Central Europe — have proved a permanent loss.[1]

It is said that there are not enough productive projects in the low-income countries to absorb much more money than is now going out. It is pointed out that the Marshall Plan, which accustomed the world to the sight of a large dollar outflow, was not a plan of new development so much as one of reconstruction, in an area where a solid industrial foundation and the 'know-how' of a skilled population already existed.[2]

No doubt this point has considerable force. But if there are not enough projects, can we not ask for international technical assistance to design them and to draw up the blueprints? Lack of basic services, such as transport, power and water supply, is a particularly serious bottleneck in the poor countries. Because of this the *physical* environment — quite apart from the obvious difficulties arising from the political or social climate — is unfavourable to private investment. A large foreign firm producing

---

[1] Cf. the Gray Report 1950, p. 62.

[2] It will be remembered, however, that some of the Marshall Aid was in effect passed on to 'underdeveloped' countries (especially by way of the United Kingdom, whose overall balance was in equilibrium in 1948–9 and in surplus in 1950).

raw materials for export may find it profitable to set up incidental facilities such as roads or waterworks, of which the local economy, too, can make some use. But the general utility of such things often depends in haphazard fashion on the technical features of the firm's main activity. It may be fairly high in the case of a railway built by a mining company from the interior of Peru to the sea-coast. It is virtually zero in the case of the pipe-line in which Arabian oil is pumped to the Mediterranean.

In the United States a hundred years ago public authorities, as well as private promoters, played a leading role in the drive for 'internal improvements', financed in part by foreign capital. There is no question that ample scope exists for international financing of public improvements in the poor countries today. Until these countries have acquired a skeleton framework of such facilities, conditions will not be particularly attractive for the more varied and smaller-scale business investments there. Even with such basic improvements, of course, the individual business investments, domestic as well as foreign, may fail to materialize, because of other obstacles. It is conceivable, therefore, that some of these public works would turn out to be white elephants. But the risk has to be taken; any form of capital investment is, in the last analysis, an act of faith. However hard it may be for the pioneering spirit that opened up the new countries to apply itself to the low-income areas today, not much can be achieved without that spirit, and no international organization concerned with development can remain untouched by it.

Apart from the distribution of the promoter-function, there still remains the question of finance. If the profitability of American business at home has kept down direct investments abroad, a simple comparison of bond yields does not explain why 'portfolio' lending cannot get started again. However, while the private investor has been standing on the side-lines, we may have witnessed the beginnings of a system of international grants-in-aid and low-interest loans from government funds. The reference to the principle of Equal Sacrifice with which Roosevelt defended the Lend-Lease programme may some day appear significant in retrospect. I need not point to other signs and landmarks. Let me just quote a few recent expressions of opinion. The man who gave his name to the Marshall Plan, in accepting the Nobel peace prize last December, said that it was 'of basic importance to any successful effort towards an enduring peace that the more favoured nations should lend assistance in bettering the lot of the poorer '.[1]

Dr. Herbert Feis, the historian of nineteenth-century foreign investment, has expressed himself as follows:

A sense of obligation has won its way in the world to the effect that a wealthy country has a call of vague dimensions to provide means to assist poorer and suffering countries. To give free admission to [it] would bankrupt us and demoralize others; but to ignore the obligation wholly would be . . . out of accord with the effort in which we are engaged, to bring together the nations of the world in peaceful and co-operative understanding.[2]

Even if we hesitate to accept the assumption that world peace can be bought or that material progress makes for contentment, the fact of growing pressures for international income transfers must nevertheless be recognized. It may be precisely because the problem of international investment is now, unlike what it was in the Victorian era, concerned in the main with the backward economies that the need for such transfers is felt to arise.

The difficulties which American trade policy encounters in following the British nineteenth-century example might also be taken to point to unilateral income transfers as more in accord with the underlying situation. With commercial foreign investment an adjustment of the trade balance to the return flow of interest and dividends cannot normally be long postponed, while gifts permit an export surplus indefinitely.[3]

[1] *The Times*, 12 December, 1953.

[2] 'International Economic Outlook', *Proceedings of the Academy of Political Science*, New York, May 1953, p. 59.

[3] However, I cannot fully share the view that, just because of the growing return flow to which it normally gives rise, foreign investment of the orthodox sort can be no more than a short-period remedy for international imbalance. When in support of this view it is said that the increase in Great Britain's foreign assets from 1880 to 1913 'was due wholly to the reinvestment of a part of the income derived from earlier investments' (Salter, op. cit., pp. 9, 53) it seems to me that a somewhat arbitrary causal attribution is made between two items on opposite sides of the balance of payments, a procedure always of doubtful validity, and particularly so when one of the items represents payments on capital account, while the other belongs to the income account. That the individual British investor, on the one hand, was under no obligation to reinvest the interest he got from abroad is obvious. From the national viewpoint, on the other hand, all one can say is that the British current account,

The idea of international grants-in-aid is essentially a consequence of the increased gaps in living standards and of the closeness of contact that is creating at the same time an increasingly acute awareness of these gaps — a situation without historical precedent. This awareness is perhaps the most fundamental obstacle to the resumption of private international lending. In contrast to the position of the backward economies today, income per head in the principal debtor countries of the nineteenth century — the newly settled regions — can never have been far below European levels. Interest payments from poor to rich are now, it seems, not only basically unwanted by the rich countries but indeed are felt to be somehow contrary to the spirit of the age. And although public grants (for 'social overhead capital') and private foreign lending (for more specific investments) can ideally be looked upon as complementary rather than conflicting sources of finance, it is easy to see why in practice the two do not mix at all well. This applies not only to grants but also in some degree to international loans from government sources.

Persistent attempts in the United Nations Organization to set up a system of international grants under U.N. auspices — from the UNEDA proposal of 1948 to the SUNFED report of 1953 — have foundered on the rocks of American opposition. Yet American practices and pronouncements alike have kept world expectations alive, and this has continued to some extent under the Republican administration. Two notable declarations by President Eisenhower last year attracted wide attention: one was the statement in April about 'devoting a substantial percentage of the savings achieved by disarmament to a fund for world aid', the other being the so-called 'Atom Bank' proposal for the international provision of atomic energy for peaceful purposes.

It must be recognized that international unilateral transfers have no necessary connexion with the subject of foreign *investment*. They may be for current consumption or for military use. Even

including foreign interest earnings as well as earnings from merchandise exports and shipping, showed a surplus, which was balanced by the outflow of capital. Britain had an excess of merchandise imports over exports throughout the period 1880–1913. Yet it is conceivable that if British foreign lending had come to a complete stop in (say) 1890, a disequilibrium in the international balance of payments — a 'sterling shortage' — might have been felt in the succeeding quarter of a century.

if they are intended for, or tied to, particular capital projects, a net increase in the overall rate of accumulation is not always assured. If they are to make an effective contribution to economic development, they call for domestic action in the receiving countries — fiscal, monetary and other policies designed to withhold resources from immediate consumption and to direct them into capital formation.

But once the receiving countries are capable of devising the necessary controls for the productive use of outside aid, they should be equally capable of using such policies for the mobilization of potential *domestic* sources of capital (e.g., skimming off resources now absorbed by luxury consumption, making use of labour set free from the land through better farm methods or recruiting any surplus labour already existing on the land). It is far from my intention to suggest that in these circumstances foreign aid becomes unnecessary. Yet this consideration does shift the emphasis upon the need for domestic policies to ensure that in the overall use of resources, domestic as well as external, investment is given top priority.[1] Here is the main criterion, and a body such as the World Bank has in this respect an even more vital role to play in the backward economies than that which the E.C.A. and the O.E.E.C. performed under the Marshall Plan.

These remarks on international grants and their possible uses may all be idle speculation, for which, perhaps, I should apologize. The practices alluded to may turn out to have been temporary devices related to particular emergency conditions. What I have said on these controversial matters should have been put in the form of questions — and extremely tentative questions at that. But they are, I think, questions which a survey of the present state of international finance inevitably draws to our attention.

[1] This theme is developed in my *Problems of Capital Formation in Underdeveloped Countries*, Oxford, 1953.

THE SERVICING OF FOREIGN CAPITAL INFLOWS BY UNDERDEVELOPED COUNTRIES*

by **Gerald M. Alter**

I. INTRODUCTION

An underdeveloped country wishing to secure foreign capital to accelerate its economic development faces various tests by potential investors. These tests — whether they relate to the likelihood of war, revolution, civil strife, expropriation without compensation, the availability of suitable investment projects, or the future balance of payments position of the country — stem from the fact that the ordinary investor expects to receive a return on the funds committed to a country. The entity receiving such funds, if it is a private enterprise or a public corporation operating along business lines, is willing to pay the required return when the use of such funds in a specific project is expected to yield the required surplus over cost directly. If the receiving entity is the government, a specific project may or may not be expected to yield the required surplus over cost directly. The government requires, however, that the overall yield to the whole economy from employing the funds should in some sense justify payment of the return required by the investor.

The fact that both parties to the use of regular investment funds must find it mutually and directly rewarding is well recognized, both in the domestic and in the international sphere. In the international sphere, however, investors recognize special risks which are associated in their minds with the transferability of the return they require. These risks induce investors to appraise the future balance of payments position of the country to which they commit their funds. The individual enterprise in the capital-importing country wishing to secure funds from abroad may be able fully to demonstrate that the employment of funds will yield the necessary surplus, at

* H. S. Ellis, and Wallich (eds.), *Economic Development for Latin America*, Macmillan & Co., London, 1961. Reprinted by permission of the International Economic Association, and the author.

The paper does not necessarily reflect the views of the International Bank for Reconstruction and Development with which the author is associated.

least at present exchange rates, and such a surplus may indeed be earned. Yet, the future balance of payments of the country may be such that interest, dividend, or principal payments due the investor cannot be transferred, or can only be transferred, if denominated in local currency, at a greatly depreciated exchange rate. Similarly, a government borrowing abroad may be able to give adequate assurance that the country's real income will be sufficiently increased by the employment of additional investment resources to justify a payment to the foreign lender. Yet serious obstacles to the transfer of service payments on such loans may be encountered when such payments are to be made.

The economic conditions which must be fulfilled if foreign debt service payments (interest, dividends, or principal) are to be met can be stated in terms of the familiar equation on total resource availabilities and uses. If an economy is to make service payments in any year equal to X, the output produced plus capital inflow, including any net use of foreign exchange reserves, must exceed domestic consumption and investment by X. This proposition may also be put in terms of the saving and investment equation. Domestic saving plus foreign capital inflow must exceed domestic investment by the volume of service payments.

In addition to these equations relating to total resource availabilities and uses, there is the equation relating to foreign exchange availabilities and uses. Total foreign exchange receipts, including gross capital inflow and net use of foreign exchange reserves, must exceed imports of goods and services by the volume of service payments. It is obvious that the payment of debt service requires the fulfilment of all three conditions: other claims on total resources, other claims on savings, and other claims on foreign exchange resources must be less than availabilities by the amount of debt service.

These elementary equations can also be reformulated in terms of increments and decrements. If, for example, there is a decline in national income, no change in capital inflow, and no decline in required debt service payments, domestic consumption and investment must decline by the amount of the decline in national income. Further illustrations are unnecessary. They only serve to emphasize the point that the fulfilment of debt service obligations is dependent on the economy's capacity to adjust the claims on total resources, saving, and foreign exchange in any given year and over time so as to release the amount required for debt service.

In appraising the capacity of a country to service foreign capital inflows, the first problem, therefore, is to determine the conditions under which these competing claims are likely to be resolved in favour of debt service. If such conditions do not exist, even a small amount of debt service is not safe. At the opposite extreme, if conditions in a country are such that the resolution of these competing claims in favour of external debt service can be taken for granted, the capacity of such a country to service foreign capital inflow is dependent only upon its ability to employ additional capital effectively. In this case an upper limit is imposed on external servicing obligations by a case by case examination of the projects and programmes proposed or considered for foreign financing. In between these two extremes there is a third alternative: the conditions under which these claims will be resolved in favour of debt service may involve a complex relationship between the amount of debt service payments which are owed and the overall economic performance of the country. In this case some appraisal must be made of the country's future economic performance, taking into account varying levels of capital inflow and associated debt service payments.

With respect to the first alternative, it is clear that there is nothing in the economic mechanism as such which makes it impossible to adjust the claims on total resources, on saving, and on foreign exchange, so that debt service payments can be met. This is true either under the assumptions of the gold standard and the classical adjustment mechanism, or under the modern panoply of fiscal and monetary policy with or without direct controls. But such a formal solution has only limited significance. The environment of policy objectives in which the economic system must operate and the economic performance which is in fact achieved necessarily condition the process through which competing claims on resources are adjusted.

Under the gold standard and the classical adjustment mechanism it can be taken for granted that so long as the system is adhered to and the government sticks to the rules of the game, competing claims on resources will, under all conditions, be adjusted in favour of debt service. Very few countries today are willing to accept the implications of the classical adjustment mechanism as a primary principle of economic management. Its unconditional acceptance is often believed to be in conflict with many of the primary objectives of modern governments, including the objective of relatively full employment, accelerated economic development, more equitable income distribution, and so forth.

Let us, therefore, consider the conditions under which competing claims are likely to be resolved in favour of debt service and whether in the modern day such conditions can ever be taken for granted.

Discussion of the major situations giving rise to balance of payments difficulties in which the priority of debt service is likely to be challenged and of the problems which may be encountered in adjusting competing claims may conveniently be divided into two parts. The risk of a world depression and the problems posed by short-term variations in the real value of exports will be considered first. Most of the subsequent discussion will deal with the risks that arise in the longer-term context of economic growth and with the relationship between debt service capacity and overall economic performance in the long term.

II. IMPORTANCE OF SHORT-TERM DISTURBANCES

The balance of payments problems which led to a suspension of service payments in the past were frequently associated with worldwide depressions. While some countries continued to service external debts even in the depression of the 'thirties, many countries did not. Since the 'thirties governments have become more intent on maintaining high levels of economic activity, consumption, and investment, and if a depression of similar magnitude and duration should occur in the future the balance of payments problems initiated in the first instance by a decline in exports are likely to be compounded by an even more active domestic compensatory policy. Debt service is unlikely to be given a high priority in such circumstances unless the capital resources available to debtor countries are increased substantially by governmental and inter-governmental action. This might provide an incentive to maintain debt service. Of course, to the extent that debt service consists of dividends paid out of current earnings, debt service claims are likely to decline, particularly when a foreign-owned enterprise is producing primarily for the export market.

Thus, the risk of a major world depression, if such an occurrence is deemed highly probable, severely limits the international flow of

private capital, particularly fixed-interest capital. At the time that
the International Bank for Reconstruction and Development was
established it is clear that such a contingency was taken into account.
The Bank, in effect, considers that it was authorized to bear the risk
of suspension of debt service payments in a world depression and
the Bank has stated that it assumes this risk.[1] The risk of a major
world depression does not appear, at the present time, to be very
great. The pressure to continue to maintain high levels of economic
activity in the major economic centres and the history of the post-
war period give some assurance even to the private investor abroad
that future down-turns in economic activity may be limited in depth
and duration.

Let us then dismiss the risk of a major world depression, at least
in so far as it affects the capacity of underdeveloped countries
to service loans from such agencies as the International Bank.
There are shorter-term risks which cannot be so easily dismissed,
particularly in Latin America, where all countries export only a
few primary commodities and where in many countries exports
constitute a large percentage of the national product. These risks
include temporary reductions in real export receipts resulting
from minor recessions abroad, harvest failures at home, and sharp
drops in export prices resulting from the return to more normal
supply and demand situations, often accentuated in its impact on
export receipts by accumulation of stocks in exporting countries.

A country which experiences great variability in its real export
receipts — and this is characteristic of most of the Latin American
countries — has a special problem in adjusting claims on total
resources, saving, and foreign exchange. The performance of the
country in meeting this problem is significant in judging its capacity
to service foreign debt in two senses. First, a country which succeeds in maintaining some degree of stability (preferably along a
rising trend) in domestic consumption and investment is likely to
enjoy a sounder and more rapid growth over the longer term than
a country which alternates between periods of rapidly increasing
consumption and investment and periods of enforced curtailment
of consumption and investment. Second, a country which is forced
to curtail domestic consumption and investment rapidly is likely

---

[1] *The International Bank for Reconstruction and Development, 1946–53,*
Baltimore, 1954, p. 42.

to experience difficulty in reconciling all of the competing claims on resources, including the claims of foreign creditors.

In the face of a considerable fluctuation in real export earnings, some degree of stability in consumption and domestic investment can be achieved by building up foreign exchange reserves and repaying external debts in periods when real export receipts are above the longer-term trend and by reducing reserves and incurring external debts in periods when real foreign exchange receipts are below the long-term trend. The policies that are required to pursue this course and the practical difficulties that may be encountered are well known.[1] The adoption of such compensatory policies is, nevertheless, advisable in countries eager to accelerate development and particularly so in countries wishing to attract foreign capital for this purpose.

Of course, if a country is willing to permit a reduction in export receipts to exert its full deflationary effect on domestic income and if foreign suppliers of capital expect such a policy to encounter no opposition in the future, creditors need not fear that a temporary reduction in foreign exchange receipts will jeopardize debt service claims. Only to the extent that extreme variability in domestic consumption and investment leads to an environment unfavourable to long-term development will such a non-compensatory policy be interpreted as an unfavourable course.

There is, moreover, a third method of dealing with fluctuations in real export earnings. This is the practice, if not policy, of stretching available resources to the limit, and beyond. This practice involves, in the extreme case, an expansionary fiscal and monetary policy in periods of abnormally high and rising export receipts, accompanied by the drawing down of international reserves and, in some cases, by the indiscriminate incurring of short- and medium-term external debts. Expansionary fiscal and monetary policies are continued when export receipts decline, but every effort is made to limit the decline in consumption and investment by rationing foreign exchange resources. Such a practice, experience has shown, strains to the utmost the policy-making and administrative capacities of even the best-equipped government. Consumption, investment, and all direct

---

[1] See Bruno Brovedani, 'Latin American Medium Term Import Stabilization Policies and the Adequacy of Reserves', International Monetary Fund, *Staff Papers*, February 1955, vol. IV, No. 2.

claims on export receipts are ultimately reduced, but in an inflationary environment in which all claimants to a share of the income produced fear that their share is in constant jeopardy, it is no wonder that the suppliers of foreign capital share this fear. Fortunately, there is evidence that this extreme policy of straining resources to the breaking point in economies where export receipts are subject to considerable fluctuation is being rejected by one country after another.

It must, however, be conceded that the policy of straining resources to the limit, if not beyond, is particularly attractive to, and it is widely practised by, countries enjoying a fast rate of growth and by countries aspiring to a fast rate of growth. This policy will now be considered as a part of the problem of the role of foreign capital in accelerating economic development, and of the conditions which determine the capacity of underdeveloped countries to service capital inflow in the long term.

III. DEBT SERVICE AND LONG-RUN GROWTH

The analysis so far has been restricted to the short-term balance of payments difficulties that may jeopardize external debt service claims, particularly in economies where exports are high relative to the Gross National Product and where the real value of export receipts is subject to substantial variation from year to year. The performance of an economy which is subject to volatile changes in adjusting competing claims on total resources, saving, and foreign exchange resources in the short term is important in judging its capacity to reconcile such claims over the long term. This is, however, only one part of the picture. While debt service claims do not vary with year to year changes in resources there is at least a presumption that the increased debt service claims arising out of capital inflows used for productive investment can be met over the long term from the increased income which the investment produces. Why should one be concerned over the long term with the competing claims on total resources, savings, and foreign exchange resources?

The economist, educated in the tradition of classical economics, may be disposed to argue that the problem arises simply from the unwillingness of countries to follow the classical blueprint. On the other hand, he recognizes that the automatic adjustment process envisaged by the classical system may involve unemployment and shifts in income distribution which governments are today loathe to tolerate. It may also require reductions in the volume of investment which development-minded governments accept with great reluctance. The automatic adjustment process also presupposes an economy in which capital is invested in a manner which will promote external and internal equilibrium. While the classical blueprint was able to handle with ease the principles which private investment will and should follow to secure this result, it never developed operational guides for government investment or for the policies which government must adopt in the economic sphere if private investment does not respond properly to the guide-posts of changing relative prices. When we add to all this the short-term instabilities which the classical mechanism imposes on countries exporting a few primary products, it is no wonder that the classical adjustment mechanism is regarded with distrust. Thus, the classical adjustment mechanism frequently conflicts with some primary objectives of government policy and the blueprint for action which it provides is inadequate in several respects. At the same time, the experience of the last ten years, particularly in Latin America, indicates that a country which violates completely the doctrines of financial responsibility and the guide-posts of a functioning price system does so at its own peril, simultaneously increasing the risks faced by foreign creditors!

Thus deprived of the fully automatic adjustments of the classical economic system, how can we appraise the capacity of a country to reconcile the competing claims on total resources, saving, and foreign exchange resources? What conditions must be fulfilled in order to develop a margin for debt service, and under what conditions can this margin be substantial?

A minimum condition for developing even a small sustainable margin for debt service over the long term would appear to be some increase in *per capita* income. Even for countries where neither the populace nor the political leaders have experienced the revolution of aspirations which characterizes so many underdeveloped countries today, it may be assumed that the revolution is highly contagious. In countries where the revolution has not occurred and where it is not expected to occur for some time, the claims of foreign debt service may be met even in the absence of a rise in *per capita* income if the yield on the foreign capital invested is sufficient to permit complete repayment of debt in a relatively short period or to permit a very high rate of return on an equity investment. Additional assurance is provided if the foreign capital finances a project which itself produces not only the necessary surplus in local currency but also in foreign exchange. In such a case one need not even rely on the classical adjustment mechanism.

In countries where the revolution of aspirations has occurred — and I suspect this is true in varying degrees of virtually all Latin American, most South-east Asian, and some Middle Eastern countries — some increase in *per capita* income over the long term appears to be a necessary condition. Unless *per capita* income rises it will become increasingly difficult to reconcile the claims of some economic groups to a larger share of the national income and the aspirations of the populace for higher consumption levels. Debt service payments, particularly if they increase relative to national income, saving, or exports, are likely to be jeopardized. It seems clear that where the basic conditions for economic development and for a rise in *per capita* income are absent — even if investment is stepped up — either the rising aspirations will be frustrated or grants must be made available by other countries. The risks facing a supplier of foreign capital expecting a return are too great.

This case, however, need not detain us, for it seems quite evident that despite the high rate of population growth now prevailing in Latin America some growth in national *per capita* income will continue in virtually all countries in the area so long as the economic growth in the outside world continues. In seventeen countries in Latin America for which some data on growth are available for the post-war period it appears that six have enjoyed a rate of growth of *per capita* income of over 3 per cent, five of between 2 and 3 per cent, one between 1 and 2 per cent, and only five below 1 per cent. Even if some part of the growth of income which Latin America has enjoyed is directly and indirectly attributable to the effects of a favourable turn in the terms of trade, which may not last, growth in *per capita* income is likely to continue. In so far as Latin America is concerned, therefore, one is justified in being relatively optimistic. One can assume that in most countries economic growth will continue at a rate in excess of population growth. This conclusion is strengthened if the current trend towards modification of policies which have hampered the growth of the external sector continues.

What then imposes an upper limit on the amount of external service payment obligations which can be incurred over the long term? To what extent can these limitations be determined by a case by case examination of the projects and programmes proposed for foreign financing and to what extent *must* they be determined by analysis of future economic prospects along aggregative lines ?

Starting with the assumption that a given rate of growth of *per capita* output is required to satisfy the aspirations of the populace for rising living standards and to resolve the competing claims on available resources, it is possible to set forth the conditions which must be fulfilled in order that both debt service claims and the income growth target be met. Assuming that the income growth target is in excess of what the country can achieve on the basis of domestic savings and that in order to achieve the target foreign capital inflows are necessary for a period, a model was constructed which yields these conditions.

The mathematical model provides a method for considering primarily the availability of, and claims on, total resources and saving in the context of economic growth. The availability of foreign exchange and the claims on foreign exchange do not enter explicitly, although we shall consider this aspect too in the discussion that follows.

The following variables were incorporated into the mathematical model :

p — projected rate of growth of population, assumed to be constant.

r' — target rate of growth of *per capita* real income, or output.

r — target rate of growth of aggregate real income or output.

K — projected incremental capital-output ratio, assuming a one-year lag between investment and income.

$S_0{}^a$ — initial average savings ratio.

i — projected rate of return on foreign capital, for interest and dividends.

n — year after start of process in which foreign debt must be completely repaid, or alternatively reach a maximum, or alternatively year in which rate of growth of debt rises no faster than rate of growth of national income.

s' — required marginal savings ratio, with required growth of *per capita* savings in the numerator and target growth of *per capita* income in the denominator.

Formulae have been derived[1] employing these variables which permit us to appraise the conditions under which a country can

---

[1] See Appendixes I and II.

develop a margin for debt service, and to determine how much the margin for debt service and the corresponding volume of capital inflow is influenced by the values which are assigned to the variables.

Certain characteristics of the definitions, assumptions, and structural relations incorporated in the model should be noted.

The following variables — the projected rate of growth of population, the target rate of growth of *per capita* and aggregate income, the incremental capital-output ratio, and the rate of return on foreign capital — are treated in the model as constants *over time*. This was done solely in the interests of mathematical simplicity. It is quite evident that they might well be expected to vary substantially over time. The values assigned to these variables may thus be looked upon as weighted averages of values which in fact vary over time.

The incremental capital-output ratio is an admittedly broad concept since it carries within it *all* of the factors affecting growth of output, not only investment. Included, for example, are the effects of the growth of the labour force (even though population growth as such is introduced as a separate variable for other purposes), the abundance or scarcity of national resources, technological progress, the availability of labour and managerial skills, and even changes in the terms of trade! Our only excuse for using such a concept is that we have been unable as yet to develop any simple yet more appropriate mathematical concept in which the influence of investment is clearly separable from the influence of the other factors.

The marginal savings ratio is treated in the formula as the derived variable or the dependent variable, that is, the variable whose value is derived after assigning values to the other variables. We could as well project the marginal savings ratio and treat *one* of the other variables, such as the incremental capital-output ratio, as derived or dependent. An important characteristic of the marginal savings ratio is that it is defined in *per capita* terms, as noted above. It can be argued that the growth of savings, to the extent that it is determined primarily by corporate savings, is more likely to be related to the growth of aggregate income than to the growth of *per capita* income. If this is the case, the concept employed here is awkward. On the other hand, the *per capita* concept is useful because it takes better account of the possibilities for saving by individual households and governments.

Let us now consider some of the implications to be derived in applying the formula which yields the marginal savings ratio required to meet debt service claims and investment requirements associated with different rates of income growth. It is perhaps obvious that all other things being equal the target rate of increase of *per capita* income, compared with the rate that can be achieved in the absence of foreign capital inflow, may be put at a higher level and a larger volume of foreign capital inflow is permitted when:

(1) the marginal savings ratio is higher;[1]
(2) the incremental capital-output ratio is lower;
(3) the rate of population increase is lower;
(4) the required rate of return on foreign capital inflow is lower;
(5) the degree of independence of foreign capital that must be achieved within a given time period is lower;
(6) the time period in which a given degree of independence must be achieved is longer.

Some word of explanation may be required on the last two points and on the inter-relationships which may in fact exist among these variables. The independence criterion was introduced into the formula to reconcile two propositions on capital inflow. First, foreign capital inflows must be available on a net basis for some period of time if they are substantially to accelerate development. Second, it is impossible to assume that new capital inflows will be available to any one underdeveloped country in unlimited amounts for an indefinite period. Both of these propositions are incorporated into the model by judging the capacity of a country to service a series of additions to its external indebtedness extending over a number of years and by posing the requirement that the country must, within a prescribed period, achieve a complete or partial independence of foreign capital inflow. The proviso that a country must be capable of achieving complete independence of capital inflow within a defined period of time is, in a sense, analogous to the repayment requirement on a specific loan. While individual loans may have to be repaid, equity investment and the total of loans may not. Therefore, formulae have also been derived to show what is required to achieve a situation where *net* capital inflow is no longer

---

[1] This is not universally the case. When the initial savings ratio is less than *Kp*, which is equivalent to the rate of investment required to maintain *per capita* income, a higher rate of growth of income may actually permit some reduction in the marginal savings ratio.

required or where the rate of increase of net capital inflow is progressively reduced. It is particularly interesting to note that all
three criteria — complete repayment of external debt, achievement
of independence of further net capital inflow, and progressive
reduction of the rate of net capital inflow — require exactly the same
performance, except for the time period. To put it more exactly, a
country which is capable of repaying debt completely in twenty-five
years will have reached a maximum volume of external indebtedness
somewhat earlier and will have reduced the rate of net capital inflow
even earlier. In other words, one can state a more liberal repayment
requirement either in terms of complete independence to be achieved
over a long-time period or a lesser degree of independence to be achieved over a shorter-time period.

An additional note on the possible inter-relations among the
variables is in order. In countries with abundant natural resources
relative to the present size of population, a high rate of growth of
population and consequently of the labour force may contribute to a
low capital-output ratio. But with a high rate of population growth
the growth of income must also be high in order to increase *per
capita* income, and it may be necessary to undertake investments
which tend to raise the capital-output ratio in order to maintain this
high rate of growth of income. Moreover, the terms on which external capital is available may become less favourable if a greater
volume of foreign capital, associated with a higher rate of growth of
income, is to be attracted. Most important, the feasibility of achieving a required marginal savings ratio is likely to be positively
associated with the rate of growth of *per capita* income.

Given the political pressures contributing to a rise in the government's current expenditures, and the economic pressures leading to a
demand for increased real wages and increased levels of personal
consumption; and assuming that the capital-output ratio and the
projected rate of return on foreign capital do not increase with
higher rate of growth of income — it can be shown with this model
that the likelihood of being able to service a larger volume of foreign
capital is greater than the likelihood of servicing a smaller volume of
capital inflow. This follows from the fact that very small increases
in the required marginal savings ratio are associated with very large
changes in *per capita* income, particularly in countries where population is increasing at a rapid rate. This is illustrated in the model
where the required marginal savings ratio has been calculated for a

country in which population is growing at a rate of $2\frac{1}{4}$ per cent per year, the initial average savings ratio is $8\frac{1}{2}$ per cent, and the incremental capital-output ratio is $3 \cdot 5 : 1$ and is invariant with respect to the rate of growth of income.[1]

MARGINAL SAVINGS RATIO REQUIRED TO SERVICE CAPITAL INFLOW
ON CERTAIN ASSUMPTIONS

Target Rate of Growth of *per capita* Income	Required Marginal Savings Ratio	Capital Inflow as ratio of	
		Initial National Income	Aggregate Net Investment
$\frac{1}{2}$%	0·23	0·23	0·07
1%	0·28	0·61	0·14
2%	0·31	1·42	0·22

Under these assumptions capital inflows over six times as large can be serviced with an increase in the marginal savings ratio from $0 \cdot 23$ to $0 \cdot 31$. Moreover, with the incremental capital-output ratio invariant with respect to the growth of income, the rate of growth of *per capita* consumption goes up from less than $\frac{1}{2}$ per cent to $1\frac{1}{2}$ per cent,[2] with a higher rate of growth of income and larger capital inflows. Clearly in this case it should be much easier for the country to reconcile the conflicting claims on resources, including both the claims represented by debt service payments, and investment required to maintain a continued rate of growth, with larger capital inflows than with smaller capital inflows. This case illustrates the highly favourable savings effect which a big push makes possible.

Now let us consider the risks which have been removed by our assumptions. If we assume that with a rate of growth of *per capita* income of 2 per cent it will be possible to save $0 \cdot 31$ and no more of the increments, debt service claims of the magnitude associated with a 2 per cent growth of *per capita* income will be met only if the capital-output ratio does not rise above $3 \cdot 5$. If the incremental capital-output ratio should rise to $4 : 1$, more than a third of the

---

[1] Also, we assume that the required return on foreign capital is $4\frac{1}{2}$ per cent and that external debt will reach a maximum in twenty-five years.

[2] Since a constant *per capita* savings ratio over time is assumed, the rate of increase in *per capita* consumption at the beginning is equal to $\dfrac{r'\,(l - s')}{l - S_0{}^a}$. The rate of growth of *per capita* consumption accelerates over time and approaches the rate of growth of *per capita* income.

increments in *per capita* income must be saved.[1] Also, the model assumes that net foreign capital inflows will be available to the country in question over a twenty-five-year period. If they were actually available for a shorter period and debt had to be completely repaid, for example, in twenty-five years, the required marginal savings ratio would exceed one-half. A still higher marginal savings ratio would be required if population growth was accelerated, or if the required rate of return on capital were increased. Clearly, the risks facing the supplier of capital in this highly artificial model are formidable!

This model demonstrates that it is possible to define — albeit in a highly mechanical way — the upper limits of debt service capacity in an environment where debt service claims are not necessarily given the highest priority. The practical significance of this model is limited by the difficulty of assigning realistic values to the variables, small but lasting changes in which are found to produce substantial differences in the final outcome. Nevertheless, the model illustrates that a creditor secures some assurance that debt service claims will be met if *per capita* income can be expected to increase at a fairly high rate. If, in addition, an environment is created which is favourable to a high marginal savings rate in the private sector and if government tax systems can be adapted to contribute to a high marginal savings rate in the public sector, the stage is set for accelerating economic development through foreign capital inflow. On the other hand, the model also indicates the great risks which the creditor faces wherever the politically, socially, and economically determined targets of income growth are set in an unrealistic fashion and then inflexibly adhered to.

The creditor's expectation of a high rate of growth of income is a favourable factor. If, however, the debtor country rigidly insists on maintaining — in the interests of a higher target rate of growth — a rate of investment which is beyond its capacity to finance, this frequently results in a lower capacity to service foreign debt and may even raise doubts as to whether the country will be willing to service foreign debt in times of strain. Even in this case, if the higher rate of investment desired by the debtor country is associated

---

[1] It should be noted that the incremental capital-output ratio in the postwar period has averaged close to 3 : 1 in Latin America. An increase to 4 : 1 is not likely in the short term but cannot be excluded if we look ahead twenty-five years.

with attainable income targets, why should not foreign capital in-flows fill the gap as an alternative to eliminating the gap by reducing investment? Whether the adjustment is more appropriately accomplished by increasing capital inflow or reducing investment depends on whether the income target associated with the higher rate of investment is feasible.

It is particularly in judging whether a target rate of growth of income is reasonable that it becomes important to consider the growth of foreign exchange availabilities and claims in the context of long-term growth. This model subsumes but does not illuminate these foreign exchange aspects of debt servicing capacity. It is, of course, clear that a country must produce sufficient additional goods for export or sufficient import substitutes, so that as income rises the increase in demand for imported goods (or for goods that used to be imported) plus the service on debt can be met from the available flow of foreign exchange. This directional aspect of economic growth has many dimensions, not just the foreign exchange dimension. Thus, form of investment and the composition of output must be adapted to the structure of demand sector by sector, if any given rate of increase of output is to be maintained over time. The foreign sector, however, can play a crucial role because foreign exchange is a highly flexible resource. It can be used to fill any temporary gaps in the adaptation of the domestic supply to changing domestic demand, gaps arising in some cases from improper directional policies. It can also be used to secure any of the goods and services which income growth requires but which the domestic economy can produce, at a given stage of development, only at a high or even prohibitive cost. A tight foreign exchange situation may arise because such a temporary gap has occurred or because of a structural deficiency, that is, the rate of growth of the economy is being pushed so fast that the economy cannot produce all of the particular kinds of goods and services, including exports, which the economy requires at this rate of growth.

The balance of payments deficits which recur periodically in countries seeking to accelerate their development rapidly may thus reflect not only the difficulties encountered in adjusting to year to year variations in the real value of exports; they may reflect not only the inability or unwillingness of the country to live within its means over the long term; they may also reflect an inability or unwillingness to produce within its means.

In this last case, the main problem is to determine whether a gap in the adaptation of domestic supply to changing domestic demand is temporary so that the target rate of growth of income can be achieved if foreign capital inflows are increased, or whether the gap reflects deficiencies in national resources, labour skills, and management abilities upon which the projected rate of growth also depends. If the gap is temporary and will be corrected fairly quickly by market forces without government action, there is no reason for concern. If, however, the gap is itself attributable to government policies which, for example, penalize the growth of the export sector, or if the gap reflects the inability of the economy to produce the types of goods and services which are required to sustain the rate of growth, corrective action is required. The country must reconcile itself to a lower rate of growth or, if the gap is attributable to government policy, it must change those policies which influence the direction of resource use. It has no alternative but to reduce the rate of growth if the more fundamental limitation is present.

IV. CONCLUSION

Let us now return to our original question. To what extent are the limitations on the amount of external debt service obligation which can be assumed over the long term subject to determination by a case by case examination of the various investment projects and programmes proposed for foreign financing and to what extent must these limitations be determined by some kind of aggregate analysis of future economic prospects?

It seems clear that in countries where the revolution of aspirations has already occurred or where it may be expected to occur the case by case approach is not sufficient. Some type of aggregative analysis of future economic prospects is essential.

In the case of many Latin American countries, where a rapid rate of growth has been achieved in recent years, it may, however, be possible to move toward greater reliance on case by case examination of projects and programmes. The dynamic character of these economies is being demonstrated and case by case examination of investment projects and programmes should itself reveal to some extent potentialities for future economic growth. However, unless many of the countries in this area show a better capacity to adjust to short-term variations in available resources by the use of appropriate monetary and fiscal policy, foreign investors will tend to discount heavily the potentialities uncovered by investigations of investment projects and programmes. Perhaps part of the difficulty of adjusting to short-term variations will be removed as tax structures are improved and governments become able to discharge their modern-day responsibilities without inflationary excesses. Moreover, in some countries there is already a growing appreciation of the damage produced by inflation, and the example of growth with stability may prove even more attractive than the example of growth with inflation. The continued expansion of the world economy is already producing a revaluation of government policies on the use of resources, particularly as between exports and the home market. Reliance upon improving terms of trade to increase real export earnings is giving way to a search for ways to increase the volume of exports.

If a greater degree of financial responsibility is firmly established as a conscious policy and if positive measures, including proper exchange rate systems, are taken to encourage the economy to produce the types of goods and services which are required to sustain growth rates, it may be possible to secure some of the advantages of the classical mechanism of foreign investment. Foreign investors may feel less compelled to centre their attention on general uncertainties concerning the debtor country's economy and more able to concentrate on the merits of the projects and programmes proposed for financing.

APPENDIX I[1]

DERIVATION OF DEBT FORMULA (FORMULA A)
DERIVATION OF S_n

Symbols :

Primes (') denote *per capita*. Subscript ($_n$) refers to time-period; first period denoted by subscript ($_o$).

S_n — aggregate domestic savings.
$S_o{}^a$ — initial average savings ratio.
Y — national income (geographical).

[1] The author wishes to acknowledge the assistance of Mr. Charles Goor and Mr. Kenneth Bohr.

P — population.

p — rate of increase of population, a constant.

r' — target rate of increase of *per capita* income, a constant.

r — target rate of increase of aggregate income, a constant.

s' — *per capita* marginal savings ratio, a constant.

Thus by definition :

$$1 \cdot 0 \qquad \begin{aligned} Y_n &= Y_n' \, P_n. \\ S_n &= S_n' \, P_n. \end{aligned}$$

$$r' = \frac{Y_n' - Y'_{n-1}}{Y'_{n-1}},$$

$$\text{or } r'Y'_{n-1} = Y_n' - Y'_{n-1}.$$

$$s' = \frac{S_n' - S'_{n-1}}{Y_n' - Y'_{n-1}}.$$

Then, substituting the above in the denominator,

$$1 \cdot 1 \qquad\qquad s' = \frac{S_n' - S'_{n-1}}{r'Y'_{n-1}}.$$

From compound interest formula :

$$\begin{aligned} Y_n' &= Y_0'(1+r')^n. \\ P_n &= P_0(1+p)^n. \end{aligned}$$

Then, from $1 \cdot 1$:

$$\begin{aligned} s'r' \, Y'_{n-1} &= S_n' - S'_{n-1}. \\ S_n' &= S'_{n-1} + s'r'Y'_{n-1}. \end{aligned}$$

$$1 \cdot 2 \qquad\qquad S_n' = S'_{n-1} + s'r'Y_0'(1+r')^{n-1}.$$

For initial period by definition $S_0' = S_0{}^a Y_0'$.

From definition for $S_n(1 \cdot 0)$ and from $1 \cdot 2$:

$$\begin{aligned} S_0 &= S_0{}^2 Y_0' P_0. \\ S_1 &= (S_0{}^a Y_0' + s'r'YY_0')P_0(1+p). \\ S_2 &= [S_0{}^a Y_0' + s'r'Y_0' + s'r'Y_0'(1+r')]P_0(1+p)^2. \\ S_3 &= [S_0{}^a Y_0' + s'r'Y_0' + s'r'Y_0'(1+r') + s'r'Y_0'(1+r')^2]P_0(1+p)^3. \end{aligned}$$

After factoring out $Y_0'P_0$, the general expression S_n becomes,

$$S_n = (Y_0'P_0)\,(1+p)^n[S_a{}^o + s'r' + s'r'(1+r') + \ldots + s'r'\,(1+r')^{n-1}].$$

Using formula for summing geometric progression and substituting Y_0 for $Y_0'P_0$,

$$= Y_0(1+p)^n \left[S_0{}^a + s'r' \; \frac{(1+r')^n - 1}{r'} \right].$$

$$1 \cdot 3 \qquad\qquad S_n = Y_0(1+p)^n \left\{ S_0{}^a + s'[(1+r')^n - 1] \right\}.$$

By definition, $(1+r')\,(1+p) = 1+r.$

$1 \cdot 4$ Thus, in $1 \cdot 3$,
$$(1+p)^n[(1+r')^n-1] = (1+r)^n-(1+p)^n.$$

Substituting $1 \cdot 4$ in $1 \cdot 3$, we obtain :
$$S_n = Y_0(1+p)^nS_0{}^a-Y_0s'[(1+r)^n-(1+p)^n].$$
$1 \cdot 5$ $S_n = Y_0\{(1+p)^nS_0{}^a+s'[(1+r)^n-(1+p)^n]\}.$

DERIVATION OF I_n

I — Net domestic investment required to secure target rate of increase of income.

K — Incremental capital-output ratio.

By definition : $K = \dfrac{I_n}{Y_{n+1}-Y_n}$.
$$I_n = K(Y_{n+1}-Y_n).$$
$1 \cdot 6$ Since $Y_n = Y_0(1+r)^n$, from $1 \cdot 6$,
$$I_n = KY_0[(1+r)^{n+1}(1+r)^n] = KY_0(1+r)^n(1+r-1).$$
$1 \cdot 7$ $I_n = KrY_0(1+r)^n.$

DERIVATION OF F_n

F — Excess of gross capital inflows over all service payments on foreign debt (interest, dividends, and amortization) rerequired to secure target rate of increase of income. F is thus the gap between domestic investment requirements and domestic savings, equivalent to the required surplus in the balance of payments on capital account, under the geographical concept of national income.
$$F_n = I_n-S_n.$$

Substituting $1 \cdot 7$ and $1 \cdot 5$, we get

$$F_n = KrY_0(1+r)^n-Y_0\{(1+p)^nS_0{}^a+s'[(1+r)^n-(1+p)^n]\}$$
$$= Y_0\big(Kr(1+r)^n-\}(1+p)^nS_0{}^a+s'[(1+r)_n-(1+p)^n]\}\big).$$
$1 \cdot 8$ $F_n = Y_0[(Kr-s')(1+r)^n-(S_0{}^a-s')(1+p)^n].$

DERIVATION OF D_n

D — Foreign debt at the end of each year.

i — Required rate of return on foreign debt, a constant.

X — Interest and dividend payments on foreign debt.

We assume that interest and dividend payments begin in the second year and that interest and dividend payments for any given

year are computed from the debt at the end of the preceding year —
or $X_n = iD_{n-1}$.

Since debt is the sum of the required surplus in the balance of
payments on capital account in the present year, interest and
dividend payments on the volume of debt outstanding at the end
of the previous year, and the volume of debt at the end of the
previous year, we get

$$D_n = F_n + X_n + D_{n-1}$$
$$= F_n + i(D_{n-1}) + D_{n-1}.$$

1·9 $$D_n = (1+i)D_{n-1} + F_n.$$

It is assumed that no debt is outstanding at the beginning of the
first year. Hence, given 1·9 :

$$D_0 = F_0.$$
$$D_1 = F_0(1+i) + F_1.$$
$$D_2 = F_0(1+i)^2 + F_1(1+i) + F_2.$$
$$D_3 = F_0(1+i)^3 - F_1(1+i)^2 + F_2(1+i) + F_3.$$

2·0 $$D_n = F_0(1+i)^n + F_1(1+i)^{n-1} + F_2(1+i)^{n-2} + \ldots + F_n.$$

From 1·8, $F_n = Y_0[(Kr-s')(1+r)^n - (S_0{}^a - s')(1+p)^n]$.

Let : $$Kr-s' = A : S_0{}^a - s' = B$$

Therefore, from 2·0, we get

$$D_0 = Y_0[A(1+r)^0 - B(1+p)^0].$$
$$D_1 = Y_0\{(1+i)[A(1+r)^0 - B(1+p)^0] + A(1+r) - B(1+p)\}.$$
$$D_2 = Y_0\{(1+i)^2[A(1+r)^0 - B(1+p)^0] + (1+i)[A(1+r) - B(1+p)] + A(1+r)^2 - B(1+p)^2\}.$$

2·1 $$D_n = Y_0\{(1+i)^n[A(1+r)^0 - B(1+p)^0] + (1+i)^{n-1}[A(1+r) - B(1+p)] + (1+i)^{n-2}[A(1+r)^2 - B(1+p)^2] + \ldots + A(1+r)^n - B(1+p)^n\}.$$

Thus, we have in 2·1 two geometric progressions, the first, with
the 'A' term is added, and the second, with the 'B' term is subtracted ; each term in turn has two geometric series which are multiplied.

2·2 $$D_n = Y_0 A[(1+i)^n(1+r)^0 + (1+i)^{n-1}(1+r) + (1+i)^{n-2}(1+r)^2 + \ldots + (1+i)^0(1+r)^1] - Y_0 B[(1+i)^n(1+p)^0 + (1+i)^{n-1}(1+p) + (1+i)^{n-2}(1+p)^2 + \ldots + (1+i)^0(1+p)^n].$$

In both progressions the first term is $(1+i)^n$; in the first progression the common ratio is $\dfrac{1+r}{1+i}$ and in the second progression
the common ratio is $\dfrac{1+p}{1+i}$.

We assume here that r is not equal to i.[1]

Thus, from the formula for summing a geometric progression, when $i \neq r$, $2 \cdot 2$ becomes

$$2 \cdot 3 \quad D_n = Y_0 \left\{ A(1+i)^n \left[\frac{\left(\frac{1+r}{1+i}\right)^{n+1} - 1}{\frac{1+r}{1+i} - 1} \right] B(1+i)^n \left[\frac{\left(\frac{1+p}{1+i}\right)^{n+1} - 1}{\frac{1+p}{1+i} - 1} \right] \right\}$$

Simplifying, we obtain,

$$D_n = Y_0 \left\{ A \left[\frac{(1+r)^{n+1} - (1+i)^{n+1}}{r-i} \right] - B \left[\frac{(1+p)^{n+1} + (1+i)^{n+1}}{p+i} \right] \right\}$$

Substituting for A and B,

$$= Y_0 \left\{ (Kr-s') \left[\frac{(1+r)^{n+1} - (1+i)^{n+1}}{r+i} \right] - (S_0{}^a - s') \left[\frac{(1+p)^{n+1} - (+i)^{n+1}}{p-i} \right] \right\}.$$

Or, if the first year is denoted by the subscript$_1$ instead of $_0$,

$2 \cdot 4$ Formula A[2]

$$D_n = Y_1 \left\{ (Kr-s') \left[\frac{(1+r)^n - (1+i)^n}{r-i} \right] - (S_0{}^a - s') \left[\frac{(1+p)^n - (1+i)^n}{p-i} \right] \right\}.$$

APPENDIX II

DERIVATION OF REQUIRED MARGINAL SAVINGS RATIO

THE required marginal savings ratio is derived by imposing a prescribed constraint upon the volume of debt in a future year and solving Formula A, subject to this constraint, in terms of s'. The following solution is for the common case, where $i \neq r$.

From Appendix I we have Formula A $(2 \cdot 5)$:

$$D_n = Y_1 \left\{ (Kr-s') \left[\frac{(1+r)^n - (1+i)^n}{r-i} \right] - (S_0{}^a - s') \left[\frac{(1+p)^n - (1+i)^n}{p-i} \right] \right\}$$

(When first year is denoted by subscript $_1$.)

---

[1] If $i = r$ the 'A' term becomes $nA(1+r)^n$.

[2] If $i = r$, we use the above for the A term and get

$$D_n = Y_1 \left\{ n(Kr-s')(1+r)^{n-1} - (S_0{}^a - s') \left[\frac{(1+r)^n - (1+p)^n}{r-p} \right] \right\}.$$

A. Debt to reach zero in nth year :

Denoting the first year by $_1$, if debt is to reach zero at the end of n years, D_n must equal zero. Placing $D_n = _0$, we solve for s'.

$$Y_1 \left\{ (Kr-s') \left[\frac{(1+r)^n-(1+i)^n}{r-i} \right] (S_0{}^a-s') \left[\frac{(1+p)^n-(1+i)^n}{p-i} \right] \right\} = 0.$$

Simplifying and rearranging terms, we get

Formula I :

$$s' = \frac{S_0{}^a \left[\dfrac{(1+p)^n-(1+i)^n}{p-i} \right] - Kr \left[\dfrac{(i+r)^n-(1+i)^n}{r-i} \right]}{\dfrac{(1+p)^n-(1+i)^n}{p-i} - \dfrac{(1+r)^n-(1+i)^n}{r-i}}.$$

B. Debt to reach absolute maximum in nth year.

Denoting the first year by $_1$, for debt to reach a maximum at the end of n years, the increased debt between the year n and $n+1$ must equal zero. Placing $D_{n+1}-D_n = _0$, we solve for s'.

$$Y_1 \left\{ \frac{Kr-s'}{r-i} [(1+r)^{n+1}-(1+i)^{n+1}] - \frac{S_0{}^a-s'}{p-i} [(1+p)^{n+1}-(1+i)^{n+1}] \right.$$

$$\left. - \left[\frac{Kr-s'}{r-i} [(1+r)^n-(1+i)^n] - \frac{S_0{}^a-s'}{p-i} [(1+p)^n-(1+i)^n] \right] \right\} = 0.$$

Simplifying and rearranging terms, we get

Formula II :

$$s' = \frac{S_0{}^a \left\{ i \left[\dfrac{(1+p)^n-(1+i)^n}{p-i} \right] + (1+p)^n \right\} - Kr \left\{ i \left[\dfrac{(1+r)^n-(1+i)^n}{r-i} \right] + (1+r)^n \right\}}{i \left[\dfrac{(1+p)^n-(1+i)^n}{p-i} \right] + (1+p)^n - \left\{ i \left[\dfrac{(1+r)^n-(1+i)^n}{r-i} \right] + (1+r)^n \right\}}$$

C. Ratio of external debt to national income to reach maximum in nth year.

For ratio of debt to national income to reach maximum at the end of n years, the rate of increase of debt between the nth and the $n+1$ year must equal the rate of increase of national income.

Thus $\dfrac{D_{n+1}}{D_n} = 1+r$. From Formula A $(2 \cdot 5)$,

$$\frac{Y_1\left\{(Kr-s')\left[\dfrac{(1+r)^{n+1}-(1+i)^{n+1}}{r-i}\right]-(S_0{}^a-s')\left[\dfrac{(1+p)^{n+1}-(1+i)^{n+1}}{p-i}\right]\right\}}{Y_1\left\{(Kr-s')\left[\dfrac{(1+r)^n-(1+i)^n}{r-i}\right]-(S_0{}^a-s')\left[\dfrac{(1+p)^n-(1+i)^n}{p-i}\right]\right\}} = 1+r.$$

Simplifying and rearranging terms, we get

Formula III :

$$s' = \frac{S_0{}^a[(1+p)^n(p-r)+(1+i)^n(r-i)]-Kr[(p-i)(1+i)^n]}{[(1+p)^n(p-r)+(1+i)^n(r-i)]-(p-i)(1+i)^n}.$$

INTERNATIONAL AID FOR UNDER-DEVELOPED COUNTRIES*

by P. N. Rosenstein-Rodan

The purpose of an international programme of aid to underdeveloped countries is to accelerate their economic development up to a point where a satisfactory rate of growth can be achieved on a self-sustaining basis. The function of outside capital in a development programme is not directly to raise standards of living in the recipient countries but to permit them to make the transition from economic stagnation to self-sustaining economic growth. The principal element in this transition must be the efforts that the citizens of the recipient countries themselves make to bring it about. Without these efforts, outside capital will be wasted. Thus the general aim of aid (loans, grants, and technical assistance) is to provide in each underdeveloped country a positive incentive for maximum national effort to increase its rate of growth. The increase in income, savings, and investment which aid indirectly and directly makes possible will shorten the time it takes to achieve self-sustaining growth. Economic progress is measured primarily by increases in income per head over a period of time, say one or two five-year periods. The overall aim of development aid is not to equalize incomes in different countries but to provide every country with an opportunity to achieve steady growth. Aid should continue not until a certain income level is reached in underdeveloped countries but only until those countries can mobilize a level of capital formation sufficient for self-sustaining growth.

Ideally, aid should be allocated where it will have the maximum catalytic effect of mobilizing additional national effort or preventing a fall in national effort. The primary criterion is thus to maximize additional effort, not to maximize income created per dollar of aid. If this last were the aim, dollars invested in developed countries might easily show better results. Nor would a criterion of maximum increase in income suffice even if only underdeveloped countries

* *The Review of Economics and Statistics*, May 1961. Reprinted with the permission of the Harvard University Press, the publishers of this journal, and of the author.

were considered. In different stages and different phases of development more investment may be required to produce a unit of additional income than in others. This is invariably the case where, for instance, social overhead capital has to be built up first. Such investment in economic infra-structure yields directly only small increases in income. It creates, however, a framework necessary to the profitability of more immediately lucrative subsequent investments. Direct increase in income is less important here than the increase in investment opportunities. Income created per dollar of aid may, therefore, at first be low; far from being an argument for *less* aid, there are circumstances in which this might well be an argument for *more*.

Capital aid should be offered wherever there is reasonable assurance that it will be effectively used. A positive incentive to increased national effort will be present only if it is believed that all requests which meet functional criteria of productivity will be granted. Knowledge that capital will be available over a decade or more up to the limits of the capacity to absorb will act in many cases as an incentive to greater effort. Assurance of continuity of aid is, therefore, as important as the amount of aid.

The main function of foreign capital inflow is to increase the rate of domestic capital formation up to a level (for instance, 12 per cent, yielding an increase of income of 2 per cent per head per annum) which could then be maintained without any further aid. Additional resources and know-how provided by foreign capital inflow produce an additional product. The proportion that can be saved out of this additional product can be very much higher than average savings at the pre-existing income level. While the *average* rate of savings is, for instance, 7 per cent in Asia, the *marginal* rate of savings can be stepped up to 20–5 per cent.

Absorptive capacity. A marginal rate which is much higher than the average rate of savings is the main lever of a development programme and should be the principal condition of aid to underdeveloped countries. The extent to which increased investments with a high marginal rate of savings can be realized depends on the country's technical absorptive capacity. The capacity to absorb capital is more limited on a low level of development, where a higher proportion of technical assistance must precede a large capital inflow. With a rising level of development the marginal rate of savings will increase. The habit of ploughing back undistributed profits in

industry prevails today already and accounts in this sector for a
marginal rate of savings of 30–40 per cent in India as well as in the
United States. An effective fiscal policy can also provide increased
savings.

Absorptive capacity relates to the ability to use capital productively. While not every single investment project need be 'self-
liquidating', total investment must not only cover its costs but
must also yield a reasonable increase in income. Total investment
entails a multitude of projects, a diversified investment programme
which requires variegated managerial and technical resources. While
some single projects may use foreign consultants and experts, the
bulk of the administrative and organizing effort must be undertaken
by the country's own personnel if it is to develop successfully.

The various projects comprising a development programme are
inter-related and reinforce each other. This balance depends on
whether complementary activities have been planned on the required
scale. It is therefore practically impossible to judge the soundness
of any particular project without knowledge of the whole programme
of which it is a part. A programme approach, not a project approach,
must determine the criteria of productive use of aid capital. Foreign
aid capital increases the range of the programme as a whole. Since
this may require a reshuffle and changes in several projects, a single
loan cannot with any exactness be said to have been given to one
specific project only — it should be considered as a contribution
to the whole programme.

While the capacity to absorb capital is a limiting factor, it can,
within a few years, be stepped up in many underdeveloped countries
by 20–30 per cent above the presently realized level of investment.
There are, however, narrow limits to the pace and extent at which
a country's absorptive capacity can be expanded. Education in the
long run and revolution of habits in the short run may widen the
scope. But it is not true to say that absorptive capacity depends
entirely on the amount of effort one is willing to put into massive
technical assistance. Foreign experts and managers may best be
used without compromising domestic control and without stifling
the growth of domestic entrepreneurs. Outside skills and knowledge
may well supplement but cannot entirely substitute for domestic
abilities to organize and to administer.

If a country's additional effort ('sufficient' or 'deficient') and
absorptive capacity could not be measured, assessed, or estimated, it

could not be the basic criterion of aid. Fortunately no exact measurement is needed, and three indexes can be used to estimate absorptive capacity. The first two refer to 'objective' verifiable facts, while the third relies on rough commonsense rules of thumb which may indicate a ranking order of magnitudes. (1) We may ascertain by how much a country has succeeded in increasing her volume of investment during the past five or more years. If a rate of increase of investment could be realized in the past, then a slightly higher rate made possible by technical assistance can be plausibly projected for the future. (2) We may also ascertain whether a country has succeeded in the recent past in raising her savings, notably in maintaining or in widening the deviation between the *average* and the *marginal* rates of savings. A similar spread for the next five-year period may constitute the lower limit of a possible savings effort. Judgement on the country's ability to mobilize additional taxes when incomes are rising may justify a projection above the recently realized lower limit of the country's ability to save. A changing composition of output (more industry with high marginal rates of savings) will lead in many cases to foreseeably higher savings rates for the country as a whole. (3) Finally a judgement on a country's overall administrative and developmental organization is by no means as 'arbitrary' as it may seem. There is not much difference of opinion on the relative 'push' or 'potential' of, say, India, Ceylon, Indonesia, or Brazil, Guatemala, Paraguay, among businessmen, economists, or even average tourists, although unforeseeable shake-ups, positive or negative, may either lower it or raise it. The longer the time distance the less certain is the judgement. On the assumption of historical continuity, however, agreement can be obtained on a ranking order of magnitudes.[1]

Capacity to repay. The foreign capital inflow mobilized by international action should be within the limits on the one hand of technical absorptive capacity, and on the other hand of the *capacity*

---

[1] For a fuller elaboration, see M. F. Millikan and W. W. Rostow, *A Proposal: Key to an Effective Foreign Policy*, Harper and Brothers, New York, 1957, Chs. V and VI; and *The Objectives of U.S. Economic Assistance Programs*, Section VI, a Study prepared at the request of the Special Committee to Study the Foreign Aid Programme, U.S. Senate, by CENIS, M.I.T., January 1957.

A rough judgement of the underdeveloped countries' absorptive capacity is shown in those countries' assumed rates of growth 1961–76 in Appendix Tables 2, 3, and 4.

to repay of underdeveloped countries. While the first limit should preponderantly determine the amount of aid, the second limit should largely determine the method of financing it. Where the capacity to repay in low-income underdeveloped countries is below their absorptive capacity, a proportion of aid will have to be given in grants, or 'soft loans', 40-99 year loans with a ten to twenty years grace period and a low rate of interest, or loans repayable in local currency which will be re-lent for subsequent investment. The capacity to repay should not be assessed by a static projection of the present situation but should take into account the increase in income and the increase in the rate of savings which will result from the adoption of a soundly conceived development programme. Nor is it sensible to assume that the whole ('hard') foreign debt of each country should be amortized within twenty or thirty years. It is by no means rational for each country to reduce its foreign indebtedness to zero. The rational question to ask is: 'How much foreign indebtedness can a country maintain in the long run?' After ten to twenty years of aid the net capital inflow to underdeveloped countries will come to a stop. The gross capital inflow, however, will continue, while at the same time old loans will be repaid. In exactly the same way in which any national debt (or corporate debt) need not be reduced if it is within sound limits, the foreign debt of debtor countries need not be amortized to zero in a sound world economy.

What is 'Aid'? 'Foreign capital inflow' and 'aid' are not synonymous. Aid, properly speaking, refers only to those parts of capital inflow which normal market incentives do not provide. It consists of:

(i) Long-term loans repayable in foreign currency. 'Long-term' conventionally means loans of more than ten years maturity; longer maturing loans (twenty years or more) should preferably constitute the bulk of such loans. The annual burden of amortization of such loans is only a fraction (one-quarter to one-half) of the burden imposed by short- and medium-term loans.

(ii) Grants and 'soft loans', including loans 'repayable in local currency'. Soft loans are in fact contingent part grants. There can be many varieties of them, e.g., very long-term (ninety-nine year) loans repayable in foreign currency at a low rate of interest, loans with a long grace period (ten or twenty years) for payment of principal and/or interest, loans repayable in local currency which is then re-lent to the borrower for further domestic investment. According to the future success of development, which is unforeseeable and uncertain for each country separately at the beginning of her development, a part of the local currency loans may be repaid at a later date, while a part will, in fact, have to be written off.

(iii) Sale of surplus products for 'local currency' payments (P.L. 480 in the United States). Not only 'capital' (equipment) goods but also consumption goods can constitute capital. In fact agricultural products can form an important part of capital in its original sense of a subsistence fund. If sufficient foodstuffs could not be supplied in a country to meet the demand from the additionally employed working on construction or other investments, then either more investment capital ('circulating') would have to be spent for imports, or the amount of additional investment would have to be reduced. It cannot be said in reality, however, that the whole of imported surplus products will be used for additional investment. A good economic development policy can see to it that a major part is used for raising investment, but a part will merely bolster domestic consumption. In practice, therefore, a withdrawal of surplus product sales would lead to a reduction in both consumption and investment. We assume in this study that *two-thirds* of surplus product sales can be considered investment aid, while one-third goes into increased consumption. Even on that basis up to one-fifth of total aid to underdeveloped countries can be rendered in this form. In the United States two-thirds of P.L. 480 sales may form up to 30 per cent of American 'aid' to underdeveloped countries. We assume an annual surplus products investment-aid figure of $700 million, which implies total P.L. 480 sales of $1 billion per annum.

(iv) Technical assistance is undoubtedly a most important part of aid to underdeveloped countries, but it is not counted in our study as 'capital inflow'. It must form part — and an increasing part at that — of budgetary appropriations for aid; it should be added to the total amount of aid required in the wider sense, but it is not included in the Appendix Table 4 as 'Foreign Capital Inflow'. Estimates of present national and international public and private expenditure on technical aid vary from $250–300 million per annum. In view of its importance, especially for underdeveloped 'pre-take-off' countries, it should certainly be increased to, say, $400 million per annum. The United States contribution through national and international channels should amount to around $250 million per annum.

What is not 'economic aid'? Economic aid was defined above as that part of capital inflow which normal market incentives do not provide. Accordingly neither short- or medium-term loans nor private foreign investment should be counted as aid. They are 'trade not aid'. Short- and medium-term loans are mostly selling devices for (tied) exports of equipment goods. They are not included in our estimates of the foreign capital inflow into underdeveloped countries, nor are other short-term capital movements. They are not tools of an international aid policy. Private foreign investment is undertaken in response to normal market incentives. In this sense it is not 'aid', but it is included in our estimates of 'Foreign Capital Inflow required for Underdeveloped Countries' (Appendix Table 4). To this rule there is one partial exception. Oil and mineral investment into 'foreign enclaves' in 'dual economies' is only counted at half its amount. For that reason Bahrain and Kuwait, for instance, are excluded in the calculation of economic aid; anyway they do not require it. In countries where foreign private investment largely but not wholly flows into extractive industries, only one-half of that investment is counted as foreign capital inflow. This somewhat rough assumption is based on the fact that — although such industries provide important tax and other revenues — their diffusion and complementarity effects are markedly smaller than those of other industries.

'Defence support' is, in principle, not included in economic aid. Parts of it may well contribute to the receiving countries' economic development. To that extent present United States economic aid may be slightly underestimated in our calculation, although 20 per cent of defence support is actually counted as economic aid.

THE BURDEN OF INTERNATIONAL AID

General principles. General principles of how the burden of international aid should be divided among developed countries have not yet been agreed upon. The social philosophy of the free world provides nonetheless some clear indications. A tentative proposal may be outlined here.

(i) All developed countries — say those with income per head above $600 — should contribute to aid either a proportion of their

GNP (perhaps one-half per cent per annum) or preferably specific contributions (which should add up to the total aid required). An estimate of total aid required might be, for each of the years 1961–6, $3·8 billion of capital aid, plus $0·4 billion for technical assistance, plus $0·3 billion for emergencies, totalling $4·5 billion. To get a figure for specific contributions, apply the United States income tax progression to the number of families of each developed country — counting a family as having four times the country's income per head. A 'real' GNP indicating the purchasing power of the GNP compared to United States prices may be computed (see Table 1–A) instead of the nominal one.

Neither short- or medium-term loans nor private foreign investment should be included in 'aid'. Long-term loans of the International Bank are certainly aid, but they are treated as private foreign investment, i.e., they are not included in the computation of each country's contribution.

Appropriations for aid should, if possible, be 33–50 per cent higher than the amount which will probably be disbursed. This would provide an incentive and encouragement to underdeveloped countries for vigorous development efforts. In our calculation in Appendix Table 5 only prospective disbursements, not the desirable appropriations, are counted.

(ii) All long-term loans and grants should be, in principle, untied [see exception under (iii) and (iv)].

(iii) Up to one-third of each country's contribution to aid can be tied, however, to the grant or sale of surplus products for local currency repayment. Only two-thirds of each country's total surplus product grants or sales are counted as capital aid.

(iv) During a year of balance of payments difficulties, a contributing country may invoke a special clause (analogous to GATT provisions), tying her loans and grants — for other than surplus product sales — during this year.

The United States Share. Since only high-income countries with GNP per head above $600 should be contributors to economic aid, Japan and South Africa should not be included among them. Japan should certainly provide short- and medium-term loans, but she is not yet a structural capital-export country.

The total nominal GNP of the contributing developed countries is $855 billion in 1961. The United States proportion of it amounts to 60 per cent.

The total real GNP of these countries is $953·2 billion; the United States proportion of it amounts to 54 per cent.

Applying the progressive income tax principle to the real GNP of the rich countries would attribute to the United States 65 per cent of the total aid, and 35 per cent to Europe and Oceania and Canada (see Appendix Table 6).

We shall accordingly assume that the United States should contribute around 65 per cent of the free world total economic aid.

How the burden of aid should be shared among the developed countries is shown in Appendix Table 6.

RATES OF GROWTH IN UNDERDEVELOPED COUNTRIES

High- and low-growth countries. The classification of countries is based on their *rate of growth per head*. 'High-growth countries' have an increase in income per head of 2 per cent per annum or more. 'Low-growth countries' have an increase in income per head per annum of 0·6–1·9 per cent. Stationary countries have either no increase in income per head, or an imperceptibly low one of under 0·5 per cent per head per annum. (See Table 1 and Chart 1.)

High growth per head of population — chosen here as the principle of classification — does not always coincide with a high 'development potential', which refers to the aggregate rate of growth. Brazil, for instance, has a higher development potential than Chile or Uruguay, but Chile has a smaller population and a lower increase in population.

Estimates of *African* countries are even more speculative than those of other regions. Rhodesia and Nyasaland have a high rate of growth due to an 'enclave' mineral investment in a dual economy. Non-economic factors will decide whether a sustained growth — even if on a somewhat lower level — can be reached in the future. Algeria's prospects depend on political developments and a possibly large French capital inflow. Libya's temporarily (1961–6) good growth is due to petroleum investment. Of the other countries, prospects of good — though neither high nor sustained — rates of growth seem to appear for Tanganyika, Nigeria, Kenya, Uganda, and Ghana.

Latin America with one-sixth of the population of underdeveloped countries has one-third of their income and 37 per cent of their investment. The region consists, however, of three unequal groups.

CHART 1

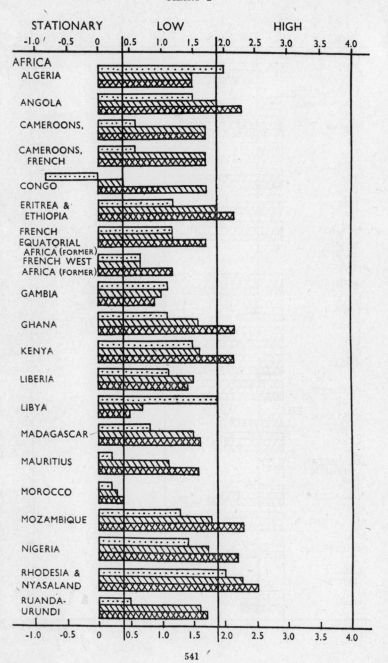

CHART 1—continued

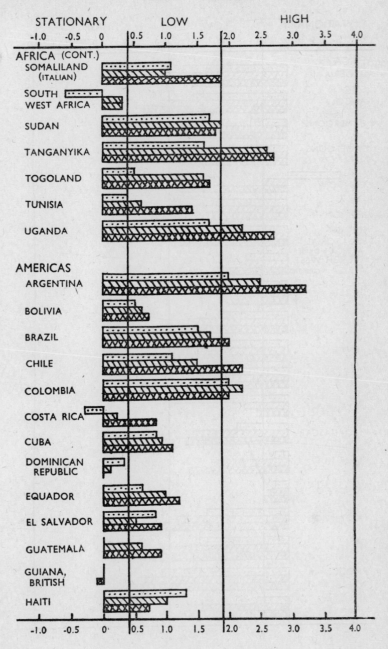

CHART 1—*continued*

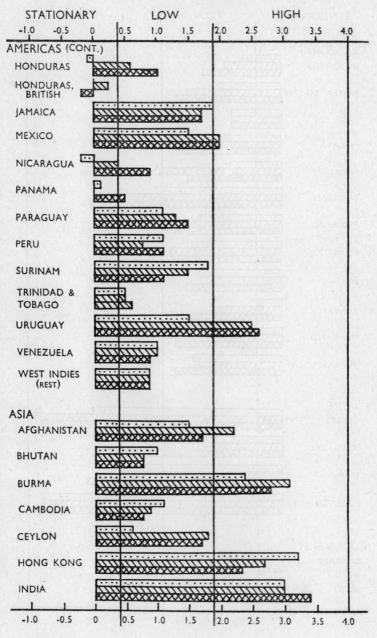

CHART 1—*continued*

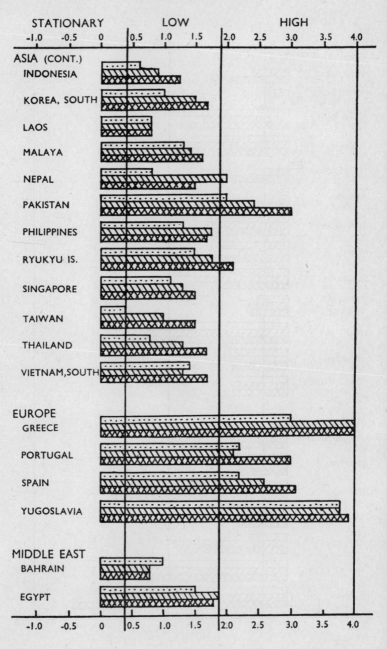

CHART 1—*continued*

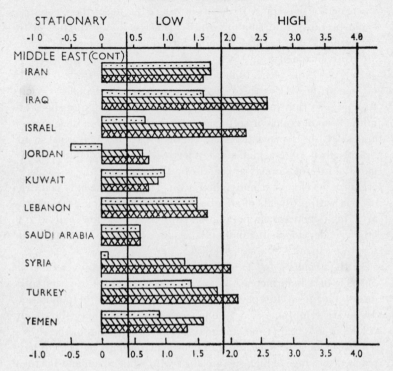

First there are five countries with a high and sustained rate of growth: Argentina, Brazil, Chile, Colombia, and Mexico, to which within a few years Uruguay and probably Jamaica can be added, and within a decade possibly Ecuador (and may be Cuba). Secondly, there are countries with a satisfactory rate of growth like Peru, Ecuador, and Venezuela. Thirdly, there is a large group of stationary countries in *Central America* with very high rates of increase in population, which partly for that reason cannot get off dead centre. It may well be that the population projections are too pessimistic for the later periods (after 1966 or 1971), when the rate of population increase may fall, and that in this case our forecast is unduly pessimistic. Costa Rica has a special position among those countries, having a relatively high level of income, but no growth. A high rate of increase in population is a powerful but not an insuperable obstacle to growth. The example of Mexico — and in the future perhaps of Iraq, Egypt, and Turkey — shows that such an obstacle can be overcome. If the absorptive capacity of these countries could be raised, aid should be provided. Our low estimates of the aid required for Central America are due to the present limited absorptive capacity.

In *Asia*, India seems to be in a 'take-off' stage, in spite of her low income per head. Her absorptive capacity is higher than her capacity to repay, so that more than one-half of the aid required should be in the form of grants or soft loans. Pakistan's tempo of development appears to be somewhat lower, but it is promising. Burma should be able to initiate a higher rate of growth. The 'economic factors' like the rate of savings appear to be favourable — the capacity to organize development may follow soon. These are the only countries in Asia with prospects of a high rate of growth. Ceylon has obstacles in a high increase in population and relatively low capacity to organize development. Indonesia is an example of a limited absorptive capacity.

In the *Middle East*, Turkey, Egypt, and Iraq may overcome the obstacle of a high increase in population — the task appears to be most difficult in Egypt because of a high density of population. There are symptoms of development vigour which may show same results in five years time, and may consolidate success in the 1970's.

Finally, in *Southern Europe*, Yugoslavia and Greece seem to have reached the stage of high sustained growth, while Spain and Portugal may follow within five and ten years. (For more details see Notes to Appendix Tables 3 and 4.)

Sustained growth. The distinction between a once-for-all movement and a sustained (cumulative) process is fundamental, but it is not easily applied for purposes of a diagnosis or a prognosis. 'Economic factors' are a necessary, but not sufficient condition of sustained growth.[1]

At a low stage of technology some once-for-all increases in agricultural productivity may often be obtained without being followed by further increases in the same sector, and without any 'sparking' or catalytic effect on productivity in other sectors. Important

---

[1] For a discussion of the multiple causation and inter-relation of social, economic, and political factors involved we may refer to *Economic, Social, and Political Change in the Underdeveloped Countries and its Implications for U. S. Policy*, a Study prepared at the request of the Committee on Foreign Relations, U.S. Senate by CENIS, M.I.T., 30 March, 1960.

symptoms of sustained growth are, on the one hand, the ability to imitate and to absorb other countries' methods of production — frequently referred to as 'technological progress'— and, on the other hand, a differentiated structure of production and investment, notably including a minimum quantum and growth of industrial production.

None of the countries in Africa has reached or is highly likely to reach this stage during the next decade. In Latin America, Argentina, Brazil, Colombia, and Mexico have almost certainly reached this stage already, Chile is on the verge of it, while Uruguay may soon reach it. In Asia, India almost certainly and Pakistan most probably have reached it, while the Philippines and perhaps Burma may reach it in the 1970's. Malaya's satisfactory but not high growth does not yet show symptoms of being sustained. No other country in Asia appears likely to reach the stage within the next decade. In the Middle East, Egypt, Turkey, and Iraq are possible candidates in five or ten years' time. In Southern Europe, Yugoslavia certainly and Greece most probably have reached the stage. Spain may reach it in a decade.

Self-sustaining growth. Self-sustaining growth marks a stage where aid is not required any more, while normal capital imports — private foreign investment — may continue. Countries in this stage are marked with an asterisk in Table 1. In Latin America several countries will probably reach this stage in five or ten years' time. Colombia will reach it in 1965, Argentina and Mexico will gradually approach it in the decade 1965–75, with increasing proportions (more than half) of total capital inflow provided through private investment. Chile's progress is less clearly foreseeable — she may need more capital imports than is indicated in Appendix Table 4-A in 1966–71 and less than shown for 1971–6. In Asia, India should reach this stage in the early 1970's, if her third and fourth Five Year Plans are implemented. While realization may lag behind the austere and ambitious targets, she may reach the self-sustaining growth stage with a few years' delay, say in 1976. Pakistan may reach this stage three to five years later, the Philippines probably only after 1975. None of the countries of the Middle East appears probable to reach this stage within 1960–75, with the possible exception of oil-rich Iraq. In Southern Europe, Yugoslavia should reach it by 1966, Greece toward the end of the 1960's.

TABLE I. — HIGH- AND LOW-GROWTH COUNTRIES, 1961-76

(Rate of growth per head)

	High Growth			Low Growth			Stationary		
	1961-6	1966-71	1971-6	1961-6	1966-71	1971-6	1961-6	1966-71	1971-6
AFRICA									
Algeria	2·0				1·5	1·5			
Angola			2·3	1·5	1·9				
British Cameroons				0·6	1·7	1·7			
French Cameroons				0·6	1·7	1·7			
Belgian Congo			2·2	1·2	1·9				
Eritrea and Ethiopia				1·2		1·7		0·4	
Former Fr. Eq. Africa				0·7	1·2	1·7			
Former Fr. West Africa				1·1	0·7	1·2			
Gambia					1·0	0·9	-0·8		
Ghana			2·2	1·1	1·6				
Kenya			2·2	1·5	1·6				
Liberia				1·1	1·5	1·4			
Libya				1·9	0·7	0·5			
Madagascar					1·5	1·6	0·2		
Mauritius							0·2	0·25	0·4
Morocco				0·8	1·1	1·6			
Mozambique			2·3	1·3	1·8				
Nigeria	2·0	2·3	2·2						
Rhodesia and Nyasaland			2·5	1·4	1·75				
Ruanda Urundi				0·5	1·6	1·7			
Italian Somaliland					1·0	1·9	-0·6		
South West Africa				1·1				0·3	0·3
Sudan			2·7	1·7	1·9				
Tanganyika		2·6	2·7	1·6					
Togoland				0·5	1·6	1·8			
Tunisia				1·7	0·6	1·7			
Uganda		2·2				1·4	0·4		
AMERICA									
Argentina	2·0	2·5*	3·2*						
Bolivia				0·5	0·6	0·7			

TABLE 1 (*continued*)

	High Growth			Low Growth			Stationary		
	1961–6	1966–71	1971–6	1961–6	1966–71	1971–6	1961–6	1966–71	1971–6
Brazil			2·0*	1·5	1·7		0	0	−0·1
British Guiana		2·2	2·2*	1·1	1·5		0	−0·2	−0·2
British Honduras			2·0*						
Chile	2·0						−0·3	0·2	
Colombia				0·8	0·9	0·8	0·3	0·1	
Costa Rica				0·6	1·0	1·1	0		0
Cuba						1·2	0		0
Dominican Republic				0·8		0·9			
Ecuador					0·5	0·9			
El Salvador					0·6	0·7			
Guatemala				1·3	1·0	1·0	−0·1		
Haiti				1·9	0·6	1·7			
Honduras									
Jamaica				1·5	1·7				
Mexico		2·0*	2·0*	1·1	1·3	0·9	−0·2	0·4	
Nicaragua				1·1	0·8	0·5	0·1	0	
Panama				1·8	1·5	1·5			
Paraguay				0·5	0·5	1·1			
Peru				1·0	1·0	1·1			
Surinam				0·9	0·9	0·6			
Trinidad and Tobago		2·5*	2·6*	1·0	1·0	0·9			
Uruguay						0·9			
Venezuela						0·9			
West Indies (rest)									
ASIA									
Afghanistan		2·2		1·5		1·7			
Bhutan				1·0	0·8	0·8			
Burma	2·4	3·1	2·8	1·1	0·9	0·8			
Cambodia				0·6	1·8	1·7			
Ceylon	3·2	2·7	2·3						
Hong Kong	(2·5) 3·0	3·0	2·3						
India		3·0	3·4*						

TABLE I (continued)

	High Growth			Low Growth			Stationary		
	1961–6	1966–71	1971–6	1961–6	1966–71	1971–6	1961–6	1966–71	1971–6
Indonesia				0·6	0·9	1·2			
South Korea				1·0	1·5	1·7			
Laos				0·8	0·8	0·8			
Malaya				1·3	1·4	1·6*			
Nepal		2·0		0·8		1·5			
Pakistan	2·0	2·4	3·0*	1·3	1·8				
Philippines				1·3	1·8	1·7*			
Ryukyu Islands			2·1	1·5	1·3				
Singapore				1·1	1·0	1·5			
Taiwan				0·8	1·3	1·5			
Thailand						1·7	0·4		
South Viet Nam				1·4	1·3	1·7			
EUROPE									
Greece	3·0	4·0	4·0*						
Portugal	2·2	2·1	3·0						
Spain	2·2	2·6	3·1						
Yugoslavia	3·8	3·8*	3·9*						
MIDDLE EAST									
Bahrain				1·0	0·8	0·8			
Egypt				1·5	1·9	1·8			
Iran		2·6	2·6*	1·7	1·7	1·6			
Iraq			2·3*	1·6	1·6				
Israel				0·7	0·6	0·7			
Jordan				1·0	0·9	0·7	−0·5		
Kuwait				1·5	1·5	1·7			
Lebanon				0·6	0·6	0·6			
Saudi Arabia				1·4	1·3	1·3	0·1		
Syria			2·0		1·9				
Turkey			2·1*		1·6				
Yemen				0·9					

* Countries marked thus are assumed to have sustained growth (see above).

550

Capital and Aid for Underdeveloped Countries

United States aid and capital outflow to underdeveloped countries amounted in 1959 and 1960 to around $2·75 billion and consisted of the following items :

		$ billion
Development Loan Fund		0·7
Export-Import Bank (gross 0·375)	net	0·275
P.L. 480 (total sale 0·9)	⅔	0·6
¼ of 'defence support'		0·2
Total Economic Aid		$ 1·75
Private Foreign Investment		
Gross 1·0 billion		
Net 0·9 billion		
Minus ½ oil investment 0·35		0·65
Total Capital Outflow		$ 2·4

Technical assistance amounted moreover to $ 0·2 billion and Emergency Fund to $ 0·2 billion.

Other sources account for a capital outflow of $1·25 billion :

	$ billion
International Bank (gross 0·42) net disbursement	0·35
United Kingdom public (0·2) and private investment (gross 0·6 net 0·52 minus ½ oil investment 0·17)	0·35
France public (0·50) and private investment (gross 0·7 net 0·65 minus ½ oil investment 0·2)	0·45
Other countries of the Free World	0·1
Total	$ 1·25

Technical assistance expenditures other than the United States (including the United Nations) amounted moreover to around $0·15 billion. The total capital outflow into underdeveloped countries amounted therefore to $3·65 billion; total expenditure on technical assistance to around $0·35 billion. The U.S.S.R. supplied economic aid of around $0·5 billion.

The underdeveloped countries' total gross capital formation is estimated at around $28·7 billion in 1961. The total capital inflow from the Free World is around $3·65 billion. Adding to it one-half of oil investments of $0·7 billion and one-third of P.L. 480 sales of $0·3 billion (omitted in the above calculations) raises the long-term capital inflow to $4·65 billion — and the U.S.S.R. aid raises it further to $5·15 billion. In addition to the long-term capital inflow, around $2 billion net of short-term capital inflow must be remembered. The domestic gross capital formation of underdeveloped countries amounts to around $21·6 billion.

Aid required in the future is illustrated in Tables 5-A-B-C in the Appendix, and, according to our definition, include only one-half of oil investments and two-thirds of P.L. 480 sales. The total increase in capital inflow required amounts to $2 billion per annum for 1961–71 (from $3·65 per annum at present to $5·7 billion per annum for the next decade) and to around $1 billion per annum in 1971–6 (if the more probable Alternative Asia Total II, Appendix Table 5-C is considered). Economic aid should increase by $1·64 billion from the present $2·65 billion to $4·290 billion (see Appendix Table 5-A). The United States share should increase by $0·7 billion (i.e., by 40 per cent) from the present $1·75 billion per annum to $2·46 billion per annum. Economic aid from other sources should increase by $0·73 billion from the present $1·1 billion to $1·83 billion (i.e., by 66 per cent). Private investment (excluding one-half of oil investments) should increase by $0·45 billion per annum (i.e., by 50 per cent) from the present $0·96 billion to $1·41 billion in 1961–6 and by a further $0·5 billion per annum in 1966–71, thus doubling the present level of private investment in underdeveloped countries and reaching a flow of $1·91 billion per annum.

The total United States expenditures on aid to underdeveloped countries may thus amount to :

	1961–6 $ billion	1966–71 $ billion	1971–6 $ billion
Economic Aid	2·46	2·13	1·41
⅔ of P.L. 480	0·34	0·3	0·2
Technical assistance	0·25	0·25	0·2
'Social development' (not treated in this study) possibly	0·3	0·3	0·2
Emergency Fund	0·2	0·2	0·1
	3·55	3·2	2·1

It should consist of around 75 per cent of 'soft' and 25 per cent of 'hard' loans for 1961–6,

65 per cent of 'soft' and 35 per cent of 'hard' loans for 1966–71, and

50 per cent of 'soft' and 50 per cent of 'hard' loans for 1971–6, in order to match the low-income countries' (mainly in Asia) limited

capacity to repay. Over 40 per cent of the 'soft' loans (i.e., 30 per cent of economic aid) will consist of P.L. 480 sales or grants. The criteria of eligibility for soft loans are low income per head and a 'foreign exchange gap' which is greater than the 'resources gap'.

The allocation in typical years might be as follows :

	1961–6 $ billion	1966–71 $ billion	1971–6 $ billion
Development Loan Fund	1·5 (1·2 soft) (0·3 hard)	1·2 (0·8 soft) (0·4 hard)	0·8 (0·3 soft) (0·5 hard)
Export-Import Bank	0·26	0·33	0·21
⅔ of P.L. 480	0·7	0·6	0·4
	2·46	2·13	1·41

The hard-loan portion of the Development Loan Fund and the Export-Import Bank Development Loans are interchangeable. Expenditures on technical assistance, Emergency Fund and 'social development', as well as ⅓ of P.L. 480 sales, will require additional appropriations of around $1·1 billion per annum in 1961–71 and $0·7 billion per annum in 1971–6.

METHOD OF COMPUTING CAPITAL INFLOW REQUIREMENTS

The method of computing the capital inflow requirements of underdeveloped countries and the single steps in applying it are shown in the Appendix and its Explanatory Notes (notably those to Appendix Tables 3 and 4). Each underdeveloped country's Gross National Product (Y_0) and its rate of growth (r) — assumed according to its estimated absorptive capacity — are shown in Appendix Table 2-A-1. The average savings rate of the initial year 1961 (S_0/Y_0) as well as gross and net investment are shown in Table 3-A. The marginal savings rate (b) is shown in Table 4-A. We assume a capital-output ratio (k) of 3 : 1 (see Appendix Explanatory Notes to Table 4). The formula for calculating the foreign capital inflow for a five-year period is :

$$F = (kr - b) \Sigma Y + 5 Y_0 \left(b - \frac{S_0}{Y_0} \right).$$

The sensitiveness to change of each of the above parameters can be examined by partially differentiating the above expression, keeping everything else constant. With respect to k, b, and S_0/Y_0 we get the following expressions :

$$\frac{\delta F}{\delta k} = r\Sigma Y \tag{1}$$

$$\frac{\delta F}{\delta b} = -\Sigma Y + 5\,Y_0 \tag{2}$$

$$\frac{\delta F}{\dfrac{\delta S_0}{Y_0}} = -5\,Y_0 \tag{3}$$

Capital inflow is obviously very sensitive to initial GNP, to the initial year's average savings rate, and to the capital-output ratio. If the capital-output ratio were, for instance, 10 per cent lower ($2 \cdot 7$ instead of 3) while the rate of growth was 4 per cent, the foreign capital inflow would be about 21 per cent lower. The marginal savings rate has a relatively smaller influence over a short period of five years — but the influence grows the longer the period considered. The assumed marginal savings rates are relatively high; in some cases they may represent desirable targets rather than present trends (see Appendix Explanatory Notes to Table 4). In spite of their poverty, however, many countries have realized such savings rates. Italy, for instance, with one-fifth of the United States income per head had in the last decade the same average savings rate of 14 per cent and a marginal savings rate of 25 per cent. A marginal savings rate considerably higher than the average is the main lever of economic development of underdeveloped countries. Once the level of self-sustaining growth is reached, with average savings of 12–15 per cent, the marginal savings rate need no longer be higher than the average rate.

The capital inflow required is subdivided between aid and private investment in Appendix Table 4-B.

In view of the nature of the statistical information available the margin of error in our computations may be estimated at $\pm$ 25 per cent.

APPENDIX

Explanatory Notes For Tables 1-A and 1-B (*see pp. 556-7*)

The Gross National Product figures were taken from *World Income, 1957* by Mikoto Usui and E. E. Hagen (M.I.T., November, 1959) and from the U.N. *Yearbook of National Accounts Statistics 1959* (United Nations, New York, 1960).

The Gross National Product estimates have been calculated as follows:

Western Europe:

Derived from the 1958 figures of the U.N. *Yearbook of National Accounts Statistics 1959*, with the following growth rates:

Common Market (except Belgium)	5 per cent per annum
Belgium	$3\frac{1}{2}$,, ,, ,, ,,
Free Trade Area	$3\frac{1}{2}$,, ,, ,, ,,
Rest of Europe	3 ,, ,, ,, ,,

Oceania:

Derived from Usui and Hagen, op. cit., with a 3 per cent per annum growth rate. These figures seem to underestimate Oceania's income. They show the GNP per family (see Table 6) for Oceania equal to 72 per cent of those of Sweden, Switzerland and Luxembourg, 82 per cent of those of Belgium and the United Kingdom, 92 per cent of France, and less than that of Western Germany. With a real wage higher than that of Germany and the United Kingdom and a relatively more even distribution of income, as well as high farm incomes, the GNP per family in Australia and New Zealand should come out at only slightly less than that of Sweden or Switzerland. The nominal and real income of Oceania should, therefore, be raised by 33 to 35 per cent.

Canada:

Estimate taken from D. E. Armstrong, *Canada's Prospects — A Reassessment* (Moorgate & Wall Street, London, 1960) giving a 1960 figure. A growth rate of 2 per cent is assumed for 1960–1.

United States:

Direct estimate of $505 billion for 1960 and an assumed 2 per cent growth rate.

Table 1-A. — World Gross National Product and Population, 1961

	GNP ($ U.S. million)	% of World total	Population (thousand)	% of World total	GNP Real Terms ($ U.S. million)	% of World total	GNP Per Head	Real GNP Per Head
							(U.S. dollars)	
DEVELOPED COUNTRIES:								
Western Europe	284,774	20·6	260,999	8·7	384,898	22·0	1,091	1,472
Oceania	17,781	1·3	16,095	0·5	24,360	1·4	1,105	1,513
United States	515,000	37·3	184,566	6·2	515,000	29·4	2,790	2,790
Canada	37,506	2·7	18,313	0·6	37,506	2·1	2,048	2,048
Japan	36,326	2·6	94,791	3·2	58,122	3·3	383	613
South Africa	6,495	0·5	15,215	0·5	9,093	0·5	427	598
	897,882	65·0	589,979	19·7	1,028,979	58·7		
COMMUNIST BLOCK:								
U.S.S.R.	175,960	12·7	214,968	7·2	212,032	12·1	818	986
Eastern Europe	54,745	4·0	99,556	3·3	82,117	4·7	550	825
China	57,844	4·2	693,957	23·2	115,688	6·6	83	167
North Korea	989	0·1	9,418	0·3	1,978	0·1	105	211
North Viet Nam	1,749	0·1	16,661	0·6	3,323	0·2	105	199
	291,287	21·1	1,034,560	34·6	415,138	23·7		
UNDERDEVELOPED COUNTRIES:								
Africa	20,565	1·5	205,814	6·9	33,657	1·9	100	164
America	65,292	4·7	210,145	7·0	89,344	5·1	311	425
Asia	65,309	4·7	779,800	26·1	119,765	6·8	84	154
Europe	20,943	1·5	66,845	2·2	33,509	1·9	313	501
Middle East	19,906	1·4	106,136	3·5	29,293	1·7	187	257
	192,015	13·8	1,368,740	45·7	305,568	17·5		
WORLD TOTAL	1,381,184	100	2,993,279	100	1,749,685	100		

TABLE 1-B. — WORLD INCOME DISTRIBUTION

Countries with GNP Per Head	'Money' GNP		'Real' GNP	
	% of World Population	% of GNP	% of World Population	% of real GNP
$100 or less	50·1	8·5	0·4	0·1
($150 or less)	(57·1)	(10·2)	(26·6)	(6·3)
$101–$300	15·7	6·1	59·9	16·6
($151–$300)	(8·7)	(4·4)	(33·7)	(10·4)
$301–$600	10·7	10·1	8·7	6·4
$601–$1,200	16·7	35·3	15·1	21·9
Above $1,200	6·8	40·0	15·9	55·0

Japan :
Usui and Hagen, op. cit., and a growth rate of 7 per cent per annum from 1957 to 1961.

South Africa :
Usui and Hagen, op. cit., and a growth rate of 3 per cent per annum from 1957 to 1961.

China :
Calculated from a direct estimate for 1961 Gross National Product of $83 per head.

U.S.S.R.:
Calculated from a direct estimate for 1961 Gross National Product of $813 per head.

North Korea and North Viet Nam :
Calculated from a direct estimate for 1961 Gross National Product of $105 in both cases.

Eastern Europe:
Calculated on the following direct estimates for 1961 Gross National Product per head:

Albania	$240
Czechoslovakia	$650
Bulgaria ⎫ Poland ⎬ Rumania ⎭	$440

Hungary $475

East Germany

(Including E. Berlin) $700

Real GNP per head (last column) indicates the purchasing power
of the GNP compared to United States prices. It is a rough estimate
of an order of magnitude. The purchasing power of various countries
has been increased by rates varying from 20 per cent to 100 per cent.
Western Europe, according to Milton Gilbert & Associates, *Comparative National Products and Price Levels, A Study of Western
Europe and the United States* (Paris, O.E.E.C., 1958). *U.S.S.R.* + 20
per cent, *India* + 100 per cent. For details about the increase of
each underdeveloped country, see the last column of Table 2-A-1.
For an alternative calculation of 'Real' GNP estimated globally,
see Everett, E. Hagen, 'Some Facts About Income Levels and
Economic Growth,' in *The Review of Economics and Statistics*,
February, 1960.

EXPLANATORY NOTES FOR TABLE 2-A-1 *(see pp. 559-64)*

Unless otherwise indicated the Gross National Product figures for
1961 have been calculated largely on the basis of the estimates in
Usui and Hagen, op. cit., on the basis of an assumed rate of growth
in 1957–61, and the U.N. *Yearbook of National Accounts Statistics
1959*. For many data on separate national income accounts of African
countries and some data' on the rate of population increase, the
writer had the opportunity of obtaining the use of valuable data
contained in Mrs. Ona B. Forrest's *Capital Formation and Economic
Growth in Africa South of the Sahara, 1950–9*, published by the
Center for International Studies, M.I.T.

National income statistics for Africa are, in many cases, still in
the nature of rough 'guesstimates'. Within the range of various
estimates available, we assumed a Gross National Product per head
(see Table 2-C) and calculated the aggregate GNP by multiplying
by the total population.

Sudan : Department of Statistics, Khartoum, 1958, estimates the
Gross National Product at 1955–6 prices at $61 per head. Our
estimate for 1961 assumes $75 per head.

Kenya : Gross National Product per head estimate of 1958 in the
official accounts assumes $82 per head compared with ours of $94.

Rhodesia and Nyasaland : Our estimate is taken from the *Monckton
Report*, 1960, based on figures of the Central Statistical Office of the

TABLE 2-A-1. — GROSS NATIONAL PRODUCT PROJECTIONS IN UNDERDEVELOPED COUNTRIES

($ U.S. million)

	1961 GNP	1961-6 Rate of growth p.a., per cent	1966 GNP	1966-71 Rate of growth p.a., per cent	1971 GNP	1971-6 Rate of growth p.a., per cent	1976 GNP	1961 Real GNP
AFRICA								
Eritrea and Ethiopia	1,149·1	2	1,268·7	3	1,470·8	3·5	1,746·8	1,953·4
Ghana	966·3	2·5	1,093·2	3	1,267·3	3·5	1,505·1	1,449·4
Liberia	113·7	2·5	128·6	2·5	145·4	2·5	164·5	1,819·2
Libya	76·8	4	93·4	3	108·2	3	125·4	122·8
Morocco	1,539·3	2·5	1,741·5	2·75	1,994·3	3	2,312·0	2,308·9
Sudan	847·8	2·5	959·2	3	1,112·0	3	1,289·1	1,356·4
Tunisia	654·0	2·5	739·9	3	857·7	4	1,043·5	981·0
Belgian Congo	1,482·0	1	1,557·5	2	1,719·6	3	1,993·5	2,223·0
Gambia	15·6	2	17·2	2	18·9	2	20·8	28·1
Kenya	624·2	3	723·6	3	838·8	3·5	998·2	998·7
Nigeria	2,920·4	3	3,385·6	3·25	3,967·9	3·5	4,712·6	4,672·6
Rhodesia and Nyasaland	1,341·0	4	1,631·5	4	1,985·0	4	2,415·1	1,877·4
Mauritius	147·3	2·5	166·6	3	193·1	3	223·8	220·9
Uganda	436·0	3	505·4	3·5	600·2	4	730·2	763·0
Algeria	2,063·4	4	2,510·5	4	3,054·5	4	3,716·4	3,095·1
Former French West Africa	2,159·1	3	2,503·0	3	2,901·7	3·5	3,446·3	3,238·6
Former French Eq. Africa	560·1	3	649·3	3	752·7	3·5	893·9	840·1
Madagascar	558·8	3	632·2	3	732·9	3	849·6	838·2
Angola	301·8	2·5	341·4	3	395·7	3·5	469·9	528·1
Mozambique	491·0	2·5	555·5	3	643·9	3·5	764·7	736·5

TABLE 2-A-1 (continued)

	1961 GNP	1961-6 Rate of growth p.a., per cent	1966 GNP	1966-71 Rate of growth p.a., per cent	1971 GNP	1971-6 Rate of growth p.a., per cent	1976 GNP	1961 Real GNP
AFRICA (contd.)								
British Cameroons	109·4	2	120·7	3	139·9	3	162·1	185·9
French Cameroons	345·5	2	381·4	3	442·1	3	512·5	552·8
Ruanda Urundi	351·0	2	387·5	3	449·2	3	520·7	596·7
Ital. Somaliland	77·4	2	85·4	2	94·2	3	109·2	139·3
Tanganyika	699·2	3	810·5	4	986·1	4	1,199·7	1,188·6
Togoland	63·0	2	69·5	3	80·5	3	93·3	113·4
South West Africa	58·2	2	64·2	3	74·4	3	86·2	104·7
Territories, etc.								
Other British	297·1	2·5	336·1	3	389·6	4	474·0	519·9
Other French	38·2	2·5	43·2	3	50·0	4	60·8	66·8
Other Portuguese	54·6	2·5	61·7	3	71·5	4	86·9	95·5
Spanish	23·9	2·5	27·0	3	31·3	4	38·0	41·8
	20,565·2	2·8 −	23,591·0	3·2 +	27,569·4	3·5 +	32,762·8	33,656·8
AMERICA								
Argentina	11,447	3·75	13,759·3	4·25	16,944·5	4·75	21,383·9	17,170
Bolivia	308	2·5	348·4	3	403·9	3·5	479·7	431
Brazil	18,082	4·25	22,267·9	4·5	27,750·2	5·0	35,417·5	25,315
Chile	2,679	3·25	3,139·7	3·5	3,729·0	4·0	4,537·1	3,483
Colombia	4,170	4·5	5,195·8	5	6,629·8	5	8,461·6	5,421
Costa Rica	330	3	382·5	3·5	454·3	4	552·7	429
Cuba	2,850	3	3,304·0	3·25	3,872·2	3·5	4,599·0	3,562

TABLE 2-A-1 (continued)

	1961 GNP	1961-6 Rate of growth p.a., per cent	1966 GNP	1966-71 Rate of growth p.a., per cent	1971 GNP	1971-6 Rate of growth p.a., per cent	1976 GNP	1961 Real GNP
AMERICA (*contd.*)								
Dominican Republic	737	3	854·4	3	990·5	3	1,148·2	921
Ecuador	700	3·5	831·4	4·0	1,011·5	4·25	1,245·6	980
El Salvador	513	3	594·7	3·7	713·2	4	867·7	718
Guatemala	715	3	828·8	3·7	993·9	4	1,209·3	1,001
Haiti	356	3	412·7	3	478·4	4	554·6	534
Honduras	360	3	417·3	3·7	500·4	4	608·8	504
Mexico	10,460	4·5	13,033·2	5	16,630·4	5	21,225·4	14,644
Nicaragua	313	3	362·8	3·5	430·9	5	524·3	438
Panama	305	3	353·6	3	409·9	3·5	486·8	396
Paraguay	230	3	266·6	3	309·0	3	358·2	345
Peru	1,952	3·5	2,318·4	3·75	2,786·7	4·0	3,390·5	2,928
Uruguay	1,270	3	1,472·3	4	1,791·3	4	2,179·4	1,587
Venezuela	4,451	4	5,415·5	4	6,589·0	4	8,016·8	4,451
20 Latin American Republics	62,228	4·0 —	75,559·3	4·3+	93,419·0	4·6+	117,247·1	85,258
British Guiana	136	3	157·6	3	182·7	3	211·8	204
British Honduras	13·6	3	15·7	3	18·2	3	21·0	20
Falkland Islands	0·2	3	0·23	3	0·26	3	0·30	0·3
Jamaica	621	4	755·5	4	919·2	4	1,118·3	807
Trinidad and Tobago	365	3	423·1	3	490·4	3	568·5	474
West Indies (rest)	190	3	220·2	3	255·2	3	295·8	247
French Possessions	94	2·4	105·8	2·5	119·7	2·5	135·4	141

561

Table 2-A-1 (continued)

	1961 GNP	1961-6 Rate of growth p.a., per cent	1966 GNP	1966-71 Rate of growth p.a., per cent	1971 GNP	1971-6 Rate of growth p.a., per cent	1976 GNP	1961 Real GNP
AMERICA (contd.)								
Greenland	3·3	2	3·6	2	4·0	2	4·4	4·9
Netherlands Antilles	32	2	35·3	2	38·9	2	42·9	48
Surinam	48	4	58·4	4	71·0	4	86·3	72
Canal Zone	25	3	28·9	3	33·5	3	38·8	33
Total South and Central America	63,756	3·9+	77,363·6	4·3+	95,552·0	4·6+	119,770·6	87,500
Puerto Rico	1,533	3	1,777·2	3·5	2,110·8	3·5	2,507·0	1,839
Virgin Islands	3·3	3	3·8	3	4·4	3	5·1	4·9
TOTAL AMERICAN UNDERDEVELOPED COUNTRIES	65,292	3·9+	79,144·6	4·3-	97,667·2	4·6-	122,282·7	89,344
ASIA								
Afghanistan	760·3	3	881·4	4	1,072·3	4	1,304·6	1,520·6
Bhutan	32·5	3	37·6	3	43·5	4	50·4	65·0
Burma	1,276·2	4	1,552·7	5	1,981·7	5	2,529·2	2,552·4
Cambodia	384·8	3	446·0	3	517·0	3	599·3	769·6
Ceylon	1,243·7	3	1,441·8	4	1,754·2	4	2,134·3	2,176·4
Taiwan	1,255·3	3·5	1,490·9	3·75	1,792·0	4	2,180·3	2,196·8
India	29,600·1	5	37,778·6	5	48,216·8	5	61,539·1	59,200·2
Indonesia	9,165·4	2·5	10,369·7	3	12,021·5	3·5	14,277·9	13,748·1
South Korea	2,531·3	3	2,934·5	3·5	3,485·3	3·5	4,240·5	3,796·9
Laos	93·3	3	108·1	3	125·3	3	145·2	186·6

TABLE 2-A-1 (continued)

	1961 GNP	1961-6 Rate of growth p.a., per cent	1966 GNP	1966-71 Rate of growth p.a., per cent	1971 GNP	1971-6 Rate of growth p.a., per cent	1976 GNP	1961 Real GNP
ASIA (contd.)								
Malaya	2,614·6	4	3,181·1	4	3,870·4	4	4,709·1	3,921·9
Nepal	444·5	3	515·3	4	626·9	4	762·7	889·0
Pakistan	5,612·6	4	6,828·8	4·5	8,510·0	5	10,861·3	11,225·2
Philippines	4,796·0	3·50	5,696·2	4·0	6,930·5	4	8,432·3	7,194·0
Thailand	2,320·6	3	2,690·2	3·5	3,195·1	4	3,887·4	4,641·2
South Viet Nam	1,515·9	3·5	1,800·4	3·5	2,138·3	4	2,601·6	2,880·2
North Borneo	44·2	3	51·2	3	59·3	3	68·7	88·4
Sarawak	77·7	4	94·5	4	114·9	3	139·7	155·4
Neth. New Guinea	32·4	3	37·5	3	43·4	3·5	50·3	64·8
Ryukyu Islands	180·9	3·5	214·8	3·5	255·1	4·5	302·9	289·4
Hong Kong	482·7	4·7	607·2	4·5	756·6	4	942·8	868·9
Singapore	615·0	4	748·2	4	910·3	3·5	1,107·5	922·5
Macao	35·5	3·5	42·1	3·5	50·0	5	59·3	60·3
Portuguese India	100·4	5	128·1	5	163·4	2·5	208·5	180·7
Portuguese Timor	80·5	2·5	91·0	2·5	102·9	4	116·4	144·9
Other*	12·8	4	15·5	4	18·8		22·8	25·6
	65,309·1	4·1	79,783·4	4·4	98,755·5	4·5	123,274·1	119,765·0
EUROPE								
Greece	3,217·1	4	3,914·2	5	4,995·7	5	6,376·0	5,147·4
Portugal	2,204·2	3	2,555·3	3	2,962·3	4	3,604·2	3,526·7
Spain	9,722·9	3	11,271·7	3·5	13,378·7	4	16,268·9	15,556·6
Yugoslavia	5,799·0	5	7,401·2	5	9,446·1	5	12,056·0	9,278·4
	20,943·2	3·7+	25,142·4	4·4—	30,782·8	4·7—	38,305·1	33,509·1

* Maldive Islands and Brunei.

563

Table 2-A-1 (continued)

	1961 GNP	1961–6 Rate of growth p.a., per cent	1966 GNP	1966–71 Rate of growth p.a., per cent	1971 GNP	1971–6 Rate of growth p.a., per cent	1976 GNP	1961 Real GNP
MIDDLE EAST								
Bahrain	28·1	3	32·5	3	37·6	3	43·5	42·1
Iran	2,526·9	4	3,074·5	4	3,740·7	4	4,551·3	3,790·3
Iraq	1,142·2	4	1,389·7	5	1,773·6	5	2,263·6	1,599·0
Israel	1,710·1	5	2,182·6	5	2,785·6	5	3,555·2	2,394·1
Jordan	214·3	2	236·6	3	274·2	3	317·8	321·4
Kuwait	678·5	3	786·5	3	911·7	3	1,056·9	658·8
Lebanon	536·5	4	652·7	4	794·1	4	966·2	804·7
Muscat and Oman	35·7	2	39·4	2	43·5	2	48·0	71·4
Saudi Arabia	1,154·6	3	1,338·5	3	1,551·7	3	1,798·6	1,731·9
Turkey	6,326·2	4	7,697·0	4·5	9,582·8	4·5	11,929·6	9,439·3
Egypt	4,004·5	4	4,872·2	4·5	6,056·6	4·5	7,539·2	6,006·7
Syria	815·9	3	945·9	4	1,150·7	4·5	1,434·0	1,223·8
(U.A.R.)	(4,820·4)		(5,818·0)		(7,369·0)		(9,370·4)	(7,230·5)
Yemen	243·4	2	268·7	3	311·5	3	361·1	486·8
Aden	106·9	3	123·9	3	143·6	3	166·4	160·3
Cyprus	281·2	3	325·9	3	377·8	3	437·9	393·6
Gaza Strip	19·0	3	22·0	3	25·5	3	29·5	38·0
Other*	82·2	2	90·7	2	100·1	2	110·5	81·0
	19,906·2	3·9	24,079·2	4·5+	29,534·8	4·6—	36,509·5	29,293·2

* Trucial Oman and Qatar.

Federation, indicating Gross Domestic Product (GDP) per head of £19 for Nyasaland, £82 for Northern Rhodesia, and £89 for Southern Rhodesia.

Libya: The Gross National Product per head may involve a considerable underestimate. A recent evaluation of the income per head by a mission of the International Bank for Reconstruction and Development is of $90 to $100 per head instead of ours of $63. Libya's Gross National Product is probably an underestimate. It may easily amount to $100 million for 1961 instead of $76·8 assumed by us.

Latin America:

The figures are calculated on the basis of the U.N. Economic Commission for Latin America *Reports* for 1958 in 'constant dollars' of 1950. If one applied the United States gross national product deflator to one constant dollar of 1950, it would be equivalent to $122 in 1961. We believe, however, that the E.C.L.A. estimates in constant dollars of 1950 are an over-estimate and have, accordingly, translated their constant dollar 1950 estimates into a current 1958 dollar by adding 12 per cent. In addition, three modifications have been introduced:

For Argentina: E.C.L.A. estimate of Gross National Product for 1958 has been reduced by 18 per cent; for *Panama*, by 10 per cent; and for *Venezuela*, by 40 per cent.

Recent country studies all seem to imply that previous Argentine income estimates (as well as the estimate of the rate of gross investment — see remarks to Table 3) overvalued the Argentine income. It is also highly probable that Panama's income per head is lower rather than higher than that of Mexico and, accordingly, a 10 per cent reduction appeared indicated. In Venezuela the translation of a Gross National Product in national currency at the previously obtaining official rate of exchange would have given Venezuela a Gross National Product per head of around $1100, which clearly implied a gross overvaluation. The correction for purchasing power is indicated in the estimate for the 'real' GNP. In Venezuela's case, however, the correction was also made for Nominal Gross National Product in order to preserve the proper ranking order of income per head of different countries. The correction of −40 per cent of Gross National Product applied to the rate of exchange which was valid until the end of 1960. By the end of 1960 a *de facto* devaluation by 20 per cent took place, so that at the present rate

of exchange only half of the reduction which we applied would be
necessary.

The Gross National Product for 1961 has been calculated on the
basis of the 1958 E.C.L.A. estimate adjusted as described above
and adding to it a rate of growth from 1958 to 1961 (see below).
During the last three years these rates of growth in Latin America
have been admittedly lower than in previous years due to losses
in terms of trade as well as other internal economic difficulties.
The E.C.L.A. 1958 estimates in constant dollars are indicated in
column one below. Column two shows the three changes for Argentina, Panama, and Venezuela, and indicates, in addition, the +12
per cent conversion from constant 1950 dollars to current 1958
dollars. Column three shows the Gross National Product of each
Latin American country for 1958 in current dollars. Column four
shows the rate of growth realized for each country during the years
1958–61.

	1958 ECLA GNP Estimates (constant 1950 dollars)	% addition for transfer to current 1958 dollars	In current 1958 dollars	% addition for growth 1958–61
Argentina	11,628	−18+12	10,679	7·2
Bolivia	260	12	291	5·8
Brazil	14,944	12	16,737	8·0
Chile	2,319	12	2,597	3·2
Colombia	3,385	12	3,791	10·0
Costa Rica	273	12	306	7·8
Cuba	2,413	12	2,703	5·4
Dominican Republic	610	12	683	8·0
Ecuador	563	12	631	11·0
El Salvador	422	12	473	8·5
Guatemala	602	12	674	6·1
Haiti	300	12	336	6·0
Honduras	300	12	336	7·1
Mexico	8,416	12	9,426	11·0
Nicaragua	261	12	292	7·2
Panama	280	−10+12	282	8·1
Paraguay	192	12	215	7·0
Peru	1,599	12	1,791	9·0
Uruguay	1,050	12	1,176	8·0
Venezuela	6,131	−40+12	4,120	8·0

The Gross National Product for Jamaica has been calculated from
the U.N. *Yearbook of National Accounts Statistics 1959* of which,
however, $18·5 million had to be deducted since undistributed
profits of foreign-owned companies were erroneously included in the
estimate. The 1959 figure corrected for this error is taken directly

from the estimates of the Department of Statistics, Jamaica, to which 9 per cent has been added for estimated growth in 1960 and 1961.

Asia:

The figures for *India* and *Pakistan* have been taken directly from the Development Plans of these countries which result in both cases in slightly lower figures than those given in Usui and Hagen, op. cit.

Philippines: The figures have been calculated from the 1958 figures given in the U.N. *Yearbook of National Accounts Statistics 1959* and using a rate of exchange of 2·4 pesos to the dollar (instead of the official rate of 2) and a 10 per cent addition has been made for growth in the period 1958 to 1961.

Figures for the following countries have been calculated from the national currency figures given in Usui and Hagen, op. cit., but using the following different exchange rates:

Cambodia	43·75 riel to the U.S. dollar
Taiwan	32·21 NT dollars to the U.S. dollar
Korea	650 hwan to the U.S. dollar
South Viet Nam	50 piastre to the U.S. dollar
Indonesia	12·53 rupah to the U.S. dollar

For the years 1957–61 a very low rate of growth of 1 per cent per annum has been assumed for *Indonesia* which implies that income per head in Indonesia has been falling by 1 per cent per annum during the last four years. No growth in income per head for the last three years has also been assumed for *Ceylon.*

Gross National Product figures for *Hong Kong* have been calculated from data given in E. Szczepanik, *The Economic Growth of Hong Kong,* Oxford, 1958.

Singapore: Figures assuming a Gross National Product per head the same as that of Malaya.

Middle East:

Iran: The figures for Iran assume a rate of growth of 5 per cent in the years 1957–61.

Turkey: The figure for Turkey assumes no growth in income per head for 1958 and 1959 (3 per cent rate of growth) and a 5 per cent rate of growth for 1960 and 1961.

Egypt and *Syria:* Our figures are taken from Usui and Hagen, op. cit., and the U.N. *Yearbook of National Accounts Statistics 1959.* We use them with a slight reservation since the resulting 15 per cent Gross National Product per head differential between Egypt and

Syria seems somewhat exaggerated. No other reliable information is available, however.

Lebanon: Our figures have been calculated from the U.N. *Yearbook of National Accounts Statistics 1959* estimate of net domestic product at factor cost (1,325 million Lebanese pounds) to which 17·7 per cent has been added to obtain the Gross National Product estimate (as indicated in Table 2-A-2).

Europe:

The figures are those from Usui and Hagen, op. cit., and the U.N. *Yearbook of National Accounts Statistics 1959* to which the following rates of growth have been added for 1960 and 1961:

Greece	4%	per annum
Portugal	3% ,,	,,
Spain	3% ,,	,,
Yugoslavia	6% ,,	,,

The official gross investment rate for Spain is 17·7 per cent of GNP. We consider this to be an over-estimate and have reduced it to 16·5 per cent. Similarly we have also reduced the official estimate of gross investment for Portugal (17·2 per cent) to 16 per cent.

EXPLANATORY NOTES FOR TABLE 2-B (*see pp. 570-5*)

Unless otherwise stated, population figures have been calculated from the U.N. *Demographic Yearbook 1959*, New York, 1960, while the rates of increase have been calculated from the U.N. *Future Growth of World Population*, New York, 1958 (henceforth referred to as *Predictions*).

The exceptions are as follows:

Africa:

Ethiopia: For Ethiopia a figure of 15 million for population for 1960 has been assumed. The official Ethiopian estimate of population of 20 million for 1958 (reproduced in U.N. *Demographic Yearbook* and in other international agencies, like the International Monetary Fund) is widely and reliably believed to be a considerable over-estimate. An Italian rough estimate of 1938 put the population at 10 million. Another estimate in 1947 also calculated the figure then as 10 million. The United Nations *Future Growth of World Population* assumes 12·2 million for 1960. Our estimate is 15 million and may, if anything, be on the high side.

TABLE 2-A-2. — RELATION BETWEEN GROSS NATIONAL PRODUCT AND NATIONAL INCOME AS GIVEN IN USUI AND HAGEN, *World Income, 1957*

$$\left(\frac{GNP - NI}{NI}\right)$$

Country	$\frac{GNP-NI}{NI}$
AFRICA	
Eritrea and Ethiopia	10·0
Ghana	11·7
Liberia	13·4
Libya	9·7
Morocco	17·0
Sudan	9·2
Tunisia	13·7
Belgian Congo	27·0
Gambia	7·7
Kenya	13·7
Nigeria	6·3
Rhodesia and Nyasaland	10·0
Mauritius	13·6
Uganda	13·4
Other British	9·2
Algeria	13·6
Fr. W. Africa	13·6
Fr. Eq. Africa	13·4
Madagascar	13·6
Other French	10·0
Angola	8·7
Mozambique	13·1
Other Portuguese	9·1
Spanish Guinea	8·3
Other Spanish	8·3
Br. Cameroons	9·3
Fr. Cameroons	13·6
Ruanda Urundi	13·1
Ital. Somaliland	11·9
Tanganyika	8·7
Togoland	12·2
S.W. Africa	13·0
ASIA	
Afghanistan	12·1
Bhutan	11·5
Burma	18·4
Cambodia	13·4
Ceylon	10·7
Taiwan	26·7
India	14·1
Indonesia	13·9
Korea (South)	5·6
Laos	12·1
Malaya	13·7
Maldive Islands	33·3
Nepal	12·2
Pakistan	11·1
Philippines	13·5
Thailand	9·1
South Viet Nam	15·5
Brunei	16·7
Hong Kong	9·2
North Borneo	14·3
Sarawak	14·3
Singapore	..
Neth. New Guinea	..
Macao	14·8
Portuguese India	14·1
Portuguese Timor	14·1
Ryukyu Islands	14·3
EUROPE	
Greece	16·8
Portugal	13·8
Spain	18·7
Yugoslavia	17·8
AMERICA	
Argentina	21·9
Bolivia	17·8
Brazil	22·4
Chile	23·6
Colombia	16·5
Costa Rica	21·4
Cuba	19·1
Dominican Republic	17·7
Ecuador	19·7
El Salvador	17·8
Guatemala	16·6
Haiti	16·8
Honduras	15·4
Mexico	12·8
Nicaragua	13·3
Panama	20·9
Paraguay	14·0
Peru	44·5
Uruguay	17·7
Venezuela	21·2
Br. Guiana	13·1
Br. Honduras	20·0
Falkland Islands	(16·7)
(Fed. of W. Indies)	16·1
Jamaica	..
Trinidad & Tobago	17·8
West Indies (rest)	13·1
Guadeloupe	15·1
Martinique	14·7
Fr. Guiana	25·0
St. Pierre et Miquelon	..
Greenland	15·4
Neth. Antilles	13·8
Surinam	10·0
Canal Zone	19·2
Puerto Rico	..
Virgin Islands	..
MIDDLE EAST	
Bahrain	13·6
Iran	13·6
Iraq	15·2
Israel	20·7
Jordan	17·8
Kuwait	11·5
Lebanon	17·7
Muscat and Oman	13·8
Qatar	12·5
Saudi Arabia	13·4
Trucial Oman	14·8
Turkey	20·1
Egypt	13·6
Syria	11·4
Yemen	20·2
Aden	17·4
Cyprus	13·3
Gaza Strip	..

Table 2-B. — Population in Underdeveloped Countries

(Thousands)

	1958	% rate of increase 1958-61	1961	% rate of increase 1961-6	1966	% rate of increase 1966-71	1971	% rate of increase 1971-6	1976
AFRICA									
Eritrea and Ethiopia	..	..	15,120·0	0·8	15,733·8	1·1	16,618·0	1·3	17,720·4
Ghana	..	..	6,902·5	1·4	7,399·4	1·1	7,932·1	1·3	8,461·1
Liberia	..	..	1,337·8	1·4	1,434·1	1·0	1,507·2	1·1	1,591·9
Libya	1,153	1·9	1,219·8	2·1	1,353·4	2·3	1,516·4	2·5	1,715·6
Morocco	10,330	2·1	10,995·2	2·3	12,320·1	2·4	13,871·2	2·6	15,771·5
Sudan	11,037	0·8	11,304·0	0·8	11,762·9	1·1	12,423·9	1·2	13,186·7
Tunisia	3,852	2·0	4,087·7	2·1	4,535·7	2·4	5,106·7	2·6	5,806·3
Belgian Congo	13,559	2·0	14,388·8	1·8	15,731·2	1·6	17,029·0	1·3	18,164·8
Gambia	277(57)	0·7	284·7	0·9	297·7	1·0	312·8	1·1	330·3
Kenya	6,351	1·5	6,641·2	1·5	7,155·2	1·4	7,670·3	1·3	8,181·9
Nigeria	33,052	1·7	34,767·3	1·6	37,635·6	1·5	40,548·5	1·3	43,253·0
Rhodesia and Nyasaland	7,780	2·3	8,329·2	2·0	9,196·2	1·7	10,004·5	1·5	10,778·8
Mauritius	603	2·8	655·0	2·3	733·9	1·9	806·2	1·4	864·2
Uganda	6,356	1·3	6,607·0	1·3	7,047·6	1·3	7,517·6	1·3	8,019·0
Algeria	10,265	1·9	10,860·3	2·0	11,990·8	2·5	13,566·3	2·5	15,348·9
Former French W. Africa	(20,189)	(2·3)	(21,591·7)	(2·3)	(24,156·8)	(2·3)	(27,042·8)	(2·3)	(30,277·5)
Dahomey	1,725	1·8	1,819·8	1·8	1,989·5	1·8	2,175·1	1·8	2,378·0
Guinea	2,508	2·1	2,669·5	2·1	2,962·0	2·1	3,286·6	2·1	3,646·8
Ivory Coast	3,090	2·5	3,327·6	2·5	3,764·8	2·5	4,259·4	2·5	4,819·0
Mauritania	640	3·5	709·5	3·5	842·6	3·5	1,007·5	3·5	1,196·6
Niger	2,490	2·8	2,704·8	2·8	3,105·1	2·8	3,564·6	2·8	4,092·1
Senegal	2,300	2·4	2,469·5	2·4	2,780·4	2·4	3,130·4	2·4	3,524·5
Sudanese Republic	3,700	2·0	3,926·4	2·0	4,335·1	2·0	4,786·3	2·0	5,284·5
Upper Volta	3,736	2·0	3,964·6	2·0	4,377·3	2·0	4,832·9	2·0	5,336·0

TABLE 2-B (continued)

	1958	% rate of increase 1958-61	1961	% rate of increase 1961-6	1966	% rate of increase 1966-71	1971	% rate of increase 1971-6	1976
AFRICA (*contd.*)									
Former French Eq.	(4,971)	(1·8)	(5,235·2)	(1·8)	(5,709·8)	(1·8)	(6,230·5)	(1·8)	(6,802·2)
Central Afr. Rep.	1,177	1·2	1,219·8	1·2	1,294·6	1·2	1,374·0	1·2	1,458·3
Chad	2,580	2·0	2,737·8	2·0	3,022·8	2·0	3,337·4	2·0	3,684·8
Gabon	420	0·8	430·1	0·8	447·5	0·8	465·6	0·8	484·5
Republic of the Congo	794	2·2	847·5	2·2	944·9	2·2	1,053·5	2·2	1,174·6
Madagascar	..	..	5,533·1	1·7	6,019·4	1·5	6,485·3	1·4	6,952·2
Angola	4,508	1·0	4,644·5	1·0	4,881·3	1·1	5,155·6	1·2	5,472·1
Mozambique	6,234	1·2	6,460·9	1·2	6,857·5	1·2	7,278·5	1·2	7,725·3
British Cameroons	1,591	1·4	1,658·7	1·4	1,778·1	1·3	1,896·6	1·3	2,023·1
French Cameroons	3,187	1·4	3,322·7	1·4	3,561·9	1·4	3,799·4	1·3	4,052·8
Ruanda-Urundi	4,700	1·6	5,087·7	1·5	5,481·4	1·4	5,876·0	1·3	6,267·9
Italian Somaliland	1,330	0·7	1,358·0	0·9	1,420·1	1·0	1,492·5	1·1	1,576·3
Tanganyika	8,916	1·5	9,323·4	1·4	9,994·6	1·4	10,714·2	1·3	11,428·8
Togoland	1,100	1·4	1,146·8	1·5	1,235·5	1·4	1,324·4	1·3	1,412·7
South West Africa	539	2·6	582·1	2·6	661·8	2·7	756·1	2·7	863·8
Territories, etc.									
Other British	4,399	1·3	4,572·0	1·4	4,901·1	1·5	5,280·4	1·7	5,744·5
Other French	562	1·5	587·9	1·4	630·2	1·5	678·9	1·3	724·1
Other Portuguese	808	1·3	840·2	1·3	896·2	1·3	955·9	1·3	1,019·6
Spanish	359	0·9	368·9	1·1	390·3	1·5	420·5	1·6	456·0
			205,814·3		222,903·6		241,818·3		261,999·3
AMERICA									
Argentina	20,248	2·0	21,487·1	1·7	23,375·8	1·7	25,430·5	1·5	27,398·8
Bolivia	3,369	1·5	3,522·9	2·0	3,889·6	2·4	4,379·3	2·8	5,027·4

Table 2-B (continued)

	1958	% rate of increase 1958–61	1961	% rate of increase 1961–6	1966	% rate of increase 1966–71	1971	% rate of increase 1971–6	1976
AMERICA (contd.)									
Brazil	62,725	2·5	67,548·5	2·7	77,174·7	2·8	88,596·5	3·0	102,709·9
Chile	..	..	7,688·1	2·1	8,530·7	2·0	9,418·7	1·8	10,297·4
Colombia	13,522	2·4	14,518·5	2·5	16,426·2	2·8	18,857·2	3·0	21,861·1
Costa Rica	1,076	3·3	1,186·0	3·3	1,394·9	3·3	1,640·6	3·2	1,915·8
Cuba	6,466	2·2	6,902·4	2·2	7,696·1	2·3	8,623·4	2·4	9,709·0
Dominican Republic	..	..	2,942·3	2·7	3,361·5	2·9	3,878·1	3·0	4,495·8
Ecuador	4,048	2·8	4,397·3	2·9	5,073·1	3·0	5,881·2	3·0	6,818·0
El Salvador	2,434	3·3	2,682·9	3·2	3,133·0	3·2	3,658·7	3·1	4,262·0
Guatemala	3,546	3·1	3,883·2	3·0	4,501·7	3·1	5,244·0	3·1	6,108·7
Haiti	3,424	1·5	3,580·4	1·7	3,895·1	2·0	4,300·5	2·3	4,818·7
Honduras	1,828	3·1	2,001·8	3·1	2,331·8	3·1	2,716·3	3·0	3,149·0
Mexico	32,348	2·9	35,246·3	3·0	40,861·0	3·0	47,370·1	3·0	54,916·1
Nicaragua	1,378	3·3	1,518·9	3·2	1,773·7	3·1	2,066·1	3·1	2,406·7
Panama	995	2·7	1,077·7	2·9	1,243·3	3·0	1,441·3	3·1	1,670·8
Paraguay	1,677	2·1	1,784·9	1·9	1,960·8	1·7	2,133·1	1·5	2,298·2
Peru	10,213	2·2	10,902·3	2·4	12,274·8	2·9	14,161·4	2·9	16,338·0
Uruguay	2,700	1·6	2,831·4	1·5	3,050·5	1·5	3,286·6	1·4	3,523·2
Venezuela	6,320	3·0	6,905·8	3·0	8,005·8	3·0	9,281·1	3·1	10,811·5
20 Latin American Republics			202,608·7	2·6	229,954·1	2·7	262,364·7	2·8	300,536·1
British Guiana	..	..	576·1	3·0	667·8	3·0	774·1	3·1	901·7
British Honduras	..	..	95·7	3·0	110·9	3·2	129·5	3·2	151·2
Falkland Islands	..	..	2·0	..	2·0	..	2·0	..	2·0
Jamaica	1,637	2·0	1,737·1	2·1	1,927·4	2·3	2,159·6	2·3	2,419·8
Trinidad and Tobago	789	2·6	852·1	2·5	964·0	2·5	1,090·6	2·4	1,227·9

TABLE 2-B (continued)

	1958	% rate of increase 1958–61	1961	% rate of increase 1961–6	1966	% rate of increase 1966–71	1971	% rate of increase 1971–6	1976
AMERICA (contd.)									
West Indies (rest)	693	2·1	737·6	2·1	818·4	2·1	908·0	2·1	1,007·5
French Possessions	..	..	571·2	1·2	607·5	1·7	662·1	2·2	737·2
Greenland	..	..	28·4	1·5	30·5	1·5	32·8	1·2	34·8
Netherlands Antilles	193	2·3	206·6	2·4	232·6	2·4	261·8	2·4	294·7
Surinam	241	1·9	254·9	2·2	284·2	2·5	321·5	2·9	370·9
Canal Zone	..	..	59·1	2·0	65·2	2·4	73·4	2·6	83·4
Total So. and Cen. America	..	..	207,729·5	2·6–	235,664·6	2·7–	268,780·1	2·7+	307,767·2
Puerto Rico	2,321	0·9	2,384·1	1·3	2,543·1	1·8	2,780·3	2·2	3,100·0
Virgin Islands	..	..	31·2	0·8	32·4	1·5	34·9	2·1	38·7
TOTAL AMERICAN UNDERDEVELOPED COUNTRIES			210,144·8	2·5+	238,240·1	2·7–	271,595·3	2·7+	310,905·9
ASIA									
Afghanistan	..	..	12,992·0	1·5	13,997·5	1·8	15,303·4	2·3	17,147·4
Bhutan	..	..	702·7	2·0	775·8	2·2	865·0	2·2	964·4
Burma	20,255	1·3	21,055·0	1·6	22,792·0	1·9	25,039·2	2·2	27,918·7
Cambodia	4,740	1·6	4,970·8	1·9	5,460·9	2·1	6,059·4	2·2	6,756·2
Ceylon	9,388	2·6	10,139·9	2·4	11,416·5	2·2	12,729·3	2·3	14,263·1
Taiwan	9,851	3·2	10,827·2	3·1	12,612·6	2·7	14,409·8	2·5	16,303·2
India	..	..	423,000·0	2·0	467,034·3	2·0	515,662·5	1·6	558,193·8
Indonesia	87,300	2·1	92,922·1	1·9	102,084·2	2·1	113,272·6	2·3	126,921·9
South Korea	22,505	2·1	23,954·3	2·0	26,447·9	2·0	29,201·1	2·3	32,719·8

TABLE 2-B (*continued*)

	1958	% rate of increase 1958–61	1961	% rate of increase 1961–6	1966	% rate of increase 1966–71	1971	% rate of increase 1971–6	1976
ASIA (*contd.*)									
Laos	1,690	2·0	1,793·4	2·2	1,999·6	2·2	2,229·5	2·2	2,485·8
Malaya	6,515	2·9	7,098·7	2·7	8,110·2	2·6	9,221·2	2·4	10,382·1
Nepal	8,910	1·8	9,400·0	2·2	10,481·0	2·0	11,572·0	2·5	13,092·5
Pakistan	..	..	90,000·0	2·0	99,000·0	2·1	110,000·0	2·0	121,000·0
Philippines	24,010	2·0	25,479·4	2·2	28,409·5	2·2	31,676·5	2·3	35,493·5
Thailand	21,474	2·2	22,923·4	2·2	25,559·5	2·2	28,498·8	2·3	31,932·9
Viet Nam (South)	12,900	2·0	13,689·4	2·1	15,189·7	2·2	16,936·5	2·3	18,977·3
North Borneo	409	2·7	467·2	2·6	531·2	2·5	600·9	2·3	673·3
Sarawak	655	2·0	695·0	2·1	771·1	2·2	859·7	2·3	963·2
Neth. New Guinea	..	..	721·1	1·0	757·8	0·9	792·5	1·8	866·4
Ryukyu Islands	838	2·2	894·5	2·0	987·6	1·7	1,074·4	1·4	1,151·7
Hong Kong	2,748	1·1	2,839·7	1·5	3,059·4	1·8	3,344·8	1·4	3,729·4
Singapore	1,515	3·3	1,669·9	2·9	1,926·5	2·7	2,201·0	2·5	2,490·2
Macao	..	1·7	221·4	2·0	244·4	2·1	271·1	2·3	303·7
Portuguese India	648	1·1	669·6	1·2	710·7	1·6	769·2	2·1	853·6
Portuguese Timor	490	1·7	515·4	1·9	566·2	2·1	628·2	2·3	703·8
Other†	155	0·7	158·1	1·9	173·5	1·7	188·7	2·2	210·9
			779,800·2	2·0	861,099·6	2·1	953,397·5	1·9	1046,498·8
EUROPE									
Greece	8,173	0·9	8,395·3	1·0	8,823·4	1·0	9,273·3	1·0	9,746·2
Portugal	8,981	0·8	9,198·3	0·8	9,571·7	0·9	10,010·0	1·0	10,520·5
Spain	29,662	0·7	30,287·8	0·8	31,517·4	0·9	32,960·8	0·9	34,470·4
Yugoslavia	18,189	1·4	18,963·8	1·2	20,128·1	1·2	21,363·9	1·1	12,564·5
			66,845·2	0·9+	70,040·6	1·0	73,608·0	1·0	77,301·6

TABLE 2-B (*continued*)

	1958	% rate of increase 1958–61	1961	% rate of increase 1961–6	1966	% rate of increase 1966–71	1971	% rate of increase 1971–6	1976
MIDDLE EAST									
Bahrain	139	1·9	147·0	2·0	162·3	2·2	180·9	2·2	201·7
Iran	19,677	2·2	21,005·1	2·3	23,536·2	2·3	26,372·3	2·4	29,692·5
Iraq	6,590	2·5	7,096·7	2·4	7,990·1	2·4	8,996·0	2·4	10,128·5
Israel	1,997	5·3	2,331·6	4·3	2,877·1	3·4	3,400·7	2·7	3,885·2
Jordan	1,580	2·4	1,696·4	2·5	1,919·3	2·4	2,160·9	2·3	2,421·2
Kuwait		..	227·0	2·0	250·6	2·1	278·0	2·3	311·4
Lebanon	1,550	2·7	1,678·9	2·5	1,899·5	2·5	2,149·0	2·3	2,407·9
Muscat and Oman	..	..	564·4	0·8	587·3	1·4	629·5	2·0	695·0
Saudi Arabia	..	..	6,799·3	2·4	7,655·3	2·4	8,619·1	2·4	9,704·2
Turkey	26,163	2·8	28,420·8	2·6	32,314·4	2·6	36,741·4	2·4	41,367·1
Egypt	24,781	2·5	26,686·6	2·5	30,193·2	2·6	34,329·6	2·7	39,221·5
Syria	4,283	3·2	4,707·4	2·9	5,430·9	2·7	6,204·8	2·5	7,020·1
United Arab Republic	..	..	(31,394·0)	(2·6)	(35,624·1)	(2·6)	(40,534·4)	(2·7)	(46,241·6)
Yemen	..	..	3,033·0	1·1	3,203·4	1·4	3,434·0	1·7	3,735·8
Aden	..	..	658·0	2·5	744·4	2·5	842·2	2·4	948·2
Cyprus	549	1·6	575·7	1·8	629·4	2·0	667·9	2·2	744·7
Gaza Strip	346	2·9	377·7	2·4	425·2	2·4	478·7	2·4	538·9
Other*	124	1·6	130·5	2·0	144·0	2·3	161·6	2·2	179·8
			106,136·1	2·5	119,962·6	2·5	135,646·6	2·5	153,203·7

† Maldive Islands and Brunei.
* Trucial Oman and Qatar.

575

Ghana: The figures are taken from the latest population census in March, 1959, published in the *Ghana Economic Survey 1959*, Accra, June, 1960, which is inconsistent with the indications in the U.N. *Demographic Yearbook*. The rates of increase are from *Predictions*.

Liberia: The figures are calculated from a starting point of the 1960 figure given in *Predictions* (the new U.N. *Demographic Yearbook* gives no figure for Liberia).

Nigeria: A new population census is to take place in 1961. It is probable that the population increase has been higher in recent years, and that the population figure may prove to be about two million higher than the figure indicated in the U.N. *Demographic Yearbook*.

Former French West Africa and constituent countries: The 1958 figures are from the U.N. *Demographic Yearbook* 1959 except that for *Guinea* and the *Ivory Coast* which were taken from a 1958 sample census in *La Zone Franc* 1958 (Rapport du Comité Monetaire de la Zone Franc, Paris, 1959).

Former French Equatorial Africa and constituent countries: The 1958 figures are from *La Zone Franc* 1958, ibid. The rates of increase are from the U.N. *Demographic Yearbook*. The figure for *Gabon* has been changed since the U.N. *Demographic Yearbook* rate of $0 \cdot 3$ per cent, stated to be subject to minimum error of $+ 0 \cdot 5$ per cent, was obviously too low; $0 \cdot 8$ per cent adopted by us makes it comparable with the lowest rates for Africa.

Gambia: The figures are calculated from the latest figure (1957) in the *Demographic Yearbook*.

Other British, French and Portuguese: Other British = Sierra Leone (2,120 thous.); Basutoland (651 thous.); Bechuanaland (331 thous.); Br. Somaliland (650 thous.); Zanzibar & Pemba (285 thous.); Swaziland (260 thous.); Seychelles (41 thous.); and St. Helena (5 thous.). *Other French* = French Somaliland (68 thous.); Comoro Islands (180 thous.); and Reunion (306 thous.). *Other Portuguese* = Cape Verde Island (182 thous.); Port. Guinea (554 thous.); and Sao Tomé and Principe (62 thous.).

The figures for these groups are calculated from the 1957 figures in Usui and Hagen. The rates of increase are calculated from *Predictions* rates for the constituent countries.

Latin America:

Chile and the Dominican Republic: The figures both for population and the rate of increase are taken from the Report of the U.N. Economic Commission for Latin America 1959.

British Guiana, British Honduras, Falkland Islands, French possessions, Greenland, Canal Zone and the Virgin Islands: These figures have been calculated from *Predictions*.

West Indies (other): The rate of increase was taken from the U.N. *Demographic Yearbook*.

Other: Comprises Falkland Islands, French Guiana, St. Pierre and Miquelon, Greenland, Canal Zone, Virgin Islands.

Asia:

Afghanistan, Bhutan, Netherlands New Guinea: The 1960 figures in *Predictions* were taken as a basis and the rates were also those in *Predictions*.

India and Pakistan: The figures for *India* were calculated in accordance with the assumption of the *Third Five Year Plan* but for 1971–6 the per annum increase is assumed to be 1·6 per cent while the estimate in the official Indian Third Five Year Plan was 1·4 per cent. The figures for *Pakistan* are in accordance with the official Pakistan *Second Five Year Plan* estimates.

The preliminary results of the new Pakistan census at the beginning of 1961 put the population figures at 93·81 million instead of our figure of 90 million. This represents an annual rate of population increase of 2·2 per cent instead of the 1·8 per cent assumed in the Second Plan.

The preliminary results of the population census in India at the beginning of 1961 show that the Indian population figure is around 438 million instead of 423 million assumed in our Table.

Macao: The 1957 figure in Usui and Hagen was taken as a basis and the rates of increase those in *Predictions*.

Other: Comprises the Maldive Islands and Brunei.

Europe: The figures for *Greece, Portugal,* and *Spain* have been taken from U.N. *The Future Growth of World Population*. They may imply an underestimate for later periods.

Middle East:

Lebanon, Muscat and *Oman, Saudi Arabia, Yemen, Aden:* The 1960 figures given in *Predictions* were taken as a basis and the rates were also those in *Predictions*.

Other: Comprises Qatar and Trucial Oman.

TABLE 2-C. — GROSS NATIONAL PRODUCT PER HEAD
($ *U.S.*)

	1961	1966	1971	1976	1961 Real GNP p.h.
AFRICA					
Eritrea and Ethiopia	76	81	89	99	129
Ghana	140	148	160	178	210
Liberia	85	90	96	103	136
Libya	63	69	71	73	101
Morocco	140	141	144	147	210
Sudan	75	82	90	98	120
Tunisia	160	163	168	180	240
Belgian Congo	103	99	101	110	154
Gambia	55	58	60	63	99
Kenya	94	101	109	122	150
Nigeria	84	90	98	109	134
Rhodesia and Nyasaland	161	177	198	224	225
Mauritius	225	227	239	259	337
Uganda	66	72	80	91	115
Algeria	190	209	225	242	285
Former Fr. W. Africa	100	104	107	114	150
Former Fr. Eq. Africa	107	114	121	131	160
Madagascar	101	105	113	122	151
Angola	65	70	77	86	114
Mozambique	76	81	88	99	114
Br. Cameroons	66	68	74	80	112
Fr. Cameroons	104	107	116	126	166
Ruanda Urundi	69	71	76	83	117
Ital. Somaliland	57	60	63	69	102
Tanganyika	75	81	92	105	127
Togoland	55	56	61	66	99
S.W. Africa	100	97	98	100	180
Territories :					
Other British	65	69	74	83	114
Other French	65	69	74	84	114
Other Portuguese	65	69	75	85	114
Spanish	65	69	74	83	114
	100	106	114	125	164
AMERICA					
Argentina	532·7	588·6	666·3	780·4	799·0
Bolivia	87·4	89·5	92·2	95·4	122·3
Brazil	267·6	288·5	313·2	344·8	374·6
Chile	348·4	368·0	395·9	440·6	452·9
Colombia	287·2	316·3	351·6	387·1	373·4
Costa Rica	278·2	274·2	276·9	288·4	361·6
Cuba	412·8	429·3	449·0	473·6	516·0
Dominican Republic	250·6	254·1	255·4	255·3	313·2
Ecuador	159·1	163·9	171·9	182·7	222·7
El Salvador	191·1	189·8	194·9	203·6	267·5
Guatemala	184·1	184·1	189·5	198·0	257·7
Haiti	99·5	105·9	111·2	115·0	149·2
Honduras	179·8	178·9	184·2	193·3	251·7
Mexico	296·7	319·0	351·1	386·5	415·4

TABLE 2-C (*continued*)

	1961	1966	1971	1976	1961 Real GNP p.h.
AMERICA (*contd.*)					
Nicaragua	206·0	204·5	208·5	217·8	288·4
Panama	283·0	284·4	284·4	291·3	371·0
Paraguay	128·8	135·9	144·8	155·8	193·2
Peru	179·0	188·8	196·7	207·5	268·5
Uruguay	448·7	482·6	545·0	618·5	560·9
Venezuela	644·5	676·4	709·9	741·5	644·5
20 Latin American Republics	307·1	328·6	356·1	390·1	420·7
British Guiana	236·0	236·0	236·0	234·8	354·0
British Honduras	142·0	142·0	140·5	138·8	213·1
Falkland Islands	100·0	115·0	130·0	150·0	150·0
Jamaica	357·5	392·0	425·6	462·1	464·7
Trinidad and Tobago	428·3	438·9	449·6	462·9	556·7
West Indies (rest)	257·4	269·0	281·0	293·5	334·6
French Possessions	164·5	174·1	180·7	183·6	246·7
Greenland	116·1	118·0	121·9	126·4	174·1
Netherlands Antilles	154·8	151·7	148·5	145·5	232·2
Surinam	188·3	205·4	220·8	232·6	282·4
Canal Zone	423·0	443·2	456·4	465·2	549·9
Total South and Central America	306·9	328·3	355·5	389·2	421·2
Puerto Rico	643·0	698·8	759·1	808·7	771·6
Virgin Islands	105·7	117·2	126·0	131·7	158·5
TOTAL AMERICAN UNDERDEVELOPED COUNTRIES	310·7	332·2	359·6	393·3	425·2
ASIA					
Afghanistan	58·5	62·9	70·0	76·0	117·0
Bhutan	46·2	48·4	50·2	52·2	92·4
Burma	60·6	68·1	79·1	90·5	121·2
Cambodia	77·4	81·6	85·3	88·7	154·8
Ceylon	122·6	126·2	137·8	149·6	214·5
Taiwan	115·9	118·2	124·3	133·7	202·8
India	69·9	80·8	93·5	110·2	139·8
Indonesia	98·6	101·5	106·1	112·4	147·9
South Korea	105·6	110·9	119·3	129·6	158·4
Laos	52·0	54·0	56·2	58·4	104·0
Malaya	368·3	392·2	419·7	453·5	552·4
Nepal	47·2	49·1	54·1	58·2	94·4
Pakistan	62·4	69·0	77·4	90·0	124·8
Philippines	188·2	200·5	218·8	237·6	282·3
Thailand	101·2	105·2	112·1	121·7	202·4
South Viet Nam	110·7	118·5	126·2	137·1	210·3
North Borneo	94·6	96·3	98·6	102·0	189·2
Sarawak	111·7	122·5	133·6	145·0	223·4
Neth. New Guinea	45·0	49·5	54·7	58·0	90·0

TABLE 2-C (continued)

	1961	1966	1971	1976	1961 Real GNP p.h.
ASIA (contd.)					
Ryukyu Islands	203·1	217·4	237·4	263·0	324·9
Hong Kong	170·0	198·4	226·2	252·8	306·0
Singapore	368·2	388·3	413·5	444·7	552·3
Macao	160·3	172·2	184·4	195·2	272·5
Portuguese India	150·0	180·2	212·4	244·2	270·0
Portuguese Timor	156·1	160·7	163·8	165·3	280·9
Other *	80·9	89·3	99·6	108·1	161·8
	83·7	92·7	103·6	117·7	153·5
EUROPE					
Greece	383·2	443·6	538·7	654·2	613·1
Portugal	239·6	266·9	295·9	342·5	383·4
Spain	321·0	357·6	405·4	472·7	513·6
Yugoslavia	305·7	367·7	442·1	534·2	489·1
	313·3	359·0	418·2	495·5	501·3
MIDDLE EAST					
Bahrain	191·1	200·2	207·8	215·6	286·6
Iran	120·3	130·6	141·8	153·3	180·4
Iraq	160·9	173·9	197·1	223·4	225·3
Israel	733·4	758·6	819·1	915·0	1,026·8
Jordan	126·3	123·2	126·8	131·2	189·4
Kuwait	2,988·9	3,138·4	3,279·4	3,394·0	2,988·9
Lebanon	319·5	343·6	369·5	401·3	479·2
Muscat and Oman	63·2	67·0	69·1	69·1	126·4
Saudi Arabia	169·8	174·8	180·0	185·3	254·7
Turkey	222·5	238·1	261·1	288·8	333·7
Egypt	150·0	161·3	176·6	192·1	225·0
Syria	173·3	174·1	185·4	204·2	259·9
(U.A.R.)	(153·5)	(163·3)	(181·7)	(202·6)	(230·2)
Yemen	80·2	83·8	90·7	96·6	160·4
Aden	162·4	166·4	170·5	175·4	243·6
Cyprus	488·4	517·7	565·6	588·0	683·8
Gaza Strip	50·3	51·7	53·2	54·7	100·6
Other †	629·8	629·8	619·4	614·5	629·8
	187·5	200·7	217·7	238·2	256·9

* Maldive Islands and Brunei.
† Trucial Oman and Qatar.

TABLE 2-D. — SUMMARY BY REGIONS, GROSS NATIONAL PRODUCT OF
UNDERDEVELOPED COUNTRIES

(*$ million*)

	1961	1966	1971	1976
Africa	20,565·2	23,591·0	27,569·4	32,762·8
America	65,292·0	79,144·6	97,667·2	122,282·7
Asia	65,309·1	79,791·6	98,756·1	123,178·0
Europe	20,943·2	25,142·4	31,118·3	39,126·8
Middle East	19,906·2	24,079·2	30,063·8	37,614·9
	192,015·7	231,748·8	285,174·8	354,965·2
POPULATION (*thousands*)				
Africa	205,814·3	222,903·6	241,818·3	261,999·3
America	210,144·8	238,240·1	271,595·3	310,905·9
Asia	779,800·2	861,099·6	953,397·5	1,046,498·8
Europe	66,845·2	70,040·6	73,608·0	77,301·6
Middle East	106,136·1	119,962·6	135,646·6	153,203·7
	1,368,740·6	1,512,246·5	1,676,065·7	1,849,909·3

EXPLANATORY NOTES FOR TABLES 3-A AND 3-C (*see pp. 582-6, 592*)

Estimates of Gross and Net Investment, as well as those of Savings shown by region in Table 3-C, and for individual countries in Table 3-A, are taken from the Reports of the U.N. Economic Commissions for Latin America and for Asia and the Far East, from the U.N. Statistical Yearbooks and World Surveys, from Development Plans and Programmes of various countries, from some International Bank Reports as well as from individual country studies. The figures are not strictly comparable since both the degree of accuracy and the methods of social accounts vary widely from country to country. Data on Savings are even less reliable than those on fixed capital formation and increase in inventories. Net investment frequently refers, therefore, to 'capacity created' rather than 'Savings plus Imports minus Exports'. In some cases the author's subjective judgement led to the selection of one among several varying estimates mainly guided by a 'hunch' about relative orders of magnitude in each region. Even this vague orientation was not possible in the case of Africa where, in spite of many studies in recent years, most figures about the Gross National Product, Investments and Savings, are more or less enlightened 'guesstimates'. It is hoped nonetheless that the general picture presents on the whole a good perspective of the relative orders of magnitude.

TABLE 3-A. — INVESTMENT AND SAVINGS IN UNDERDEVELOPED COUNTRIES

	GNP 1961 ($ million)	% of GNP assumed for gross investment	Gross investment 1961 ($ million)	Proportion of gross investment assumed for net investment	Net investment 1961 ($ million)	Average savings rate 1961 (%)	Savings 1961 ($ million)
AFRICA							
Eritrea and Ethiopia	1,149·1	9·0	103·4	2/3	68·9	5·0	57·45
Ghana	966·3	11·0	106·2	3/4	79·6	6·0	57·97
Liberia	113·7	10·0	11·3	2/3	7·5	6·0	6·82
Libya	76·8	12·0 m	9·2	2/3	6·1	3·0	2·30
Morocco	1,539·3	10·0	153·9	3/4	115·4	5·0	76·96
Sudan	847·8	9·0	76·3	3/4	57·2	5·5	46·62
Tunisia	654·0	10·0	65·4	2/3	43·5	5·0	32·70
Belgian Congo	1,482·0	5·0 m	74·1	1/2	37·0	1·0	14·82
Gambia	15·6	7·5	1·1	3/4	0·8	3·5	0·54
Kenya	624·2	14·0	87·3	2/3	58·1	7·5	46·81
Nigeria	2,920·4	10·0	292·0	3/4	219·0	6·5	189·82
Rhodesia and Nyasaland	1,341·0	30·0 m	402·3	3/5	241·3	12·0	160·92
Mauritius	147·3	12·7	18·7	3/4	14·0	7·5	11·04
Uganda	436·0	14·0	61·0	3/4	45·7	7·0	30·52
Algeria	2,063·4	16·0	330·1	2/3	220·0	7·0	144·43
Former Fr. W. Africa	2,159·1	12·5	269·8	3/4	202·3	5·5	118·75
Former Fr. E. Africa	560·1	15·0	84·0	3/4	63·0	6·5	36·40
Madagascar	558·8	8·4	46·9	3/4	35·1	4·5	25·14
Angola	301·8	7·5	22·6	3/4	16·9	4·5	13·58
Mozambique	491·0	8·5	41·7	3/4	31·2	5·5	27·00
British Cameroons	109·4	9·0	9·8	3/4	7·3	4·0	4·37
French Cameroons	345·5	11·5	39·7	3/4	29·7	5·0	17·27
Ruanda Urundi	351·0	9·0	31·5	3/4	23·6	4·0	14·04
Somaliland	77·4	9·0	6·9	3/4	5·1	4·0	3·09

m Countries in which extractive industries (oil or minerals) form the preponderant part of investment.

582

TABLE 3-A (*continued*)

	GNP 1961 ($ million)	% of GNP assumed for gross investment	Gross investment 1961 ($ million)	Proportion of gross investment assumed for net investment	Net investment 1961 ($ million)	Average savings rate 1961 (%)	Savings 1961 ($ million)
AFRICA (*contd.*)							
Tanganyika	699·2	14·5	101·3	3/4	75·9	7·0	48·94
Togoland	63·0	9·0	5·6	3/4	4·2	4·0	2·52
South West Africa	58·2	10·0	5·8	3/4	4·3	4·0	2·32
Other British	297·1	7·5	22·2	3/4	16·6	4·5	13·36
Other French	38·2	7·5	2·8	3/4	2·1	4·5	1·71
Other Portuguese	54·6	7·5	4·0	3/4	3·0	4·5	2·45
Spanish	23·9	7·5	1·7	3/4	1·2	4·5	1·07
	20,563·1	12·1	2,488·6	69·7	1,735·6	5·9	1,211·74
AMERICA							
Argentina	11,447	18·5	2,117·6	3/5	1,270·6	10·0	1,144·7
Bolivia	308	15·5	47·7	2/3	31·8	6·0	18·5
Brazil	18,082	15·5	2,802·7	2/3	1,868·5	9·5	1,717·7
Chile	2,679	11·0	294·7	3/5	176·8	7·5	200·9
Colombia	4,170	18·0	750·6	2/3	500·4	10·0	417·0
Costa Rica	330	16·5	54·4	2/3	36·3	9·0	29·7
Cuba	2,850	15·0	427·5	2/3	285·0	7·5	213·7
Dominican Republic	737	16·0	117·9	2/3	78·6	7·5	55·3
Ecuador	700	15·0	105·0	2/3	70·0	7·5	52·5
El Salvador	513	15·0	76·9	2/3	51·3	6·5	33·3
Guatemala	715	14·5	103·7	2/3	69·1	6·5	46·5
Haiti	356	9·0	32·0	2/3	21·3	3·0	10·7
Honduras	360	14·2	51·1	2/3	34·1	6·5	23·4

TABLE 3-A (*continued*)

	GNP 1961 ($ *million*)	% of GNP assumed for gross investment	Gross investment 1961 ($ *million*)	Proportion of gross investment assumed for net investment	Net investment 1961 ($ *million*)	Average savings rate 1961 (%)	Savings 1961 ($ *million*)
AMERICA (*contd.*)							
Mexico	10,460	17·0	1,778·2	2/3	1,185·5	11·0	1,150·6
Nicaragua	313	14·9	46·6	2/3	31·1	6·5	20·3
Panama	305	15·0	45·7	2/3	30·5	6·0	18·3
Paraguay	230	12·0	27·6	2/3	18·4	5·5	12·6
Peru	1,952	17·5	341·6	2/3	227·7	8·0	156·2
Uruguay	1,270	15·0	190·5	2/3	127·0	8·0	101·6
Venezuela	4,451	22·0 m	979·2	3/5	587·5	9·5	422·8
20 Latin American Republics	62,228	16·7	10,391·2	64·5	6,701·5	9·4	5,846·3
British Guiana	136·0						
British Honduras	13·6						
Falkland Islands	0·2						
Jamaica	621·0	23·1	143·5	3/5	86·1	10·0	62·1
Trinidad and Tobago	365·0	25·0 m	91·2	1/2	45·6	10·0	36·5
West Indies (rest)	190·0						
French Possessions	94·0						
Greenland	3·3						
Netherlands Antilles	32·0						
Surinam	48·0	16·0	7·7	2/3	5·1	9·0	4·3
Canal Zone	25·0						
Total S. and Cen. America	63,756·0		10,633·6		6,838·3		5,949·2

m Countries in which extractive industries (oil or minerals) form the preponderant part of investment.

TABLE 3-A (continued)

	GNP 1961 ($ million)	% of GNP assumed for gross investment	Gross investment 1961 ($ million)	Proportion of gross investment assumed for net investment	Net investment 1961 ($ million)	Average savings rate 1961 (%)	Savings 1961 ($ million)
AMERICA (contd.)							
Puerto Rico	1,533·0	20·7	317·3	2/3	211·5		
Virgin Islands	3·3						
TOTAL AMERICAN UNDER-DEVELOPED COUNTRIES	65,292·0		10,950·9		7,049·8		
ASIA							
Afghanistan	760·3	14·0	106·4	2/3	70·9	6·0	45·6
Bhutan	32·5	9·0	2·9	2/3	1·9	5·0	1·6
Burma	1,276·2	16·0	204·2	2/3	136·1	8·5	108·5
Cambodia	384·8	12·0	46·2	2/3	30·8	5·0	19·2
Ceylon	1,243·7	11·5	143·0	2/3	95·3	6·5	80·8
Taiwan	1,255·3	18·2	228·5	2/3	152·3	8·0	100·4
India	29,600·1	15·0	4,440·0	2/3	2,960·0	8·5	2,516·0
Indonesia	9,165·4	8·0	733·2	2/3	488·8	5·0	458·3
South Korea	2,531·3	13·8	349·3	2/3	232·9	6·5	164·5
Laos	93·3	9·0	8·4	2/3	5·6	4·0	3·7
Malaya	2,614·6	18·0	470·6	2/3	313·7	11·0	287·6
Nepal	444·5	9·0	40·0	2/3	26·7	5·0	22·2
Pakistan	5,612·6	15·0	841·9	61·70	519·4	7·8	437·8
Philippines	4,796·0	15·0	719·4	2/3	479·6	7·5	359·70
Thailand	2,320·6	13·5	313·3	3/3	208·9	7·5	174·0
South Viet Nam	1,515·9	9·0	136·4	3/4	102·3	5·0	75·8
Ryukyu Islands	180·9	15·0	27·1	2/3	18·1	8·0	14·5

TABLE 3-A (continued)

	GNP 1961 ($ million)	% of GNP assumed for gross investment	Gross investment 1961 ($ million)	Proportion of gross investment assumed for net investment	Net investment 1961 ($ million)	Average savings rate 1961 (%)	Savings 1961 ($ million)
ASIA (contd.)							
Hong Kong	482·7	18·0	86·9	2/3	57·9	10·0	48·3
Singapore	615·0	18·0	110·7	2/3	73·8	11·0	67·6
Other	383·4	14·0	53·7	2/3	35·8	7·5	28·8
	65,289·1	13·9	9,062·1	66·3	6,010·8	7·0	4,591·7
EUROPE							
Greece	3,217·1	18·6	598·4	2/3	398·9	9·5	305·6
Portugal	2,204·2	16·0	352·7	0·6	211·6	7·0	154·3
Spain	9,722·9	16·5	1,604·3	0·6	962·6	7·5	729·2
Yugoslavia	5,799·0	23·3	1,351·2	2/3	900·8	12·0	695·9
	20,943·2	18·6	3,906·6	0·63	2,473·9	9·0	1,885·0
MIDDLE EAST							
Iran	2,526·9	20·0	505·4	3/5	303·2	8·0	202·1
Iraq	1,142·2	20·0 m	228·4	1/2	114·2	10·0	114·2
Israel	1,710·1	26·5	453·2	2/3	302·1	12·5	213·8
Jordan	214·3	8·0	17·1	2/3	11·4	3·0	6·4
Kuwait	678·5	16·0 m	108·6	1/2	54·3	10·0	67·8
Lebanon	536·5	14·0	75·1	2/3	50·1	8·5	45·6
Saudi Arabia	1,154·6	14·0	161·6	1/2	80·8	6·0	69·3
Turkey	6,326·2	12·0	759·1	2/3	506·1	7·5	474·5
Egypt	4,004·5	11·5	460·5	2/3	307·0	7·0	280·3
Syria	815·9	10·0	81·6	2/3	54·4	6·5	53·0
(U.A.R.)	(4,820·4)	(11·2)	(542·1)	(2/3)	(361·4)	(6·9)	(333·3)
Cyprus	281·2	15·0	42·2	1/3	28·1	6·5	18·3
	19,390·9	14·9	2,892·8	62·6	1,811·7	8·0	1,545·3

m Countries in which extractive industries (oil or minerals) form the preponderant part of investment.

586

TABLE 3-B. — NET INVESTMENT MINUS SAVINGS (1961) AND CAPITAL INFLOW PER ANNUM (1961-6) AS PERCENTAGE OF NET AND GROSS INVESTMENT

	Net investment minus saving ($ million)	Column 1 as % of net investment (%)	Column 1 as % of gross investment (%)	Capital inflow, yearly average ($ million) 1961-6	Capital inflow as % of net investment (%)	Capital inflow as % of gross investment (%)
AFRICA						
Eritrea and Ethiopia	11·4	16·6	11·1	10·12	14·7	9·8
Ghana	21·6	27·2	20·4	29·16	36·6	27·4
Liberia	0·7	9·1	6·0	1·64	21·9	14·5
Libya	3·8	62·3	41·3	7·30	119·7	79·3
Morocco	38·4	33·3	25·0	38·16	33·1	24·80
Sudan	10·6	18·5	13·8	15·06	26·3	19·7
Tunisia	10·8	24·8	16·5	16·22	37·3	24·8
Belgian Congo	22·2	59·9	29·9	29·68	80·2	40·0
Gambia	0·3	32·5	23·6	0·40	50·0	36·4
Kenya	11·3	19·4	12·9	8·28	14·2	9·5
Nigeria	29·2	10·0	13·3	71·32	32·6	24·4
Rhodesia and Nyasaland	80·4	33·3	20·0	..	..	..
Mauritius	2·9	21·1	15·8	..	..	..
Uganda	15·2	33·2	24·9	8·46	18·5	13·9
Algeria	75·6	34·3	22·9	17·2	7·8	5·2
Former French W. Africa	83·6	41·3	31·0	75·56	37·3	28·0
Former French Equat. Africa	26·6	42·2	31·7	14·00	22·2	16·7
Madagascar	9·9	28·4	21·2	25·48	72·6	54·3
Angola	3·3	19·6	14·7	8·98	53·1	39·7
Mozambique	4·2	13·5	10·1	9·70	31·1	23·3
British Cameroons	2·9	40·1	29·9	2·12	29·0	21·6
French Cameroons	12·4	41·8	31·3	3·16	10·6	7·9
Ruanda Urundi	9·5	40·5	30·3	7·02	29·7	22·3

587

TABLE 3-B (continued)

	Net investment minus saving ($ million)	Column 1 as % of net investment (%)	Column 1 as % of gross investment (%)	Capital inflow, yearly average ($ million) 1961-6	Capital inflow as % of net investment (%)	Capital inflow as % of gross investment (%)
AFRICA (contd.)						
Italian Somaliland	2·0	39·4	29·1	1·54	30·2	22·3
Tanganyika	26·9	35·5	26·6	13·56	17·9	13·4
Togoland	1·7	40·0	30·0	1·26	30·0	22·5
South West Africa	2·0	46·0	34·1	1·16	27·0	20·0
Other British	3·2	19·5	14·6	8·84	53·2	39·8
Other French	0·4	18·6	13·9	1·42	67·6	50·7
Other Portuguese	0·5	18·3	13·7	1·64	54·7	41·0
Spanish	0·1	10·8	7·6	0·72	60·0	42·3
	513·8	29·0	20·6			
AMERICA						
Argentina	125·9	9·9	5·9	198·76	15·6	9·4
Bolivia	13·3	41·8	27·9	22·70	71·4	47·6
Brazil	150·8	8·1	5·4	563·40	30·1	20·1
Chile	−24·1	−13·6	−8·2	58·52	33·1	19·8
Colombia	83·4	16·7	11·1	115·50	23·1	15·4
Costa Rica	6·6	18·2	12·1	2·04	5·6	3·7
Cuba	71·3	25·0	16·7	60·36	21·2	14·1
Dominican Republic	23·3	29·6	19·8	10·60	13·5	9·0
Ecuador	17·5	25·0	16·7	22·46	32·1	21·4
El Salvador	18·0	35·0	23·4	12·48	24·3	16·2
Guatemala	22·6	32·7	21·8	17·44	25·2	16·8
Haiti	10·6	49·8	33·1	22·18	104·1	69·3
Honduras	10·7	31·4	20·9	8·80	25·8	17·2

TABLE 3-B (continued)

	Net investment minus saving ($ million)	Column 1 as % of net investment (%)	Column 1 as % of gross investment (%)	Capital inflow, yearly average ($ million) 1961-6	Capital inflow as % of net investment (%)	Capital inflow as % of gross investment (%)
AMERICA (contd.)						
Mexico	34·9	2·9	1·9	198·96	16·8	11·2
Nicaragua	10·8	34·7	23·1	7·60	24·4	16·3
Panama	12·2	40·0	26·7	9·14	30·0	20·0
Paraguay	5·6	30·4	20·3	3·30	17·9	11·9
Peru	71·5	31·4	20·9	79·32	34·8	23·2
Uruguay	25·4	20·0	13·3	9·02	7·1	4·7
Venezuela	164·7	28·0	16·8	100·06	17·0	10·2
20 Latin American Republics	855·0	12·7	8·2			
Jamaica	24·0	27·9	16·7	10·43	12·1	7·3
Trinidad and Tobago	9·1	19·9	10·0	6·66	14·6	7·3
Surinam	0·8	15·6	10·3	1·36	26·7	17·7
ASIA						
Afghanistan	25·3	35·7	23·8	22·80	32·1	21·4
Bhutan	0·3	15·8	10·3	1·30	68·4	44·8
Burma	27·6	20·3	13·5	47·8	35·1	23·4
Cambodia	11·6	37·7	25·1	15·56	50·5	33·7
Ceylon	14·5	15·2	10·1	30·36	31·8	21·2
Taiwan	51·9	34·1	22·7	29·0	19·0	12·7
India	444·0	15·0	10·0	1,677·72	56·7	37·8
Indonesia	30·5	6·2	4·2	172·3	35·2	23·5
South Korea	68·4	29·4	19·6	63·30	27·2	18·1
Laos	1·9	33·9	22·6	4·86	86·8	57·8

TABLE 3-B (continued)

	Net investment minus saving ($ million)	Column 1 as % of net investment (%)	Column 1 as % of gross investment (%)	Capital inflow, yearly average ($ million) 1961-6	Capital inflow as % of net investment (%)	Capital inflow as % of gross investment (%)
ASIA (contd.)						
Malaya	26·1	8·3	5·5	17·34	5·5	3·7
Nepal	4·5	16·8	11·2	18·18	68·1	45·4
Pakistan	81·6	15·7	9·7	331·6	63·9	39·3
Philippines	119·9	36·1	24·0	a) 147·78	30·8	20·5
Thailand	34·9	16·7	11·1	b) 123·88	25·8	17·2
South Viet Nam	26·5	25·9	19·4	30·74	14·7	9·8
Hong Kong	9·6	16·6	11·0	86·3	84·3	63·4
Singapore	6·2	8·4	5·6	17·44	30·1	20·1
Other	7·0	19·5	13·0	4·08	5·5	3·7
	989·5	16·5	10·9	0·56	1·6	1·0
EUROPE						
Greece	93·3	23·4	15·6	72·32	18·1	12·1
Portugal	57·3	27·1	16·2	41·5	19·6	11·8
Spain	233·4	24·2	14·5	128·92	12·4	8·0
Yugoslavia	204·9	22·7	15·2	143·80	16·0	10·6
	588·9	23·8	15·1			
MIDDLE EAST						
Iran	101·1	33·3	20·0	96·8	31·9	19·2
Iraq	0	0	0	20·0	17·5	8·8
Israel	88·3	29·2	19·5	30·9	10·2	6·8
Jordan	5·0	43·8	29·2	6·6	57·9	38·6
Kuwait	−13·5	−24·9	−12·4	..	..	..

TABLE 3-B (*continued*)

	Net investment minus saving ($ million)	Column 1 as % of net investment (%)	Column 1 as % of gross investment (%)	Capital inflow yearly average ($ million) 1961-6	Capital inflow as % of net investment (%)	Capital inflow as % of gross investment (%)
MIDDLE EAST (*contd.*)						
Lebanon	4·5	9·0	6·0	18·8	37·5	25·0
Saudi Arabia	11·5	14·2	7·1	34·0	42·1	21·0
Turkey	31·6	6·2	4·2	231·8	45·8	30·5
Egypt	26·7	8·7	5·8	173·3	56·4	37·6
Syria	1·4	2·6	1·7	19·9	36·6	24·4
(UAR)	(28·1)	(7·8)	(5·2)	(193·2)	(53·5)	(35·6)
Cyprus	·9·8	34·9	23·2	6·8	24·2	16·1
	266·4	14·7	9·2			

TABLE 3-C. — SUMMARY BY REGIONS, INVESTMENT AND SAVINGS, 1961
($ *million*)

	Gross Investment	Net Investment	Domestic Savings
Africa	2,488·6	1,735·6	1,211·7
America (Total South and Central America)	10,633·6	6,838·3	5,949·2
Asia	9,062·1	6,010·8	4,591·7
Europe	3,906·6	2,473·9	1,885·0
Middle East	2,892·8	1,811·7	1,545·3
	28,983·7	18,870·3	15,182·9

The estimates of Gross Investment and of Savings involve in many cases (some examples follow) an upward bias. Realized Gross Investment and Savings often lag behind planned target estimates. It is felt that the underdeveloped countries total Gross Investment of almost $29 billion may involve an overestimate of around 5–6 per cent. Domestic Savings may involve an overestimate of 6–10 per cent.

The estimates of Net Investment as a proportion of Gross Investment may also involve a slight overestimate. In many publications Depreciation is estimated as 40 per cent of Gross Investment, extrapolating Kuznets' estimate for the U.S. in the mid-19th century. We assumed that in countries with a small capital stock and a *recent* relatively high rate of growth Depreciation may be less — and assumed accordingly in most cases only one-third of Gross Investment for it (see Table 3-A). In some very poor and only very recently developing countries of Africa only one-quarter was assumed for depreciation. In countries with a considerable capital stock in extraction industries (oil or minerals) marked 'm' like Rhodesia, Belgian Congo, Venezuela, Iraq, Saudi Arabia, as well as in Iran, Argentina, Portugal and Spain, 40 per cent of Gross Investment was assumed for Depreciation. Our judgement is that the overestimate, if any, is less than 5 per cent.

Africa :

Libya : The relatively high Investment is due to recent oil discoveries.

Belgian Congo : In recent years mineral investments from Belgium were exceptionally high (over 30 per cent of GNP) while in the second half of 1960 they were certainly nil. For actual 1961 the estimate is a pure guess. The savings estimate of 1 per cent also applies to this 'exceptional' year.

Ghana's and *Nigeria's* Investment figures are probably too low. While *Uganda's* and *Tanganyika's* Investment figures may be overestimates.

America :

Argentina : The official Gross Investment estimate is of 23½ per cent scaled down in our study to 18½ per cent which, if anything, seems still to be rather an overestimate. It may be noted that the depreciation rate in Argentina is assumed at 40 per cent of Gross Investment.

Brazil : Brazil's absorptive capacity — if grants besides repayable loans were forthcoming — is higher than her present rate of investment which, owing to losses in terms of trade, may well be a 6-8 per cent overestimate.

Chile : Had very low investment and savings rates in recent years. The official investment estimate quotes a figure of 10·4 per cent for Gross Investment which is undoubtedly too low. We raised it to 11 per cent which may well be an underestimate by up to 10 per cent. On the other hand, Chile's average savings rate of 7½ per cent — although extraordinarily low at that level of income — may, in spite of it, be a slight overestimate. The presently low rate of investment is partly due to recent monetary stabilization efforts.

Costa Rica : Her published Gross Investment figure (23 per cent) seems to involve a considerable overestimate. We have scaled it down accordingly to 16½ per cent. If a higher Investment and Savings were possible, Costa Rica could have a rate of growth of higher than 3 per cent, at which level the income per head is not increasing.

Cuba : All estimates about the present situation in Cuba are, in the nature of things, pure guesses.

Haiti : The Gross Investment rate has to be interpreted in conjunction with Table 3-B which shows that 50 per cent of her Net Investment is covered by a foreign capital inflow. A great deal of it is 'budget support'. The investment figure — although low — may therefore still represent an overestimate.

Jamaica : The investment figure for Jamaica is very high, which is largely due to high foreign alumina investment in recent years. It is not sure whether investment at that rate can or will continue. The quoted figure for 1961 may, therefore, well involve an overestimate.

Peru : The relatively high Gross Investment rate has to be read in conjunction with the great difference between Gross National Product and National Income shown in Table 2-A-2.

The total Investment figure for Latin America seems on the whole, however, to be realistic.

Asia :

Burma : The National Accounts of Burma show a consistently high Investment estimate in recent years. It is difficult to believe, however, that they do not involve a considerable (20–25 per cent ?) overestimate. If they were correct, we should have to assume that for some reasons the capital-output ratio in Burma was considerably higher (for instance 4 : 1) than in other countries. We have reduced the official estimate (21 per cent) of Gross Investment in Burma to 16 per cent.

Ceylon : Had a very much higher Investment and Savings rate in the first half of the 1950's. Those have gradually fallen, in consequence of which Ceylon has not been able to increase her income per head in the past three years. The assumed Gross Investment rate of $11\frac{1}{2}$ per cent and the average savings rate of $6\frac{1}{2}$ per cent for 1961 reflects this situation and may be over-pessimistic, i.e., may be an underestimate.

Taiwan : Our figure of $18 \cdot 2$ per cent as a rate of Gross Investment is based on the 1958 figures in the U.N. *Yearbook of National Accounts Statistics 1959.* Other estimates give an even higher figure of $21 \cdot 1$ per cent, which seems to us to be an overestimate.

India : The estimate of Investment and Savings is that of the *Third Five Year Plan.* It may well be that in actual 1961 the targets will not be fully met, that the average savings rate may well be 8 per cent instead of $8\frac{1}{2}$ and Gross Investment $13\frac{1}{2}$ or 14 per cent instead of 15 per cent. In Table 4-A, the consequences of such an alternative are indicated resulting in a rate of growth for 1961–6 of $4\frac{1}{2}$ instead of 5 per cent.

Indonesia : Has a low Investment and Savings rate and has not been able to maintain her income per head in the last three years. Owing to her limited absorptive capacity of capital and her low savings rate, a low rate of growth of $2\frac{1}{2}$ per cent per annum for the next five-year period had to be assumed.

South Korea : The published accounts of this country give a Gross Investment rate of $14 \cdot 9$ per cent. We have scaled this down to $13 \cdot 8$ per cent.

Pakistan : The estimate of Investment and Savings is that of the official *Second Five Year Plan.* The original Gross Investment figure was 13·4 per cent instead of 15 per cent. The Indus Water Agreement foresees, however, an inflow of $700 million for the five-year period of which 20 per cent ($140 million) constitutes Net Investment while the bulk of it (80 per cent = $560 million) constitutes replacement and maintenance. Accordingly, Net Investment in Pakistan forms 61·7 per cent (instead of 66 per cent) of Gross Investment.

Philippines : Have a very low savings rate of 7½ per cent which, moreover, may still involve a slight overestimate. Their Investment and Savings rates could and should be raised considerably by a more vigorous development policy. For a more optimistic alternative for the future, see the notes to Table 4-A.

Thailand : Our Gross Investment percentage figure is 13·5. Other reports for 1959 give 14 per cent and in view of the Mekong River operations, this may be reasonable.

South Viet Nam : Our Gross Investment percentage figure is 9. Our sources give 11 per cent, which does not appear probable.

The Total Investment figure for Asia may well involve a 6-10 per cent overestimate.

Europe :

The underdeveloped Mediterranean countries of Europe show remarkably low estimates of increase in population. Even if they were correct for 1961, they may well increase in the future. The Investment figures for Portugal and Spain may well involve an overestimate.

Middle East :

Iran : The figures, although rough estimates, are based on recent reports about the Iranian Development Plan.

Iraq : Could well increase its at present very low productivity in agriculture, which might then lead to a successful part-industrialization. An optimistic estimate of her rate of growth is therefore given (see the *Reports of the International Bank,* Johns Hopkins Press, 1951, and of the Mediterranean Project of the FAO, 1959).

Turkey : Due to her high increase in population and a recently slowed down rate of growth, Turkey has not been able to increase markedly her income per head in recent years (see notes to Table 2-A-1). Her savings and investments could be stepped up, however.

Even for 1961 the low investment figure may represent a slight underestimate.

Egypt : Information on present Investment and Savings is not sufficient. The investment figure of 11·5 per cent may well be an underestimate.

EXPLANATORY NOTES FOR TABLE 3-B (*see pp. 587-91*)

The purpose of this Table is, first, to check (from column one— Net Investment minus Saving) whether our estimates of domestic savings and domestic investment are compatible with estimates of the capital inflow into each country. The second purpose is to identify those countries in which the capital inflow is, in a very large proportion, 'budget support' rather than a direct increase in net investment. Whenever the second column shows very high percentages, as in Libya, Belgian Congo (in the present situation), Former French West Africa and Former French Equatorial Africa, British and French Cameroons, Ruanda Urundi, Togoland, South-West Africa, in *Africa*; Bolivia and Haiti in *Latin America ;* and Jordan in the *Middle East*; there is *prima facie* evidence that the high percentage of what appears in the balance of payments account as foreign capital inflow is 'budget' and other support rather than investment. The last two columns, on the other hand, where the figures are very high cover two different cases, either those of the 'budget support' countries mentioned above or those where the absorptive capacity is so high that capital inflow has to cover both the resources gap and, in some cases, also over and above that, the foreign exchange gap.

EXPLANATORY NOTES FOR TABLES 4-A AND 4-B (*see pp. 598-604*)

Method of calculating capital inflow requirements :

Gross National Product is assumed to increase by r per cent over a five-year period. Denoting GNP by Y, we get for a five-year period :

$$\sum_{0}^{4} Yt = Y_0 \left\{ \frac{(1 + r)^5 - 1}{r} \right\}$$

If the capital-output ratio is assumed to be k, then for a constant rate of growth equal to r per cent we need kr per cent (I) as a ratio of national income at each time period. Thus

$$\Sigma I_t = k_r \Sigma Y.$$

The savings function is assumed to have the usual linear shape :
$$S_t = bY_t - a.$$
$$\therefore \Sigma S_t = b\Sigma Y_t - \Sigma a.$$

The marginal savings rate b is assumed to be given; a is determined by putting $t = 0$.

For $t = 0$, we have
$$S_0 = bY_0 - a$$
$$\therefore a = (b - S_0/Y_0)\ Y_0$$
where S_0/Y_0 is the initial average savings rate.

Hence, total aid requirements
$$= \Sigma I_t - \Sigma S_t = k_r \Sigma Y - b\Sigma Y + \Sigma a$$
$$= (k_r - b)\ \Sigma Y + \Sigma a$$
where k, r, b, a, are all known magnitude. (The formulas have been worked out by Dr S. Chakravarty of M.I.T.).

The capital: Output ratio k is throughout assumed to be 3 : 1. It should, of course, refer to increased net output obtained by investment, while our data compel us to apply it to Gross National Product. The difference between GNP and NNI for each country is indicated in Table 2-A-2. For most countries the difference is of 10 to 13 per cent and there the true capital-output ratio is around 2·8 : 1. In those countries in which the difference is 20 per cent or more, our capital-output ratio has been raised. It has been thus assumed to be 3·2 in *Argentina*, *Brazil*, and *Chile*, while for *Peru* it has been calculated at 3·5 : 1.

The total Capital Inflow required for Underdeveloped Countries in 1961–6 is determined by each country's GNP and assumed rate of growth (Net Investment) — which in turn reflects absorptive capacity — her initial average rate of savings and her marginal rate of savings during each five-year period, which determines the initial average savings rate for the subsequent five-year period. The marginal savings rate depends on each country's : (*a*) Capacity to organize development, (*b*) Income level, (*c*) Composition of Investment (for instance, the marginal savings rate is higher when industry absorbs a higher proportion of investment). In the majority of cases the marginal savings rate was assumed as roughly twice as high as the average rate. The assumed capital-output ratio of 3 : 1 (or rather 2·8 : 1) involves, of course, an over-simplification. It may well vary in different five-year periods for different countries, so that the projection for many particular periods may have a considerable margin of error. Where the existing railway capacity,

TABLE 4-A. — FOREIGN CAPITAL INFLOW REQUIRED FOR UNDERDEVELOPED COUNTRIES, 1961-76

	1961-6					1966-71					1971-6				
	Rate of growth (%)	Average savings rate (%)	Marginal savings rate (%)	Capital inflow 1961-6 ($ mill.)	Capital inflow per annum ($ mill.)	Rate of growth (%)	Average savings rate (%)	Marginal savings rate (%)	Capital inflow 1966-71 ($ mill.)	Capital inflow per annum ($ mill.)	Rate of growth (%)	Average savings rate (%)	Marginal savings rate (%)	Capital inflow 1971-6 ($ mill.)	Capital inflow per annum ($ mill.)
AFRICA															
Eritrea and Ethiopia	2·5	5	9	50·6	10·1	3	5·4	12	217·3	43·5	3·5	6·3	16	278·3	55·7
Ghana	2·5	6	10	145·8	29·2	3	6·4	13	129·3	25·9	3·5	7·3	20	157·2	31·4
Liberia	4	6	8	8·0	1·6	3	6·3	8	16·2	3·2	3	6·9	10	39·5	7·9
Libya	2·5	3	8	36·5	7·3	2	3·5	12	233·9	46·8	2	4·1	15	26·2	5·2
Morocco	2·5	5·5	8	190·8	38·2	3	5·8	12	145·3	29·0	3	6·3	15	234·5	46·9
Sudan	2·5	5·5	8	75·3	15·0	2·75	5·3	10	134·7	26·9	3	6·6	15	114·1	22·8
Tunisia	1	1	5	81·1	16·2	3	6·5	15	no aid		3	5·9	14	246·5	49·3
Belgian Congo	2	1	6	148·4	29·7	3	8·1	9	2·0	·4	3	6·9	12	147·2	29·4
Gambia	3	3·5	6	2·0	·4	3	3·6	15	20·0	4·0	4	3·9	18	2·1	·42
Kenya	3	7·5	12	41·4	8·3	3	8·1	14	335·0	67·0	3	3·9	16	39·1	7·8
Nigeria	3	6·5	10	356·6	71·3	3·25	7·5	20	no aid		3·5	8·4	20	440·7	88·1
Rhodesia	2·5	12·5	20	no aid		4·0	13·4	12	9·0	1·8	3·5	14·6	16	no aid	
Mauritius	3	7·0	10	42·3	8·5	3	7·8	16	75·4	15·1	4	8·1	16	2·7	·54
Uganda	4	7	10	85·9	17·2	3·5	7·5	12	522·7	104·5	3	9·0	20	106·9	21·4
Algeria	3	7	10	377·8	75·6	3	7·5	12	353·6	70·7	4	9·0	16	356·6	71·3
Fr. F. W. Africa	3	5·5	9	70·0	14·0	3	6·9	12	62·0	12·4	3·5	6·7	16	491·0	98·2
Fr. F. Eq. Africa	2·5	5·5	9	127·4	25·5	3	6·2	12	141·7	28·3	3	5·9	15	156·7	31·3
Madagascar	2·5	4·5	8	48·5	9·7	3	4·9	12	66·8	13·3	3	5·8	15	107·2	21·4
Angola	2·5	4·5	8	10·6	2·1	3	5·8	10	83·9	16·8	3·5	6·6	15	84·7	16·9
Mozambique	2·5	5·5	8	15·8	3·2	3	4·3	10	27·6	5·5	3	5·1	14	114·6	22·9
Br. Cameroons	2·5	5·5	8	35·1	7·0	3	5·3	10	69·4	13·9	3	5·9	14	25·2	5·0
Fr. Cameroons	2·5	5·0	7	7·7	1·5	3	4·5	8	92·0	18·4	3	5·0	12	60·1	12·0
Ruanda Urundi	2·5	5·0	8	67·8	13·6	3	4·2	8	171·8	34·4	3	4·9	18	85·7	17·1
It. Somaliland	2	4·0	6	6·3	1·3	2	4·2	8	16·5	3·3	3	8·8	10	18·6	3·7
Tanganyika	3	4·5	8	5·8	1·2	4	7·5	15	15·2	3·0	4	4·8	13	132·8	26·6
Togoland	2	4·0	6			3	4·2	8			3	4·7		17·3	3·5
S. W. Africa	2	4·0	6			3	4·2	8			3			15·8	3·2
Other British															
Other French	2·5	4·5	10	63·1	12·6	3	4·9	12	76·4	15·3	3	5·2	15	209·7	41·9
Other Port															
Other Spanish															
AMERICA															
Argentina	3·75	10	18	993·8	198·8	4·25	11·5	23	1029·4	205·9	4·75	13·7	23	822·4	164·5
Bolivia	2·5	6	11	113·5	22·7	3	6·5	14	38·5	7·7	3·5	7·6	18	47·6	9·5

TABLE 4-A (continued)

Country	Rate of growth (%) 1961-6	Average savings rate (%) 1961-6	Marginal savings rate (%) 1961-6	Capital inflow ($ mill.) 1961-6	Capital inflow per annum ($ mill.) 1961-6	Rate of growth (%) 1966-71	Average savings rate (%) 1966-71	Marginal savings rate (%) 1966-71	Capital inflow ($ mill.) 1966-71	Capital inflow per annum ($ mill.) 1966-71	Rate of growth (%) 1971-6	Average savings rate (%) 1971-6	Marginal savings rate (%) 1971-6	Capital inflow ($ mill.) 1971-6	Capital inflow per annum ($ mill.) 1971-6
AMERICA (contd.)															
Brazil	4.25	9.5	20	2817.0	563.4	4.5	11.3	22	2065.3	413.1	5	13.5	23	1692.9	338.6
Chile	3.5	7.5	15	292.6	58.5	3.5	10.1	20	220.0	44.0	4	10.4	20	254.4	50.9
Colombia	4.5	10	16	577.5	115.5	3	11.6	18	802.1	160.4	5	12.9	16	490.7	98.1
Costa Rica	3	9	12	10.2	2.0	5	8.1	16	36.4	7.3	4	10.1	20	39.6	7.9
Cuba	3	7.5	12	301.8	60.4	3.25	8.0	18	344.1	69.0	3	9.5	18	248.5	49.7
Dominican Republic	3	7.5	10	53.0	10.6	3	7.9	14	34.1	6.8	3	8.96	18	no aid	
Ecuador	3.5	7	12	112.3	22.5	4	7.9	15	181.6	36.3	4	9.2	16	181.8	36.4
El Salvador	3	6.5	10	62.4	12.5	3	7.0	15	109.6	21.9	4	8.4	17	168.2	33.6
Guatemala	3	6.5	10	87.2	17.4	3	7.7	15	157.4	31.5	3	8.3	12	177.7	35.5
Haiti	3	3	5	110.9	22.2	3.5	3.8	15	116.2	23.2	4	6.1	16	115.6	23.1
Honduras	3	6.5	10	44.0	8.8	3	6.6	22	81.0	16.2	5	14.7	23	91.6	18.3
Mexico	4.5	11	20	994.0	199.0	5	12.8	15	959.0	191.8	4	8.3	17	no aid	
Nicaragua	—	6	10	38.0	7.6	3	7.0	13	68.8	13.8	3	7.6	16	71.4	14.3
Panama	3	6.5	9	45.7	9.1	3	6.4	18	44.3	8.9	3	6.5	15	57.0	11.4
Paraguay	3	5.5	8	16.5	3.3	3	5.5	18	39.6	7.9	4	10.4	18	28.4	5.7
Peru	3.5	8	14	396.6	79.3	3.75	8.9	20	425.9	85.2	4	12.3	20	443.2	88.6
Uruguay	3	8	14	45.1	9.0	4	8.8	16	198.2	39.6	4	11.4	22	83.1	16.6
Venezuela	4	9.5	16	500.3	100.1	4	10.6	18	490.6	98.1	3	11.2	18	36.6	7.3
Jamaica	3	10	15	33.3	6.7	3	10.7		14.4	2.9	4		18	no aid	··
Trinidad	4	10	14	6.8	1.4	4	9.8		no aid					no aid	··
Surinam		9							4.9	1.0				0.09	·02
ASIA															
Afghanistan	3	6	9	114.0	22.8	4	6	12	264.5	52.9	4	7	15	254.6	50.9
Burma	4	8	15	239.2	47.8	5	9.6	22	362.6	72.5	5	12	22	225.1	45.0
Cambodia	3	5.5	8	77.8	15.6	3	5.5	10	87.9	17.6	3	6	14	70.1	14.1
Ceylon	3	6.5	10	151.8	30.4	4	6.9	15	349.6	69.9	4	8	18	306.6	61.3
Taiwan	3.5	8	13	145.2	29.0	3.75	9.4	15	120.1	24.0	3	10.4	18	98.1	19.6
India	(4.5)	8.5 (8)	23 (18)	8388.6 (7528.0)	1677.7 (1505.6)	5	10.2 (9.97)	25 (20)	5591.0 (8261.7)	1118.2 (1652.3)	5	14.5 (12.1)	25 (23)	no aid (5103.0)	(1020.6)
Indonesia	2.5	5.5 (5.0)	10 (10)	861.4 (1134.9)	172.3 (226.9)	3	6.2 (5)	14 (12)	1301.0 (1983.8)	260.2 (396.8)	3.5	7.1 (6)	18 (16)	1759.0 (2453.3)	351.8 (490.7)
South Korea	3	6.5	9	316.5	63.3	3.5	6.8	14	503.9	100.8	4	8	18	609.2	121.8

39

TABLE 4-A (concluded)

	1961-6					1966-71					1971-6				
	Rate of growth (%)	Average savings rate (%)	Marginal savings rate (%)	Capital inflow ($ mill.)	Capital inflow per annum ($ mill.)	Rate of growth (%)	Average savings rate (%)	Marginal savings rate (%)	Capital inflow ($ mill.)	Capital inflow per annum ($ mill.)	Rate of growth (%)	Average savings rate (%)	Marginal savings rate (%)	Capital inflow ($ mill.)	Capital inflow per annum ($ mill.)
ASIA (concld.)															
Laos	3·5	4	6	24·3	4·9	3	4·6	7	27·5	5·5	3	4·6	10	27·2	5·4
Malaya	4	11	16	86·7	17·3	4	11·8	18	no aid	··	4	13	20	no aid	36·6
Nepal	4	5	8	90·9	18·2	4	5·1	10	184·8	37·0	4	6	14	182·9	··
Pakistan	4	7·8	15	1667·9*	331·6*	4·5	9·1	20	1668·0*	333·6	5	(11·2)	23	1732·7	346·5
Philippines	3·5	7·5	16	619·0	123·9	4	8·8	20	720·1	144·0	(4·5)	10·8	(23)	(607·0)	(121·4)
Thailand	3	(7)	12	(738·9)	(147·9)	3·5	(8·4)	18	(833·5)	(166·7)	4	(10·4)	23	95·5	19·1
South Viet Nam	3·5	7·5	8	153·7	30·7	3	8·0	10	259·5	51·9	4	9·6	—	(234·0)	(46·8)
Hong Kong	4·7	10	18	431·4	86·3	—	5·5	—	453·4	90·7	4	6·2	20	276·0	55·1
Singapore	4	11	16	87·3	17·4	—	—	—	—	—	—	—	14	602·3	120·5
EUROPE															
Greece	4	9·5	15	361·6	72·3	5	10	23	815·7	163·1	5	12·8	23	341·9	68·4
Portugal	3	17·5	11	207·6	41·5	3	7·5	16	139·8	28·0	4	8·7	20	389·1	77·8
Spain	3	—	12	644·6	128·9	3·5	8·7	18	1114·4	222·9	4	15·4	22	1070·4	214·1
Yugoslavia	5	12	20	719·1	143·8	5	13·7	22	211·67	42·3	5	—	23	no aid	··
MIDDLE EAST															
Iran	4	8	14	484·2	96·8	4	9·1	18	383·7	76·7	4	10·7	18	149·0	29·8
Iraq	4	12·5	15	99·8	20·0	5	10·1	22	296·9	59·4	5	12·7	22	139·2	27·8
Israel	5	13·6	20	154·3	30·9	5	14·1	22	29·7	5·9	—	15·8	22	no aid	··
Jordan	2·4	3·5	4	33·0	6·6	3	3·0	6	73·0	14·6	3	3·0	10	81·5	16·3
Lebanon	3	8·5	12	94·0	18·8	3	8·3	20	108·6	21·7	3	10·0	20	52·7	10·5
S. Arabia	4	6	10	169·8	34·0	4	6·5	14	147·9	29·6	3	7·6	18	68·3	13·7
Turkey	4	8	16	1159·0	231·8	3	9·4	20	1347·8	269·6	4·5	11·5	23	539·9	108·0
Egypt	4	7·5	14	866·4	173·3	4·5	8·6	18	1092·9	218·6	4·5	10·5	22	673·2	134·6
Syria	3	6·5	10	99·3	19·9	4·5	7·0	15	224·7	44·9	4·5	8·4	18	269·8	54·0
Cyprus	3	6·5	10	34·1	6·8	3	7·0	12	29·8	6·0	3	7·7	18	14·6	2·9

* $560 million added to $1107·9 to obtain the total aid figure.

($ million)

	1961–6			1966–71			1971–6		
	Capital inflow	Aid	Private investment	Capital inflow	Aid	Private investment	Capital inflow	Aid	Private investment
AFRICA									
Eritrea and Ethiopia	10·1	7·1	3·0	43·5	31·5	12·0	55·7	37·7	18·0
Ghana	29·2	15·2	14·0	25·9	11·9	14·0	31·4	14·4	17·0
Liberia	1·6	1·0	0·6	1·3	0·7	0·6	7·9	4·9	3·0
Libya	7·3	2·3	5·0	3·2	1·7	1·5	5·2	3·2	2·0
Morocco	38·2	20·2	18·0	46·8	24·8	22·0	46·9	24·9	22·0
Sudan	15·0	10·0	5·0	29·0	18·0	11·0	22·8	12·8	10·0
Tunisia	16·2	10·2	6·0	26·9	15·9	11·0	49·3	20·3	29·0
Belgian Congo	29·7	4·7	25·0	..	..	..	29·4	4·4	25·0
Gambia	0·4	0·3	0·1	0·4	0·3	0·1	0·4	0·3	0·1
Kenya	8·3	5·3	3·0	4·0	1·0	3·0	7·8	3·8	4·0
Nigeria	71·3	55·3	16·0	67·0	47·0	20·0	88·1	58·1	30·0
Rhodesia	..	..	..	..	..	..	..	..	..
Mauritius	8·5	5·5	3·0	1·8	1·0	0·8	0·5	0·5	..
Uganda	17·2	15·2	2·0	15·1	9·1	6·0	21·4	12·4	9·0
Algeria	75·6	57·6	18·0	104·5	84·5	20·0	71·3	51·3	20·0
Former Fr. W. Africa	14·0	8·0	6·0	70·7	50·6	20·1	98·2	62·2	36·0
Former Fr. Eq. Africa	25·5	16·5	9·0	12·4	5·4	7·0	31·3	11·3	20·0
Madagascar	9·0	6·0	3·0	28·3	16·3	12·0	21·4	11·4	10·0
Angola	9·7	5·7	4·0	13·3	8·3	5·0	16·9	9·9	7·0
Mozambique	2·1	1·6	0·5	16·8	8·8	8·0	22·9	11·9	11·0
Br. Cameroons	3·2	1·7	1·5	5·5	3·5	2·0	5·0	3·0	2·0
Fr. Cameroons	7·0	4·0	3·0	13·9	5·9	8·0	12·0	4·0	8·0
Ruanda Urundi	1·5	1·4	0·1	18·4	10·4	8·0	17·1	9·1	8·0
It. Somaliland				1·4	1·3	0·1	3·7	3·2	0·5
Tanganyika	13·6	9·6	4·0	34·4	24·4	10·0	26·6	14·6	12·0
Togoland	1·3	1·0	0·3	3·3	2·3	1·0	3·5	2·5	1·0

Table 4-B (continued)

	1961-6			1966-71			1971-6		
	Capital inflow	Aid	Private invest-ment	Capital inflow	Aid	Private invest-ment	Capital inflow	Aid	Private invest-ment
AFRICA (contd.)									
So. West Africa	1·2	0·7	0·5	3·0	2·0	1·0	3·2	2·0	1·2
Other	12·6	8·6	4·0	15·3	10·0	5·3	41·9	21·9	20·0
	429·3	274·7	154·6	606·1	396·6	209·5	741·8	416·0	325·8
AMERICA									
Argentina	198·8	103·8	95·0	205·9	90·9	115·0	164·5	..	164·5
Bolivia	22·7	17·7	5·0	7·7	2·7	5·0	9·5	3·5	6·0
Brazil	563·4	283·4	280·0	413·1	113·1	300·0	338·6	..	338·6
Chile	58·5	32·5	26·0	44·0	15·0	29·0	50·9	10·9	40·0
Colombia	115·5	70·5	45·0	160·4	65·4	95·0	98·1	..	98·1
Costa Rica	2·0	1·5	0·5	7·3	4·3	3·0	7·9	4·0	3·9
Cuba	60·4	30·4	30·0	69·0	30·0	39·0	49·7	9·7	40·0
Dominican Republic	10·6	6·6	4·0	6·8	2·8	4·0	..	..	..
Ecuador	22·5	12·5	10·0	36·3	18·3	18·0	36·4	16·4	20·0
El Salvador	12·5	8·5	4·0	21·9	12·9	9·0	33·6	18·6	15·0
Guatemala	17·4	12·4	5·0	31·5	20·5	11·0	35·5	19·5	16·0
Haiti	22·2	21·2	1·0	23·2	20·2	3·0	23·1	20·1	3·0
Honduras	8·8	5·8	3·0	16·2	11·2	5·0	18·3	10·3	8·0
Mexico	199·0	100·0	99·0	191·8	41·8	150·0	..	..	..
Nicaragua	7·6	5·0	2·6	13·8	8·8	5·0	14·3	7·3	7·0
Panama	9·1	5·6	3·5	8·9	4·9	4·0	11·4	6·4	5·0
Paraguay	3·3	2·3	1·0	7·9	4·9	3·0	5·7	2·7	3·0
Peru	79·3	55·3	24·0	85·2	55·2	30·0	88·6	48·6	40·0
Uruguay	9·0	5·0	4·0	39·6	22·6	17·0	16·6	..	16·6

	1961-6			1966-71			1971-6		
	Capital inflow	Aid	Private investment	Capital inflow	Aid	Private investment	Capital inflow	Aid	Private investment
AMERICA (*contd.*) Venezuela	100·1	45·1	55·0	98·1	38·1	60·0	7·3	..	7·3
20 Latin Amer. Republics	1522·7	825·1	697·6	1488·6	583·6	905·0	1010·0	178·0	832·0
Jamaica	10·4	7·4	3·0	2·9	..	2·9	..	..	..
Trinidad	6·7	3·7	3·0	..	..	..	..	..	..
Surinam	1·4	1·0	0·4	1·0	0·5	0·5	·02	..	·02
TOTAL AMERICAN UNDER-DEVELOPED COUNTRIES	1541·2	837·2	704·0	1492·5	584·1	908·4	1010·02	178·0	832·02
ASIA									
Afghanistan	22·8	20·8	2·0	52·9	44·9	8·0	50·9	40·9	10·0
Burma	47·8	38·8	9·0	72·5	52·5	20·0	45·0	22·0	23·0
Cambodia	15·6	15·1	0·5	17·6	15·6	2·0	14·1	11·1	3·0
Ceylon	30·4	25·4	5·0	69·9	60·9	9·0	61·3	51·3	10·0
Taiwan	29·0	22·0	7·0	24·0	16·0	8·0	19·6	10·6	9·0
India	1677·7	1577·7	100·0	1118·2	988·2	130·0	..	..	..
	(1505·6)	(1425·6)	(80·0)	(1652·3)	(1452·3)	(200·0)	(1020·6)	(800·6)	(220·0)
Indonesia	172·3	142·3	30·0	260·2	190·2	70·0	351·8	251·2	100·6
	(226·9)	(176·9)	(50·0)	(396·8)	(306·8)	(90·0)	(490·7)	(350·7)	(140·0)
South Korea	63·3	55·3	8·0	100·8	85·8	15·0	121·8	95·8	26·0
Laos	4·9	4·7	0·2	5·5	5·0	0·5	5·4	4·6	0·8
Malaya	17·3	8·3	9·0	..	..	..	..	..	..
Nepal	18·2	17·7	0·5	37·0	35·0	2·0	36·6	33·6	3·0
Pakistan	331·6	291·6	40·0	333·6	283·6	50·0	346·5	266·5	80·0
Philippines	123·9	83·9	40·0	144·0	80·0	64·0	19·1	..	19·1
	(147·8)	(87·8)	(60·0)	(166·7)	(96·7)	(70·0)	(46·8)	(..)	(46·8)

TABLE 4-B (continued)

	1961-6			1966-71			1971-6		
	Capital inflow	Aid	Private investment	Capital inflow	Aid	Private investment	Capital inflow	Aid	Private investment
ASIA (contd.)									
Thailand	30·7	23·7	7·0	51·9	40·9	11·0	55·1	38·1	17·0
South Viet Nam	86·3	66·3	20·0	90·7	65·7	25·0	120·5	85·5	35·0
Hong Kong	17·4	2·4	15·0	..	..	..	..	..	..
Singapore	4·1	1·1	3·0	..	..	..	..	..	..
(alt. India)	2693·3 (2521·2)	2397·1 (2245·0)	296·2 (276·2)	2378·8 (2912·9)	1964·3 (2428·4)	414·5 (484·5)	1247·7 (2268·3)	911·2 (1711·8)	336·5 (556·5)
EUROPE									
Greece	72·3	45·3	27·0	163·1	123·1	40·0	68·4	18·4	50·0
Portugal	41·5	31·5	10·0	28·0	18·0	10·0	77·8	52·8	25·0
Spain	128·9	98·9	30·0	222·9	142·9	80·0	214·1	114·1	100·0
Yugoslavia	143·8	128·8	15·0	42·3	22·3	20·0	..	..	..
MIDDLE EAST	386·5	304·5	82·0	456·3	306·3	150·0	360·3	185·3	175·0
Iran	96·8	66·8	30·0	75·7	40·7	36·0	29·8	..	29·8
Iraq	20·0	10·0	10·0	59·4	29·4	30·0	27·8	..	27·8
Israel	30·9	20·9	10·0	5·9	..	5·9	..	..	..
Jordan	6·6	6·5	0·1	14·6	14·4	0·2	16·3	15·7	0·6
Lebanon	18·8	9·8	9·0	21·7	11·2	10·5	10·5	..	10·5
Saudi Arabia	34·0	24·0	10·0	29·6	18·6	11·0	13·7	2·7	11·0
Turkey	231·8	171·8	60·0	269·6	199·6	70·0	108·0	38·0	70·0
Egypt	173·3	143·3	30·0	218·6	170·6	48·0	134·6	80·6	54·0
Syria	19·9	15·9	4·0	44·9	36·9	8·0	54·0	40·0	14·0
Cyprus	6·8	5·3	1·5	6·0	4·0	2·0	2·9	0·9	2·0
	638·9	474·3	164·6	747·0	525·4	221·6	397·6	177·9	219·7

604

as for instance in the case of Indonesia, is not fully utilized, railway investment for another five years may be very small and the capital-output ratio in such cases of excess capacity can be easily $2 \cdot 5 : 1$ or even slightly lower. The capital-output ratio obviously also depends on each country's capacity to earn foreign exchange. Where this is limited so that the foreign exchange gap is larger than the resource gap, recourse must be had to import-saving investments which are costly and which raise the capital-output ratio. In large markets like *India*, or even *Brazil*, the increase in the capital-output ratio may not be very large. For small countries it would be very large if each were to substitute imports individually. It is assumed, however, that institutions like the Latin American Common Market will provide for some international co-ordination of investments. It is only on such an assumption that the 'true' capital-output ratio of $2 \cdot 8 : 1$ can be assumed for the smaller Latin American countries. The margin of error can only be reduced by more detailed specific country studies. It is felt, however, that for a longer run the assumed capital-output ratio will not be far off the mark.

Africa :

Ghana's gross investment figure may be an underestimate. Her rate of growth of $2\frac{1}{2}$ per cent for the next five-year period may also, therefore, understate Ghana's potential. It may well rise to 3 per cent.

Kenya's gross investment in recent years has been somewhat higher than the 14 per cent assumed for 1961. The cautiously lower rate has been assumed in view of the fact that Kenya was able to draw heavily on her sterling balances in recent years which she will not be able to continue at the same rate. She has also suffered during the last two years from a markedly smaller capital inflow and perhaps even some capital flight.

Belgian Congo : Figures for the *Belgian Congo* are sheer speculation; nothing else is possible in the present political situation. It is assumed that the uncertain and unstable situation will clear up. The average savings rate for the period 1966–71 is, therefore, arbitrarily assumed and not calculated on the basis of her previous average and marginal savings rate.

The territories of *Former French West Africa* and *Former French Equatorial Africa, Madagascar, French Cameroons, Togoland* and *Other French* possessions received ample aid and support from France in 1959–60. Their present assumed investment rates were made

possible due to that aid. Since a high proportion of the capital inflow
may be of the nature of 'budget support' (see Notes to Table 3-B)
there may be some doubt whether all of them will be able to maintain
their average and marginal savings rates if that aid were not to
continue at a similar rate.

Due to the nature of the statistical information about *Africa* the
figures assumed in Table 4-A are in many cases 'guesstimates'.

Latin America :

Chile's average and marginal savings rates assumed in our Table
are, to some extent, in the nature of a target figure rather than an
actual description of the present situation (see Notes to Table
3-A). We assumed, however, that at Chile's level of income a minimum effort of raising the initial savings rate from 7 per cent (or
perhaps even slightly under 7 per cent) to $7\frac{1}{2}$ per cent should be
possible. Chile's absorptive capacity is assumed to be somewhat
lower than that of other Latin American countries due to the low
savings and investment rates of recent years. This is the reason why
the rate of growth assumed is $3 \cdot 25$ per cent for 1961 and $3 \cdot 5$ per
cent for 1966 to 1971.

Cuba : Since detailed information is not available our assumptions
are, in the nature of things, speculative.

Jamaica had a very high foreign investment in recent years. The
continuance of it at a similar rate cannot be taken for granted.
Under circumstances, therefore, a somewhat higher capital inflow
and a much higher percentage of aid than private investment (see
Table 4-B) might be called for.

Asia :

Ceylon's low average and marginal savings rates reflect her recently
reduced investment effort (see Notes to Table 3-A). If her development effort and absorptive capacity were to improve, a higher capital
inflow might be justified.

India : The first line in our Table reproduces the assumptions of
the *Third Five Year Plan* as far as the rate of growth, of gross
and net investment, and of the average and marginal savings rates
are concerned. We suspect, however, that underlying assumptions
about a lower capital-output ratio may not be fully justified and
that the capital inflow required is higher than that assumed in
India's *Third Five Year Plan* ($\$6 \cdot 5$ billion of aid to which $400 to
$500 million for private investment may be added). On our assump-
tions a 20 per cent higher capital inflow would be required. It is

only on those assumptions that India would reach the stage of self-sustaining growth in her *Fifth Five Year Plan* period of 1971–6. The alternative shown in brackets assumes that at present India's average (8 per cent) and marginal (18 per cent) savings rates may be still somewhat lower than the target figures in the Plan and that, accordingly, the rate of growth in 1961–6 is more likely to be 4½ per cent. On those assumptions the amount of aid required to realize a 5 per cent rate of growth during the *Fourth Five Year Plan* period would be considerably higher than is shown in the projections of the *Third Five Year Plan*. In addition, substantial aid will still be required in the *Fifth Five Year Plan* period of 1971–6.

If India received $6·5 billion aid for the *Third Five Year Plan* and her average and marginal savings rates were only 8 and 18 per cent respectively, the rate of growth realized would be 4·3 per cent.

Indonesia: The assumed average and marginal savings rates (however low) may still be slight overestimates. If the present situation were to continue with the lower savings rates shown in brackets in the alternative to Indonesia, a higher capital inflow would be required to secure the low assumed rate of growth. It might then become a question of policy judgement whether the higher capital inflow would not constitute a 'negative incentive' instead of being, as it should be, an encouragement for increased development effort.

Pakistan: The average and marginal savings rates are those of Pakistan's *Second Five Year Plan*. About her gross and net investment, see Notes to Table 3-A. The capital inflow computed by us is considerably lower than the assumption of the Plan. Pakistan's *Second Five Year Plan* postulated foreign aid of $2 billion. Adding to it our assumption of private investment (see Table 4-B) of $200 million, the target for capital inflow would amount to $2·2 billion. We assume instead a total capital inflow of $1667·9 billion. If aid alone without private investment is counted then aid would amount to $1·458 billion instead of $2 billion. The foreign aid assumed in the *Second Five Year Plan* appears to us to be an overestimate.

Pakistan's rate of growth is assumed to increase to 4½ per cent for the period 1966–71 and 5 per cent for the period 1971–6. It may well be, however, that the capital inflow in 1971–6 required to secure a 5 per cent rate of growth may be too high and also that Pakistan's absorptive capacity may, under circumstances, remain lower than 5 per cent. Amounts of aid for an alternative assumption of a rate of growth of 4½ per cent for 1971–6 are therefore shown in brackets.

Philippines : The assumed average savings rate of 7½ per cent, although low at the Philippines' level of income, may be an over-estimate. Some studies suggest that the present rate may not be more than 7 per cent, in which case the higher amounts of aid required to secure a 3½ per cent rate of growth are indicated in brackets. It is, again, a matter of policy judgement whether such a negative incentive to an insufficient development effort should be given. It is in view of this low savings and investment effort that a rate of growth of only 3½ per cent has been assumed for 1961–6. A better development effort could secure a higher rate of growth of 4 per cent for 1961–6 and 4½ per cent for the subsequent decade.

Europe :

Greece may well be able to have a higher rate of growth of 4½ per cent in 1961–6. Our figure may, therefore, involve an underestimate.

Middle East :

Israel : The figures may underestimate the capital inflow since continuation of the presently high flow is taken for granted. Since we were not able to check the capital account, our figures are too low and should be treated with utmost caution.

In Table 4-B the foreign capital inflow is tentatively divided for each country between aid and private investment. The figures may have considerable margins of error in the case of many single countries. It is felt, however, that they add up to a plausible picture for regions as a whole shown in Tables 5-A-B-C.

EXPLANATORY NOTES TO TABLES 5-A-B-C (*see pp. 609-11*)

The total capital inflow required for underdeveloped countries 1961–6 consists of both Aid and Private Foreign Investment. Those are shown separately in tentative projections in the Tables 5-A-B-C which are derived from Table 4-B. Private investment amounts to around 25 per cent, 30 per cent, and 50 per cent of total capital inflow in the successive three five-year periods. It is necessarily unequally distributed between different regions, forming a high proportion in Latin America, Africa, and Europe and a low and slowly rising proportion in Asia.

TABLE 5-A. — CAPITAL OUTFLOW PER ANNUM INTO UNDERDEVELOPED
COUNTRIES, 1961–6

(*$ million rounded*)

Region	Capital inflow	Aid	Private invest- ment	U.S. private invest- ment	Other countries' private invest- ment
AFRICA	430	275	155	40	115
LATIN AMERICA	1550	840	710	620	90
ASIA	2695	2395	300	190	110
ASIA (alt. India)	(2520)	(2240)	(280)	(190)	(90)
MIDDLE EAST	640	475	165	100	65
EUROPE	385	305	80	40	40
TOTAL I	5700	4290	1410	990	420
TOTAL II (alt. India)	(5525)	(4135)	(1390)	(990)	(400)
TOTAL III					
(I minus Europe)	5315	3985	1330	950	380

Total Aid		4290	Technical Assistance	400
International Bank		500	Emergency Fund	300
Aid to be provided by				
Governments		3790		700
U.S. Share	65%	2460	Total Aid (excluding 'Social	
Other Countries' Share	35%	1330	Development' and Surplus	
			Products for Consumption) :	4490
			U.S. Share 65%	2920
			Other Countries' Share 35%	1570

TABLE 5-B. — CAPITAL OUTFLOW PER ANNUM INTO UNDERDEVELOPED
COUNTRIES, 1966–71

(*$ million rounded*)

Region	Capital inflow	Aid	Private investment
AFRICA	605	395	210
LATIN AMERICA	1495	585	910
ASIA	2380	1965	415
ASIA (alt. India)	(2910)	(2430)	(480)
MIDDLE EAST	750	525	225
EUROPE	455	305	150
TOTAL I	5685	3775	1910
TOTAL II (alt. India)	(6215)	(4240)	(1975)
TOTAL III (I minus Europe)	5230	3470	1760

Total Aid		3775	Technical Assistance	400
International Bank		500	Emergency Fund	300
Aid to be provided by				
Governments		3275		700
U.S. Share	65%	2130	Total Aid (excluding 'Social	
Other Countries' Share	35%	1145	Development', and Surplus	
			Products for Consumption) :	3975
			U.S. Share 65%	2585
			Other Countries' Share 35%	1390

TABLE 5-C. — CAPITAL OUTFLOW PER ANNUM INTO UNDERDEVELOPED
COUNTRIES, 1971–6

(*$ million rounded*)

Region	Capital inflow	Aid	Private investment
AFRICA	740	415	325
LATIN AMERICA	1010	180	830
ASIA	1250	910	340
ASIA (alt. India)	(2270)*	(1710)*	(560)*
MIDDLE EAST	400	180	220
EUROPE	360	185	175
TOTAL I	3760	1870	1890
TOTAL II (alt. India)	(4780)	(2670)	(2110)
TOTAL III (I minus Europe)	3400	1685	1715

	I	II		
			Technical Assistance	300
Total Aid	1870	2670	Emergency Fund	200
International Bank	500	500		———
Aid to be provided by				500
Governments	1370	2170	Total Aid (excluding 'Social	
U.S. Share 65%	890	1410	Development', and Surplus	
Other Countries'			Products for Consumption) :	
Share 35%	480	760		I	II
				1870	2670
			U.S. Share 65%	1215	1735
			Other Countries'		
			Share 35%	655	935

* If Pakistan's rate of growth were only 4·5% per annum the Capital-inflow
in Asia (alt. India) would be reduced by $ 225 million per annum.

TABLE 6. — SHARING THE BURDEN OF AID[a]

	Nominal GNP					'Real' GNP					
	GNP per family (dollars)	Number of families (thous.)	Tax per family (dollars)	Contribution[b] by each (%)		Weights for 'real' GNP	'Real' GNP per family (dollars)	Tax per family (dollars)	Contribution[b] by each (%)	
				With U.S.S.R.	Without U.S.S.R.				With U.S.S.R.	Without U.S.S.R.
Belgium	5392	2303·2	495	1·0	1·1	1·23	6632	729	1·2	1·4
Canada	7954	4578·2	1002	4·1	4·3	1·00	7954	1002	3·4	3·7
Denmark	4774	1152·7	380	0·4	0·4	1·33	6349	676	0·6	0·6
Finland	3573	1128·5	164	0·2	0·2	1·44	5145	449	0·4	0·4
France	4815	11478·0	389	4·0	4·2	1·20	5778	568	4·8	5·3
W. Germany	4452	14072·0	326	4·1	4·3	1·43	6366	679	7·0	7·7
Italy	2491	12385·7	0	0	0	1·44	3587	164	1·5	1·6
Luxemburg	6084	83·0	626	0·04	0·04	1·23	7483	900	0·05	0·06
Netherlands	3815	2910·5	209	0·5	0·6	1·55	5913	594	1·3	1·4
Norway	4895	906·7	398	0·3	0·3	1·29	6315	670	0·4	0·5
Oceania	4419	4023·7	317	1·1	1·2	1·33	5877	585	1·7	1·9
Sweden	6228	1889·7	653	1·1	1·2	1·30	8096	1033	1·4	1·6
Switzerland	6222	1343·5	652	0·8	0·8	1·25	7778	944	0·9	1·0
United Kingdom	5383	13075·0	493	5·8	6·1	1·30	6998	799	7·7	8·4
U.S.A.	11161	46141·5	1728	71·3	75·2	1·00	11161	1728	58·6	64·4
U.S.S.R.	3274	53742·0	110	5·3	··	1·20	3928	227	9·0	··

a On basis of progressive income tax schedule of U.S.A. Also assuming GNP per family as a measure of income and a family as consisting of 4 members.

b May not equal 100 because of rounding.

INDEX

absorptive capacity, 292n, 301, 533-6,
  546, 553, 593-7, 606f
accelerator, 50
Ackley, G., 443n
Aden, 564, 569, 575, 577, 580
adjustment mechanism, classical, 510,
  514f, 516
Adler, J. H., 114, 158n, 422n, 424n,
  428n
Ady, P., 141n
Afghanistan, 543, 549, 562, 569, 573,
  577, 579, 585, 589, 599, 603
Africa, 115, 160, 212, 433, 435, 541f,
  547f, 556, 558f, 568ff, 578, 581, 587,
  592, 596, 598, 601, 605f, 608ff
—— British West, 424n
—— French Equatorial, 541, 548, 559,
  569, 571, 576, 578, 582, 587,
  596, 598, 601, 605
—— French Possessions, 561, 573, 577,
  579, 584
—— French West, 541, 548, 559, 569f,
  576, 578, 582, 587, 596, 598,
  601, 605
—— Other British, 560, 569, 571, 576,
  578, 583, 588, 598
—— Other French, 560, 569, 571, 576,
  578, 583, 588, 598, 605
—— South, 385, 496n, 539, 556f
—— South West, 541, 548, 560, 569,
  571, 578, 583, 588, 596, 598,
  602
—— Spanish, 560, 569, 571, 578, 583,
  588, 598
Agarwala, A. N., 199n
agriculture, 6, 12, 31, 41, 54, 71f, 78,
  80, 97f, 100ff, 106, 112ff, 120f, 127f,
  133, 134n, 148, 160f, 168f, 190, 192,
  202, 204, 206, 209, 280, 284, 287f,
  296f, 325, 342, 348, 414, 419, 423f,
  425n, 430, 454, 456-65 *pass.*, 470,
  537, 546
Ahn, C. S., 355n
Albania, 557
Algeria, 540f, 559, 569f, 578, 582, 587,
  598, 601

Alter, G. M., 110
amortization, 110, 166, 173, 243n,
  270, 371, 527, 536
Angola, 541, 548, 559, 569, 571, 578,
  582, 587, 598, 601
annuities, 268
Arabia, 504
Argentina, 32, 43, 141, 357f, 376,
  379, 381, 387f, 390-400 *pass.*, 424,
  433, 435, 493, 496n, 497f, 542, 545,
  547f, 560, 565f, 569, 571, 578, 583,
  588, 592f, 602
Arkwright, R., 38, 42
Armstrong, D. E., 555
Ashton, T. S., 37n
Asia, 64, 66, 114f, 146, 160, 212, 327,
  433, 435, 543f, 546f, 549, 552, 556,
  562, 569, 574, 579, 581, 585, 589,
  592, 595, 599, 603, 608-10
—— South, 52n, 56, 58, 60n, 516
Atom Bank, 506
Aubrey, H. G., 155n, 303n, 328n
Australia, 32, 43, 141, 152n, 391, 393f,
  397f, 400f, 421n, 434, 436, 463, 493,
  496n, 500, 502n, 555
Austria, 391, 434, 436
autarky, 105, 180, 475, 489n

backward linkage effect, 8, 58
backwash effect, 62
Bahrain, 538, 544, 550, 564, 569, 575,
  580
balance-of-payments, 109, 135f, 138n,
  140, 147, 150n, 151, 154-80 *pass.*,
  185, 216n, 296, 338, 375-80 *pass.*,
  384, 413, 424, 426, 481, 483, 488,
  505n, 506n, 508f, 511, 514, 523,
  527f, 539, 596
Baldwin, R. E., 15n, 27n
Balogh, T., 16n, 83ff, 92, 155n, 484n,
  488n
Balopoulos, E., 444n
banking (system), 154, 320, 325n, 413,
  429f
bank loan (credit), 138, 291f, 353, 371
bankruptcy, 366, 488